Spies in Arabia

Spies in Arabia

The Great War and the Cultural
Foundations of Britain's Covert Empire
in the Middle East

PRIYA SATIA

OXFORD
UNIVERSITY PRESS
2008

Oxford University Press, Inc., publishes works that further
Oxford University's objective of excellence
in research, scholarship, and education.

Oxford   New York
Auckland   Cape Town   Dar es Salaam   Hong Kong   Karachi
Kuala Lumpur   Madrid   Melbourne   Mexico City   Nairobi
New Delhi   Shanghai   Taipei   Toronto

With offices in
Argentina   Austria   Brazil   Chile   Czech Republic   France   Greece
Guatemala   Hungary   Italy   Japan   Poland   Portugal   Singapore
South Korea   Switzerland   Thailand   Turkey   Ukraine   Vietnam

Copyright © 2008 by Oxford University Press, Inc.

Published by Oxford University Press, Inc.
198 Madison Avenue, New York, New York 10016

www.oup.com

Oxford is a registered trademark of Oxford University Press

Library of Congress Cataloging-in-Publication Data
Satia, Priya.
Spies in Arabia : the Great War and the cultural foundations of
Britain's covert empire in the Middle East / by Priya Satia.
   p. cm.
Includes bibliographical references and index.
ISBN 978-0-19-973480-1
1. Middle East—Foreign relations—Great Britain.   2. Great Britain—Foreign
relations—Middle East.   3. Espionage—Great Britain.   4. Espionage—Middle East.
5. World War, 1914–1918—Secret service—Great Britain.   I. Title.
DS63.2.G7S28 2008
940.4'86410956—dc22   2007028405

Printed in the United States of America
on acid-free paper

For Amann

Acknowledgments

This book began when, in the course of researching the British Indian development of Mesopotamia during World War One, I came across frequent complaints from local British officials about their difficulty gathering information about the areas in their charge. I assumed their problems arose partly out of a cultural mind-set that had long seen the Middle East as essentially inscrutable, an interesting story in itself of the power of cultural representations to influence the practical unfolding of empire on the ground. However, the project truly seized my attention when I came across the Air Ministry files on air control in Iraq, with their obsessive dual emphasis on "ubiquity" and invisibility of surveillance. My hunch was that there must be some connection between the wartime complaints of blindness and the panoptic ambitions of aerial control, and between the diffident early efforts to gather intelligence and the postwar insistence on covert imperial rule. I am grateful for the opportunity to acknowledge some of the many debts I have accumulated in the course of finding the evidence to support these hunches and putting it all together in this book.

My thank-yous must begin where the book began, at the University of California, Berkeley. Tom Metcalf was an early source of encouragement and belief and provided crucial comment during his meticulous reading of my often painfully long early drafts. I could not have written a book at all without the help of my adviser, colleague, and friend, James Vernon, whose incisive insights into British history and into my own writing and arguments have left their mark all over this book.

To the extent that I have successfully exercised them, writerly and analytical discipline—in fact, *the* discipline—I learned from Tom Laqueur, whose knowledge and wisdom gently tamed my excesses even as his exuberant imagination helped me challenge the limits of my own. Alex Zwerdling saved me from numerous errors, both factual and grammatical, and helped me think about how to write about literature and history. Margaret Anderson, Beshara Doumani, Carla Hesse, and Martin Jay helped in myriad unforgettable ways, as guides and mentors. The comradeship, friendship, and feedback of Arianne Chernock, Kate Fullagar, and Andrew Jainchill have been—and remain—indispensable. I owe special thanks to my friend Rebecca Manley for her constant support, ever-ready ear, and painstaking criticism. Her penetrating mind has on countless occasions shown me the way forward.

In England, many friends opened their homes to me and helped arrange my stay: my warmest thanks to Helima Croft; Berta Figueras and Giulio Federico; the community of the Notting Hill gurdwara; and my cousins. I owe a special and unrepayable debt to my dear friend Abhi Katyal, who gave me a home, music, and side-aching laughter and single-handedly banished loneliness from my research experience. In Princeton, Gaurav Majumdar was an encyclopedic resource on literary modernism.

Conversations with and critical feedback from my colleagues at Stanford have been invaluable. I want particularly to thank Bart Bernstein, David Como, Bob Crews, J. P. Daughton, Zephyr Frank, Sean Hanretta, Libra Hilde, Jessica Riskin, Jim Sheehan, Peter Stansky, Amir Weiner, and Caroline Winterer. The members of the European History Workshop (2004) provided much insight into the book's last chapter. Joel Beinin and Richard Roberts went far beyond the call of collegial duty, ploughing through the entire manuscript at an early stage. In the world of British history, I must thank in particular Roger Louis for his wise counsel and stimulating critical engagement. I would also like to acknowledge the input I have received at the regional and North American Conferences on British Studies. A timely encounter with Peter Sluglett allowed me to correct at least some lingering obscurities. I am also grateful to Phillip Knightley for kindly allowing me to pick his brain about the Philbys.

This book also depends heavily on the research expertise of librarians and archivists on both sides of the Atlantic, including the staff at the Public Record Office, the British Library, the Liddle Collection at Leeds University, the Middle East Centre at St. Antony's College in Oxford, the Liddell Hart Centre for Military Archives at King's College in London, the National Army Museum, Firestone Library in Princeton, Bobst Library at New York University, and Green Library and the Hoover Institute Library at Stanford (especially Ben Stone). Financial support came from the Smithsonian Institute, the Mabelle

MacLeod Lewis Memorial Fund, the British Library's Helen Wallis Fellowship, and the History Department at UC Berkeley. At Stanford, Nancy Falxa-Raymond and Peder Roberts provided energetic research assistance during the final stages of the writing.

The task of turning my roughly hewn manuscript into a finished product fit for consumption was eased considerably by the expertise of Susan Ferber at Oxford University Press. I am indebted as well to Linda Donnelly, the staff, and the anonymous readers at the press. My thanks also to the editors and anonymous readers at the *American Historical Review* and *Past and Present* for their insights into segments of my research that have appeared in those journals. Bill Lewry graciously provided his father's stunning photograph for the book's cover; and Don Pirius Cartographic Services created the map. Many thanks to Michael Engelbach for permitting me to quote from the private papers of H. St. John Philby and to the family of David Hogarth for allowing me to cite the Hogarth collection.

I owe my greatest debt to my friends and family, especially my brother and sisters, who lovingly and often hilariously sustained (and tolerated) me for the duration of this often consuming and seemingly endless process. I thank my parents for giving me my first taste of the enchantment of the past and making it possible for me to make a career of perpetual pursuit of it. Their belief in me has been constant from my very first hesitant steps in the world of the written word that they always knew I wanted to enter. I owe a tremendous debt of gratitude also to my parents-in-law, not only for their love and example but for crossing the seven seas to look after Amann at her littlest, and the whole house too, so that I could finish my manuscript. My family in India, especially Mummyji, provided loving and memorable respite from Microsoft Word each year. Lastly and mostly, I want to thank Aprajit Mahajan for imperiling his very soul as an economist (a tribe disposed to classify history as a "consumption good") to cheer me on indefatigably, fight my battles with my computer, indulgently scrutinize countless drafts, assure me continually that the book will one day be done, and for everything else under the sun.

Contents

Note on Arabic Spellings, xiii

Reference Map, 2
Introduction, 3

Part I: War and Hope
1. The Foundations of Covert Empire, 23
2. The Cultural World of the Edwardian Agent, 59
3. The Failure of Empiricism and How the Agents Addressed It, 99
4. Cunning in War, 137
5. Imperial Expiation, 165

Part II: Peace and Terror
6. Official Conspiracy Theories and the Wagers of Genius, 201
7. Air Control, 239
8. Covert Empire, 263
9. Seeing Like a Democracy, 287

Conclusion, 329

Notes, 339
Selected Bibliography, 409
Index, 443

Note on Arabic Spellings

Throughout the text I have opted for common English spellings of Arabic words and names rather than the more precise formal transliterations of Arabic spellings. I have eschewed all diacritical marks for the sake of readability, with apologies to specialists in the field.

Spies in Arabia

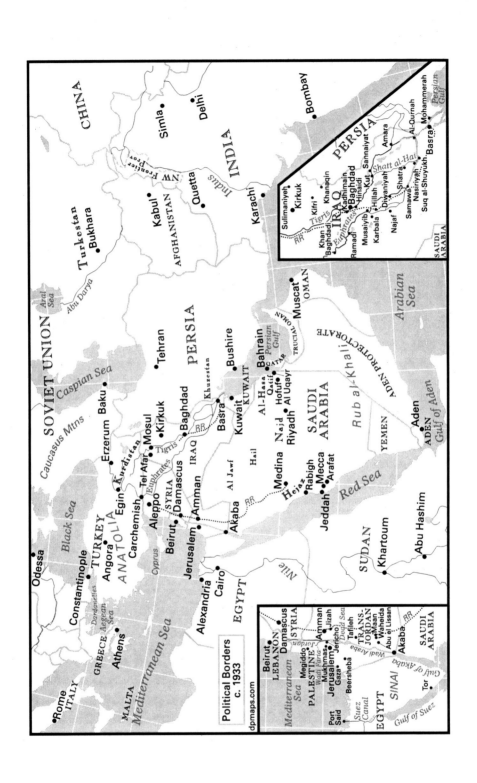

CHINA

Simla
Delhi
Bombay

INDIA

NW Frontier Prov.

Indus

Quetta

Kabul

AFGHANISTAN

Karachi

PERSIA

Sulimaniyeh
Kirkuk
Kifri
Khanaqin
Khan-i-
Baghdadi
Baghdad
Kadhimain
Hinaidi
Kut
Sannaiyat
Amara
Al-Qurnah
Mohammerah
Basra
Persian Gulf
RR
Tigris
Euphrates
Ramadi
Musaiyib
Hillah
Karbala
Diwaniyah
Samawa
Shatra
Nasiriyeh
Najaf
Suq al-Shuyukh
Shatt al-Hai

IRAQ

SAUDI ARABIA

Turkestan

Bukhara

SOVIET UNION

Abu Darya

Aral Sea

Tehran

PERSIA

Caspian Sea

Baku

Erzerum

Caucasus Mtns

Khuzestan

Bushire

Bahrain
Persian Gulf
QATAR
Qatif
Al-Hasa
Hofuf
Al Uqayr
KUWAIT
Kuwait

TRUCIAL

Muscat
OMAN

OMAN

Arabian Sea

ADEN PROTECTORATE

Rub al-Khali

Odessa

Black Sea

Constantinople

TURKEY

Angora

ANATOLIA

Dardanelles
Aegean Sea
GREECE

Athens

Rome
ITALY

MALTA

Mediterranean Sea

Cyprus

Mosul
Kirkuk
Tel Afar
Kurdistan
Egin
Carchemish
Aleppo
Beirut
SYRIA
Damascus
Jerusalem
Amman

Baghdad
IRAQ
Tigris
RR
Euphrates
Basra

Al Jawf

Hail

Najd
Riyadh
SAUDI ARABIA

Medina

Rabigh
Mecca
Arafat
Hejaz
Jeddah

Akaba

RR

Red Sea

YEMEN

Aden
ADEN
Gulf of Aden

Cairo
Alexandria

EGYPT

Nile

SUDAN

Khartoum

Abu Hashim

Political Borders
c. 1933

dpmaps.com

Mediterranean Sea

Beirut
LEBANON
Damascus
SYRIA

Amman
Jizah
TRANS-JORDAN
Maan
Waheida
Abu el Lissan
Akaba
RR
SAUDI ARABIA

Megiddo
PALESTINE
Mukhmas
Jericho
Jerusalem
Gaza
Beersheba
Tafileh

Jordan
Dead Sea
Wadi Faria

Wadi Araba
Gulf of Akaba

Port Said
Suez
Suez Canal
EGYPT
SINAI
Tor
Gulf of Suez

Introduction

I wonder why Arabia is the best-looking land, however you see it.
I suppose it is the name that does it.

—T. E. Lawrence, 1916

These gentlemen have formed a plan of *geographical morality*, by
which the duties of men ... are not to be governed by their relation to
the great Governor of the Universe, or by their relation to mankind,
but by climates, degrees of longitude, parallels, not of life, but of
latitudes: as if, when you have crossed the equinoctial, all the virtues
die ...; as if there were a kind of baptism, like that practised by
seamen, by which they unbaptize themselves of all that they learned
in Europe, and after which a new order and system of things
commenced.

—Edmund Burke, 1788

At the start of the twentieth century, British intelligence agents first
began seriously to venture into the region they knew as "Arabia." They
were drawn there by two objectives: the desire to secure the land route
to India and the hope of finding in a proverbially mystical and antique
land the metaphysical certainty they no longer felt at home. These
competing objects created a dilemma for them as agents: How were
they to gather practical information and serve the British state in a
region they were attracted to because of its legendary inscrutability
and promise of escape from Britain? The agents' grappling with this

conundrum in the era of the Great War and the manifold consequences of the tactical and methodological choices they made form the subject of this book. This is a story about a state that could not see, that depended on equivocal agents groping blindly through a fog of cultural representations about the new region it sought to control and the unique epistemological and technological remedies they evolved to soothe their consciences and cure their blindness. Their work cast a long shadow over imperial statecraft and metropolitan culture in the twentieth century.

How states see—or don't see—is, in my view, a matter intricately bound up with cultural history; it may even be that all states are unseeing, or at least intensely myopic, without the benefit of a cultural lens to bring into focus the otherwise elusive space and people they rule. In most instances, this is the lens that concentrates the illuminations of the Enlightenment into a shaft powerful enough to strip a place of all idiosyncrasy and opacity, rendering it universally intelligible, empirically graspable. There are other places, however, in which the modern state's knowledge-gathering practices are refracted through different cultural lenses, places deemed beyond the domain of the universally accessible, rational, secular world—perhaps, in Edmund Burke's terms above, those places beyond the equinoctial. Burke was writing about India in the era of the notorious trial of Governor-General Warren Hastings, but questioning the ways of the empire and the limits of universalism was again the fashion on the eve of the Great War, when the gaze of the British state had fallen intently upon the region known as the Middle East.[1] The story of British intelligence-gathering in the Middle East reveals the extent to which cultural representations mattered in the epistemological strategies the British state employed there and the extent to which the varying standards of the empire's "geographical morality" flowed from epistemological principles. This is a story of a state so conscious of the particular illegibility of the terrain it sought to control that it forsook empiricism for intuition, with critical consequences for both Britain and the Middle East as the war and its violent aftermath unfolded in the region.

I am interested in this book in piecing together the world of British intelligence in the Middle East. More importantly, however, I want to unpack the enduring fascination with Arabia as a spy-space which colored this British effort (and has perhaps even attracted readers to this book).[2] My focus is on the formation and fallout of the cultural imagination that shaped agents' approach and methods, rather than on the efficacy of the information order as such—on thinking about intelligence and agents' skills rather than on the agents' actual abilities (a subject better left to intelligence experts).[3] Nor is my purpose to hold British representations of Arab views up against the Arab reality but to demonstrate that the activities of the modern state are shaped by the cultural imagination.[4]

Indeed, given received wisdom about the power of European cultural representations of the Orient, the cultural formation of intelligence agents must lie at the heart of any effort to understand British intelligence-gathering in the Middle East. The cultural imagination mattered especially in a region conceived in its very essence as a space for the imagination. As it happens, the intelligence agents wandering in the Middle East were among those early-twentieth-century Britons questioning the reliability of sense perception at a time when what Weber famously called the "disenchantment of the world" had triggered an almost desperate interest in matters spiritual. These were not the obscure, anonymous intelligence workers of a later, more bureaucratic era, but social, political, and, in some cases, cultural elites emerging from a range of professional backgrounds, from military to diplomatic to scholarly. As a community, they shared almost without exclusion an intense literary ambition—many were prolific—and social contact with the British cultural and political establishments. Their personal searches for spiritual and cultural redemption, coupled with their practical difficulties in navigating desert topography, profoundly shaped their methods as agents, and their mixing with the worlds of letters and politics at home ensured that awareness of their work in the Middle East was diffuse. In a sense I am trying to bring the history of perceptions of the Orient together with the history of perception as such, for, the social world of Edwardian Britain ensured that imperial statecraft and metropolitan culture were mutually influential.

These agents' most important methodological innovation was an intuitive intelligence epistemology modeled on their understanding of the "Arab mind." Long immersion in the desert would, they thought, allow them to replicate the apparently intuitive knowledge-gathering and navigational practices of nomadic Arabs.[5] The premium this modus operandi placed on "genius" guaranteed them an enormous influence over the planning and execution of the Middle East campaigns of the Great War and over the postwar administration of the British-controlled Middle East. In the influence of their tactical imagination and epistemological outlook, this book argues, lies the explanation for the gradual transformation of British intelligence-gathering in the region from the informal, even accidental, work of world-weary Edwardians to the paranoid preoccupation of a brutal aerial surveillance regime after the war. If, as James Scott has recently urged, local knowledge can serve as an antidote to the imperialism of the modern state's flattening gaze, in this instance agents of the British state fetishized local knowledge as the foundation of a violent effort to render nomad terrain legible. Their story is a reminder that imperialism is a political relationship more than a perspective; intimacy does not make it go away.[6]

British intelligence in the Middle East was, in short, *different* from British intelligence projects in other parts of the world in this period. Certainly, British agents were also venturing into Germany, Japan, Persia, North America, India, and elsewhere. No other region, however, possessed such a combination of geopolitical cachet, cultural resonance, and utter unfamiliarity potent enough to indelibly mark intelligence practices and profoundly influence British popular and official culture. The intuitive mode was also a radical departure from the dogged empiricism of earlier and contemporary efforts to gather information in other regions perceived as essentially deceptive and disorienting, such as India, Australia, the Poles, and central Africa. Furthermore, the peculiarities of British relations with the Ottoman Empire and of the political organization of that empire meant that the intelligence project was itself interested in unique objects, as we shall see. Perhaps the most important evidence of the peculiarity of this intelligence project is Britons' frequent remarking of the fact, a theme that runs throughout what follows.[7]

To be sure, the British were not the only Great Power spying on the Middle East in this period; their concern about improving their intelligence sources was partly intensified by news of the exploits of Continental spies. An unsigned secret memorandum of 1909 among the papers of Vernon Kell, founder of the British Security Service (later MI5), urged the British state to emulate the German, French, Russian, and other foreign intelligence organizations in the lengths of deceit to which they were willing to go.[8] That said, in the end, no other European country sent as many agents or made as large a cultural investment in agents who went to Arabia. Nor did any other power eventually obtain a stranglehold over the region that allowed the logic of its intelligence system to play out in such dramatic ways. I am not making a claim for British cultural exceptionalism but for exceptional opportunity. Indeed, Germans shared many of the same cultural fascinations with the Middle East, but German withdrawal from the region after the war makes it a less useful case for exploring the relationship between those fascinations and statecraft. Russia's ultimate domination of Persia and Central Asia make a Russian version of the story more promising, not least for the light it might shed on what, if anything, is exceptional about the cultural fascinations with "Arabia" as opposed to the Middle East more broadly construed. The French story might also be usefully told, given the intensely brutal nature of postwar French rule in Syria, but the cultural significance of French agents in the Middle East is less clear. They never made the kinds of claims Britons, Germans, and Russians did to a special sympathy with the inhabitants of the region, and in British eyes at least, they were remarkably "clumsy." Historians, too, have called them "poor competitors"; in Edward Said's succinct phrase: "There were no French Lawrences or Sykeses or Bells."[9] In short, the British story is the big story about European intelligence-gathering and colonial control in the Middle East in the twentieth century, but its usefulness in helping us understand empire is general.

Thus, I am offering here a cultural history of the interwar British imperial state, of imperial information systems, the tactics of conquest, and the mechanisms of colonial rule, of how the colonial state sees, and the drastic steps it takes when it thinks it cannot see. Ultimately, as we shall see, the state that could not see became a state that could not be seen. The aerial surveillance regime in the Middle East was the ethereal outcropping of a style of imperial rule I call "covert empire." The constitutional monarchies established in the British Middle Eastern mandates after the war are usually classed as instances of "indirect rule," a style originally evolved in the Indian princely states.[10] This book argues, however, that the British did not so much rule through these potentates as sideline them for all matters pertaining to "imperial security"—a highly elastic rubric—by creating a parallel state, entirely informal and in the hands of intelligence officers who held real executive power. This was a new form of imperial rule, invisible, barely existing on paper, designed for an increasingly anti-imperialist postwar world, both at home and abroad. This was more than a case of the (unsuccessful) application of old imperial ideas—orientalist stereotypes, Indian experience, and so forth—in a new imperial space;[11] certainly there are continuities with the past, but there is also a historical specificity to British ideas about the Middle East and the style of imperial rule they underpinned. Racist constructions of Arabs go only so far in explaining the origins of the covert state and its technological infrastructure of air control, both considerable departures in British imperial practice. The explanation lies, I think, in British ideas about the kind of place Arabia was, historically contingent ideas informed by the cultural concerns of early-twentieth-century Britain and generating a commitment to a particular epistemological framework for knowing and governing the Middle East.

The Great War is the pivot of this story and must lie at the heart of any effort to understand the way affective knowledge informed state practice in the Middle East. It was the moment when the agents and their methods were bestowed with an official legitimacy and began to extend their reach into the realms of military operations and colonial administration. In recounting the story of the agents' growing influence within official circles, and, increasingly, with the public at home, this book inevitably expands our understanding of the military, political, and cultural legacy of the war—which has for the most part been understandably but nevertheless narrowly focused on the Western front—and of Britain's imperial project in the Middle East, of which we know very little beyond the apparently idiosyncratic popularity of Lawrence of Arabia.[12] If intelligence agents were shaped by the cultural anxieties of British modernity, British modernity was itself touched by the shadow of the surveillance tactics applied in the Middle East. The state's blindness was part of a wider contagion—as even the term, the "state," refers not to a discrete entity, but to "a whole network of people and institutions," a shifting organism whose assorted appendages are dispersed into the substrate of society.[13] I argue in this book that the cultural fascinations of the Middle East and of the agents who made their mark in it ensured that at a time when Britain hungered for heroes, imperial confidence, and the remains of a lost civilization, their traces could be found as much in contemporary literary modernism as in the romantic military tactics of the Middle Eastern theaters and the wartime turn to "development" as a means of reestablishing the constructive benevolence of the British Empire. Imperial expansion in and development of the Middle East helped blunt the sense of total rupture with the prewar past.[14]

In other words, in an increasingly mass democracy, how the state saw was a matter of public contention; the state's growing invisibility in the Middle East was partly intended to evade this political flashpoint. Covert empire came into its own in the Middle East *because* a self-assertive mass democracy was coming into its own in Britain; in this sense, too, did it differ from the older paradigm of indirect rule. In a postwar political moment shaped by the campaign to assert democratic control over the state—to make the institutions of the state a mere administrative machinery manned by an actually governing citizenry—some segments of the British public were desperate to see what their state was up to in the land of imperial redemption. As they squinted at the desert horizon for evidence of their government's good faith, a coarse critique of state secrecy gathering in their parched throats, they ensured not only that the state would twist into ever new shapes to avert and avoid their gaze, but that wider cultural perceptions of the Middle East would continue to shape its activity in the region. The point for my purposes is not whether ordinary Britons knew about or cared anything for their Middle Eastern empire but that there was a conversation about how much they knew, could know, should know—and why.

Thus, despite conventional wisdom about the relative absence of a culture of paranoid politics in Britain,[15] it was in fact doubly present: in the conspiracy thinking about "Eastern unrest" that underpinned the government's obsessive surveillance of the Middle East and in the public's growing suspicion of its government's covert imperial activity once the promise of an affordable developmental empire was proven false. In Britain, as on the Continent, political paranoia played a fundamental role in the unfolding of interwar violence—albeit displaced, in this case, onto colonial theaters—as the state strained under the triple burden of an increasingly recalcitrant empire, straightened means, and a critical public at home. Neither the exclusive intellectual property of the Right or the Left, political paranoia was the product of a certain epistemological outlook in which the intelligence agents at the heart of this book figured centrally, as servants of that state and symbolic proof of its ability to wage war and covertly conquer vast terrain by means of a single, intrepid genius.[16] This book thus seeks to illuminate some of the interwar ramifications of the British state's much-remarked "culture of secrecy" and the public's critique of it, particularly their joint influence on the shape of interwar empire, whose unique material and ideological forms have not been much recognized. Certainly, the critique evolved partly from an older tradition of populist working-class suspicions of a corrupt and conspiratorial state, a kindness returned by the state's habitual interpretation of domestic subversion as the work of foreign agencies, whether in the assumption of a French hand behind working-class discontent during the Napoleonic Wars, the fears of German espionage that produced the security state of 1909–11, or the paranoia about Soviet manipulation of labor and the British Communist Party between the world wars.[17] The cultural history of British intelligence-gathering in the Middle East reveals the centrality of the Arabian imaginary, and the particular epistemology it produced, to the interwar state's conspiracy thinking, even its focus on Bolshevism. What distinguished this moment of the state's and the public's mutual suspicions was its commentary on the democratic conditions of the postwar period. The apparent elusiveness and mystery of the region at issue permitted expression of the public's and the government's shared skepticism about the authenticity and viability of mass democracy from the moment of its inception. Britons insisting on democratic control, particularly over foreign policy, remained unconvinced that their assertions would translate into real power; they were less anti-imperialist than concerned about what the covert, because brutal, pursuit of empire did to democracy at home. By the same token, government officials, despite lip service to the principle, remained doubtful that an empire could be managed democratically without succumbing to manipulation by anti-imperial forces—the self-fulfilling anxiety that produced covert empire. This episode of political paranoia thus produced a powerful impact in both imperial state practices *and* domestic political culture. The covert and brutal form of interwar empire was a product of the British state's imbrication with wider British culture in its enthrallment to certain cultural conceptions about Arabia but also in its theoretical accountability to a democracy. This was not only a state that couldn't see but a *democratic* one in the throes of coming to terms with itself.[18]

In short, this book describes how particular intelligence and military practices and, ultimately, a particular kind of imperial state emerged from a particular cultural construction of the Middle East.[19] In doing so, it argues that violence and culture were more closely and literally allied in imperial rule than has generally been recognized. That Europeans derived power from cultural knowledge about the "Orient" is a commonplace; this book examines how representations shaped the practical knowledge-gathering projects of intelligence and surveillance in the Middle East. Recent literature has told us a great deal about the cultural violence done by the construction of colonial knowledge, in censuses, ethnographies, museums, and so forth. However, cultural representations also perform a more literal, physical kind of violence; Said argued from the outset that "representations have purposes,... they accomplish... many tasks." This is a book about how representations mattered in the creation of material structures of power in the Middle East, how they *functioned*, how they underwrote the horrific episode of state-sanctioned violence that was the air control regime.[20]

By attending to cultural conceptions, this story sheds light on the continuities between the violence of imperialism and total war, as urged in the recent work of Mark Mazower, Isabel Hull, Hew Strachan, and others.[21] Hannah Arendt long ago implicated the British secret agent in the origins of European totalitarianism, although ultimately acquitting the British Empire itself of the "real" horrors of the twentieth century:

> When the British Intelligence Services (especially after the First
> World War) began to attract England's best sons, who preferred
> serving mysterious forces all over the world to serving the common
> good of their country, the stage seemed to be set for all possible
> horrors.... The happy fact is that... cruelty played a lesser role [in the
> British Empire] between the two World Wars than ever before and a
> minimum of human rights was always safeguarded.[22]

It is time, I think, to reexamine received wisdom about the relatively benign nature of the British state and to begin to understand how British officials reconciled genuine ethical scruples with the actual violence of imperial policing in the Middle East. Indeed, there remains a tendency to belabor Britain's *relative* sanity, compared to the excesses of the Nazis, Soviets, and other goons of the twentieth century,[23] but this is an argument from false premises: it depends on uncritical acceptance of the empire's self-representation as the Solomonic creator of a rule of law to whose authority it humbly, gracefully, and yet patronizingly submitted even itself. But this "rule of law" was in many ways a Trojan horse of codified and normalized exceptions that underwrote the coercions, corruptions, expropriations, and various forms of abasement that made the empire possible. "Perversion of the law" (in Richard Price's phrase), including the rules of war and any notion of the rights of "civilians," was part of the empire's daily functioning; atrocity was endemic to the "policing," "pacification," "punitive expeditions," "counterinsurgency," and "small wars" (small in the manner that the Himalayas were "hills") that were routine aspects of imperial government, security, and expansion.[24] Air control, too, was a system of everyday violence. The crime was empire, air control merely its most technologically advanced instrument. This book strives to understand how Britons squared the belief that a unique ethical scrupulousness anchored their liberal empire and its compassionate counterinsurgency with the violent reality on the ground. These are weighty historical myths that continue to guide the unfolding of international military intervention. Some time after World War One, Britain forgot it was a "warfare state," David Edgerton has shown; even while pioneering offensive air warfare, it packaged its bomber as a force for peace. It is not, I think, incidental to this forgetting that British airpower first stretched its wings in the mythical terrain of Arabia; it is there that we must search for the door to oblivion.[25]

Given my cultural preoccupations, readers looking for a guide to British *policy* in the Middle East might instead look to the extremely rich and sophisticated historiography on that subject, cited throughout this work. While this book does seek to increase our understanding of some policies, such as air control and the decision to hold on to the Middle Eastern mandates, it is essentially about the realm of state *practice*—military, diplomatic, intelligence. It does not dispute the historiography on policy so much as provide a cultural-historical explanation of the particular institutional environment in which it was formed and in which the knowledge it was based on was assembled. It argues that intelligence is a product of far more than a few professionals' search for objective, if hidden, facts about another country. Its collation and interpretation occur in a far broader context than we have generally imagined, something our present discontents seem only to confirm. Information, its analysis, and its military and political fallout are culturally embedded phenomena.

A qualifying word about one of the key protagonists of this story is perhaps also in order. Scores of authors have minutely dissected T. E. Lawrence, although perhaps no one more than himself. I am less interested in the truth of his claims and his military insights than in the way contemporary Britons understood and valued them. Unique as he was in many ways, he was also a man of his time, and our understanding of him can only benefit from contextualization. I have tried here to embed the Lawrence phenomenon—both his self-fashioning and his popular reception—in the context of the cultural and political exigencies of early-twentieth-century Britain by restoring him to an ensemble cast in what is at one level a prosopography. As Lawrence himself put it, others "could tell a like tale": "My proper share was a minor one, but because of a fluent pen...I took upon myself...a mock primacy."[26]

As for my own epistemological practice—apart from the perhaps ironic intuition of a connection between prewar musings on Arabia's inscrutability and the postwar aerial surveillance regime—I have tried to tell this story about intelligence-gathering by drawing on an assemblage of intelligence records, correspondence, memoranda of the Foreign, India, Colonial, and War offices, the Air Ministry, and other official records, assuming that their language emerges out of a particular cultural formation, for, such documents are, in the last analysis, written by individuals shaped by a particular set of ideas and cultural concepts, a *mentalité*. My temporal focus has been fortunate in terms of source recovery in that intelligence was far from professionalized during much of the period. This means that intelligence reports, while not organized in an easily accessible manner, are usually not censored or blacked out when one does stumble upon them. Most wartime materials have been declassified, and where individual documents *were* blacked out, I was often able to find stray duplicates in the serial correspondence of the Foreign Office. As Yigal Sheffy has pointed out, many of the gaps in the paper trail are due to the actually ad hoc nature of intelligence collection in the Middle East in this early period and to the deliberate efforts to keep information within "a small circle of privileged functionaries 'in-the-know'"—I am partly after the history of these methodological predilections.[27] Interwar intelligence documents might have posed a more difficult problem, as it was then that the permanent peacetime organizations of MI5 and MI6 fully came into their own. Indeed, files containing documents about such arrangements sometimes end abruptly, with the final decisions impossible to uncover. The enduring exceptionalism of intelligence practices in the Middle East, however, ensured that MI6 (then known as the Secret Intelligence Service) became active in the region only toward the end of my period, so that methodical mining of other departmental papers has proved successful for the postwar era as well. I have juxtaposed this wealth of official documents with personal papers and published works by the same individuals as well as novels, periodicals, publications of scholarly societies, and other contemporary literature relating to the questions these officials and agents were interested in. This range of archival material has enabled me to trace the epistemological change that marked official and popular thought about Arabia in this period, as well as some of the broader cultural, institutional, and political ramifications of that change. Still, this is a method not unrelated to the story at hand, as we shall see in the conclusion.

Of course, the very meaning of "intelligence" continued to change through-out this period, partly as a result of increased professionalization. In the beginning, it referred to information of any kind—whether secret or not—gathered by Britons of any kind for their government's perusal. By the end of the period, it included counterintelligence and deception and possessed a considerable military dimension. Part of my effort in this work is to trace the evolution in British understanding of and accommodation to the more violent and "ungentlemanly" aspects of intelligence-gathering.[28]

Let me also provide some geographical definitions. "Arabia" is a classical word whose initial and terminal "a's" seem to gesture in their purity of tone and open-endedness to all that is romantic, past, magical, and far away. The Britons I examine strove repeatedly to define the term but continued to use it imprecisely without much compunction, for what was the use of being precise about a region of shifting sands and people? Time and again, avowed experts on the region refrained from specifying its borders; some frankly stated, "no definite boundaries exist." The crudest definition was that it was the region made up of "all those eastern races which speak Arabic," an area inaccurately delimited as that between the Mediterranean, the Suez Canal, the Red Sea, and the line of the Tigris and the Persian Gulf. Some urged that the term be used to refer to a somewhat more expansive "Arabia of the Qu'ran." For many Britons, "Arabia" was the "land of Holy Writ, from Jerusalem to Babylon, and from Babylon to Shush." The one thing that was clear was that its "mentality" and "civilization" were vastly different from India's. It gestured to the sublime in a way that India and even Persia could not; comparing it to the latter, Lawrence judged it "the better": "Persia is all hills and looks wet." All other bounds remained contentious. At times, Yemen was the quintessence of Arabia, at times "a world apart." Some agents determined Anatolia was neither ethnographically nor geographically part of Arabia but still thought of Constantinople as the gateway to Arabia, a political and spiritual capital for Arabs who might never venture elsewhere in Anatolia. Egypt and the rest of North Africa were also off and on part of this imaginary; Cairo, like Constantinople, figured as an island city where Arabs mixed with others in a borderland. In general, "Arabia" connoted a vaguely defined desert domain of Bedouin; it had coasts—on the Red Sea and the Persian Gulf—but near the Mediterranean it became something else. In intelligence contexts, it initially bled into Africa and Persia but was eventually reined in from those regions for practical reasons. Defining it was ultimately deemed a somewhat "academic question," for topographic and ethnographic continuity belied any attempt at drawing lines in the sand. During the war, however, the problem acquired a practical urgency. If more people began to appreciate the question, the answer remained elusive, with dire consequences that are still being played out. I am referring here to the infamous correspondence in which Henry McMahon, the British high commissioner in Cairo, and Sherif Hussein, ruler of the Hejaz, attempted to define the borders of the "Arabia" that Hussein's followers would inherit in exchange for their help in ousting the Ottomans from the region. The deliberate imprecision of these exchanges ensured that various powers in the Middle East would remain in intractable disputes ever after. To be sure, the borders were only vaguely defined partly because they were only vaguely known—ignorance serving Machiavellian politics. It became, in Lawrence's wry phrase, "indiscreet only to ask what Arabia is."[29]

"Arabia" was, however, a word with more than a cartographic definition. It was a geographic and cultural imaginary, "a country of the mind more real than any place on a map," as Kathryn Tidrick puts it. In what follows, I use the word in that cultural sense, as a signifier for the land of mirage, myth, and imprecise borders that the British imagined it to be, but when I speak of the places in which the practical effects of its influence on the British imagination were felt, I am referring essentially to the region comprising present-day Jordan, Syria, and Saudi Arabia, but most especially Iraq, as I track the gaze of the postwar British state homing in on what it took to be the "key to the future" and the centerstage of global conflict. I venture into Egypt, Palestine, and Lebanon only when the agents' activities in the wider region take them there. Kurdistan also lingers at the margins of this story, reflecting its position in the geographic imaginary of Arabia.[30]

The "Middle East" was an equally fraught neologism that tended to spill willy-nilly over the borders it was assigned. Coined in 1902 by the American Captain Mahan in the British *National Review*, it referred to "those regions of Asia...bound up with the problems of Indian...defence."[31] Those exercised by the newly christened "Middle Eastern Question" were at pains to explain why they could not refrain from investigating the Young Turks, Korea, and Persia too, given the impossibility of confining the "political interests of the Middle East within their geographical boundaries." Indeed, at the most fundamental level, the "Question" was inspired by the region's dangerous lack of geographical discipline. The East "all hangs together," in the epigrammatic words of Gertrude Bell. Sir Mark Sykes warned his colleagues in Parliament in 1913: "The break-up of the Ottoman Empire in Asia must bring the powers of Europe directly confronting one another in a country where there are no frontiers....That very awkward geographical situation troubled the mind of Alexander the Great, the mind of Diocletian and the mind of Constantine." He thus summed up both the geopolitical quandary posed by the region and the epic proportions in which the British conceived the struggle for hegemony in it. This was "a

Debatable Land... prone to involve in its own unrest those responsible for the peace of the world," warned the eminent David Hogarth; it was a no-place, a mere "thoroughfare... between the West and the West-in-East."[32] For what it may be worth, the domain of the Middle East Department established at the Colonial Office after the war included the Arabian peninsula, the mandates in Palestine, Transjordan, and Iraq, but *not* Syria, Persia, or Egypt, although this was likely as much for practical reasons as for any pedantic attempt at precision.

The frantic efforts to define the "Middle East" and "Arabia" signal the general apprehension at the turn of the century of a new need to reckon with the region between Europe and South Asia. Up to that point, the relatively poor establishment of British military intelligence had been partially compensated by the sheer size of the empire, which stretched Britain's diplomatic tentacles to all the corners of the world. Its enormous network of expatriates and loyal imperial citizens formed an information system critical to the empire's power and stability. The turn-of-the-century war in South Africa irrevocably shattered faith in this ad hoc system. A protracted affair during which guerrillas almost managed to bring the British military to its knees, it made intelligence reform an urgent matter. Whitehall responded immediately with the creation of a new Directorate of Military Operations in charge of intelligence. Many of the nervously flitting eyes in this nascent security state began to settle on the Middle East, for two reasons.[33]

First, the rise of German power and imperial ambition had manifestly altered the geopolitical balance by the turn of the century. Germany was aggressively pursuing closer relations with the Ottoman Empire, Britain's traditional ally, and through its dominance of the Baghdad Railway project, from which the British retreated in 1901, continually provoked British insecurities about the route to India. This was a pivotal moment: in 1904, the geographer Halford John Mackinder famously named that wedge of "Euro-Asia which is inaccessible to ships, but in antiquity lay open to the horse-riding nomads, and is to-day to be covered with a network of railways," the "pivot region of the world's politics." The geopolitical centrality of the Middle East was partly heralded by the relative calm in old zones of inter-imperial contest: the Anglo-Russian Convention of 1907 and the Entente Cordiale of 1904 diffused Great Game tensions in Central Asia and "Fashoda mentality" in Africa.[34]

The second factor urging improved intelligence-gathering in the Middle East were the political rumblings within the Ottoman Empire. Burgeoning Arab nationalist movements such as Sayyid Talib's in Basra, the rise of new provincial rulers such as Abdul Aziz ibn Saud in Najd, and the Young Turk revolution recommended diplomatic preparation for the demise of the allegedly long "sick man of Europe," lest, as Sykes feared, the various empires—Russia, Britain, British India, British Egypt, France, and Germany—found themselves facing each other across a no man's land. This required knowing something about the emerging provincial powers. To be sure, the old diplomatic priorities, like the sick man, had not yet expired: an Anglo-Turkish Accord of 1901 committed both parties to the status quo. Even this, however, recommended more intensive intelligence-gathering, for, as the British chargé d'affaires in Constantinople put it, "it is somewhat hard to say at the present moment what is the true state of affairs in the Nejd." At the same time, creeping actions behind the scenes—like the secret British arrangements with Sheikh Mubarak of Kuwait—undermined the status quo and stoked Ottoman paranoia about British commitment to the accord. The Ottomans banned British travel in the region, just when Britain was growing keen to know more about it—a move with which some British officials, long sensitive to interlopers in the North West Frontier, sympathized. That their imperial alliance was foundering was most blatantly evident in the Taba affair of 1906, when threats were exchanged during the joint effort to delineate a British-Ottoman border in the Sinai peninsula.[35]

Thus, the lack of knowledge about this geopolitically crucial zone was increasingly remarked after the turn of the century and the time deemed a fitting one for "taking stock of knowledge." In 1901 and 1903, official proposals to expand intelligence into the peninsula were seriously entertained for the first time, if ultimately postponed in view of the region's "disturbed" condition. Following the Gulf tour of Indian Viceroy Lord Curzon, a new Political Agency opened at Kuwait, specifically to address intelligence needs, and the Indian government's twin projects of the *Gazetteer of the Persian Gulf, Oman, and Central Arabia* and a new map of Arabia were launched. Geographical exploration of Arabia received a new impetus. Douglas Carruthers, a naturalist and agent who traveled in the peninsula in 1909, would later write:

> The era of the Great Arabians from Ibn Batuta to Doughty and
> Huber was complete in itself. There followed a long pause during
> which no voice spoke of the great desert peninsula.... Unwittingly
> I was to open up the second phase of Arabian exploration, which
> culminated eventually in the part Arabia played in the Great War,
> and the almost exaggerated interest aroused since then in all things
> appertaining to Arabia.

Arabia emerged on, indeed dominated, the British stage in the period after the turn of the century. It is thus then that I begin my story.[36]

The turn of the century also signaled a new era for Britons at home. The end of the South African War and of Victoria's reign heralded a new epoch. The incipient rise of the new security state was formalized with the 1909 foundation of the secret service and the 1911 Official Secrets Act. Mirroring the new appreciation for the need to develop British intelligence systems, the spy emerged for the first time as a heroic figure in novels like Rudyard Kipling's *Kim* (1901) and Erskine Childers's *The Riddle of the Sands* (1903), entwining his cultural and institutional careers from the outset. These developments were part of a new cultural fascination with investigation, also manifest in journalism, social investigation, and police work. One of the period's most prominent social investigators, the playwright Florence Bell, was stepmother of the agent Gertrude Bell, with whom she carried on an intimate correspondence throughout the period (her edited volumes of Gertrude's letters appeared after the latter's death in 1926). Her husband, the steel magnate Hugh Bell, introduced Gertrude to travel in the Middle East. Gertrude's *The Desert and the Sown* and Florence's study of Middlesbrough, *At the Works,* both appeared in 1907. This was by no means an exceptional coincidence. After the war, the agent Wyndham Deedes embarked on social work in the slums of Bethnal Green. And, as we know, late-nineteenth-century and early-twentieth-century investigators of urban Britain drew on the vocabulary of imperial explorers and were invested in tactics of cultural immersion, masquerade, and "intrapsychic incorporation," as Judith Walkowitz has put it. This taste for deceptive practices was but London's homage to the investigatory world from which they were seen to have derived and which was their primary setting. The whole culture of turn-of-the-century social investigation was orientalized, as Seth Koven has recently pointed out: "street arab" and "nomad" were common synonyms for the homeless, and incognito investigators dubbed their work "going 'Haroun Al Raschid,'" after the Baghdadi caliph of the *Arabian Nights* who nightly masqueraded as a poor man to learn more about his subjects' needs.[37]

Despite these tactical similarities, intelligence-gathering in the Middle East remained a world apart epistemologically. As Walkowitz points out, social investigatory work of this period continued to aspire to the "'grand tradition of English empiricism', which assumed that facts spoke for themselves, that they were perceived by the senses and gathered by an impartial mind." It remained allied with the classificatory impulse that drove the rising interest in criminology and anthropology as disciplines integral to the process of defining social and cultural identity.[38] The agents in this book were certainly also animated by a positivistic ambition, but one adulterated by other intellectual motives: their very desire to travel in a region that seemed to defy all fixity in its places, persons, and information was the mark of their engagement with the cultural and epistemological questioning of an avant garde increasingly suspicious of Victorian positivism. That their intelligence project was shaped by the intellectual trends that informed new attitudes toward knowledge more generally is one of the arguments I press in this book, although the agents themselves were always careful to attribute their methodological choices to the stage on which they worked. Their work thus acquired its own cultural significance as a special, Arabian strand of contemporary grappling with epistemological questions.

While these various domestic and international factors set the stage for the start of this story of intelligence-gathering in Arabia, its end remains elusive. At some level, we are still witnessing its unfolding climax, as similar fascinations with Arabia continue to guide both the tactical imagination governing the U.S. and British war in the Middle East and the post-9/11 conversation about the apparent practical and epistemological peculiarities of intelligence-gathering there. Nevertheless, the tale of the *genesis* of the unseeing British state in the Middle East unfolded in a discrete time period and distinct social, cultural, economic, and political context, before its repercussions began to echo down the tunnels of time. This was the period when Britain was paramount in a region of inchoate states, before the political and economic crisis of 1931, before Iraq joined the League of Nations as an ostensibly independent country in 1932, and before the emergence of the modern state of Saudi Arabia and the rise of the American star in the peninsula in 1933. These events were all linked in some way to the emergence of oil as the central geopolitical concern in the region.

Certainly, oil had long been a growing concern, motivating much of the imperial interest in the region. The Anglo-Persian Oil Company on the Persian Gulf was an asset requiring protection immediately upon the outbreak of war in 1914; the suspected oil wealth of Mosul ensured its inclusion in British-mandated Iraq after the war; oil concessions were a critical component of the negotiations leading to Iraq's "independence" in 1932; and foreign oil prospectors were a constant source of unease to British officials anxious to maintain exclusive surveillance of the region. However, oil began to flow in Mosul only near the end of our period, was discovered in Saudi Arabia only in 1933 under American auspices, and remained a decidedly secondary factor—after the Bolshevik threat and the security of the route to India—among those that made the Middle East a crucial sphere for intelligence-gathering in the early twentieth century. When Britons talked about the promise of Iraqi wealth during and after the war, they were almost always talking about its agricultural potential as a restored granary of the world. In 1921, just after serving as civil commissioner in Iraq, Arnold T. Wilson attested publicly that "there is oil in Mesopotamia" but that it would be unwise to "bank too much" on it; the infrastructure required to extract it was so complicated that "we must wait, perhaps a long time."[39]

Bookended by the turn of the century and the turn of the imperial tide, the story will unfold in two parts. The first, covering the period through the war, describes how British hopes for spiritual, cultural, and, eventually, military redemption in the Middle East found fulfillment in the emergence of an intelligence community whose peculiar methods and unique wartime achievements shimmered with the aura of authentic heroism at a time when it was most desperately needed. Part II tells the story of the terrors unleashed when, following postwar rebellion in the region, the scales fell from the eyes of the British state and public. As hopes for redemption were dashed, the petrified British state turned to the agents for help in devising a regime of terror in the Middle East, and the British public began to fear for the soul of their state.

PART I

War and Hope

I

The Foundations of Covert Empire

As the Pentagon takes on new roles collecting intelligence, initiating information operations and conducting other "self-assigned missions,"...some embassies have effectively become command posts, with military personnel in those countries all but supplanting the role of ambassadors in conducting American foreign policy.

—*New York Times*, December 20, 2005

The new focus on intelligence resulted eventually in the 1909 establishment of a Secret Service Bureau under Mansfield Smith-Cumming ("C"), in charge of overseas intelligence-gathering, and Vernon Kell ("K"), in charge of domestic counterespionage. The Middle East, however, remained beyond the pale of this system. With official efforts to gather intelligence constrained by the policy of maintaining the status quo, intelligence in Arabia went underground rather than simply undercover. Its practitioners emerged from a variety of backgrounds because the British were interested not only in military and diplomatic developments in the Ottoman Empire but also in the ethnography, territories, history, and languages of the various political forces likely to emerge from its rubble, if and when it crumbled. In the shadow of official policy, in a semicovert and thus semiautonomous sphere, the diplomatic, administrative, and military representatives of the Indian and British governments and an assorted group of civilians formed a community whose bonds crossed departmental lines and whose common interest succeeded in emasculating official directives against intriguing in the Middle East.[1] This chapter describes the coalescence of this community before and during the war; their methods and objects will be the focus of a later chapter.

The Prewar Intelligence Community

As elsewhere, the administrative machinery of the empire was the primary source of intelligence on the Middle East, but there the overlap of the administrative spheres of the London and Indian governments complicated things: the Indian government's Residencies and Political Agencies were, in many cases, also posts in the British government's Levant Consular Service.[2] This service extended to Ottoman Europe in the north, the Arabian peninsula in the south, Morocco in the west, and Mesopotamia in the east. Now, consuls everywhere were responsible for producing commercial intelligence and protecting British citizens in their districts, but in the Ottoman Empire they were also entrusted with political functions, including collection of political intelligence, normally left to the more prestigious diplomatic service—since working with "Oriental" authorities in any capacity was held to require "all the tact and intimate knowledge of men that are supposed to be the essential qualifications of the trained diplomatist." Officials also gained flexibility by serving two masters; the Baghdad Residency, for instance, had been established in the eighteenth century to serve intelligence needs generated by Great Power rivalry, and when London incorporated it in the consular service in the 1830s, it retained its original functions. Consulates in the Ottoman Empire were also larger, more numerous, and more lavishly appointed than could be justified by the needs of the few British people in the region because of the extraordinary judicial and administrative responsibilities stipulated under the Capitulations and the perceived need for frequent consular intervention in a society not "constituted on the basis of European civilization." The range of new developments that required watching and the closure of the area to most European travel made the consuls even more vital to intelligence. "I trust that the momentousness of the parting of the ways which has been reached in the history of the Middle East will be held to justify my remarks," J. G. Lorimer, consul-general at Baghdad from 1910 to 1914, prefaced one of his many unsolicited reports. "They perhaps go beyond the ordinary scope of a local representative." The Levant service emerged in this period as the most prestigious service for prospective recruits; new consulates were opened with alacrity all over the region.[3]

The very density of the consulates helped transform them into intelligence centers. Having little to do—few Britons to assist—consuls filled their time with intelligence, at times creating minor diplomatic incidents. "I often wish we had no vice consul at Mosul," wrote the chargé d'affaires in Constantinople, for he "has nothing to do and so gets into scrapes...and all with the best intentions in the world." In a manner recalling their predecessors on the Indian frontier, bored consuls frequently endangered the official policy of non-entanglement. Still, the Foreign Office felt consuls could with considerable impunity attend to certain intelligence tasks, such as geographical surveying, which it considered, somewhat disingenuously, a harmless scholarly task. Crucial as it was that a consul "not be caught by the Turks sketching fortresses or making maps even in his own consular district," it was also true, the ambassador explained to the foreign secretary, Sir Edward Grey, that "the case of one of HM's [His Majesty's] consular officers undertaking a journey within...his own district is very different from that of a British military officer travelling in Mesopotamia for a special purpose...which may...give rise to a certain amount of suspicion in a country...as sensitive to the idea of foreign penetration as Turkey." By quietly relying on consuls for intelligence, the Foreign Office rendered the ban on military officers in Mesopotamia a merely formal gesture. Hesitating to admit topographical work was objectionable, the office pushed it into the realm of undercover work because it was, after all, objected to.[4]

Consuls took enthusiastically to this work, taking it well beyond the realm of their tours. We find, for instance, the Baghdad consul asking a friend, "a scientific man and not a politician," to pick the brains of the officers on a Hamburg American ship he would board in Basra and transmitting the resulting notes on German designs to the Foreign Office. Consuls called on their staffs and each other for such sleuthing purposes and took initiative in mapping and recording conversations with Great Power rivals. Some developed enduring relationships with informants reporting on various Arab potentates and German agents.[5]

To these agents, there remained a blurry but critical line between such work and "intrigue," between being a spy and an agent provocateur. Their object, the secret collection of information about commerce, geography, and politics, remained unimpeachable, unlike that of their rivals—gathering information with a view to *altering*, rather than merely observing the situation. In view of the Anglo-Turkish Accord, the avowed object of British intelligence was merely ascertaining the "status quo," despite the fact that their new interest in gathering intelligence stemmed from a perception that the status quo was in great flux. When a sheikh from Hofuf sought British protection in an uprising against the Turks, the political agent in Bahrain explained haughtily that it was not his government's custom to intrigue with the subjects of a sovereign, friendly state but added that the sheikh could write to him, for "I would be glad always to receive any authentic news of the interior." Hence also the objections of the government's Gulf resident at Bushire to sending an intelligence agent to Najd: even if he were sent "without any political mission," the Turks and local potentates would see it as an open commitment to Ibn Saud. Such scruples, British officials thought, separated them from the rest: the vali of Basra complained to the consul, F. E. Crow, of the Arab nationalist Sayyid Talib's incessant "consorting with foreign consuls to bring about a state of things which will end in a revolution."[6]

Still, it was disingenuous of Crow to presume that the vali's denunciation excluded him, for, when a sheikh of the Beni Lam visited him in secret to request British protection against the Turks, he was hardly discreet in his enthusiasm, warning his superiors that "a rebuff might cost us dearly if their plans materialize." Indeed, British consuls were not always successful in keeping to the straight and narrow in intelligence-gathering, as others noted: Lorimer at one point took an American consul and engineer on tour to show them his work was "of a perfectly open and above-board character" and dispel the impression "that it consists chiefly in political intrigues—Heaven knows for what purpose—with Arab sheikhs and Persian mujtaheeds." However, as he knew well, the vice-consulate at nearby Karbala had been established in 1903 for the very purpose of acquiring influence over the Persian mujtahids there, and thus over Persia. So it is no surprise that consuls' frequent protestations about the innocent nature of their travel and talk did not impress Turkish officials, whose suspicions were potent enough to interfere with even their ostensibly legitimate work. Consuls convinced themselves, at least, that they merely *appeared* to intrigue because of Arabs' inveterate habit of drawing them into subversive conversations to elicit sympathetic responses, which they broadcast "in a garbled form."[7]

"Special duties" did disrupt the consuls' regular work. The Foreign Office defended Lorimer against the Lynch Steamship Company's complaints of his lengthy absences (approximately half the year) by explaining that they were due to special duty rather than incompetence or neglect. At times, however, the Foreign Office did express unease about the increasing intimacy between consuls and the military intelligence establishment, which threatened to upset their own more delicate manipulation of their men on the spot. One such official insisted, "I don't think military attachés should call on consular officers for information, to obtain which they have to make hazardous journeys, without the knowledge of the head of the mission." But consuls were themselves committed to an intelligence-gathering role: the particular journey the official objected to was *not* in fact undertaken at the military attaché's illicit request but on the consul's own initiative. As the distinctly unrepentant consul put it,

"Consuls have often to make journeys in wild regions where no one else would go." The Foreign Office's prudish attitude toward intelligence-gathering further obscured the position of the Levant consuls, leaving much of the initiative to them, and pushing the work further undercover, so that even the Foreign Office did not know who directed it.[8]

The consul and political agent at Kuwait, Captain William Shakespear, was central to the tightening of the community of Middle East intelligencers across departmental and governmental lines. The remarkable expertise of his tour reports and his success at establishing friendly relations with local sheikhs attracted the attention of Indian Army intelligence officers in Simla, who requested, "If you have an opportunity of doing anything when you happen to be on tour we shall be very much indebted for your efforts." The Indian government informed the Gulf resident, "Political Officers may correspond with Intelligence Branch on matters relating to a) details of routes, b) enquiries of a specially secret character respecting persons employed...for reconnaissance purposes." Shakespear's connection with Simla put the imperial intelligence work of political agents on a more regular footing.[9]

So too did Lorimer's *Gazetteer of the Persian Gulf, Oman, and Central Arabia*, an encyclopedic project undertaken by the Indian government to update its information on the Middle East. Ultimately running to thousands of pages and encompassing a historical section and a geographical dictionary, it was the impetus behind the surge in consular touring in the period. Percy Cox, as Gulf resident, helped Lorimer coordinate the project, asking local officials to send him copies of their tour reports. The iterative process tightened the bonds between the nascent community of consuls and Indian political officers. For instance, for the Iraq section Lorimer first toured Zubair, Basra, Baghdad, Musaiyib, Karbala, and Hillah, then added information gathered by Colonel L. S. Newmarch, Baghdad resident in 1905, and other consuls in Iraq. The resulting draft of the topographical article was sent to local officers and the embassy for revision, producing so much new material that the entire work was redrafted and revised by the new resident, Major Ramsay. The imperial bureaucracy provided a framework in which local information acquired its proper significance and place, while personal contacts, frequent rotation in posts, and tours of contiguous hinterlands generated an increasingly full map and fostered independent communication networks among regional officials. Shakespear was frequently in touch with Lorimer "through a newsletter which circulated only to the most trusted of their colleagues." The Basra consulate remained in "demi-official" touch with Lorimer and Shakespear, who was also in regular contact with the Royal Indian Navy in the Gulf and with Colonel Francis Richard Maunsell, the former military attaché in Constantinople now employed at the Directorate of Military Operations (DMO), although mostly to be found in the map room of the Royal Geographical Society. The *Gazetteer* also provided cover for more illicit missions such as the otherwise unauthorized peninsular exploration by Captain F. Fraser Hunter of the Survey of India. Lorimer himself took advantage of the opportunity to explore sensitive political questions. "I have been put on another job outside the gazetteer," he told Cox in 1906, "one however which works in with one of my appendices, viz., that on religions: the subject is pan-islamic activity." He soon roped other consuls into this project. The community was developing its own investigative momentum, agenda, and methods of communication.[10]

Military organizations, as already suggested, were fast becoming part of this mix. Despite the commitment to intelligence reform, a peacetime military intelligence corps remained elusive as long as the British military establishment (unlike the French and German) remained unsure who its next enemy would be. In the interim, the military attaché at the embassy was, in the words of Alfred Vagts, "the most advanced, most open, most permanent observer for his home service abroad," and Constantinople was the fulcrum of the imperialist competition these agents waged. Although attachés were generally not expected to engage in "secret service," this rule was not strictly enforced in Constantinople, where British attachés were known to travel extensively and provide considerable information to their government. Maunsell, attaché from 1901 to 1907, was critical to the invigoration of intelligence in the Ottoman Empire. He coordinated compilation of the DMO's new *Military Report on Syria*, which replaced the old *Military Report on Arabia*. His successor, Major Tyrell, also interpreted his job description loosely, acting unilaterally in his relations with consuls and the ambassador, who invariably excused—even facilitated—his unauthorized trespasses into the diplomatic domain.[11]

Maunsell compiled the secret guide in collaboration with the Admiralty, the honorary attachés at the embassy (of whom more later), and a handful of other agents best described as "special duty" officers, usually run by the DMO but as likely affiliated with Cairo or Indian intelligence or the Admiralty. When, in 1907, the Indian chief of staff intimated "an opportunity 'for non-official travellers to explore inner Arabia,'" particularly civilians traveling as businessmen, the DMO turned primarily to military officers on leave, such as Gerard Leachman of the Royal Sussex Regiment, who had just arrived in London overland from India. He was followed by the naturalist Douglas Carruthers, Captain C. M. Gibbon of Simla intelligence, Richard Meinertzhagen from Quetta Staff College, Ely Soane (formerly of the Imperial Bank of Persia and at one time a vice-consul in Persia), Captains S. S. Butler and Leycester Aylmer from East Africa, Indian Army officers Norman Bray and Hubert Young, Captain Stewart

Newcombe of the Royal Engineers, and several others. These individuals often traveled under the cover of the Survey of Egypt. Indeed, Middle Eastern policy and intelligence was, to be entirely precise, caught between three rather than two imperial governments: Lord Kitchener, the Egyptian high commissioner, and Reginald Wingate, sirdar of the Egyptian Army, together directed an intelligence network extending all over Africa and western Arabia. Special duty officers from Egypt were also likely to travel under cover of the Palestine Exploration Fund (PEF), whose devotion to the study of the Holy Land compelled its support of military contributions to that study—it had sponsored Kitchener's survey of Sinai in the 1870s, a treasure for Biblical scholars *and* military geographers. Special duty agents, positioned by their status and geographies in the interstices of the military establishments of India, Britain, and Cairo, formed the nomadic core of the Middle East intelligence community. To be sure, British intelligence in other parts of the world, like Germany, was also conducted semiofficially and by amateurs, even within the overarching organization under C. What set the Middle East community apart were its interdepartmental and intergovernmental ties, which allowed agents to draw on a wide array of institutional resources and establish their own contacts, priorities, and distinctive techniques. Just as the world's great empires collided in the Middle East, so too did the governments of the British Empire, and out of that collision emerged a contact zone for various functionaries with overlapping interests in intelligence about Arabia.[12]

Instructions issued to these officers demanded silence about their true assignments. The officer "should understand that he...can only be considered as traveling on his private affairs." Given the casual nature of intelligence-gathering and intelligence employments, it is difficult to discern which officers were thought of as agents, as opposed to ordinary officers patriotically passing on information that happened to come to hand. The naturalist G. Wyman Bury said paradoxically of his work in Aden, "I was traveling unofficially (in connection with certain matters pertaining to Intelligence)." Although agents' work was undertaken "on behalf of the government," they were, as Bury put it, "invariably without official sanction and liable to repudiation if involved in difficulties, even when actually carrying out government orders or instructions." Needless to say, they also usually went without special pay since most were technically "on leave."[13]

Unsurprisingly, the Foreign Office was not entirely supportive of these War Office interlopers. While it expected diplomats to collect intelligence from within their offices, through their intercourse with their foreign counterparts, and by limited touring, it looked less benevolently on intelligence work of a purely footloose sort. Its sensitivity to Turkish suspicions caused it on several occasions to refuse even those requesting permission to travel for ostensibly unobjectionable purposes, fearing not only that such journeys "might act as an encouragement to other travellers, with less innocent objectives in view," but that "an assumed obligation to protect [the prospective traveler] might serve the Porte as a pretence for asserting or reviving claims in portions of Arabia which HMG [His Majesty's Government] do admit them." The Foreign Office could not risk exposing the fraud of British support of the Ottomans. The case of Captain Teesdale illustrates how widely the Foreign and War Office views diverged: When a Turkish gunboat caught him wandering around Mesopotamia in Arab dress, the Foreign Office asked the India and War offices to deny all permission for such journeys in the future; but Tyrell, articulating War Office priorities, commended Teesdale's enterprise, urging his name be "noted for employment on this sort of work in Turkey, should the occasion arise." Perhaps more importantly, the thing to note here is Teesdale's very presence in the region, which testifies to the intelligence community's collective ability to circumvent the interdepartmental contest for control over the gates to Arabia. As Baghdad resident in 1910, Lorimer reported several "tours by British military officers" stoking Turkish suspicions, "the more so that Mr. Leachman and Capt. Teesdale avoided observation as much as they could and wore Arab clothes"; two years later he reported, "British officers continue to arrive here on leave, and I generally know nothing of their presence in the country until they have left Basrah for Baghdad."[14]

These officers had used various ploys to circumvent Foreign Office orders. For instance, when Leachman was chosen as London's agent to Riyadh, rather than go through the proper channels—apply to Gulf Resident Cox for India's and London's unlikely approval—he met with Cox, then on leave in London, and arranged for Shakespear's private assistance near Kuwait. He departed with the authority of the War Office and the Indian General Staff and without having consulted the Foreign Office. This kind of subversion strengthened the unofficial bonds among the community of Middle East intelligencers, who saw it only as patriotism pragmatically exercised. Thus, in 1914, when Ibn Saud, trusting in Shakespear's then unofficial standing, showed the latter his confidential correspondence with local rivals, Shakespear passed his notes of the meeting to Whitehall, despite the fact that he had had to struggle against official obstruction to make the trip. His accompanying letter explained, "I did my best to discourage his confidence, seeing that I had no official status, but as he insisted they may now be useful."[15]

Determined agents also took advantage of the divided loyalties produced by the peculiar overlap of the Levant Consular Service with the Indian Political Service. Many consuls were willing to circumvent Foreign Office orders and facilitate illicit intelligence-gathering by taking shelter in the administrative blind spot created by imperial overlap. When the vali of Basra asked the consul, Crow, what Leachman was doing near the Shammar camp, Crow covered with: "He's an English dervish studying botany in the desert." DMO agents such as Norman Bray and Hubert Young began their researches by consulting local consuls; from Karachi to Baghdad, Leachman stayed with the consul at each stopping place, wandering into the desert from these safe havens. Lorimer was especially instrumental to such journeys, despite his concern about Turkish sensitivities: he had tried earnestly, he reported in 1910, to *prevent* the sudden departure at the vali's insistence of an Indian officer who had arrived in Baghdad to study Arabic and conduct surveys. He also dealt leniently with Teesdale and Leachman, despite the ambassador's request that they be suitably rebuked. He regularly recommended Leachman's reports to the Foreign Office as highly exciting and informative, affirming "[Leachman's] journeys have no other motive than love of travel and adventure." In one instance, he shielded Leachman and another officer by assuring the vali they were merely tourists and would avoid "the unprofitable discussions into which Arabs sometimes sought to draw them." Oddly, given that travel was still banned in the region, he hoped this assurance would end suspicion of officers "who are merely traveling within…the three vilayets or…on their way to Europe." In 1911, two more officers from India, apparently unaware of the prohibition against visiting Mesopotamia on leave, roamed freely, for, Lorimer explained, they had arrived before he knew of their coming and he had therefore not felt obliged to restrain them. The first, Gregson, was with the Punjab Police, employed on the Gulf arms blockade, and the second, Captain J. C. More, performed translation duties with the Indian General Staff; both later served in wartime intelligence. In 1912, Lorimer reported the arrival of two more traveling officers who were unaware of having transgressed any regulation and to deter whom he again did nothing.[16]

The Foreign Office was thus concerned not only with military authorities' transgressions but also with legitimate officials' disregard for their instructions. Shakespear proved to be one of the most intractable, and not merely because of Simla's blandishments. The breadth of his wanderings increased inexorably, as did the slack between his and the official line of noninterference. He was personally so intrigued by the new political force represented by Ibn Saud that he stole away on several occasions to meet him, without reference to his superiors and fully aware he was acting against his orders. By wartime, the Foreign Office suspected him and Cox of "all sorts of designs."[17]

Upon closer inspection, however, it appears that these agents connived to evade the Foreign Office with the Foreign Office's knowledge and perhaps even tacit approval. In 1910, when Stewart Newcombe, a Cairo staff officer on special duty, applied to travel in Mesopotamia, ostensibly to carry out irrigation and railway surveys, the Foreign Office deprecated the visit in view of Turkish suspicions. When he reapplied, asking merely to travel as a private individual, the Foreign Office remarked shrewdly, "We may assume that the purposes of the journey remain unchanged though the form of the application is modified." This suggests the Foreign Office knew the DMO was behind avowedly "private" requests and that some of the officers who slipped by must have done so because the Foreign Office turned a blind eye. This was not interdepartmental subterfuge; the intelligence community was being *allowed* to act autonomously, fulfilling unofficially tasks the Foreign Office could not consent to officially. While the Foreign Office was careful to ensure that it was, to all *official* appearances, doing its best to bar prospective travelers and agents from entering Ottoman territory, it knew some slipped by and, when push came to shove, protected them from the wrath of the Turkish government by retroactively upholding the fiction that their missions were harmless tourist and scientific enterprises. The very fact that officers continued to arrive in Basra and Baghdad without difficulty and apparently entirely unaware of the prohibition suggests the prohibition was somewhat nugatory. Stray remarks on particular cases betray this position. When Bury contrived to reach the desert in 1909, an India Office official noted privately that there were "obvious advantages to shutting our eyes" but that they had to act lest official silence be construed as consent. In 1905, when Turkish officials suspected Lorimer and Lieutenant Gabriel of designing to visit Najd to encourage Ibn Saud to resist a Turkish expedition gathering at Najaf, the British chargé d'affaires, having consulted the Foreign and India offices who were equally in the dark about the officers' plans but considered it entirely possible that they *could* be en route to Najd, whatever their approved itinerary, indignantly asserted that they were only collecting topographical information. The Foreign Office knew the community of intelligence-gatherers was silently, unofficially pursuing its goals, without their official knowledge but presumably with the unofficial knowledge of local consuls.[18]

The Foreign Office tolerated these missions because of its own desperate need for intelligence. They thought it "most unlucky," for instance, that Teesdale was caught in 1910, perfunctorily reminded the War and India offices not to allow such journeys, and then devoured his report, assailing only its more technical and military than political focus. In 1914, when Shakespear finally wrested permission to travel across Arabia as a private person, he was requested on his return to comment on official correspondence about Ibn Saud and submit reports to the Foreign and India offices. The government was in such earnest denial of its knowledge of the avowed purposes of these journeys that when Richard Meinertzhagen finally obtained permission for an *intelligence mission* in Mesopotamia, he was asked "in *return* for this permission...to collect information about road and river transport...the Railway." It would seem that if the Foreign Office sincerely wanted to stop British officers going to Mesopotamia, they might have empowered the Basra consul to turn back officers intending to travel without permission. The basic tension governing Foreign Office behavior was that between its growing impatience of an opportunity to promote intelligence work in an increasingly restive and important region and its obligation—to both the Ottoman government and the policy of paramountcy without entanglement—to combat that volatility by refusing entry to visionary foreigners nurturing dreams of revolution in Arabia. The organic formation of an unofficial community of intelligencers resolved this tension, ironically also giving agents nurturing such dreams a wider berth.[19]

On the eve of war, the balance of power in Arabia began to shift as a result of Ibn Saud's gains and Turkish losses at Hofuf and the coastal towns of Uqair and Qatif, and the Foreign Office's official scruples diminished. It yielded without much struggle to Hubert Young's request to travel in Turkish Arabia to practice languages for intelligence purposes. Hence also Shakespear's authorized private journey in 1914. The office also let Lieutenant E. W. C. Noel proceed to his post as second assistant to the Gulf resident via Baghdad, as "he would derive useful knowledge and experience from the journey." Matters were further simplified when the Turkish government recognized Ibn Saud as mutessarif of Najd, making visits to him legitimate. The diplomatic arm of the British government had also grown resigned to the fact that, "desirable as it may be not to throw open Central Arabia to exploration, it is probably not in the power of HMG to exclude any traveller who is determined to enter."[20]

In the meantime, another breed of agent had begun to venture into Arabia. The Foreign Office ban on travel ensured that the unofficial sources that had been the staple of nineteenth-century intelligence everywhere remained all-important in the Middle East into the twentieth century. Civilians provided the intelligence community with a range of institutional resources and a conduit for the exchange of official and scholarly knowledge about the region. The need for such agents grew partly from dissatisfaction with the consuls as too locally focused and DMO agents as too suspicious to the Turks. Indeed, it is hard to identify precisely which ordinary Britons traveling through Ottoman territory were working for their government, officially or unofficially; any Englishman in the region was a potential agent, as even the officials in the region knew. The very diversity of British commercial, industrial, and diplomatic life in the region helps maintain the ambiguity surrounding these individuals. While it would be anachronistic and simply inaccurate to label all of them intelligence agents, it is crucial to note the extent to which some of their efforts resulted in real intelligence gains to the government and the espionage-like behavior many of them indulged in just by virtue of being in the Middle East. T. E. Lawrence, for instance, collected "intelligence" about Kurdish insurgency near the archaeological site at Carchemish for reasons of "self-preservation."[21]

The honorary attachés at the embassy operated somewhere between designated and voluntary intelligence officers in Ottoman territory. George Lloyd, Aubrey Herbert, and Mark Sykes were all aristocratic Oxbridge graduates on their way to illustrious political careers. All three were drawn to Constantinople for its exciting place in the unfolding drama of European rivalry. Sykes had been used to traveling in Ottoman territories since childhood and, after the Boer War, worked his connections to obtain a post there. While there, whenever he traveled, whether for personal or official reasons, he compiled intelligence reports for the Foreign Office. Through his close personal friendships with Maunsell and Ambassador Nicholas O'Conor, he also drafted many embassy dispatches and reports outside his brief. He and Lloyd continued their travels—and their reporting—after their stints at the embassy.[22]

Journalists and businessmen also provided intelligence. Submitting notes on the Baghdad Railway to the DMO, David Fraser of the *Times of India* explained, "They told me in the WO [War Office] that you had practically no very recent information on the Anatolian railways, so I have embodied my notes...in the hope that they may be useful." The Lynch Company was sometimes the only source of information on both commercial *and* political developments in Mesopotamia. Rendel Harris of an Anglo-American industrial plant at Egin privately sent news of Kurdish unrest to Secretary Grey, assuring, "There is no need to trouble over a reply....I understand that I may send you from time to time information which may lie outside the view of our Consuls." When an American licorice exporting company sent an English representative to Mosul, the residency rejoiced that "he may be able to supply the Vice-consulate with valuable information." The Jewish Colonization Association in Paris sent agents to explore possible settlement areas, and their reports on Mesopotamia's economy, politics, and topography also found their way to Whitehall.[23]

Most legendary among civilian agents in Ottoman territory were the scholar-archaeologists whose work received a new impetus from both the European rivalry in the region and late-nineteenth-century revisions of received wisdom about the Bible. Many historians have claimed David Hogarth's team at Carchemish, including Lawrence, Leonard Woolley, and Reginald Campbell-Thompson, was more focused on the Baghdad Railway than on digging, but many of these claims have been refuted; archaeology was not merely cover for secret service work.[24] Nor, on the other hand, was it entirely innocent. It was partly funded by members of the PEF, on which Hogarth also served and which regularly underwrote intelligence activities masquerading as scholarly endeavors. Furthermore, archaeology was a prestige issue impinging on geopolitical considerations. The British ambassador saw the opening of a German vice-consulate at Mosul, ostensibly for the assistance of German diggers nearby, as a disturbing and "unmistakable symptom of the increasing interest of Germany in these regions." As resident, Lorimer, regretting the relative lack of British archaeologists in Mesopotamia, urged the India Office to request a learned society or private munificence to step into the breach, as it was crucial that no means of establishing British interests be neglected. Unsurprisingly, then, when they eventually began to embark on archaeological explorations in earnest, diggers and scholars maintained close relations with the intelligence network. Hogarth sent Gerald Fitzmaurice, chief dragoman at the embassy and something of a self-styled spymaster, copies of his museum reports, and Grey was a childhood friend through whom he kept the Foreign Office informed about German activity. He exhorted "wandering scholars" to interpret their brief ecumenically,

> for the Ottoman Empire has been shut against the West so long and
> so closely that...the Scholar had best take not too professional a view
> of his ostensible calling: maps and political reports, customs and
> types and folk-lore, eggs and bulbs and butterflies and rocks—all
> these fill his day with amateur occupations for which his professional
> interest is probably not the worse; for...catholicity will serve him
> even within the limits of Archaeology.

Intelligence-gathering fell comfortably and innocently within the wider domain of oriental scholarship.[25]

On at least one occasion, Lawrence and Woolley were engaged on a clearly defined military intelligence mission. In 1913, the DMO urged the Foreign Office to seek Turkish permission for an intelligence survey of Sinai by falsely applying in the name of the PEF. The PEF, which was informed only after the fact, recommended sending along an archaeologist, and the British Museum offered up Woolley and Lawrence, who remarked, "We are obviously only meant as red herrings, to give an archaeological colour to a political job." Their subsequent friendship with Newcombe of Cairo intelligence involved them in yet another mission. On their suggestion, Newcombe visited the dig on the excuse that the trip would yield useful information. From there, he traveled to the Taurus mountains to gather information on the Baghdad Railway, writing to his friends to follow his route to fill in any gaps. On the eve of war, Lawrence and Woolley were just finishing *The Wilderness of Zin* for the PEF, which

Kitchener, then Egyptian high commissioner, had ordered "pdq, as whitewash" and which they dedicated to Newcombe for showing them, as Moses did his flock, "the way wherein they must walk, and the work that they must do."[26]

Gertrude Bell's friendships in the upper reaches of Whitehall allowed her to fuse polite travel and amateur archaeology with (unpaid) information-gathering. "Mr. Lorimer says that he has never met anyone who is in the confidence of the nations in the way I am...!" she wrote from Baghdad. The Foreign Office dealt with her illicit journeys in the same way that it dealt with those of renegade officials—by doing all it could, on the surface, to rein her in, while hoping she would manage to elude its reach. It was Bell's childhood friend, Ambassador Louis Mallet in Constantinople, who first uselessly passed on official advisories against travel and, afterwards, excitedly submitted her journey report, praising her "remarkable exploit." Such personal connections helped further the Foreign Office's unofficial ambition to access the secrets of Arabia.[27]

Bell's best friend was Hogarth's sister Janet. This is no isolated coincidence, but a common factor behind the creation of the community of Middle East intelligence experts. The bonds that drew them together were based as much on social, class, and family as on professional relationships. Take Hogarth: through his family's clerical connections, he was a good friend of the first director of naval intelligence, Admiral Reginald "Blinker" Hall. He also knew the head of the London School of Oriental Studies, Denison Ross, who was to become a "special advisor" on military intelligence in the Middle East. His Oxford connections opened the doors of the India Office library to him, where he researched his history of Arabian exploration, *The Penetration of Arabia* (1904), which itself became a key reference for the intelligence world. His professional ambit put him in a position to write to a publisher seeking his opinion of Bury: "I have read a long report of his, made to the Secret Service Department of the Indian Government, which was quite good."[28]

Hogarth's relationships with other archaeologists were primarily forged in the academy. He recruited Lawrence and Woolley at the Ashmolean Museum. Campbell-Thompson was a fellow at Merton College, famous for his translations of ancient Babylonian legends. Prospective diplomats and consuls also gathered at the feet of E. G. Browne, Arabic professor at Cambridge.[29] The academy also fostered political connections. At Oxford, Aubrey Herbert became close to Raymond Asquith, son of the future prime minister. His friendships with Lloyd and Sykes, dating from Oxbridge, carried through their parliamentary careers when he and Sykes were both members of the Conservatives' Tuesday Club (the "Hughligans"). At Oxford, the novelist Compton Mackenzie met many of his future colleagues in intelligence, including Herbert, Woolley, and Harry Pirie-Gordon, whom he had known earlier and who went on to gather intelligence on the Syrian coast and write for the London *Times*. Pirie-Gordon was related to Hogarth, through whom he met Lawrence, also en route to Syria.

This community also met socially. Herbert's wife regularly complained about his endless hospitality toward "drunken consuls," with whom her own fashionable set was condemned to mix.[30] Herbert and Lloyd were family friends of Gertrude Bell's; in Constantinople, she dined with Philip Graves, then a *Times* correspondent who also sent intelligence to Whitehall. Many of those involved in Middle Eastern politics and intelligence gathered at her home as summer guests, including the journalist and former Foreign Office hand Valentine Chirol. He had facilitated Bell's first journey to the Middle East by tapping into his network of friends among the consuls, and she sent him her travel reports, which he drew on for his editorials and supplied to government officials.

Aspiring travelers took pains to contact their forerunners in the field of Arabia exploration. In need of advice on travel in Syria, Lawrence initiated a correspondence with the legendary Charles Doughty, then an aging and impecunious poet. Bell's greatest unconsummated love affair was with Doughty's nephew, Charles Doughty-Wylie, a military vice-consul in Turkey. She was also friendly with Lady Anne Blunt in Cairo. The mutual adulation among this group is also evidenced by their incestuous authoring of biographies about one another, cited throughout this book. The exploration fraternity extended to the Royal Geographical Society, which provided an important extraofficial institutional framework for the interaction of the civilian and official components of the community. Hogarth, Bell, Bury, the Blunts, Leachman, Carruthers, Butler, Shakespear, and others were all at various times at the society—many of them nominated by each other for membership—as were key figures in the DMO's mapping section. The society's president could openly remind "English officers in distant parts of the world of the admirable opportunities they have when going on leave of exploring some hitherto unknown part of the world." Besides scholarly cover and financial backing for officially discouraged trips, the society also provided a store of expertise and references.[31]

The social world and institutions of this community extended abroad in the empire. In 1902, at the Delhi Durbar, Bell "met all the world." It was there, with Lorimer, Chirol, and Cox, that she learned the latest news about the peninsular feud between the Houses of Saud and Rashid. In Cairo, that other imperial crossroads, we can find Graves working for the *Egyptian Gazette* and sharing a flat with his future intelligence colleague, Ronald Storrs. Socializing between travelers and residency and consular staffs in the Middle East was also routine. At the Mohammerah consulate, Leachman met fellow DMO agent Ely

Soane and Arnold Wilson, the Indian officer on special duty in Persia and future civil commissioner in Iraq. In Constantinople, he met Shakespear, also fresh from the overland journey from India, and struck up friendships with the embassy attachés. At the embassy, the Foreign Office hand Lancelot Oliphant also joined this group, as did British advisers to the Turkish Ministry of the Interior such as Wyndham Deedes. Leachman, Shakespear, Lloyd, Herbert, Fraser, Chirol, and Bray all passed through the Gulf residency, attracted partly by Cox, who was universally admired as a great authority on Arabia. Archaeologists were integral to this network of intimates; Lawrence and Woolley were especially close with the author-consul at Beirut, James Elroy Flecker. The paths of these diggers, diplomats, and explorers also intersected in Damascus, the "gateway between East and West," where many of them acquired guides, often the same ones. Carchemish was also a common curiosity, drawing agents and diplomats alike. So too were other archaeological sites: Bell and Hogarth had worked at different times with William Ramsay in Turkey; Lawrence for Flinders Petrie in Egypt; and Woolley knew Lord Carnarvon, also in Egypt. Now, Carnarvon was the brother of Aubrey Herbert, a central node of "the digging fraternities of Egypt, Syria and Mesopotamia." These encounters were partly the Middle East version of the expatriate imperial social world but also the result of a deliberate effort to build a network of intelligence relationships, to exchange the information and contacts essential to successful exploration and intelligence work in Arabia.[32]

The very nomadism of intelligence in the Middle East strengthened ties among the agents, despite their far-flung posts and the slow travel and communication separating them. (Even fortuitous meetings in the desert were not unheard of.) As John Mackenzie writes, contemporary history was for this group "like a series of spectacular entertainments and they were often theatrical people who filled the stage they found for themselves." Bell romped her way through the sites and celebrations of British imperial power; witness her excitement after a meeting with Chirol: "We drew out maps and discussed his Persian journey and our hidden plans.... We want to meet in Delhi!" The spatiality of this spectacular stage was mirrored in the agents' relations as a community, for what bound them, and the Middle East, was their and its position at the nexus of governments, departments, and empires. Movement across it was movement across institutional lines, a lateral motion that produced a community of Middle East intelligencers with its own agenda and priorities, its own casual coordination and exchange of information, and its own archive, however spatially dispersed.[33]

The community mainly relied on physical mobility, telegraph, and the post to communicate. Consuls could exchange telegrams in cipher from 1910. Naval ships in the Gulf, the Red Sea, and the Mediterranean also provided important relay facilities with the connivance, especially, of the military attaché and Fitzmaurice at the embassy. Information was also communicated through the heavy circulation of certain key documents that attempted to pool together the results of the community's effort to construct a composite view of the region—like the six blind men and their elephant. Among these, Lorimer's *Gazetteer* acknowledged debts not only to consuls and agents but to the irrigation engineer William Willcocks, Lynch Company captains, Dr. Bennett of the American Presbyterian Mission, W. D. Cumming of the Indo-European Telegraphy Department, Charles Doughty, and Hogarth. Such documents testified to the existence of an intelligence community straddling the worlds of diplomacy, the military, commerce, and scholarship.[34]

Wartime Evolution

Two major campaigns were fought in the Middle East during the Great War. The Mesopotamian campaign began as a small operation for the defense of Indian frontiers and British interests in the Persian Gulf. However, once at the Gulf, the Indian Expeditionary Force D began to rapidly advance north along the Tigris and Euphrates rivers in a characteristic effort to shore up what it already held. After an ill-fated first attempt at taking Baghdad forced them to a disastrous retreat on Kut, the campaign was taken over by the War Office and, after capturing Baghdad in March 1917, ultimately routed the Turkish Army near Mosul. Farther west, troops guarding the Suez Canal embarked on an offensive assault in the Sinai and then into Palestine and Syria, absorbing the remnants of the Gallipoli campaign into an enlarged Egyptian Expeditionary Force and coordinating its push north with the Arab Revolt launched by Sherif Hussein of the Hejaz and led by two of his sons, Faisal and Abdullah.[35] Almost immediately on the outbreak of war, the informal agents' contacts opened official doors through which they passed unhindered—not the least among their champions was "their spokesman," Lord Kitchener, the new head of the Ministry of War, whom Roger Adelson hails as "the first major figure in London to be clearly identified as an Arabist." Cox was deputed chief political officer with the force in Basra; Shakespear was stopped on his way to France and posted as political officer on special duty under him, ultimately dispatched to Riyadh to secure Ibn Saud's friendship. The civilians too were brought under the official umbrella, the perception being that archaeologists' "familiarity with out-of-the-way localities ... and ... close relations, ... more intimate, than a consul's ... to native populations, obviously fit them for special missions." Hogarth, through his friendship with the director of naval intelligence, landed in the new Geographical Section of that directorate. Through Captain Deedes, who joined the DMO, Bell submitted her views to Whitehall. Woolley wrote to the Foreign Office, confident that "my name has come before you in connection with work in North Syria," and offered his and Lawrence's services. (He later referred rather disingenuously to his and Lawrence's crossing of the Taurus as the reason they "were both shoved by the War Office into the Intelligence as soon as the war began.") Lawrence, likely through Hogarth's intervention, secured a position in the Geographic Section of the General Staff. Angling for a position through 1914, Mark Sykes finally obtained, through old Constantinople contacts, an introduction to Kitchener and a position at the DMO. As Kitchener's personal representative on the Interdepartmental Committee on the Future of Asiatic Turkey, popularly known as the De Bunsen Committee, he attained an anomalously influential position for a junior official, on the merits of being the only one with firsthand experience of the East.[36]

Many of these agents soon coalesced into the intelligence departments of Sirdar Reginald Wingate's Egyptian Army at Cairo and Indian Expeditionary Force D in Basra. By late 1914, Hogarth had arranged for Woolley, Lawrence, and Lloyd to join the Cairo staff under the command of Newcombe, plucked from the Western front for "special assignment" under Gilbert Clayton, in charge of General Staff Intelligence (GSI) at Cairo. Philip Graves and his uncle, Robert Graves, formerly consul at Salonika and adviser in the Turkish Ministry of Interior, arrived from Constantinople and provided names of "a number of British residents obliged to leave Turkey, who would be glad to give their services as Intelligence Officers and Agents, or Interpreters." Herbert, wounded at Mons, became a staff officer. Intelligence, military planning, and other tasks were not precisely apportioned among these old friends. Through Hogarth's and Admiral Hall's intervention, the circle was soon completed with the arrival of Bell, who had until then been helping Lord Robert Cecil trace the wounded and missing with her old friend, Janet Hogarth. As parliamentary undersecretary for the Foreign Office, Cecil remained a key Whitehall contact for Bell and Sykes; his brother, Edward, the financial adviser to the Egyptian government, was virtually prime minister of Egypt under martial law.[37]

In Basra, besides the Indian cavalry and the spy networks of the sheikhs of Mohammerah and Kuwait, whose friendship Cox had long cultivated, General Headquarters relied on the embryonic intelligence section headed by Captain W. H. Beach, in whose charge were several prewar agents, including Reginald Campbell-Thompson, J. C. More, W. H. Gribbon of Simla intelligence, and Captain G. F. Eadie. Cox's Political Department, however, seems to have been the primary site of intelligence collection. Designation aside, the political officer was first and foremost a member of the General Staff, "and only in a very subordinate degree the local representative of the CPO [Chief Political Officer] in his capacity as head of the civil administration." Levant consuls were impressed into this service, as were former Gulf and Middle East officials from India: H. R. C. Dobbs, who had traveled in Mesopotamia and was intended consul general of Baghdad when war broke out, headed the new Revenue Department; S. G. Knox, former Gulf resident, formed the judicial system; D. L. R. Lorimer, former political agent in Bahrain and brother of the late Baghdad resident (who accidentally shot himself in 1914), was a political officer; and Reader Bullard, who had evacuated the Basra consulate at the beginning of the war, was assistant political officer under Dobbs. Experts on neighboring precincts—central Arabia, Persia, and Kurdistan—also gathered in Basra, such as Captain Noel of the Anglo-Persian Oil Company and Leachman, who had been languishing with his regiment on the North West Frontier. Soane, released with other British refugees from Turkish imprisonment at Baghdad—trusting in their friendships with the provincial government, few Britons had evacuated—trekked to Aleppo and made his way to London and then Cox's staff. Some political officers were seconded from the army, including the Indian Army officers Harold Dickson, son of the former consul at Jerusalem, and Hubert Young, who arrived from the North West Frontier. The Indian Civil Service answered an urgent call for political personnel, particularly those with demonstrated linguistic ability, sending H. St. John Philby among the first batch. By the end of the year, of the seventeen "gazetted" members of the "civil administration," all but one spoke Arabic fluently and had traveled in Arabic-speaking countries. "These men...made a group whose collective knowledge was unrivalled," wrote Cox's deputy, Arnold Wilson, and under Cox's guidance, "it was possible to make their knowledge subserve our military purpose."[38]

Newly official and backed for the first time by the financial and material might of the empire, the wartime intelligence world nonetheless remained strikingly informal and ad hoc, fading at its edges into the familiar unofficial world of local European businessmen, Christian missionaries, former consular employees, the agents' former guides, itinerant traders in essential items like ointment for curing mange in camels, and corpse carriers—particularly ubiquitous in wartime. Agents struck by the anachronism of their disorganization in the midst of a total war marked by efficient bureaucratic coordination of massive actions periodically tried to reform their organization but had to struggle against the tendency produced under the peculiar conditions of prewar intelligence-gathering of collapsing all intelligence work into the hands of a small band of intrepid agents willing to breach official directives. Their influence grew ever larger as they claimed an ever larger domain of political matters as part of intelligence work.

From the beginning, military and political intelligence were difficult to separate. Besides keeping tabs on local sheikhs and running Arab scouts and spies, political officers were entrusted with a range of more military tasks. "Though I am nominally here for political duties," wrote Wilson, "I have actually spent the whole time on purely military reconnaissances as I have mapped every yard of the country and know it thoroughly, and the Brigade Commanders always insist on having me with them when they go out." At Suq al-Shuyukh, Dickson had "spys [sic] and agents everywhere, some...in touch with the centre of Arabia," but also trained the Nasiriyah Arab Scouts and employed them on patrol work and military intelligence. The generals' dependence on political officers like him meant "fellows are continually picking our brains and coming round for news." The political officer was generally "of the nature semi military semi political." Beach officially recognized the political officers' position at "the forefront of affairs," particularly in assisting the military system. This was partly, as many pointed out, the result of the lack of people with the requisite linguistic skills but also inevitable in a campaign between two competing imperial powers, in which the political sentiment of the occupied population was itself a factor of military consequence. Mesopotamia was the only place in the Great War where British forces were confronted with a hostile or indifferent occupied population; as one scholar puts it, "Intelligence had a different battle to fight." As before, the nature of British priorities in the region—now, the need to "battle for hearts and minds"—tended to subsume political and administrative work into military intelligence. Thus, while, in European theaters, according to Keith Neilson, wartime intelligence entailed a conspicuous abandonment of "political, as opposed to military, intelligence," in the Middle East, as one agent put it, it was "impossible to dissociate the Political and Military problems." This overlap undermined bureaucratic differentiation of tasks. "A political officer's duties are various, the underlying idea being that all dealings with the natives (except killing them) should be done through him," wrote the political officer and historian C. J. Edmonds, formerly of the Levant Service. He had to "[interview] sheikhs who come in to submit...heat up the countryside to get transport, do a certain amount of intelligence work, pronounce on the value (before death) of a dead donkey, answer conundrums about the tribes at a moment's notice as if one had been in the country all one's life." The political officer also functioned as a makeshift quartermaster or "universal provider": at Amara, Leachman provided the army fresh meat, grass, firewood, transport ponies, guides, eggs, milk—"anything that anyone does not know how to get." "I am supposed to know every Arab in the country by name and face," he went on in exasperation, "Also exactly when the river will rise and by how much. If it is going to rain, how much? and how long?"[39]

Wartime exigencies and the skills agents acquired before the war meant intelligence also shaded into administration. As the Indian Army rushed north in 1915, "liberating" Mesopotamia, it created a pressing need for officials to pacify, govern, and watch the occupied regions. Cox's duty was to keep the Indian government informed of the situation but also to set up an administration in the occupied regions through his political officers.[40] Administrative and intelligence work were both concerned with making Arabia legible to the emerging colonial state by surveying the land and population—particularly for tax assessment—for which both relied on political officers.[41] Political officers employed in the Revenue Department worked closely with their counterparts governing occupied districts; many rotated between these posts. Dobbs, the head of Revenue, regularly submitted intelligence reports. The centrality of the rivers to the fighting and their susceptibility to enemy manipulation made the services of George Buchanan, the conservator general of the rivers, equally crucial to intelligence and the work of political officers in riverain districts. The amalgamation of intelligence and administration produced a manifestly weird regime. Cox affirmed, "The [Indian] Political Branch...with this Force is performing functions which it has never had occasion to perform before in the history of the country or of the Department." So managerial did the political officers become that their cozy arrangements with the military loosened over time. In Basra in 1916, Lawrence pronounced "Political Department" a rather "false name," as the organization was "really a civil service...mostly taken up with administration." Cox was high commissioner in all but name and an "absolute dictator in the Gulf." He would take orders only from London but knew London "so well that...this is only a diplomatic way of taking no orders at all." Despite the "strict divorce" between Cox's and Beach's establishments, Cox remained a colonel on the general's staff to "preserve a fiction of control." Moreover, he worked well with Beach "personally," and they kept each other "au fait" with their doings.[42]

Such personal cooperation outside bureaucracy facilitated agents' multitasking, even across the chasm between the Basra and Cairo establishments where formal cooperation was mooted by political differences and the ambiguous division of spheres between the Egyptian and Indian governments.[43] Continual migrations of intelligence personnel between the two establishments preserved the informality of Middle East intelligence and kept substantive decisions in that informal sphere. While Force D had mostly absorbed experts from the Indian side and Egypt those based in London—there were battles over some bodies—both sides knew each other informally from before the war. When Mesopotamian intelligencers traveled to London, they inevitably stopped at Cairo and rekindled old contacts, smoothing the exchange of

information. Hogarth, for instance, although tightly bound to the Cairo establishment, also received information from Leachman and Shakespear through
the War Office, the Royal Geographical Society, and Indian Army intelligence.

This makeshift organization came under sharp scrutiny after the Gallipoli
debacle and the investment of Kut at the end of 1915. Nine thousand soldiers
and thousands of noncombatants ultimately surrendered to the Turks after
more than twenty thousand men were lost in botched rescue attempts, heralding "the British Army's greatest humiliation in the First World War" and that
too in "the one theatre of the war where we could least afford a fluctuating standard."[44] The intelligence world was thoroughly shaken up, partly to launch an
Arab revolt that would break the deadlock in the East and inextricably link the
affairs of Mesopotamia, Egypt, and India. Sykes's influential position in London
was critical in the design of the new intelligence regime. In 1915, he embarked
on a special War Office mission to report on the military and political situation
throughout the East. His peregrinations through the imperial bureaucracy
stretching between the Mediterranean and East Asia convinced him of the need
for unified intelligence organization *and* unified policy for the Middle East. He
was as impressed with the long-distance connections between anti-Turkish
groups in the region—a perception I will have more to say about later—as with
British officials' isolation from each other in "water-tight compartments" held
apart by tortuous channels of communication (whereby Aden, for instance,
had to consult with Bombay and Delhi for instructions, and they, in turn, with
the India Office, which had to meet jointly with the War and Foreign offices,
which had to report to the War Committee, which usually sought the opinion
of the high commissioner in Egypt, who had then to report back to the Foreign
Office and the War Committee, a process consuming sixteen days and some
£250, according to Sykes). He urged centralization. The otherwise admirable
autonomy of the man on the spot "was alright in the past when such sectors
dealt with varying problems which were not related, but is bad now that each
sector is dealing in reality with a common enemy." Moreover, whatever special
insight the man on the spot possessed, there were no clear channels through
which he could leverage the entire bureaucratic machinery. Policy went wrong
in the hands of bureaucrats; it required the expertise of *intelligence agents*.
A central agency would also keep the Indian and British networks from "doing
the same work twice over," Bell affirmed. It would formalize the mingling of
political and military intelligence, coordinating reports from agents in
Mesopotamia, the Gulf, the Indian Criminal Investigation Department (CID),
Sudan intelligence, Mediterranean Expeditionary Force intelligence, and the
Athens intelligence organization. Sykes's proposed "Islamic Bureau" at Cairo
would coordinate not only intelligence, but also propaganda *and* policy in the

Middle East, laying the groundwork for a new covert empire in the hands of intelligence personnel.[45]

Sykes, whom a contemporary immortalized as "that strange romanticist who flitted from campaign to campaign as a half-official, half unofficial free-lance," arrived in London with his proposal in the wake of the debacles in the East and on the eve of a major government shake-up and general restructuring of intelligence that resulted in the creation of a new Directorate of Military Intelligence, under which C's organization became MI1c (renamed MI6 in the 1930s), and K's section, MI5. Whitehall was highly receptive to his ideas; in any case, the interdepartmental meeting in January 1916 at which his proposal was approved was made up of intimates of the community of Arabia agents, including Oliphant, Herbert Asquith, Arthur Hirtzel of the India Office, and others. The Arab Bureau's establishment was finalized, substantially as he wanted.[46]

Despite the hope for order, the bureau remained an unbureaucratic bureaucracy without clear standing, so that policy on the Middle East effectively emanated from the shadowy interstices of the British government rather than from a clearly defined and accountable department. In the first place, Sykes could not find a space for it in the existing bureaucracy. It was so unique in its conception—at once a military and political intelligence, propaganda, and policy unit—that simple absorption into any existing intelligence structure proved impossible. Technically a section of the Sudan Intelligence Department at Cairo (at Kitchener's insistence), it was formally attached to the General Staff, bankrolled by the Admiralty and the Exchequer (although staff salaries were paid by their original departments), and responsible to the Foreign Office through the high commissioner. Its operations remained so obscure that in 1923 a perplexed Public Accounts Office made inquiries at the Foreign Office, where W. J. Childs, a former agent, explained that although only "a few with inner knowledge" could divulge its "decisive" role, in general it had served as "no mere collecting...agency for general intelligence" but had "advised with authority upon the highest and most delicate questions affecting British policy" and diplomacy.[47]

This wide brief was partly the inevitable product of the habits of an intelligence community so used to a free hand and informal organization that it simply could not adapt to strict bureaucracy. Personal, unofficial contacts were fundamental to the bureau's operation from the outset. Hogarth, its sometime head, urged that it "stay close" to GSI and retain its "indefinite status" rather than become "independent and distinct," as it could thus cover a wider field and draw on the activities and knowledge of "several officers not strictly on its staff." In January, when Bell was invited to India by her old friend Viceroy Charles Hardinge, Clayton encouraged her to go. A bit nervous about the responsibility, she nevertheless reasoned, "the pull one has in being so unofficial is that if one doesn't succeed no one is any the worse." Moreover, her dear friend Chirol was in Delhi, "which will make everything easy." (It was he who had convinced Clayton that she, as "a quite unimportant and unofficial person," accept the invitation.) In the event, so successful was her informal turn at pulling "things straight a little between Delhi and Cairo" that she became convinced "nothing will ever keep them straight except a constant personal intercourse" and insisted on continual "exchange of people in the various Intell. Depts." The bureau's George Lloyd, deputed to Basra on intelligence, agreed on the need of "constant personal touch." Informal communication remained the network's modus operandi, not least because the bureau's awkward fit between the profusion of existing agencies threatened to undermine the confidentiality prerogatives of each. Having paid lip service to the importance of proper communication, even Clayton considered "some unofficial channel of communication...desirable to send information for the private information of" the director of military intelligence. It was on behalf of Simla's new gazetteer of Arabia that Bell next stopped in Basra although she also worked as an informal liaison for the bureau, using Beach's bedroom as her office. There she insisted that work such as hers could not be carried out "without free and private intercourse with one's chief" and that she "be able to write to you [Hogarth] privately about the work here, personal impressions and personal judgements which have no official value and no official weight." Since a formal request for such an arrangement might arouse suspicions, she urged that the arrangement be allowed to come about gradually. As she squeezed herself between Cox's and Beach's organizations, Cox requested the wider Mesopotamian and Gulf network to cooperate with her and the bureau. Thus, functionally, the bureau was a queer mix of the formal and informal. It fulfilled Sykes's objectives by availing itself of the material and financial resources of bureaucracy, but without subjecting itself to its hierarchical and procedural constraints. After all the minute planning for its surgical insertion into the existing bureaucracy, it evolved its own channels of communication, designed to evade the controls of the potentially paralyzing number of its sponsors.[48]

Constant touring also kept the bureau's staff amorphous and fluid. Officially, Hogarth was head, but because he was often required elsewhere was soon replaced by an (equally nomadic) acting director, Kinahan Cornwallis of GSI. At one point in 1916, Cornwallis and a single clerk were left alone to man the office. But it hardly mattered: Lawrence and Graves, then at GSI, worked closely with him on propaganda and the bureau's intelligence digest, the *Arab Bulletin*. When the bureau's increasing dominance of diplomacy and military preparations made it such a thorn in GSI's side that Clayton was effectively sacked as head of GSI and the two institutions separated, GSI agents such as Newcombe, Deedes, and Woolley continued to work closely with it. Non-bureau members including J. W. A. Young at Jeddah, Lieutenant L. F. Nalder of the Sudan government at Aden, and Alfred Parker at Rabigh collected information for its handbooks. Perhaps the truest statement about the agency was Hogarth's rather portentous admission, "Well—in a sense I *am* the Arab Bureau," which assumes proper proportion when we realize that he made it at a time when he had *no official standing* at the bureau, an arrangement, he explained, designed primarily to assure Cornwallis's salary. The Treasury's discovery in 1918 that the bureau, whose budget was £3000, had been spending £14,000 annually bespeaks the agency's near autonomy, which assured its political influence, regardless of institutional change. Unlike any other intelligence staff, the bureau members devised their own campaign plan, chose their own chiefs, established and pursued their own objectives, and shaped policy at Whitehall.[49]

Such institutional suppleness eased the bureau's takeover of military and diplomatic work in the region. The Red Sea Patrol employed Lieutenant Nalder, who would later serve as a political officer in Mesopotamia, and G. Wyman Bury, whom the Foreign Office had in fact banned from travel in Arabia after 1909, to monitor Arab views of its blockade. It also worked closely with a new agency in Jeddah, tied elliptically to and bankrolled by the bureau. Established at the urging of Lawrence and Colonel Cyril E. Wilson, former governor of Khartoum, Port Sudan, and Red Sea Province, the Jeddah agency's ostensible purpose was to improve communication with Sherif Hussein, but it was in fact entrusted with a much larger role, "it being almost impossible to separate the military operations from the political side." Wilson was in charge (but addressed only as "Mr." or "Pasha" to avoid the impression that he was not an ordinary pilgrim officer). Advisers to the Sherifian forces—Lawrence, Newcombe, Pierce Joyce—were under his command but also had their own idiosyncratic connections to the bureau, roaming more or less free, often with nothing but their own inspiration to rely on for orders. Thus, Newcombe worked a field extending "from Yanbo North," and at one point Lawrence found himself *explaining* to Clayton, "I regard myself as primarily Intelligence Officer, or liaison with Feisul," adding that, as there was no further need for him at Yanbo, he was going to Joyce "to see if he can suggest anything worth doing." Wilson himself was technically a member of Wingate's staff but generally communicated with London through McMahon, who used him to exercise political control over the revolt. When General Edmund Allenby took command of the Palestine campaign in the summer of 1917, the Jeddah agency was absorbed into a new Hejaz Operations Staff at General Headquarters, which relieved the bureau from responsibility for the military needs of the revolt. Nevertheless, as Bruce Westrate puts it, the two entities remained virtually "indistinguishable, with officers used almost interchangeably." Thus, Alan Dawnay was officially chief staff officer, but Joyce, who was on Wilson's staff but not the Hejaz Operations Staff, was officially senior British officer with Faisal's army *and* officer commanding Hejaz operations. In any case, as Hubert Young explained with hindsight, Lawrence "really counted more than either of them with Allenby and Feisal." By then, Lawrence had actually rejoined GSI, noting presciently that although he "should properly have no more to do with the Arab Bureau," "so eccentric a show as ours is doesn't do anything normal." All this overlap was eased by Wingate's appointment as high commissioner while retaining authority over relations with the Sherif and Hejaz operations.[50]

The obscurity of the bureau's network helped it fulfill its anomalously wide brief but also tended to pull its political work out of the light of public scrutiny. It quickly became entangled with MI5, whose very existence, unlike ordinary intelligence units, was secret and whose wartime responsibilities had expanded to include oversight of imperial counterespionage, for which it was christened the Central Special Intelligence Bureau, since "special intelligence" seemed less impolitic than "counterespionage" in imperial communications. The interaction between this bureau and the community of agents in Arabia dated to 1915, when the Mediterranean Expeditionary Force had stopped in Cairo—its intelligence and map base—en route to the Dardanelles. Many Cairo agents, including Robert Graves, Herbert, Lloyd, Newcombe, and Lawrence, had temporarily migrated to Greece with the force. There they encountered many of their old friends, such as Deedes, Pirie-Gordon, and Doughty-Wylie, employed in a subbranch of the Eastern Mediterranean Special Intelligence Bureau under the Central Special Intelligence Bureau. This subbranch was founded on the networks of prewar consular officers and was headed by Major "R" (Rhys Samson, prewar military consul at Adrianople). After the Gallipoli disaster, many of R's agents joined Cairo intelligence. Then, just as the Arab Bureau was being established, the Central Special Intelligence Bureau contacted Clayton privately to inform him of its existence and its officers' desire for closer contact with his " 'vital intelligence center' for the Near and Middle East." The Eastern Mediterranean Special Intelligence Bureau was soon placed under the head of the Cairo section of MI1c, apparently Colonel Holdich, also head of GSI. Eventually that bureau's headquarters were moved from Alexandria to Cairo to "work more centrally," creating a "New Jerusalem of Intelligence." In short, the visible intelligence and policy-making establishments of GSI and the Arab Bureau were co-opted into the ultracovert networks of MI5 and MI1c, although arrangements remained fluid and informal. As intelligence began to widen its domain to include administration and operations planning, it also sank further into the recesses of the covert world.[51]

The contact zone created by informal connections between the covert and open worlds dragged intelligence's new political responsibilities into obscurity. Agents shuttling between intelligence and policy-making centers drew politicians and bureaucrats into their circle of intimates, keeping policy making diffused through an informal rather than formal network. Take, for instance, Bray's easy movement between these worlds late in 1916 when he was recalled from the Western front, briefed by Sykes, and deputed as intelligence officer under Colonel Wilson. He soon returned to London to meet with Sykes; attend a War Cabinet meeting; dine with Austen Chamberlain, the secretary of state for India, who wanted to hear all about the revolt; and discuss the revolt with the director of military intelligence and the new chief of staff, returning to Jeddah via Cairo. Cairo also deliberately sent a steady stream of visitors into Cox's domain to undermine official Indian policy. Although India grew alarmed at the invasion of "Instrusives," the oddly apt telegraphic address by which GSI Cairo was known, the visits were all sanctioned by Kitchener (until he died at sea just as the revolt was launched). In one extraordinary covert operation in April 1916, Lawrence and Herbert arrived in Basra to mix with old friends in the intelligence departments and then, with Beach, proceeded upriver to try (unsuccessfully) to bribe the Turks into releasing Kut. The director general of the Survey of Egypt claimed that Lawrence's visit—particularly his ability "to get inside the skin of the participants"—wound up infecting Beach's mapping section with the "short-circuitings of official hierarchy which the kaleidoscopic situation demanded." Such visits ensured that, despite the Indian government's efforts to emasculate the bureau's Basra branch, a remarkable amount of exchange of information, methods, and policy ideas persisted between Cairo, London, Basra, Jeddah, and Delhi. The campaigns' incompletely delineated operational spheres, partly the result of the manifest usefulness of intelligence from one theater to the other, encouraged this informal intertheater influence.[52]

The contest over the bureau's Basra branch illustrates the extent to which the intrusions allowed the agents to keep policy-making about Arabia in an unofficial zone. Cox was initially against the bureau as a policy center encroaching on his own sphere, and his suspicions were wise: a prototypical agency of covert empire, the bureau was determined to access the revenue and tribal information gathered by his establishment. As George Lloyd explained, the bureau preferred liaison with Cox's department rather than Beach's as the one that would remain in place after the war and the one in closest touch with civil officials "who will be left dotted about this country." Its civilian status provided long-term cover for what was projected as a long-term surveillance project. Bell was particularly useful in this regard, Lawrence felt, as she could "work up the connections we require" with the political officers, thanks partly to "her sex and energy and lack of self-consciousness." The bureau, like the Political Department, viewed intelligence expansively, as an advanced guard of and even enduring proxy for the imperial state. Singling out Leachman, Young, Eadie, and Dobbs—a mix of Beach's and Cox's men—for praise, Lawrence wrote to the bureau of their "magnificent work in keeping in friendly touch with the people, and winning their respect for our administration," what he called the "social side" of intelligence work—"the particular province" of the bureau and the side military intelligence tended to miss. He hoped the Indian nominee for bureau liaison, Major W. F. Blaker, would serve as "a sort of pillar-box" and let Bell do the real work. Lloyd, then in Basra on intelligence, agreed Bell was the best person for the job, mainly "because *as a civilian* she more naturally works in the political department." He cautioned against hasty "precising" of the question and defining "the actual position of the correspondent vis a vis either the military or the civil authorities here."[53]

Keeping control of Arabia in the hands of agents was synonymous to these agents with keeping themselves free of Whitehall's control. Bell, who ultimately retained the liaison position alone, confessed she preferred working in Basra, particularly as she had been given a "free hand" to recast the intelligence publications. Lloyd, who had also chivalrously offered himself for the position, was relieved at having escaped any degree of restriction—his visit was sandwiched between a flying mission to Russia and raiding in the Hejaz. Lawrence himself, who languished in GSI until the fall, ultimately used a mix of skillfully targeted pedantry and intellectual snobbery to obtain transfer to the bureau, where he found "the atmosphere of being one's own master... pleasant." These agents wanted to be "free agents." Cox, as we have seen, seldom reported to or consulted his superiors. Leachman communicated erratically and whimsically, partly because he operated in places from which it was difficult to communicate but partly because he had a very free hand. Perhaps most tellingly, Lawrence justified his irregular communication by citing Whitehall's own secrecy about its plans for Arabia, of which he got wind thanks only to his friends there: information came to him "not officially... but privately." This was the condition of work these agents were used to: an embattled position vis-à-vis their own government, to which they adapted because of their confidence in their own authority and patriotic dutifulness. Bell transmitted volumes of confidential information in lengthy private letters to everyone from her family to the director of naval intelligence (she had her father ascertain discreetly whether the latter liked her missives) with the express aim of reforming the pervasive ignorance of the "High and Mighty" about Middle Eastern affairs. This was the style of the

Middle East intelligence world, where the personal lubricated and kept pliant a system straining under manifold bureaucratic, financial, and political pressures, a legacy of the prewar period when these agents had learned to circumvent procedural constraints to serve their vision of a greater national good. The patriotic subversiveness that had licensed illicit intelligence-gathering before the war now licensed covert policy-making. And, apparently, with considerable success: Whitehall's respect for their opinions is evident in their constant referral of even those questions concerning operations in north Persia to Cox, Bell, and Arnold Wilson, valuing their opinions, as one scholar has pointed out, "more than those of... personnel... actually in north Persia."[54]

Official standing only fortified their position as free agents. Witness the fallout from Bell's discreet indiscretions: A few weeks into her job, she began to find its informality uncomfortable, particularly when Hogarth published extracts of her *private* letters in the *Arab Bulletin*. Incensed at this transgression of her otherwise seamlessly unofficial existence, she reminded him that she was in Basra under Indian, if any, auspices, and that her letters were the result of a special dispensation from Cox. As the genie could not be put back into the bottle, she requested him to define her duties more clearly. *Cox* then made her an assistant political officer with the title "Liaison Officer, Correspondent to Cairo" and did so without seeking the bureau's approval, for, as Philip Graves later recalled, "though she took it for granted that she was a member," she had "joined the staff in Mesopotamia as a free-lance." Such was the flexibility conferred by membership in the nebulous Arab Bureau. Bell's quest for official standing was not a retreat from her freelance style but an attempt to protect it with a veneer of formality. Initially concerned that Cox's "chief motive was to give himself a much firmer hold over me," she was soon assured that her new position need neither stem the flow of her pen nor diminish her freedom of movement. It merely gave her freelance status an official impress and the backing of institutional power; she now had "the right to be lodged and fed, and looked after when I'm ill." In any case, as a rule, political officers were fairly autonomous. Bureaucracy empowered rather than constrained agents' autonomy in the Middle East.[55]

The new intelligence order impressed its staff with its panoptic potential. Bell was confident she could "keep an eye on all the developments in the Near East." "Our office is the clearing house through which every report and item affecting the Near East has to pass," marveled Lawrence. "The mass of Stuff is amazing, and it all fits into itself like a most wonderful puzzle. If we had only begun in peace time there would have been almost nothing we had not known." However, to Sykes, at a new desk in Whitehall, the new order's enduring informality spelled utter pandemonium for policy-making, turning it into a "perfect babel of conflicting suggestions and views," he grumbled in his weekly intelligence digest, the "Arabian Report." The *"dramatis personae"* of the intelligence world acted "in a piece in which it is impossible to observe the unities." Thus, for instance, "Sir R. Wingate, Sirdar, nominally lives isolated in Khartoum, now in charge of whole of the military and part of the political conduct of affairs in Hejaz. Corresponds with FO [Foreign Office] through McMahon but does not see him." He mused that "the relations of London, Simla, Basra, and Cairo are perhaps clearer to these...desert folk than to British officers themselves" and that the "evils" of Arab craftiness and fractiousness had begun to feed on "our natural British tendency to team rivalry." In a word, British intelligence in the Middle East had become "oriental," inscrutable and mysterious, and had taken Middle Eastern policy with it.[56]

The picture quickly grew more obscure. Late in 1916, captured documents revealed the existence of the Silk Letter Plot to create an "Army of God" that would liberate Islamic countries under infidel rule; the plan was communicated on scraps of silk circulated between the so-called Hindustani Fanatics across the Indian frontier; Pan-Islamic leaders in India, the Hejaz, and Kabul; and German and Turkish collaborators. Other documents exposed the abortive von Stotzingen mission to the Hejaz—apparently forced to retreat by the timely launch of the revolt. Both revelations were harrowing in retrospect for their implication of Arab cooperation just when the thousands of Arabs expected to join the Sherif failed to materialize. In Bray's analysis, the Silk Letter Plot revealed an anti-British effort "spread over...the whole mohammedan world," to guard against which "we must watch and study...Persia, Afghanistan, Turkestan, Java and Arabia as well as within the empire." The German mission put British agents in an unusual position as orientalists—anxious not over the Sherif's honesty but about his being hoodwinked, in Lloyd's words, by *Europeans* who "by means of intrigue...seek to poison his mind." Reconfiguring all Arabs as potential enemy collaborators and spies, these events inspired a new conceptualization of intelligence as a tentacular network, with multiple centers of surveillance, designed as much to watch the German and Turkish enemy as to authenticate Arab loyalty. "The whole question is an Imperial one," Bray explained, requiring "perpetual interchange of views, intelligence, of affairs, of policy" from India to Egypt to Aden. On a map of the area between the Mediterranean and Burma, he marked the places that Pan-Islamism was taught as the basis for "an Intelligence Service that would cover the whole area." Bray's recommendations, which circulated among the highest echelons of government thanks to the express interest of Robert Cecil, argued that merely channeling information toward a single center like Cairo would no longer do; a *network* of centers was required, conforming to its subversive counterpart.

Moreover, this network was designed with a longer term in view; it called for a Consular Service that would collect information and possess "a military as well as a civil side."[57]

British intelligence also expanded into the political project of *fostering* an Arab unity that remained otherwise inchoate. Cox wrote with satisfaction after a British-sponsored durbar at Kuwait and Ibn Saud's visit to Basra:

> The dream of Arab unity which engaged the imagination of the
> Liberals of Damascus...has been brought nearer fulfilment than
> dreams are wont to come, but the role of presiding genius has been
> recast. Instead of the brilliant, unscrupulous Saiyid Talib...the
> Chiefs of Eastern and Western Arabia have united at the instance of
> the British Government.

In his original description of the Arab Bureau's functions, Sykes had not included what he now claimed as its very raison d'être: "the fostering of arab unity and the arab movement." If his new intelligence organization was mirroring a mirage, or, worse, a lie, he simply transformed it into the cause of which, now, Arab unity was to be the effect and reflection.[58]

Loosely linked agencies now began to coalesce into an intensely collaborative network that spied not only for, but on Arabs, ensuring they joined only in pro-British unity. The bureau had long taken care to decipher the Sherif's communications with his sons and the Arab Party to authenticate their bona fides as allies, but from 1917 the object was to acquire information about the Arab allies as a nascent independent military and political force. Hogarth's task in Allenby's intelligence organization was to collect all knowledge about the Arab world, *"especially* the Arab armies which are fighting in cooperation with us." Likewise, Alec Kirkbride's position as an intelligence officer with the Arab Army at Waheida was considered particularly valuable as a window onto the Arab intelligence staff. Covertness was key: the British staff nearby at Abu el Lissan, from whom Kirkbride took orders, forbore from visiting Waheida since any indication of "inspection" would be extremely resented. The advisers and agents under Cyril Wilson's command prodded the Sherif repeatedly to employ more spies—reluctant imperialists egging on reluctant oriental intriguers— eventually extracting special dispensation to take over the task themselves, thus extending their surveillance to the Hejazis they were ostensibly helping to free. At the same time, Wilson's agency worked closely with the Indian CID and the Arab Bureau to apprehend the organizers of the Silk Letter Plot, ultimately deporting a clutch of suspects to Malta. Spying on ostensibly friendly Arabs was part of the plan "To Keep the Arab Movement Alive," Sykes explained in a memo urging the creation of "an intelligence organisation capable of keeping politically in touch with the Arabs" through a "political depot" where "messengers should rendezvous, representatives be entertained, councils held and plans discussed." Through it, they could organize a "secret service" in Syria, based on the natural spy network that was Arab society. "To Employ the Nomad Bedouin to the Best Advantage," he suggested creating a mobile system of posts through the tribes which would eventually put them in contact with tribes in Mesopotamia. These ideas were most substantially taken into account in the new Jerusalem branch of the Arab Bureau, whose tasks included registering and tracking Bedouins "who after delivery of their messages, disappear...and fade away without notice unless more hold is kept on them than it has been possible hitherto to keep." It would also function as "a place of reunion, where some hospitality can be extended Arab-wise...and the necessary mediation with the British administration can be exercised.... *Secondarily*, the Bureau will serve as a centre for Intelligence...and *incidentally*, for propaganda." The bureau's political brief now took precedence over tactical intelligence, making intelligence about Arabs in the occupied territory, whose nomadism now seemed intrinsically subversive, the ultimate priority. Intelligence would have to be further "orientalized": the new office would not function as a "European office," but "like a semi-Arab house run by a staff jointly British and native." Counterespionage entailed concentration of "natives" in fixed areas and prohibition of movement, while "all roving Arabs were arrested and searched." The Eastern Mediterranean Special Intelligence Bureau became integral to this effort, cooperating with GSI Palestine partly to extend its counterespionage work east upon the *cessation* of military operations; intelligence was evolving into covert peacetime surveillance for purposes unrelated to proximate military needs. Deedes, who was in the special intelligence bureau, also headed the political section of the new Intelligence Corps under Richard Meinertzhagen (back from East Africa) and the Jerusalem branch of the Arab Bureau. Near the end of the war, the Eastern Mediterranean Special Intelligence Bureau and GSI Palestine merged to eliminate by then obvious redundancies, GSI becoming a "unit in the Imperial chain of other Special Intelligence Bureaus such as South Africa, Melbourne, India and Singapore, while maintaining the centralization and coordination of imperial *policy* with MI5 London." This reorganization signaled the official absorption of a military intelligence agency and occupation regime into the ultra-secret world of C and MI5; the informal concentration of all intelligence into but a few indispensable hands had fast made "specialized" agencies redundant with each other.[59]

To the east, where General Maude had again banished "defeat" from Force D's vocabulary, tribal pacification and surveillance had always been intrinsic to intelligence. Outposts at the desert frontier were "the eyes and ears through which [the political officer] can see and hear ... beyond his borders." Increasingly, however, political officers watched local Arabs not merely as pawns of the Turks but as threats in and of themselves, partly because the uneven British perfor- mance in the campaign had prevented them from winning over Arab loyalty wholesale. When a local agent informed him that Amara was being made a "spy-base," Philby, the local political officer, instituted a new practice requiring all visitors to register at his office and certify they would not leave without per- mission. Dickson admitted spying was "not a very nice job," but since even submission did not preclude treachery by local sheikhs, "I am in turn watching them." Here, too, nervousness about Arab loyalty derived partly from an increasing dependence on Arabs militarily—besides political officers' bands of irregulars, levies were raised to police roads and occupied villages and towns— which presented them in newly alarming aspect. Surveillance was made easier as the net of the Political Department was widened and made denser in the wake of Maude's advance. The "civil commissioner," as Cox was now styled, headed a Secretariat in Baghdad with departments for revenue, finance, judi- cial, public works, health, and so on, that communicated directly with political officers administering their territories. General Maude's indifference to the "political" side of the occupation (on the grounds that France had no political officers, even though, Bell pointed out, the French had no occupied territory to administer) compelled Cox and Bell to secure, through private channels, an independent status for their regime, in practice if not in fact. In the agents' hands, a covert colonial state grew up under cover of the actual military occupa- tion. The liberation of Mesopotamia was a sleight-of-hand by which a mas- sive counterespionage regime was configured as a "civil administration"; indeed, counterespionage was made "difficult," according to Beach's staff, "by the policy of reconciliation which we had to adopt towards the inhabitants of territory under British occupation." For them, "a primary necessity from an Intelligence point of view" was to "restrict the movements of civil inhabitants as far as possible" and, ideally, prohibit all movement. "Bureaux" were estab- lished all over, and political officers employed to create a system of passes, per- mits, and control posts. This "vast political Intelligence organization" watched over the population—and also governed it.[60]

The parallel developments in Mesopotamia and western Arabia were no accident. The two campaigns had begun increasingly to impinge on each other, agents facilitating much of their coordination. For instance, Sykes created a chief political officer analogue in Palestine to advise Wingate and the com- mander of the political situation farther east. Geographically, too, the cam- paigns encroached on each other. The fall of Jerusalem at the end of 1917 forestalled the German Operation Yilderim against Baghdad; both campaigns were heading north to an imprecisely delineated region, inspiring thoughts of military cooperation; and Cairo was increasingly interested in Najd as the Sherif consolidated his position in the Hejaz. This rapprochement was aided by a bout of agent criss-crossing between the two campaigns, also intended to control the diplomatic damage caused in 1917 by the Balfour Declaration (which promised Palestine to the Zionists), Russian exposure of the secret Sykes-Picot Accord (in which Sykes, acting as a diplomat, had arranged the postwar division of the Arab lands between the Allies), and Russian withdrawal from the war. By opening up Central Asia to attack and utterly shaking Arab faith in British intentions, these events also intensified the commitment to regionwide surveillance. The danger now seemed not so much of German attack but of German use of small forces and propaganda to set increasingly willing local movements in motion against the British. In the shadow of this insecurity, British agents launched an effort to blanket the region with their presence and prevent any weak spot, geographic or diplomatic, from pulling down the web of British power.[61]

Key agents were literally in a perpetual state of motion. Leachman was in charge at Karbala while also darting back and forth to help pacify occupied areas in the north. After the fall of Khan Baghdadi, he also joined a unit of armored cars in pursuit of the Turks. For the next few months he was in charge of both Karbala and the Dulaim region. On the eve of armistice, he was called to join the advance whilst keeping up his other duties. When Mosul fell, he was appointed military governor, in charge of a staff of assistant political officers including Bullard, who was something of a roving administrative jump starter, dispatched to each newly occupied part of Mesopotamia—Khaniqin, Baghdad, Kifri, Kirkuk—before joining Cox, who served in Tehran from 1918 to 1920. The informality of the administrative and intelligence worlds encouraged such hovering between posts. Lawrence having chosen him as an "understudy," Young left Mesopotamia for Cairo, but as Lawrence showed no sign of giving out, he began to roam the field of operations in search of a job, ultimately assisting in the organization of the nascent departments of Faisal's short-lived government in Damascus while technically attached to the Desert Mounted Corps. Meanwhile, Bray, thoroughly fed up with the Hejaz, left for France, only to be shunted back to replace Leachman at Karbala. Through Deedes, Kirkbride wound up in the employ of the Eastern Mediterranean Special Intelligence Bureau, although for all *public* purposes, he remained associated with his department at General Headquarters, liberally sharing information he gathered as a special intelligence bureau agent. The original Arab Bureau assumed a spatially attenuated existence; its staff was reinstalled in various new agencies but continued to maintain contact with the Cairo office. It resumed control of military operations in October 1918 when the Hejaz Operations Staff was disbanded. Arnold Wilson's abolishment of the Basra branch changed little in practice; that branch was never more than Bell (informally), who continued to pour out volumes for Cairo when the administration moved to Baghdad, while the stream of visitors showed no sign of abating. Agents' connections to any particular organization were often tenuous to the point of nullity; they remained ever freelancers, albeit responsible to a clear set of authorities, whose authority derived not from their institutional placement but from their own freelance claim to it.[62]

The shifting patchwork of wartime organization was essentially a single staff made up of the old, prewar community of agents circulating through a bewildering redundancy of agencies. It is difficult to overstate the importance of personal relationships to the form of this organization. Personal contacts buoyed Sykes, Hogarth, and Bell to ever loftier positions, ensuring their ability to shape and direct policy well beyond the scope of the usual intelligence worker. Outright nepotism was rank. There was Kitchener's nephew Parker, the Dawnay brothers, the Kirkbride brothers (Alec's brother took over his intelligence post at Beersheba when he joined the Eastern Mediterranean Special Intelligence Bureau), and even the Philby brothers (Tom Philby was with Basra Marine Transport, another sent a friend in the Royal Flying Corps to fly St. John around Amara, a third with the Royal Indian Marine visited). Lawrence would have gotten his brother into the Arab Bureau but for the war's end. Philip Graves's initial usefulness to Hogarth rested as much on his expertise as on his prewar friendship with Storrs and his relationship to Robert Graves. Wingate's son, Ronald, was a political officer in Mesopotamia. These intimacies underwrote the sharing of adventures, methodological approach, and assumptions about the elision between the military and the political in the Middle East.

As the agents prepared for the transition to peacetime occupation, Sykes, with Cecil's help, moved to the Foreign Office as "Acting Adviser on Arabian and Palestine Affairs." Although he would soon become a casualty of the Spanish flu, he and his colleagues had already laid the foundation for a covert empire in the Middle East in which officials technically affiliated with intelligence institutions would wield an almost unchecked executive power. Prewar coyness about the presence of British agents in Arabia launched the ship of official secrecy about the entire British endeavor in the region. But before unfolding that story, we need to know more about their presumption of authority and flaunting of their expertise, as well as their taste for the covert style. While the conditions of prewar intelligence-gathering shed light on this ethos, it is to the agents' cultural world that we must turn for fuller illumination.

2

The Cultural World of the Edwardian Agent

The intelligence community working on the Middle East was peculiar not only for its informal organization and vexed relationship to White-hall, but also for the motivations and provenance of its members. As Edwardians disillusioned by the direction of turn-of-the-century life, this group of men—and one woman—were drawn to the region as much for personal as for patriotic reasons; they offered their services partly as cover for their dearer hope of finding spiritual and artistic inspiration in the cradle of civilization. The Arabian blank spot on Edwardian maps was to them as much a "screen on which European fantasies may be projected" as a stage on which they could actually attempt to enact the fantasies repressed by bourgeois Britain. When the war came, it seemed to them to fulfill all their artistic and spiritual cravings with real, world-historical action. As cultural actors, these agents shared the sensibility of contemporaries fascinated by primitivism, the occult, and a minimalist aesthetic; the British intelligence effort in the Middle East was part of the mainstream early-twentieth-century effort to come to terms with modernity and produced for those at home a utopian Arabian counterpoint to all that disturbed them about the direction of British culture and society. In short, the intelligence project in Arabia was shaped as much by Edwardian cultural concerns as by geopolitical ones. The agents' personal preoccupations, of which they left a rich record, were not merely incidental but attest to their profoundly anti-empirical disposition while on their missions. As their imaginations ran amuck in the Arabia of their dreams, empiricism had hardly an opportunity in which to flex its atrophying muscle.[1]

Intelligence in the Name of Literature

The geopolitical circumstances that inspired official interest in intelligence about the Middle East also inspired a more popular interest in recording imperishable images of Arabia at a time in which it appeared to be undeniably and very quickly *changing*, threatening, as one journalist put it, to "make this 'unchanging East' but the memory of a dream." As railways began to roll back "the domination of caprice and temporal decay," countless books, newspapers, and lecturers strove to capture "this lost land of dead Empires, while yet its sleep remained unharmed." Indeed, the controversy surrounding the Baghdad Railway itself kept the region in the papers, while the opening of another "sacred railway" from Damascus to the holy cities occasioned the printing of the first European photographs of Medina in the *Illustrated London News* in 1908. That year's Young Turk revolution and its aftermath kept the Middle East in the headlines for the remainder of the period. Comment on Sir William Willcocks's high-profile plans to reconstruct the Mesopotamian irrigation system milked to fullest advantage the object lesson embodied in British reclamation of the putative site of the Garden of Eden from devastation at the hands of the feckless Turks. The infant cinema industry, projecting itself as a magical medium best suited to capturing the fantastic, depicted Arabs from the very outset, drawing on the rich supply of universally familiar tales in the *Arabian Nights*. Tourism and religious revivals dating from the previous century produced an enduring fascination with the Holy Land as a "living museum" of the Bible. In short, as one commentator noted on the 1908 release of a new edition of Charles Doughty's classic travelogue, *Arabia Deserta* (1888), "A new breath moves over the face of Asia, a new curiosity has awakened in Europe." This curiosity was only intensified by Arabia's relatively greater inaccessibility compared to the days in which Doughty and his famous forbears such as Alexander Kinglake had traveled.[2]

Intelligence agents were part of this cultural industry. Almost all of them eventually produced books based on their experiences, writing with a particular audience in mind, one that relished tales of mystery and adventure in the Orient. The construction of the explorer as author is especially important in this case, for unlike their forerunners elsewhere, many of these agents traveled to Arabia either with the intention of fulfilling their dream to become writers "first and foremost" or with the preconceived notion that travel in Arabia was *primarily* of literary interest. Gathering information was incorporated into their hope of finding in Arabia a means of launching their literary careers. "I am gathering a store of Arab News and notions, which some day will help me in giving vividness to what I write," wrote the young archaeologist T. E. Lawrence. Most prolific and famous in the community were David Hogarth, G. Wyman Bury, Aubrey Herbert (under the pseudonym "Ben Kendim"—Turkish for "I, myself"—to accommodate embassy rules against disclosures by active diplomats), Leonard Woolley, Mark Sykes, and Gertrude Bell, who used her highly popular works to finance her travel. The inspiration of these literary ambitions lay in the Edwardian view of Arabia as an essentially fictional place, a trope the agents' works did much to reinforce, as will become clearer below.[3]

As authors and heroes of their accounts, these agents maintained an increasingly high profile in Edwardian society. Their mixing with the world of writers, artists, and other cultural figures was predicated on their status as independently respected and popular men and women. Their exploits were hyped in their widely read, much-publicized books as well as in newspapers—indeed, many of their adventures, such as Valentine Chirol's, Angus Hamilton's, and David Fraser's, were sponsored by papers like the *Pall Mall Gazette* and the *Times of India*. Sykes's *Dar-ul-Islam* received rave reviews in 1904 and established him as a writer of importance, and *The Caliph's Last Heritage* (1915), a tome that combined a rare attempt at a general history of the Ottoman Empire with his unedited tour diaries, was an acknowledged publishing sensation. James Elroy Flecker, the poet, playwright, and consul, single-handedly made small villages near Beirut famous with his poems. Accounts of travel in Arabia, by both anonymous tourists and famous explorers, filled the pages of publications like *Blackwood's Magazine*. The pages of the newly founded *Times Literary Supplement (TLS)*, to which many agents contributed, were so full of books on various Arabic matters that one anonymous reviewer (none other than Hogarth) remarked, "Asiatic Turkey seems to occasion more entertaining books of travel than any other land." That the genre was reaching the point of super-saturation is evident from frequent prefatory apologies for "having added yet another gallon" to that "ocean of literature." Explorers also profited from their access to other prominent public platforms, including offices of government; universities; organizations such as the Royal Anthropological Institute, the Royal Geographical Society, and the Central Asian Society; and museums such as the Ashmolean (Captain Shakespear's Arabia specimens remain on display at the Natural History Museum). As they painstakingly disinterred the great cities of antiquity, Woolley and Hogarth became celebrated and eminent figures, both among and beyond their own circle of academics. Bell was an illustrious guest when she called at Carchemish in 1911, and the story of her prewar trip to Hail remained a favored topic for school essays in England until the 1930s. Sykes was fêted at home in Sledmere, where he received numerous invitations to speak about his travels at neighboring villages and towns. In 1904–1905, Sledmere's schoolmaster prepared slides to accompany the show, and in Sykes's parliamentary campaign of 1908, his lectures took him well beyond the Yorkshire lecture circuit. There were also singular sensations, such as that caused by Lawrence and Woolley in 1913 when they made a mutual exhibit of Britain and two Arabs from the site, Hamoudi and Dahoum, taking them to a show at Earl's Court and commissioning Francis Dodd to sketch Dahoum.[4]

This commission was not an exceptional transgression by the community of agents into the mainstream of Edwardian artists, intellectuals, and writers. They were intimately connected with that world, both socially and professionally. Aubrey Herbert, an agent, member of Parliament, and poet (his *Eastern Songs* appeared in 1911), counted among his intimates the spy novelist John Buchan, the poet Rupert Brooke, the politicians Maurice Baring and Raymond Asquith, and the social commentator Hilaire Belloc, who had coached him at Oxford. James Elroy Flecker regularly sent his work—much of it Middle Eastern in theme and locale—to magazines and publishers and to the likes of G. K. Chesterton and George Bernard Shaw, who gave him critical feedback. He, too, was close with Rupert Brooke. Sykes actively cultivated relationships with literary figures. After a brief spell at *Granta* and his own satire journal, *Snarl*, the Middle East route to literary fame proved felicitous. Fawning letters of appreciation of *Dar-ul-Islam* arrived from H. G. Wells, who referred to it extensively in his massively popular *Outline of History* (1919), and from Rudyard Kipling, who praised its authentic depiction of all the sights, smells, and confusion of Turkey, offering the notably narcissistic compliment, "You ought to have been born in the East." Sykes was also friends with Belloc and George Wyndham, the politician and man of letters under whom he briefly served at the Irish Office. Shakespear's cousin was Olivia Shakespear, herself of Indian Army background, a novelist and longtime intimate of W. B. Yeats, with whom she had an affair and shared an interest in occultism. Her daughter, the artist Dorothy Shakespear, married Ezra Pound, and their son, Omar, is a poet who has translated much Arabic and Persian poetry and traveled extensively in the Middle East. Richard Meinertzhagen, the prewar agent who would become Allenby's intelligence chief during the war, grew up in intellectual society through his mother's family, the Potters. Beatrice Webb was his aunt, but Herbert Spencer, Sir Francis Galton, Aldous Huxley, George Eliot, Bernard Shaw, and Oscar Wilde (of whom he severely disapproved), among others, were also family friends. Clement Atlee was a playmate, Winston Churchill a schoolmate, Joseph Chamberlain his aunt's unsuccessful suitor, and Charles

Darwin a revered acquaintance. It was at Huxley's daughter's instigation, and with Spencer's encouragement, that he launched into and remained devoted to writing his notorious diaries.[5]

Gertrude Bell, as usual, outdid everyone, even in her social reach, partly thanks to her father's position as a country gentleman, industrialist, and Liberal politician. Hence, for instance, her flattering dedication of *Amurath to Amurath* (1911) to Lord Cromer. Distantly related to Bertrand Russell—his uncle was married to her aunt—she was also friendly with Lady Ottoline Morrell, Russell's well-known correspondent and mistress. Bell's sisters were definitely known to Virginia Stephen, whose brother was apparently smitten by these "most brilliant girl conversationalists in London" and whose social and family relations overlapped considerably with that of imperial administrators, even before her marriage to Leonard Woolf, then an administrator in Ceylon. (This was, notably, the era of the famous "orientalist" practical jokes perpetrated by the Stephen siblings: the 1905 "Zanzibar Hoax" and the 1910 "Dreadnought Hoax"). Bell was also close with later affiliates of the Bloomsbury clique: Vita Sackville-West and her diplomat husband, Harold Nicolson, who was one of Bell's relations, were two of the very few people she dined with in Constantinople upon her return from Hail in 1914; Sackville-West would write the foreword to Elizabeth Burgoyne's 1958 biography of the explorer. Bell's brother-in-law was George Trevelyan, who along with another relative, Cecil Spring-Rice of the Foreign Office, was among her summer guests in 1905. In 1913, Trevelyan traveled to Greece with the Indian Army intelligence officer Hubert Young (then on his way to Arabia) and Young's cousin, an editor of the *Morning Post*.[6]

Hogarth's friends among an older generation of Arabia explorers, the Blunts, were pivotal figures in this web of relations between "Arabists" and the rest, particularly since Sir Wilfrid was both a famous, if declining, poet in his own right and a fashionably vocal critic of the government and Lady Anne was Lord Byron's granddaughter. Sir Wilfrid was close with Belloc and a slew of emerging modernist poets, including Pound and Yeats, whose friendship he actively cultivated as early as 1902, and whose appreciation for Blunt's vehement opposition to British rule in Ireland was expressed in "The Peacock" (1916). Yeats and Blunt initially met at the home of Lady Gregory, Yeats's closest collaborator, Blunt's mistress of many years, and a writer and Irish nationalist whose eyes were first opened to the powers of cultural nationalism in Cairo during the revolt of Urabi Pasha in 1882. Bernard Shaw was also a friend of Wilfrid Blunt and consulted him on his work. The Blunts also socialized with Lord Alfred Douglas, Arthur Balfour, G. K. Chesterton, and Churchill, whose particular fascination with the world of cloak-and-dagger had been sharpened by his experiences on the North West Frontier. In short, if the late-nineteenth-century cult of Arabia was, in Kathryn Tidrick's words, "esoteric and exclusive," by the Edwardian era, it had become part of the mainstream.[7]

In this social world, and with their publications, the agents propagated a view of Arabia as a space for "illicit adventure"; their accounts are marked by a curious slippage between reportage and storytelling. If, as scholars say, the shared cultural environment of spy agencies, writers, and readers produced the artifice of apparent realism at the heart of the attraction of Edwardian spy fiction, the "true fiction" of Arabia explorers, set in a fictionalized Arabian spy-space, played on the same conceit.[8] Many of these works—such as G. Wyman Bury's *The Land of Uz* (1911), Mark Sykes's *Dar-ul-Islam*, Arthur Wavell's *A Modern Pilgrim in Mecca* (1913), and David Fraser's *The Short Cut to India* (1909)—were cast in the mold of traditional imperial adventure novels, recalling especially those familiar "tales of the North-West Frontier." Fraser's book, for instance, while full of technical detail about the route, was capped off by an account of his adventure at the hands of a Shammar robber, for which reviewers reserved their highest praise: "Even those who are not interested in the political and commercial questions will find it an engrossing narrative of adventure." A tourist's account of her travels in Arabia was *criticized* for attempting to pass on too many facts: "We do not want any of that sort of thing...no information, indeed, whatever, but just the enthralling story of their daily contact with the incongruous Eastern society in which...they were adventuring themselves." Now, the anonymous reviewer in both these instances was Hogarth; writing in the *TLS* and other journals, agents were doubly influential in shaping British ideas about Arabia. Their books' frequent disavowal of scientific pretensions reinforced their status as accounts of adventure, as did their use of such literary devices as scenic dialogue. In general, the more serious and less imitative of fiction the account, the more polite the public reaction. By the anonymous hand of the celebrated geographer Halford John Mackinder, the *TLS* affirmed that Arabia was a land best known imprecisely: noting the discrepancies between the text and maps of Hogarth's *The Penetration of Arabia* (1904), a book assessing *scientific* exploration of the region, it observed indulgently that Arabia was "a land which as a whole is so vaguely known that it is better fitted for the half light of literary description than for the hard and inevitably definite expressions of cartography."[9]

Adventure was not, however, the summit of the agents' literary ambition. They were even more intensely invested in the Romantic view of Arabia as an essentially artistic space, a catalytic space where the poet could abandon himself to reverie. This Romantic egoism may have been somewhat offset by Doughty's vision of the desert as "the place where man regained a proper sense of his own weakness and unworthiness" and other late-nineteenth-century efforts to reconstruct Arabs as basically earthy and earthly, but Edwardians craving a fusion of art and life continued to see Arabia with what Hogarth's sister called "a poet's imagination." They took up Doughty's struggle to use Arabia as a site for undoing "the decadence of the English language"; the Romantics had found inspiration in the desert, but not linguistic redemption of this sort.[10] The desert's minimalism was key; to Edwardians, it was an atypical heart of darkness, a "void" they knew to be a palimpsest of ancient civilizations, whatever its superficial blankness. The desert horizon had "nothing to show and nothing to tell you," wrote a tourist, "and yet [its] very emptiness is so full of secret possibilities and hidden wonder." "However flat and colourless" the landscape, remarked Edmund Candler as the London *Times'* war correspondent in Mesopotamia, there was "always food for imagination in the air." Bedouin knowledge of this, British commentators reasoned, was the root of their undyingly poetic nature. Their fanciful place-names invested empty spaces with meaning and provided their poets with what Bell called the great "changeless theme of the evanescence of desert existence." Aspiring agents hoped they too might arrive at a transcendental understanding of existence by tapping into creativity kindled by contemplation of the desert. This thinking was in keeping with the modernist fascination with the primitive and the contemporary anthropological belief in "savage survivals," which associated poetry with the mythology of primitive people. Edwardian agents hoped to attain the fusion of art and life they so desired by using a sojourn in the desert to exhume the vestigial primitive in themselves.[11]

Sykes's frequent litanies against the banalities of modern, bourgeois civilization provide perhaps the best example of the Edwardian view that Bedouin life was both more advanced (in a sense) and creatively inspiring because of its barrenness. In an acerbic footnote to his assertion that Arabs, as rhetoricians and poets, have no place in a "civilised community," he defined the latter as, "a community living in towns and in houses, suffering from infectious and contagious diseases, travelling in railway trains, able to read and write, possessing drinking shops, reading newspapers, surrounded by a hundred unnecessary luxuries, possessing rich and poor, slums and palaces, and convinced that their state is the most edifying in the world." Alternating the alleged virtues with the emerging vices of modern European life, he damned the whole system as lacking the genuinely civilized, albeit primitive, sensibility of the Arabs, which was the key to art. In Arabia, the authentic poetic sensibility could thrive. Poets, heroes, laments, dirges, councils of war, women's shrill cries—the stuff of noble desert warfare: "These things are the very salt of a life which knows nothing of old age pensions, Nonconformist consciences, suffragettes, maffickings, professional politicians, trusts, excursions, halfpenny papers, hysteria, and appendicitis." He encouraged the imperial hero, artist, writer, and veteran spy Robert Baden-Powell to adapt Bedouin poetic culture to Boy Scouting to provide precisely the spirit of vitality Britain needed to instill in its youth. Lawrence shared this obsession with the desert's superior aesthetic qualities. "I feel very little lack of English scenery," he wrote to his brother. "Here one learns an economy of beauty which is wonderful. England is fat—obese." He agreed absolutely with Doughty's claim that he who has once been to the desert "is never the same." "My books would be better," he affirmed, "if I had been for a time in open country: and the Arab life is the only one that still holds the early poetry," since it, unlike the Sahara, was "Semitic" in its atmosphere and past. His first foray into writing was a piece for the Jesus College magazine titled "The Gospel of Bareness in Materials," in which he celebrated austerity as an aesthetic principle.[12]

Arabia was thus not merely an aesthetic space, but *the quintessential* space for twentieth-century art, a physical manifestation of the emerging aesthetic of the day. Lawrence and Sykes, despite their own fairly conservative literary tastes, were in tune with emerging trends of European culture. *Arabia Deserta* was ubiquitous on the shelves of Edwardian agents, but also on those of many modernists, such as William Morris, Henry Green, W. H. Auden, Yeats, Wyndham Lewis, D. H. Lawrence, and Aldous Huxley. T. S. Eliot ranked it along with the novels of Henry James and Joseph Conrad as indicative of future directions of English prose. In it, the desolate landscape emerged for the first time as a metaphor for man's inner state and a transcendent space that could induce mythic consciousness, a shift that, according to Richard Bevis, signifies Doughty's break with the Victorians and anticipation of the modernists, for whom the void was a central literary concern. Without Doughty's invocation of the Desert Sublime, argues Bevis, *The Waste Land* remains inexplicable; moreover, where else but the desert would a minimalist want to live?[13]

James Joyce completed *Ulysses* in 1918, and although Stephen Daedalus never quite leaves Dublin, it is worth recalling that there was a wider context of travel literature framing this fascination with Doughty's work and that of self-styled "Near East Kiplings" such as Flecker and Herbert. Novelists were using travel, metaphorically and practically, as a device for exploring psychological states and the writer's craft, so much that by the Edwardian period, "the modernist poem and the scientific paper were crowding in on territory once a part of travel writing." Indeed, other writers were also venturing, at least figuratively, in the agents' direction. Virginia Woolf, who got as far as Constantinople in 1906 and 1911, was experimenting with travel to vast, unfathomable spaces in her first novel, *The Voyage Out* (1915), which she began in 1908. Though its imaginary Amazonian setting is a long way from Arabia, she had already begun to signify in this, as in later novels, those characteristically Woolfian moments of surreality with a sudden vision of the "outlines of Constantinople in a mist." (A Constantinople enshrouded in mist and "opalescent cloud" also appears in a contemporary poem by Vita Sackville-West, who, like the agents, was a writer initially shaped by her experiences in the Middle East.) The novel's horizonless Amazonian landscape echoes the agents' Arabia in its lack of place-names, dizzying oceanlike vastness, and mountains resembling a "great encampment of tents." It dominates the novel's mood, frequently providing the object of the characters' drowsy philosophical contemplation. All the excitement of "the voyage out" derives from precisely the same sense of exaltation, vitality, and freedom that marked much of the travel writing on Arabia, expressing which, Woolf deploys the desert metaphor. As Rachel Vinrace's ship pulled away from England, "a shrinking island in which people were imprisoned," she became "an inhabitant of the great world, which has so few inhabitants, travelling all day across an empty universe, with veils drawn before her and behind. She was more lonely than the caravan crossing the desert...infinitely more mysterious...in her vigour and purity she might be likened to all beautiful things." Joyce's *Dubliners* (1914) reaches explicitly for the Middle Eastern metaphor to express the surreality of the world. Similarly, Joseph Conrad's *Lord Jim* (1900) sets out on a voyage—to Aden, in that remote, Middle Eastern sphere of the world, "beyond the end of telegraph cables and mail-boat lines," where "the haggard utilitarian lies of our civilization wither and die, to be replaced by pure exercises of imagination, that have the futility, often the charm, and sometimes the deep hidden truthfulness, of works of art." This space "off the map" was the ideal space in which the fantastic, melodramatic, and deeply philosophical tale of the disastrous fate of the sailor Jim could unfold. Popular novels experimenting with evocative styles and arcane plotting were also set in the Orient. Witness the applause for a novelist who had abandoned a setting in "the more trivial and vulgar side of London society" in favor of allowing his soul to be "stirred by the desert, its immensity and freedom and solemnity," thus imparting to this book "more emotion, more vigour, more sense of life" than any of his previous.[14]

Contemporaries remarked the sudden emergence of this new "literary and artistic cult" of the desert. One reviewer asserted: "No sensitive soul before the nineteenth century ever regarded the Sahara as anything but a horrid waste. Now hotels are built in it, ladies camp upon it, tourists meander about it, and the chorus of its praise ascends daily." He speculated on the cause:

Our civilization has grown so complex that a long dormant instinct of revolt is awake. The individual, chafing under his burden of social observance, wants to return, for however short a time, to more primitive life and feel his self-sufficiency. The desert, which is the most primitive thing on earth, offers an opportunity; so into it he goes and finds there beauty and health, things which were there always, but used to make no more appeal to him.

Agents were both shaping and diagnosing this aesthetic shift: this commentary in the *TLS* was anonymously authored by Hogarth. The fetishistic interest in the desert suggests that the craving for escapist descriptions of Arabia was more than the old hankering after an exotic and mysterious East. A reviewer of *The Desert and the Sown* (1907) praised Bell for forbearing to describe the famous sights of Damascus: "Unless one realizes that Damascus is the gate of the desert...one misses all its significance. The wild desert life, with its uncertainty and vicissitudes, haunts Damascus, and nothing appeals more to the imaginative traveller." Edwardians had shifted their focus from the exotic-erotic bazaars, mosques, and palaces of Arabia to the desert idyll.[15]

Perhaps unsurprisingly, the Arabian desert also provided a particularly useful setting in contemporary espionage fiction. Rudyard Kipling addressed the Royal Geographical Society in 1914, an event emblematic of the coeval evolution of the British spy novel and British intelligence in this period. In the area of Middle East intelligence, that mutual influence was perhaps most memorably manifested by Aubrey Herbert's inspiration of Sandy Arbuthnot, the fictional hero of John Buchan's *Greenmantle* (1916), written the year before Buchan was appointed wartime director of information and then director of intelligence. The enormously popular novel chronicles Richard Hannay and Sandy Arbuthnot's journey to Constantinople and, abortively, to Mesopotamia, as they attempt to uncover and crush a giant German-Islamic conspiracy against the empire. But even where Arabia was not the spy novel's actual setting, its imagery hovered in the background. That Buchan described Constantinople as "pure Arabian nights" on his 1910 visit and then depicted the England of *The Thirty-Nine Steps* (1915) as "a sort of *Arabian Nights*" can be read as an attempt to orientalize that familiar landscape, to render the *heimlich unheimlich* and thus fitting for an espionage tale. An "unenhanced" English landscape would not have sufficed, for the very infrastructure of storytelling had vanished from that settled and thus disenchanted space. An innkeeper in the novel explains why he, unlike his ancestors, could not regale visitors with wondrous tales:

Maybe in the old days when you had pilgrims and ballad-makers and highwaymen and mail-coaches on the road. But not now. Nothing comes here but motor-cars full of fat women, who stop for lunch, and a fisherman or two in the spring, and the shooting tenants in August. There is not much material to be got out of that. I want to see life, to travel the world, and write things like Kipling and Conrad.

To revive storytelling, the aspiring writer had to travel where itinerant "pilgrims and ballad-makers" might still be found. Buchan named Erskine Childers's *The Riddle of the Sands* (1903), set on Germany's northern coast, the best adventure story ever written, largely because its "atmosphere of grey northern skies and...wet sands is as masterfully reproduced as in any story of Conrad's." It too transformed an ordinary occidental landscape into an exotic wasteland of infinite oriental mysteriousness. Indeed, Childers, who would serve in wartime intelligence on the coasts of Syria, Sinai, and Asia Minor, explicitly evokes the spy-space of Arabia: the adventure in the surreal northern German landscape unfolds on "a desert of sand," and Davies, one of the agents, is a "street arab." Basil Liddell Hart, the military theorist, later noted that "the title of that famous story of spying on the German coastline...might have been coined still more aptly to fit" Lawrence's activities in Sinai on the eve of the war. While some thought it typically incompetent of the authorities to assign Childers, an expert on the North Sea, to intelligence on the eastern Mediterranean, perhaps his North Sea was something of a proxy for Arabia all along. Other classic spy fiction, such as G. K. Chesterton's *The Man Who Was Thursday* (1908) and Conrad's *The Secret Agent* (1907), also took place in deceptive and murky surroundings obliquely referring to the Middle East. In the popular imagination, even espionage transpiring far from the East tended, by its very nature, to "orientalize" all settings, to render them obscure and inscrutable.[16]

The spy novel was a genre rooted in imperial insecurity, and Arabia was, as we have seen, the focus of many imperial anxieties in this period. In general, Edwardian writers drew on the desert motif to express not only anxiety about the direction of British culture and society but also their concern about the seemingly aimless trajectory of the empire, which threatened, like all modern, capitalistic, only outwardly solid creations, to simply "melt into air" and squander its potential to achieve the majestic immortality and imperishable meaningfulness of its ancient predecessors, whose glories were then being rediscovered in the Middle East, often by the agents. "Ah, if there shall ever arise a nation whose people have forgotten poetry or whose poets have forgotten the people, though they send their ships round Taprobane and their armies across the hills of Hindustan, though their city be greater than Babylon of old, though they mine a league into earth or mount to the stars on wings," warned Flecker, "they will be a dark patch upon the world." The very surroundings of the ancient empires bespoke a broader civilizational indestructibility. Vita

Sackville-West's "Nomads" described in enchanted tones Bedouin wandering, "frontiers falling as we went," over all Asia and all time: "the old forgotten empires, which have faded turn by turn,/ From the shades emerging slowly to their ancient sway return,/ And to their imperial manhood rise the ashes from the urn." Edwardian writers found in the desert theme a means of expressing the danger to a civilization that had gone adrift from the safe harbors of faith, austerity, grandeur, and elemental liberty into a hedonistic ocean of sophistry, overabundance, mediocrity, and conformity.[17]

The view that "Primitiveness inhered in the Orient, *was* the Orient," was, Edward Said has told us, a touchstone of orientalist thought, but Said is not entirely on the mark in his claim that travelers like Lawrence and Bell saw Arabia as historically and geographically "barren and retarded" and the Arab as possessed of "centuries of experience and no wisdom." The racist perception of Arab primitivism was not an entirely negative depiction *to the Edwardian mind*, nor was it mere romanticization of their noble savagery. It was also, during the weary Edwardian era, envious, however speciously in our view. Edwardians did not see Arabs as entirely lacking in wisdom, but as possessed of a different, more seductive, intuitive rather than intellectual wisdom. They wanted to know, as the journalist Meredith Townsend put it, "What gives the Arab alone, even among Asiatics, that perfection of mental content," for "suppose...that Mecca survives Manchester, that when Europe is a continent of ruins, the Arab shall still dwell in the desert...living on like the Pyramid." Adepts at "rhetoric, subtle argument, poetry and histrionism," in Sykes's only partly patronizing words, Arabs were alleged to have greater insight into matters abstract. This was a period in which primitivism was *trendy*, however racist.[18]

Intelligence in the Name of Escape

Early-twentieth-century works by Conrad, Kipling, Woolf, Buchan, and others were invested in forestalling the "disenchantment of the world" unleashed by Western expansion and together constituted a distinct turn-of-the-century genre that John McClure calls "late imperial romance." Seeking to once again open up unmapped spaces, Buchan and Kipling suggested that imperialism in its very triumph produced such a space—in the deterritorialized zone of espionage, a world in which mystery is rediscovered and the disillusioned hero dramatically and redemptively lost from the realm of politics to the realm of spirit. The fascination with Arabia as an artistic and even culturally redemptive space was rooted in its special significance as just such an unmapped, unexplored space, one that also happened to have emerged as *the* zone of Edwardian espionage. The very consciousness of ignorance that inspired new intelligence initiatives in the region at this juncture at once clouded those initiatives with an aura of romance especially compelling to Edwardians. "As the visible world is measured, mapped, tested, weighed," wrote the anthropologist and occultist Andrew Lang, "we seem to hope more and more that a world of invisible romance may not be far from us." A sense of "belatedness" marked European exploration in this period, a sense that all the dark places of the earth had already been explored and con-quered, producing in Britain what one scholar describes as an obsessive search for "an 'elsewhere' still unexplored." The exploration "theme" became ubiqui-tous, pervading children's books as a form of play and attracting followers through Baden-Powell's Scouting movement. The agents were among those bored of the jungle, shikars, and, most of all, old India hands, as Walter Stirling, an Egyptian Army officer who served in intelligence and as chief staff officer to Lawrence during the Arab Revolt, would later recall; they yearned for new expe-rience. In this expectant atmosphere, the political situation in Arabia also began to draw the British public's eye repeatedly toward it: the *Times* noted that, while little was known about Arabia, "stories reach the bazaars of Bombay and Cairo of strange fights between mail-clad warriors, of armies still contending with bows and arrows, of moonlight battles, of siege and sortie, and attack and sur-prise." To temper the disheartening announcement of the end of the age of romantic exploration, the Royal Geographical Society instituted a special series called "The Still Unknown," focusing on places that continued to offer scope for the pioneer explorer, beginning first with Hogarth's lecture on Arabia. The *Times* frequently hailed the relief Arabia offered to those fearing that "the old type of adventure into the absolutely unknown" could now transpire only on the South Pole; the *TLS* called Arabia "the one country whose secrets still elude [archaeologists]." Arabia offered a reassuring continuation of the glories of nine-teenth-century imperial exploration at a time when projecting imperial glory had become especially crucial to British prestige (witness the spate of ceremo-nial durbars, tours, and other such spectacular pageantry). The fact that much of the region was blank by virtue of being forbidden, both by local and British authorities, enhanced its appeal, allowing journeys in it to morph into "quests" of a higher order. The Suez Canal and railways having brought the region closer, its inviolateness became even more agitating. Hogarth pointed to the irony that Mecca's "very pretension to secrecy" tended to "excite in many Europeans so strong a curiosity of the forbidden as to impel them to Arabia." Indeed, Arthur Wavell excused his 1909 trespasses into Mecca on these very grounds. So criti-cal was Arabia's enduring inaccessibility to its attraction that some despaired at its imminent incorporation, via the Hejaz railway, into the realm of the accessi-ble world.[19]

An intelligence assignment in Arabia was thus framed within the *fictional-ized*, because consciously anachronistic, terms of the old imperial adventurism, rather than within the terms of, say, a contemporary intelligence mission to Germany; hence in part the fictional aspirations of the agents' works. Agents projected onto the practical task entrusted to them their personal fantasies of repeating the legendary coups of Richard Burton and David Livingstone. Meinertzhagen grew up infatuated with such figures, not least because of his awesome boyhood encounters with Blunt; Henry Stanley; Cecil Rhodes, who invited him to Africa (his father forbade him to go); and Sir Harry Johnston, who introduced him to Burton and thrilled him with descriptions of Africa (and perhaps even more inspiringly, tales of his bureaucratic insubordination). Hogarth may have thought that "to repeat Burton's exploit in these days would be to effect a mere *coup de théâtre*," but that was precisely what many agents wanted to effect. Wavell, for instance, determined to enter Mecca in disguise, knowing his intrusion would not result in any information gains. On his death, Soane's journey was also compared to Burton's and Doughty's. Renewal of the Victorian script of imperial adventure in forbidden Arabia produced that increasingly rare imperial perquisite, fame. Bell was thrilled to discover in Mesopotamia: "I am a Person in this country....Renown is not difficult to acquire here." Hubert Young later reminisced about his youthful daydreams about "the fame that would one day be his for his journeys in the trackless wastes of Central Arabia." Somewhat perversely, but crucially for the evolution of intelligence practices, these individuals became agents not to become anony-mous ciphers but to garner a more traditional imperial fame. In this, their mind-set was notably different from the humble "public service mentality" of, say, contemporary explorers of Australia's deserts.[20]

Agents were also attracted to the region by another kind of nostalgia: a longing for Britain's preindustrial past. Certainly, the Romantics too had sought redemption from industrial life in the East, particularly India, but Edwardians did not so much urge Europe to copy Arabia as seek escape *from* Europe into Arabia and combined fulfillment of this wish with intelligence work. In Najd, "the gateway of an unknown land," wrote the Aden agent, G. Wyman Bury, "one may step straight from this modern age of bustle and chicanery into an era of elemental conditions...back into the pages of history to mediaeval times." Likewise, Lawrence first stepped into the Middle East to research his Oxford thesis, "The Influence of the Crusades on European Military Architecture to the End of the Twelfth Century," which his brother later described as "a dream way of escape from Bourgeois England." In Arabia, jaded Edwardians found a living stage set, where the deceit of modern life was replaced by the glittering mirage of medievalism and literature, a more alluring deceit, perhaps less oppressive, but in any case not conducive to a measured, empirical approach to intelligence-gathering.[21]

Unlike their Victorian predecessors, these agents hoped not only to escape the ugliness of industrial society, but also the decadence and discord of a society of warring classes. The enduring tribal order of the cradle of civilization seemed to offer a glimpse of their own, increasingly mythical, organic medieval past. The frustrated upper-class affinities many of them shared—Sykes was an aristocrat disturbed by the seemingly inexorable decline of his class; the bastard-child Lawrence felt cheated of his aristocratic patrimony—informed their sense of alienation from England and attraction to Arabia, their marginality at once serving as a badge of authentically eccentric Englishness. Bell followed in a line of aristocratic women travelers in the desert, explicitly bucking bourgeois Victorian gender stereotypes.[22] Together, they romanticized Arabia as an oasis of nobility in an otherwise debauched world, whatever its faults as an admittedly oriental society. It was on a space-time continuum outside the reach of a real world laboring under the unenviable burdens of history, modernity, and "progress." The disasters of the South African War brought a new intensity to the mourning for Britain's lost valor. Serving on the front, Sykes pined, "O for the East, the East and real feelings. *Allah! Ho Akbar, Din we el Mohamed!* There fighting is real fighting." In the twentieth century, the fascination of Arabia was less a desire for the exotic than, to borrow Peter Brent's phrase, "nostalgia for the standards of Sir Lancelot." The region's agitated political state, manifested in a series of tribal clashes, seemed to confirm the myth that it was the last refuge of a chivalric order, its very proximity stirring the European's hankering after a way of life lost to him. Agents went to Arabia in search of escape from the harsh reality of life, into a *utopia*, a no-place; witnessing or taking notes on the reality of life in Arabia was not uppermost in their minds.[23]

In this utopia of aristocrats, agents hoped to rediscover a personal sovereignty crushed by the oppressive conventions of bourgeois society. Arabs seemed "a free people...on the very edges of a Europe more and more bound in the chains of industrialism, prudishness and economic necessity." The desert was, to Sykes, a haven for individuals who prized "boundless liberty" above all else, whether they had been born there or had fled civilization's relentless smothering of their instincts to be there. Extending their romanticization of the noble Arab to *themselves*, Edwardian agents hoped in Arabia to resurrect their authentic selves and allow their intrinsic nobility as free-born Englishmen of legend to surface uninhibited by bourgeois convention. Soane's "unorthodox ways" shocked his deskbound chiefs at the Imperial Bank of Persia when he embarked on his journeys. The DMO agent Douglas Carruthers compared his "escape from the bonds of civilization" to "running away from school!" "From now on we were ourselves," he rejoiced. "We acknowledged no master, we obeyed no rules....We paid no taxes...we answered no letters; civilization could go bang for aught we cared." Instead, "A new responsibility developed upon us—that of self-discipline in its most exacting form."[24]

Ostensibly stripped of artifice in the desert, the agents worked their surreptitious, undercover behavior into an imaginative vision of their primordial identity. Arabia became the space to which traveler-agents came to be *free* from their governments, to be, as Bell called herself, an *outlaw*, especially given that their missions were often undertaken in defiance of official orders. Besides being the quintessential space for unfettered movement, it was also sovereign, beyond "the longest arm of the law" (particularly for Europeans protected by the Capitulations). To many, it recalled the sea, that traditional space of English liberty. The fact that it was Ottoman territory, without, evidently, being under effective Ottoman control, made it a sort of "no man's land." A Hobbesian state of nature beyond any legal, societal, or bureaucratic gaze, it was invisible, a space into which the agents too could vanish, disappear. There, "silence and solitude fall round you like an impenetrable veil." Collecting intelligence— serving and representing a government by being its *eyes* abroad—was a task requiring subtle characterization in a space whose freedom from servitude, governments, and any sort of surveillance was celebrated. Agents coped with these incongruous obligations by conceiving their work more in mythopoeic than in mundane terms, their dispositions more visionary than pragmatic. They strove to become *part* of this utopia of free nobility, especially while fulfilling the intelligence missions that took them there. Their missions would thus be awash in the glow of the code of honor, loyalty, and duty that was the region's demiurge, raising their fact-finding missions to epic quests—with some success, evidently: Herbert was unanimously described as a "knight"; Norman Bray titled his biography of fellow agent Leachman, "*A Paladin of Arabia*"; and Lawrence, according to his friend and biographer, the poet Robert Graves, never outgrew playing at knights, actually binding himself to the same codes of conduct. This was partly the source of their social capital at home: Buchan considered his muse, Aubrey Herbert, a "survivor from crusading times," possessing "the most insane gallantry" he had ever known.[25]

Indeed, at home, Arabists drew the romantic aura of Arabia to themselves, constructing themselves as eccentrically mysterious people worthy of entry to the world of artists and writers. Even before his travels, Lawrence's ascetic eating habits were much remarked, as was his reputation as "a strange undergraduate who never appeared in the daytime but spent hours of the night walking round the quadrangle by himself." A friend described his austere rooms as "the most silent place I have ever been in," since Lawrence believed, "only in silence can the soul hear its own accents, and...only a withdrawal from the world can ensure...integrity of his purpose." In the Officers' Training Corps at Oxford, he was known to keep a copy of the *Odyssey* in his pocket at all times. Thus, by 1909, writes one of his biographers, "Lawrence was already creating in the substance of his life and his vivid accounts of it material for legends about his adventures and exploits, activities which were, *in reality*, extraordinary." His wartime colleague, Wyndham Deedes, would also be lionized for his peculiar love of the desert and its silences and an "asceticism of habit" that enabled him to do without food and rest and to bend his "pain-wracked body" to his will. Likewise, during the war, officers' hearts leapt at the sight of Aubrey Herbert, whom they knew well from his prewar days scrambling across Oxford "by roofs, gutters, parapets, pipes, window-sills." In Buchan's literary representation, Herbert/Arbuthnot "was a man of genius...but he had the defects of such high-strung, fanciful souls. He would take more than mortal risks....Let him find himself in some situation which in his eyes involved his honour, and he might go stark crazy." However heroic, they were vulnerable in a way that the typical phlegmatic British gentleman was not. (Thus, the evil mastermind behind the German plot at the heart of *Greenmantle* aroused only hatred in the average Briton, but could, by appealing to Arbuthnot's imagination, find in him "an unwilling response.") The dramatic value of such individuals lay in their complexity as barely bona fide Englishmen, eccentrics and near-rogues at once bound by a unique, overweening sense of honor putting them beyond the pale of ordinary moral exactitude. They were sovereign, laws unto themselves— ideal heroes of spy novels in which the ethical-moral dimension is fundamental. The agents celebrated their own and their region's shared peculiarity. A consul avowed, "The geographical zone combined with the somewhat irrational conditions of work produced a marked professional deformation"; in short, all the members of the Levant Service "were slightly mad," forming "a rather eccentric fraternity." In donning the mantle of wise eccentricity, the agents and other Edwardian elites looked again to Doughty and, especially, to Blunt, who periodically wandered the south of England with a tent "as though reliving the desert journeys of the past" and kept his "Baghdad robes" handy on social occasions, dressing Churchill in them in 1912 and presenting a similar set (kaftan, waistcoat, and abbeyeh) to Sir Sydney Cockerell, curator of the FitzWilliam Museum at Cambridge. He could be seen in his Bedouin garb most famously at the Peacock Dinner of January 1914, at which Pound, Yeats, Richard Aldington, Frederic Manning, and other poets honored him as the prophet of modernist poetry. "It seems very unlikely this [lunch] was just about Blunt's poetry," wagers Helen Carr. "It was more the heady mix that Blunt represented: virile, poetic, anti-establishment, anti-Empire and aristocratic."[26]

The "desert aura" seemed to distinguish travelers in Arabia from even the most romantic of explorer-authors in other regions. Their special fascination with the desert, a veritable obsession to a proud few, was held to set them apart from the ordinary information-gatherer abroad, investing their missions with deeper purpose. They claimed a congenital "restlessness," an atavistic wander-lust that drove them to "return" to a nomadic existence that had become impossible in the restrictive, settled, urban life at home. These sensitive souls felt they alone could recognize, in a time of slavish materialism, the austere beauty and vitality of the desert: Bell greeted news of another's equally eccentric love for it with an ebullient "Welcome and kinship!" Through the war, their taste for the desert was echoed in legends of their peculiar abstemiousness and devotion to learning. They seemed to be after a greater prize than the usual interloper abroad. Whether "pilgrims to its holy places, or archaeologists confessed and disguised, or passing observers of its actual societies," affirmed Hogarth, explorers in Arabia were a breed apart from the soldiers, adventurers, missionaries, and traders who had "opened out most dark places of the earth," "impelled to the peninsula by their own curiosity." The motley crew in Arabia shared a pursuit of knowledge beyond an assortment of facts that could be assimilated via the usual taxonomies; they were after the knowledge that came of the journey itself, especially in the land of "pilgrimage"—a word frequently bandied about in this context. A reviewer paid tribute to Hogarth himself as "a man of the world in the best and broadest sense of the term—the sense in which Herodotus and Kinglake were men of the world," which was the epic status to which Arabia explorers aspired and which they attained partly by recalling these classical forbears in the very nomenclature of the region they crossed. That they assiduously cultivated this heroic reputation is evident from the occluded perspective of their narratives: H. V. F. Winstone notes that the members of this intimate community "hardly ever referred to their fellow travellers, even in private correspondence, though they stayed in the same hotels and crossed paths in the same barren stretches of country." Explorers tended to portray their adventures as solitary forays into a land that remained untouched even by their colleagues and unmarked by the overlapping domains of the various agencies involved in intelligence in the region.[27]

The Edwardian agent in Arabia was also distinct from his Victorian proto-type in the very important sense of being a self-consciously heroic figure in what he thought of as a world of make-believe and delighting in his awareness of being a hangover from the actual era of exploration. The new type of explorer-agent—such as Bury, Bray, Shakespear—was a nostalgic gentleman of military background, a *government* agent acting out an expired Victorian ideal of free-lance exploration. They were avatars of Colonel Creighton in Rudyard Kipling's

Kim (1901), exemplar of the power-is-knowledge trope in Edwardian fiction. A man of action armed with an encyclopedic grasp of his domain, he was, above all, a disciplined English gentleman. Agents in Arabia maintained that "the right spirit for a traveller to enter Arabia" was "as a gentleman of quality" and aspired to play, with consummate skill and honor, a very great game. Other agents—disguise aficionados such as Lawrence, Leachman, Soane, and Major Noel (an agent in Kurdistan)—were more like Kim himself, liminal figures capable of "passing" and with a taste for life on the lam. They, too, fit in with the ethos of the "great game" propagated by Victorian and Edwardian public schools as the critical metaphor for the colonial mission. Indeed, St. John Philby, who would emerge during and after the war as one of the most notorious members of this community of agents, fatefully named his even more notorious son after his literary hero. It was thus no accident that by the twentieth century, Britons no longer saw espionage as incompatible with Englishness and gentlemanliness and that for the first time secret agents emerged as *heroic* protagonists in popular literature: if the twentieth-century English gentleman was, above all, a *performer*, someone driven to conceal in order to impress, a crucial pillar of the official culture of secrecy, the spy in the East, according to Kipling, *as quoted* in a foundational intelligence memorandum of 1909, was the consummate gentleman-hero who concealed all behind an immovable mask of rectitude, played the game discreetly, and died quietly and honorably.[28]

While, aside from the Great Game itself, almost everything in *Kim* relating to the organization of British agents passing as Indian natives was the product of Kipling's imagination,[29] in the decade after the book's publication, reality began to imitate it in Arabia, in a critical evolutionary moment in the mutual shaping of the world of real spies and the genre of the spy novel. The 1909 intelligence memorandum treated the novel as a veritable guidebook, accepting its world and even its bureaucracy literally and elaborating its lessons with characters from the *Arabian Nights*; conceptually, Arabia had been incorporated into the world of the Great Game, not least because Arab tribal warfare was considered "really very like playing a game." Arabia was conceived as a geographical and political extension of the similarly barren and tribal North West Frontier. The entire swathe was thought to be controlled by the same "vast and mysterious agencies...incomprehensible to rational minds"—the arcane political universe at the heart of *Kim*. (Not that the overlap was entirely imagined: while the British Indian government reached into the Middle East and the Persian Gulf, Indian and Arab trade and Shia pilgrimage to Najaf and Karbala ensured close regional ties, as did the social and financial connections fostered by the Oudh Bequest, which since the mid-nineteenth century had channeled millions of rupees to the holy cities through British mediation.)

Elision of the North West Frontier with Arabia compounded to colossal proportions both the domain of inscrutability and the stage on which mythic imperial
heroes with a preternatural insight into these "mysterious agencies" had for
generations confronted their nemeses and become larger than life.[30]

The real-life agents in Arabia relished the apparently authentic resemblance of their work to the intelligence world of espionage fiction. Many
reported, and some reveled in, the atmosphere of intrigue in Arabia, in which,
despite the Turks' precautions, it was *easiest* "to travel secretly, or hatch plots."
It was generally agreed that all travel in Arabia called for a furtive deportment
that rendered even tourism casually espionage-like. The leniency of consular
officials towards illicit British travelers, described in chapter 1, was partly rooted
in the idea that innocent British travelers could not help but comport themselves like spies and intriguers; it was simply the way of the place. Arabia was
a stage, a place for "making believe," and *escaping*, rather than simply recording, reality.[31]

The feeling of fictional enactment set intelligence-gathering in Arabia
apart, crucially shaping the agents' willingness and ability to function as empir-
icists. The Romantics had recoiled from the real Orient, failing to find in it the
escape promised by the Orient of imagination, but Edwardians, recoiling from
the grotesque reality of their *own* country, nurtured a need for aesthetic experience so desperate that they did not even see mundane Arabia when they got
there, only their prefiguring vision of it. Their ostensible purpose may have
been to gather precise intelligence, but, Brent observes, "deep down they pursued no such practicalities; instead they moved through the landscape of an
ancient reverie, emissaries of a collectively held illusion, links between a Europe
that had become incomprehensible and an Arabia that had never existed."
Sykes reveled in "How pleasant it is to be absolutely ignorant of geology," for it
left one to dream up explanatory theories of the strange landscape, shaped by
the chatter of his "philosophic muleteer." For such agents, however charmless
the real Baghdad, "Baghdad is a magic word, as the place itself was magic in the
days of long ago." Whatever its dilapidated state, "memory and imagination,
too, are faithful genii easily summoned" and would conjure "from the pages of
the Nights the most gorgeous palaces, the most impregnable castles, and the
most beautiful gardens...like a dream." Similarly, Bell confided to Hogarth
that whatever she actually felt while there, "I *say* I love the Desert." Travel in
Arabia was a matter of fashioning reality from the stuff of fiction—from "the
pages of the Nights"—rather than appraising reality by the standard of fiction.
Indeed, agents doubled their missions for fact with searches for fictions:
Carruthers coupled his intelligence mission with a quest to find the oryx, presumed unicorn of Biblical fame, in "a region as fantastic and wild as himself."

When he finally encountered his "treasure" "behind the veil," he rejoiced, "Imagination has become a reality." He had gone through the wardrobe into an enchanted world.[32]

Playing knights, explorers, or spies seemed appropriate on a desert stage where Arab thespians provided a model of uninhibited and unending perfor- mance. "The Bedawi is to a great extent a histrion," explained Sykes's compan- ion, Captain Smith, "and much as I like and respect him, I must admit that his ferocity, his chivalry, and his generosity are to a large extent myths—myths that he has created himself, and propagates persistently and well." If Arabs filled the monotony of desert life with illusions of their grandeur, British travelers battled an otherwise somber existence by joining what they knew for only illu- sorily grand company. Storytellers, jugglers, poets, and magicians were among the ubiquitous, peripatetic entertainers of the desert they encountered, a web of yarn-spinners that seemed to immerse the entire region in an ocean of stories. Only in the Syrian desert, Sykes said, could the traveler find an old man "dressed in rags, equally prepared to extemporize poetry or travel six days' journey for 1s.6d. per diem." The agents' own journeys, they knew, would become part of this endless storytelling. Bell took heart when a guide told her: " 'In all the years when we come to this place we shall say: "Here we came with her, here she camped." It will be a thing to talk of, your ghazzu. We shall be asked for news of it and we shall speak of it and tell how you came.' "[33]

Ultimately, information in the desert could only be magically real, secreted in a labyrinth of tales. Desert politics were merely episodes in a land of unend- ing (and, implicitly, pointless) epics. Bell rejoiced upon her return to the desert in 1906 when she heard the latest installments in the Rashid-Saud feud around the campfire: "So the tale ran through the familiar stages of blood feud and camel lifting, the gossip of the desert." The desert was full of such "long stories . . . without beginning, without end." This idea acquired the immutability of an axiom. The title of Bell's travelogue *Amurath to Amurath* is an homage to Shakespeare's pithy comment on the serially unchanging imperia of the Turkish court. The timelessness of the East is, of course, a familiar orientalist trope, but, carried around in the minds of intelligencers in Arabia, it acquired a special significance. While ostensibly collecting facts, they confronted the rather counterproductive notion that there could be no real "news" in the des- ert, that all that transpired was part of an endlessly unfolding epic and that the epic repeated itself ad nauseam. One could only enjoy retelling the tales within the tales, so that intelligence in Arabia began itself to resemble a mission akin to Scheherazade's yarn-spinning nights with Shahriyar.[34]

Indeed, agents generally compared entering Arabia to entering the pages of a great book. Many felt the Bible was "one of the few books that one can read in this sort of wandering life....Any other book made too great a demand on one's mental powers." It functioned as an eternally relevant guide to the region, placing travelers as much in the mythological past as in the real present. Epic literature like the *Odyssey* was also held to provide insight into Arabia, speaking as it did to what was universal and timeless, and thus to the essence of the desert. Consuls' training in the classics did not merely build character; for those sent to the Middle East, it was seen as practical knowledge. Some, like Bell, traveled by the light of Doughty's archaic new-age bible *Arabia Deserta*, feeling "as if I were on a sort of pilgrimage, visiting sacred sites." Even Shakespear's fiancée at home found the book, her guide and textbook, an almost religious experience. Exploration was not merely travel in the physical space of Arabia but in the imaginative space of books. This is not to say agents felt espionage was impossible in Arabia but that they conceived of their work in fictional terms. Certainly, the fictional world conjured up by the *Odyssey* and the Bible, the sources of the cliché that ranks spying as the world's second oldest profession, situated them in an espionage world that was epic and mythic rather than quotidian. It is no wonder that their own published works were so riddled with pretensions to fiction.[35]

To many of these agent-authors, the war offered an opportunity to fulfill to the utmost their dreams of vital experience and storybook romance in the Middle East. Then, too, literature remained an important source of information about the region, rendering agents' work and the campaigns themselves even more pointedly mythic. Kipling's stories, Edward Gibbon's *The Decline and Fall of the Roman Empire*, and the works of Xenophon, Herodotus, and Thucydides were all regularly consulted for parallels with their own situation. With these grand narratives framing their outlook, it is no surprise that agents continued to define their own work in mythopoeic terms. *Arabia Deserta* remained a cherished *daily* source of inspiration and intelligence, and the Bible was ubiquitous. Archibald Wavell (cousin of the interloper in Mecca), a member of Allenby's staff (laying the foundations for his more illustrious career as World War Two commander in the Middle East and viceroy of India), later recalled how Allenby studied the Bible "with the passionate absorption of Cromwell's Ironsides, and...based his plans on the study of the wars of Joshua." He also devoured histories of the Crusades, "so convinced that in the unchanging East history would repeat itself that from the beginning he said that the decisive battle of the campaign would be fought at the Pass of Meggido." His troops "used the Bibles as guide books to Palestine, and remarkably fine ones they turned out to be!" affirmed Major Vivian Gilbert. En route to Jericho, and lacking any other information on the area, Gilbert planned the attack on Mukhmas by studying the tactics Jonathan used there, as recorded in the Book of Samuel.[36]

This epic and mythological sensibility shaped the entire British war effort in the Middle East, in a manner above and beyond the imaginative uses of literature on the Western front.[37] Agents took the war as an opportunity to fulfill the literary and mythopoeic impulses that had attracted them to the region, conceiving of it as the moment when the region's romantic qualities would be sharpened and their own, until now only provincial, heroism emerge on a world-historical stage. After all, an epic war in a land of epics could hardly take place without adventure heroes, which was the reputation agents from Arnold Wilson to Leachman to Lawrence acquired during the war, certainly among their own military followers. Compton Mackenzie, for one, dreamt of the formidable Deedes "in as many shapes and sizes as Jim Hawkins dreamed of that one-legged mariner who according to Billy Bones was the most dangerous of Flint's unemployed pirates." When this community met, the literary potency of their combined genius was electric: at a dinner in Cambridge attended by Ronald Storrs, the editor of the *TLS*, and others, Mackenzie exclaimed, "What a night it was!...woven out of Persia and Arabia, out of Egypt and Mesopotamia...Athens...and Rome." It was this romance that colored the war for those in the Middle East, in sharp contrast to the grim news from the Western front.[38]

Agents made sense of their wartime experiences through literary allusion, particularly to juvenile adventure fiction. If Lawrence took the part of the impish hero, his colleagues took that of his happy sidekick. Lloyd described his experiences behind enemy lines as an "adventure rather like a Henty novel—my companion was Lawrence." Even far from Lawrence's shadow, the circumstances of the Arabia agent recalled fiction time and again. In Mesopotamia, Harold Dickson felt "like the successful wanderer of musical comedy, who finds himself king in some unknown country." He was carrying on "in quite novel style—Captain Kettle and his adventures would perhaps be nearer the mark....I am acting the part in rare style." What made it all so "fictional" was his configuration of the Arab population as a den of spies: "hobnobbing with men you know are downright rascals....It is quite like one of Fennimore [*sic*] Cooper's story books and to be living through it all is great." Arab talk was "in the form of a parable....One feels quite biblical." He soon adopted such a rhetorical style himself, recounting, for instance, the story of the Prodigal Son while settling a tribal boundary dispute. In time, he took to calling his experiences "my 'oddysy'." He, like many of his colleagues, definitively placed himself in a fictional landscape; precedents for his bizarre tasks as an agent and governor were to be found only in the world of adventure fiction.[39]

As intelligencers, these individuals continued to feel like spies of lore rather than bureaucrats dealing with the practical exigencies of wartime information collection. To Lawrence, Herbert's unmasking of "futile conspiracies" was "like the man who was Friday." Wandering about Athens at night in a black mask and black silk domino, Mackenzie fancied himself "the Caliph in the *Arabian Nights*." Storrs recorded an incident during his abortive journey to Riyadh when the political agent at Kuwait, thinking him an intruder at the consulate, pointed a gun at him, so that he "dreamt for the rest of the night that I was a spy flying for my life." Storrs *was* in fact a spy, but, in this episode in the Arabian interior, found himself transformed from the functionary that a real-life agent was to the adventurer-spy of fiction. (Significantly, Storrs's reading material in those days was the Bible, in Arabic, and the *Odyssey*.) Even while spying, agents aspired to the fictional ideal of espionage that they thought befit the Arabian spy-space. "Life is really quite like a page out of a novel," wrote an intelligence officer at Port Said:

> The air vibrates with hushed whispers, the stairs...resound with the stealthy tread of stage villains, corpulent Egyptians with tarbooshes, down-at-heel Greeks.... We keep invisible ink, secret drawers and insoluble ciphers. Letters arrive by special messengers enclosed in two or three envelopes covered with mystical seals, while the least member of the organization is known by a number and the greatest by a single letter.... We pass to outsiders as ordinary staff officers about whose occupation the civilian may speculate, but only superficially fathom. Little do they realise that their every movement is watched, and that, as we sit in the hotel bars of an evening, we are gathering the threads of a case into our hands.

The spies' prewar literary efforts, together with novelists' engagement with Arabia and espionage, inspired wartime agents to fit their experiences to the scripts of fiction. Arabia was simply the most glamorous stage for intelligence. Hence, a proposal to gather intelligence in Romania elicited from Hogarth "the expression of a dramatist being invited to go out to Hollywood and work for the movies" (a demotion by contemporary standards). Bell thrilled at the opportunity the war offered to mold events into an epic scale: "We have had great talks and made vast schemes for the government of the universe," she exulted after Lawrence's visit to Basra in 1916. Dickson, on hearing of his posting to Kuwait, wrote home, "This time next year I expect you will find me at Hail in central Arabia leading a revolution and marrying the Amir of Najd's daughter!! Shades of Burton and Doughty."[40]

That agents actually strained to shape their wartime experiences in the image of literature, particularly epic literature, is perhaps most evident in the case of Lawrence, who remained stubbornly attached to Doughty's *Arabia Deserta* and, even more tellingly, a dog-eared copy of *Le Morte D'Arthur* during the war. Medieval texts certainly informed experience on the Western front, but here they actually shaped the running of the campaigns. His head full of medieval mythology and "the poignant knowledge of his own aristocratic birth," Lawrence went to Arabia determined to fulfill a secret destiny worthy of anything in the works dearest to him; he behaved, in Tidrick's words, "as though he was one of that small group of people singled out for special attention by the gods, liable at any moment to be called on to perform some heroic task—or suffer some special degradation." In him, all the medievalism and literariness cultivated by prewar agents came together to produce a vision of the ideal Arabia agent, whose escapades would be worthy of the most colorful memorialization. His coy communication was designed to preserve both his own heroic autonomy and that of the epic movement he purported to lead. "To make [Egypt] continue in sacrifice we must keep her confident and ourselves a *legend*," he insisted. The epic quality of the revolt, its mythic appeal, what made all of London wait breathlessly for the latest intelligence digest from Cairo, was the product of the fertile mind of the agent who went to Arabia in search of adventure and did not rest until he had shaped events into one. Albert Hourani compellingly describes Lawrence's postwar account, *The Seven Pillars of Wisdom* (1926), as

> an attempt to write an epic work about activities that themselves had been moulded by a person who intended to write about them. Lawrence's ambition to write, his view of epic action based on his reading of ancient epics and of medieval romances, to some extent moulded his actions during the war. He later remoulded the epics in his book.

Indeed, Lawrence allegedly confided to a friend during the campaign that "if he [Lawrence] ever should feel as he contemplated the book he would write one day about it all, that a little heightened colour was needed here or there, he could always contrive a raid, or...goad Auda a little, and that would give him the 'copy' he needed in just that place." The impulse to use intelligence in Arabia as a springboard for a literary career remained potent and became, if anything, even more effectual during the war. So, too, did the impulse to fulfill dreams in Arabia: the war offered Lawrence the ultimate opportunity to fulfill his schoolboy dreams of leading a personal crusade to liberate a people from bondage "as a kind of contemporary armed prophet." He stated unequivocally that the revolt—which he billed as the "biggest thing in the Near East since 1550"—allowed him to give expression to his artistic urges and resurrect the "epic mode":

> I had had one craving all my life—for the power of self-expression in some imaginative form—but had been too diffuse ever to acquire a

technique. At last accident, with perverted humour, in casting me as
a man of action had given me place in the Arab Revolt, a theme ready
and epic to a direct eye and hand, thus offering me an outlet in
literature, the technique-less art. Whereupon I became excited only
over mechanism. The epic mode was alien to me, as to my generation. Memory gave me no clue to the heroic, so that I could not feel
such men as Auda in myself. He seemed fantastic as the hills of
Rumm, old as Mallory.

Like his prewar colleagues, Lawrence's "strongest motivation" during the war
was "a personal one." His awareness of the peculiar coincidence of man and
moment, of his power to convert fantasy into reality, eventually alarmed him:
"Those who dream by night in the dusty recesses of their minds wake in the
day to find that all was vanity," he would write, "but the dreamers of the day are
dangerous men, for they may act their dream with open eyes, and make it possible. This I did." This was what the war allowed many an agent enchanted with
Arabia to do—so completely in Lawrence's case that it cured him of "any desire
ever to do anything for myself."[41]

Intelligence in the Name of God

Besides functioning as a space for artistic escape and fulfillment, the region's
biblical topography also cast a mystical aura around the war in the Middle East
for many of its British participants. "Our eyes were often on the past," recalled
the *Times* war correspondent (and novelist) Edmund Candler in Mesopotamia.
"The arid tracts where our own troops and General Allenby's were fighting,
and the desert between spanned the whole land of Holy Writ.... We had a supply dump not a hundred yards from the...spot where Jonah was cast up by the
whale." The map they followed was sacred, not profane. The fall of Jerusalem
and Baghdad were seen as more than events of modern history; they belonged
to older narratives of the Crusades and ancient Rome. In their roles as administrators and intelligence-gatherers, agents like Dickson felt "Biblical." These
were not the spontaneous fascinations of wartime but the product of the
Edwardian period of intelligence-gathering in the region; the momentum of
that early history owed as much to escalating geopolitical and cultural tensions
as to a mounting sense of spiritual crisis among elite Britons.[42]

In Kipling's moral universe, "espionage in the service of empire and the
quest for spiritual harmony are complementary activities," to borrow the words
of Jon Thompson. And in this, too, it provided an early model for agents in

Arabia. They combined their intelligence adventures with a search for spiritual illumination. They did this as Edwardians, for the mind of turn-of-the-century cultural elites was wracked by uncertainties about politics, aesthetics, and social mores but also about basic conceptions of space and time. Modernity, in the form of such globe-shrinking technologies as steam power and electricity, had its disconcerting side. The historian and philosopher Edwyn Bevan wondered in 1918 "whether any increased acceleration in the rate of progress is possible— or even desirable for the mental stability of mankind" and pointed hopefully to the new Mesopotamian colony as a site for redemption. Uncertainties were also evoked by geologists, archaeologists, biologists, and physicists, whose work had destabilized faith in the ideas that had been the foundation of nineteenth-century faith in progress. In just over a century, explains Stephen Kern, "the age of the earth had oscillated from the cramped temporal estimates of Biblical chronology to the almost unlimited time scale of Lyell, down to Kelvin's meager twenty million years, and then back up to hundreds of millions of years." Within this infinite span, the history of humankind appeared parenthetical indeed.[43]

This atmosphere of profound uncertainty about the meaning of life and the universe, pervaded by regret at the passing of the old order and revulsion against the materialism and commercialism that seemed to be taking its place, produced in the late nineteenth century a mystical revival, which among the educated middle and upper classes took the form of a new interest in medieval and Renaissance Christian mysticism and various forms of spiritualism and the occult. Hence, for instance, the remarkable number of conversions to Roman Catholicism in this period, from which agents such as George Lloyd and Gerald Fitzmaurice were not exempt, making them even more sympathetic to Catholics Aubrey Herbert, Mark Sykes (converted at age three), and the wartime director of military intelligence George Macdonogh. Those inclined toward mysticism sought, as Alex Owen writes, an "immediate experience of and oneness with a variously conceived divinity." Their interests extended to philosophical idealism and European vitalism and, in a cultural moment that was also the high watermark of popular interest in empire, spiritual alternatives derived from the East, broadly conceived, not least as a result of increasing exposure to the written works of colonial explorers and administrators abroad.[44]

All occultisms are founded on a claim of historical continuity, and it was on Arabia's ancient past, in particular, that many turn-of-the-century occultists staked their claim. The occultist G. R. S. Mead compared the "rising psychic tide" in London to that which had inundated the Alexandria of Hellenistic times, "where Egypt and Africa, Rome and Greece, Syria and Arabia met together," and philosophy, science, religion, and theosophy of every sort swirled together in a mystical melting pot. This was by no means an arbitrary comparison, but one founded on, literally, groundbreaking research on the topic, for the cataract of books on Arabia was partly composed of a raft of popular works, such as W. St. Chad Boscawen's *The First of Empires: "Babylon of the Bible"* (1904), R. Campbell-Thompson's *Semitic Magic, Its Origins and Development* (1909), and Bell's *Palace and Mosque at Ukhaidir* (1914), about or derived from contemporary archaeological coups in the region, often perpetrated by members of the intelligence community. This is not to minimize the importance of interest in Arabia's purely biblical past—Thomas Cook's "Holy Land Excursions" remained popular—but to place it within the larger framework of interest in Arabia as a spiritual place in a more general sense, where the syncretic, polytheistic, iconoclastic world of the occult survived, despite the monotheistic civilizations that serially held sway over it. Discoveries of ancient Babylonian myths, in which were recognized earlier versions of Biblical tales, only confirmed this view of the Arabian palimpsest.[45]

The new awareness of Arab contributions to "Western civilization"—Arab preservation of classic Greek scientific texts during the Dark Ages and the shared adulation for Aristotle, for instance—underwrote the Edwardian view of Arabia as European patrimony, a place where Britons might find their lost past and faith. Of late, remarked Campbell-Thompson in an anonymous review, people were happy "to admit to the people of those lands their proper position in the ancient world." In Arabia's complacent, anti-intellectual endurance was embodied an ironic affront to that old shibboleth "progress." Meredith Townsend's immensely influential *Asia and Europe* (1901) mused:

Imagine a clan which prefers sand to mould, poverty to labour,
solitary reflection to the busy hubbub of the mart, which will not earn
enough to clothe itself, never invented so much as a lucifer match,
and would consider newspaper-reading a disgraceful waste of time.
Is it not horrible, that such a race should be? more horrible, that it
should survive all others? most horrible of all, that it should produce,
among other trifles, the Psalms and the Gospels, the Koran and the
epic of Antar?

The Arabian counterpoint seemed to invalidate all European claims to superiority during a period beset by a sense of imminent social and spiritual crisis. Archaeology and works such as J. G. Frazer's *The Golden Bough: A Study in Magic and Religion* (1890) helped turn received wisdom about civilizational difference on its head, strengthening an incipient cultural relativism over nineteenth-century theories of progressive development, which had seen Western civilization as the vanguard of Civilization as such. This "change in sensibility," in T. E. Hulme's words, enabled Britons to appreciate the art and symbolic systems of ostensibly more primitive societies not only for its own sake but also, as Elleke Boehmer argues, as a means to "interpret the cataclysmically expanding and collapsing modern world."[46]

In short, " 'the will to believe" was very much in the air," as Samuel Hynes puts it, quoting William James, in his classic description of *The Edwardian Turn of Mind*. The Edwardian tourist, Hogarth likewise observed, sought not the "intelligible," but visions of "the half-known, the unknown, and even the not to be known, craving the stimulus of infinite possibilities behind a half-drawn veil"; he looked to be reminded, "by finger-posts pointing into darkness, of the existence of a Beyond, but has really no sort of desire that the cloud should lift." Hence his interest in Egypt, "where nothing is more than half known." Here, "Egypt" functioned as a synecdoche for the entire spread of unmapped, unknown, phantasmagoric Arabia; it owed its magnetism to its position, "penned between illimitable silences. How little we know of those deserts!...the Arabian and Libyan bluffs...peopled with chimaeras and griffins." Since the Romantics, Arabia's infinite horizons had offered Britons a balm for personal sorrows, but in the twentieth century they offered an antidote to a society-wide nostalgia for faith.[47]

The admixture of spiritual and escapist fascinations with Arabia is evident in the fictional analogue of the agents' real world. John Buchan wrote his Richard Hannay books partly out of a fascination with "the notion of hurried journeys," from Homer to "the penny reciter," which appealed to a "very ancient instinct in human nature." For, he felt, it was when the "twin categories of time and space" came into conflict that "we get the great moment....Life is sharpened, intensified, idealised." He turned to Arabia as more than the exotic Orient; he was attracted to it as an austere space, ideally suited to a journey-quest structure and thus an espionage tale. Arbuthnot, who, as an agent in Arabia, albeit fictional, can be counted on to "know" such things, describes the dawning of this new vision of Arabia:

> The West knows nothing of the true Oriental. It pictures him as lapped in colour and idleness and luxury and gorgeous dreams. But it is all wrong....It is the austerity of the East that is its beauty and its terror....The Turk and the Arab came out of big spaces....They want to live face to face with God...to prune life of its foolish fringes and get back to the noble bareness of the desert....It is always the empty desert and the empty sky that cast their spell over them....It isn't inhuman. It's the humanity of one part of the human race.

He adds, "It isn't ours" but then, remaining true to his liminal status, exclaims, "There are times when it grips me so hard that I'm inclined to forswear the gods of my fathers!" A better statement of the new desert orientalism, resounding with Edwardians' own helpless attraction to it, would be difficult to find. The immense popularity of Buchan's novel—its reminder that "fiction has often a basis of fact"—is a testament to the currency of these ideas at the time. Painting for the first time on such a vast geographical canvas, Buchan also liberally exploited the landscape's biblical resonances, not least with the apotheosis at the climax: the image of the prophet Sandy leading the Russians to Erzurum.[48]

Other novelists also quietly fit desert Arabia into their armory of setting atmospherics and metaphors—not merely as an exotic setting or minimalist canvas, but as a vision of the occult world to which many of them were increasingly drawn. Yeats, for instance, would criticize Flecker's *Hassan* (1922) for using the Orient as merely an exotic backdrop rather than a means for achieving greater philosophical depth. Modernists like Eliot, Pound, and Yeats found in Arabia a route back to "genuine mythic consciousness," a space that seemed to invite abandonment of historical time and immersion in myth. They subscribed to the notion that the journey-quest was critical to attaining real metaphysical knowledge. In 1909, Yeats described his old longing "to disguise myself as a peasant and wander through the West.... Some day, setting out to find knowledge, like some pilgrim to the Holy Land, [the artist] will become the most romantic of characters." The pilgrimage—journeys, quests, paths, and so forth—forms a leitmotif of his oeuvre, and its frequent destination "the shining holy city of Byzantium." Yeats's Arabic interests were part of his more general interest in the East—in China and India, especially—occasioned by his incessant dabbling in mysticism and the occult, but he saw Arabia in particular as the homeland of Magic. This is not to say that he looked to *Islam* for the sort of mystical inspiration he found in other religions, such as Hinduism and Buddhism; rather, Arabia itself seemed to him the kind of place in which the spiritual and physical worlds coincided, where the mythic ethos he espoused actually existed, and where the roots of Western mysticism, both pagan and Biblical, were to be found. This is evident from his debt to Swedenborg's doctrine of "the desolate places," which described "a world of spirits" like the real world, but inhabited by itinerant souls. In this "other world of the early races"—presumably the ancient occult world of the Middle East—the imagination could thrive, while "our life in the cities, which deafens or kills the passive meditative life" renders "our souls less sensitive." Primitives, he felt, "live always on the edges of vision." Yeats's effort to access this occult world of the *spiritus mundi* became critical to his entire ambition as an artist and was partly an attempt to resurrect the primitive within him, that visionary primordial essence that possessed "knowledge innate." He sought "an asceticism of the imagination" and urged the destruction of "Law and Number, for where there is nothing, there is God." Once in the space of pure spirit, he enjoyed the company of an Arab daimon he met during a 1912 séance with Olivia Shakespear—the ghost of al-Hasan ibn Muhammad al-Wazzan al-Zayyati, a Renaissance explorer from Granada known in the West as Leo Africanus, whose works had recently come back into circulation (as part of the tide of interest in things Arabian) and would have been familiar to Yeats's Arabist friends in the occultist order, the Golden Dawn. Communion with this daimon was critical to his formulation of the theory that artistic inspiration emanated from the interaction between the physical and spiritual worlds, that poetry was divine. This theory he took on faith, stating simply "like the Arab boy that became Vizier: 'O brother, I have taken stock in the desert sand and of the sayings of antiquity.'" Arabia recalled for Yeats a vision of precolonial Ireland, where unspoiled Celts had also worshiped poetry as something divine. His, Pound's, Buchan's, and other authors' admiration for the agents was based partly on the latter's apparent substantiation of the supposed affinity between Britons' subjugated mythic consciousness and Bedouin still embodying that ancient ethos. Indeed, Celtic sentiment ran equally high in agent circles: many insisted that only a Briton of "Celtic blood" could get on well with the Arabs. In a sense, Yeats's ideas naturally echoed those embraced by the agents, given that, as one scholar puts it, he "lived at a time when it was natural for him to be aware of [the raft of new books on Arabia and the news of rising Arab nationalism], and he moved in the literary circles to which most of those who were enthusiastically interested in Arabia belonged."[49]

Despite the influence of her social world, Virginia Woolf was not much of an occultist; however, her literary allusions to the desert were similarly concerned with matters of the spirit. In the Amazon, Rachel Vinrace finds escape from everyday life into a more profound reality when, for the first time, she opens the pages of Gibbon's history of the Roman Empire to the part about "Aethiopia and Arabia Felix." The incomparably "vivid" and "beautiful" words "seemed to drive roads back to the very beginning of the world, on either side of which the populations of all times and countries stood in avenues, and by passing down them all knowledge would be hers, and the book of the world turned back to the very first page." Arabia was an archive of all time and knowledge, a bible spread out in space. Rachel dies by the end of the novel, fulfilling Woolf's artistic aim of portraying "a vast tumult of life…which should be cut short for a moment by the death, and go on again," most likely inspired by her brother Thoby's sudden death from typhoid on their 1906 trip to Constantinople.

The head-space, if not the actual space, of Arabia, the land of the oldest such journeys, as Edwardians thought of it, seemed only appropriate to the descriptions of quests for profound existential knowledge and authentic lived experience that were central to much of contemporary literature.[50]

On the whole, occultists and modernists were probably more socially progressive than the agents, but both sought an opportunity to escape the strictures of modern life and enter the spirit-world of ancient Arabia. Agents were among those who looked to the Land of the Bible and the Tree of Knowledge as a metaphysical utopia. They did not go to Arabia in search of the sensual indulgence the Orient is generally supposed to have offered Europeans but to escape what they saw as the moral decadence of their *own* society. In Arabia, the supposed secularization of modern European travel seems to have unraveled under the suggestive power of the region's very nomenclature. There, as elsewhere, travel was conceived as a journey into the past, but this past was not merely further back on the secular time scale of modern history, but on a different scale altogether, outside secular time. Moving in the desert itself allowed the mind "wander into the past and...pry into the future," explained Sykes. In its supreme continuity, the queer way different eras continued to coexist in it at once, the desert was time spread out in space—a space in which the reality of the past endured in the present. Arabia's antiquity, its status as the site of the foundational myths of Western civilization, enveloped it in a mystique from which agents found it difficult to extricate their work. Carruthers wrote of his feeling, despite the absence of visible evidence, "that man has known this road from earliest antiquity," that he walked in a region "smothered with the dust of the ages...amongst a people...just stepped out of Genesis." Others were similarly disoriented and spent as much time investigating Biblical lore—Jonah's route, his tomb, the Tower of Babel, the Garden of Eden, Eve's tomb, Abraham's final resting place, among others—as they did gathering intelligence. Contemplation of this biblical topography invariably inspired musings on a luminously ethereal realm out of the ordinary, material world of the intelligence operative. Of course, enough havoc had been wreaked by nineteenth-century geology, archaeology, and biology to convince these travelers that the Bible was meant to be taken somewhat less than literally; to find the actual, historical Biblical sites on the ground was to locate themselves in a mythological landscape, in a time and space that, they knew, existed somewhere in the shadow of reality.[51]

Islamic holy sites, such as Mecca, were equally eerie. "It awes one by its strangeness" and the "almost tangible presence of the deity," testified Arthur Wavell, notorious intruder in the city. "One feels instinctively that one is looking on something unique: that there can be nothing else in the world the least like it." The effect of the "*genius loci*" was "almost uncanny." "Something in the atmosphere," affirmed Captain Bray, "appeals strongly to the imagination." Likewise, in Karbala, Bell noted that nothing she *saw* but "the sense of having reached those regions which saw the founding of imperial Islam" was what "made the strongest assault on the imagination." This sense removed agents' missions from the realm of the real to the mythic, awesome, and unfathomable. What impressed them was Arabia's *aura*, in the sense that Walter Benjamin would soon give to the word; there, unlike mechanical Europe, they found things that seemed utterly unique and embedded in local tradition. There, art remained intact and authentic. Travelers were beset by the difficulty of finding words adequate to, rather than braced for a "mechanical reproduction" of, what they saw and heard.[52]

The Biblical and Koranic were only two layers in the topographical accretion of Arabian mythologies. Intelligence agents proved as susceptible to the region's occult traditions as their compatriots at home. Desert travel was travel back in historico-mythical time, but also into the "mysterious yet familiar world of childhood," which for a generation raised on the *Arabian Nights*, was most often a pantheistic world of genies and spirits. Sykes was convinced of the supernatural powers of wandering poets, mystics, madmen, and dervishes of the desert—and told friends at home so. The origen Carruthers sought were "phantom beasts moving in a silent and supernatural world," vanishing in the darkness "as if by magic!" "Peopled mainly by the spirits of the Arabian Nights, where little surprise would be occasioned in...seeing a genie floating in a stream of thin vapour out of a magic bottle," this landscape possessed, to the military attaché Colonel Maunsell, "a fascination of scenery...unlike any other part of the world." At once a nightmare and a dreamland, it was wreathed in "an atmosphere of unreality." There they could find intact all the world's forgotten fiction: "beliefs which have been driven out with obloquy by a new-found truth, the half-apprehended mysticism of the East, echoes of Western metaphysics and philosophy, illusive memories of paganism." This "occult world, or ghost-land" was the template that generated all religions, the "immovable" source of Arabia's essential changelessness. In the war, the numinous landscape continued to resist incorporation into the material world. "Of Azrak, as of Rumm," Lawrence explained, "one said *'Numen inest.'*" The peninsular desert was "fantastic to the point of unreality." Jeddah was "a strange and uncanny place," recorded Hogarth, "rather what one sees in a disordered dream." In this hallucinatory Arabia, agents' wartime work took on a mythic quality; the British arrival at Baghdad, the city of the *Arabian Nights*, itself appeared a "kind of mirage trick." "Even the East itself provides no true analogy to Arabian conditions," affirmed Captain William Ormsby-Gore of the Arab Bureau: "Arabia we must approach with an open mind." Wartime agents endorsed prewar inclinations toward epistemological broadmindedness in understanding this utterly ineffable place.[53]

What they knew from their experience in the mundane world, at least, was useless. Wandering deeper and deeper into Arabia, a "new world," a "Valley of the Genii," Carruthers told himself, "We are now in Arabia.... We have to forget that we ever saw green woods, and flowing rivers.... These things are forbidden." Its "uncanniness" made it positively extraterrestrial. He felt "suddenly transplanted to the...moon." To function there, affirmed another traveler, you had to "disentangle" yourself from the "net in which you have all this time been unconsciously enveloped." During the war, agents continued to remark this otherworldly quality and its provocation to the imagination. Unlike India, they pronounced, Arabia was "still unknown, unwritten and romantic," "another universe." As a political officer with the Muntafiq, Dickson felt "quite at the End of the World, regularly cut off." Just as occultists were making their astral journeys to barren planets with winged guides, Arabists were journeying to Arabia and found themselves beyond the pale of the planet they called home.[54]

If this kind of astral travel rendered their existing knowledge useless, it did promise—for agents as much as occultists—a new kind of knowledge: greater insight into the nature of that increasingly incomprehensible contrivance, reality. In Baghdad, Bell reflected on the colorful sights and people she had witnessed, "and...truth, which lies somewhere concealed behind them all." Arabia transported agents from the real to the mythical world and their missions from the physical to the metaphysical realm. It attracted agents seeking refuge from Edwardian science as much as those in search of faith. Bell told an Iraqi *kadi* that "prophets alone," which Europe did not have, could "distinguish the true from the false." When the *kadi* pointed to Europe's men of science, she replied: "They know nothing.... Their eyes have explored the stars, yet they cannot tell us the meaning of the word infinity." She and other agents looked to Arabia's deserts for the existential certainty denied by European life. The birthplace of three monotheistic religions, all of which began with prophets who saw visions and heard voices, it was *the* place for miraculous conviction. As Sykes put it, if certainty could not be found in the cradle of civilization, which had produced the longest lasting certainties of all time, then perhaps it could not be found anywhere.[55]

The desert's minimalism was thus ideal for spiritual as much as aesthetic redemption. There, wrote Bell, "the mind ranged out unhindered...and thought flowed as smoothly as the flowing stream." Its vastness and changelessness "filled the eyes, and satisfied, for the moment, the most restless mind." There, affirmed a tourist, "you are conscious of battling against primeval forces akin to the unknown elements of your own being.... All the little accessories with which we have learnt to shield ourselves fall away, and you are just there, stripped yourself, and in the middle of naked realities." In "naked" Arabia, one was closer to, because more aware of, the Creator. There one could glimpse a topographical manifestation of divine cosmic order and penetrate the "great abiding truths" that were buried at home where everything was "dressed up." With "mingled fascination and terror," it also produced a feeling of being "lost in the immensity of a silent death-like solitude of infinitely sinister aspect," wrote Soane. Sykes described the "horror" of this "one great stretch of dead, forgotten desolation" and considered, "Some day when the world dies its corpse will be like this." Even the desert's more decadent phenomena, such as mirages, seemed visions vouchsafed by God—"Can we not forgive the error in mistaking the wondrous works for the builder's hand itself?" asked Sykes. The desert's unique natural phenomena inspired a suspension of disbelief and invited credulity based on faith rather than scientific proof. The Creator's unseen power was expressed physically "in these barren regions of the earth," whence it appealed "through our eyes and ears to the regions in us beyond these senses." The agents were after a knowledge which, for all its physicality, was ultimately beyond empiricism. Sykes reasoned, "It is not strange that a man who lives in a desert—where there is one day, one night, one silence, one sky and one horizon—should know that there is one God." The dramatic landscape seemed to confirm what they had thought of as the more fantastical elements of the Bible. Bell noted, "The Ark and all the rest become quite comprehensible when one sees Mesopotamia in flood time." The Bible's topographical nomenclature, such as "the oak which is in [unreadable]," seemed less odd, for "one often in official descriptions noted similar landmarks—'the village with the tree', because there was not another tree for twenty miles." The Saidian school's saga of unremitting, European "othering" of the Orient, premised on a secularization which "loosened, even dissolved, the Biblical framework," glosses over the lingering perception, at least among Edwardians, that Arabia was an ancient biblical homeland to which they *returned* in their travels, in an act that was at once a reclamation of an ancient past and of a flagging contemporary faith (and an important element in their proprietary attitude toward the place). Time and again, travelers were reminded of Mohammed's epiphany in the desert—of how, under circumstances strikingly similar to their own solitary wanderings, he must have moved from feeling "trivial" to a sense of his own share in the "primeval forces" as "the Silence of the desert" responded to the silence in "the region you are dimly conscious of beyond your senses." Thus too did the tourist Louisa Jebb come to feel what she could not feel in the crowds of London—undeniably *significant*. The desert could restore the faith sacrificed to centuries of enlightenment and materialism, a faith based not on proof or scientific reasoning, but on an innate knowledge given free rein in an essentially liberating landscape. Yeats's views of primitives and Arabia find an echo not only in the work of contemporary anthropologists, but also in Sykes's: "The desert is of God and in the desert no man may deny Him. In the bazaars the voices of men...kill the knowledge innate." The Edwardian would never proclaim, as had the audacious Victorian Alexander Kinglake, "I was here in this...desert, and I myself, and no other, had charge of my life."[56]

An at least temporary exchange of the Victorian ideal of progress for the life of aimless drift seemed critical to gaining metaphysical insight to this generation. Many described how cutting loose from civilization enabled them to live and enjoy the present, content without any particular desire to *reach* anywhere. "Existence suddenly seems to be a very simple matter," Bell discovered, "and one wonders why we plan and scheme, when all we need to do is to live and make sure of a succeeding generation." Wandering itself unraveled the knots of the overcivilized mind and opened up that mystical space outside the senses. Hogarth insisted:

> To be at once a Scholar and a Wanderer is to indulge the least
> congruous desires....For the "wandering fever" is in a sense a
> temptation of original sin, still heard across the ages, and the scholar
> finds a subtle joy in the returning to the wilderness rather in spite
> than because of his being a scholar.
> And therein lies the danger to him....He is an agent of science, a
> collector of raw material for the studies of other men. But the life of
> the Wanderer, himself a law to himself, conduces to a certain
> Bohemian habit of mind.

The very fulfillment of their missions, through travel, entailed the forsaking of those missions in favor of profounder quests. The desert could "brace and quicken the spirit"; it could restore the deadened soul to a vitalized state. There, where meaning was never superficial, physical activity, gestures, acquired meaning; the very act of going to the desert to witness the faith was intended to counter geologists' arguments against Biblical truth with symbolic action; even prayer, otherwise "a ritual of empty words," became "strangely relevant" in "Nature's loneliness."[57]

The interest in primitivism was thus as much a spiritual as an aesthetic fascination. These troubled souls—for that is how many of the agents thought of themselves—explicitly hoped to emulate Arabs' primitive certainties, as they understood them, for to be primitive was to *know*, without resorting to Cartesian proofs and the rest of rationalist Western philosophy, whether human existence mattered and whether, regardless of the latest scientific discoveries, there was a God. Desert travel was held to be transformative; agents believed themselves to come back utterly changed, even estranged from European society. Bell both quailed at and gloried in the alteration the desert had wrought on her senses and mind. It had turned her into a "savage," she wrote dramatically to Valentine Chirol, for she had "seen and heard strange things, and they colour the mind....I come back...with a mind permanently altered....Don't...tell anyone that the me they knew will not come back in the me that returns." Surely, a unique metamorphosis in the annals of intelligence history. Agents made belief and made believe in Arabia; they framed their intelligence journeys as philosophical odysseys, partly as cultural legatees of the Romantics, but more importantly, as Edwardians dealing with the peculiar social and cultural malaise that marked that time. Their sense of their experience echoed the closing lines of Walter de la Mare's famous 1912 poem, "Arabia" (which Flecker greatly admired): "Still eyes look coldly upon me,/ Cold voices whisper and say—/ 'He is crazed with the spell of far Arabia,/ They have stolen his wits away.' "[58]

This philosophical bent of mind colored the agents' literary output; however much they appealed as adventure stories, their works also touched the spiritual nerve of Edwardian readers. In *Blackwood's*, Bell urged inclusion of enlivening details in any "tale" of serious archaeological enterprise in a country "where unrecorded chapters of history...enrich every path" and distract even the "gravest explorer," for, in such places, "awakened memory" returned to "the great majesty of the waste, to the encompassing silence of its nights and days, to the unbroken passage of its sun and stars from verge to verge of the world." Accordingly, whereas Bury's otherwise well-received book was criticized for devolving frequently into "a series of anecdotes," Hogarth's *Accidents of an Antiquary's Life* (1910) was praised for its lessons on enduring and enjoying "the delightful privations and exciting perils of rough and frugal travel across regions of Asia and Africa rarely trodden by European feet." Edwardian audiences, too, longed for the experience of the journey-quest with all its insights into existence. They looked to these works for a record of the mental inversion wrought by the desert sublime, for the very escape from science that had driven the agents to the region. Bell's *The Desert and the Sown* was thus better received than her later work *Amurath to Amurath* (1911), which was said to contain "maturer science and less careless rapture." Philip Baldensperger's *The Immovable East* (1913) was lauded for its inclusion of various "tales"—anecdotes of weeks spent in the black tents of the Bedouin, parables drawn from local folklore, the visions of a dervish—and thus its reproduction of

the very atmosphere of an untutored society, wherein the frontier
lines between the real and the supernatural are so shadowy as to be
almost negligible; and whether he...listens to an acquaintance
telling of adventures in the company of the Jinn, or...describes his
own feats of endurance in the waters of Jordan...we accept all as
reasonable items of human experience. His stories have the aroma of
the camp fire and of the village hearth.

Edwardians wanted to consume records of travel not in actually existing Arabia
but in the Arabia of legend, of the Bible and the ancient seat of occultism, conjured up by storytellers' smoke and mirrors—at least so they were told by the
TLS's anonymous reviewers, who were of course none other than the agents
themselves. Indeed, some narratives even took stylistic inspiration from the
Bible.[59]

However inspired it was by fiction, the real world of Arabia intelligence,
with all its outpouring of philosophical and metaphysical insight, was critical to
the creation of latter-day fictional odysseys like *Greenmantle*. Arabia travelogues—and the agents' sensibility—were framed by a wider set of literature
dealing with travel and, especially, ruminative travel in the vicinity of Arabia;
their accounts, in turn, framed the Edwardian public's idea of Arabia. To be
sure, Russia also featured in spy fiction as a vast playground for secret agents,
passions, and those with an occult knowledge of the universe, such as the iconic
Madame Blavatsky, but it appealed precisely because these qualities made it
more Asian than European in British eyes—its fascination was derivative. In
any case, its utter topographical worldliness and the image of a drunken and
ignorant populace made it a decidedly secondary fascination.[60]

In this feeble tracing on the vast topography of early-twentieth-century
British culture is evident the ubiquity of the association of a hazy, surreal, otherworldly, and yet more *real*, because less mundane, reality with Arabia. In
multifarious formats and fora, the rising tide of interest in Arabia flooded
Edwardian society, just as that society had begun to steep itself in the deep
waters of metaphysical enquiry. At the confluence of these two cultural cur-
rents was a vision of an occult space of pure spirit in which agents and other
Edwardians found escape. The Orient had always served as a counterpoint in
Western literature, but in this period authors used their idea of Arabia in a new
way, to evoke a new vision of existence as such. If Edwardians rummaging
through Eastern philosophies in search of an antidote to spiritual angst admitted a new sense of relativity that rendered their own image and world strange
and dreamlike (as Elleke Boehmer has argued), Arabia, by implication, began
to appear less strange, more natural even, a place that precluded existential

confusion, historical meaninglessness, and civilizational captivity. While modernists condemned the cold quantification of time and the annihilation of the natural rhythm of human experience as harmful of human creative potential, British agents in the Middle East showed the world a living space of nomadism where they had successfully excavated their own buried creative potential. In short, the intelligence project in Arabia was inflected with a metaphysical and affective dimension—and a solipsism—that set it quite apart from information-gathering projects elsewhere in the world: British spies in the Middle East were as interested in the deepest secrets of creation as in politically and militarily useful information. A particular cultural lens refracted what they saw and, as we shall now see, how they saw it and reported it.[61]

3

The Failure of Empiricism and How the Agents Addressed It

The landscape of his poetry was still the desert, the shifting dunes with the plumes of white sand blowing from their peaks. Soft mountains, uncompleted journeys, the impermanence of tents. How did one map a country that blew into a new form every day? Such questions made his language too abstract, his imagery too fluid, his metre too inconstant. It led him to create chimeras of form... whose shapes felt obliged to change the moment they were set.

—Salman Rushdie, *The Satanic Verses* (1998)

Doubts of all things earthly, and intuitions of some things heavenly; this combination makes neither believer nor infidel, but makes a man who regards them both with equal eye.

—Herman Melville, *Moby Dick* (1851)

Dozens of men worked on the nitty-gritty of wartime intelligence work in the Middle East—intercepting telegraphic traffic, translating captured documents, interrogating prisoners—but, as Captain W. H. Beach, head of General Staff Intelligence (GSI) in Mesopotamia explained, these routine activities shrank in significance next to more remarkable work undertaken because of "certain difficulties... peculiar to the country," namely, lying natives and the "abnormal characteristics" of the terrain. The illegibility of Arabia called for the attention of a special kind of agent. Illegibility, James Scott has observed, is usually a "resource for political autonomy," but in Arabia the British had recourse to what contemporaries and historians alike have termed a "handful of brilliant and resourceful eccentrics" who promised to bring the region within the pale of British rule.[1]

The sources of their exceptionalism is a question of some weight, not least since intelligence has been blamed for the campaigns' failures as much as it has been credited for their brilliance.[2] There is in fact no riddle in this eccentricity; it was a conscious tactical preference, which developed in the years before the war when British agents first deemed the region fundamentally unfathomable and invented a new intelligence epistemology that prioritized the intuition of gifted persons over, and in default of, mere, unverifiable "fact." Their antiempirical frame of mind was vindicated, they felt, by the impediments to empiricism that seemed to emanate from the region's very topography. Not only was Arabia a place of escape and myth-making, it was "so misty and unreal, incomprehensible...unfathomable," in Gertrude Bell's words, that an ordinary fact-finding mission seemed a pipe dream at best, an oxymoron at worst. Experiences on the ground encouraged their development of an intuitive epistemology and reliance on an impressionistic style of reporting, which they in any case favored on aesthetic grounds. By intuition, they meant the *acquired* ability to *think like an Arab*, an empathetic mimicry of the "Arab mind"; they determined to know enigmatic Arabia as the Arabs seemed to know it—that is, intuitively—by reforming their minds through long immersion in Arabia. Those who earned a reputation for possessing an intuitive genius about Arabia were in an influential position when war broke out, as we have seen, and oversaw the hardening of their epistemological practice into an official tactic.[3]

The recovery of faith as a basis for knowledge thus served as an antidote to their spiritual cravings as Edwardians *and* a practical solution to their intelligence-gathering difficulties. Their epistemology bore a strong affinity with the intuitive modes under exploration in contemporary philosophy, science, and literature. It was part of a broader struggle to come to terms with a general perception of the world itself as a hazy, mystical cosmos beyond empiricism's reach but open to psychic intervention.

In the Sea of Stories

Agents' difficulties in extracting information from the region's people and topography confirmed their impression of Arabia as an essentially fictional place. "The difficulty of dealing with Orientals and savages, whether as informers or spies," was a standard topic in textbooks on intelligence. "The ordinary native," proclaimed Colonel C. E. Callwell's classic text *Small Wars*, "lies simply

THE FAILURE OF EMPIRICISM 101

for the love of the thing, and his ideas of time, numbers, and distance are of the vaguest, even when he is trying to speak the truth." The Baghdad Resident J. G. Lorimer customarily editorialized reports with warnings about the "extraordinary exaggerations which pass current so easily in this country." Gerard Leachman affirmed, "There is no place or people in the world for hatching fabulous stories like the Arabs; one cannot believe a word of anything one hears." Newspapers were held to be unreliable; the telegraph a beacon of fiction. Even the Turkish government seemed determined to create "a land of make-believe" and prevent Europeans from knowing anything about the empire. Its raison d'être was not to inform but to misinform, explained Arthur Wavell, for "nothing, to the Turk, is what it seems to be.... It is better to lie at first, he thinks, than speak the truth, even though there is nothing to conceal." To some extent these statements are merely the usual passing, orientalist assessment of native character, but, in the present context, they impinged crucially on intelligence work. If the region's own rulers were suspicious of appearances and propagators of misinformation, the agents reasoned, it would be naïve, if not reckless, for the solitary European to be any less skeptical of superficial data.[4]

Suspicion of surface appearances was also shaped by an abiding belief in a magical Asia-wide (dis)information network. Information flowed in the "speedy and mysterious manner of the East." Some tried to identify its source—the Machiavellian politics of the Ottomans; the power of Islam, at whose "meeting places" pilgrims mixed and news circulated; the unique phenomenon of "desert gossip"; or the more mundane mischief of "rumour"—but most found it frankly inexplicable. "By a kind of instinct," explained Callwell, people devoid of courage or fighting capacity could interpret "military portents" and ended up "far more observant than the dwellers in civilized lands," uncannily knowing one's movements before they had even begun. The enemy had "no organized intelligence department, no regular corps of spies, no telegraphs—and yet...knows perfectly well what is going on." The information flow seemed psychic, divorced as it was from the usual modern technologies for accelerating the transmission of information. It also seemed to thrive on twisting fact into fiction. Lorimer composed a paper on the "Difficulty of obtaining reliable information in this country," in which he described anecdotally the remarkable credulousness of Mesopotamians, compared even with Indians, in matters of information. While rumor spread like wildfire, *real* news seemed hardly to penetrate the region at all. Whatever its putative motive power, the mysterious flow of information seemed to confirm the futility of British efforts at creating an intelligence archive. The would-be intelligence agent would have to summon up from the wells of his own creativity the means for mining the truth content from its tales.[5]

During the war, agents continued to blame the distorting information network and lying natives for their trouble gathering real intelligence. Bell pronounced, "Words in the East are just words—signifying nothing." Arabia's inhabitants, alleged a number of reports, lacked any sense of time, space, or number. In short, the situation in Arabia simply could not be understood objectively, for it was "never logical," explained Aubrey Herbert: "The natural consequence constantly does not follow the parental cause." It was so mercurial that, one exasperated political officer forewarned, "What we write today about a situation or relations may be completely out of date by to-morrow." The fact of the matter was "accurate information is not easy to get, and one must rely principally on a lucky brainwave for inspiration."[6]

This view was reinforced by perceptions of the deceptions of Arabian topography. Geography had always been "the material underpinning for knowledge about the Orient" and was also central to intelligence work anywhere, but it acquired a special importance in the Arabian peninsula, an infamous "white spot" on Edwardian maps. Theories of environmental determinism also suggested agents could learn much about Arabs simply by studying their landscape, in any case the primary factor in a region of "small wars," which were "in the main campaigns against nature." The urgent need to obtain details of the Baghdad Railway made mapmaking even more central, and turn-of-the-century agents found in geography a suitably scholarly cover for other kinds of intelligence work in Arabia. Together, these factors made geography the foundation of all other intelligence work.[7]

Geographical exploration of unknown regions was commonly conceived of as submission of the land to the European gaze, vision being the key element in the construction of "discovery"; and "Arabia," the opening pages of Hogarth's 1904 history of Arabian exploration tantalized, was "still in great part withdrawn from western eyes." Geographers' emphasis on vision was grounded in a faith in scientific empiricism, the use of sense data as the basis of knowledge. At the turn of the century, geographers were actively promoting scientific practice and tools—theodolite, sextant, artificial horizon, barometer, chronometric watch, prismatic compass—to cement geography's uncertain disciplinary status. "Exploration," they declared, "now requires, not the pioneer, but the surveyor and the student." In Arabia, however, British agents encountered a series of stumbling blocks in the way of their cartographic ambitions, which collectively created the impression that it was impossible to map by scientific methods, thankfully perhaps, given their antiempirical predisposition and predilection for pioneer-style exploration. The sheer physical exertions of desert travel, coupled with British and Turkish official obstructions, made it exceedingly difficult even to lay eyes on the region. Those who did gain access to it had still to contend with the "lies" of the land. Agents unanimously pronounced "the topography...difficult to grasp," its "infinite and immeasurable," "interminable, featureless," distances rendering it unmappable. Far from grasping the lay of the land, expert explorers had great difficulty simply determining where they were. Reporting on his travels, DMO agent Douglas Carruthers thematized "the ease with which one could lose one's self." The mist, mirages, and lack of "atmosphere" made it hard to judge distances, while even discernible features either lacked names or changed "from convenient landmarks" into "perplexing distractions"—slight hills becoming gigantic objects "suspended in the air at nearly double that distance." The protean landscape was "alive," its dunes changing shape daily. In the end, one could only cease "thinking geographically"; this applied to the region as a whole, for, as Peter Brent puts it, Arabia had become "neither more nor less than the desert....The landscape had become everything."[8]

In short, vision encountered defeat in Arabia. Explorers found it difficult as much to trust and describe what they saw as to find something to see: "one's eyes ranged north, south, east and west to the horizon, and found no rest—no object to alight on." The limitless horizon made it impossible to know precisely when an object disappeared: "You think it is still there, and you slowly realise that it is not." Suspending belief in the constant "atmospheric delusions," as many agents did, Bell confessed, "It is excessively bewildering to be deprived of the use of one's eyes in this way." Indeed, all the senses were paralyzed: "It was a waking sleep," said the traveler Louisa Jebb. "One's senses were numb because of the absence of anything to call them into play, though one might 'see, hear, feel, outside the senses.'" And the realm "beyond the senses," as the last chapter has shown, was the very realm to which the region made its greatest spiritual appeal.[9]

The prewar consensus with respect to maps of Arabia was that "none worth possessing exists." During the war, frequent complaints about the absence of landmarks and trustworthy maps continued—the first half of the Mesopotamia campaign was fought entirely without maps. On the way to Kut, "No one knew exactly where we were," recorded Captain H. Birch Reynardson. Agents and soldiers continued to point to the region's vastness, its "absolute flatness" and lack of "perspective," its "unbroken circle of horizon," its sandstorm-induced atmosphere of "opaque and rushing veils," all of which, taken together, made "ones [sic] eyes ache." They complained frequently about "the dearth of news" and the impossibility of putting in place a "system of Secret Service...comparable with that on the Western front" owing to "the nature of the country." "The mirage played the strangest tricks with our sight," attested Alec Kirkbride, an intelligence officer in the Hejaz, and a wireless officer pronounced Mesopotamia "a country of topsy-turveydom as regards the subjective estimate of the eyes." Captain William Leith-Ross of GSI Basra catalogued for posterity "The Physical and Climatic Difficulties of Waging War in the Mesopotamian Theatre of War," among which the mirage featured as "an insuperable obstacle to reliable observation," no minor vexation given that "in Iraq all military problems…are affected by climate and physical conditions to an extent rarely met with in any theatre of war." It so succeeded in "falsifying the whole aspect of the country" that observers were never sure whether to put discrepancies in daily observations down to change or illusion. "The atmosphere is most deceptive," pronounced Candler, "and in the haze or mirage it is difficult to tell if the enemy are on horse or foot, or to make any estimate of their numbers.…All that is gained in scouting by the flatness of the country is discounted by the eccentricities of the mirage." Dust haze and other atmospheric phenomena only amplified these distortions. The country was "astonishing…one minute a desert and the next a garden"; everything, including houses and villages, was fleeting. The rivers shifted course daily—their windings "so intricate that they cannot be shown on a small scale map"—and the marshes were unnavigable. Nomenclature "in a land of flat mud" remained impossible. Herbert complained, "I have got a 'Who's Who', for Arabia, but I want a 'Where's Where'" (the Indian General Staff issued a two-volume *Where's Where in Arabia, Mesopotamia and Persia* that year). In general, agents agreed, ordinary topographical reconnaissance was distinctly less effective in Mesopotamia than elsewhere; the problems faced by surveyors were "very different from [those] in most other theatres."[10]

Not least among the obstacles to mapping these shifting sands was their shifting population, which, in a manner "in keeping with the country," defied efforts at demographic surveying. Somewhat less ignored than other nomadic indigenous populations were by European explorers, given Britain's interest in at least mapping their general ambit for diplomatic purposes, the Bedouin population remained an elusive quantity through the war. Even the strength of the British-backed Arab army remained a mystery, its composition varying on a daily basis; likewise, the extent and strength of Arab political organization, whose far-flung groups, Hubert Young conjectured, could remain in "uninterrupted communication" across the desert through "camel-riders pass[ing] freely in all directions," lacking any occupation besides "talking incessantly" or a notion of "Time" that might prohibit long rides. Scattered dissidents were "in as close communication…as if they had been on the telephone." The information network could support *infinitely* large and dispersed networks of subversives. Agents attempting to gauge their strength and organization had to assume that any rebels they contacted were but a fraction of a whole too vast for comprehension or representation.[11]

In view of these various difficulties, the Royal Geographical Society conceded early on that certain vast spaces called for "wilder and, in some sense, looser methods of surveying" than a scientific standard would normally allow. Still, Arabia explorers insisted that atmospheric conditions and Turkish sensitivities made it impractical to use or conceal any instrument more ostentatious than a compass. To be sure, some continued to hope for a more scientific survey of Arabia, recalling Colonel Chesney's successes in Mesopotamia in the 1830s under Turkish auspices and seeing in the new railways future base lines for triangulation. Colonel Wahab, speaking from his experience delimiting the Aden boundary, reminded the Royal Geographical Society that Indian explorers had never had to rely only on compasses, given the ease of camouflaging instruments in "uncivilized countries." But Hogarth pointed in response to Arabia's comparatively civilized nature and Turkish officials' discerning eyes, in addition to their secrecy about the railway charts and sensitivity to open surveying of their territory. Four years after he had heralded a new era of Arabian exploration, Hogarth declared Arabia still "almost wholly unsurveyed in any scientific sense," and put the failure down to the region itself—its lack of obvious landmarks, points to triangulate, or elevated points from which to survey the landscape. He speculated, rather presciently, that only "some air pilot in the future" would realistically be able to survey areas like the Rub al-Khali, the "Empty Quarter" of the peninsula. In the end, agents resigned themselves to the fact that "in Oriental countries there are many obvious difficulties in the way of detailed or accurate surveys, and maps therefore have to be compiled from reconnaissance work and less perfect data."[12]

This is not to say that they entirely abandoned scientific attempts at surveying, rather that the standard at which a survey qualified as scientific reached a nadir. For instance, the Royal Geographical Society praised the DMO agents Captains S. S. Butler and Leycester Aylmer for having "wiped one white spot off the map," even though their report was not in the least "scientific"—in the sense of endeavoring to triangulate or even provide positions for key points—but rather a familiar "pioneer"-style narrative including descriptions of the landscape and characters met on the journey, the advantages of Arab costume, and an adventurous meeting with the emir of Al Jawf. Other agents made similar presentations on subjects whose only apparent claim to being "geographical," if they did not explicitly deny any, was their setting in little-known areas. To be known, this place, unlike others, did not have to be thoroughly subjected to the Western gaze; after all, said Hogarth, "Arabia is very much the same everywhere." If the War Office and the Survey of India considered Captain Fraser Hunter's map of Arabia "a crime against science," he was content that "great authorities" like Hogarth and H. St. John Philby thought highly of it.[13]

The low bar for scientific exploration of Arabia helped configure *all* Edwardian travelers in Arabia as spies, producing the community of amateur talent from which the wartime "experts" would be drawn. Because existing maps of even allegedly well-known areas were so poor, possessing only a "specious appearance of precision," Hogarth recommended all travelers in such areas make detailed topographical notes; there was no need for exact charts made with tools. Likewise, it was said that whoever performed the feat of exploring Najd would have accomplished "a work of great scientific value" almost despite himself, for "it demands no special qualifications." Since so little was known about Arabia, even the most romantic and untrained of travelers could marshal patriotic duty as "cover" for an exercise in escapism. Bell, for instance, felt useless in much-mapped and much-seen Turkey: "This is not my country.... I have not the training for it.... I shall go back to Arabia, to the desert where I can do things and see things that...[the] learned...could scarcely do and see." There, intelligence work could be combined with adventure: at one point in her frustration with mapping on an Arabian journey, she fell to wishing desperately that "something would happen—something exciting, a raid, or a battle!" In Arabia the agent could contribute to science almost unwittingly; *any* observation, however inexpert and unscientific, significantly increased the stock of knowledge. "If you are not a scientist or an archaeologist or a politician...if, in fact, you have no particular knowledge of any sort, but your pores are wide open to receive passing impressions," explained a traveler, "what you get is a vivid idea of the appearance of things." Such an "idea" was what agents ultimately sought to convey and what they thought would ultimately provide more insight into inscrutable Arabia than a mere catalogue of facts. In such a space, they agreed, "geography was a necessary but not sufficient tool for realizing the territory" and must always be accompanied by "thick" description. The apparent limitations on empirical approaches to intelligence-gathering thus tended to open the door to a breed of explorer-agent glad to experiment with "unscientific" ways of knowing, indeed, a breed drawn to Arabia, as chapter 2 has shown, partly to escape the unsettling sense of cosmic entropy produced by modern science. An unabashed "amateur" such as Sykes (untrained in Arabic, Persian, Islamic civilization or history, or as a diplomat or consul) suffered no disadvantage: so little was known, and so much made of the lay, impressionistic style suited to knowing the region, that his claim to a natively contemplative nature was sufficient for him to come off as expert.[14]

The consensus around impressionism as the only practicable mode of description for the region was buttressed by the trope of Arabia's sublime ineffability. The Desert Sublime endured partly because it continued to resist

mapping (the Arctic and Alpine Sublimes were by contrast already demysti-
fied). Bell, an accomplished mountain climber, tellingly compared the silence
of the desert to the Alps', only "more intense," without even the "echo of
sound." Judged against the Texan and Mexican plans, the veldt, and the deserts
of Africa and Central Asia, the Arabian deserts seemed to Edwardian explorers
most sublimely impervious to verbal explication: the "very curious optical illusion" produced by their "atmosphere, which is at once clear and hazy," created
"an impression of vastness and space...difficult to describe in words." Terror
and awe strengthened the sense of verbal hopelessness: "There are no words to
tell you how bare and forbidding is this land." In the war, too, agents and soldiers deemed it "a profound enigma," "the hardest in the world to describe"
(despite the inevitable pages of lengthy description). In any case, detailed observation seemed futile to a type of agent more interested in plumbing the depths
of this essentially wonderful space. "Why should one write and take snap-
shots?" asked Sykes. "Is it not better to sit and gaze, and wonder?" Of course,
agents did take photographs and write but deemed these modes of representation ultimately inadequate to the desert's sublime surreality. Like all sublime
spaces, it challenged their linguistic abilities, at the same time inspiring them,
after all, to write. Like Australia a century before, Arabia's blankness inspired
plans for its regeneration within the fold of European empire, but it also triggered a new, *happy* admission of the defeat of Western powers of observation.
Edwardians were relieved to find in Arabia a place that did not collapse beneath
their imperial gaze, one that retained its power to exalt the imagination.[15]

The impressionistic style that solved the cartographic quandary dovetailed
neatly with agents' hopes that travel in Arabia would make them writers. This
ambition found an outlet not only in their popular published works. Their
lengthy and quite literary intelligence reports were farragoes of landscape
description, personal meditations, accounts of amusing incidents on the way,
together with reports on routes, recent developments on the railways, and the
like. Sykes's in particular were full of fantastic set pieces, elaborate characterizations of those he met, lengthy disquisitions on the terrain and ancient sites,
and fabulous dialogue in which archaic English substituted for Arabic. They
were so "literary" that he often reproduced them verbatim in his published
accounts. As a genre, exploration reports had long exhibited a tension between
realism and fiction, but in Edwardian reports from Arabia, this elision was the
rule rather than the exception and was fully intended.[16]

Aside from their patently literary style, intelligence reports also included
overt "fictions" as relevant "information." Fantastic local legends were submitted without comment. For instance, when one agent could discover no information about a site, he simply referred to his guide, who was "full of information,

explaining all antiquities, as is his wont, by a book of Bedawin fairy stories."
Employing the conventions of storytelling, intelligence reports often reproduced such stories in full. In a report on a journey in Mesopotamia, Sykes submitted as intelligence the story a sheikh told in reply to an inquiry about
agricultural works in the area:

> After the death of Haroun-al-Rashid a certain khalif ruled over this
> country: and about that time two owls dwelt in this neighbourhood.
> Now the youngest owl fell in love with the daughter of the elder. So
> after some thought he approached the senior and begged of him his
> child in marriage. Quoth the old owl "my daughter is accustomed to
> live in great comfort; have you a deserted village wherein to entertain
> and another with which to endow her." Now when the young owl
> heard these words he rejoiced and replied "O owl, at present I have
> only eighty ruined villages in my domain, but if God wills our Lord
> the Khalif live another three hundred years I shall be the sole pos-
> sessor of all the villages between here and Bagdad."

Sykes's official duty was to research agricultural developments and attitudes
toward the sultan's high taxes. He wove another sheikh's views into a folklorish
tale featuring a magic wolf and the fountain of Abraham. Reporting this way,
he played on the incongruity of a fabled land being thrust into the world of real
economies and politics by the sultan's repressive policies. He could hardly
admit, much less find, hard facts in this fictional utopia without first swathing
them in the softness of a good yarn. (The Foreign Office knew Sykes was using
his intelligence work to lay the foundation of his literary career: his reports'
"poetic description" was generally appreciated, and even Sir Edward Grey found
them "interesting and lively.")[17]

Agents included stories not merely for amusement; it was generally
believed that, in this region, even the patently fantastic contained useful information. Winston Churchill, freshly returned from fighting and reporting at the
Indian frontier, held that part of playing the "game" was dealing with the
improbable stories that passed as "facts" in the East, for "amid all this falsehood, and idle report, there often lies important information...the germ of
truth." Many were convinced that a suspension of *dis*belief in reported information (as much as a suspension of belief in visual data) was a basic precondi-
tion for their work in Arabia; it was the only way to participate authentically in
the magic information network. After recounting the story of a man from
Jerablus who had lost his memory and then regained it on the expiration of an
afrit's curse, exactly as prophesied by a certain religious sheikh, Leonard
Woolley submitted: "All I can say is that I heard the story from good sources

and knew the actors...but I cannot explain it. But that's the sort of thing that does happen, or at least that one must accept."[18]

In wartime intelligence documents this literary timbre crystallized into an official style. In the matter of nomenclature, "confusion became the mother of invention, and the Old Testament, more especially the book of Genesis, was called in with its none too fanciful associations," recorded Candler. "We had 'The Walls of Jericho', 'Eve's Crossing', 'Serpent's Corner', 'Sodom and Gomorrah'...'Jacob's Ladder' and 'The Tower of Babel.'" The stories of the Bible and the *Arabian Nights* that had long informed agents' idea of the region were inscribed onto a contemporary map. More concretely, the Arab Bureau was, from the beginning, designed to function as an analytical clearinghouse and "a kind of museum of up to date knowledge on affairs geographical, political economic and archaeological in the ares [sic] in which it operated," for which it required "an expert political *and literary* staff." The contents of the bureau's main organ for transmitting intelligence, the *Arab Bulletin*, were highly eclectic, including intelligence reports and appreciations, captured documents, and the like, but also journey reports from laymen, histories of events leading up to the revolt, and extracts from academic works. The bureau's unique mission derived partly from the longstanding overlap between academic and intelligence work in the region—wartime intelligence continued to allow the simultaneous pursuit of academic knowledge, not least because "voluntary assistance from travellers and other visitors" continued to be expected and because the war offered the "opportunity of a lifetime" for exploration formerly constrained by diplomatic scruples. Agents' duties included research into and education of soldiers on the ethnography and history of the region, partly to enable them to understand the local population and to convince them of the otherwise not entirely obvious purpose of their sacrifices in a desert far from home. The *Bulletin* included a record of "all fresh historical data concerning Arabs and Arab-speaking lands" and strove to rescue "from oblivion older facts which may help to explain the actual situation: likewise, any data of geographical or other scientific interest, which may be brought to light by our penetration of the Arab countries during the present war." Bell's fortnightly reports on intelligence in Mesopotamia were also intended to provide "the record of our work here." The intelligence record was conceived as a concurrently produced epic account of what could only unfold as epic events. It morphed into a serialized literary narrative of the war in Arabia rather than a mundane record of abstruse military facts. The *Bulletin*'s purpose, according to Hogarth, was to provide "intelligence...compiled by those in possession of all news, secret or otherwise, but not necessarily to contain all that news." Furthermore, as "it was as easy to write in decent English as in bad, and much more agreeable," the

Bulletin had "from the first a literary tinge not always present in Intelligence Summaries." Its reports were stripped of facts that its trusted authors had already processed into a literary narrative. As Malcolm Brown observes of Lawrence's famous report on the leader of the Howeitat, Auda is introduced "almost with the kind of flourish one associates with the first appearance of a major character in a Dickens or Trollope novel—or, perhaps, more aptly, the arrival on the scene of a heroic figure in Malory or William Morris." He invariably included lengthy descriptions of natural phenomena which possessed no inherent military or political relevance but "contributed to that 'literary tinge'....In writing it Lawrence was looking to the future as much as the present." Indeed, during the war itself he wrote of his intention to write a book on the "Hejaz show, the like of which has hardly been on earth before," "to make other people see it," for which he would draw on his wartime reports. He too felt that "Army prose is bad" and feared "contamination" by it. He was asked to edit the *Bulletin* in 1916 when he was still at Cairo GSI largely in view of his writing talent. Reports by other agents working in various official capacities, such as Philby, Bell, Ronald Storrs, Arnold Wilson, the demolition expert and Arab adviser Herbert Garland, and Political Agent Robert Hamilton in Kuwait, shared this literary tinge. So digressive were some that the agent-author had to abruptly recall himself with "I seem to have wandered from the point." This "agreeable" literary style was the product of a longer stylistic tradition and shared taste among agents drawn to Arabia. A literary style simply seemed suited to the place and its people: Auda, Lawrence reported, "sees life as a saga and all events in it are significant and all personages heroic. His mind is packed (and generally overflows) with stories of old raids and epic poems of fights." The Koran, the classical poets, and a "dim distortion" of the glorious past of the Arabian Khalifate—ideas savoring "rather of the Arabian Nights than of sober history"—held Arabs together, he explained.[19]

This literary tinge earned the *Bulletin* a larger and more eager following than was normally the due of any intelligence digest. In London, it was read as much as an intelligence missive and collection of "considered appreciations" as the latest installment in an epic adventure in the making. "Even the Whitehall Treasury, sick as it was of Arabia and Arabs...looked forward to reading Gertrude's compositions [in the *Bulletin*]," writes Winstone. "Along with Hogarth and Lawrence, she provided war-time reading which has certainly never been equaled in intelligence documents, and seldom in any kind of official paper." In 1917, Sykes demanded the *Bulletin* be printed in larger runs as it was being read by more than ninety people in London. Popularity quickly compromised its confidentiality, which in turn watered it down into an increasingly anodyne summary of news avoiding especially the controversial issues between the Allies. More important, for my purposes, its resemblance to a serialized adventure story reinforced the predilection for fantastical schemes led by genius agents in the campaigns in Arabia. The agents' literary turn is usually seen as an incidental fault of overarticulateness to which much of the discord in Britain's Arabian policy can be traced—John Connell famously wrote in 1958, "It would have been better for our country, and probably for the world, if C. M. Doughty, T. E. Lawrence and Gertrude Bell had not been such able and persuasive writers"—but the entire intelligence-gathering project in Arabia had from the first been conditioned by literature and literary interests. They were the reason the revolt happened in the first place.[20]

"Outside the Senses"

The literary reporting style was part of an epistemology that attempted to dispense with the empirical methods that seemed neither suitable to the agents' state of mind nor appropriate to the bizarre properties of Arabia. By turns wondering at and admiring what they saw as the special, magical epistemology of the nomads, who seemed to mystically divine truth, identify invisible landmarks, and grasp the meaning of things, the agents determined to immerse themselves in desert life and learn to think like the nomads, "outside the senses," for intelligence as much as personal purposes.

While disguise was a standard tool of agents in foreign countries, in Arabia mere camouflage would not do. There the problem was not only access but also comprehension of another universe, one that was, in the orientalist vision, cosmically ordered, a closed system of meanings. Witnessing a scene at the Jiza station where diverse elements of Ottoman life had fortuitously come together, Sykes exclaimed: "What a combination! A man might write till doomsday trying to describe what it all means.... Each is a symbol pent up with meaning." To understand a cosmological system is "to perceive patterns," Isaiah Berlin once observed, something requiring a "profoundly anti-empirical" attitude—what the agents had. Unlike the Australian case, Arabia's apparent blankness did not signify actual blankness to British explorers but rather their inability to discern its symbolic meanings. Its serial production of prophets and poetry had convinced British agents ex ante that its emptiness concealed riches. There, even nomad encampments had a "contradictory" but "extraordinary feeling of endurance and permanence." It was widely assumed that, despite their primitiveness, ancient populations had left the marks of their "fleeting sojourn" on "every stone...every hill...every rock"—inscriptions many agents collected. Unlike the Sahara "with its dismal solitude" or the veldt "with its miserable emptiness...unmeaning, where man is an uninteresting cipher," noted Sykes, the Arabian desert "was once teeming with life and wealth, business and war." This desert could be read, if only the mind were conditioned appropriately to interpret its signs.[21]

Islam too appeared a closed system, a "visionary cosmology," rendering the region a self-contained otherworld. It was "as much a society, as a religion," declared Arthur Wavell, with "certain rules binding on its members, as in Freemasonry... certain peculiarities of dress, certain salutations, and distinctive habits, by which members may know each other." The European had to immerse himself entirely in its secret society and learn its ceremonies, greetings, gestures, and postures to access its encrypted knowledge. These rules constituted "the real obstacle" to passing in the Middle East. The 1909 memorandum on secret service in "uncivilized countries" illustrated the importance of learning the full body of authentic Eastern knowledge with an example from the annals of Arabian exploration: Burton's dead-giveaway European-style micturition in Mecca.[22]

By aping Arabs, agents could fling open the doors of the Arabian archive, for, as one traveler put it, "Only by Orientals—*or by those whose long sojourn in the East has formed their minds after the Oriental pattern*—can the Orient be adequately described." In other words, a European who immersed himself long enough in Arab life might begin to alter internally as well; he might be able to *think like an Arab* and perceive the cosmic pattern governing Arab life. There was a limit to what Europeans qua Europeans could learn about Arabs. Contemporaries identified as the secret of Lawrence's later power his prewar "immersion in [the Arabs], by sympathetic projection," which produced a profound understanding of "native ways," "different from, the acquired knowledge of the outside observer." Abandoning the conventions of "civilized life," he became a "naturalized Arab instead of merely a European visitor to the Arab lands." His tramp habits, rooted in his own impecuniousness, helped him to make the easier transformation "from a 'street Arab' to a 'white Arab.'" Bell's powerful "sympathy with [Arabs]" likewise enabled her "to penetrate into their minds." Time was essential to successful reshaping of the mind. Bell was disappointed at her mere two-day stay in Aleppo, for "an Oriental city will not admit you into the circle of its intimates unless you spend months within its walls, and not even then if you will not take pains to please." Indeed, a new attitude toward time was part of the necessary transformation. Carruthers was retroactively grateful for his unplanned long stay with the Beni Sakhr, which taught him Arab manners and dress, how to drink coffee "*a la* Arab, and most of all, how to sit all day long doing nothing."[23]

During the war, lengthy immersion was official practice for agents and officials in the region. Lawrence coached novitiates: "Watch...your companions all the time: hear all that passes, search out what is going on beneath the surface.... Bury yourself in Arab circles, have no interests and no ideas except the work in hand, so that your brain is saturated with one thing only." He himself may have had the desert in his blood, but, stressed his colleague Pierce Joyce, "It is his intimate and extensive knowledge of the history and the tribes and the language that really counts." Or, in Liddell Hart's more visceral terms, "He got inside the Arab's skin first, and then transcended it." Colleagues similarly admired Political Officer Harold Dickson's "unstudied ease [in] an Arab setting," thanks to his Kim-like childhood in Jerusalem where his father had been consul (with Iraqis, he embellished the truth by claiming he had had an Arab foster mother). "He seemed to the manner born," recalled Philby enviously, "and in a sense he was." He could "walk blindfold without faltering" among the "intricacies" of the Arabian universe, thanks to his "peculiar...understanding [of] the...Arab's mind." In the Middle East for the first time himself, Philby seized the opportunity to frequent "the respectable and less respectable purlieus of the city [Basra]" and learn to speak Arabic like a native. The more seasoned Leachman allegedly lived in the desert all year "dressed as an Arab, and with his boy Hussein wandered about amongst the tribes...organizing, compelling, acquiring priceless information." Immersion in the "crosscurrents of intrigue" soon enabled Deedes to join a secret society in Cairo, through which he reached "men who would never have cared to call at his office or be seen talking to him in public, and...collected a vast amount of information from the talk of bazaars, native cafés and brothels and *all of those underground and hidden sources debarred to an Englishman.*" Immersion was critical because real information was too esoteric to be merely observed.[24]

Because the object of protracted immersion was not simply to "pass" but to become part of the Arabian cosmos, the practice of adopting Arab dress had a complicated purpose. From the outset, Arab clothing was used as disguise—Bury dressed as a dervish while eavesdropping at wells, Leachman as a Levantine jewelry peddler on a visit to Kuwait—but as often merely as part of the desert experience; to journey to Arabia "openly" did not preclude donning Arab dress. Indeed, the stagey furtiveness of agents' behavior could even undermine their efforts at discretion—Leachman's identity and mission were well known to local authorities and tribes before the war. In Arab dress even before he became an agent, Lawrence was convinced, despite his "obvious incongruities," that he was "the only European who knows [Aleppo]," since the clothes allowed him to "get inside an Arab's skin." Indeed, without them, averred Ely Soane, "a European would be an alien, a stranger without acquaintance, in an isolated position and a dangerous one, hampered in his movements." Arab dress conveyed the stranger's awareness that he was trespassing on forbidden terrain and doing his best to banish incongruous sights from it. "There can be really no such thing" as disguise in Arabia, Carruthers explained. "A European who...has studied the manners and customs of the Arabs, may pass more freely and without offence if he wears native clothes...but...is always known to be what he really is." "The aim of anyone entering Arabia," he explained, was "to pass as *unnoticed*....Therefore he should appear as near like his hosts, and do as they do, in so far as he can." The idea of an Arabian *order* requiring preservation made immersion a necessary part of intelligence work and made the Edwardian delight in "vanishing" in the desert a tactical as much as a fanciful move; immersion overlapped neatly with agents' desire to make believe.[25]

To be sure, overly zealous immersion in Bedouin life could invite suspicion of the agent's Britishness. Bury had "really lived in Arabia as an Arab," Hogarth advised Bury's prospective publisher. "I have photos of him in a skin with castor oil in his hair. I fancy he has explored some depths of Arab custom not usually plumbed by Europeans....He told me he belonged to an old Devonshire farm, but he looks like a goanese and must have much the Eurasian in him." Radical physical transformation—the "disreputable" sight of an Englishman in "Arab costume, very dirty, hair very long, bosom very manly and exposed," as the Baghdad resident twitted one such apparition—invited the disapproval of the more straightlaced among the community. "Indeed, it is not a good thing to know too much of orientals" was Sykes's mordant pronouncement. "If you do, perhaps you may wake up one morning and find that you have become one....Any one who has seen an oriental European usually retires to a convenient distance to be sick." Still, there were assurances that Europeans could brave this occupational hazard without risking total racial and cultural perdition. Besides the limits on actually disguising one's true identity, the banner of patriotic duty also shielded agents from impugning of their Europeanness. Soane struck a bitter note as he exited the fantasy land of his journey, renouncing the, admittedly illusory, cosmic completeness he had found:

> I felt stranger and more lonely than I had done ever before. Gone was the coffee-house and the bazaar, of the multitudes of which I was one, and equal, with whom I spoke and laughed, and fought and wrangled. They were far away, and I must learn to look upon them as upon strange and inferior beings, if such were now possible, and taking place again on the platform of Western birth, once more go on my way.

His imperial melancholy points to both the impossibility of ever attaining a permanent position in the Arabian order and the Edwardian hankering after Europe's own long-shattered cosmic order. Those most earnestly dedicated to "passing" were thus heaped with the greatest praise—for the sheer romance of their exploits, their success at having secured a position in one remaining British social cosmology: the mythology of empire. Hence also were disguise and deception no longer perceived as egregious offenses against British gentlemanliness in this period.[26]

Thus, although disguised British agents in India were primarily the stuff of myth, the early-twentieth-century view of Arabia as a cosmically ordered otherworld ensured that, in Rana Kabbani's words, "the mode of disguise became the classic method through which the British related to the Arab world." By Said's own reckoning, Richard Burton *stood out* in the nineteenth century as the one explorer who immersed himself in Arab life on the assumption that "to be an Oriental or a Muslim was to know certain things in a certain way." Edwardians went further, following Kim, for, as Thomas Richards points out, while disguise gave Burton access to Mecca, Kim infiltrates a community *by actually joining it*. He is no mere master of disguises but "a master of identities." There were exceptions—although careful to learn "the strict etiquette of the desert," Shakespear refused to travel in anything but his uniform—but most could not resist the thrill of "simply dressing up." Arabia was simply the sort of place where one did that sort of thing. There, unlike in India, the British insisted on accessing the "deep knowledge" that comes from "inhabiting the same moral realm"; as Edwardians they were more disenchanted with their own world and attracted to the idea of immersion in another and, moreover, perceived Arabia even more than India as an entirely different planet, governed by utterly different codes. As they often pointed out, the basic disguise—as little as a kaffiyeh and sheepskin coat—was also easily adoptable, while racial barriers to "passing" were rendered negligible both by fitful perceptions of racial affinity with Arabs and by the cosmopolitanism of the Middle East, to which Islam regularly and legitimately drew every race.[27]

During the war, disguise evolved into an official policy of being "as little out of the Arab picture" as possible. Philby admonished "those who would travel in Arabia...to do as Arabs do," dismissing the prejudice against dissimulation as ungentlemanly—a scruple, he pointed out, that had cost Shakespear his life at the start of the war (deputed to Najd, he was killed in January 1915 while observing a battle between the armies of Ibn Saud and Ibn Rashid). Arab "head-gear" was standard issue for officers in the desert, "to give the proper 'silhouette' effect." Disguise also remained critical to entering the desert archive. In "Arab kit," explained Lawrence to his wartime disciples, "You will be like an actor in a foreign theatre, playing a part day and night for months, without rest.... Complete success, which is when the Arabs forget your strangeness and speak naturally before you...is perhaps only attainable in character."

Successful deportment in Arab clothing became a measure of ability as an agent, although Lawrence discouraged disguise intended to repudiate the agent's British and Christian identity as likely to damage Arab trust. Nevertheless, some agents' ability to "pass" was lionized as evidence of their prodigious powers. Norman Bray's description of Leachman's transformation recalls comic-book superheroes:

> He never paraded himself in Arab dress before his countrymen, but
> would change into his faded khaki the moment he reached the
> borders of civilization, so that few had the privilege of witnessing the
> remarkable transformation from the long, lanky, British officer,
> always beautifully clean, always fastidious, into a wild-looking
> Bedouin so perfect in disguise that not even his closest friends could
> penetrate it.

Despite his disavowal of any intention to pass—"No easterner could have taken me for an Arab, for a moment"—Lawrence's skill at disguise also grew legendary. For his part, he considered *un*-disguise the key to his security, given his status as a kind of superhero in Arabia:

> My burnt red face, clean shaven and startling with my blue eyes
> against white headcloth and robes, became notorious in the desert.
> Tribesmen or peasants who had never set eyes on me before would
> instantly know me, by the report. So my Arab disguise was actually
> an advertisement. It gave me away instantly, as myself, to all the
> desert: and to be instantly known was safety.

If he saw danger, he would "get into a soldier's cap, shirt and shorts, and get away with it, or draw my headcloth over my face, like a visor, and brazen it out." The appeal of such stories of disguise (even within officialdom) lay (and lies) in their adumbration of a Kim-like existence, of complete entry into fictional Arabia.[28]

From the outset, agents stressed that attire alone could not open up the desert archive; it was but the first step in total adaptation to nomadic existence. To know the desert and collect information that moved in tandem with its nomadic population, they would have to inhabit it the way nomads did, continually roving, in the mode they also found most conducive to meditative attainment of metaphysical knowledge. Sykes put it bluntly, "In the desert everything moves, and that which cannot move dies." The peripatetic Lorimer stressed, "Really good work cannot be done in Mesopotamia and Kurdistan without a great deal of travelling....The intimate first-hand knowledge...which is the secret of success in political work, is not to be acquired except by actual moving."

Immersion in the desert was, to the agents, like immersion in the sea, in something vast, seemingly infinite; to grasp the whole of its spatially disperse system of information, one had to be literally absorbed in the whole thing. District tours, a peculiarly British consular activity, became an important (and politically expedient) means of acquiring local political and military intelligence and spying out the terrain (with the exception of the consul at Jeddah, whose travel outside town walls elicited considerable local official displeasure). A mobile harvester of intelligence, Bell collected "what falls from the lips of those who sit round our camp fires, and who ride with us across desert and mountains, for their words are like straws on the flood of Asiatic politics, showing which way the stream is running." Words uttered on the move could provide real insight because politics too were a matter of *flow*, movement: she strung their words "upon the thread of the road." The extent of an agent's travels therefore provided a measure of the quality of intelligence. Sykes proudly introduced his list of Kurdish tribes as the result "of about 6000 miles of riding and innumerable conversations with policemen, muleteers, Mullahs, Chieftains, sheep-drovers, horse-dealers, carriers, and other people capable of giving one first-hand information." In their romantic conception of themselves and of travel, Englishmen seemed particularly destined for such work, as a "race...given to wandering over the face of the earth."[29]

Leachman's posting as "OC Desert" is perhaps most symbolic of the official sanction gave this mode of work during the war (his command was no army but the desert itself, where he was to enforce a blockade, another odd task that had fallen into the hands of political officers.) In general, wartime political officers and agents were licensed to wander, not least to circumvent the distortions of the magical information network. Ronald Storrs, oriental secretary to the Cairo Residency whose work included intelligence, warned, "Syrian and Arab intermediaries cannot transmit a message without causing it to undergo a sea-change." Itinerancy was also encouraged by the continued commitment to pioneer-style exploration, for a mix of tactical and scholarly purposes, Arabia offering even in wartime "just sufficient spice of danger to enliven the monotony of a lonesome desert life." Rudimentary techniques remained the favored style for surveying. Agents remained enchanted by the possibility of vanishing into the void, despite war duty: on his first mission to Najd and filled "with that restless longing for the vast spaces," Philby took every opportunity to vanish into the blue for long stretches of time.[30]

The crux of the immersion strategy as it was cemented into an official tactic was development of the intuition, in the sense of "immediate apprehension of an object by the mind without the intervention of any reasoning process." Early on, agents concluded that Arab grasp of the seemingly ungraspable politics of the region derived from a special insight into the flux of truth and lies. Bell wrote,

> Their statecraft consists of guesses, often shrewd enough, at the
> results which may spring from the clash of unknown forces, of which
> the strength and aim are but dimly apprehended; this wisdom is that
> of men whose channels of information and standards for comparison
> are different from ours, and who bring a different set of preconcep-
> tions to bear upon the problems laid before them.

They drew conclusions about politics almost magically, the absence of facts proving no obstacle. Indeed, "The nature of evidence is not clearly grasped in the East." The Arab's wisdom, his "strangely subtle mind," was beyond scientific check; it took the place of, rather than coexisted with, the potential to think rationally. "The European thinks, the Oriental only reflects," Meredith Townsend ruled more generally, "and if left to himself the idea, turned over and over endlessly in his mind, hardens into the consistency of steel. Thenceforward it is part of the fibre of his mind." Nevertheless, the agents conceded, this sort of reflection invariably led the Arab to the correct conclusion. Their appreciation for the accuracy of Arab intuition even in reason's sacred sphere of politics went well beyond the Romantic admiration of oriental wisdom in spiritual matters. In a place utterly devoid of rationality, it would be reckless to persist in relying on reason alone, for, in Churchill's words, "So extraordinary is the inversion of ideas and motives among [tribesmen] that...those who know them best know them least, and the more logical the mind of the student the less he is able to understand of the object." In a realm of miraculous insight, there was no place for the fundamentals of Western scientific thought—proposition, evidence, deduction, theorem. During the war, Lawrence felt he had succeeded in surrendering to the subtle ways of the desert archive:

> My business was to see everyone with news, and let him talk himself
> out to me, afterwards arranging and combining the truth of these
> points into a complete picture in my mind. Complete, because it gave
> me certainty of judgment: *but it was not conscious or logical,* for my
> informants were so many that they informed me to distraction, and
> my single mind bent under all its claims.

This was partly the nature of the beast: Arabia's reality was itself not objective but subjective; the desert possessed the suggestive power of Solaris. A wireless officer in Mesopotamia who was confident that he understood the science of mirages remained baffled that "several men would experience exactly the same illusion." He concluded: "Mirage, like Rumour, is a curious thing. It may have some inner connection with the set of a man's feelings." The Mesopotamian marshes, too, yielded only to subjective penetration: going through them was "the weirdest feeling in the world," avowed Dickson. "You could get lost for ever and easily.... Marshmen know the place with their eyes shut"—which, ultimately, was the only way to know it. The war correspondent Edmund Candler agreed that "the absence of colour, form, and light, was subjective," the product of "the inward eye." Those who knew how to discipline this psychic organ might, like the Bedouin, overcome the obstacles to surveying. Hence perhaps the irrelevance to their work of the much-remarked myopia of Aubrey Herbert and J. Hope-Johnstone, another prewar traveler in Mesopotamia who wound up in wartime intelligence; eyesight was not the vision that mattered.[31]

In other words, agents did not link the intuitive mode strictly to race or to any factor inherent in the indigenous population. Rather, it was *contagious*, something that originated in the numinous landscape itself. Echoing Townsend's description of oriental thought processes, a traveler explained, "In very slow travelling through desert countries, where day after day the same trivial events occur in similar yet different settings, the essential facts of that country sink into you imperceptibly, until at the end they are...woven into the fibres of your nature." Where information seemed to flow of its own accord, instinctively, and science collapsed unceremoniously, more "scholarly" information-gathering might be less effective than meditative surrender. The desert could get into one's brain, Bell observed; if Arabs preferred "to sleep, and smoke, and contemplate," argued the journalist-agent David Fraser, this was "the type evolved by the environment." Sykes was adamant that "no townsman, no European, can live for any appreciable time in a desert without becoming intuitively aware of a fact which may seem doubtful in the midst of the distractions of a crowded city." The desert seeped into the mind, not only resurrecting faith, but altering the senses and smothering clarity, rationality, the intellect. Bell found it difficult to keep her own mind "steadily fixed upon" certainties based on evidence. In the war, soldiers similarly complained of the desert's "softening effect" on their brains and described the "meditative mood" it induced: "One of the fellows...dream [sic] regularly of armies of mail clad warriors marching through wonderful cities...curious effect of environment." Desert travel "[lapped] one into a trance," affirmed Candler; the cries of the marsh boatmen on the way upriver had a "strangely hypnotic effect" on the troops. "We dreamed ourselves into the spirit of the place," wrote Lawrence. "This escape of our wits from the fettered body was an indulgence against whose enervation only change of scene would avail." This entrancement left an indelible mark on intelligence; identifying landmarks was for Philby "a matter of inference rather than conviction."

In Iraq, Dickson lost "all idea of dates or days of the week." "Instead of facts and figures," attests Lawrence, "my note-books were full of states of mind, the reveries and self-questioning induced or educed by our situations, expressed in abstract words to the dotted rhythm of the camels' marching." The desert distracted the agent from a quest for objective, empirical knowledge toward the discovery of subjective self-knowledge. The "large mental element" induced by this "flat and uniform" place forced its inhabitants to "become sensualists or seek a higher path and become mystics," a soldier intoned. The pathology of Arabian information created an officially sanctioned space for the authority of the "genius" on Arabia, for experts who considered reverie an aid rather than an impediment to their work.[32]

And this, after all, was why many of the agents had come to Arabia in the first place—to wander and escape the disciplining power of Enlightenment rationality. Sykes had early on exhorted other aspiring travelers "to divest yourself of all preconceived notions. Wipe John Stuart Mill, Omar Khayyam, Burke, Ruskin, Carlyle, and Bernard Shaw out of your mind" and instead, "learn the Book of Job by heart for philosophy, the Book of Judges for politics, the 'Arabian Nights' (Burton's translation) for ethics." By excavating an older form of knowledge from repressed cultural memory—from the biblical past that located their roots in Arabia—British travelers would be able to surrender to intuition, to "ride by balance, not by grip" and "learn a good deal." Travelers' literary hopes, spiritual cravings, and intelligence work shared a common epistemological objective, the recovery of intuition as the basis of knowledge. Their distinctive attraction to Arabia signaled to them their likely success at this strategy. It was easy for Lawrence to get inside an Arab's skin, a contemporary explained, "because he already shared the Arabs' deep-rooted desire for untrammelled freedom, and had no more desire than they had for the material possessions." The scope for immersion, the apparent contagiousness of the desert way of knowing, was a boon to an intelligence project otherwise paralyzed by the apparent inaccessibility of knowledge in a fictional land.[33]

A "guide, philosopher and friend" was the "first essential" in British agents' imaginary apprenticeships in "nomad science." Many were regulars with British travelers, serving as route navigators and prophets of future raids. They were ideally hyper-nomadic, "omniscient" Arabs whose occupations led them to wander abroad of their traditional tribal ambit, the best, according to Sykes, being robbers, religious mendicants, or odd men (a course that would be sanctified in a wartime handbook). Bell wrote fondly that her guide "knew the name of every hill and every bare furrow—I was surprised to find they had names." These names meant little to her undistinguishing eye then; she continued dryly, "This was the sort of conversation.... 'Oh, Lady, this is the Valley of the

Wild Boar'. There didn't seem to be anything to say about it except that it was a horrid sandy little place." She did not remain skeptical for long. Five years later her words betrayed a new respect for Arabs' discriminating eyes: "The map is blank, and when you reach the encampment the landscape is blank also," but "a rise in the ground, a big stone, a vestige of ruin, not to speak of every possible hollow...these are marks sufficiently distinguishing to the nomad eye." It was not that she had missed the features that more careful observation would have revealed but that nomads had a peculiar way of seeing, behind the landscape's objective blankness. Elsewhere during this journey, she "looked out beyond him...and *saw the desert with his eyes*, no longer empty but set thicker with human associations than any city. Every line of it took on significance." The DMO agent Norman Bray likewise determined to "merge myself in the Oriental as far as possible, absorb his ideas, *see with his eyes, and hear with his ears*, to the fullest extent possible to one bred in British traditions." Having let the desert transform his senses, Carruthers too noted that emptiness was no longer "as it first appeared":

> The sense of smell is rested while the sight and hearing are quickened to a pitch that is unbelievable. One's eyes are forever searching over immense spaces, and by practice they become accustomed to focusing on to objects at a distance they had never been able to focus before. The range of sight and sound is multiplied by ten, and one's power of observation is increased in like proportion.

Sensory transformation had opened the door to the Bedouin universe.[34]

These agents had in all likelihood simply learned with practice to distinguish topographical variations on the minute scale of the desert, but they understood their skill as the product of a more profound transformation. Bury allowed his hair to grow "bedouin-fashion" for warmth, and, "like all the rest, I had the usual 'desert stare' (sunken eyes and over-hanging brow), with a...complexion of duskier hue than most of the Nisabis." His feeling of oneness with his companions is evident from his use of the collective pronoun: "Our faces were all sharp-featured and grimly set...with pinched prominent noses and emaciated frames...a villainous and abandoned set of crocks." Agents understood their new skill as the result of their effort to remake themselves as nomads. The effort to read the landscape did not, *to them*, constitute a reversion to empiricism or strip them of their fundamentally cosmological vision of Arabia; it was motivated by a desire to penetrate that cosmos, which was, by definition, not empirically accessible, insofar as empiricism is based on the presumption that there is no reality beyond appearances. Agents interpreted their work not as unmediated recording of sense data but as an effort to grasp theories and patterns, to intuit hidden realities. The nomad eye was to them a sixth, mystical sense, beyond ordinary vision. Liddell Hart would explain Lawrence's peculiar abilities: "His senses are very highly developed—but different." To Philby, "the ordinary Arab—and how much more so the expert?—[was] equipped with an almost instinctive power to read the signs of the desert." Carruthers explained to the Royal Geographical Society that although he often had no way of finding out where he was for days at a time, his guide could invariably determine their bearings exactly, with next to no data. S. G. Knox, while political agent in Kuwait, described how Bedouin found their way in an "absolutely featureless plain" by almost imperceptibly "wavering uncertainly to right and left." By apparently losing their way, they miraculously kept their direction. Shakespear remarked his guides' idiosyncratic way of studying the compass "long and deeply whenever placed on the ground." In his notes, he marked bearings pointed out by his guides as "invisible approximate...merely to show how very good a reliable bedouin's sense of direction really is." Rather than interpret Bedouins' adept use of scanty astronomical data as proof of unusual empirical ability, he presumed the data so meager as to preclude rigorous empiricism without recourse to an innate "sense of direction." To him, they looked for *signs*, not data; hence, one leg was accomplished "with 'the North Star in your left eye', as the bedouin phrased it," which "references to the compass showed...to give about 38' to 42' as our direction." Translating Bedouin knowledge into Western scientific fact, he admitted both as accurate—a departure from late-nineteenth-century trends—but acknowledged the relative success of the former. Carruthers spoke admiringly of Bedouin tracking as "a science" and an "art," but their astonishingly precise extraction of information from camel tracks and dung remained to him a miraculous phenomenon he could verify with "real" science: thus, "on each occasion I proved him correct." "Scientific" did not imply "empirical," but methodical, governed by rules, albeit with the object of recovering signs, not data—something like the occultist commitment to science. Included in Carruthers's account of "nomad science" was a description of the Sherrarat's fortune-telling tactics—drawing marks in the sand and reading them for good or bad omens—when in doubt as to the way.[35]

Thus, by wartime, the consensus was that what made experts on Arabia *expert* was their ability to see, like Arabs, beyond surface deceptions to the buried, deeper truth, to discern the real from the unreal, the mirage, the lie. Lord Kitchener, then high commissioner in Cairo, who acquired his own desert aura as an intelligence officer in disguise in Sinai in the 1880s, possessed an "Oriental habit of keeping his ear close to the ground," to which contemporaries attributed his preternatural grasp of the situation in Arabia. The Aden

Residency employed Bury on the grounds that he could perform the work of a native assistant—namely, ascertaining the truth of local people's statements— "equally well," and more safely, since "he is besides an educated Englishman, in whom...complete confidence may be placed." The Orient was "second nature" to Sykes; his "powers of mimicry, and an occasional flash of genius or wisdom often enabled him to penetrate further into Eastern matters than a more exact student." Intuitive ability to grasp the Arabian reality was *preferable* to rigorous academic training; it was a matter of genius. Skill in acting, invention, "making-believe," gained Sykes, like the endlessly theatrical Arabs, access to knowledge of Arabia. James Elroy Flecker likewise confessed self-pityingly that, despite his animus against all that was Eastern, "yet it seems—even to hardened Orientalists—that I understand." The claim to intuitive ability was prized among agents such as Lorimer, Shakespear, Sykes, and the Basra consul F. E. Crow. Knox was confident he could assess the truth of talk in Kuwait simply "from the way the story was told." Reginald Wingate, the governor-general of the Sudan and sirdar of the Egyptian Army who would head the Arab Bureau, was said to possess an uncanny ability to cope with "that mysterious child of lies, the Arab." He could "converse with him for hours, and at the end know not only how much truth he has told, but exactly what truth he has suppressed." Meanwhile, tyros earnestly declared their commitment to learning "to keep clear of most of the facts and reports which in reality are only bazaar rumours." The claim to special ability enhanced the aura of the predestined hero attached to these agents; the intuitive intelligence epistemology helped them fulfill the mythopoeic impulse animating much of their work.[36]

It also secured them positions of influence when the war broke out. Those considered most gifted were consulted as oracles rather than as well-informed bureaucrats—hence Sykes's sway in London, Bell's in Mesopotamia, Lawrence's in the Hejaz, and Hogarth's everywhere. "The value of Lawrence in the position which he has made for himself with Feisal is enormous," wrote Gilbert Clayton, head of Cairo intelligence, regretting that it was "extremely difficult to get" such men "to act in the same way with Ali and Abdulla." He eventually asked that no Europeans be sent into northern Hejaz, "beyond Lawrence, who is of course essential and unique." He seemed to possess the "uncanny ability to sense the feelings of any group in whose company he found himself...[the] power to probe into their minds and divine the well-spring of their actions." Reflective by nature, Lawrence explained his powers in words that recall Yeats: "Though my sight was sharp, I never saw men's features: always I peered beyond, imagining for myself a spirit-reality of this or that." To British subalterns otherwise mistrusting and loathing their "fierce-looking" Arab allies, Lawrence's fluid consciousness solved the "riddle" of their role, furnishing what one captivated soldier called "a visible link between us and the Arabs...between us and our own British Army, between us and England, between us and home." In Basra, Bell's skill made her similarly irreplaceable. "I do know these people," she admitted. "I have been in contact with them in a way which is possible for no official, and it is that intimacy and friendship which makes me useful here now." She, too, would be memorialized as "a connecting link between the British and Arab races." Cox and Meinertzhagen ignited similar sentiments; Pierce Joyce, commander of the Hejaz operations alongside Lawrence (and postwar military advisor to the Iraqi Army) was said to be natively skilled at coping with "the maddening uncertainties of the Arab character"; and the "idealist" Deedes to possess "a cold and penetrating eye which can perceive the flaw in a man's character behind the most skilful screen of words." "The Arab talent for elaborate fiction" was likewise wasted upon Leachman, "the quiet-looking man who...probably knew before he asked any questions." Thus, during the war, "Espionage that mattered was," on the testimony of intelligence memoirist Captain Ferdinand Tuohy, "primarily the preserve of a few resourceful officers...who masqueraded...and wandered about collecting information. *Next* in the list of honour—or dishonour?—came the Bedouin." A Briton who had surpassed the Arabs at their own game was a real asset. After the war, the Arab Bureau agent Captain Ormsby-Gore continued to stress the importance and difficulty of finding others who were "particularly gifted" and "have got the feeling of the Middle East in their blood." Even mastery of Arabic required "more than knowledge and learning—something in the nature of a gift." An ideology of inspired genius had come to dominate the British intelligence world in the Middle East.[37]

Under the influence of these elite members of the intelligence community, the goal of imitating Bedouins' subjective apprehension acquired the status of an official tactic. Bedouin, wrote Lawrence, "showed a completeness of instinct, a reliance upon intuition, the unperceived foreknown, which left our centrifugal minds gasping." He officially enshrined the goal of rivaling these abilities in his famous "Twenty-Seven Articles," a compendium of advice to officers and agents working with Bedouin. The articles, which were published in the *Bulletin*, postulated: "Their minds work just as ours do, but on different premises. There is nothing unreasonable, incomprehensible, or inscrutable in the Arab experience of them." The agent had to discover those "premises" to understand the Bedouin and to become as naturally skilled at intelligence as they were. At once committed to the possibility of interracial understanding and the scarcity of those capable of it, he vacillated, as one scholar points out, between the reality of a common humanity and the illusion of the difference of the genius order. Intelligence work in Arabia was "curious," Lawrence insisted; it demanded "a sort of twisted tact, which many people do not seem to possess." That immersion was the only route to acquire that tact (for the few who ever could) was no longer the eccentric belief of the casual agent but validated as corporate best practice. Political officers may not have had the requisite book knowledge, explained Bray, "but, from a certain knowledge of men and man- ners…we 'sensed' the essence of a matter." Candler witnessed unseasoned political officers gradually master the language and, with it, acquire "an insight into the Arab mind, possibly in time the habit of oblique thought, so that one could…understand a great deal that is hidden and implied and never passes the lips." Cox's Political Department rather than GSI earned Lawrence's ulti- mate approval because of its patently literary taste and deep understanding of the "natives." Even ordinary officers were encouraged to acquire this ability in some measure, according to the syllabus of an "Intelligence Course" held at Baghdad near the end of the war—probably as a result of Lawrence's denuncia- tion of Beach's entire establishment as "amateurs" lacking knowledge of local customs and languages and thus unable to differentiate "between obvious truth and falsehood" in their examinations of agents, refugees, and prisoners. Only men "accustomed to dealing with orientals" could sift reports by compulsively mendacious "native agents." Tactical failures were put down to a failure to apply intuitive skill: Arnold Wilson accused General Townshend, who com- manded the initial unsuccessful attempt to capture Baghdad, of profoundly misunderstanding "Arab psychology," and Bray attributed Leachman's failure to prevent the murders of British officials in Kurdish Iraq to his inability to grasp the Kurdish mind in the way he had the Arab.[38]

The emphasis on rare skill supported the preference for informal rather than bureaucratic collection and transmission of intelligence for the duration of the war. The "personal impressions and personal judgments" that Bell insisted on conveying reflected the unique insight of the expert Arabia agent; they were what made intelligence about Arabia intelligible. Meinertzhagen was "delighted to find that my reports were not only read but acted on" in Palestine, for, in East Africa, commanders had remained unperturbed by his efforts to impress upon them that "when I stated information about the enemy as a fact it was indeed a fact" and not mere gossip. Respect for intuitive genius was de rigueur in Arabia. A handful of distinguished agents' opinions carried weight regardless of evidence. Rumors were confirmed by reference to them. They, like their prewar guides, were considered omniscient—"Leachman…knew everything"—possessed of an occult knowledge of an occult region. Lieutenant Fielding, erstwhile secretary of the Psychical Research Society, reputedly approached intelligence in Cairo as "one investigating a house alleged to be haunted" and hoping the ghosts were real. It was this sense of confidence that made the "Mesopotamian Breakdown" at Kut so shocking. "In the East there is not excuse for bad intelligence," one critic insisted, "least of all in a country so familiar to us as Mesopotamia." Genius had literally done wonders for a land so recently advertised as "Still Unknown."[39]

The willful legend-building around these agents bespeaks contemporaries' understanding of intelligence in Arabia as something outside the ken of ordinary men. Lawrence was "no ordinary man," attested his colleague Stirling; it was "an amazing thing that an Englishman should have beaten all the records of Arabia for speed and endurance...of the dispatch riders of the Caliph Haroun al Raschid which had been sung for centuries in the tribal sagas." At the same time, according to the air commander J. E. Tennant, flying officers carried special cards in case of a forced landing, on which were printed "Lijman" [Leachman] in Arabic: "Such was the magic of his personality." Bray termed him a "super man," while Major C. S. Jarvis, postwar governor in the Sinai, reserved the same epithet for Lawrence, who "saw to everything personally with his strange forceful personality." The armored-car driver S. C. Rolls joined this awestruck legend-making about Lawrence as a "super-human" with "power over all" whose words and acts had "a prophetic quality." This superhero quality set certain agents apart; witness Storrs's desperate but ultimately foiled attempts to join that exclusive club by journeying in the peninsula. This was, of course, the legendary status that these agents had reached for; the war allowed them to fulfill the mythopoeic impulse behind their work. As one contemporary aptly put it, Leachman's "perilous journeys" and "still more perilous behaviour on them" were rooted in his feeling that "he had to keep on doing the most desperately reckless things simply because that was how he had made his name and imposed himself on the Arabs." The Bible's uncanny reliability as a guide to Arabia strengthened the view that intelligence was an act of divination, the work of heroes, not mortals—perhaps for this reason Lawrence put his "Twenty-Seven Articles" in "commandment form."[40]

The most consequential instance of recourse to agents' prophetic powers was the effort to assess the significance of the Arab nationalist movement. Before the war, Young, Bray, and other agents had begun to communicate secretly with what was termed the "Arab Party." Through shady and informal contacts with what they presumed was the fringe of a substantial core organization, they had divined the existence of a militarily formidable party sprawling from Damascus to Baghdad, Basra, and the Hejaz. During the war, as Kitchener's secret diplomacy with Sherif Hussein gained momentum and Aziz al-Masri and other nationalist exiles in Cairo began to solicit British support, partly through agents like Philip Graves whom they had known in their more unofficial capacities before the war, Cairo grew confident that "there has been a distinct tendency towards combination on the part of the more powerful chiefs...with a view to throwing off the Turkish domination and working towards an Arabia for the Arabs." The Foreign Office decided, "Every possible encouragement should be given to the Arab Movement." By 1915, thanks partly to Mohammed al-Faruqi's desertion to British lines at Gallipoli, Cairo was sure in its "belief in the existence of a strong arab party, both in the army and among the leading chiefs of Arabia, which is ready to join the British if it gets its terms, or in the alternative to join the Germans and the Turks." (The British fear that the Arabs would be co-opted into the network of German spies operating between Constantinople and Delhi was the kernel of truth at the heart of *Greenmantle*.) How the British arrived at this conclusion—that the various groups they had met were part of one Arab Party—only makes sense in light of the official emphasis on the oracular intuition of key agents. The evidence was considered far from conclusive in some quarters. "There is a feeling in London that the Arab movement is unreal, shadowy and vague," acknowledged Alfred Parker, Kitchener's nephew and Cairo intelligence agent on duty at the War Office in 1915, but "the reality and possible force of the movement is not doubted by any person of experience in the Near East." Used to thinking of the region as superficially deceptive and ever ready to suspend disbelief, agents trusted their hunch that the Arab movement was real and substantial. This difference of opinion was in a sense most convenient, for, if in London the prevailing view was that "the Pan-Arab idea is a mirage," as Arthur Hirtzel of the India Office put it. "*If it had not been, we could not have supported it.*" Its seeming inchoateness made it at once an ideal cause for self-described experts confident that they knew better and a safe gamble for a government wary of unwittingly consolidating rather than dividing Islam. In the end, such was the influence of the accepted experts in the field of Arabia intelligence that any doubts about the wisdom of supporting the Arab Party were swept aside, for, in the words of an India Office official, "we have to accept the word of Colonel Clayton, General Maxwell and Sir H. McMahon, who profess themselves satisfied after long inquiries that there is a large and solid Arab party."[41]

The Arab Party's ultimate failure to muster the military strength the experts expected did not engender doubts about their views. When many allegedly proBritish Mesopotamians sided with the Turks, the experts explained that these *sedentary* Arabs, as opposed to Bedouin, had succumbed to Pan-Islamist propaganda. At the same time, the natural elusiveness of the "real" Arabs on their side made assessment of their true strength meaningless. In 1918, the Arab Bureau agent Osmond Walrond (Kitchener's prewar assistant) produced a memorandum on secret societies "to try and find out why the Arabs and Syrians had no heart in the business." He concluded that the societies "have only been and still are in reality parts of a huge machine," whose "motive power" remained unknown to all except their leaders. This hidden "Arab Committee" coordinated their "preparation of a serious movement towards the realisation of the Arab Ideal." But, he explained, "It would be useless to seek to know more, to pretend to arrive at fuller details about this Committee, its organization and power"; one had to "be content" with his assurance that it was indeed "stronger than ever" and that "its adherents...can be found in every family, every tribe, every branch of the administration...every unit of the army and in the schools. All would obey the first signal which came to them from the Committee." It was on the basis of these memoranda that the British made their fresh promise to the Arabs in June 1918 in the Declaration to the Seven—the reply to a memorial by seven Syrians assuring that Arab territories that had been independent before the war would remain so and that the "complete and sovereign independence" of territories liberated by the Arabs themselves would be recognized. The pervasive belief in Arabia's fundamental inscrutability tended to encourage credence in a phantom political world despite evidence to the contrary simply because those who could know—the experts—knew what they knew based not on evidence but on their intuition. It is irrelevant for my purposes whether the secret societies in the oppressive Turkish regime were substantially large, well connected, or truly secret. What I am interested in is how the British arrived at their assessment of them. An abiding view of the Middle East as a spy-space bound by a magical information network fathomable only by the intuitive expert made them fatally susceptible to belief in the existence of extensive, efficient Arab secret societies. In default of incontrovertible information on the point, agents in Arabia trusted their instinct, and their reputations as gifted appraisers of the region ensured that their view held sway despite skepticism at home. "The WO [War Office] people are very easily to be deceived into a respect for special knowledge loudly declared aren't they?" mocked Lawrence.[42]

Genius was not, however, without its burdens. Besides omniscience, a reputation for a kind of oriental inscrutability became a common feature of the rising legend of many agents and, as we shall see, of their eventual fall. Deedes, for instance, was said to possess some indefinable quality: "I don't know that I should call it courage," wrote Compton Mackenzie, the novelist and spy; "it was something quite different from what other men have." He and Lawrence were "hard to understand for ordinary folk." Similarly, there was "always...something queer" about Dickson, "something missing." Fitzmaurice, to whom Sykes's anxieties were sometimes traced, had high-strung nerves, which his admirers construed as an uncanny ability to foresee danger. Their maverick carelessness about uniforms and other protocol raised eyebrows but was more often indulged as the fallout of genius. The same was true of their idiosyncratic handling of information. In Italy, the British minister complained of Sykes's "eccentric behavior," his "tendency…to 'discover' facts which have long been known to the officials on the spot and to place exaggerated or erroneous interpretations on them." But Sykes's sway in London was such that the matter was immediately dropped and the *minister's* impudence excused on the grounds that, "Sykes' manner might mislead someone who has never seen him before." This license would ultimately produce dire consequences—for the British Middle East and the agents themselves.[43]

Intuition at Home

In their gesturing to a universal mind of the desert, the agents gestured to a philosophical monism being articulated in this period by William James, Bertrand Russell, and others. To Lawrence, enduring desert existence entailed the collapse of mind and body:

> The conception of antithetical mind and matter, which was basic in
> the Arab self-surrender, helped me not at all. I achieved surren-
> der…by the very opposite road, through my notion that mental and
> physical were inseparably one: that our bodies, the universe, our
> thoughts and tactilities were conceived in and of the molecular
> sludge of matter, the universal element through which form drifted
> as clots and patterns of varying density.… My perverse sense of
> values constrained me to assume that abstract and concrete, as
> badges, did not denote oppositions more serious than Liberal and
> Conservative. The practice of our revolt fortified the nihilist attitude
> in me.

The revolt was an enactment of the abstract in concrete form, of imagination in reality. As a willful enactment of the epic, it was a real event outside reality, one situated in the no-place of the desert, or, perhaps, in the *spiritus mundi*. Lawrence's exposition, to me, encapsulates the metaphysics behind much of the intelligence-gathering project in Arabia. The perception of a continuity of mind and matter, of the *spiritus mundi* and the desert's physicality, of philosophy and the desert, lay at the core of the project. Immersion in the desert was tantamount to entry into an occult world in which information could be accessed through meditation, and meditation stirred the agent to *action*.[44]

Notions of heroism change over time; the agents' mystical insight held particular appeal to the Great War generation, among whom experimentation with new epistemologies was far from the exclusive hobby of intelligence agents. The agents' answer to methodological problems in Arabia bore striking affinities with the new modes of perception explored by modernists and philosophers dealing with the very existential uncertainty that had sent them to Arabia. This symmetry was bred partly of the agents' intimacy with cultural elites at home and speaks to the source of their appeal among contemporaries.

The appeal of the literary cult of the desert extended beyond musings on social and cultural anxiety to the broader constellation of turn-of-the-century efforts to deal with a new perception of the world. The new appreciation of the universe's vertiginous scale was compounded by an at once wondrous and dreadful confrontation with the invisible forces powering it. The eccentric poet and mystic Edward Carpenter wrote in 1912 that "the existence of the X and N rays of light, and of countless other vibrations of which our ordinary senses render no account" but which powered the marvelous phenomena of wireless telegraphy, hypnotism, and telepathy, "have convinced us that the subtlest forces and energies, totally unmeasurable by our instruments, are at work all around us." At the heart of the worldview of the Edwardian avant-garde was a new conception of existence in which tranquil surfaces concealed a world of activity and profound truth. The "Edwardian turn of mind" was, in a sense, globally "orientalist"; the aura of strangeness previously confined to the Orient now hung over the world as such.[45]

The agents' emphasis on intuition resonated perhaps most deeply and obviously with the popular current of Bergsonism. Around 1909, the French philosopher Henri Bergson—whose mother was an English Jew—emerged as "a cultural phenomenon" both inside and outside the British academy, which saw him as a champion of the spirit in an otherwise materialistic and progress-obsessed world. The agents' work may have been far from philosophy, but their social reach took them to Bergsonism's core. For instance, Wilfrid Blunt's friend Arthur Balfour—prime minister before 1906, leader of the Conservatives until 1911, and amateur philosopher—was an ardent fan. Bergsonism's appeal extended beyond the academic world to literary circles and individuals whose place in society revolved around their knowledge of important movements, issues, and personalities of the day.[46]

By radically reorienting conceptions of time and space, Bergson offered a new theory of knowledge that emphasized intuitive insight into otherwise inaccessible, concealed essences. "Sympathetic communication" between each individual and the rest of the world was made possible by the binding force of the *élan vital*. Bergsonism acknowledged that "there are forces beyond empirical understanding that nonetheless help to explain the universe." It viewed the whole world through the haze that rendered Arabia opaque to intelligence-gatherers, condemning Cartesianism "for falsely claiming to 'mirror' the world by rational means." Intuition would permit knowledge of unrepresentable, pervasive objects like God and the *durée*. Like the agents in Arabia, Bergson felt that to really know a thing, the philosopher must *enter* it; subjective experience mattered more than any objective perspective or "representation." By accessing the hidden realm of deep meaning, Bergsonists would be "liberated from the habits of everyday life" and restored to authentic humanity. In a sense, Arabia was Bergson's *durée* writ large—a space in which the past was prolonged into the present. It was more easily grasped by an experience of "spatial extensity," "as a feeling, say, of direction," than by vision alone.[47]

Sanford Schwartz insists that we view Bergson "as one participant in a development that includes other philosophers." Indeed, William James, Friedrich Nietzsche, and John Buchan's favorite, F. H. Bradley, "believed that they were forging a fundamentally new theory of knowledge." Bertrand Russell and the rest of Bloomsbury were likewise preoccupied with epistemological questions. The appearance in 1914 of Russell's essay "Mysticism and Logic" attests to the currency of the topic. His philosophy, which anathematized Bergsonism as irredeemably anti-intellectual, also grappled with the failings of scientific knowledge. Reflecting on the two ways of knowing the external world, "one direct apprehension of it through the senses and the other scientific knowledge," he concluded that all we ever know immediately is not matter, but our own sensations of it. If empiricism itself rested on subjective foundations, "the correlation with objects of sense, by which physics was to be verified, is itself utterly and for ever unverifiable." He turned to logic as a way out of this epistemological impasse, as a form of knowledge "which starts out from observation but radically differs from it," and in which "the unobserved becomes a necessary feature of the things knowledge arrives at." Thus, he too traded vision for other cognitive methods. His and Bergson's strands of thinking share a fundamental doubt in the independent effectiveness of empiricism as a source of knowledge and a recourse to other means of extracting meaning from sense data.[48]

Despite his aggressively rational posture, Russell's eyeless logic also tended to converge on the kind of blank, uncomprehending amazement usually produced by mysticism. Ann Banfield points out that his "mystical impulse to discover 'a Reality behind the world of appearance and utterly different from it' shares something with logical analysis, which can . . . 'show the strangeness and wonder lying just below the surface even in the commonest things of daily life' and suggest 'that even the strangest hypotheses may be true.' " While exercising logic to derive meaning from sense data, the "belief in the unreality of the world of sense arises with irresistible force," and we are back in a world gone oriental. The whole external world appears a "dream," and we alone seem to exist. Thus, even logic was a sort of mysticism; even science, whose aim was to render the unfamiliar familiar, produced strangeness: "Not an unfamiliar phantasy world but the real world becomes unreal." That the mind knows things is itself a miracle, Russell concluded; in the end, we believe what we believe owing to "animal faith," and only our disbeliefs are due to science. The paradoxical similarity of the world as apprehended by logic and by mysticism in Russell's philosophy points to a fundamental characteristic of the leading edge of the Edwardian turn of mind—that it could not reconcile itself to relying entirely on its senses in order to understand a world that was known to be essentially miragelike. Epistemology had become a miraculous affair of faith and intuition—and of the mystical hunt for patterns that characterizes logic. Russell, like Bergson, believed artists and poets *ought* to use the mystical faculty, as that best suited to attaining the kind of profound knowledge they sought. Thus, despite Russell's countervailing influence, and perhaps because of his own unwitting endorsement of the intuitive mode, his Bloomsbury associates remained intrigued by Bergsonism. The sense of unreality that haunted writers from Woolf to Joyce to Eliot, at times encouraging them, as we have seen, to reach for Middle Eastern metaphors, was grounded in an epistemological speculation—a feeling that sensory perception could not be relied upon to reveal the truth about existence.[49]

To take a relatively middlebrow example, the novel *Uncle Hilary* (1910) by Yeats's confidante and Captain Shakespear's cousin, Olivia Shakespear, revolves around the Buddha-like figure Hilary, who enlightens his niece on the matter of unconscious knowledge: "There are two methods of gaining knowledge; one is through observation and experience; the other is through intuitions" which miraculously migrated from consciousness to consciousness. Humans were not bounded by their own personalities; a spark of universal consciousness resided in each. In this world of letters, Enlightenment skepticism had been turned on its head and suspension of *disbelief* become mandatory. The Arab hero of Flecker's *Hassan* pronounced as a universal maxim, "Men who think themselves wise believe nothing till the proof. Men who are wise believe anything till the disproof." The search for what Jon Thompson describes as a "remoter 'something'—a hidden truth, a concealed clue to existence...an underlying pattern of meaning," was a standard paradigm in much modernist writing. Besides an interest in minimalism, modernists shared the epistemological curiosity of agents in Arabia.[50]

The heroes of spy fiction in particular shared the agents' preference for a "magic epistemology" (in Thomas Richards's phrase) ideally suited to the orientalized spaces in which they moved—spaces "orientalized" partly because, in

Buchan's concise summation, "a clue may be dumb in London and shout aloud at Bagdad." "I wasn't any kind of Sherlock Holmes," explains Richard Hannay in *Thirty-Nine Steps*, "but I have always fancied I had a kind of instinct. . . . I used to use my brains as far as they went, and after they came to a blank wall I guessed, and I usually found my guesses pretty right." He is chosen for the Greenmantle mission not for any particular skill, but because he has "a nose" for finding things out. On the road to Erzurum, his sidekick, the Boer Peter Pienaar, formerly an intelligence agent during the Boer War, has "a 'feel' for the landscape, a special sense which is born in savages and can only be acquired after long experience by the white man." Hence his disregard for compasses: he could "smell where the north lay." Pienaar's talents echo Buchan's understanding of space in a remarkable short story of 1912, pithily titled "Space," which recounts the tragic end of an enigmatic genius whose intellectual tastes lay "on the borderlands of sciences, where mathematics fades into metaphysics." This character, Holland, poses the fateful question: "How if Space is really full of things we cannot see and as yet do not know? How if all animals and some savages have a cell in their brain or a nerve which responds to the invisible world?" Such thoughts send him into a panic about "civilized man": "*Don't you see it is a perception of another kind of reality that we are leaving behind us?*" His effort to regain this perception takes him into the world of séances and psychical research. Having forfeited shelter from hidden realities, he perceives "'the Desolation . . . spoken of by Daniel the prophet,'" and, scribbling on a postcard, "I know at last—God's mercy," plunges to his death in the Alps. Buchan, like his friends, the agents, was intrigued by the idea of emptiness as a mere artifact of sense data and the notion that with knowledge of the "contents of the void" came an apocalyptic knowledge of God. His fictional heroes were among those who had learned to see the world as the "uncivilized" did. In *Greenmantle*, his homage to the silent crew of spies at work in Mesopotamia, carrying "their lives in their hands," was explicit. It was they who substantiated his belief that "we are the only race on earth that can produce men capable of getting inside the skin of remote peoples," echoing the view of his friend and the model for Sandy, Aubrey Herbert, that a few Englishmen alone possessed the "quality . . . which produces unique relations between themselves and the people of the East."[51]

Buchan was not alone in testing the practical, if fictional, uses of intuition. G. K. Chesterton's heroes also worked in a distinctly occult sleuthing paradigm. Gabriel Symes was "subject to spasms of singular common sense . . . poetic intuitions, and they sometimes rose to the exaltation of prophecy." Flecker's great favorite, the detective Father Brown, also uses intuition and imagination to solve mysteries. Unable to rely on vision, Davies of Childers's *Riddle of the*

Sands, feels his way through the sands, resorting to touch, reflex, sound, and smell. In the sands of the North Sea, as in Arabia, nomadism was the key to a new mode of perception. Thus, to remark, as has one historian, that, in their bizarre reliance on intuition, agents like Wingate, Clayton, and Storrs "acted as though they understood the natives of the Ottoman Empire as well as did the...hero of [*Greenmantle*]" is rather to miss the point. They were not "acting"; they inhabited the world of spy fiction where only intuitive tactics would work, even as they were inspiring the novelists conjuring that world.[52]

Bergson's sister was married to the chief of the Hermetic Order of the Golden Dawn, a social link between modernist philosophy and occultism that was not unique. Bergsonists like Arthur Balfour and Arabists like Yeats also shared an interest in the occult, and the secretary of the Society for Psychical Research would serve in Middle East intelligence during the war. Indeed, the desert and the universe of modernist imagining were penetrable by similar epistemologies because both were understood as basically occult worlds, in which, to borrow Alex Owen's words, "all of creation is interrelated and part and expression of a universal soul or cosmic mind." At the heart of occultism, according to G. R. S. Mead, was the belief that "the range of the senses can be enormously extended psychically" to access this *anima mundi*—automatically accessible to nomads, who, in Vita Sackville-West's poetic phrase, knew "the secret, the value, and the might" of every place they passed. The coeval interest in occultism and the desert was epistemological as much as aesthetic and spiritual; both stemmed from the emergent awareness of a hidden reality beyond ordinary sensory perception. In short, "Arabia" was not only one of the major canvasses on which occultists projected their spiritual dreams; it also offered an immediate renewal of that realm "outside the senses." It was a physical manifestation of the occultist and modernist vision of the world as an encoded realm whose hidden truths could be apprehended with sufficient intuitive genius. Mead wrote in 1912 that "the idea of the adept and initiate in secret knowledge, the ideal of the divine man or woman, of the god-inspired, or at any rate of the human with superhuman powers, is in the air." And, to be an explorer, perhaps more than anything else, was to Edwardians to be "almost a superman." Explorer-agents in Arabia shared with modernists, Bergsonists, and occultists a belief that artists, like mystics, could provide insight into the otherwise unfathomable world.[53]

Indeed, the contemporary response to the agents' own artistic concoctions reveals that Edwardians looked to travel writing on Arabia for instruction in escape from the weary European mind into the sensitive, impenetrable soul of the Bedouin. "It is seldom that a European can read the imaginings of the Arab mind, and see the desert with Arab eyes like this," applauded a review of Bell's

The Desert and the Sown, "To most travellers the talk of the camel drivers is meaningless, but in these pages a conversation in Arabic becomes a live thing." The secret of Bell's success, the reviewer explained, was her "full sympathy with the Arabs," bred by her avoidance of "well-beaten" tracks in favor of the desert, which was "the king to their souls." The author of *The Witness of the Wilderness: The Bedawin of the Desert; In Their Relation to the Bible* (1909) was likewise praised for possessing "what most European scholars lack, the faculty to understand Orientals," particularly their proclivity to " 'clothe their thoughts in a dress of their own weaving, and in a way that obscures their real meaning to one who is unaccustomed to this form of speech.' " While Soane was castigated for his dull adherence to the "beaten" track, his book was redeemed, in one reviewer's eyes, by the fact that, at the eastern frontier, "he is at home. He knows and understands the Kurd, and that is a great deal more than can be said for most travellers." Unsurprisingly, this anonymous reviewer was Bell herself.[54]

   A new intuitive epistemology reverberated through Edwardian culture, among intelligence agents, philosophers, and novelists of various sorts. The orientalism of British intelligence agents in the Middle East was not the positivistic, secular, nineteenth-century project of amassing and arranging facts, but an antiempiricist, metaphysical epistemology that allegedly allowed them to "know" the Orient in new, participative rather than distancing, ways through emulation of what they thought of as the intuitive, mystical knowledge of the Oriental. They attempted to solve the epistemological difficulty posed by the spectacle of the Orient by "orientalizing" themselves, a tactic partly premised on a lingering perception of racial affinity and a shared past rather than a view of Arabia as entirely "other."[55] By flaunting their privileged insight into Arabia, they rose above the level of mere functionaries and became part of a cultural-philosophical avant-garde. Inspired by the same disaffection with empiricism as were the new philosophy and poetics, intelligence in Arabia, in its metamorphosis from a simple collection of data to a more artistic enterprise, seemed to prove the new epistemology could indeed *work*. But the war did not only confirm the dominance of their modus operandi in the work of gathering and analyzing intelligence in the Middle East; it also saw the proliferation of that mode in the political and military spheres that the claim to genius had allowed the agents to penetrate.

4

Cunning in War

The full story of the part Arabia played in the war remains to be written. It will be a stirring tale, full of romance and of all the glamour of guerilla warfare.... The success attained is due largely to men who, of their own initiative, had prepared themselves beforehand, and who, when the time came, were able to take their places in what must surely be one of the most extraordinary epics, not only in the Great War, but in the whole intercourse between Europe and Asia.

—Douglas Carruthers, 1922

"War upon rebellion is messy and slow, like eating soup with a knife." This grim assessment of quelling armed insurrection...comes from the book which graces the...office of Rory Stewart, the British diplomat who runs the province around the city of Amara.... The same book is also a favorite of Major John Nagl—one of the US Army's top counter-insurgency experts—who is based near...Falluja.... The book, *Seven Pillars of Wisdom*.

—BBC News, April 9, 2004

During the war, the immersion tactic subtly morphed from a method for acquiring information to a means of acquiring influence and control over the agents' Arab charges; the quest for knowledge became entangled with a quest for power. As they strayed into administration and operations, agents who saw "cunning" as the demiurge of Arabian politics, history, warfare, and communication found in immersion supple license for ethical lassitude in all their various responsibilities. In the licentious atmosphere of the war, the agents instituted an *avowedly* conscience-less approach to intervention in the Middle East, in the realm of military as much as diplomatic and intelligence practice.

Knowledge Becomes Power

A handful of British officers were deployed as advisers with the Sherifian forces. It is among them, as much as the political officers–turned–governors in Mesopotamia, that we see the gradual morphing of immersion from a purely intelligence to a political strategy. That immersion was the key to political control was a notion grounded in theories of Arabian medievalism. "The happiest master," wrote an agent in the *Bulletin*, "is he who knows the names and relationship of all his men, for under such conditions the feudalism latent in the sedentary tribes attaches them to him: his ascendancy becomes...almost instinctive." "Unremitting study" of Arabs was the key to intelligence, but also, Lawrence explained, "the secret of handling" them. "Leave your English friends and customs...and fall back on Arab habits entirely...to beat the Arabs at their own game," he advised in a familiar refrain, with the new objective of becoming "their leader." The need was not for the Englishman who became "more rampantly English" away from home, but for a more "subtle and insinuating" type who imitated those about him and "directed men secretly." Tacit fealty engendered by the agent's immersion in the community would permit his covert control of it—since his participation in the community, he knew, was pragmatic rather than sincere. Disguise, too, evolved from a technique of intimacy to a means of acquiring influence: the agent should wear Arab clothes of the best quality, Lawrence insisted, famously dressing like a sherif himself. His colleague, Hubert Young, affirmed that without "gorgeous" dress, the desert would quickly reduce the agent to a sunburnt, bearded, "rather seedy Bedouin," "a nonentity." Nomadism was as critical to impressing the Arabs with the Englishman's superior powers as it was to gathering knowledge; the perpetual motion of certain agents was predicated on the conviction that "the only influence of any use among Arabs is personal influence." The Bedouin thought Leachman possessed "miraculous powers of movement," boasted his colleague Norman Bray, given his ability to materialize "on the same day at...places...so far apart as to make a journey between them...appear an impossibility." His "uncanny gift of retaining a mental picture" of the land enabled him to know the desert "as the chief sheikh of the Anaiza states, 'better than the Arabs themselves.'" Exploration was transformed by a new connection to occupation, which allowed access to areas formerly barred to Europeans. The political officer Harold Dickson fulfilled his vow to "occupy and open up the town of Samawa," where "to date no British have been," and used as his "excuse to get there" a fellow officer's need for assistance in pacification operations. His heart's next ambition was to get to Shatra: "If I am not the first white man there I'll eat my hat"—a gastronomic experiment that proved unnecessary. Thus immersion relied on and acquired a *political* role as the foundations of covert empire were laid. It was the key not only to understanding but impressing and "pacifying," as the agents' roles expanded in wartime from intelligence workers to advisers and governors. After four years, Dickson was emphatic: *I am the only white man who at the present day can manage the Muntafik.* Immersion produced an instinctual knowledge that was now politically effectual. Thus, Bell felt that, despite his "limited intelligence," "knowledge of and sympathy with Arabs" enabled Colonel Knox, head of occupied Mesopotamia's judicial system, to apply the Indian-derived Iraq Code almost whimsically without demur.[1]

It was through immersion, agents alleged, that they learned how to be unscrupulous; that was the local political modus operandi. They were merely applying the lessons of counterespionage to espionage: in an intelligence report, Captain Leith-Ross moved seamlessly from describing GSI's use of cautionary placards and pamphlets to curtail loose talk in Baghdad's messes, clubs, camps, restaurants, and shops into an admiring discussion of the talent of "certain trading classes"—especially coffee-shop keepers—for insinuating themselves into their occupiers' lives. "None of these men were Intelligence agents," he stressed. "But they had managed to acquire much useful information purely in the carrying out of their ordinary business." Similarly, traveling jugglers' "innocent adherence" to an "ancient Oriental custom" of demanding a chit from the audience enabled them to collect enough information to assemble the British Order of Battle. "This method of obtaining information, whether by actual juggling or otherwise, is calculated to produce good results anywhere in an Eastern theatre of war," he concluded, pressing the need for British intelligence officers who knew colloquial Arabic and Turkish, possessed "an understanding and liking for the people," were "adepts at distinguishing truth from falsehood," and "absolutely conversant with the topography of the country." The hope, in short, was that immersion would produce agents capable of mimicking local cunning—in a version of the age-old nostrum, "When in Rome..." Similarly, instructions for appropriate communication with local agents—by means of "electric carpets" and concealed "Dictophones"—were irradiated with the inspiration of fiction and an orthodox vision of oriental intrigue.[2]

As representatives of an occupying power, the agents now strove as much to manipulate as to access the regional information network. "Please don't fail to keep me posted," Bell implored Hogarth, "for I'm up against native opinion . . . and it's difficult to walk wisely and warily unless you are pretty well informed." Indeed, she could do more than walk: "A good many people drop in and talk to me and it's a useful medium for propaganda." Ely Soane edited the *Basra Times*. The Arab Bureau was also intended to function in this dual capacity. Sykes urged that it be used to "promote the spread of rumours, prophecies, saws, rhymes, cryptograms . . . by means of native agents," cautioning against investing in a library at the expense of these stratagems, since "propaganda in the East is a matter of atmosphere."[3]

Individual agents took seriously and literally this brief to meet intrigue with intrigue, plot with plot. Dickson mocked the futility of discretion in his letters home: "The Arabs are ubiquitous and they know everything that goes on." "It is our policy to treat them as friends," he explained to his mother, "yet among them there must be scores nay hundreds . . . who are spying on us and reporting everything . . . to the Enemy." "I'm all right though," he assured her, "I meet cunning with cunning." In due course, he gained a reputation for his skill at keeping "the Arabs of his district guessing." Parker's "motionless face and steady gaze" also famously puzzled the Bedouin, and Lawrence's sway over Arabs was likened to "the hypnotic influence of a lion-tamer." This inscrutability, which, as we have seen, was much remarked as a quality that set these agents apart from ordinary mortals (or Europeans), was understood as merely another artifact of the immersion strategy. Leachman "gossiped, as an Arab among Arabs . . . he heard, as though the wind had told him, of the activities . . . far away in the desert," wrote a fellow officer on Leachman's death in 1920. "The ways of the Political Officer are mysterious, his manner quiet and inscrutable, like the Arab's. . . . The desert gets a hold on some white men, as it does upon the Arab." The construction of Arab cunning thus underwrote an ethic of deception among Britons in the region. Meinertzhagen's perhaps bitter condemnation of his colleagues provides precisely this excuse for the corruption of the British mind: Lawrence's "meek schoolboy expression hides the cunning of a fox and the intriguing spirit of the East," and Storrs's "close connection with the Arab" had "orientalized his mind, introducing an exceptionally strong element of intrigue and intellectual dishonesty." There was not room for scruples in wartime Arabia, in either pacification operations or intelligence. After six months of "humbugging the arabs," Dickson was boasting, "I'm a regular Sultan in my own small kingdom. I do the most outrageous things, but tell nobody and the results are good for I keep my people quiet." In his report on intelligence in Mesopotamia, Lawrence described admiringly how one agent, Captain J. C. More, who knew Arabic and understood Arabs, dealt with the condition of being besieged by spies spreading "wild fictions" by single-handedly setting up a secret service at Amara, for which he had "unlimited funds and carte blanche" and was "willing to do everything or anything."[4]

The *official* construction of Arabia as a spy-space licensed any amount of unscrupulous covert activity, rendering irrelevant the regard for social and cultural mores and legal conventions that may have constrained, or at least engendered doubts about, their activity elsewhere. Intrigue is probably a permanent feature of politics anywhere, always, but in this instance, perhaps for the first time, the British freely *admitted*, without recourse to euphemism, that they were intriguing without scruple and were doing so because the place they operated in provided them with a ready excuse for dishonorable and certainly ungentlemanly behavior. In a sense we have missed the most obvious implication of orientalism: it not only empowered the British to dominate the "Orient"; it armed them, through the agents' immersion strategy, with an excuse for their unscrupulousness in doing so. It normalized intrigue in the Middle East. Representations of a mysterious Orient produced a truly mysterious Orient. In the agents' hands, the imaginary Arabian spy-space became real. This is not to minimize the real threats to British preeminence or the amount of intrigue actually afoot but to point to the British contribution to this instance of reality imitating fiction. The biggest imperial intrigue of all was, after all, the British effort to conspire with Ottoman subjects in the destruction of the Ottoman Empire. The British had, as Lawrence knew, "entered their country like sphinxes."

The frisson of fiction in the Arabian spy-space conveniently redeemed the scheming agent-governor. "Yea, sometimes that which was done east of Suez in the name of the British Raj would be odd in the extreme," conceded one eyewitness of Leachman's efforts to divide-and-rule tribes by, for instance, arranging for one tribe to carry off the women of another. But then, Leachman, the witness explained, was "the Romantic of the 'White Tabs'" (white tabs on the collar being the distinguishing mark of the political officer). His excesses were excusable, as those of an artist. Dickson's equivocation on the moral standing of the spy epitomized the same ethical conundrum. When his police captured a Turkish spy, he wrote, "If he is, he'll hang. I've no patience with that type," but confessed in the same breath, "Yet when all is said and done 'spys' are the pluckiest of all men." In the Arabian spy game, humbuggery was not ungentlemanly; it was an art. "Crossing the Mediterranean one entered a new realm of espionage," explained Captain Ferdinand Tuohy, "full of Eastern patience and cunning and subterfuge...in which the spy no longer emerged bogey-like as in the West." The "liberating" forces in Iraq left a ruthless occupying regime in their wake, in the hands of political officers whose status as heroic agents transformed their disciplinary actions into episodes in the ever-unfolding, charming epic of Arabian intrigue. First imagination, and then the epistemology it inspired, produced this particular geographical morality.[5]

As the agents stretched themselves into ever more reaches of official power, they carried the virus of cunning with them. Most famous was its infection of the always susceptible, lofty world of diplomacy. With hindsight, secret diplomacy would be blamed for triggering this destructive war, but in wartime Arabia the British indulged in intrigue of a different order, as the agents knew. In Riyadh, Philby scoffed at Balfour's "silly" speechifying against "secret diplomacy," given what they were doing in Arabia at that very moment. Indeed, from the outset officials advised "profound secrecy...regarding the participation of HMG in an Arab revolt" and warned not to "commit ourselves in writing." Lawrence, Storrs, and Clayton were key players in Whitehall's slide down the slippery slope to unrestrained intriguing with various segments of the Arab Party by means of a bizarre flow of secret messengers and veiled, enigmatic language. Most famously, Sykes, a novitiate when it came to diplomacy, was, by virtue of his status as an expert on Arab affairs, allowed to reach an understanding with the French on the postwar settlement of the Arab lands. He negotiated without reference to anyone else, for, as Jeremy Wilson observes, "to consult Cairo would be to admit that there were greater experts than himself on the Arab question." Indeed, when he stepped into the Foreign Office, "it was felt that some of the mysterious atmosphere of the Sublime Porte had descended upon stolid English diplomacy," in the nostalgic words of a contemporary. The principles of intelligence in Arabia constructed the agent as an actor, but one always hidden from view, as was his primary stage—the Arabian desert. Lawrence "conceived of himself as the power behind the scenes," writes Kathryn Tidrick. In Hannah Arendt's more chilling assessment, his was "precisely the story of a real agent...who actually believed he had entered...the stream of historical necessity and become a functionary or agent of the secret forces which rule the world." Other agents shared in varying degrees this will to occult power, the desire to pull the strings of Arabia's fate from behind the scene of official diplomacy, with secret agreements and operations that took them far afield of their original province. It was thus that "every part of [Arabia] was involved in...'the fine mesh of a network of skilfully drawn but ambiguous documents.'"[6]

Cunning in Battle

Agents adopted cunning as a political style that would make covert empire viable and acceptable, but they also adapted it to the military operations with which, as we have seen, their intelligence work increasingly began to merge. It was thanks to their involvement in the planning and prosecution of the Middle East campaigns that those campaigns remained strangely mobile and creative affairs in a war generally known for the Sisyphean struggles of soldiers and the torpidity of generals on the Western front. Allenby's masterful ability to coordinate "infantry and cavalry, artillery and Air Force, Navy and armoured cars, deceptions and irregulars" earned Lawrence's hard-won praise, and in the amphibious Mesopotamian campaign, Candler delighted, "all the five arms of the Force—the Navy, Cavalry, Infantry, Artillery, and Flying Corps—were working together in a way that was new in war." Intelligencers played a greater role in these campaigns "than in any other campaign of the First World War," notes one scholar, and this, I think, was because the Arabist agent was in thrall to an ethic of adventure and was, at once, constructed as a kind of oracular figure to be consulted on all matters pertaining to the region. Their involvement in military operations signaled the creation of a new sphere of operational intelligence whose full-blown incarnation would be the postwar aerial surveillance regime, the technological expression of covert empire. In the field of military as much as intelligence operations, these agents felt standard methods ill suited to Arabia and advised mimicry of local practice. They saw in this consummate modernist space a stage for an ultramodern warfare that would restore the possibility for the individual heroism they so desperately sought. In their newly defined operational sphere, cunning and genius were indispensable; contemporaries noted Allenby's staff's "ever-readiness...to get along with their war by every piece of craft and cunning they could think of," so much so that "they approached much nearer to how the spectral 'next war' may open (in the brain line) than did any of the others." Indeed, deception, irregular warfare, and airpower, which have become basic to twentieth-century warfare, achieved their greatest level of development in the Middle East campaigns.[7]

The agents' sense of cunning is most evident in their turn to deception tactics as a military extension of the disinformation lessons they had absorbed as intelligencers. The most famous such operations were performed before the Third Battle of Gaza at the end of 1917 and the Battle of Megiddo in 1918. In the first, the "haversack ruse," Meinertzhagen, Allenby's intelligence chief, rode into no man's land, where he pretended to be hit by Ottoman fire and dropped a sack of carefully faked "confidential" documents suggesting a major British attack at Gaza. False wireless messages also hinted that the activity in anticipation of the real attack on Beersheba was merely reconnaissance movement. Prime Minister David Lloyd George credited this ruse with the success of the battle; Allenby, with the success of the entire campaign. In the visual deceptions before Megiddo, agents such as Lawrence, Young, and Joyce were critical to the concealment of the main effort in the western sector and diverting of Ottoman attention to the eastern flank. Camps were built in the Jordan Valley and filled with unfit soldiers and fifteen thousand dummy horses; bridges were thrown up across the river; battalions marched east by day, returning secretly by night in trucks. Meanwhile, movement was actually going the other way: troops poured into camps near the coast, which had been built extra large in anticipation. Dust clouds were created by sand sleds to cover up activity or convey an impression of feverish activity, as needed. Overt preparations were also made for the imminent "transfer" of General Headquarters to Jerusalem; a hotel was vacated, and signs, telephone lines, and the like installed. These legendary deceptions were the *only* successful modern deceptions of the First World War and the only attempt during that war to use deception as a strategic principle, in an entirely modern way. Allenby's staff officer Archibald Wavell praised the campaign's inventive use of "almost every form of operation in almost every variety of climate and terrain"; as Middle East commander in World War Two, he would draw on Allenby's deceptions in the design of the Battle of El Alamein, which would in turn inspire the deceptions leading to the invasions of Sicily and Normandy. The Mesopotamia campaign was likewise full of "attack by indirection," "the ruse, the left hook." Cox complained of Maude's commitment to Western front tactics and general lack of sympathy with the agents—he was "purely a soldier . . . without any previous experience of the East or of Orientals." Nevertheless, the initial attack against Sannaiyat, for instance, was a bluff, covering the real assault along the Shatt-al-Hai, and many of the advances, including that on Khan Baghdadi, also involved ruses. Others certainly considered him a "great man for mystifying and misleading" who knew "how much he could accomplish by surprise."[8]

The general theory behind deception is that of a force multiplier for the desperate, numerically inferior combatant. In this campaign, however, the British had a preponderance in strength and still went to great lengths to deceive the enemy; deception was clearly inspired by other considerations. The intelligence community, we know, had long been fascinated by the region's biblical and ancient epic associations, in which the earliest and archetypal deceptions also happened to be recorded—before deception became dishonorable in the Middle Ages. According to these sources, which, we know, the agents consulted regularly, the country was practically designed for invention. Arabia's deserts made Allenby, too, "feel carried far beyond this world to something or some place I can't understand." He, too, found instruction in the Bible, specifically Judges VII, in which is described the first recorded night attack by Gideon's three hundred. As Wavell would put it in the next war, "The lessons it teaches—the value of discipline, the need for personal reconnaissance, the moral effect of surprise—are applicable to any night attack to-day." Allenby's staff was also much struck by a passage in Sir George Adam Smith's *Historical Geography of the Holy Land* (1894): "Everything conspires to give the inhabitants easy means of defence against large armies. It is a country of ambushes, entanglements, surprise... where the essentials for war are nimbleness and the sure foot, the power of scramble and of rush." Romantic deception tactics seemed fitting, even fated, in Palestine, especially given the atmosphere of superstition and romance in which the troops felt enveloped: "It would be a short... step in this superstitious country to translate Allenby into a Messiah," proposed Meinertzhagen. Every circumstance of the campaign heightened the "romantic setting," observed another, and "prophecy after prophecy was fulfilled." It was in this pregnant atmosphere that agents and other military personnel planned the deception operations.[9]

Besides the land of ancient mystique, there was the desert of stupefying physical aspect. It was, ironically, in a desert famously devoid of cover that the British first attempted to hide an entire offensive. Indeed, the lack of cover seemed initially to eliminate the possibility of surprise. "Where we are had is, by the flatness of the country," complained Dickson in Mesopotamia. "For miles and miles it is like a table and... the Enemy... can see us coming hours before." At the same time, the desert's natural subterfuges compounded the tactical puzzle as much as they had complicated intelligence-gathering. "There is not a cavalry regiment... which has not at some time or other mistaken sheep for infantry," grumbled Candler. Soldiers on reconnaissance became lost, visual signaling failed, and ranging was impossible in "a fairyland that danced and glimmered." Soldiers could scarcely observe their own fire or its results. Indeed, General Townshend's misadventures were partially excused by "the deception emanating from desert mirages."[10]

But what made the mirage truly menacing and, ultimately, inspiring was the enemy's clever tactical use of it—in a manner befitting Arabia's spirit-world. In his memoir, Martin Swayne described how "hostile Arabs, knowing the mirage areas, would *get into them* and make ranging impossible." Vanishing in and out of it, "like a minuet," they used it for surprise: when approached, they "disappeared into the mirage as if the ground had opened and swallowed them up," recounted a reconnaissance officer. "No sooner had a group vanished on our right, than another would appear like a cinema picture on our left, also to vanish and have its place taken by another elusive spectre, perhaps straight ahead. So, chasing phantoms, we continued towards our destination." Like "magic," when he had seen "*nothing* for hours and hours," attested Dickson, Arabs would attack "from behind mirages... employing a thousand and one other stratagems." They could thus invent cover where there was none.

He tried to convey the "élan dash mystery and picturesqueness" of the "lightening" warfare of these *"whil o the whisps [sic]"*:

> Picture...a perfectly flat sandy desert....A white man would see not an atom of cover, but these desert men make use of these weird folds in the ground in diabolical fashion....An officer...scanning the horizon for a sign of the enemy is in the foreground, his halted squadron completes the picture. Suddenly...in the far distance, commences the dust storm....It strikes in full force at last and God in Heaven what comes to. Five thousand howling fiends, wild desert arabs, with faces wrapped up all except the eyes come with the storm. Like a whirlwind they are upon you—flowing robes, firing from the saddle whilst at full gallop, never pausing a moment on they come. Before you can count sixty they have surrounded you.

And then, "they simply disappear no one knows where." Under air attack too, they could invent cover: an astonished correspondent described them spread out, each "quite still beside his camel," when, "withdrawing into the stony wadis...they lay down on the shady side of their crouching 'mounts', and from the air could not be distinguished from the surrounding rocks." In such "subtle ruses" could be found "lessons...of the greatest interest," he advised. The entire Arab approach to war seemed a lesson in flexibility: in flood-prone southern Mesopotamia, their quick mounting of boats and rebuilding of villages inspired Force D's floating air bases and patrol boats. Perhaps, a soldier speculated, the loneliness of the desert "sharpened...ingenuity."[11]

Bedouin ingenuity—their ability to turn to tactical advantage the very phenomena that seemed to render regular, modern warfare impossible—was enchanting, threatening, and instructive all at once. They posed a "new enemy question," and their traditional warfare seemed bafflingly modern to a British army ordinarily sure of its own supreme sophistication. "We can take no risks with these men of mystery," avowed Dickson. "We understand the Turk but I'm blessed if we can quite fathom our latest enemies." They had to be *studied*, he insisted. Lawrence likewise admired Arab forces in the west, "riding about in small parties, tapping the Turks here and there, retiring always when the Turks advance, to appear in another direction immediately after," causing "the enemy not only anxiety, but bewilderment." Far from seeing Bedouin as primitive combatants because of their unsophisticated technology, agents who were painfully aware of British forces' frustrations in the desert and already amenable to adapting to desert ways began to see in the "cunning" of Bedouin tactics a possible way forward. Among themselves, they concluded that it was not the strong but "the man who uses his wits...who is most likely to win."[12]

Immersion would ultimately help them defend *against* Bedouin deceptions. "We of us who have been here some time are beginning to grasp it
slowly," attested Dickson. "It is the new Regts that are continually being fooled."
But more important, for my purposes, the Arab example inspired the construction of the British forces' own "strategic mirage." The desert's particular vul-
nerability as a spy-space justified the turn to deception as a necessary evil in
Arabia when it remained beyond the pale of honorable combat elsewhere.
"British intelligence had need of imagination and ingenuity" among "an assortment of peoples" of unclear loyalties and whose "wandering habits...made it
easy for them to carry on extensive spying," explained a contemporary.
Deception tactics emerged as part of the agents' ongoing effort to beat the
Arabs at their own game by "going native," militarily speaking. Take, for
instance, the use of false camps: Where billeting was primarily in camps,
explained Leith-Ross, "tent-checks" were central to tactical intelligence; signs
such as the absence of transport animals, wheel-marks, or tracks would awaken
"the suspicions of the Intelligence officer." Here again, his discussion of counterespionage morphed into a positive lesson, shading into the field of operations: "The possibility of false camps, erected with the idea of misleading the
opposing side as to the location or strength of troops in any area, must not altogether be lost sight of. A clever piece of bluff of this sort will stand a good
chance of success if not tried too often." The nature of the country and its
people made guarding against deception and perpetrating deception equally
crucial.[13]

Spreading rumors likewise became as central to deception operations as it
had become to the political-intelligence work of maintaining British popularity
in the region. In the capture of Akaba, the difficulty of maintaining secrecy
inspired the Arab forces to instead profit from the desert's inbuilt rumor network. Since, as Lawrence put it, "the Turks seem unable to discriminate the
true from the false, out of the flood of news unquestionably brought them by
the local Arabs," the British would spread faulty information about their activities; signalers would make hay with their wireless sets. If the incessant inter-
mixing between the Turkish and Arab spheres, an ineradicable feature of
nomadic life, tended to undermine secrecy, by the same token it also made
"our intelligence service...the widest, fullest and most certain imaginable"—
since Lawrence and his colleagues were confident in their own ability to identify what was true and false and since the meaning of "intelligence" in this
particular region had expanded to encompass the active dissemination of false
information by means of the naturally expert nomad population. It was not difficult "*in a country like Iraq* to start the circulation of misleading and inaccurate
information with a view to such information reaching the enemy," attested

Leith-Ross. This notion was enshrined in the War Office's postwar handbook on intelligence, which stated unequivocally that in "semi-civilised" regions, "races are able to transmit news to each other over great distances with astounding rapidity and by means which are sometimes difficult to explain," and that this facility offered certain advantages in the form of the "comparative ease with which false information can be spread," "an effective weapon," since, "although most irregulars are adepts at setting snares, they are seldom sufficiently wary to avoid them." Far from bewildered in the face of the local's information advantage, the British military establishment was now confident of its ability to take a feather from the native's own cap and flaunt it unashamedly.[14]

Newcombe, Deedes, Lawrence, and Meinertzhagen were closely involved in the invention and planning of the major deception schemes before Gaza and Megiddo. Meinertzhagen's great originality lay, according to a biographer, in "his ability to turn the conventional intelligence officer's task on its head." Instead of merely collecting information, he "deliberately went out in search of his opponents to provide them with...carefully doctored falsehoods. In his hands, *intelligence became almost a weapon of attack*." Deception was part of the new conception of intelligence as inseparable from operations themselves. Lawrence confirmed, "After the Meinertzhagen success, deceptions, which for the ordinary general were just witty hors d'oeuvres before battle, became for Allenby a main point of strategy." Meinertzhagen's originality was hardly idiosyncratic; it was, as we have seen, cultivated by the entire British intelligence world in Arabia. His close sympathizer, Guy Dawnay, the alleged "brain behind the titular chief," particularly in planning the deceptions before Megiddo, was cut from the same cloth. A student of Greek history, a poet, and a reputed eccentric, his prototype, Compton Mackenzie avowed, "must be sought in a Trojan scene of the middle-ages...perhaps in the corner of a picture by Crivelli where one of those small figures of warriors in the foreground seems to have detached itself from the crowded scene of chivalry behind and to have stepped forward from the past to commune with ourselves." Then there was Lawrence, who, with his "unwitting arab agents," was placed under Allenby's command and used primarily for deception purposes. He also invented his own "local" deception strategies, for instance in the false preparations for an attack on Amman—a deception-within-deception that Liddell Hart termed a "Lawrentian mirage." "So long as they didn't let him down," Tuohy wrote, "Allenby gave carte blanche to his Intelligence Staff to go ahead and bamboozle the Turk to the limit of their art." Their unusual influence with their commander was largely the product of the ideology of genius that dominated the Middle East intelligence and military establishment and Allenby's particular sympathy with their sensibility. As Tuohy pointed out, which other commander would have tolerated Lawrence for ten minutes? Allenby turned to the agents for their ability not only to track down information but to cope with the strange ways of the desert and desert warfare. So impressive was their success that Meinertzhagen and Dawnay were eventually shunted to the Western front to infect it with their genius because the local intelligence establishment "was in a groove and stagnant."[15]

For deception to work, the British had to know how to present an intelligible, albeit false, picture to Turkish intelligence; they had to know, in other words, how the enemy tracked them. British agents would have pursued such a strategy only in a place in which they felt knowledge could be acquired intuitively and could therefore approach omniscience. Deception evolved from the notion that Arabia was an encrypted space; it entailed the inscribing of false signs, the deliberate broadcast of a false cipher. If deception works by feeding on the enemy's "basic concept," the British fed on the alleged Turkish and Arab assumption that all appearances deceived and therefore that *double* bluffs would be the best course of action. It was thus that under Allenby, "Intelligence in the field reached its fullest, and it may well be its final expansion—namely, that of pulling the enemy's leg clean off regarding what we intended doing."[16]

Irregulars in an Irregular Land

The British also co-opted the irregular tactics of "wild desert horsemen," creating what in modern parlance is termed a "special operations force" despite an actual preponderance in numbers. The military establishment had generally viewed guerrilla warfare as the unsophisticated but gallingly vexatious warfare of tribes, Boers, and other backward peoples. With the Arab Revolt, however, it was naturalized as a modern British tactic. Even Arab support of the enemy ceased to be labeled "tribal harassment" and was recognized as "a kind of irregular arm for the Turk." The agents, primarily Lawrence in this case, drew on their understanding of Bedouin military tactics—"desert tactics"—in their formalization of modern irregular tactics, taking intelligence a step further into the field of operations.[17]

Typically, fascination presaged mimicry. Candler, like Dickson, was awed by the way "a horde of Arabs emerge from the dark masses and spread in a fan-like movement over the whole horizon." "These irregulars are eternally swooping about for no apparent reason," he mused, "unless it be bravado or the instinct of the kit, in complicated movements and figures of eight." "Instinct of the kit": something about this desert stage and its "men of mystery" costumed in billowing robes demanded a fittingly romantic style of warfare in the eyes of agents already dreaming of adventure. These Bedouin knights were too individualistic to endure an ordinary command structure, thought Lawrence, himself incorrigibly insubordinate. He insisted, "The Hejaz war is one of dervishes against regular troops—and we are on the side of the dervishes. Our text-books do not apply to its conditions at all." This was not a casual assessment, but an article of faith—the twenty-second of his twenty-seven articles on working with Arabs: "The Hejaz confounds ordinary tactics. Learn the Bedu principles of war."[18]

Adaptation to Bedouin warfare was not merely whimsical indulgence of a romantic sensibility but was presented as the product of careful reflection on what kind of warfare was appropriate to Arabia. Lawrence would later explain: "Savage warfare seems never to have been thought out in English from the savage point of view, and the Arab revolt would have been a great opportunity for a thinker to test its possibilities on a grand scale. Our war was so odd and so far away that coy Authority left us to ourselves." Left to his own devices, as it were, he grew determined to "prove irregular war or rebellion to be an exact science, and an inevitable success." True understanding followed the "self-education" of immersion: "Only by graduating in the Beduin [sic] school could [I] gain the competence and the prestige to modify its practice." (His object was not to merely imitate Bedouin practice, but, as always, improve it.) His tactical epiphany came not when his senses were intact but during an episode of psychic intensity, a series of "reveries" lasting eight feverish nights early in 1917. Fever, "as usual," cleared his mind, made his senses "more acute," and allowed him to dispense with the "pompous, professorial" path of "algebraical, biological, psychological" approaches. "My wits, hostile to the abstract, took refuge in Arabia again," he explained, gesturing to Walter de la Mare's "Arabia." He presented the results of his theorizing as "The Evolution of a Revolt" in the first issue of the postwar *Army Quarterly*.[19]

Central to his theory was the desert's effect on perception. Nomadism, the ability to dwell by moving, was now adopted as the essence of desert *warfare* as much as of desert intelligence-gathering. Unlike fixed, immobile armies, Lawrence reasoned, "we might be like vapour," "an influence, an idea, a thing intangible, invulnerable, without front or back, drifting about like a gas." He pointed to Bedouins' "assiduous cultivation of desert-power," their ability to control with scattered parties "the desolate and unmapped wilderness…of Arabia." Their small number was, paradoxically, their strength, making them "the most elusive enemy an army ever had." Arguing strenuously against the formation of regular Arab forces at fixed positions, he explained that not the attack, but the *threat* of attack would arrest the enemy; thus, for instance, had they kept a Turkish force holed up in Medina without yet doing anything "concrete." Smeared through space, they and their threat were coextensive with the desert itself. "Our war should be a war of detachment [rather than contact]," he concluded. "We were to contain the enemy by the silent threat of a vast unknown desert, not disclosing ourselves till the moment of attack." Their purpose, he explained to Clayton, was not to engage the Turks but impress them "with the fact that behind the Beduin screen lies an unknown quantity." In Arabia, in short, "space [was] greater than the power of armies." Liddell Hart would later agree that the Arabs' success derived from topography: "Retained with the army in Palestine this handful would have been merely a drop in the ocean. Sent into the desert they created a whirlpool that sucked down almost half the Turkish army."[20]

In the desert, as Lawrence saw it, action and information became one; a small movement could expand through rumor into an epic event, with important political implications in an inter-imperial campaign that was implicitly a battle for hearts and minds. There, every action and individual had a disproportionate effect because there everything became *larger than life*, the mythic proportion to which Lawrence himself aspired. Irregular warfare exploited the information fog of the desert; disorder became a virtue. In sharp contrast to the Western front, the Arabs' circumstances "were not twice similar, so no system could fit them twice," and their enforced organizational "diversity"—their strength depending on "whim"—threw enemy intelligence off. They went about in bands, their "minds not bodies" arranged in a battle order; neither enemy aircraft nor spies could count them, since they themselves "had not the smallest idea of [their] strength at any given moment." Irregular warfare, like deception, turned the desert's information problems to advantage; the objective was to "orientalize" British tactics. Lawrence advised, "The more unorthodox and Arab your proceedings, the more likely you are to have the Turks cold." The desert would allow them to camouflage the capricious Sherifian forces as a massive "national" uprising. The crux of irregular warfare was *bluff*. It went hand in hand with deception.[21]

In the Great War, this sort of military thinking was nothing short of revolutionary. It is for this reason that contemporaries and historians characterize Lawrence as ahead of his time in his military thought. His work was a "prototype of what may become a commonplace in the future wars," wrote Meinertzhagen presciently on the eve of World War Two. "I see no reason why every army in the future should not have an element of highly trained regular guerrillas as part of their normal organization." Much of the value of his contribution, according to contemporaries like Meinertzhagen, Hubert Young, and Basil Liddell Hart (who as military correspondent for the *Daily Telegraph* wielded influence well beyond his military and political circle), lay in its open condemnation of traditional approaches and promise of restoring vitality and individuality to warfare; Lawrence insisted, "Irregular war is far more intellectual than a bayonet charge." This new form of warfare might recapture the glory of prewar combat. Without any other form of discipline, the Arabs' "only contract was honour," which made their war "simple and individual" and their "ranks a happy alliance of commanders-in-chief." Even among the British contingent, so many officers diluted the pool of rank and file that, a subaltern recalled, over time "rank fell into abeyance." They ceased to look like regulation soldiers, outfitted in a ragged ensemble of drill shorts, open-necked shirts, kaffiyeh, and heavy army boots without socks—certainly the "worst-looking soldiers in the British army," he boasted, and thus better fit for the work at hand. In the Arabian desert, war, like intelligence, allowed recovery of individuality and liberty of action. "Those who have experienced war in France only do not know what war is," declared a soldier in Mesopotamia; there, experiencing the "funny feeling being alone...in the desert" with "these bloody arabs coming in from nowhere," he found the epitome of warfare, with all its felt element of myth and the individual quest, all that had been banished from the Western front. In the covert operations of the Middle Eastern war, the independent style of warfare of those "gifted amateurs" that had built up the empire merged with the new world of professional, organized intelligence, offering a way out of "the horrible de-humanisation" of contemporary warfare. And happily the British were natively suited to such tactics, for, Lawrence assured, "nearly every young Englishman has the roots of eccentricity in him." Moreover, Arab tactics were "like naval warfare...in their mobility, their *ubiquity*, their independence of bases and communications...with a sure retreat always behind them into an element which the Turks could not enter." The desert-as-ocean motif, itself ubiquitous in the agents' writings, suggested that, however oriental desert warfare, the British were destined to succeed at it. Echoing agents' prewar delight in Arabia's deserts, Lawrence invoked the old English maxim (as framed by Francis Bacon), "He who commands the sea is at great liberty, and may take as much or as little of the war as he will"; command of the desert would give them an equal liberty. Military historians have followed him and Liddell Hart in domesticating irregular warfare as a quintessentially "British way in warfare," rooted in Britain's ancient past.[22]

That deliverance from modern warfare was on Lawrence's mind is perhaps most evident in his hope that desert war might be bloodless. Since the Arab aim was "geographical," "killing Turks" would serve no tactical purpose; their victory "lay not in battles, but in occupying square miles of country." In a typical modernist move, Lawrence tried to look beyond attrition and the fixed positions and massive supplying of modern warfare—he was particularly stirred by the Kut disaster—by searching backwards in the medieval past. His colleague

Walter Stirling warranted that he "would have been more at ease in the period of the early Italian Renaissance *or* possibly two hundred years hence." Lawrence's theorizing had evolved from his fidelity to the medieval pursuits that had drawn him to Arabia. Deeming "empirical practice" and the canonical military theorists of the West—Clausewitz, Foch, Napoleon—irrelevant, he turned to the only campaigns he had studied "step by step"—those of "Hannibal and Belisarius, Mohammed and the Crusades!" His purpose was, as always, to wed "metaphysical" ruminations to action, "to find an immediate equation between my book-reading and our present movements." Formulating a theory of irregular warfare was part of his effort to enact the epic in Arabia, to recover the poetic, now mythic, past in contemporary practice. Fascinated as he was with the Crusades, which were certainly bloody, "his ideal of waging war" was, Alec Kirkbride claimed, actually "based on the professional condotieri [*sic*] of medieval Italy" in its insistence on gaining "one's objectives with a minimum of casualties *on both sides*." (Lawrence's own words reveal a more qualified humanity: after the war he confessed himself proudest "that I did not have any of our own blood shed. All our subject provinces to me were not worth one dead Englishman.") That Lawrence had a "horror of bloodshed"—or at least professed one—is evident from his war letters. While to Stirling he described raiding trains as "the most amateurish, Buffalo-Billy sort of performance," he confided more darkly to a friend at home: "I hope when this nightmare ends that I will wake and become alive again. This killing and killing of Turks is horrible." After the war, he grew more attached to the pacific implications of his theory. The revolt was far from bloodless, and one of its gorier episodes, the Tafileh massacre, he insisted was "an exception in my practice, undertaken in bad temper as a sardonic jest," throughout which he was "quoting to myself absurd tags of Foch and the other blood-fighters, and ... parodying the sort of thing they recommended.... Killing Turks was no part of our business."[23]

This abhorrence of violence—I speak here of his tactical tastes, not his psychology—and attraction to a warfare of evasion fit neatly with his and other agents' romantic conception of their work in Arabia. "I love the preparation, and the journey, and loathe the physical fighting," Lawrence confided to a friend. "Disguises, and the prices on one's head, and fancy exploits are all part of the pose." Killing was a kind of decadence, the ultimate debauchery, the very sort of thing from which he had sought escape in Arabia. Austerity had become a military as much as an aesthetic objective: "The Arab appealed to my imagination," began his explanation of his tactics. "The old, old civilization ... has refined itself clear of household gods ... which ours hastens to assume. The gospel of bareness in materials is a good one, and it involves apparently a sort of moral bareness too.... This is a very long porch to explain why I'm always trying to blow up railway trains and bridges instead of looking for the Well at the World's End." Both were equally bardic ventures to his mind. To a generation of agents in thrall to the principle of austerity, the streamlined logic of Bedouin warfare seemed aesthetically appropriate to the desert. "This show is splendid," Lawrence wrote. "We win hands down if we keep the Arabs simple.... To add to them heavy luxuries will only wreck their show, and guerilla [*sic*] does it. It's a sort of *guerre de course*, with the courses all reversed. But the *life and fun and movement* of it are extreme." Minimalism was now the key to recovering the authentic experience of war denied to those on the Western front. Large numbers of regular forces would be futile at best, Lawrence argued, pointing to the Turkish Army which had lost its "efficiency for rough-and-tumble work" the more it had been "improved" by the Germans.[24]

Lawrence was not alone in this thinking. Even before the Arab Bureau was founded, others were advocating an Arab revolt as a purely tactical initiative. Bray's early conception of the revolt as a campaign organized through the medium of British officials and imported arms, ammunition, and money was substantially the system ultimately adopted. Eventually invited to the Hejaz to help train Arab irregulars, Bray affirmed that they were "far more powerful than at first appears" and that their strength derived from their ability to deny the enemy a target. Ever renewable, they could be dispersed but never destroyed: "Given a rallying point they will appear again as strong as ever." The contrast with the Western front, where forces were continually being decimated and never scattered, was obvious. Storrs, Young, Sykes, and Deedes voiced similar opinions. (The latter in fact had tried inconclusively to use irregular Cretan forces to cut Turkish lines of communication in the Gallipoli campaign.) They appreciated especially the democratic, improvised, and distinctly *unbureau-cratic* nature of the revolt.[25]

The agents' involvement in the articulation of this new style of warfare derived partly from that warfare's evident overlap with intelligence work. Indeed, its success, like deception's, hinged on perfect intelligence; it was because the Arabs knew the terrain so well that they could threaten the enemy so economically. Hence Lawrence included in Bedouin principles of *warfare* scouting, mobility, and familiarity with the terrain—the skills of effective *intelligence* work in the region. And in this instance, for once, the region's dissembling propensities were no disadvantage, for, as Joyce said, "Bedouin intelligence amongst themselves is as quick and accurate as it is the reverse when passed on to us." As a commander, Lawrence found an ideal application for the knowledge and skills he possessed as an agent. "We became adepts at that form of *geographical intuition*, described...as wedding unknown land to known in a mental map," he explained; in any case, "I had traversed most of it on foot before the war many times, working out the movements of Saladin or Ibrahim Pasha." The new warfare was the brainchild of a front in which intelligence concerns had always been paramount, in which the struggle to gather accurate information had been a major preoccupation for so long that the final solution to the problem—intuition—had produced a sense of omniscience where there had hitherto been an anxious uncertainty.[26]

This prototypical special operation was the first instance of covert military activity waged primarily by an intelligence outfit. Political considerations—particularly fear of offending worldwide Muslim opinion—meant that British support for the revolt was, from the outset, shrouded in secrecy. The entire strategy of attaching British advisers, a "small expert military staff" with experience in Arabia, to the Arab rebels was based on the intelligence principle of immersion. This was the birth of a new matrix of operational intelligence that fused knowledge-gathering and military activity into a single band of experts or "special forces" unit. On a visit to the Cairo intelligence establishment, Leachman called it "an absolutely new world of soldiering." Lawrence was struck by the anomaly of his unclassifiable role: "The position I have is such a queer one—I do not suppose that any Englishman before ever had such a place." Despite agents' metamorphosis into operatives, Henry McMahon continued to protest GSI Cairo's noninvolvement with operations, insisting that it merely watched "the course of events" in order to comply with the Sherif's requests for assistance. In fact, as we have seen, GSI was deeply involved in the supply, planning, and staffing of operations, its organizational informality easing its illicit forays into the battlefield. Covertness was an almost obligatory military style in such a place, as the imperial intriguers saw it. The Hejaz's forbiddenness continued to raise the profile of agents permitted entry in it, cloaking their military operations with the same aura of romance as it had their intelligence missions. In the revolt, agents found both a military application for their intuitive skills and fulfillment of the mythopoeic impulse behind their acquisition of it. Hogarth wrote home, "T. E. L. is still away and writes from time to time that he wishes to stay away from Europe and all things European for ever and ever, and get thoroughly Arabized. Things are going pretty well in his part of the world." Initially drawn to intelligence work in Arabia for the opportunity to roam the terrain of the Crusades and other ancient glories and to gain, at least vicariously, a measure of authentic experience, the agents found in irregular warfare a chance to actually join a crusade using the skills they had acquired as intelligence-gatherers. The space the Middle East military establishment created for their influence in the formulation of these tactics meant that it was only there that "mobility was given opportunity, and the opportunity taken," as Liddell Hart noted. Indeed, the British forces' charge some 350 miles north beyond Aleppo during the last stretch of the Palestine campaign was one of history's most stupendous cavalry actions, instantly bringing down the Central alliance and precipitating "the end of the greatest war that the world has ever known," as the *Journal of Royal United Service Institute* memorialized it. It occurred, as Archibald Wavell noted, very near to "the battlefield of Issus (333 BC), where Alexander the Great first showed how battles could be won by bold and well-handled horsemen." The advance was historic but was rendered categorically epic by the ancient parallel. Ancient precedent and the lack of contemporary parallel conspired to fulfill the mythopoeic impulse animating these campaigns.[27]

As military tactics and intelligence merged, agents unsurprisingly declared accurate intuition proof of true military understanding as much as intelligence ability. "The greatest commander is he whose intuitions most nearly happen," asserted Lawrence. "Nine-tenths of tactics are certain, and taught in books: but the irrational tenth is like the kingfisher flashing across the pool, and that is the test of generals." "The perfect general," he revealed to Liddell Hart, "would know everything in heaven and earth." As agents were elided into generals, their skills became the indispensable weapons of commanders. Lawrence reasoned from the need for "perfect intelligence" that "the chief agent had to be the general's head...and his knowledge had to be faultless, leaving no room for chance." Allenby seemed eminently suited to the task, sympathetic to experts like Guy Dawnay, although perhaps as Lawrence famously surmised, "hardly prepared for anything so odd as myself—a little bare-footed silk-shirted man offering to hobble the enemy by his preaching if given stores and arms and £200,000 to convince and control his converts." Lawrence's self-description as an eccentric prophet of a new kind of warfare underscores the central creative role he assigned to the agents in the war in Arabia—not to mention the power of a claim to genius in Arabia. Despite his proselytizing, in the end he felt Dawnay alone succeeded in "feeling instinctively the special qualities of rebellion...as...it had been my dream every regular officer would." Posterity too attributed the campaign's ingenuity not to Allenby's tactical genius but to his "instinctive" trust in Lawrence and Dawnay. An ideal commander for the new warfare, he recognized *their* genius and allowed *them* to command. Indeed, to Liddell Hart's postwar collaborator J. F. C. Fuller, the ideal *commander* was both "cunning" and "naturally intuitive," and the ideal army one man with weapons, backed by a "clairvoyant Staff"—in our terms, a *commando*.[28]

From the outset, Mesopotamia too seemed destined for irregular warfare, and early on efforts were made and schemes suggested to link the peninsular revolt with a similar movement there. Even once the revolt was under way, the western Arabian command continued to try to persuade their Mesopotamian counterparts to adopt their tactics, offering to send agents with tips on working with Arab irregulars. But nervousness about the political implications of encouraging Arab assistance, given the British government's mission to maintain postwar control in Mesopotamia, prevented Cox from following the western model. Meanwhile, that heedless government itself began to push for revolt in Mesopotamia: upon the death of General Maude, who remained loyal to "modern" principles of war to the end, the chief of the Imperial General Staff urged General Marshall to launch an Arab revolt with Cox's guidance. Still, Cox remained skeptical of its practicality in Mesopotamia, where British and Turkish competition for Arab loyalty was so fierce that he reckoned the British would require enormous subsidies and masses of supplies to persuade the local people to do anything. Despite the presence of the sort of officers required for these tactics—Arnold Wilson named in particular Dickson, Leachman, and G. F. Eadie—both Cox and Beach remained hostage to the proclivities of generals and fears about the postwar settlement. (Wilson proudly claimed this hesitation as the reason the war in Mesopotamia ended "virtually free from promises.") In another sense, the entire British effort in Mesopotamia was an exercise in covertness, the rhetoric of liberation camouflaging invasion and occupation, since, in the international climate of the Great War, the British had for the first time to conceal their imperial ambitions.[29]

Still, Mesopotamia did end up seeing its own share of irregular tactics. Many of the notoriously free-handed political officers raised "bands" of Arabs (such as the Nasiriyah Scouts) for pacification operations. Leachman in particular was "a man of stratagems and surprises...a pioneer among Politicals...generally found in some unorthodox zone." Cox's antipathy to irregular tactics was no blanket condemnation of covertness as a tactical style or of the new sphere of operational intelligence; in 1917, he dreamt up a special force for intervention in Persia and recommended that Soane and the Kurdistan agent E. W. C. Noel be absorbed into its commanding ranks, partly to ease his assumption of responsibility for it as a sort of proxy for the ambassador in Persia. Communicating, notably, through demi-official channels, he stressed to the director of military intelligence that the force should not be controlled through the commander in Baghdad, who had "little appreciation for such novelties."[30]

Cox's "mobile intelligence unit" soon materialized, consisting of handpicked officers and noncommissioned officers whose task was to raise an army of irregulars in the "utmost secrecy" from the "various races of the near east." The virtually independent force was commanded by General Dunsterville, Kipling's boyhood friend and the original "Stalky" of *Stalky & Co* (1899). "Dunsterforce," better known then as the "Hush Hush Army" or the "phantom army," began to collect in Basra and Baghdad. "These men hung together mysteriously in groups," wrote Candler, "and kept their own counsel about their future plans, of which, as a matter of fact, they knew very little indeed." They were a "band of adventurers into the unknown." Discussion of the mission was forbidden, but everyone knew "some swashbuckling game was afoot, for they were as tough a looking crowd of cheery customers as our race could produce." Between Stalky and the "hush-hush," the force possessed precisely the allure that would entice the classic agent in Arabia: the foretaste of intelligence work at El Tor having so appealed to his "sense of the cloak and dagger," Reginald Savory promptly volunteered, for "the little expedition combined the attractions of a military adventure and a crusade." Ultimately failing to find sufficient local support near the Caspian, the force became the British military's first independent special forces unit, filling the gap that the Russians had left in North Persia by "a kind of moral camouflage" explicitly designed to take advantage of presumed local exaggeration of their meager strength. Via Mesopotamia, irregular methods were exported into the Russian field, another "irregular battleground" where the shortage of men was actually a critical factor. Desert isolation allowed this force, too, to preserve its secrecy and independence from military command. In short, special operations were a product of British intervention in the Middle East where, to them, the terrain was everything.[31]

The Nomad Eye—In the Sky

If irregular warfare and deception exploited the desert's falsifying powers, the air arm offered a means of overcoming them. A Cabinet Paper of 1921 pronounced, "Great as was the development of air power in the war on the western front," it was "in more distant theatres...such as Palestine, Mesopotamia and East Africa [that] the war has proved that the air has capabilities of its own." These were discovered in the course of coping with desert topography and the intelligence problems it posed. Aircraft were, of course, a new technology, their tactical uses not yet fully imagined. Their usefulness in the desert was thus a gradually dawning realization, one that proved crucial in shaping notions of their possible postwar role in the Middle East.[32]

In an unmapped and unmappable desert, the aircraft's bird's-eye view seemed, like intuition, to offer vision beyond the mirages, sandstorms, and horizonlessness that bedeviled two-dimensional observation. Early on, agents pined: "Oh for some aeroplanes. If there was a country in the whole world eminently suited to these machines this one is: Flat flat as your hand." A naval officer confirmed that only aircraft would permit reconnaissance of the "dangerously deceptive" and "incalculable" landscape. By early 1916, Force D was urging the provision of aircraft for artillery observation and reconnaissance. On their arrival, air personnel affirmed their indispensability to "obtaining quick and accurate information" in Iraq. Commanders learned to rely on guidance from distant observers. Since "in Mesopotamian battles, little can be trusted that is seen," explained Brigadier General A. G. Wauchope, "commanders are bound to rely on reports by aeroplane." In the desert, aircraft allegedly made it "impossible for an enemy to alter his dispositions without discovery; the movement of a few tents or shelters can be spotted at once, and there are no woods or buildings in which to hide his men." In the Hejaz too, they were deemed "the only means of overcoming the mirage" and the prevarications of native agents and prisoners; indeed, their information was "the only sort that can be relied on." Aircraft, like the intuitive expert, could extract truth from an essentially deceptive land (in theory—in fact, there were real limits on using aircraft in the desert, as we shall see).[33]

Of central importance in the Royal Flying Corps' ability to improve geographical knowledge was aerial photography, a technique developed largely thanks to the informal liaising and experimentation of agents such as Lawrence and Newcombe. It was Gertrude Bell who, having witnessed her colleagues' work in Cairo, inspired GSI Basra to learn more about the technology. Hence, during his visit to Mesopotamia in 1916, besides trying to ransom the force at Kut, Lawrence also advised Basra on the uses of aerial photography. The hitherto ineffectual mapping section was soon able to turn out hourly editions of maps before attack, distributing them at the front by air. In a summary of wartime advances, the freshly rechristened Royal Air Force explained that aerial photography in Mesopotamia differed from that done on the Western front, since "in Mesopotamia...no reliable maps exist, and...all new mapping...is done by means of aeroplane photography." The technology would be useful, they concluded, in all such "flat countries." Historians too consider the technology to have "exerted its greatest influence in Mesopotamia" where aerial mapping was "the most advanced in the world."[34]

Aircraft also promised to ease communication with tribes and officers marooned in the desert and cooperation between distant bands of irregulars, since "a good pilot could generally land by the unit itself, give them their accurate position and inform the commander of the situation personally," in the words of air commander J. E. Tennant. The desert offering endless landing grounds, pilots could function as dei ex machina, restoring a lost unit's bearings and ending its isolation from news. Thus, a squadron might be out of action by nightfall in France, but not in Arabia:

In this far land, where, without aerial observation, shot might as well not be fired; where maps were insufficiently accurate for troops to

march by; and where, unless guarded and forewarned by the Air unit,
men might walk into unknown and ambushed nullahs; it would have
been a sorry tale to tell GHQ [General Headquarters] that there could
be no flying on the morrow because of casualties to-day. The risks
had to be taken and we backed our luck; it never failed.

Without airpower, the troops were literally nowhere. Its centrality was dictated
by the special kind of warfare in use in the Middle Eastern theaters. A commander in the Hejaz extolled the air force "as a new factor in warfare" that also
had "enormous political possibilities," given its effect on morale and potential
for establishing officers with distant friendly tribes. By establishing a network
of landing grounds in the desert, the British might coordinate the operations of
tribes in the entire western desert and synchronize pressure on the Turkish
flanks in Mesopotamia and the Hejaz with the general strategic offensive. An
air network could provide the material sinews for the vaporous Arab network
and annihilate distance altogether. This plan was appreciated partly because
"the value from an Intelligence point of view would be very great." It would
physically link up not only the Arabs, but the agents deputed to both advise
and, as we have seen, spy on them. Aircraft provided the infrastructure that
enabled agents like Leachman and Wilson to be almost everywhere at once. In
the end, organization of the Royal Flying Corps' Middle East command, in
which each squadron was equipped with its own intelligence section, was such
that "the spoke of communication led direct to the hub, there was no need to
delay or refer to others, we could act at once." Airpower also provided access, of
a kind, to otherwise forbidden sites. Whereas British forces would not be welcome in the Hejaz, Lawrence explained, the same objections did not exist to
aircraft, which Arabs found "delightful." Thus, an air reconnaissance of
Medina, where the Turks were holding out, was conducted in 1917. Aircraft
generally impinged on intelligence work in the Middle East in a way they never
did on the Western front.[35]
    This new technology did not by any means render intuitive experts obso-
lete. Only a few wartime agents were ever thought to have developed the geographical intuition expected of the ideal agent, namely Lawrence, Leachman,
and perhaps Philby. The best supplement, since, despite their powers, they
could not in fact be everywhere at once, was the hyper-nomadic airplane.
Moreover, one of aircraft's purposes was to enhance the expert's instinctual
grasp. Philby confessed that his "altogether astonishing" first flight "impressed
itself deeply on my mind"; in a mere quarter-hour, the "magnificent bird's-
eye panorama...doubled my knowledge of Mesopotamia." Air patrolling was
also so inchoate as a system, because of the lack of landing grounds, and

pilots so *in*expert in deciphering the terrain that ground agents remained crucial guides, not least because of the endless possibility of deception in the
form of haze and mirage as much as false camps and camouflage. Intelligence
agents were urged to scrutinize the "personal idiosyncrasies" of the air force's
observing officers to ensure, for instance, that a claimed increase in tents at a
camp was not merely the result of a novitiate's misperception. That desert
signs could be only subjectively interpreted remained the intelligence orthodoxy. Similarly, when aircraft took over reconnaissance duties, they were
instructed to rely on the ground experts for the accompanying political work,
such as feeling out the intentions of local Arabs. In any case, as demonstrated
by the case of aerial photography, the agents were central in the practical
development of air potential; it was a technology associated with their peculiar work and methods. Indeed, aircraft were such an "eccentric mode of
transport for a high official" that the agents' (as much as the Arabs') oft-
expressed "delight" in them only fed their reputation as unique, heroic, indeed
superheroic, figures.[36]

In short, the air force absorbed the reigning intelligence outlook on the
Middle East. It was because the intelligence community viewed Arabia as an
inscrutable, encrypted space that aircraft, like deception tactics, were used in
this way, at this time, in this region. Control of the air gave control over this
enciphered space; it was deemed integral to the campaigns' other innovations.
Without it, Sykes reasoned, the Arabs would not have had confidence in their
ability to conceal their movements and effect surprise, nor would the staged
routine in the run-up to Megiddo have been concealed. For this reason, too, it
was in the Middle East campaigns that aircraft signaling was first thoroughly
formalized: for purposes of communicating with the cavalry, artillery, and
infantry, aircraft were instructed to move in a circle, draw arrows in the sand,
place ground-sheets in certain positions, or use Véry lights and wireless signals
in a particular way. After the war, the Royal Air Force in Mesopotamia issued a
booklet on aerial photography, providing examples from Mesopotamia with
instructions on how to interpret them, especially tracks and roads, for "nothing
affords fuller insight into the enemy's daily life than tracks." The manual also
provided instructions on how to discriminate truth from deception from on
high, particularly by reading shadows. As always, the key was to face such tactics with an equal knowledge, "complete knowledge of the appearance of the
ground from the air." Leith-Ross's tactical guide also offered instructions in
recognizing the signs of such phenomena as invisible pools of water in the
desert. The insights that underwrote the ascendance of the intuitive expert
were adapted for the new vehicle of omniscience, whose special uses in Iraq
were generalized to produce a new science of airpower.[37]

While air cooperation with other arms helped meet the unique requirements of "a moving battle over unchartered [*sic*] country," especially in "operations in a country of this kind," as Tennant put it, they also began to seem
capable of mimicking the very arms they supplemented; for instance, they
might "themselves effectively make raids on the railway." Indeed, if Cox
remained reluctant to import the Arab Revolt into Iraq, he did permit the air
force to replicate Lawrence's train-wrecking exploits on the Baghdad Railway.
In other ways, too, aircraft began to function as a kind of aerial irregular force,
taking warfare to a new, mythic, almost biblical level through demonstrations
of their extraordinary destructive capacity, particularly in the "aerial trap" created when Turkish troops and transports retreated through the steep, narrow
canyon of Wadi Faria in September 1918, spearheading the fall of Damascus.
There had been no precedent "for such effective use of air superiority against
ground forces in a maximal exploitation of the topographic conditions." The
Cabinet Paper I mentioned earlier stressed this new lesson in aircraft's uses in
"operations against the enemy's ground forces" and in the "attack and disper-
sal of considerable bodies of ground troops." It was to this "solitary exception
of the War," this "military disaster wrought exclusively by bombs," that Lionel
Charlton directed postwar Britons "to witness air power really in the working"
in his 1940 book-length celebration of the air force's "deeds that held the
Empire." Famous for his outraged resignation from the Royal Air Force's
regime in postwar Iraq, Charlton nevertheless considered Wadi Faria "a classic
instance of the proper application of air power." Indeed, the air force was credited with much of the success of this part of the Palestine campaign: "We were
butchers," admitted the commander, Geoffrey Salmond, "but the good thing
was that all plans for retirement were completely upset by this attack from the
sky.... It is a new feature in war, and I do hope it can be made use of." (He was
apparently so appalled [yet still impressed] by the site afterward that he prohibited pilots from returning to the scene and contemplating the results of their
action.) Aircraft, like irregulars, configured the entire desert/sky as a battlefield. Appearing from nowhere like magic, denying the enemy a target, and
focusing on wearing the enemy down, their power stemmed as much from the
actual destruction they wreaked as from the awesome and ubiquitous threat
they embodied. Unlike irregulars, however, they suspended all notions of "fair
play" and reconfigured war as a visitation.[38]

"Ground troops" were not the only bodies attacked and dispersed. The
political officer's policing responsibilities required close collaboration with disciplinary air expeditions. Airpower complemented not only their mapping and
reconnaissance work but also the "political" work grouped under "counterespionage." In this sense too, intelligence became operational. The task known as

"tribal reconnaissance by air" referred to surveillance not of tribes fighting with the enemy, explains Leith-Ross, but of tribes "both within and without the territorial boundaries which we control" who at times "get out of hand and require a lesson" in the efficient form of "an aerial raid with bombs and machine guns." Aircraft were useful substitutes for the grueling night marches ordinarily used for attacking villages in "small wars": Tennant found that "if a tribe got out of hand a raid could leave the next morning and bomb and machine-gun any village within a 100-mile radius. Such immediate and drastic action inspired terror in the Arabs." This was the germ of the postwar air control regime, and of the concerns it would produce: "In a country where nomad tribes are dispersed broadcast over the face of the land," cautioned Leith-Ross, "to send out a bombing raid without the most accurate and easily followed instructions may only result in considerable damage being inflicted on some friendly and unoffending tribe." On the other hand, an airplane's visit to an offending tribe's territory, if it did not culminate in a destructive "Straf," tended to "cheapen" the airplane in their eyes and lose its "moral effect." He concluded that, when used judiciously, airpower was a great asset and labor-saving device in "tribal operations." This more tentative position, at once recognizing aircraft's particular suitability to "tribal operations," while remaining circumspect about their omnipotence, was already somewhat revisionist, for many "Politicals," Leith-Ross noted, already regarded them "as a panacea for all the ills to which tribal situations give rise."[39]

Agents' ready resignation to such carnage seems at first to fit awkwardly with, say, Lawrence's idealistic efforts to banish killing from warfare. However, it is important to recall that, despite his military reasoning, Lawrence, who approved this use of airpower, did see plenty of bloodshed during the Arab Revolt, and seeing it was part of what made the revolt authentic experience for him: "The whole business of the movement seemed to be expressible only in terms of death and life." The agents did not go to Arabia in search of mere adventure but for the experience of the journey-quest. For this, they had to come back *having seen things*. They did not actually seek escape; they wanted to *enact* the role of the unknowing knight seeking escape but stumbling into great events that yielded real knowledge—following a romantic script of medieval adventure. Magnifying "both defeat and victory," aircraft impressed Bedouin with British power, Bray explained to his superiors. Indeed, they magnified the British effort in Arabia to the epic proportions in which agents habitually conceived it; they were *ennobling*. Aircraft, despite and perhaps because of their lethal power, were their technological counterparts, "knights of the air," vehicles on a hyper-quest. Then, too, this was a biblical land—British pilots called Wadi Faria "the Valley of Death." From on high, the British pilot, a deus *in* machina, could enact the divine retribution that was fitting in such a land, of which more in a later chapter.[40]

Between aircraft and intuitive expertise, the British felt they had overcome the intelligence obstacles of the Middle East. Near the end of the war, Candler could point to the "uncanny" certainty with which "our Intelligence ... forestalled every movement of the enemy." In the course of acquiring this confidence, the agents became, if anything, even more eccentric, despite the measure of bureaucratization. Leachman's work, Bray attested, "could not be judged by any known standard." As they expanded the domain of intelligence into the realm of operations, they were transformed from exceptions to exemplars of the reality of the British intelligence world. As Tuohy foresaw, intelligence would never be the same; rather than merely concentrate on discovering what the enemy was doing and prevent the enemy from finding out what you were doing, agents would deliberately deceive the enemy. "This final development of 'Intelligence' will rule supreme in any future war," he foretold. "Things will verily not be what they seem." The romance the intelligencers injected into these campaigns resonated deeply with the hope of Britons at home for some sign of the survival of the passing Victorian order, as we shall see next.[41]

5

Imperial Expiation

The war in the Middle East fulfilled not only the hopes of British agents but also those of many of their countrymen at home. Britons who had hoped war would bring release from a decade of decadence and complacency witnessed the shattering of this illusion during the continually unfolding debacle of 1914–1917, but two conspicuous bright spots on the map of this global Armageddon, located not entirely providentially near the actual site of Armageddon, offered something of a narrative of compensation. For a brief moment, as the agents found fulfillment of their dreams of authentic experience in the Middle Eastern campaigns, the British public glimpsed a shimmering vision of the old world rising, like a phoenix, from the ashes of total war, and stripped of the decadent veneer that had sent so many of them in search of authentic experience and redemption—ultimately in war itself. Central to this vision was the survival of individual heroism in the modernist shape of Lawrence of Arabia and of the British imperial idea, reinvented as technocratic developmentalism on the ground in Mesopotamia.[1] Indeed, if technology had unleashed disorder and desolation in France, in the able hands of experts in the Middle East, it was held to have dispelled chaos and deception. As the Middle East became central to British hopes for postwar redemption, the agents acquired a mass celebrity—it was this position that would make them pivotal to criticism of the government when development was ultimately traded for a punishing discipline, as we shall see in Part II. To get there, however, we need first to examine just how development and heroism came to dominate postwar constructions of the Middle Eastern campaigns.

The Romance of Development

Soldiers transferred to the Middle East from the Western front were invariably relieved, even during the grim operations to relieve Kut, because these "side-shows" held out the hope at least of escape, of adventurous journeys in fabled locales. With a sparkling vision of Baghdad before them, they wondered about their "ultimate destiny" and were grateful to be on this "interesting adventure." The excitement of arriving in "terra incognita" was only amplified by what one soldier described as the

> wealth of legend, rumour, and history attached to this unknown country, sufficient to light a spark in the most unpromising imagination. Who could possibly resist some whisper of romance at the thought that we were heading towards the homeport of Sinbad the Sailor, and that beyond lay the ruins of great Babylon, Ur of the Chaldees, Nineveh of the Assyrians; a land crowded with great and terrible ghosts, full of strange history and mysterious legends?

A didactic, morale-boosting pamphlet titled *The Land of the Two Rivers* attested, "Mesopotamia stirs the curiosity of the troops more perhaps than any other of the theatres of war." Even the poet and memoirist of the Western front, Robert Graves, brother of the agent Philip Graves, sought transfer to the Middle East. Once there, soldiers hoping for romance were not disappointed by the "strange land of mystery," a "Fairyland" that was "hard to imagine, impossible to describe," wrapped in an atmosphere of "melodrama, of romance, of imagination." The agents' idea of Arabia had sunk deep roots. In their letters home, soldiers strove to convey the endless fascination of the region, directing loved ones to the agents' by then classic accounts, although many anxious relatives were already immersed in such works for their own edification. Some asked their families to send them new copies of these books along with that ubiquitous prerequisite, the *Arabian Nights*. Even a decade later, the Mesopotamia campaign's peculiar conditions prompted reminiscences of a "queer war," over which hung "an 'Arabian Nights' quality of enchantment by desert djinns." In his 1927 novel based on his war-time experiences as an army chaplain with the Leicestershires, Edward Thompson described a landscape of eternal drift in which the protagonist, a medical missionary, is visited by epiphanic realizations about reality and unreality. Anything can be believed in a place where naval soldiers "see unicorns and fabulous things all day long," he explains. "A couple of years here would turn the whole army into mystics," he adds. "You simply *can't* take this show for real."[2]

Of the many reasons that Baghdad became a military objective, the least controversial was that its fabled past ensured almost everyone at home had heard of it, which, one scholar points out, was more than could be said of any other place in the country: "It was the Arabian nights," in the pithy words of one enchanted soldier. It was a *glamorous* place to be sent to (if repulsive once encountered). The very word was "a moral factor": soldiers despairing of toiling uselessly in a vast "nowhere" now had a goal, whose name "all knew and had known almost since we could remember." More than the *Nights*, it conjured up the "background" of those memories: "flickering firelight and a quiet room and a gentle voice reading of old Baghdad.... Who would not fight to get there and really see it?" Officers got goose bumps thinking of the ancient footsteps they followed: "This was not... 'miles on miles of F. A. [Fuck-All],' but a mine of historical interest." They lived in "a state of constant wonder." Thompson's nonfictional account *The Leicestershires beyond Baghdad* was likewise marked by an awareness of uncanny parallels with the ancient adventures of Xenophon (his fictional characters in the later novel also carry Gibbon and *Anabasis* in their packs, transporting themselves to their schooldays as they read at the foot of the Median Wall). In the first year of the occupation, the Army's Young Men's Christian Association of India distributed tourist guidebooks about Baghdad to the troops to "supply a demand increasingly evident." Laid out as a series of walking tours, its stated purpose was to enable "visitors" to see efficiently the city's many points of interest.[3]

Baghdad's glamour caught the imagination of Prime Minister Lloyd George himself, inspiring him to make Jerusalem Britain's next objective in a campaign hailed as "the Last Crusade" and in a country "steeped in the romanticism of the old crusades." Palestine, too, was "far from being a strange country": soldiers looked forward to seeing places they had learned of "at our mother's knees," where they felt "at home and not lost as... in Gallipoli and Salonika." There, too, "'we travelled in the print of olden wars,'" explained Major C. S. Jarvis—who saw in the white-robed Lawrence atop a white camel a vision of the messenger who had rushed to Medina to announce the great Arab victory over the Romans in Yarmuk in 636. This campaign, too, would be remembered as "the most romantic episode of a war which had little romance." These two campaigns offered a glimpse of prelapsarian imperial adventure and the comfort of cherished bedtime stories. If, as Paul Fussell has told us, soldiers on the Western front drew ironically and tragically on the quest motifs of (pseudo) medieval romances, those in the Middle East drew on them as still valid metaphors for their own experiences.[4]

As these fascinations suggest, the information void about the Middle East was filled with references from the history of Christianity that infused the campaigns with a unique moral fire. The crusade motif may have been used primarily by "a privileged few" from public schools speaking metaphorically about "fighting a just cause" (partly because of the official ban on references to the Crusades that might alienate Muslim opinion), but, as Eitan Bar-Yosef has argued, ordinary Britons also found in the Holy Land a reminiscence of Christian history and an echo of familiar, domestic religious practices. Troops arriving in Mesopotamia routinely sought out the Garden of Eden, Ezra's tomb, the Tower of Babel, Ur of the Chaldees, and other Biblical sites (although, by the end, scarcely a humorist or cartoonist had resisted milking the irony of Eden's paradisiacal reputation given Qurnah's present state). Edward Kinch, a soldier who would learn Arabic and join the civil administration at the end of the war, felt "immensely moved by the close contact with many Old Testament places and Legends" which produced "an affinity with the country...quite unexplainable but nevertheless strong." Familiarity with such sites was "absolutely necessary," it was thought, "to look upon anything with eyes of intelligence." The ranks reportedly sat around for hours with Bibles and maps working out natural explanations for what they had taken to be legends. Though not all were convinced, the experience of Biblical sites "brought to many...the realization that the tales of the Old Testament were *based on fact*." There, affirmed a war correspondent, "you live the story of the Bible, and you do not wonder in the least if it is true; you know it is." It even seemed fitting that the only British surrender should have occurred at Kut, making Mesopotamia a place of pilgrimage for Britons as it had long been for myriads of people. In the Palestine campaign too, God's palpable presence was a "splendid incentive." Major Gilbert found the "cockney soldiers'" open displays of piety increasingly attractive as his "outer layers of supersensitive insincerity and decadent refinement" wore thin, allowing his "true nature" to shine through. In this campaign, soldiers found a reminiscence of the classic personal quest for a "fuller and more vital" life, punctuated by solitary communion with the infinite at famous sites of pilgrimage. In light of the wisdom gained and the knowledge that this final crusade had brought "peace and freedom" to the Holy Land after five hundred years, "it all seemed worth while." As the London *Times* memorialized it, Allenby's consummately "artistic" achievement was fought over country that "enshrined the most sacred memories and traditions, whose familiar place-names stir the deepest emotion of all who read the dispatch." Even to the more secular-minded, the biblical austerity of Bedouin life offered an exemplary counterpoint to the decadence that had, some suspected, landed the British in this nightmare. "It is the poverty of Arabia," as Lawrence said, "which makes them simple, continent and enduring."[5]

The Middle East campaigns seemed episodes in a longer history of valiant, righteous, and *meaningful* crusading that made the war, for a moment at least, seem worthwhile. Resurrecting a style of clever warfare recalling their classical predecessors, they confirmed the endurance of British military prowess, wit, and valor, providing "a little flash of humour across the grim darkness of war." In a theater in which agents and aircraft were dispatched to do the work of occupying forces, individual heroism stood out in sharp relief against the backdrop of anonymous mass slaughter at home. "In exile from the world," the "Invincibles," as Force D was dubbed, fought "war as we used to imagine it," with the old, "humane" implements, pondered the American secretary of the Young Men's Christian Association serving with the British troops. This was the "good old fighting" that had vanished from France; it proved that "in the right place war even to-day can be a romance." "Would that the whole war could be fought in the desert lands," he pined. Comparatively poor living conditions and supplies made their "side-show" feel all the more like a penance promising expiation, especially since the one, considerable advantage was that "one was not being shot at." Many soldiers who fought in the Middle East, perhaps alone among that sacrificial generation, felt their hopes for adventure and authentic experience reach fulfillment, especially *after* experiencing the futility and beastliness of war in France.[6]

Even the tragedy that checked the force's first surge upriver did not break this faith. After a reverse at Ctesiphon, the force fell back on Kut, where it was besieged through the winter of 1915–1916 and eventually surrendered after sacrificing thousands of troops in ill-fated rescue efforts. To be sure, "the conditions of France were repeated in Mesopotamia," to borrow Candler's ominous words, but the trench warfare that followed the siege and preceded the campaign's magnificent rush north to Mosul was its rite of passage to a modernity no longer diminished by its colonial quality. Whatever difficulties the troops had experienced were in retrospect put down to their *lack* of access to modern technology—the wire-cutters, water-carts, Véry lights, rockets, mosquito nets, periscopes, and medical facilities essential to "war carried on under modern conditions"—or to the inappropriateness of modern technology in a deceptive land that morphed cars into a "few filmy lines," rendered signaling useless, and whose "fickle lady," the Tigris, prohibited use of modern riverboats. The Indian government had simply failed to recognize "the immense differences between…an Indian frontier and a Mesopotamian campaign." Indeed, the campaign's initial mobility—recalling a frontier escapade—had only frustrated "the business of range-finding and registering, so easy in the stationary conditions on the Western front"—however fruitless the ability in those stationary conditions. Modern warfare had come to mean the *mobile* supply of an *immobilized* army in a clearly demarcated battlefield. The campaign's eventual resumption of its breathless pace, after the War Office and the chastened Indian military establishment began to provision everything from aircraft to harbors, seemed to prove there was life after trench warfare, that stalemate could end. Candler attested, "bloody, remorseless trench fighting…was a thing of the past." Armed with all the paraphernalia of modern warfare, the force waged *"war as it should be waged,* with the spirit of movement in it, the new scenes a background to the drama of battle…waiting to be explored." At Ctesiphon, a naval officer mused on the great armies and historic figures that "had passed this way before the coming of men in khaki, with their aeroplanes and wireless." The ubiquitous aircraft in particular seemed to herald an ultramodern warfare in which even chivalry and individual heroism were restored to technological warfare, as we have seen. The copious ad hoc innovations that marked this small operation made a similar promise. An officer insisted that the troops never felt cast in a sideshow precisely because the presence of fewer battalions made each feel more important. "You couldn't have a more interesting show," he assured his mother, what with the cavalry, armored cars, pontooning—"all these fancy corps alongside us." And people noticed: Palestine and Mesopotamia "were not the minor struggles of the war," affirmed a war correspondent, "but an imposing spectacle, especially seen together." Because "after thousands of years, the tactics of Saul and Jonathan were repeated with success by a British force," the Palestine campaign could be classed, along with older wars of substance, as *historic*. In short, defying the wisdom from France that "modern warfare" had rendered long advances impossible without "a certain calculated sacrifice which is generally prohibitive," here the British were modern and yet highly mobile.[7]

It was French conditions that now appeared "abnormal." These campaigns seemed to prove the reigning military science was sound—the cavalry certainly was "saved…from utter extinction." Indeed, it was perhaps such counterpoints that kept the British military establishment committed to the "cult of the offensive" despite the news from France. General Townshend, who commanded the force besieged at Kut, later affirmed:

> The Napoleonic war of manoeuvre or movement was rendered
> practically impossible, after the Battle of the Marne, and…a war of
> entrenchments, more suited to a secondary theatre, became the order
> of the day.…On the other hand, the operations in the secondary
> theatres of the war, such as Palestine and Mesopotamia, were wars of
> manoeuvre and movement.

The *Times* declared "no example of the war of movement…better worth study" than that in "Mesopotamia To-Day." The epic tenor of the events in the Middle

East—the crusade in western Arabia and the classic scenic structure of the Mesopotamian campaign (glory–tragedy–even more glory)—provided a continual narrative of relief to Britons at home. The fall of Baghdad in March 1917 was hailed as "the most triumphant piece of strategy... since war started" and "the first big place we've taken in this war," while the fall of Jerusalem incited unprecedented public euphoria—the Bell of Westminster chimed for the first time in three years—and captured the British imagination. Postwar military journals noted the "perfectly reasonable reversal in the importance of the various campaigns" of the war: during the war, France and Belgium had preoccupied military theorists, but since then, the innovatory, so-called sideshows, especially Mesopotamia and Palestine, had seized attention—for their demonstration that new technologies practically guaranteed that all future warfare promised to be "small" and that, as at Waterloo, "mobility and power" could still be "rightly correlated." Moreover, these Middle Eastern campaigns suggested warfare might still be a productive enterprise. If technology's dark side was exposed in France, a new aspect of it was unveiled in Mesopotamia: in the hands of "experts," it could resurrect a military campaign and, at once, a devastated civilization.[8]

Indeed, after Kut, reclaiming Mesopotamia for the modern world was the new call to arms. A parliamentary inquiry into the disaster produced a scandalous report in June 1917, in which the Mesopotamia Commission severely censured the Indian government and army for rashly deciding to advance on Baghdad, especially without adequate transportation and medical facilities. Though public exposure of Indian blunders triggered something of a regime change, bringing to power Edwin Montagu as secretary of state for India and Lord Chelmsford as viceroy, it also renewed that government's determination to prove it could competently dispense the blessings of imperial rule and stake out the land of two rivers as a material object with modern transportation technologies: the oft-repeated list of materials—timber, steel, dredgers, electrical plant, cable, engines—laborers, and technical experts sent to Mesopotamia for the construction of ships, wharves, railroads, dams, canals, harbors, telegraphs, and so on became a proud inventory of British imperial beneficence transferred via India. Not least among the contingents to appease with this activity was the enraged British public. Montagu was soon acclaiming the force in Parliament for "gradually changing the appearance of the country and eradicating the blight of Turkish misrule." Whatever its everlasting wonder, in this vision Mesopotamia was at bottom a vast, autarkic wasteland, so void of diversion that even "Adam and Eve might well have been excused," as one soldier derisively remarked. Its "Physical and Climatic Peculiarities," as catalogued in the Commission Report (echoing intelligence surveys), spoke to its fundamental remoteness "far away from home, civilization, and comfort," in the rueful words of a naval captain. It was a fallen Eden requiring reintegration into the global economy, a land of "excess, where the elements are never moderate or in humour," wrote Candler, this careless inefficiency bespeaking its otherworldliness: "There was something almost Biblical in the way the deities of this ancient land conspired to punish us...heat and drought; hunger and thirst and flies; damp and cold, fever and ague, flood, hurricane and rain." Technology could only improve a land so far from England, so close to an unforgiving God. In a word, "development" emerged as the campaign's primary purpose, in the sense of a statist effort to use public investment for the avowed purpose of raising a colony into a modern nation-state (as opposed to earlier notions of empire as a means of, say, civilizational catch-up or moral uplift that did not presume a particular role for state investment in infrastructure). The wartime development of Iraq differed from earlier experiments and experiences in Punjab and Egypt in that it was designed to serve the immediate military need to produce battlefields and nature itself out of a disordered landscape and the pressing cultural need for proof of Britain's constructive powers. In the crucible of world war, Joseph Chamberlain's turn-of-the-century vision finally acquired traction in a government otherwise hostage to the principle of colonial financial self-sufficiency. In an important sense, the roots of the modern practice of technocratic development were military-industrial, and its purpose was to underwrite fresh imperial conquest for a people seeking renewal of the certainties crippled by world war.[9]

In Mesopotamia, technological development did not raise the preservationist fears of rapid change upsetting the indigenous social and political order that tended to undermine fulfillment of visionary wartime plans for colonial development. There, development was framed *as* preservation, as a restoration of the country's lost ancient order—in a backward-looking gesture distinct even from the modernizing "preservationists" of David Matless's interwar England.[10] The dams and canals ravaged by the Mongols, on which "some fifty centuries of prosperous civilisation had been based," would be restored, proclaimed the *Times* after the war, and Clio would return as Baghdad's lingering aura of mystery was "violated by the whirring wheels...of trains, of cars, of aeroplanes." Aircraft were seized on as a fittingly miraculous technology for restoring the country to its old prominence as a cosmopolitan entrepôt. However revolutionary, their arrival ultimately only reaffirmed the agelessness of the Orient, enthused the *Times*, recalling the sorcerers who, once upon a time, had made Sinbad the Sailor turn airman on the back of a great bird. Likewise, motor-cars were simply "snorting land monsters which rush across the deserts." "The inhabitants take these things as a matter of course," the paper affirmed, for "the age of miracles has happily returned, and we may see strange Arabian nights in the coming years." The postwar writer Richard Coke echoed that the advent of air and road transport would restore a great artery of world trade to its rightful importance. The press seized on the notion of Baghdad as the "Clapham Junction of the air." By making it so, Britain was merely obeying geography; the "natural junctions" of the world's airways and railways lay in Iraq. Its past and future destiny was to be "the world's centre." In H. G. Wells's vision of the *Shape of Things to Come* (1933), a world devastated by war is resurrected by an aerial "Transport Union" based in Basra. Developing Mesopotamia was simply a matter of refitting of it, through modern technology, to resume its *traditional* role in a reconstructed, commercial, and peaceful postwar world. As David Edgerton notes, it was liberal Britain rather than fascist regimes of the period that pioneered air warfare; and it did so by couching airpower as a force for peace and commerce, anchored in the oldest commercial center of the world. Technologies like dams and modern roads would not only produce battlefields from Mesopotamia's disordered landscape but Mesopotamia itself as a coherent geographical entity. They would both improve the fabulous and terrible country and bring it within the realm of the knowable, within the pale of the economy that development sought to make. In India, by contrast, the signs of wartime modernization were most often viewed as a violation of the colony's romantic aura, betokening social, cultural, and political chaos.[11]

In short, abject failure raised the stakes of the campaign. The refitting of the troops triggered a refitting of the country. During the war itself, it came to be seen less as a backwater, a mere sideshow, than the place where the war could find meaning; less an oriental escape from industrialism than the proving ground for industry and empire. By "reclaim[ing] a wilderness" and "rebuild[ing] a civilization after many years of anarchy and desolation" for "a new country and a new people," the force determined to give meaning to the sacrifices of British soldiers, explained an officer. Theirs was the blessed task of revitalizing not just any civilization but one of "mysterious and divine" origins. Indeed, Gertrude Bell confessed feeling "rather like the Creator." In a terrain hallowed doubly, by its past and by the sacrifice of British lives, Britons constructed a new imperial identity that could even explain away the, retrospectively charming, missteps that had landed them in such a Great War in the first place. A sailor wrote in a 1917 memoir:

> We Britons spend our lives in making blunders, and give our lives to retrieve them. But though the clouds remain, they are no longer dark and threatening; the dawn has come, and with it the confident assurance that in this new burden of Empire—the task of restoring

Mesopotamia to her former prosperity—the generations to come will gain inspiration from the long chronicle of heroic deeds which make up the story of her deliverance. The lives of Britain's sons have not been sacrificed in vain.

They were the bearers of a new "dawn" for Iraqis—and for Britons. This was a restoration of East as much as West: British representations now stressed that, far from "unchanging," this bit of the East had metamorphosed from a locus of secular power and worldly riches, tightly bound to Hellenistic-Christian culture, to a "sordid relic." "When European Christendom looks to-day at the desolation of these lands," wrote Edwyn Bevan in a wartime publication, "it is looking at a lost piece of itself." Restoring Arabia was part of the larger project of restoring the Old World after its orgy of self-destruction: in the development of this "vast, neglected" part of Asia lay the hope of a better life for "western peoples." The object of the British campaign was now nothing less than a "regenerated Babylonia, in which the ancient streams reflect once more mighty structures of men and gardens like Paradise, and in the streets of whose cities traffickers from all the earth once more meet." The conviction that they could not possibly worsen such a derelict land made the steady grind of imperial administration especially reassuring. These were by no means idiosyncratic or academic views; in Parliament, Robert Cecil, Bell's friend and the assistant secretary of state for foreign affairs, earnestly praised the "very satisfactory progress...in redeeming [Mesopotamia] from the state of ruin into which it had fallen under the Turks." Restoring Mesopotamia was "the talk of the dinner-table" even among the ranks.[12]

After all, in such constructive work lay proof of the vitality of British imperial idealism. Some may have felt "all the things one is fighting for are so far away," but others found high ideals to fight for in that breach. Major General A. G. Wauchope of the Black Watch explained in *Blackwood's*:

> Watching these columns of Englishmen and Highlanders, of
> Hindus, Gurkhas and bearded Sikhs advancing [within sight of the
> Median Wall], one felt the conviction that this struggle was being
> fought for the sake of principles more lofty, for ends more perma-
> nent, for aims less fugitive, for issues of higher service to the cause of
> humanity, than those that had animated the innumerable and bloody
> conflicts of the past.

The power of place made enduring idealism conceivable at the very moment of the gestation of the postwar ironic mode on the Western front. If the war had proven ideologically bankrupt and "mindless" elsewhere, in the Arabian desert, "the reservoir of all ideas, the birth of all prophecies," lived a population enslaved to "ideas," reminded Lawrence, in whose company they too might conceive an ideal that would redeem the war of all its apparent purposelessness. Thus, for instance, Reginald Wingate hoped that "in the theory of Arabian union...may lie not merely a partial solution of...our present difficulties but possibly the foundation of a really constructive scheme for the future." As "Patron & Protector" of an Arab federation, Britain would find a redeeming imperial role for the future—reshaping itself in the image of the ancient greats.[13]

Indeed, the ancients loomed large in discussions about British imperial redemption in the Middle East. By making man once again "master of the great waters" of Mesopotamia, Bevan explained, the British would bring to an end the wanton destruction wrought by feckless and savage imperial tyrants since the Mongol invasion. They would resurrect an older imperial tradition of *improvement*, the tradition of the Persians, Seleucids, Parthians, Sassanides, and the Saracen caliphs; in this too, modern development was styled as restoration, a revival of the forgotten practices and ideals of the strong, paternalistic imperial states of antiquity. The British army had launched a "programme of public works as has no parallel in that ancient land since...ALEXANDER THE GREAT," proclaimed the *Manchester Guardian* in stentorian tones. The fall of Baghdad inspired wonder and hope because it was no ordinary city but "Baghdad!" a place "famous for the men and armies that had crossed it." The capture of "Dar-as-Salam, the City of *Security*" instilled "confidence," inserting the British into the hallowed history of the timeless, episodic imperial struggle to rule the cradle of civilization. Candler reeled off the names of glorious past rulers of Baghdad—Nebuchadnezzar, Alexander, Cyrus, Julian, Haroun al-Rashid—"and now it was General Maude." He had become "one of the immortals." His death late in 1917 (from cholera) was compared to Julian's and Alexander's. The echo of imperial Rome was perhaps loudest among these reverberations from the past. Candler reported on the entire campaign by the light of Gibbon, drawing parallels throughout. The new governor of Jerusalem, Ronald Storrs, was acclaimed as the successor "*sed long intervallo*" of Pontius Pilate. All this history produced an unwavering optimism about the fruits of the campaign: Captain C. R. S. Pitman confidently scribbled "present" over "former" in a *Times of India* article on Baghdad titled "Scene of Former Glories." By crossing this ancient land, the British, too, had achieved epoch-making imperial greatness; far from bankrupt, the empire had finally *arrived*. However unsung, soldiers knew their "little show in Mesopotamia ha[d] done as much to save the Empire as any other."[14]

To Britons in Mesopotamia, these noble purposes saved the empire from abasement at the hands of the growing number of anti-imperialists at home

and abroad. "British seed" would make the desert "bloom as the rose," promised an officer, furnishing a fitting rebuke to "fluent decriers of their own country" who called empire "a thing of pitiless blood and iron." As in Egypt and
Punjab, explained Sykes in an official note, here too the British imperial ideal
was "not...conquest but...redemption." The development of Mesopotamia
offered proof of the queerly selfless and attractive nature of British imperialism: "Truly we are a remarkable people," Bell mused. "We save from destruction remnants of oppressed nations, laboriously and expensively giving them
sanitary accommodation, teaching their children, respecting their faiths," yet
remained cursed by subjects, who, nevertheless, "when left to themselves...flock
to our standards.... It's the sort of thing that happens under the British flag—
don't ask us why." The British presence was thus exempt from the sins ordinarily associated with an occupying regime. "It was interesting," said Montagu
knowingly in Parliament, "to compare British occupation in Mesopotamia with
German occupation in Belgium. (Hear, hear.)" Surveying the "the sound and
colour of the reviving world," Bell felt she was "really part of Mesopotamia and
not part of an army of occupation." Hogarth valiantly assured his son he was
"against imperialism" and was helping to attach the Middle East to the empire
only to prevent its occupation by anyone else. The point was not "painting
Mesopotamia red," caviled that arch-imperialist foreign secretary Lord Curzon
at the Central Asian Society, but "redeeming the country from anarchy." If the
Arabs appeared ungrateful for their deliverance, what better proof of Britons'
total selflessness as imperial improvers. Through the twenties, unabated Iraqi
intransigence was considered an "inscrutable visitation of divine wrath upon a
nation that presumed to aid a fallen land to rise phoenix-like from the dead
ashes of its past." Even domestic criticism of Britain's Middle East policy was
deflated by the press's divagations on the resurrection of irrigating Babylonia
and its "benefit to the world." To be sure, some did see in Mesopotamia's future
"untold wealth"—its projected bounty of cotton, wheat, and perhaps oil—more
material redemption of British sacrifices. (By the same logic, the state's actual
parsimony toward development projects was later justified by the unexpectedly
pessimistic official postwar assessment of Mesopotamia's agricultural potential.) But even this seemingly selfish hope was no stain on the imperial conscience, insisted one officer; for, rather than proof of "motives of 'land-grabbing'
and Imperialism in its worst aspects," the "large reward" for Mesopotamia's
"rescuers" would be but minor recompense for their redemption of the empire
from centuries of (equally selflessly) policing the Middle Eastern seas and inad-
vertently abetting the Turks' truly rapacious imperialism. That India was the
primary agent of Mesopotamia's technological recovery only redoubled faith in
the unadulterated altruism of the British Empire. Indians' monumental efforts

proved, according to one exultant parliamentary paper, that they knew Britain ruled for their good and "not to exploit India for the benefit of this country." John Stuart Mill's version of empire had been vindicated, announced the London *Times*: Britain's was a "steadfastly progressive rule...the most beneficent in design and execution known in the history of mankind." Through the Mesopotamia campaign, Britain's beneficence toward India had been "blessed not only to the giver and the receiver, but to the world at large." To the end of the mandatory period, officials held that "in the welter of world politics and imperial problems the establishment of the new State of Iraq...'shines like a good deed in a naughty world,'" pursued consistently by the Coalition, Conservative, Labour, and National governments. It showed the world that the British grudged no people their freedom, that the empire was not for the sake of "imperial domination or material rewards" but for the good of others.[15]

To some, the project of reclaiming Mesopotamia for the West and the world invested the entire war with meaning. As in the past, at this epochal juncture, Mesopotamia held "the key to the whole world's future." In an essay much circulated among the troops, Bell described how the revived ancient markets of Iraq would "add immeasurably to the wealth of a universe wasted by war," besides providing new fields for European industry. "Nowhere, in the war-shattered universe," she held, "can we begin more speedily to make good the immense losses sustained by humanity." She effused in letters home about the government's unprecedented strides in "the making of a new world." While those at home were "over-strained," "we are out of that atmosphere here." Candler too found it "comforting to think that the war which had let loose destruction in Europe was bringing new life to Mesopotamia," a sentiment echoed closely in the *Guardian* too. This promise of global salvation was further proof of the empire's true purpose. An officer confided to a fellow combatant,

> All this show of ours out here is nothing in itself.... It's a beginning
> of something that will materialise a hundred or two hundred or a
> thousand years hence. We are the great irrigating nation and that's
> why we're here now.... We'll fix this land up...and move the wheels
> of a new humanity. Pray God, yes—a new humanity! One that
> doesn't stuff itself silly with whisky and beef and beer and die of
> apoplexy and high explosives.

Mesopotamia proved that the British could still *civilize*, if they had lost civilization itself. The "great enterprise of the regeneration of Palestine" was also "one of the few fine and imaginative products of the war," vouched the *Guardian*. In 1926, Colonial Secretary Leo Amery was still speaking of the "great development in

Iraq which will bring us some recompense for the great sacrifices we made in the Great War." In what has become a painfully familiar pattern, the avowed objective of war shifted and evolved as the war unfolded, becoming more glorious and selfless the more tragedy struck. Hence in part did the myth of a uniquely "peaceable kingdom" triumph immediately after the war. Mesopotamia was central to the postwar shift in imperial propaganda, described by John Mackenzie, from militarism to more idealistic economic themes that preserved empire's respectability.[16]

In this mix of heady rhetoric and mundane technocratic activity lies the essence of that moment in the twentieth-century formation of British identity when, as Robert Colls has put it, "The traditions of an ancient realm were held aloft to signify Englishness to the world, while behind all that it was understood that modern men ran the business." The return of a king to the Baghdad of Haroun was one thing, noted one sentimental American a decade later:

> But in the shadows beside the dais stand men in green-brown
> uniforms—blue-eyed men of a tribe that had no standing in Arabia
> [before]. . . . Angles they call these men, and they are not like the other
> conquerors who flowed into Iraq with sword and torch in the days
> whose record may be read in the ash piles along the Tigris. They are
> children—fussy children—eternally worried over the removal of
> rubbish, the "improvement" of roads and bridges that for hundreds
> of years served our ancestors . . . the disciplining of the police force
> and what not.

Efficient as these imperial professionals were, they were not George Orwell's famously lamented dull "clerks" of the 1920s, the "well-meaning, over-civilized men, in dark suits" prefiguring his nightmare vision of bureaucracy. The Royal Air Force (RAF) regime in Iraq was, as we shall see, the one spot in the empire held to combine the adventure and romance of the past with the efficiency of the new order (however much it did in fact aspire to totalitarian surveillance). The sentimental American concluded: "The flying carpet of the Cairo air-mail has come to rest in the landing field beyond Hinaidi and a sergeant is inspecting its hot motors. . . . Who can say that romance is dead in a spot such as this?" Nor was it the case in the Middle East that Orwell's "older officials, who had known more spacious days" were "writhing impotently" under these changes, for the old agents remained in command, while the new joiners were unequivocally "young men of spirit," inspired by the legends of the amateurs and their recuperative vision of technology and even bureaucracy. It was Bell's unflagging ardor, Vita Sackville-West diagnosed on her visit, that made the drudgery of their mission seem like zeal. Indeed, so warmly did the light of hope glow in Mesopotamia in the dimly lit postwar world that soldiers at a loose end sought transfer there to find an assuredly constructive role. In 1920, weary from four years in France and Belgium, the legendary career of the young John Glubb was launched when he read "with something of a throb of excitement" of the need for volunteers in Iraq—the prospect of more fighting "and all the excitement and interest of adventure and a strange country." Likewise, James Mann, who became a political officer in Iraq, reasoned with his mother, "If one takes the Civil Service, or the Bar, or Literature, or Politics, or even the Labour movement, what can one do that is constructive? Here on the other hand I am constructing the whole time." Arabia's incandescent appeal was, if anything, more catholic after the war. The Middle East offered an update on the traditional image of the solitary British officer managing a vast area by sheer force of personality; it was not only the usually cited nostalgia but actual persistence that made that trope so central to interwar cinematic and literary projections of British character.[17]

Thus, after four years of hedging on the fate of Mesopotamia, Britain ultimately insisted on postwar control, despite American opinion, as restitution for its sacrifices for the country's development. A war of conquest was reconfigured as an international development effort (forgetting the empire's own historical role in the region's poverty). The wartime development effort laid the groundwork for the trusteeship imperialism of the 1920s—empire as a kind of "training academy" for modern political and economic organization—quieting some critics of empire. The occupying army did set about building bridges and railways, creating an irrigation department, draining marshes, and so on, but largely to serve army needs and make the nomad terrain legible to the emerging imperial state—as the *Guardian* noted exactingly when the cost of these works was finally debited to the new Iraqi state in apparent violation of the spirit of imperial development. In any case, many of these projects were quickly abandoned after the war, partly because of financial stringency and partly because military needs dictated another use of technology in the region: counterinsurgency, of which more in Part II, along with the new generation of critics it launched.[18]

A Culture for Redeemers

The image of Mesopotamia as an outlet for the constructive energies of the surviving young men of spirit derived partly from the legends constructed around agents who made their name in the war—not least because it was they who, morphing into local administrators, manned the ship of the Middle East's "reawakening." They were also present in full force at the Paris Peace Conference and the Cairo Conference of 1921, where the fates of the former provinces of the Ottoman Empire were finally settled, and soon found themselves drawn through the usual informal contacts into top imperial administrative positions as the British government launched its formal imperial career in the region. Thus, for instance, Hubert Young joined the Foreign Office through the good offices of George Lloyd, whom he had known in Mesopotamia and found again in Port Said en route to Bombay. After serving as governor there, Lloyd reappeared in Egypt as high commissioner. Lawrence, having become something of a minor legend among the elite and "the catch" of the London social season "long before Lowell Thomas made him famous," thanks to local Allied and British officials' reports to governments and families at home, found himself advising the cabinet at Curzon's invitation and assisting Churchill with his plans for a new Middle East Department at the Colonial Office. Along with Hogarth, Cecil, Aubrey Herbert, and others, he rallied the community of agents to petition the government to create the department, and ultimately, he, Meinertzhagen, Young, and Reader Bullard staffed it. Churchill wanted them partly for the aura of legitimacy they would bring to its work. Meinertzhagen testifies (perhaps with some jealousy) that by this time, Churchill's attitude toward Lawrence amounted to "hero-worship" (he certainly figured among Churchill's *Great Contemporaries* [1937]). Bullard later served as Jeddah consul. After a stint at the Foreign Office, the Arab Bureau's Kinahan Cornwallis served as adviser to the Ministry of Interior in Iraq. The political officer Captain Geoffrey Stephenson joined the India Office to liaise with the civil administration in Iraq; the Arab Bureau's William Ormsby-Gore joined the Colonial Office under Bonar Law; Robert Graves (senior) was at the War Office before rejoining Wyndham Deedes (military attaché) in Constantinople, and the latter was later appointed chief secretary in Palestine; Harold Dickson became political agent in Bahrein, then consulted at the Colonial Office before being exiled to Bikaner, finally serving in Bushire and Kuwait; St. John Philby worked with the India and Foreign offices before serving successively in the Iraq and Transjordan administrations; Bell, as Percy Cox's "Oriental Secretary" in Iraq, exercised an "excessive and almost mesmeric effect" on her chief's judgment. In short, agents and officers from the Middle East campaigns were catapulted to fame and distinction as the new occupiers of the highest positions of government in the empire. Arnold Wilson observed proudly that "the governments of all the British territories on the coast of East Africa" were by 1932 "in the hands of men who won their spurs either in Mesopotamia or ... Palestine."[19]

If the imperial ideal and chivalric values survived the war, it was in great part thanks to these agents' legends as redeemers from the desert embodying not only the hope that the past might survive but that the future might hold greater promise. Their association with the romantic events and locales of the campaigns, the modernist imagery of the RAF–ruled postwar Middle East, and the accompanying Faustian charge of remaking the cradle of civilization were central to their legend, as was constant news of fresh desert exploits by Philby, the political officer Bertram Thomas, and others. In other words, the development idea was one public discourse about the redemptive conquest of Arabia; ideas of heroism provided another, related mode of engagement with the region. If official circles saw in Lawrence an expert who had, for instance, dealt with the practical matters of setting up Faisal's government in Damascus, his popular image was grounded in altogether more poetic notions—the tinge of the prophetic that came to inflect development rhetoric itself. His role in the revolt was hailed "a spiritual even more than a physical exploit." Indeed, his "spiritual equipment overrode the ordinary needs of flesh and blood," pronounced Walter Stirling; he was "utterly divided from his contemporaries," as much by an unmistakable "puckish quality." He had joined the desert's cast of genies and knights and found among them a route to the epic glory of which he had long dreamt. If his political capital lay in his status as an "expert" on the region on whose development postwar society had, at least rhetorically, staked its imperial redemption, his cultural capital lay in another discourse of redemption—a discourse about the redeemer *from* the desert, which built on the image of the old imperial adventure-hero even as it envisioned a new kind of modernist prophet, imparting a heroic aura to the development notion itself.[20]

Despite—or perhaps because of—his association with an alleged "sideshow," Lawrence emerged the only unanimously adored action-hero of the war. His figure thus looms over what follows, but, as we shall see, he was not the only Arabist agent to acquire popular fame; this remains a story of a broader community and its collective place in the British cultural imagination. The need for a hero aside, postwar British society also possessed the means of generating a mythic hero of gigantic proportions, thanks to the new dramatizing media and the rapid growth of competitive mass-circulation dailies fostering a taste for the sensational. Lawrence was "the first media legend."[21] Besides dramatic popular media, the massively enlarged academic societies and broadened social networks of the literary world also underwrote the emergence of Arabist celebrities. Their celebrity was, in short, a product of the increasingly inclusive mass democratic public sphere.

Lowell Thomas's hugely popular lecture and slideshow about Lawrence broke show business records. Millions saw it in 1919, including the royal family, the cabinet, Allenby, Faisal, Philby, and Lawrence himself (apparently frequently). The show moved from Covent Garden to Albert Hall and toured internationally. His narrative of the revolt also appeared in serial form in *Strand Magazine* in 1920 under the title, "The Uncrowned King of Arabia." Lawrence's media-created popularity guaranteed him all the press space he needed to further substantiate it with his own journalism (on which more later). The Thomas show, the 1923–1924 production of James Elroy Flecker's *Hassan*, and the exhibit of Eric Kennington's portraits for *Seven Pillars of Wisdom* (the Leicester Gallery catalogue carried essays by Lawrence and George Bernard Shaw) merged with a postwar genre of films, fictional and semidocumentary, that portrayed the Palestine war with a "boys' adventure stories" approach. Indeed, boys' papers were full of Lawrence, idolized as the "Silent Sentinel of the Sand" and the "Man Who Won a War on His Own," inspiring endless imitation in juvenile fiction. Desert battle emerged as a major cinematographic theme, offering a reassuring vision of a hero and a region preserving the values lost to the West—austere, organic, chivalrous, virile, individual, timeless—a trend that culminated in Alexander Korda's ill-fated 1930s attempt to make a film about Lawrence with the help of Lawrence's brother Arnold, Siegfried Sassoon, and Stirling. Cinematographic expeditions to Iraq were also common—drawn as much by the Arabian mystique as by the mystique of a forbidden, RAF-controlled space in a period generally marked by a passion for planes and travel. There was, to visitors, "romance in this demonstration of the power of modern inventions which are able to conquer the vast open spaces of the world, as yet little known to civilised man." The 1920s also saw the emergence of an entire genre of "sheikh" films—launched with Rudolph Valentino in *The Sheik* (1921)—that romanticized the desert and Arab virility and fed the Lawrence mania. *The Sheik* was based on a 1919 novel by Edith Hull, the most successful among a "myriad of desert-passion novels" of the period. Its sales surpassed those of "all the contemporary best-sellers lumped together," with 108 editions appearing between 1919 and 1923 in Britain alone. (In Virginia Woolf's *Night and Day* (1920), Mary Datchet's daydreams of herself astride a camel in the desert and her love Ralph Denham commanding "a whole tribe of natives" invoked a romantic cliché). Robert Graves thought it a "cosmic joke" that Lawrence's legend had become entwined with this pulp genre, that booksellers had to explain that *Revolt in the Desert*, his 1927 abridgment of *Seven Pillars*, was not a sequel to "Son of the Sheik." Despite—or perhaps because of—the confusion, "no book within memory has been greeted … with such frank enthusiasm by every sort and condition of reader," remarked Cox. It generated a subgenre of works on "war in the desert" (the title of John Glubb's 1960 memoir).[22]

Indeed, many agents shared Lawrence's publishing success. Bell's articles were ubiquitous, although the public came to know her best through her letters, published posthumously in 1927. The publisher's advertisement quoted the *Daily News*'s description of her as sharing with Lawrence "the distinction of having stepped like a figure in a legend into an age of prose." Arnold Wilson published five books and countless articles on the Middle East and lectured frequently. Fame brought him election to the Athenaeum Club and exposure to a more eclectic society than his old United Services Club. He became a member of Parliament in 1933 and edited *The Nineteenth Century and After*. After gathering intelligence among the Kurds in 1919, Leonard Woolley returned to archaeology (remaining, of course, in close touch with Bell), until his appointment as Syrian inspector of antiquities. Along the way, he emerged a great popularizer of archaeology in a society increasingly mesmerized by its position as the inheritor of the ancient empires in the region. The region firmly in Britain's grasp, this was the period of the great discoveries in Egypt and Iraq. Woolley's *Ur of the Chaldees* (1929) went through eight editions by 1935 and was the first archaeology book to appear as a Pelican paperback. In his books, in the press, on the radio, and at countless clubs, universities, and institutions demanding illustrated talks on "Abraham's city," he turned spectacular archaeology into mass entertainment. Philby was a sort of lesser Lawrence, publishing in popular dailies multipart, eyewitness accounts of Arabia, including his crossing of the Rub al-Khali and dramatic conversion to Wahhabism in the early 1930s. His *Heart of Arabia* was rated most popular of travelers' tales in the fall of 1922, and his *Arabia of the Wahabis* was in "keen demand" late in 1928 (along with Vita Sackville-West's book on her Persian journey and Eldon Rutter on the holy cities of Arabia). He was praised for writing not as "an objective historian but as an enthusiastic advocate." Fame landed him a major lectureship at Oxford in 1932. Journalism also absorbed the efforts of the former agents Owen Tweedy and Philip Graves, whose work could be found in the *Fortnightly Review, Atlantic Monthly, Daily Telegraph, Daily Mail, Times, Financial Times*, and elsewhere. Alan Dawnay published poetry; Herbert, his war memoirs. The field was lucrative enough to elicit belated publications of prewar journeys, including Norman Bray's and Douglas Carruthers's. The overlap of literary talent with an attraction to Arabia did not pass unremarked: "It is surely phenomenal," observed Cox, that "so many individuals should have proved to possess the inspiration and marked literary talent which have been displayed in turn by Philby, Lawrence, Eldon Rutter, and...Bertram Thomas." A *Times* editor mused on Philby's illustrated series on his "Ride into the Unknown," which elicited dozens of readers' letters, that "something in the very air of Arabia...breeds style." Leonard Woolf's review of *Revolt in the Desert* likewise concluded with what was fast becoming a cliché, that "Arabia itself...made the style."[23]

Their fame was also spread through the scholarly societies many of them found congenial as spaces preserving something of the rarefied atmosphere that

had distinguished their knowledge before it, and they, had become public property. The Middle East became the cynosure of societies interested in Asia, particularly the Central Asian Society (founded at the start of the century and
denoted "Royal" in 1931), where there was "a great rejoicing...over the influx of
new members from Mespot," according to one political officer who had joined
the India Office. Membership swelled from 132 in 1918 to 1,082 in 1928. Besides
generals, airmen, "pro-Turks," and sundry academics, the society absorbed a
bevy of agents, including Bray, George Buchanan, Meinertzhagen, Philby,
Valentine Chirol, Gilbert Clayton, Cornwallis, Deedes, Henry Dobbs, Gregson,
Pierce Joyce, Lloyd, Henry McMahon, J. C. More, Ormsby-Gore, Alfred Parker,
Arnold Wilson, Wingate, Bullard, Cox, Dickson, G. F. Eadie, C. J. Edmonds,
E. W. C. Noel, Tweedy, and others. By 1925, the imprecision of the term "Central
Asia" had become something of a running joke. Philby pointed out the irony
that "Arabia, the extreme south-westerly corner of the great continent...and
geologically more African than Asiatic...has recently...become the *pièce de
résistance*...of the intellectual meals so lavishly supplied by a Society which owes
its inception to the Russian and other nineteenth-century bogeys." He welcomed
the new focus on Arabia as a signal of the society's sympathy with the "war on
luxury." So popular were some of the stories the newcomers recounted that on
the occasion of Bertram Thomas's lecture on his crossing of the Rub al-Khali, "it
was impossible for all to get into the lecture-hall." More than ever, this community was beset by the sense that old-style exploration—alone, by camel, and at
the explorer's own cost—was over, especially after Thomas's feat, with which,
Lawrence ominously declared, "we know the whole earth." With this and the
changes wrought by the arrival of the airplane and "the ever-present appetite for
the sensational," lamented Hogarth, "the interest and the means available for
promoting exploration are being diverted...to...'stunts.'" He and other agents
sighed over the democratic seizure of Arabia from their hands, the cars and aircraft it depended on puncturing the "air of mystery" that had first lured them to
it. Nevertheless, they carried the torch along to the Royal Geographical Society,
where they expounded on the constructive results of the war in the Middle East,
the civilizational promise of air control, and, despite their nostalgia, the real
gains in geographical knowledge about the region. The same set of experts circulated between these and other venues creating and fulfilling a demand for
information about the Middle East. A colonel marveled after a General Staff
officer's lecture at the Royal United Service Institute on Britain's responsibilities in the Middle East that the very next day the Central Asian Society would
meet in the same building to hear Robert Brooke-Popham of the RAF speak on
the Middle Eastern air route—the very route which, he pointed out, made it possible for personnel in the Middle East to join the lecture circuit.[24]

The agents' visibility spawned other nonfictional genres on the Middle East campaigns. Besides a raft of histories of the ancient Middle East, particularly of the dynamic fortunes of Baghdad, there were captivity narratives about Kut and the postwar rebellion, as well as both book- and article-length memoirs by soldiers. Many of the latter were directly inspired by Lawrence, or at least found a market because of him—Lawrence's mention of a soldier in *Seven Pillars* or brief appearance in the soldier's narrative could provide its entire justification. For instance, S. C. Rolls, who, like Lawrence, had kept a record of his experiences as an armored-car driver with the intention of writing a book afterward, opens his account with a lengthy description of himself taken from *Seven Pillars*. He then cites Lawrence's disclaimer of his ability to do full credit to the "un-named rank and file" as the "final incentive" for his book. Collectively, his and other soldiers' works reinforced a familiar set of ideas about Arabia and were marked by a taste for fabulous and Biblical literary cadences. Many took advantage of the campaigns' classical scenic structure in their telling—victory in three acts—even mixing fact and fiction. Conscripted soldiers on the Western front drew on the theatrical idiom to explain their wartime roles (Fussell tells us), but the Middle Eastern theater felt more intensely and less ironically stagelike, offering an ending, a structure, and meaning readily transformable into explicitly entertaining war narratives.[25]

The mania for Arabia permeated other aspects of postwar popular culture, from fashion and décor to music and tourism, unleashing a torrent of imitative tourist tales in which atmospheric and topographical deceptions, together with existential musings, remained standard tropes. Many tourists came via the Nairn Company's convoys, a commercial service made possible by the fact that "by 1918 there were many people who had some experience of living, travelling and fighting in the desert, including the use of motor cars." (Moreover, "the mere presence of British aircraft" allowed tourists to feel "secure" in the "unending waste.") Bell inspired a train of visitors to Baghdad—including her occultist nephew George Trevelyan—although she reserved special contempt for the "silly females, all with introductions to me." Many of these imitators traveled by the light of *Revolt in the Desert*—literally, "*In the Steps of Lawrence*," as one proclaimed—as Edwardians had by Doughty, hoping an Arabian "escapade" would satisfy their literary ambition. Veteran agents were selective in their praise for such works, preferring those inflected by the ethos that had inspired their own work. "Not more than one-tenth" of those thousands of books, wagered Wilson, "have that peculiar literary charm which is the hallmark of sympathetic observers who, by long residence and habit of mind, have not only much to tell, but much to teach their readers." The genre—and pretensions, at least, to such charm—exploded to an extent provoking mockery: in his own memoir, Major Jarvis of Palestine fame sneered at the much-vaunted "type" of the administrator sympathizing passionately with the nomad's "eleventh-century outlook" and at the copycat travel writer looking for "thrilling adventures among Lawrence's Arabs." Both, he scoffed, were "quite as expert at fiction as at travel autobiographies," projecting the desert as a romantic, lawless space even when it was under police rule—an irony whose true proportion will become clearer in Part II. Indeed, many of these literary myrmidons worked into their books novelistic descriptions of first meetings with Lawrence, a mysterious, bedraggled, prophet-like character, as instantly recognizable as the hero of any popular adventure series. Liddell Hart remarked, "If Conan Doyle had been born a generation later he would have found in Lawrence an apt model from which to create Sherlock Holmes."[26]

In fact, encounters with Lawrence were equally ubiquitous in fiction. In 1929, informed by Lawrence's *Army Quarterly* essay, John Buchan made him the hero of *The Courts of the Morning* (originally "Far Arabia"), which featured the guerrilla-style exploits of Sandy Arbuthnot, whose real-life referent now morphed, even physically, from Herbert to Lawrence (whom Buchan likely met in 1916). Lawrence also appeared as the all-knowing Private Meek in Bernard Shaw's *Too True to Be Good* (besides advising Shaw on military vocabulary). He also inspired the character Aubrey Bagot, a former RAF officer struggling to come to terms with the horrors of the war. Henry Williamson, who was fascinated by Lawrence's famous mind-reading ability, used him as the basis for the poet-aviator Major Manfred in *The Gold Falcon* (1933), and D. H. Lawrence spoofed him in *Lady Chatterley's Lover* (1928). W. H. Auden's *The Orators* (1932), and indeed, much of his work in the 1930s, including "Journal of an Airman," was indebted to T. E. Lawrence. Cecil Day Lewis also used a Lawrence figure in his early mystery novel *Shell of Death* (1936) (published pseudonymously). Yeats's "Stories of Michael Robartes and His Friends," in *A Vision* (1925), was heavily influenced by both Doughty and Lawrence: Yeats's persona, Michael Robartes, who has lived with an Arab tribe and led it in wars, confesses, "Lawrence never suspected the nationality of the old Arab fighting at his side." These fascinations had as much to do with Lawrence's role in Arabia as his role in the RAF, which he joined in 1922 under the name John Hume Ross, until his unshakable fame forced his 1927 rechristening as T. E. Shaw, in homage to one of his greatest literary patrons. Writers from Yeats to Kipling to Wells, like Lawrence, believed airpower would restore romance to war—some of them had for decades. It was Lawrence's magic combination of desert and air that appealed. Indeed, a novel about the air war on the Western front, written at the behest of and dedicated to Henry Williamson, sexes up that comparatively lackluster story by putting at its center the powerful Flying Camel, a fighter plane whose liability to spin out could be tamed only by the pilot who took to it "like an Arab," flying by "volition [rather] than conscious control" by drawing on "the all-pervasive human mind," since, the novel explains, "Reality" is only "in the mind."[27]

Simply put, "Lawrence" sold. The name's career became entwined with the explosion of postwar publishing. Lawrence submitted chapters of *Seven Pillars* to support the literary magazine of his indigent new friend and fellow veteran Robert Graves. He allowed Graves to write a popular account of him for Jonathan Cape, which established Graves on sound financial footing. Cape's successful establishment can be traced directly to his publication of *Revolt in the Desert*, which raised his profits more than tenfold in 1927.[28] The *Spectator* sought Lawrence out for book reviews. A publisher asked him to translate the *Odyssey*, for "here, at last was a man who could make Homer live again—a man of action who was also a scholar and who could write a swift and graphic English." (Lawrence did not dispute this assessment.) In the United States, where it was published under his own name, the book was a phenomenon. Frederic Manning's publisher embellished *Her Privates We* (1929) with quotes by Lawrence, and Lawrence put Cape on to publishing Roy Campbell's work in 1924. Through Lawrence's intervention on behalf of "young poets" seeking an affordable reissue of *Arabia Deserta*, Doughty was resurrected as a prophet of his age, his work finally placed "where some of us wanted it to be, but hardly expected to see it." Lawrence also became "one of the most significant private patrons of contemporary artists in Britain," in the words of one scholar, using his influence to place their work in national collections. Partly out of an altruistic notion to support struggling young artists, he involved Eric Kennington, Augustus John, William Roberts, Frank Dobson, Wyndham Lewis, and Paul Nash in the production of *Seven Pillars*, creating a kind "medieval guild."[29]

Thus, the Middle East brought Lawrence what he had sought all along—a launch into the literary firmament. E. M. Forster finished *A Passage to India* (1924) under the influence of *Seven Pillars* and adopted Lawrence's suggestions for "Dr. Woolacott." In *Good-bye to All That* (1929), Graves warmly acknowledged his many financial and literary debts to Lawrence, including his appointment as a teacher in Cairo. He included these acknowledgments in a book written to make "a lump of money," partly because people "like hearing about T. E. Lawrence." Lawrence also gave Graves critical feedback on *I, Claudius* (1933), for which he was thanked in the preface. Graves's and Laura Riding's pseudonymously published *No Decency Left* (1932) incorporated an "autogyro of the future" designed by Lawrence. Yeats elected him to the Irish Academy of Letters, explaining, "You are among my chief of men, being one of the few charming and gallant figures of our time, and as considerable in intellect." He had coveted "no man...as Aircraftsman Shaw." Eventually Lawrence's contacts also included T. S. Eliot, Joseph Conrad, Ezra Pound, Thomas Hardy, Edward Elgar, Edmund Blunden, Harley Granville-Barker, and others. So wide a swathe did he cut through literary society that Graves claimed to be able to identify those mimicking his gestures and speech. Lawrence produced *Seven Pillars*, his attempt at "an English fourth" on the titanic level of "The Karamazovs, Zarathustra and Moby Dick," in the bosom of this community. They were the audience he wrote for; hence the limited 1922 subscribers' edition of *Seven Pillars*, his intense circulation of the draft of his work on RAF life, *The Mint*, and his indifference to *Revolt in the Desert*, which was intended for mass consumption. His fellow agent and war veteran Robin Buxton took the lead in printing *Seven Pillars* after Bernard Shaw, Hogarth, Kipling, Bell, and others prevailed on him to publish it. They, Lawrence's comrades, the king, Hardy, Sassoon, Wells, Stanley Baldwin, and select others received the rare copies of what became "the decade's most talked about and least available book." Whatever posterity's estimate, contemporary literary savants from Churchill to Wells to Forster considered it an unequivocal masterpiece and an instant classic of English literature—Wells ranking it with *Robinson Crusoe* and *The Pilgrim's Progress*. Buchan called Lawrence the best prose writer of his day and owned he would have followed him "over the edge of the world." It was also in this literary company that Lawrence eventually grew disenchanted with the book's epic style and began work on *The Mint* as a more explicitly modernist work. On his death in 1935, the venerable London bookshop Foyles hosted a luncheon for 350 of his admirers, mainly authors, literary men, and pressmen.[30]

This community welcomed Lawrence as a kindred spirit. To be sure, he stood out as a heroic and intriguing figure—that was his social capital (whatever his avowed awe of artists)—but he was also one among a group of artists and reluctant soldier-heroes coming to terms with the war. If the popular Lawrence legend provided reassurance of continuity with the past, his own artistic investment was in depicting the disillusionment that so gripped his peers; in a sense, as an individual drawn to Arabia by a somewhat precocious disenchantment with modern European civilization, he had anticipated them. Though *Seven Pillars* was an epic full of heroic, individual action otherwise absent from the memory of the Great War, it also told the story of a hero's bitter disillusionment with the duplicity of his country; it is this tragic element that makes the book unmistakably *modern* and yet even more of a romance.[31] Lawrence was visited by nightmares, which he recognized as a symptom of being unable to "get away from the war" that he shared with Graves and Sassoon. He was hooked on "war books." His own was accepted by the literary world as part of the emerging war literature but one that fit awkwardly. The

Bloomsbury novelist David Garnett, who would edit Lawrence's letters, considered it "the only big book to come out of the war; the only thing to which my generation can point with certainty," despite the fact that it was "a freak in literature, a freak by virtue of its subject & the character of its author, & the nature of his achievement." Nevertheless, Sassoon was grateful "that a great war-narrative (& criticism) has been written by one who is the same sort of human being as [his initials:] SS." While Lawrence speculated that Sassoon would have written in a very different vein had he served in Arabia, Graves pointed out that that war was so "romantically appealing" that it was perhaps fortunate Sassoon, Wilfred Owen, Blunden, and the others had wound up in France. Lawrence's was a work that expressed postwar disillusionment but not the emblematic experiences of the war, which were tightly bound to the Western front. Its portrait of a reluctant hero expressed the "generation gap" but not the *experience* of the generation. (Perhaps for this reason, in it alone do we find an explicit attempt to deal with the "taboo" subjects of the war—the actual act of killing and sexuality on the front—a frankness perhaps licensed by the fantastic Middle East setting.) Lawrence's books evoked a vision of redemption from the troubled spirit of the age. Pondering his notes of *Seven Pillars*, H. M. Tomlinson strove to portray in *All Our Yesterdays* (1930) the sort of thing he felt had happened to Lawrence: "The evil that others had done caught you, & you faced it for them—was [sic] crucified." "There you are," he wrote of *The Mint*, "with the ruthless mind of this younger generation, regarding the wreckage of a world ruined by the last of the Victorians … and some scruple keeps you from sorting it out for us, as you could all right." It was a book "the young men" would instantly recognize and "the old in mind & obsolete" rail against. He beseeched Lawrence, then stationed in India, "Come over & help us!" While symbolizing the continued validity of traditional notions of heroism, Lawrence's legend was also identified with postwar forces of change and distanced from the discredited elements of the old order that were blamed for the blunders of the war.[32]

The web of private friendships Lawrence formed with the elites who gathered beneath his umbrella of fame formed an important part of the literary public sphere. Indeed, they were public relationships from the outset. Witness the many publications dedicated to him—besides the obvious literary homages to him and his writing—perhaps with an eye on the cash value of his name: Frederic Manning's new edition of his 1909 *Scenes and Portraits* (1930), including a new piece for T. E. Shaw, "Apologia Dei"; F. L. Lucas's *Cécile* (1930); Graves's "The Clipped Stater" (1929); a 1927 collection of Forster's short stories, including again a story especially for Lawrence; even Liddell Hart's *Ghost of Napoleon* (1934), which is also heavily, if silently, indebted to Lawrence's strategic thinking. Moreover, rarefied though this literary world was, it was not self-contained: he reached it through his existing affiliations with the political, diplomatic, bureaucratic, and military worlds, to which it was socially bound, particularly since the war had elided the distinction between the civilian and military worlds, producing a postwar literature ineluctably bound to the trenches. The editor of the *Army Quarterly*, which carried his essay in its first issue, was none other than Guy Dawnay. Lawrence's literary agent, Raymond Savage, had served on Allenby's staff (and authored a biography of Allenby soon after). Lawrence, along with Faisal, first met E. M. Forster at a lunch in 1921, the year Forster himself became an imperial servant in princely India— although their paths might have crossed during the war when Forster was in Alexandria with the Red Cross. John Maynard Keynes observed him intimately at the Peace Conference. Buchan, fellow author, former director of information, and friend of the prime minister, would eventually secure his entry into the RAF. Edward Marsh, Churchill's private secretary, introduced him to Sassoon. After a dinner at All Souls', he met Graves, whose poetry he knew and alongside whose brother, Philip, he had served in Cairo. Now, Graves's neighbor was the India-returned imperial critic and (after 1923, ex-) Methodist chaplain Edward Thompson, whose experiences ministering to the troops in the Middle East campaigns earned him the Military Cross and put him in a position to advise Edmund Candler in the writing of the classic war account *The Long Road to Baghdad* (1919), besides netting him his own war memoirs, *The Leicestershires beyond Baghdad* (1919) and *Damascus Lies North* (1933); a novel, *These Men, They Friends* (1927); many appearances behind the podium; and a Syrian-raised American wife. (The draft of his dissenting view of the Indian "mutiny," *The Other Side of the Medal* (1925), was read by Graves, Sassoon, and Forster before publication by the Woolfs' Hogarth Press.) Lawrence's elite social world also merged with the humbler world of servicemen. He, at least, felt he "bridge[d] the classes"—the "writers and artists" who so intoxicated him and the "fellows in the service" with whom he felt so content. The idyllic, austere habitat provided by his cottage in Dorset, Cloud's Hill, was the site of many gatherings mixing literary types, tank corpsmen, and airmen—the latter two forming an elite among servicemen.[33]

Likewise, Bell's "personality," according to Sackville-West, "held together and made a centre for all those exiled Englishmen whose other common bond was their service for Iraq." Indeed, though Lawrence was perhaps the most warmly embraced, he certainly was not the only agent mixing with literati. Bell appears in Sackville-West's *Passenger to Teheran*, published in 1926 by Hogarth Press, as another instantly recognizable character: Lawrence's female analogue, as she is so often touted, "Desert Queen" to his "Uncrowned King of Arabia." Her friendship with Sackville-West and Harold Nicolson was renewed at the

Peace Conference and in Baghdad where Sackville-West also met Woolley and Faisal, whom she described as "prey to a romantic, an almost Byronic, melancholy." While she was there, Virginia Woolf, to whom Sackville-West had presented a copy of Flecker's *Hassan* on their first meeting in 1923, continually visualized her roaming the desert and sent along her typically quixotic musings on Bell's resemblance to an Aberdeen terrier. Bell was a "masterful woman," she wrote, who "makes you feel a little inefficient." (Bell would appear in *Three Guineas* [1938].) Desperate for distraction from the "Ottolines of the world," Woolf begged Sackville-West for letters describing her romantic journey, for, cried the famously haunted soul, "I've lived in Persia half my life." Her imagination supplied her with enough material for *Orlando* (1928), her *roman à clef* about Sackville-West, in which the eponymous hero(ine), cursed with an English love of landscape and a desperate itch to write, roams Turkey with gypsies and dons Turkish clothes to facilitate her gender-bending. Woolf's interest in the quirks of Britons in the Middle Eastern dreamscape was perhaps ensured by her husband's more practical participation in the founding of and subsequent debates about the mandate system, working closely with Philby, Ormsby-Gore, Lawrence, Arnold Toynbee, and others in 1920. (Not that he was immune to more romantic notions—his *Stories from the East* (1921) betrays a similar taste for pearls of Arab wisdom—acquired, literally, from Arab pearl divers in Ceylon—and a sense that "out there you live so near to life.") A combination of adventures in the air and the desert brought Philby further notice in the literary world, especially through Sir Wilfrid Blunt's nomad-style weekend parties in Sussex (until Blunt's death in 1922). The already well-connected Aubrey Herbert found greater, if posthumous, literary intimacy in the form of his son-in-law, Evelyn Waugh. Photographs of Leonard Woolley's work in the *Illustrated London News* drew Agatha Christie, desperately searching for an escape, to Iraq, where—unsurprisingly, given the affinities between mystery, archaeology, and Arabia—she found the excavators deeply engrossed in her recent crime novel *The Murder of Roger Ackroyd*. Woolley's wife, Katherine, soon published a novel, *Adventure Calls* (1928), owing much to Christie's style, and Christie married Woolley's assistant, Max Mallowan, after which she set many novels and stories in the region, dedicating them to the Woolleys. Kipling was another fan and friend of Woolley's, casting him as one of the Kut captives in his 1917 poem "Mesopotamia." Kipling also knew James Mann and George Lloyd, whose criticism of air control inspired his poem on the subject. Lloyd and Lawrence were also friends with Noel Coward. Through Lawrence, the Shaws met Philby; Alan Dawnay came to know Robert Graves; Sassoon wrote the foreword to Stirling's war memoir; and Charlotte Shaw, Forster, Augustus John, Manning, and Eric Kennington met Faisal and other Arab soldiers and came to know or know of Cox, Allenby, Hogarth, and Bray. The Shaws were among the stream of tourists to the Middle East, as was Kennington, who went to Jerusalem to draw portraits for *Seven Pillars* and meet Lawrence, who was then touring for the Colonial Office. And, of course, the Shaws knew Meinertzhagen through the latter's uncle Sidney Webb.[34]

To the literati, this community of Arabist agents offered a vision of the coming dawn, of modernist man and perception, as prefigured in many of their Edwardian works. In Lawrence, writes Samuel Hynes, they found "evidence that a literary, modern heroism was possible." His sensibility was modernist; his heroism, another scholar points out, a paradoxically impossible one, despite its successful evocation in films and juvenile fiction. Indeed, Lawrence himself had no personal faith in his deeds or in heroic action per se—or thus in the dream of a regenerated Babylonia. What he was really after, he claimed, was something deeper. Unlike Doughty, who was devoid of "sympathy," his aim was to grasp the "final unity." Though "finite minds" could only understand infinity as an "infinite series," he explained, in reality there was but one step: "There is only one element, which is the same as the sole source of energy." His book tried to express this heroic "metaphysics," and his peers felt it succeeded. David Garnett's father, the influential editor Edward Garnett, held that Lawrence's particular contribution as an artist was his "very *special*" and "new apprehension of things." "You are one of those writers," Manning wrote, "who...try to precipitate their thought and feeling into an instantaneous act. Having a sudden completeness of vision, complete in all its detail, you try to represent it, immediately, as you see it." The secret of his apparent omniscience, revealed in Robert Graves's biography as the uncanny product of "a small knowledge...in harmony with itself," became a veritable epistemological motto, appearing in as unlikely a context as Selfridge's column in the *Times* where it was promoted as the core of the department store's business ethic (along with the enthusiasm, courage, and endurance it also claimed to share with Lawrence). His mode of perception was part of the interwar "orthodoxy" inaugurated by Bergsonism and evident in Einstein's physics and stream-of-consciousness literature. Lawrence disavowed material goals, but his existential longings in fact echoed the epistemological underpinnings of the notion of developing a new Iraq from a fallen Mesopotamia—a total vision to be instantly precipitated into a material reality by visionary experts.[35]

Contemporaries linked this mode of perception even more explicitly than before to the Arabian backdrop. Frequently to be found in the Middle East, Hercule Poirot instantly "intuits the totality of the case," to borrow the words of Ernst Bloch. Yeats's efforts to suspend the will and make the mind automatic likewise found most dramatic expression in his poems on Arabia, particularly the autobiographical "The Gift of Harun al-Rashid" (1923). The recurring Michael Robartes, he explained, was based on a friend (an imaginary one) who had "lately returned from Mesopotamia where he has partly found and partly thought out much philosophy" with the help of certain Arab tribes. Arthur Conan Doyle turned obsessively to mysticism (notably in *The Land of Mist* [1925]), claiming that an "Arabian spirit," in his case Pheneas, communicated with him through his wife's automatic writing about the coming end of the old world and the dawn of a glorious new one. Misty Constantinople, an image of "the whole world spread out," appears in Virginia Woolf's *To the Lighthouse* (1927), whose moonlike landscape of ocean and sand morphs periodically into desert. In *Orlando*, too, critical confrontations with deep truth occur in a shimmering Constantinople. An airplane figures centrally in the novel's ending (as in much of Woolf's oeuvre), restoring belief in magic. *The Waves* (1931), perhaps most literally, dramatized the percolations of the universal mind, each consciousness streaming frictionlessly into the next. The mirage world of *Seven Pillars of Wisdom* participates in these works' invocation of an evanescent reality.[36]

Writers' admiration of Lawrence's special perception was thus inseparable from their fascinations with the Arabian backdrop of his fame. Aside from his confessed nihilism, his very moniker, "of Arabia"—which lived on, despite his habitual name changes ("Rarely has a territorial title, popularly conferred, made such an impression," noted Liddell Hart)—triggered visions of a sacrificial redeemer. His native qualities, the imperial architect Herbert Baker explained, had "deepened and matured in the solitude of the Arabian desert, ever the breeding place of saint and prophet." In a sermon on Lawrence's death, Reverend L. B. Cross directly compared him to Christ, and Lawrence's own self-deprecating comparisons to the Savior in *Seven Pillars* only strengthened the allusion, as others have noted. Buchan's Richard Hannay affirms this belief that cultural "purification" would come from the desert, that "when mankind is smothered with shams and phrases and painted idols a wind blows out of the wild to cleanse and simplify life." From renewed contact with the desert would come redemption from the West's forgetfulness of being, its deafness to the universal consciousness (the *spiritus mundi*). Its power made Lawrence's heroism possible. Liddell Hart closed his hagiographic biography with the crescendoing words: "The young men are talking, the young poets writing, of him in a Messianic strain—as the man who could, if he would, be a light to lead stumbling humanity out of its troubles.... He is the Spirit of Freedom come incarnate to a world in fetters." Lawrence's asceticism acquired a Dionysian spin. "He says himself that he hunts *sensation*—in the deeper sense of the word," explained Liddell Hart, for his philosophy was that "the more elemental you can keep sensations, the better you can feel them." Whether an ascetic or a hedonist in his own strict sense, he was a figure emerging from the desert to deliver a society chained to a discredited past and an impoverished present.[37]

Lawrence admittedly fed such expectations and associations by compulsively dressing as an Arab at social functions, to his later embarrassment. He was not, however, the only agent held up as a redeemer—whether in the form of restoration of the cradle of civilization or a new prophet, redemption *would* come from Arabia. In Iraq, an officer fascinated by the desert, its Biblical past, and Childers's *Riddle of the Sands* was convinced that Arnold Wilson was "a superman, and that the Second coming is very near at hand." (Perhaps in anticipation, he converted to Roman Catholicism in 1920.) Somewhat graspingly, perhaps, Philby pointed knowingly to the "strange coincidence" that he had turned fifty at Eve's Tomb in Jeddah, was born in the shadow of Adam's Peak in Ceylon, found his soul at Arafat, began the "decisive period" of his life at Qurnah in the shade of the "Tree of Knowledge of Good and Evil," and had seen Mecca and Najaf, the supposed burial place of Adam. He wondered if any other soul, living or dead, could claim to have seen all six of the recorded links with man's great common ancestor. Moreover, his birthday fell on the exact anniversary of the Crucifixion—perhaps itself "a portent."[38]

Perhaps unsurprisingly, given their willing adoption of the mantle of superman and redeemer, some agents later revealed a sympathy with Nazism, either eliding their pro-Arabism into anti-Semitism or seeing in Nazism an embodiment of the qualities of classlessness, Spartanism, and purposefulness that had drawn them to Arabia. For instance, Philby, initially leaning toward socialism and staunchly anti-imperialist, slipped toward fascism via his ardently anti-Jewish stance on Palestine (he was imprisoned in World War Two). On the other hand, the staunchly anticommunist Meinertzhagen (despite his uncle Webb), moved from hoping Jews might furnish a useful "worldwide secret service network" to enthusiastically endorsing Hitler, whom he met several times, and dismissing Zionism as Bolshevism. As secretary of the Conservative Junior Carlton Club after leaving government service, Bray also met (and, apparently, argued with) Hitler but considered allegations of his own fascist sympathies unjustified. In 1933, a former Jeddah clerk who was apparently "third-in-command" of Oswald Mosley's Fascists was threatened with prosecution under the Official Secrets Act for his pro-Saudi speeches. During the Second World War, at the mellowed age of fifty-one, and with perhaps a tacit nod to the late Lawrence, Arnold Wilson attempted to atone for his interwar fascist flirtations by joining the RAF (incidentally, inspiring the hero of Powell and Pressburger's "One of Our Aircraft is Missing" [1942]). Lawrence himself was at once democratic and elitist but was strikingly apolitical in his social reach, although it is perhaps not surprising that fascists like Henry Williamson saw much to admire in him (he was on his way to discuss politics with Williamson when he met with his fatal accident). Another intimate, Liddell Hart, also outspokenly admired the Italian Fascist regime. Some of this elective affinity goes back to common epistemological fascinations with Bergson and Nietzsche: Mosley's fascism was grounded in an antiempiricist, occultist view of knowledge, as one scholar has pointed out.[39]

Despite all this, it is important to recall that the critique of decadence as the historic nemesis of imperial greatness also had an older lineage and a more catholic political appeal. Socialists, too, were in search of redemption from the age of anxiety and saw in Lawrence a congenial fellow traveler. Counting him among those who "want to make this present world feel the fool it is," Wells promised him a copy of *The Open Conspiracy* (1928), which set forth his program for a global movement of visionaries who would lead humankind out of the moment of crisis and competition into a utopian, scientifically managed cosmopolis. Of course, socialists like Bernard Shaw notoriously found much to admire in fascism themselves, but the point is that all those dissatisfied with the present, particularly with the new, irretrievably mass, society saw hope in certain "personalities," and the Arabist agents, who had exercised such a profound influence over Arabia apparently by sheer "force of personality," thus possessed a particular appeal. Socialists fantasizing about the modern cosmopolis as much as conservatives longing for escape from modernity found in this band of experts who had launched the epochal effort to free and (re)develop the cradle of civilization advance news of redemption from the anomie and decadence of modern life.[40]

Thus, the association with Arabia ultimately mattered in the agents' public image not for its exotic appeal but for the particular vision of interwar Englishness it expressed, in which, again, lofty traditional rhetoric was wedded to reliance on the expertise of the modern man. On the one hand Lawrence was inscrutably oriental: "When one is tempted to accuse him of being unreasonable," wrote the indulgent Liddell Hart, "the echo of his own comment on the Arabs comes as answer—'Their minds work just as ours do, but on different premises...' T. E. could not have played the Arab so well unless he had made his mind Arab." Buchan defied anyone to understand him fully, for there was no brush fine enough to capture the subtleties of his mind, "no aerial viewpoint high enough to bring into one picture the manifold of his character." It was precisely this slipperiness that made him an obvious hero for a wide array of constituencies. But at the same time, Lawrence's lionizers, including Liddell Hart, insisted on his Englishness—as did Lawrence himself—building on older notions associating the desert with (English) liberty: while the desert's native inhabitants "usually lived in heaps," remarked Lawrence, it was "a part of pride with Englishmen to hug solitude." Lord Winterton, a fellow veteran, likewise held that life could be enjoyed only "in the desert and in this country." What Arabs and the English shared in equal measure, however, was a "gift of personality." To be Arab—or rather to be the kind of idealized Arab that no real Arab could be—was to be English in a glorious old manner. Philby compared the Wahhabis to the Puritans of Cromwell's day. Fascination with Bedouin chivalry was part of an effort to recuperate Europe's own. "We find, in the bed-ouin warrior," wrote Glubb, "something of that gallant humanity which thrills us in the pages of Homer." (Such comparisons did not risk invidiously oriental-izing Britain since these storybook Bedouin were a species apart from other Others.) As Arabia supplanted Greece as the most romantic backdrop for the enactment of Englishness, Lawrence emerged the Byronic figure of his time: he too was a guerrilla and an uncrowned prince of the people he had helped liberate, Graves pointed out. The *Daily News* insisted, "There has, probably, been no English soldier so astonishing in his character and circumstances since Byron was at Missolonghi," with whom he shared "the genius of litera-ture and...adventure."[41]

The "Lawrence myth" and the development notion together recuperated Britons' dearest convictions about themselves: their extraordinary ability to overcome hardship and keep their nation in the avant garde through pluck, wit, and amateur skill. Lawrence appealed partly as an outsider formed by exotic experiences but also as someone typically English, insofar as being English meant being original, eccentric, and "the mere wishing to be an Arabian betrays the roots of a quirk." He, like Doughty, was "at once typical of his race and pro-foundly *sui generis*." Edward Said rightly claims that in this period, "the Orientalist has become the representative man of his Western culture"; Lawrence and his colleagues were at once freaks and stereotypes of Englishness, at once inside and outside the nation—and the state, given their liminal func-tion as spies. Their image brought to the old formulas of heroism the new taste for unorthodox methods, suspicion of authority, and impatience with "red tape" noted by scholars. Hence, as we shall see, their centrality to the debate on state secrecy that emerged from public scrutiny of the failure of Middle Eastern development. It has been remarked that the spy emerged in the twentieth cen-tury as a kind of everyman hero for societies in which individuals feel alienated from the large organizations that dominate public life; this was particularly true in interwar Britain when a stirring mass democracy came face to face with its limited purchase on the state's activities and where a culture of gentlemanly reserve made the spy a peculiarly English professional. If Arabia was the space for the spy's spy, it was naturally Lawrence, the top spy in Arabia, who became *the* representative Englishman of his time.[42]

For all the attempts to deify him, Lawrence was entirely in tune with his times, whatever his own doubts on the matter. His fascination with Arabia was not idiosyncratic but part of a larger trend; his fascination with airpower as much as his longing for pastoral English life (while posted in India) were of a piece with the at once modernist and conservative visions of nation and empire in the period—fused in the dream of a restored, yet refitted, Mesopotamia. His asceticism was in tune with an emerging fascination with an ethic and aesthetic of austerity that stemmed as much from postwar disillusionment with technology and materialism as from an embrace of technology and modernism. His appeal was rather like that of his fellow imperial subject Mohandas Gandhi, with whom he on occasion compared himself. A photographer who chased him down explained, "You and Gandhi are the two people I want to take." Both were known for their struggles to subject the body to the mind, through fasting, sexual abstinence (perhaps perversion), and a Morris- and Ruskin-inspired absorption in craft—Gandhi looked backward to the spinning wheel, Lawrence forward to mechanical work at the RAF for the happiness of "complete emptiness of mind"—while at the same time creating for themselves a position at the center of the maelstrom of interwar British politics and culture. Both used their spaces of hermetic withdrawal as sites for the creation of a new kind of society: Gandhi's ashram; Lawrence's cottage. Both were described as impish, inscrutable, frail of physique but possessing unexpected endurance and power; both leapt to the heads of liberation movements abroad (Gandhi embarking originally from South Africa), and both went "native" in the process, basing their conversions on a claim to racial and cultural affinity. They may have been the two most famous exemplars of this heroic type (however unequal their legacies), but they were not *sui generis*; their intellectual genealogies and appeal were integral to this particular cultural moment.[43]

Gandhi and Lawrence shared something else: both were subject to increasingly paranoid speculations about their loyalty to the empire—as were the colonial stages across which they strode. Even the adventure fiction that Lawrence inspired took as its backdrop an Arabia at the mercy of worldwide conspiracy against the empire. The wartime and postwar hopes for imperial expiation through the development of Arabia, fed by fascination with the heroic exploits of Arabist agents, began to crumble almost from their inception, as British officialdom and the British public both confronted the idea at the heart of the fascination with Arabia: it was a place that belonged to no one, not even to the material world. Could such a place be trusted to remain quietly within the empire? With so much at stake—redemption itself—some early crystal-ball gazers foresaw Britain "approaching either our greatest political achievement *or* a catastrophic conflict [with] the Oriental world." The opening gambit of the massive Iraqi rebellion of 1920 may have been greeted with the complacent assurance that "those who know most" knew it meant nothing, but its tumultuous aftermath would blight that community with a sclerotic fear of catastrophe in the Middle East.[44]

PART II

Peace and Terror

6

Official Conspiracy Theories and the Wagers of Genius

"It is an epistemological problem," one of [Paul] Bremer's senior advisers said, describing the experience of leaving the Green Zone [in Baghdad]. "You wonder, 'What's going on out there?' You sniff, and then once you're out you overanalyze."
—George Packer, *New Yorker*, November 24, 2003

Each—Wilfrid Scawen Blunt, Doughty, Lawrence, Bell, Hogarth, Philby, Sykes, Storrs—believed his vision of things Oriental was individual, self-created out of some intensely personal encounter with the Orient, Islam, or the Arabs; each expressed general contempt for official knowledge held about the East.
—Edward Said, *Orientalism*, 1978

After the war, as Lawrence backed into the limelight at home, Faisal struggled to establish a government in Damascus, the British declared their intention to leave Mesopotamia to the Mesopotamians, and the world trained its eyes on Paris with bated breath. There the mess of wartime diplomacy was laid on the table for the scrutiny of the world's elders, for the British had made many promises besides the ambiguously worded pledges to their Arab allies. In the notorious Sykes-Picot agreement of 1916, France, Britain, and Russia (which ultimately defected from and exposed the agreement) had secretly agreed to share the remains of the dismembered Ottoman Empire after the war, while the Balfour Declaration of 1917 had expressed British support for a Jewish national home in Palestine to rally international (especially American) Jewish opinion to the Allied war effort (on the assumption that Jews exercised such global power) and to secure pro-British settlement near Suez.

Ultimately, Faisal's hopes were doomed by French ambition, and Iraqi nationalists' by British pragmatism: the experts waved a wand and unveiled a new solution to the ever intractable "problem of the Middle East." Article 22 of the Covenant of the new League of Nations, an organization that British and American liberal internationalists hoped would prevent future international conflict, authorized member nations to govern former German or Turkish colonies judged unripe for self-government, something of a compromise between the Allies' enduring commitment to traditional imperialism and their diplomatic wartime declarations against annexation. In theory, mandatory control would be supervised by the Permanent Mandates Commission, but a lack of enforcement mechanisms allowed the mandatories to rule more or less at their pleasure. The British were awarded the mandates for Iraq and Palestine (not to mention the financial mechanisms of their informal control of the peninsula).

Unsurprisingly, British rule never met with the full acquiescence of the region's inhabitants, to whom "mandate" signified little more than a flimsy imperial disguise, especially when the League of Nation's main champion, Woodrow Wilson, died and the U.S. Senate failed to ratify the league. Writhing under protracted military occupation, Iraqis—both Arabs and Kurds—mounted a violent insurgency in the summer of 1920, in a long war that killed roughly a thousand British and Indian troops and ten thousand Iraqis.[1] The following decade was marked by frequent rebellion and continual contest of territorial frontiers, particularly by the Turks in Mosul (through 1926) and the Najdis in southern Iraq (even after Ibn Saud overran the Hejaz in 1924). All this evident local dissatisfaction prompted endless revision of the mandatory arrangement, first at the Cairo Conference of 1921, which, among other things, established the Iraqi constitutional monarchy under a much-chastened Faisal. From 1922 began efforts to finesse the mandate into a more agreeable form, but one that the Iraqi government nevertheless continued to suspect (rightly) as colonial control masked by semantic play: first, a renaming of the relationship under a Treaty of Alliance, then a 1923 Protocol to replace the mandate with an advisory relationship, followed by a treaty in 1927 promising early support for Iraqi admission to the league, yet another in 1930 promising admission by 1932, and finally nominal independence in 1932.[2] Middle Easterners were not, of course, the only British subjects demanding redress during this period: spurred by the postwar rhetoric of self-determination, Bolshevik example and encouragement, and expectations of political rewards for wartime cooperation and sacrifices, nationalists in Egypt, India, Ireland, Afghanistan, Somaliland, and elsewhere organized mass agitations, while Persia and the imploding Russian empire remained volatile, and Turkey was at the mercy of occupying forces and the contest between the Nationalist followers of Mustafa Kemal and the old guard of the Committee of Union and Progress (CUP).

The British effort to comprehend the postwar Middle East evolved into a furious search for a single secret center directing global unrest, which laid the foundation for the aerial surveillance regime in Iraq—to them the center stage of global conflict. It is no use arguing with hindsight that British officials should have read the myriad postwar rebellions as what they were: local movements that were certainly mutually aware and bound by the ties of region and empire but that ultimately rejected British rule in varying degrees and ways and with at most tenuous and incompetent backing by the Russians and Turks.[3] The point here is to make sense of how contemporaries made sense of these events, to explain how the intuitive mode for understanding Arabia evolved into a penchant for conspiracy theories, an epistemological paranoia in which, to borrow Thomas Richards's words, "all information, far from continually breaking apart into disjoint fragments of fact, has an invisible center and a true meaning." Such an epistemology is decidedly empirical in its reliance on an obsessive observation and recording of data but is ultimately intuitive in its assumption of a meaning *beyond* sense reality, in its treatment of data as *signs* whose deeper meaning can be accessed by a mystical insight. "What distinguishes the paranoid style," Richard Hofstadter has argued, "is not...the absence of verifiable facts...but rather the curious leap in imagination that is always made at some critical point in the recital of events." We are after that imaginative leap.[4]

Antecedents

Earlier glimmerings of conspiracy thinking were grounded in the old trope about oriental intrigue. As a counterpoint, they usefully expose the nature and extent of the postwar shift. Insecurities unleashed by the Indian rebellion of 1857 and the occupation of Egypt in 1882 had long rendered frequent polling of Muslim opinion a fundamental necessity to British officialdom. Nevertheless, when evidence of burgeoning nationalist movements in the Ottoman Empire stoked Edwardian concerns about Britain's standing in the region, even the most anxious intelligence agents retained faith in Britain's popularity, convinced that the Shia-Sunni schism, besides the sundry tribal, ethnic, and other religious divides, provided an eternal natural dam against a tide of anti-British Islamic sentiment anywhere. Even as faint echoes of the clashing of swords of new rivals in the peninsula reached Britain, officialdom, like the London *Times*, remained confident that "never again will the world see a swift outpouring of Islamic forces from the sands of Arabia." Considering natural Arab unity, particularly of an anti-British sort, a rank impossibility, British officials blithely encouraged it during the war. They did not dismiss Arab nationalism so much as view it, as we have seen, through rose-tinted glasses as a romantic expression of the Arabs' independent but irredeemably apolitical nature. Secret societies were rendered toothless by their abject orientalism, their absorption into the unending game of purposeless, fabulous, mutually eviscerating Asiatic intrigues. Pan-Islam was written off as an equally docile ideology; the prewar Baghdad resident J. G. Lorimer considered it a primarily religious movement whose political content, if any, was a "progressive" sign of the spread of secular ideas. Investigations of suspected Pan-Islamists were invariably dismissive. The haj was considered a curious but innocuous annual gathering. Agents were admittedly concerned about the threats posed by rival Europeans but ultimately shelved even those with an air of complacency—the paranoid literary genres of spy and invasion fiction strove to arouse the government from this stupor.[5]

Fitzmaurice, the shifty dragoman who dominated the embassy in Constantinople, was the main proponent of the one grand Middle Eastern conspiracy theory that was generally—but far from universally—believed: that of Jewish and Freemason control of the Turkish revolution of 1908. It however fit into a longer tradition of anti-Semitic conspiracy thinking, had little to do with mystical perceptions of the region, did nothing to generalize conspiracy thinking to all aspects of Arabian politics, and, most saliently, was not viewed as threatening to British interests. The British ambassador in Constantinople pointed out that they had only to publicize that Jews and atheists were behind the Young Turk movement to convert Indians to an even more Anglophilic and less Pan-Islamic position. In short, this prewar theory was nothing on the scale of the dire postwar visions of Arab-Turkish-Jewish combinations against the British.[6]

During the war, anxiety about Arab unity was sufficient to compel experts to urge British backing of the Arab Party lest "their machinery" be "employed against us throughout the arab countries." The Arab movement was understood as a "Separatist Conspiracy, organized by secret societies" but seriously embraced by only an educated handful: "Syrians think, write, talk; and the Arabians act," in Mark Sykes's taut summary. In any case, the timely launch of the revolt disposed of this threat to everyone's satisfaction. Pan-Islamism was considered a secular threat manufactured by the political desperation of the Turks. Even after the exposure of the Silk Letter Plot, Sir Charles Cleveland, head of the Indian secret service, who had inaugurated that somewhat precociously paranoid organization's inquiry into Asiatic conspiracies in 1911, remained convinced that scattered "unpleasant incidents" perpetrated by Pan-Islamists were "not connected to one big movement." It was all "very pathetic and ineffective." Pan-Arabism was likewise under control: "If properly handled," Cairo intelligence calculated, "[the Arabs] would remain in a state of political mosaic, a tissue of small jealous principalities, incapable of cohesion, and yet always ready to combine against an outside force. This is good for us." The Russian revolution aroused some forebodings—Sykes envisioned it steamrolling through Asia in the company of "a holy war, a pan-Turanian rising"—but in the authoritative pages of the *Arab Bulletin* Hogarth pronounced Pan-Turanianism ultimately infeasible. At the end of the war, these diverse concerns were pulled together as "Cumulative Evidence of Enemy Political Activity in Arabia" but explicitly in the manner of a catalogue of dangers averted by the opportune launch of the Arab Revolt.[7]

These early worries were not paranoid but illuminate the paranoid tendencies inherent in the agents' epistemology. The famed rarity of the genius for intelligence work on the region and its consequent concentration in the hands of a cultish community of agents expanded the scope for paranoia. The latent paranoia was perhaps most obvious in the agents' own much-remarked eccentricities. Their mystical ability to discern the signs inscribed on the landscape and its inhabitants was understood as a kind of hyper-awareness, a special sensitivity to the subtle emanations of an enigmatic region. Sykes's nervous and intense behavior in Italy, noted earlier, attracted considerable attention. Some of this paranoia he allegedly absorbed from Fitzmaurice during a meeting in Sofia. Sympathetic colleagues feared Norman Bray's health had "caused him to attach undue importance to certain ideas which he has got into his head." In retrospect, Lawrence diagnosed Bray with "persecution-delusions." It was to this set of slightly neurotic experts, now incorporated into Whitehall and the mandatory administrations, that the government turned for help in understanding the eruption of postwar rebellion. They were the fount of an elaborate and complex conspiracy-thinking culture about Middle Eastern resistance to British imperial rule.[8]

The Theories

Given general confidence in Arab Anglophilia and in the efficacy of British rule, much of the unrest caught officialdom entirely by surprise; hence, the desperate struggle to explain it and the certainty that a hidden hand was at work. Many agents assumed the "Eastern Unrest," as it was dubbed, emanated from a single grand scheme to undermine the British Empire. Men on the spot in Iraq, unwilling to accept the rebels' verdict on their skill as experts, grasped frantically for explanations. The political officer in Hillah, for instance, could not fathom the sudden "unity of purpose and lack of dissensions" among sheikhs ordinarily at each other's throats; it suggested "some strong controlling personality behind the movement." Some described an "anarchic" tribal conspiracy aimed at the "removal of all government control." Agents on the spot suspected they had front-row seats to a disorder with wider significance than merely local resentment of occupation. Gertrude Bell explained that in Baghdad they had "the very doubtful advantage of getting the news of Asia from all quarters," making them "look at the world with very different eyes from the people who didn't know that Napoleon had taken ship from Elba," since "all the secret reports from everywhere pass through our hands," leaving an impression of "unmitigated intrigue, turmoil and revolution."[9]

Those entrusted with analyzing the "Eastern Unrest" from afar came to similar conclusions. Some described the Iraqi, Irish, and Indian unrests as a single trouble perpetrated by "bolshevik money." Reports of Iraqi rebels "issuing communiqués" and treating prisoners as "a sacred trust"—"absolutely un-Arab" methods—betrayed European direction. Bray, who, after something of an inter-departmental tussle, had joined the India Office as a unique "Special Intelligence Officer," argued in a much-circulated memorandum that subversive activities throughout Asia were "inter-dependent and highly organized" and traced the Iraqi rebellion to a "violent...panislamic" conspiracy of Syrian, Mesopotamian, and Turkish nationalists with links to Moscow through Switzerland and Berlin. Military intelligence traced Kurdish unrest to Constantinople, where it was "one phase of C.U.P. [Committee of Union and Progress] activity, which may now embrace pan-Islamic, Egyptian Nationalist, possibly Bolshevic, and even Indian Nationalist activity." They elaborated: "The ostensible bolshevik, pan-islamic and nationalist propaganda are all apparently organized and controlled in the near East by Turks....[U]nder whatever name it may pass the...movement is, in its essence, really a pan-Turanian one." Other versions added, variously, the Germans, the Greeks, the Standard Oil Company, and the French to this nefarious combination. Pan-Islam was frequently invoked, as both a political force and an international movement of "religious fanaticism."[10]

Throughout the decade, the conspiracy theory remained a ready recourse to British analysts of the Middle East. When sheikhs and priests gathered at a much-dreaded but ultimately innocuous conference at Karbala in 1922, Iraqi intelligence inferred that intrigues had been carried on at "private séances." The India Office was certain "of a general plan of active hostility directed against the British empire" in the Middle East. Besides Turco-Bolshevik conspiracy, Jewish migration to Palestine seemed to offer another avenue of Bolshevik contamination of the Middle East. In 1923, a new Interdepartmental Committee on the Eastern Unrest (IDCEU) was convened, drawing heavily on the involvement and information of several former Arab Bureau affiliates. It concluded that the subjects in its original terms of reference—Turkish, Egyptian, and Indian Nationalists, the Pan-Islamic movement, the CUP, and Indian revolutionaries in Europe, North America, and Asia—were "so closely connected as to make any clear distinction a matter of the greatest difficulty." With hindsight, postwar officials traced "the Sinn Fein movement in Ireland and America, the Home Rule and seditionary movements in India, the Egyptian Nationalist, Turkish Nationalist, pan-Islamic and Greek royalist movements...with their accompanying plots and conspiracies" to the German enemy, helped by "extreme sections of the socialist party in Great Britain."[11]

Certainly, there were skeptics. Although the Foreign Office response to Bray's theories was initially warm and credulous, within months it began to criticize India Office theories as generally "going too far in attributing the trouble to the direct intervention of some mysterious external agency, rather than to conditions obtaining in the country itself." Some agents on the spot regarded as "farcical the opinion of those pessimists who talk in hushed whispers of the possibility of a united Arab, or mohammedan kingdom stretching from the Caucasus to Delhi." The agents in the Colonial Office's Middle East Department repeatedly protested their disbelief in the broader conspiracy theories, calling "this great 'united movement'" a "mere bogey." Richard Meinertzhagen soon revealed, "I have never had much faith in the potency of either pan islam or any other pan movement east of Suez." As his confessional tone suggests, this opinion was newly admissible in 1923, when the continued dormancy of the allegedly minatory conspiracies began to hearten some quarters. A Foreign Office official sneered that the War Office might enjoy "making their [own] blood creep," but they need not share this indulgence, for "with as little fact and as much imagination one could almost produce a paper on the Icelandic menace."[12]

Much of this skepticism derived from internecine departmental politics. The Foreign Office's antipathy toward the IDCEU can, for instance, be traced to its adversarial relationship with the India Office. Foreign Secretary Austen Chamberlain deplored in particular the encroachment of this "ill-informed and ill-constructed" body "on what is primarily my business." Some suspected that Bray's theories emerged from an India Office conspiracy to absolve itself of administrative failings. And some Foreign Office skepticism was rooted in reluctance in a time of retrenchment to support the costly policies that would emerge from perceptions of an immediate threat.[13]

None of this, however, removed the dissenters beyond the pale of paranoia. The Foreign Office's alternative explanation for the unrest, purveyed by its agent-bureaucrats Young and Cornwallis conceded the existence of a conspira-torial organization: "Granted that there are secret societies and that there is an organisation, such as that traced by Major Bray," Cornwallis began his assess-ment, he attributed their success primarily to "the presence in that country of a large body of semi-educated Nationalists who were discontented with our administration...and who influenced the ignorant tribesmen." Young also favored this perspective because it allowed for remedial policy changes. This did not make him more progressive—he was hostile to Bray's theory partly because, by mooting any policy change, it had become a rallying point for those calling for the evacuation of Mesopotamia. He and Cornwallis granted entirely "the completeness and ubiquity of enemy activity" and frankly and explicitly agreed with Bray's postulate of a web of secret societies dubbed the "Asiatic Islamic federation" which had been converted to Bolshevism; they differed only in assigning primary motivation to disgruntled Iraqi nationalists rather than inter-national conspirators. Others in their office confirmed, "There are anti-European, anti-British and anarchic influences all over the Middle East and doubtless simi-lar agencies in Europe and elsewhere." Organized conspiracy against the empire was *obvious*; this paranoid consensus underlay the apparent interdepartmental discord. After all, as Cornwallis noted, Bray himself was hardly consistent on the matter of the prime mover, vacillating rather incoherently between "internal" and "external" causes.[14]

To be sure, some of the conspiracy theories possessed an element of truth. Faisal's army and administration in Damascus did contain many Mesopota-mians, including former Turkish Army officers and future Iraqi statesmen, many of whom were eager to carry the torch of freedom on to Baghdad. Frontiers were ill defined between Iraq and Syria and Turkey. People did join "secret societies," and the Russians did back anti-British movements. The Wahhabis were continually raiding from the south. Pan-Islam was a political force. The Anjuman-i-Kaaba probably did nurture the outsized ambition of cre-ating an independent Muslim dominion in all Arabia. There were Arab students in Germany in contact with socialists—Husain al-Rahhal, father of the Iraqi Communist Party, was in Berlin in 1919 (and in India in 1921). The CUP and the Kemalists were in contact with the Bolsheviks. The Home Office correctly discerned that socialists, Indian nationalists, and others met in London.[15]

However, the ready flourishing of the term "conspiracy" to describe all these activities requires explanation, for most were neither covert nor illegiti-mate nor arranged by cabals. For instance, Hindu-Muslim cooperation was an unconcealed feature of Indian nationalist strategy, as the joint Khilafat and Gandhian agitations of 1920–1922 demonstrated. Indeed, the Kemalists' aboli-tion of the sultanate and the caliphate, which triggered the Khilafat movement, antagonized Pan-Islamists everywhere. Meanwhile, Kemalists and the CUP, despite their different, complex relations with the new Soviet empire, remained strictly at odds with each other—and indeed with the Soviets, too: Enver Pasha was ultimately killed by the Red Army while fighting with anti-Soviet insurgents in Bukhara, and the Turkish Republic's friendly relations with the Soviet Union could not lift the Turkish ban on the Communist Party. The conspiracy theories are also remarkable in their sheer totality—each claimed the power to explain *all* the unrest. Anti-imperialist Londoners simply lacked the kind of power required to mastermind the entire world unrest. Likewise, the Young Turks and various nationalists fraternizing with Bolsheviks and Germans in Switzerland could not have been the *only* forces involved in the mass uprisings in Egypt, India, Iraq, and elsewhere. Few British officials seem to have recognized that some of these agencies' ambitions far outstripped their actual ability to act.[16] So entrenched was the postwar belief that all politics in Arabia were secret that the politics of secret societies were deemed the only politics worth monitoring.[17] The ideas underpinning this conspiracy-thinking culture reveal the influence of the agents' perception of Arabia as a place in which energy and information coursed freely, magnifying and exaggerating the efforts of the few, creating a space in which grand conspiracies *could* be real.

Spaces of the Imagination

A belief in Arabia's underlying geographical and metaphysical unity was well established among the agents, we know; it was now pressed into practical service in their analyses of the "Debatable Land" now in their grasp. "No hard and fast line can be drawn between Kurdistan and Mesopotamia," insisted Arnold Wilson: "There are a series of imperceptible gradations between Nomadic tribal Kurds, settled tribal Kurds, settled non-tribal Kurds, settled Turcoman tribes, settled tribes half Turcoman half Arab, Nomadic Arab and settled Arab." (Hence his persistent opposition to an autonomous Kurdistan.) Iraq itself was a chimera whose "geographical limits... cannot be precisely defined." The desert was "a thing in itself," in which tribes hundreds of miles apart remained closely connected, a topographical quality that posed a practical problem for officials attempting to draw frontiers; it made international conspiracy conceivable. The entire region from the Mediterranean to the Indian frontier was, in Bell's dramatic phrase, a "devil's cauldron." An official in Beirut was certain that "propinquity and identity of political and economic interests are bound to create connections between Arab agitators in [Syria and Palestine]," though he had "no information to show how close such connections are." Hence, the futility of dealing with Mesopotamia "as a separate problem." The assumption of connection was made a priori and followed from Arabia's desert geography and society. Mesopotamia was a particular source of anxiety, "completely surrounded" as it was by the Turks, the French, Ibn Saud, and the Russians in Persia. Internal forces of subversion—tribes and nationalists—were closely intertwined with these besieging external agencies, by virtue of Bolshevik sympathy, Turkish past, Shia identity, pro-Sherifian leanings, or some such factor. The presence of Indian troops, clerks, pilgrims, and laborers provoked further concern.[18]

More important, the old connectivity began to appear sinister when Russia and Turkey, the imperial dams holding the shifting sands at bay, collapsed and, in their new, highly volatile incarnations, let subversion bleed across continental and national borders. By "imperceptible gradations" Iraq shaded into Soviet terrain: "Unless we remain in Mosul we shall have no means of preventing the extension southwards of USSR." Worse, the devious Soviets were liable to creep quietly into the no-man's-land of the Middle East: through "ethnographical overlap," they worked from the *inside*, using Central Asian "buffers" as "jumping-off places for subversive activities." Likewise, "Turkish intrigue is easy in a country where men of Turkish race or education or both are numerous." The universal historian Arnold Toynbee was then forming his ideas about civilization as an intelligence analyst, arguing that while distance, race, and history clearly distinguished the European and oriental parts of the state in European empires, "two great states, Turkey and Russia...occupy between them the land-bridge between Europe and the East, and embrace Europeans and Orientals in one political body without any clear-cut division between them....Europe and the East merge into one." This was what was so unsettling and intrinsically subversive about the seductive stretch of land and nomads between Moscow and Mecca. In it, the entire world order based on the principle of separation between oriental and European collapsed. When the two formerly stagnant, despotic empires themselves yielded to the forces of change, they became the "political conductor between Europe and the East." The realm of subversion no longer stopped at the edge of the sands of Arabia. While agents on the ground continued to complain of the difficulty of obtaining information "dimly through a distorting mirage of desert rumours," inscrutable Soviet and Turkish policy enormously compounded the domain of mystery. Bray investigated a phenomenon "spread over the whole mohammedan world" but "essentially asiatic."[19]

Russia and Turkey were also insidious because, through their porous borders, they threatened an imperceptible penetration rather than a straightforward amassing of troops on British frontiers. Swaggering pronouncements about the impoverished Russian army's inability to operate at long distances were amply rebutted by those "with local knowledge" who pointed to the dangers of regarding it as "an European and not a semi-savage Army," given its proven capability to live off the country. Moreover, "there was no telling what mad men would do." It was a more or less irregular army, liable to employ subterfuges and subtle agencies, such as propaganda and supporting local intrigues. A Royal Air Force veteran of the Russian civil war explicitly likened "the mentality of the Russian peasant and the conditions of fighting in South Russia" to "the types met with and the mode of warfare conducted in minor affairs in the out-skirts of Empire." The space between them was literally nil; after all, the British had themselves used Mesopotamia as their launching point into South Russia (via Persia) in their own frontier-style warfare against the Red Army. The Turks, "who do not usually expend more effort than is essential," would likewise "be more likely to attempt an attack mainly by rousing unrest among the tribes and by stiffening any tribal forces...with the nuclei of regular troops, guns, and machine guns." The irony was again entirely lost on the British, who had used precisely such tactics against the Turkish empire. The new, secret style of war-fare they had adapted from Bedouin tactics now threatened to haunt them indefinitely in their own Middle East empire. These were imperceptible but formidable forces functioning from within the imperium itself—a potent cause for paranoia. In such a situation, the absence of intelligence of a major Turkish or Soviet invasion plan provided little comfort, for the threat was, like so many things in this region, undetectable, something that would only be "sensed," "a matter about which we can only make guesses." Their Middle Eastern empire, with its long lines of communication and small band of functionaries, seemed an ideal target for covert warfare.[20]

Contiguity, ethnography, and irregular warfare bound the Soviet Union to the subversive Middle East; yet perhaps most disturbing was the coincidence of their ideologies. According to Toynbee, the entente between the Russians and Muslims stemmed not from mere opportunism but from the overlap in Islamic and Bolshevik sympathies among Russian Muslims: "Scratch the Tartar and you find the Bolshevik!" Both defied the emergent (rhetorical if not yet practical) order of nation-states. "Islamic consciousness" shared with the "European Labour Movement" a highly dangerous international dimension, and both worked by gradually permeating the minds of the masses. "It is...extremely difficult to tell where bolshevism ends and some other 'ism' begins (the parties are so closely allied)," one official groused in a report that Young considered "very serious."[21]

Bolshevism and Islam were both giant secret societies in the British official mind, their members following party decrees and clerical fatwas, respectively. Most striking was the functional similarity between Mecca and Moscow, those international, cosmopolitan cynosures of believers, forbidden to unbelievers and thus ideal sites for subversive contact and meetings. Both were secret

centers. Some British observers felt confident that certain factors of "government, religion, tradition, and social practice" militated against the spread of
Bolshevism in the Arab world, but then again, George Lloyd pointed out, the
Najdi theocracy might try "to use the Bolsheviks for purposes of local nationalism without admitting the communist part of the programme," corrupting their
subjects into an uncontrollable anti-British force. The ideologies also shared a
reliance on a militant avant-garde—the Bolsheviks and the Ikhwan. Most chilling
was the thought that Bolshevism might harness the fanatical power of Wahhabism
for its own ends. Lawrence warned of "a wahabi-like Moslem edition of Bolshevism" arising from Russian incursions into the Middle East.[22]

Another dangerously cosmopolitan source of overlap between the Bolsheviks
and Islamists was, inevitably, the Jew. In contemporary conspiracy explanations of the Bolshevik revolution, Bolsheviks were neither Russians nor ideological extremists but "enemy secret agents called into existence by Germans
doing the work of Jews who were devoted to the vengeful destruction of Russia,"
to quote David Fromkin. Changeling subversives, Jews possessed the power of
the catalyst, the external agency—the deus ex machina?—which, through an
almost occult power, could cause the disunited Middle East to coalesce into a
vigorously anti-British bloc. It is impossible to understand the potency of interwar anti-Semitic conspiracy theories without the context of a more general
paranoia about an Arabia surrounded by Germany, Turkey, Russia, and
Palestine—all at times perceived as the domains of Jewish conspirators—
besides fanatical Persia and Najd and a colonial nationalist fringe. What made
the Jew a threat, among sundry other characterizations, was his status as a root-
less *Semite*, as slippery and ambiguous in his loyalty as Arabia itself. It was the
Jew—in all his subversive avatars—who was responsible for stretching the
Middle East, its intrigues, and even its magic information system, into Europe:
Palestine was "connected by very live wires with the rest of the world by the
international aspect of Judaism." Any unlawful dealing with "suspects and
political intriguers" was known immediately in the House of Commons. Worse,
grumbled the chief of RAF intelligence in Iraq, "the authorities at home are
obviously afraid both of jewry and labour and their rapid system of information." The anti-Semitic and the related anti-Bolshevik paranoia of this period
was intimately connected to concern about the new colonies in the Middle East;
even intelligence about Moscow arrived via listening stations in Palestine,
Baghdad, and India. It was Norman Bray who helped write Curzon's famous
1923 ultimatum to the Soviets demanding, among other things, the recall of
Soviet representatives in Persia and Afghanistan, and it was the IDCEU as
much as domestic agencies that gathered intelligence about Communist
involvement in the General Strike of 1926.[23]

The fundamental trouble with this region was that people would not stay put. Many were nomadic by custom; others, Reader Bullard (at the Colonial Office) pointed out, had become so through their late inclusion in an enormous Turkish empire. "Semi-independent," desert nomads led "a fugitive existence," in Air Ministry language; their allegiance to government was "transitory" at best. Wartime displacement, which sent refugees from Russia to Turkey, Sherifians into Damascus, and Iraqi rebels into Persia, intensified itinerancy. Some officials also realized that the porous British Empire itself promoted the mobility of suspicious persons, from India to England, Iraq, the Hejaz, and so on.[24]

Since wartime, this incessant nomadism had been incorporated in a discourse about a vortical quality that endowed Arabian cities with special political potency as "centers" through which far-flung networks could be reached and intelligence effectively gathered. Of course, at one level, the entire region was a center of sorts, the "pivot of world rivalry" around which swung the fates of the Russian, German, Turkish, and British empires. There was something *centripetal* about the Middle East; it was a global center of gravity, the black hole of international rivalry, to which ascendant empires serially turned to face the final test and in which each was ultimately swallowed into oblivion. And within this geopolitical gyre, certain cities were believed to exercise a magnetic pull. Thus, wartime certainty of the "enormous" scope of the network of Arab nationalists had been based on the fact that "the expression of their aims has appeared sporadically in Constantinople, Syria, Switzerland, Cairo, London, Mecca and elsewhere." In the material world of the cities, otherwise nebulous and inarticulate desert subversion could become manifest. It was possible to know the desert through the network of cities superimposed on and around it, in which a continent of wayfarers ineluctably left their mark. Baghdad in particular was "an irresistible lodestar." Even the Abbasid Caliphate, explained David Hogarth, had been drawn to it from Damascus and Mecca as "the force of economic gravity in…south-west Asia." "Should Empire be there again," he argued, "the centre of gravity will swing round the same arc.…It must gravitate to the old point of rest." It was there that the fate of the entire war would be decided. On the other hand, Lawrence proffered Syria as the historic linchpin of empires and continents and the focus of a recent "centripetal nationalism." Damascus was "the lodestar to which Arabs are naturally drawn" and the key to the end of the war.[25]

The post-1916 intelligence regime was designed to take advantage of this centripetal quality by centralizing collection and analysis to mimic the flow of the desert archive. Knowing the desert would require insertion of a catch at the confluence of desert information flows. Thus might order be got out of "chaos." Gilbert Clayton and Sykes envisioned "a centre to which all information on the various questions connected with the Near East will gravitate," made up of a staff "competent to sift and catalogue this information and to bring it into a form...easily digested by those who may not be experts." They favored Cairo, where lay "all the moral and intellectual ties between the Arabs and ourselves." It was the bridge between Asiatic and African Arabia and England and India. Clayton was certain "this will be even more the case when the war is over, and many elements which now have their home in Constantinople will...gravitate here." In any case, the war had made other Arab cities more inaccessible than ever. Levant Service employees booted from enemy territory had flocked to Cairo; its sheer wartime cosmopolitanism reinforced the conviction of its Mecca-like political centrality. Wartime events retroactively rendered authentic its position at "the nexus" of the "huge web of intrigue which spread over the whole of the Near and Middle and Far East."[26]

Still, lesser cities were also understood to function as nerve centers in the regional information network described by nomadic flows. Suq al-Shuyukh (literally, suq of the sheikhs) was the starting point for Hail and Najd and the Mesopotamian pilgrimage to Mecca. "Whenever headquarters are short of news they seem to bombard me, Suk being the central meeting place of sheikhs," Dickson observed. "All kinds of good information is obtainable here, where in other places there may be nothing but 'blanks.'" Most of the desert was an informational void; only at key intersections of desert traffic could the agent tap into the ether. By the same token, Nasiriyah was "the centre from which influence can be exercised among the powerful Arab tribes...along the Euphrates." The holy cities, in particular, seemed to offer the key to knowledge of the Arabian cosmos. If Islam was a secret society, they were the dens in which the order of things was decided and promulgated throughout the region. The Shia holy cities, Young held, were "hotbeds of intrigue and...the most convenient point of contact with Damascus on the other side of the desert." They remotely controlled events in Persia. Through them the Russians might control Persia and Iraq. Pious pilgrims hailing "from all corners of the East" to Kadhimain, Najaf, and Karbala, were certainly "not indifferent to temporal affairs," wrote the shrewd Candler; they included "suspects on the political black list, men long known in the Gulf as gun-runners, jehadists and spies, and men who come with strange, unconvincing tales, leaving suspicion behind them but no evidence for arrest." And, of course, Mecca, Hogarth warned, always possessed the "potentiality of being an armed conspiracy." Through it, the Turks might poison the entire well of Muslim opinion. This chain of holy cities enabled an enemy to leverage the entire Muslim world; it possessed limitless subversive potential.[27]

While the Arab Revolt was thought to have channeled this potential in salubrious directions, postwar analysts could not rest as assured. The cities they had viewed primarily as entry points into the diffuse information network now figured as nodes in an equally diffuse conspiracy network; their very existence seemed to make regionwide conspiracy a real possibility. What made the Mesopotamian situation so "volcanic" was the "divergent location of possible storm centres." Thus began a decade-long effort to identify the secret center of regional subversion. At different times, "polyglot" Mosul, Kermanshah, Baku, and Constantinople were identified as "storm centers" of the Middle East, particularly for Bolshevik intrigues. The latter also radiated a Pan-Turanian subversion, in which "Baghdad, Syria, and Mesopotamia" figured as "centres of acute agitation and intrigue." For Lloyd, "Zionist immigration" made Palestine another "dangerous centre of Bolshevik infection" of Arabia. Karbala and Najaf were likewise frightful: holy and transnational, they were apparently the points through which Kemalists and Bolsheviks entered the desert information matrix. The holy cities might be the "key to an understanding of...the people," but, cautioned the political officer Thomas Lyell, the "streams of the faithful" also made each of those unworldly microcosms "the receiver and distorter of all the news of the world," enabling them to exercise "a malign influence *far beyond the limits of [the] town and even of Iraq.*" Thus, Young explained to new officers, had news of Faisal's expulsion from Syria run "like wildfire across the desert to Nejef and Kerbala," commingling with "the various germs of bolshevism, Turkish nationalism, and Arab nationalism" to produce a "local discontent" that actually expressed a more general discontent coursing through the desert's information network. To these analysts, Arabia was what the philosophers Deleuze and Guattari (themselves drawing on Arabia travelogues) would call a "smooth space," a single, ubiquitous place, local and universal at once (the ideal space for espionage, they note—somewhat unoriginally).[28]

No city embodied this duality to postwar observers more obviously than Mecca. More than impose a religious duty, warned the agent G. Wyman Bury in 1919, the haj "evolved a means of perpetual communication with the remotest corners of the Moslem world"; it was the "strongest factor in pan-Islam as a political movement." The entire commercial infrastructure of the Mecca pilgrimage could be used to spread Bolshevik propaganda. While a Bolshevik agent might stand little chance of success in India, in the haj, "he finds an India out of India and the few seeds he drops...may easily germinate and bear fruit in India." Agents watched anxiously for signs that the Muslim Soviet representative in Jeddah was trying to "get at" the sultan in the secret holy city that he, but not the British, could enter. They in turn employed an Indian Muslim spy, under cover as "Pilgrimage Officer" in Mecca until Hejazi suspicions rendered this tactic impolitic. As Egypt's high commissioner, George Lloyd identified the Soviet Agency as the "center of...activities directed against established order in this part of the world" and launched a protracted but discreet effort to oust it. During these years, no concrete evidence ever seems to have emerged that the Soviet consulate actually engaged in such activities with any success. Nevertheless, the idea that the pilgrimage *could* be used for such a purpose remained irresistible. "The pilgrimage offers unique opportunities," the Jeddah agent insisted, "and it would be strange indeed if Soviet Russia failed to make use of it." The absence of subversive activity at a conference at Mecca in 1926 was so unbelievable that the IDCEU began to lose faith in the efficiency of the agent on the spot; they could not shake the conviction that there was something "going on under the surface....A great deal must have happened." The cloistered atmosphere of the Hejaz was simply "different," explained the British representative; an "enclosed space in which prejudice and mis-conception would spring up rapidly," it "sharpened nerves." Before the war, this heterocosmic quality had made it a romantic spy-space; now, its suggestive powers were politically subversive.[29]

At one point, Bray ambitiously attempted to diagram the entire network of collaborating secret centers. "For the purposes of control," he explained, "the whole eastern world" had been "divided by Asiatic intriguers into certain areas, each having its centre, in which the leaders instal [sic] themselves, and from which intensive propaganda and intrigue is carried on in the sub-divisions." He tabulated the centers and their "controls":

CENTRE	CONTROL
Switzerland	Morocco, Algiers, Tunisia, Egypt, Western Arabia (to an increasing extent), India (occasionally), Constantinople
Constantinople	Asia Minor, Armenia, Kurdistan, Caucasia, Syria, Egypt, Tehran, Kabul
Kabul	Samarkand, Yarkand, Kulja, India, Tribal country of N. W. Frontier, Bokhara
Bokhara	Eastern Turkestan, Samarkand, Tehran
Tehran	Persia, Gulf Littoral, Mesopotamia (more especially Kerbala and Nejf)

An attached map showed schools where Pan-Orientalism was taught (with Pan-Germanist methods) and agents' radii from each center. Minutes on this well-received memorandum reveal that its description of a "pan-orientalist" movement centered in Switzerland was already widely accepted. The memo was thought to confirm existing information rather than "provide any new theory."[30]

But how did Arabia reach Switzerland? This was perhaps the most disconcerting aspect of the tentacular network of secret centers—like a vortex, it drew greater and greater reaches of the world into its cosmos without regard for continental propriety. The "back-door to Germany" and "an outpost of Russian Bolshevism," Switzerland was ideally positioned to enable contact among Eastern and Western collaborators. Odessa, Vienna, and Greece were also contenders. More frightening was the thought that the center was in Britain itself: Home Office spooks pointed to London, "the centre of the empire," as "the place from which these conspiracies draw their inspiration and personnel," where foreign seditionists mingled with various British undesirables—pro-Turks, socialists, and "Russians of Bolshevik tendencies." It was from London, a Foreign Office official agreed, that the "latest form of CUP Bolshevism" emanated to link up with "every form of revolutionary activity throughout the world:—CUP, Bolshevism, Indian and Egyptian nationalism, anti-Zionism, Sinn Fein, the extreme Labour party, Japanese Asiaticism, Persian 'democracy' and the Armenian Deshnakstation."[31]

Prewar certainty that it was impossible to "mould the desert sands into shape" had given way to visions of shifting sands spreading organized rebellion throughout the region. The Arab Revolt had become a Pandora's Box; through it, Muslims from all over had "met together for the first time." Like Frankenstein, Bray and others reeled at the thought that "*we* have launched the ship of Arab aspirations." In the parlous postwar world, where even the Arabs had been touched by "experience," the insouciance of the prewar era was a luxury they could no longer afford. What impressed officials were "the volcanic possibilities," the potential, through the mixing of volatile elements, for an apocalyptic end to the British Empire in a land that had buried many great empires. So stretched were the empire's resources, so vulnerably incontinent this continent; observers were overwhelmed by the sheer scope for subversion, by the what-ifs that could wreck the fragile empire in that window of opportunity and geography. Thus immediately after the war, the War Office penned these sibylline lines: "For many years to come it is the Middle East that will be our greatest source of danger and our chief military preoccupation." By 1921 military eyes were trained intensely on this region, the space in which British imperial might would, like the ancients it followed, be tested by all the gathering dark forces of the world. It was here, at the heart of the oldest world, that all the empires collided. After all the lapidary phrases about Arabia's position at the pivot of the planet and the black hole of empires, now had come the hour of reckoning.[32]

The Method to the Madness

In the spatial imagination of agents in Whitehall and the Middle East, the desert's emptiness was a deception that the expert analyst might unmask in

Arabia's cities; the conspiracy-thinking culture it underwrote was firmly rooted in their particular epistemological outlook. They analyzed the Middle East with the ex ante assumption that there was more to any particular incident than met the eye—that, say, an open conference in Karbala concealed a world of secret activity—and that even successfully apprehended plots were mere epiphenomena signaling the existence of a more general subversion. Hence the inquiry into the relatively paltry Silk Letter Plot generated Bray's gigantic memos on "the Mohammedan question" with their accompanying maps and diagrams. By tracking travel and information across the heart of Asia, he hoped to discover the hidden structure of a continent-wide subversion. Working with the a priori assumption of a hidden reality, he saw any evidence of movement, such as Swiss newspapers in Egypt or Europeans known "for their pro-this and pro-that tendencies" in Iraq, as proof of the workings of a secret organization. That the organization existed was never in doubt; he searched for facts in support of a theory that he already knew was true. His report was heavily circulated as "a model of the way in which young political officers should approach the deeper problems with which they come in contact."[33]

The assumption of "deeper problems" went hand in hand with a continued reliance on intuition for piecing together promiscuous conspiracies. Intuitive ability continued to set the experts apart from the hacks and made "evidence" less urgent than opinion. After all, the cachet of the unconventional recruits at the Middle East Department lay in their transcendental insight; the instinctive Lawrence could "grasp a situation with a clarity...which is not a marked characteristic of the average Whitehall official," explained a colleague. Bray explicitly based his theory of Pan-Islamic conspiracy on "very little reading." Though he had engaged in "innumerable conversations with people of every degree of education and standing," as an expert, he chose to submit "a sketch of an 'impression' gained of the whole" rather than the actual evidence. Elsewhere, he traced his grasp of the situation to an epiphany deep in the Himalayas, when, in "the intense solitude—the profound silence...I seemed to hear a whisper, to sense a feeling...which had drifted, intangible as vapour...over the thousands of miles of desert...and...left behind it a restlessness." It came to him while he sat immersed in the magic information network. He sensed it, the way an Arabia agent could.[34]

Indeed, entire conspiracy theories needed only be based on hunches—albeit those of acknowledged geniuses—to acquire credibility. Arnold Wilson's suspicions about Standard Oil's involvement in the Mesopotamian unrest were accepted as true not because he had proffered concrete evidence but because he claimed to be able to see through the deceptions of the American consul. The

India Office stopped short of officially approaching the American government about the matter, but Wilson's reports were incorporated into a 1921 indictment of the company. "Direct" evidence of Bolshevik influence in Iraq and "corroboration" of Bolshevik influence in the Hejaz were established by equally tendentious logic. The General Staff theory of Kemal's Greek backing was "purely conjectural and merely indicates a suspicion, which is hardening." Expert presumption also underlay the indictment of the Syrian political literary club Nadi al-Arabi, each statement about its conspiratorial activities modified by such phrases as "no doubt," "only natural to suppose," "undoubtedly," "I imagine that," and "I should not be surprised if." Similarly, the IDCEU report on Turkish intrigues relied heavily on statements by British experts in the region, particularly Cox and the India Office's C. C. Garbett, formerly of Iraqi intelligence. These consisted entirely of personal impressions about French, Bolshevik, and Turkish intrigues. Cox baldly asserted that it was simply "difficult to accept" that Iraq was not an immediate Turkish objective; Garbett, that "secret societies are without doubt at work in Mesopotamia although the full detail of their organisation has not yet been discovered." This "evidence" was marshaled to justify "the deduction that these activities are controlled from a single centre." Cox's and Garbett's statements were taken seriously as the statements of two men who *would know.* They did not need substantiation. Agents in the field often submitted unsubstantiated reports on the strength of their reputations, as intuitive divinations of "the real reasons" hidden behind the ostensible.[35]

Intuition was also enshrined in the new, more rigorous technique for distilling meaning from scanty or faulty information—the table. The General Staff's effort to determine the extent to which Arabian unrest was "spontaneous" or merely "a section of attack in a general conspiracy against the British Empire" rested on the construction of a table demonstrating the "correlation" of international events. Coal strikes in England and troubles in Ireland were aligned with evidence of Italian-Turkish-Bolshevik and other intrigues and the breakdown of trade negotiations with the Soviets. The hope was that an answer would leap out from this mass of evidence; a tabulation of concurrent events would expose the design behind only seeming coincidences. The IDCEU used a similar method in its interim report on Turkish intrigues. Bray also exhibited a partiality for tables. The technique rested on the belief that coincidence was an illusion; events, including unrest in the empire, were assumed, simply by their "striking synchronization," to be causally connected.[36]

Certainly, agents relied on hard evidence as well—reports by colleagues, intercepted communications, witnesses' statements, and the like—but in the end their own expert intuition mattered most. The overwhelmingly positive response to Bray's reports testifies to the faith in his sheer genius as an Arabia agent, regardless of his eccentricities. An India Office "oppressed and...confused by the numberless activities and intrigues in so many parts of the world directed against our rule" selected him to "[trace] the evil to its source"—apparently by sheer power of genius. With his gift for comprehending so much, simply through intuition, the Arabia agent *comforted*; he embodied the imperial archive of fantasy.[37]

Faith in intuition continued to derive from the perceived inscrutability of the region, the impossibility of ever unearthing "real" evidence, and the need, therefore, to rely on almost extrasensory powers. Philby and Bell were the "antennae of Cox, probing the impalpable air for signs of the times." Reports of conspiracy often contained disclaimers that "no absolute proof is available," or "definite evidence is of course hard to obtain." The "of course" pointed to the obvious futility of seeking proof of inevitably recondite activities. Agents frequently warned about the exaggerations and unreliability of informants, although they invariably passed on even highly dubious testimonies as "confirmation of talk that has been going on for some time." Diffident expressions of doubt did accompany some of the more embarrassingly fantastic reports. A Jeddah official noted, "While giving all such information I do not wish it to be understood that I endorse it, but it may be useful as a link with information received by you from other sources." So aware were agents of the chimerical nature of intelligence in the region that the Damascus consul, for instance, habitually used the words "news" and "information" in quotes, accompanied by frequent disclaimers of the authenticity of "facts."[38]

This style of reporting was considered distinctively British. "I am somewhat surprised that the French take the trouble to publish reports of such an improbable nature," the British liaison officer in Syria remarked of a French intelligence summary. "They publish every report received together with the source of information, *leaving others to form their own conclusions.*" He advised that they be read "with considerable reserve," and his colleagues at home took note. French reports were not mediated by genius. British reports also contained rumor, hearsay, and unconfirmed news, but passed on selectively and with the imprimatur of wise agents aware of the dangers posed by false rumors "in a country like this." The categorical preference for genius-vetted over "French" reporting was affirmed during a flap over police abstracts from Iraq. With Whitehall saturated with Arabist experts, the Foreign Office asked Arnold Wilson to send full rather than abstracted reports, but Garbett at the India Office upheld the traditional deference to the man on the spot, affirming, "He and not we are [sic] in the best position to judge of the reliability of the statements made." Wilson, for his part, peevishly pointed out that since Meinertzhagen, his counterpart in Palestine, did not normally furnish the Foreign Office with reports received from *his* assistants, he too "should be allowed discretion in the matter."[39]

An origin in genius made the conspiracy theories ultimately unverifiable against evidence. Thus, faced with the continued absence of evidence of significant Soviet activity in the Hejaz, the British political agent could only deduce that the Soviet Agency was using these early years as "a time of study, a period of observation." A similar logic obtained in the case of the unfulfilled theory of a Kemalist plot to seize Faisal's throne. When the 1922 Karbala conference proved unexpectedly serene, Cox concluded that the Kemalist and Bolshevik conspirators' efforts had merely proved "abortive." He did not consider the possibility that no conspiracy existed—remarkably, given that the original suspicion of a hidden hand derived from pure speculation. When the awaited Soviet aggression against Iraq also failed to materialize, Bray pointed feebly to the complexity of the Soviet government. Confidence in intelligence officials' intuitive understanding of the Middle East produced a tautology: agents were sure the conspiracies they intuited were true, else they would not have been intuited. Genius was its own verification.[40]

With reputations at stake, conspiracy theories were also put forward in a manner ensuring they could be neither completely believed nor refuted. Having passed on information about a terrifying Moscow-Berlin-Irish-Egyptian-Persian-Indian conspiracy, the War Office told Wilson not to lay "too much stress" on it. The chief of Air Staff Intelligence in Iraq failed to find any "real pieces of meat" regarding Bolshevik activities, but then, he added, he had not expected to. In general reports of potentially devastating conspiracies included a simultaneous dismissal, although always with a remnant of lingering danger. Bell might have hoped she was not witnessing "the crumbling of the universe," but nevertheless found it "too immensely interesting to be in such close touch with it." It is as though the agents and officials *wanted* to live in fear; part of the fun of working on and in the Middle East was the opportunity to steep themselves in extraordinary fictions and romantic scenarios, to face in theory, if not in practice, the situations faced by spies of lore. A Foreign Office official relished the news of the appointment of a Soviet consul at Jeddah: "Now we will have some fun." A novitiate, "plunged into a strange world" of bewildering complexity, relished becoming "a *real* cog in the machinery, not merely a make-believe humbug." He soon joined the chorus propounding Bolshevik conspiracy theories. After all, the British now formally occupied what they had traditionally perceived and what official comment now recognized as the consummate spy-space. What continued to make the hunt for the secret center exigent, despite the fun of it all, was the lingering fear that in this land of trivial plots a *grand* conspiracy might actually be afoot, thanks to the dangerously diluted oriental nature of Russians and Turks. The game in Arabia had become Great.[41]

A conspiracy is a plot; a conspiracy theorist, someone who discerns a plot behind what might be random events. He searches for a *story* to knit together diverse events. He is perhaps a fantasist. In the increasingly bureaucratized postwar era, intelligence reports about the Middle East continued to bear a robust literary tinge and partiality for the parable. They were still read for "interest and humour" as much as information. Arabia remained a land of stories to British agents, and conspiracy theories were perhaps the logical end of their literary efforts there. The General Staff investigation into the Mesopotamian unrest, most likely authored by Bray, consisted primarily of a lengthy narrative of events from 1919 to 1920, complete with episodic chapter headings such as, "Kurdish and Arab hopes disappointed," "Faisal loses influence," demonstrating the buildup of Moscow's "general strategic plan" against England. The habit of narrativizing intelligence in this region found its apotheosis in this hunt for the causes of the unrest: all facts and impressions were collected into a grand narrative much greater than the sum of its seemingly insignificant parts. Colleagues tellingly referred to Bray's careful collation of information as a "disquieting chronicle." The IDCEU was established ostensibly to address a threat whose geographical reach exceeded that of any one department of government and to make sense of the masses of contradictory evidence about different conspiracies, but its operating assumption was that these contradictions were only superficial, that beneath them all lay a carefully concealed, consistent story of Turkish/Bolshevik activity against Britain. They were right that the contradictory evidence about Turkish and Russian policy in the Middle East was not a mere artifact of the data but remained blind to its source—the chaotic state of affairs in revolutionary Russia and Turkey. But then, the British official mind—and its blindness—was itself conditioned by the apparent chaos of the postwar world and by the official "idea of Arabia."[42]

Stranger Than Strange Theories

In a report from Bahrein in 1920, Dickson scoffed at Ibn Saud's allegation that "we English frame our policy on the first bit of gossip we pick up"—before obligingly passing on the latest Bahreini gossip about Najd. A decade later, Andrew Ryan, the British minister in Jeddah, again vigorously denied Saudi allegations that rumors proliferated largely in response to the demand of British spies. He protested—too much, I think—that he did not root around for rumors or employ others to do so but that "they reached me in profusion through my own ears and those of my staff." In fact, every intelligence digest from the Middle East included a section on "Rumour," partly on the grounds of the sparsity of more reliable sources but also because of the old saw that gossip contained a kernel of truth about the whole region. Fantastical news, one report explained, "though not to be accepted with credulity, is nevertheless a straw which shows the direction of the wind." In the postwar era, when all this news of confessedly doubtful validity collectively created an impression of massive subversion, officials habituated to reading reports with a grain of salt saw even the *conspiracies* as a "direction of the wind," phantasmal, wraithlike things that could neither be checked nor accurately assessed. However determined the hunt for the secret center, the secret itself defied all efforts at precise exposition, its nebulousness also conveniently explaining away discrepancies between theory and observable reality. The strangeness of British conspiracy theories about the Middle East did not stop at their irrefutability; they were also, in the last analysis, ineffable—hence their prolixity, profusion, and incoherence.[43]

Since all news of conspiracy was merely a sign of the direction of the wind but nevertheless a sign of the direction of the wind, it was impossible to safely dismiss even the most glaringly incompetent subversive organization. Major Valentine Vivian had served in intelligence in India, Palestine, and Constantinople (and would soon help the War Office assess proposals for a regionwide intelligence organization in the Middle East). With all this accumulated expertise, he at once scorned the pretensions, naïveté, and laughable attendance of the Mouvahiddin Society and took seriously its claims to universal Islamic membership, which, he said, invested it with "the sinister features of a Terrorist organisation of world-wide scope." "In common with ... all Pan-Islamic schemes," he warned, "the boundless ambition of its aims and the grandiloquence of the language employed seem to detract from the practical dangers which the 'MOUVAHIDIN' Society may have in store for British interests." In this program of almost willful paranoia, stemming from a vision of notional rather than concrete conspiracy, an admittedly anemic society could still cause considerable embarrassment to the empire.[44]

British conspiracy thinking about Arabia thus diverged somewhat from standard definitions in that officials attributed little agency to Middle Easterners themselves. The passive voice runs throughout Bray's reports; agency, and the ultimate enemy, remain obscure, a sort of elemental force or spirit. After confidently dismissing the Silk Letter Plot as a pathetic attempt to manipulate an artificial Pan-Islamism, Bray still insisted on the existence of "a force tending to unite Mohammedans all over the world," an indefinable, almost unconscious unity—"a feeling, illusionary." In a sense, there could be no single "mastermind" behind the conspiracies because Orientals did not possess individual minds as such. Theirs was a collective existence, made possible by the magic information network. The "minds of the masses over a wide area" were disturbed, Bray wrote, "as the still surface of a lake is ruffled by a slight breeze." To Charles Cleveland's query about the "one brain" behind prewar Indian agitation, he replied: "Yes—but that brain is not a human one...!" This perception of a collective Asiatic mind derived both from an orientalist attitude incapable of recognizing the agency of "Asiatics" and from agents' assumption that anything observed or observable, including an uncovered plot, was only an epiphenomenon of "the underlying forces and organization." While conventional conspiracy theorists see hidden actors behind the stage, these fantasists saw a hidden force *behind* the hidden actors *behind* the stage. Bray disclosed, "Because we find the threads leading to BERLIN and MOSCOW it by no means proves that we have reached the end of our investigations, we have only commenced them." Having charted the network of subversives, named various causes, legitimate and illegitimate, he ultimately came up with an empty hand. There was always another still obscured source.[45]

It was because they focused on a subversive energy rather than on individuals that the conspiracy theories proved so capacious, accommodating Turks, Russians, the French, and sundry others in a single, formless cabal. George Kidston at the Foreign Office insisted on the "fundamental error" of thinking "there is or ever has been any dividing line between the CUP and bolshevism. The force behind all these movements is the same." These formidable bogeys were only fronts for the mother of all bogeys—a third, nameless, as yet hidden force, an abstract destructive energy. "The first object in all cases," he continued, "is the destruction of all existing institutions and the force behind the movement alone knows what is ultimately to be substituted for them." In each place, "it" manifested itself differently: in Turkey, as the CUP; in Russia, the Soviet; in Germany, Spartacism; in Ireland, the Sinn Fein; in Persia, the Young Persia Party; in the Dutch East Indies, the Sarikat al Islam; in Egypt and India, nationalist movements; in England, the Independent Labour Party, everywhere exploiting grievances against existing regimes—the czars, military defeat, "our past mistakes" (Ireland), "national conceit of a dead past" (Persia). This was a force of karmic justice and no less inimical for all its claims to righteousness. It was, Kidston asserted, unwise "to treat its varying manifestations as if they spring from entirely different sources." Kidston claimed a sort of omniscience, but what ultimately did he think he knew? Without an understanding of how he and fellow officials perceived the world, especially the voluptuous spread of it between Moscow and Mecca, his knowledge remains unintelligible. In this land of intrigue, intrigue itself was superficial, concealing an entire cosmos governed by primordial forces. To be sure, the talk about a destructive force at

OFFICIAL CONSPIRACY THEORIES   225

large was partly a rhetorical lamentation of the passing of the old order. Late in 1920, Churchill lectured to the City of London about a "world wide conspiracy...designed to deprive us of our place in the world and rob us of victory." His uplifting message was that Britain would overcome this "malevolent and subversive force" as it had others, but his metaphor quickly acquired literal political content as he enumerated the abstract force's material constituents— "the Irish murder gang, the Egyptian Vengeance Society, the seditious extremism in India...the arch-traitors...at home."[46]

While Kidston and Churchill conjured up a hydra-headed adversary, contorting the word "conspiracy" into nearly impossible shapes, others attempted to give a name to the shadowy force behind all the unrest. Some called it "Islam," a living, pulsating entity with its own earthly existence. Those proposing a special Middle East intelligence center pressed the need to know "more about Islam as a whole than its Moslem subjects themselves." Agents assumed that in reports of "this or that Pan-Islamic society or group," they received "scattered items" of the "complete Pan-Islamic programme," which existed, it seems, apart from Pan-Islamists themselves—despite, for instance, the IDCEU's catalogue of the bewildering number of positions on so-called Pan-Islamic issues such as the caliphate. Bray listed as "symptoms" of the movement the tendency of Muslims everywhere to exhibit "discontent with their status, taking [sic] offence more easily, more sensitive to their religious scruples, less friendly as a whole to ourselves." These were not, to him, causes in themselves but signifiers of a yet deeper cause.[47]

Or, the trouble was "nationalism," which, in tribal Arabia, could only be artifice. The War Office reasoned that contact among Arabs, encouraged by the war, made "a Nationalistic feeling more easily fostered" through propaganda. Therefore, if trouble emerged in Mesopotamia, "fostered and created by Arab leaders, there would probably be some sort of organisation behind it." With this non sequitur the War Office expressed its view of Arab nationalism as an artificial construct designed to promote coalescence among factious tribes, a false consciousness imposed by a hidden organization, *behind* them, whose existence had to be deduced, as if nationalism were secret and not openly proclaimed every day by masses of people everywhere. (Indeed, in their intelligence reports, agents treated public denunciations of British imperialism as covert activities they had cleverly exposed.) Hence, to watch any one nationalist movement, the agents had to watch them all, as well as their European backers. No nationalism worth watching existed outside the internationally organized sort, since "sincere," local nationalisms would naturally favor "development under British control." As late as 1930, the British minister at Jeddah described Ibn Saud's minister of foreign affairs as "anti-British in the sense of so many

Orientals who are hostile to our 'Imperialism' and administration over Moslems; but he has never shewn with me any signs of a violently anti-British virus." Putting its own empire in scare quotes, British officialdom failed to see the wood for the trees. In their rose-tinted view, those doubting Britain's good intentions had obviously been duped by external agencies: Bray was certain that ordinarily loyal Pan-Arabs had begun to suspect Britain of nurturing exploitative, "Imperialistic ambitions" in Arabia only because of "Bolshevik nationalist intrigue." All Middle Eastern avowals of nationalism were degraded and deligitimized by absorption into a grand conspiracy of indeterminate authorship. In his only public explanation of the 1920 unrest, Arnold Wilson argued that "external" forces and extremists had hijacked nationalist ideals to pursue "revolutionary, fanatical and anarchic" ends; the administration had not fallen "through any inherent defect."[48]

To others, the subversive energy signaled not so much nationalism as an epic clash of civilizations—"the antipathy of east v. west." The apparent yearning for equality was but the expression of a "hidden brain" exploiting every local argument "to upset the present order." It was a will to freedom *manufactured* to achieve a freedom it desired only for invidious purposes and was easily elided into anarchism: the uprisings were "symptoms...of that intolerance of authority...which is the characteristic feature of the world today." The East sought to oust the West not because it desired independence but because it remained committed to chaos (revealing just how much it needed the West's tutelage). The openly socialist aims of the Mouwazanat il Ibad in Palestine and Syria were disregarded as nonsense, for "the real object of the Society is to organise and join up all Mohammedan countries so as to render government by a European country impossible" (surely, a program compatible with socialist pretensions). Indeed, avowals of socialist commitments as much as nationalism were only ever "socialist camouflage" in British eyes. Anti-British conspirators had "invented fictitious socialist parties in Turkey, Egypt, India etc. where of course socialism is in reality almost unknown."[49]

Even theories clearly identifying a Russian or Turkish mastermind configured the enemy as an incorporeal adversary, an anthropomorphized wantonness. The Turks' "covert hostilities" exploited and gave "a sense of unity and direction to every unconnected form of intrigue," giving "local unrest...a different and wider significance and a new intensity and bitterness," reported the Iraqi Air Command. The Turks were a cementing force lending artificial meaning to otherwise insignificant and disconnected events. The General Staff urged all British officers to absorb this fact, in their case identifying a Soviet hand. After an exhaustive narrative of the "tangled skein in the Middle East," they pointed to the danger of regarding "events in each country as isolated and independent," since in fact it was all the result of a Bolshevik conspiracy against the British Empire, "assisted by other agencies and influences." Indeed, "far from its apparently isolated countries being allowed to work out their salvation...the whole Middle East is being kept in turmoil...on a definite plan." The conspicuous irony of the region heretofore thought of as hopelessly disunited becoming a solid block of subversive energy was explicable by recourse to a theory of diffuse conspiracy bound by Moscow's sinister activity.[50]

Who Knows Most Knows Least

Besides epistemological predilections, this peculiar brand of conspiracy thinking was also fueled by political struggles within the world of Arabian intelligence, manifested in a rancorous contest over the claim to genius. Whitehall evidently respecting "special knowledge loudly declared," it became ever more crucial for the ambitious agent to prove *unique* insightfulness, to claim possession of the most abstruse level of knowledge of the region—and thus preserve the control of policy secured during the war. Bury bewailed the "fungus-like growth of 'Arabian experts'" produced by the war, counting a bare handful of authentic experts (presumably including himself). He ridiculed the "cocksureness" with which neophytes advertised their opinions and their sublime indifference to the inaccuracies produced by a *limited perspective*. He was most offended by their "crass empiricism," which prevented them from comprehending "the rough-cut, many-sided and clouded crystal of Arabian politics." Gertrude Bell's enduring rivalry with Arnold Wilson thrived in this competitive atmosphere. Arriving on the eve of the insurrection, the new commander in chief Aylmer Haldane dismissed Wilson's dispiriting briefing about expected trouble in favor of Bell's more optimistic assessment, since she, after all, "knew the Arabs more intimately than any other member of the civil staff." (Bell had reversed her position within days, but General Headquarters only caught up months later when the crisis was recognized as a state of war.) Indeed, the Iraqi rebellion opened up a window for asserting special knowledge as part of a critique of policy. "*Those who know the country and the people* are convinced that the present state of affairs would not have arisen if the original policy of HMG had been carried out properly," Young insisted, adding, "It would be unwise to neglect individual opinions which are in some cases very strongly held." Bell likewise complained of her former underling, the India Office's Garbett, fecklessly trespassing "where *we who know* take care not to tread."[51]

The conspiracy explanations most of them offered for the unrest emerged as part of this competition, each tarring the other with the brush of paranoia as the explanation itself began to vanish into obscurity. Conspiracies unmasked by green agents handicapped by rookie credulity were dismissed as routine Arab intrigue. When Consul C. E. S. Palmer first arrived in Damascus, modesty compelled the disclaimer, "I am still too new to this milieu of intrigue and wild rumours to venture upon more than a mere statement of the two versions without making any attempt at deciding between them." Even this tentativeness was not enough to avert the condescension of his betters at the Middle East Department. Of his frequent reports about the intrigues of one Oseimi, Lawrence wrote witheringly: "Assaimi [sic] doesn't matter....Can nobody turn this tap off?" Palmer soon learned the ways of the classic Arabia agent, submitting a theory of Saudi-French conspiracy as "more a prophecy than a mere surmise." Within months, he felt sufficiently experienced to grumble that "amateur civilians" were "very apt to adopt a definite attitude towards any given political question shortly after their arrival in the Near East. They seem to—as it were—crystallize in this opinion, and are thereafter unwilling to or incapable of modifying it later even in the face of overwhelming evidence against it." This skepticism was reserved for the conspiracy theories of lesser observers; he continued to propound conspiracy theories of his own, as was his prerogative as an increasingly seasoned agent.[52]

In 1921, the Secret Intelligence Service (SIS) was made exclusively responsible for espionage on an interservice basis, although it had not yet closed in on the Middle East, the last preserve of amateurs. Nevertheless, the rise of professional agents in various intelligence institutions rankled, and many veterans of Middle Eastern intelligence blamed the conspiracy-thinking culture on their influence. For instance, Cox took it upon himself to privately submit his "personal impressions" to defuse the alarm caused by doomsaying military intelligence reports on the Karbala conference. "'Military Intelligence' like 'Scotland Yard' are rather inclined to build up a theory from a co-ordination of reports from all directions and then without realising it proceed to work up to it," he explained. Similarly, old hands in the Middle East Department pointed a guilty finger at the professionals' obsession with Pan-Islamic subversion in Palestine. Young asked his former Arab Bureau chief, now chief secretary in Palestine, Gilbert Clayton, for a "personal impression," which he forwarded to his colleagues. Clayton's advice was that they take SIS reports with "a few grains of salt":

> I have had a fairly extensive experience in intelligence work in this
> part of the world...and I have always found, as I have no doubt you
> have too, that there is a tendency in purely Intelligence Agencies to
> be attracted towards mysterious and occult organisations spreading
> their tentacles all over the world. The "Black Hand" is a very

fascinating bogey but sometimes it is advisable to look nearer home
for the real source of trouble.

The SIS was apparently hurt by these remarks, but its staff might have taken
heart from the fact that Clayton was more dismissive of the messenger than the
message: he in fact agreed that Pan-Islam was a potent force, quibbling only
with its relative importance among other forces. This exchange between Young
and Clayton was more about affirming their special ability to recognize which
unrest mattered and which was merely innocuous oriental intrigue than about
questioning the consensus around conspiracy. It worked: Clayton's standing
was such that one of Young's colleagues ultimately pronounced himself "hardly
competent to express an opinion on the same paper as Sir G. Clayton." As
before, the informal contacts among the community of agents facilitated the
communication of "personal" impressions and allowed them to reserve the
final word on Arabian affairs, even as they gradually abandoned the field itself
to the professionals. Clayton served next as high commissioner in Iraq (until
his death in 1929). Then too official respect for his special knowledge was said
to have enabled him to persuade the government to comply with Iraqi requests
for League of Nations admission by 1932: such advice "would have been disregarded at their peril by any British Government, least of all by Ministers who
had still to prove their grasp of Oriental affairs" (a *Times* jibe at the Labour
government).[53]

The new class of agent, for its part, blamed the conspiracy culture on the
entrenchment of the veterans' intelligence-gathering style. Lieutenant Colonel
Geoffrey Wheeler, who served in Iraq, Persia, and Turkey, reflected that the
glamorization of the "great game"-style had produced agents who collected little information of real value and were "disposed to clutch at every cheap scrap
of evidence which corroborated official theory, and to overlook the circumstances which should have inspired a prudent Skepticism....They seldom
brought themselves to the point of making a detached and impartial survey of
the immensely complex phenomenon of Asiatic politics." He found irritating
British officials' habit of crediting Soviet intelligence and propaganda with
"superhuman skill in manipulating eastern government" and accepting
"reports of their machinations...much too readily." From his own experience,
he knew the intelligence organization accepted a report because it "fit in with
what had by then become a habit of thought," and "its original effect persisted
even after it became known that the report was spurious." Likewise, Robert
Brooke-Popham, air officer commanding in Iraq, while recognizing the old
hands' insecurity about the new RAF intelligencers, expressed concern about
their desperate efforts to prove their superiority. Dickson, for instance, knew

a great deal, but was "far more concerned in shewing how great is Dickson's influence than in carrying out the policy of HMG. He is quite unbalanced and whilst generally he claims to have full knowledge of everything that is going on he will occasionally go to the opposite extreme and says that he is entirely in the dark." He was "one of those people who see all sides of the question equally at the same time, so he never follows a straight and firm course"—"at heart more Arab than British," came the damning phrase. Mistrustful professionals blamed charlatan veterans for generating paranoia by relying on intuition and for thus knowing all and nothing at once—precisely what the vague conspiracy theories claimed to do.[54]

While the old hands and the neophytes bemoaned each other's pernicious influence, jealous career bureaucrats panicked about the ascendancy of flamboyant agents in Whitehall. They had been worried from the outset; indeed, they had preferred situating the Arab Bureau in Cairo partly because it was better than London for "controlling free lances" like Sykes. The bureau itself was designed not only to house "a sufficient body of arab experts," but, Henry McMahon hoped, "to restore well meaning but mistaken enthusiasts to a sense of proper perspective and proportion." It would channel the experts' anarchic energies into imperially useful *political* directions; genius would check the excesses of genius. Clearly, McMahon, the much-bypassed high commissioner, had been too optimistic. By war's end, it was clear that "official harness still sits lightly on Lawrence's shoulders." Churchill felt proud of having put him into a "bridle and collar" at the Colonial Office, but his wary undersecretary of state doubted Lawrence would ever fit into the "official machine," accustomed as he was to dealing directly with ministers "and Ministers only—and I see trouble ahead if he is allowed too free a hand." Similarly, some Foreign Office hands chafed at the agents' prima donna behavior and reporting style. If his underlings saw him in the mold of the heroic Arabist agent, Arnold Wilson remained something of a stodgy old India hand as he struggled with systemic insubordination from the likes of Leachman and Noel. Noting the rise of such types in London, he and his old friends at the India Office advised, "Too much 'local colour—acquired 'on the spot'—is rather a dangerous thing in a headquarters department." He objected to the new Whitehall inductees—Garbett, Young, Lawrence—as "enthusiasts" and "out and out theorist[s]" and grew veritably paranoid about Bell's correspondence with high-level friends. (The suspicion was entirely mutual.) He insisted that his men, and not enthusiasts who had the ear of government, were the true "experts."[55]

As the decade wore on, the alleged fanatical streak of agent-administrators ran like a red thread through the bureaucracy's discussions of these parvenus—some of whom criticized the government's generosity to the Arabs and some its betrayal of promises to them. Disagreement over policy—especially if couched as an assertion of superior knowledge—could not be brooked by a state bent on making the erstwhile frontier zone a routinely administered part of empire where everyone toed the official line. Like the new class of professional agents, bureaucrats turned the blame game against the veterans, seeing any criticism of Middle Eastern policy as proof of their megalomania and paranoia (variously about Bolsheviks, Turks, Pan-Islamists, or the British government itself). If Bell "[took] some handling" and Noel was wildly overzealous, the RAF intelligence officer John Glubb was entirely "unreasonable." (He eventually "defected" to an Iraqi government post when the War Office recalled him from his work in the southern desert in 1926.) Meinertzhagen quarreled with his uncle Sidney Webb, the Labour colonial secretary in 1929, whom he found entirely lacking in "imagination." A new appointee for Jeddah was firmly discouraged from meeting George Lloyd in Cairo on the grounds that Lloyd would so excite him with a "slightly false perspective" as to incapacitate his judgment indefinitely. (Lloyd resigned in 1929 in protest against Labour's conciliatory tack toward Egypt.) Dickson, who named his son after Ibn Saud, confided to Philby, "The whole [Colonial Office] seems to look upon me as something dangerous, why I don't know." Officialdom likewise shunned Bray after his retirement in 1923 when he adopted "a more critical attitude towards Government." Having long respected him, with hindsight his Whitehall colleagues judged him "intense and misguided." Exhausted, apparently by domestic troubles, and too ill to take up a post in the colonies, he joined the SIS under cover of the Passport Control Branch and headed for Geneva—Sir Wyndham Childs, the head of Scotland Yard, shared his view of Switzerland as a "nest of Turkish-cum-Bulgarian-cum-Indian intrigue." The SIS eventually dumped him too, allegedly for reasons of temperament, and he later fell under suspicion as the "go-between" for Danish arms dealers and Ibn Saud. The reclusive Peake Pasha, the ex-Egyptian Camel Corps officer commanding Transjordan's Arab Legion, was likewise eyed with suspicion. A certain intensity seemed to set some agents-turned-officials apart, to mark them as somehow unbalanced, in their mutinously pro-Arab views, their fervid partisanship for a particular group, or their sheer paranoia about Soviet and other threats. Of these mavericks, Philby, the devoted pro-Saudian, would prove most troublesome. After serving unhappily in the new, Hashemite Iraq, he was appointed chief British representative at Amman, where his constant straining at the leash and "fanatical nature" caused enormous anxiety at the Colonial Office (he was as displeased with pro-Hashemite policy as with Jewish immigration into Palestine), until, in high dudgeon, he resigned from public service in 1924. Not that that ended official worries: he left for Najd. His adversaries' paranoid descriptions of *his* paranoia were part of an effort to delegitimize his claim to a special understanding of Arabia. Paranoia was in this sense entirely political, and the political contest ultimately enshrouded the "real reasons" behind Middle Eastern unrest as the exclusive but ultimately ineffable knowledge of a few individuals in Whitehall.[56]

Still, genius was rare enough and the Middle East inscrutable enough that government officials continued to depend on the views of these tarnished idols. Philby became a kind of forbidden oracle, whom lesser agents were obliged to spy on as a fount of exclusive information, ever more so as he became closer to Ibn Saud, as we shall see. Likewise, Foreign Office annoyance with Glubb's presumptuousness did not prevent them from avidly reading his reports, implicitly trusting his interpretation despite complaining of his refusal to "stick to the facts." After ostracizing Bray, the Foreign Office also continued to read his voluntary appreciations, calculating that "wild" as they were, "his information may be of value." Even as they were dismissed for their paranoia, these agents retained a special position within the pantheon of agent-prophets of Arabia, ensuring that the official understanding of events in the Middle East remained contradictory, impressionistic, and confused, at best.[57]

The factions asserting competing claims to superior knowledge of the region had emerged from a cleavage within the world of Arabia agents, not so much between those who supported and those who criticized the government as between those who were willing to submit to bureaucratic trespass into their beloved Arabia and those who could not. Philby aggravated the government precisely because he represented himself as "having the support of all the intelligence agents of British policy in the Near East, but that both he and they are thwarted by official obstruction at headquarters." His efforts to be friendly with the consul at Damascus were interpreted as part of a "scheme" of "getting at" colleagues who might prove sympathetic to his views. Bray's apparent discombobulation was likewise presumed to be the result of Philby's diabolical influence. An informal network grew up among the outcasts in this intelligence community: Dickson and Philby confided to each other their difficulties and their success at fulfilling the traditional, but now suspect professional goal of becoming as "badawi" as possible. Bertram Thomas traced his love for the region to Dickson, venerating him as "one of the great ones rather shamefully shelved" and his guru in "muntafiq methods of surprise." He gibed Philby for "crossing the rubicon and embracing akhwanism" but insisted he was "as big a renegade myself [for] coquetting with the sunnis." Glubb also joined this circle. A sort of mutual adoration society emerged among rogue agents bemoaning their government's stupidity in casting them off, even while they enjoyed the eminently heroic status of official outcasts. Earlier, all Arabia agents had formed a community of insubordinate—but indulgently insubordinate—agents; now a smaller group shared their transgressions and insights and commiserated over their misguided superiors.[58]

So emerged a contest between veteran agents who fell foul of the government, veterans who adapted to a complacent bureaucracy, a new class of professional agents emulating the veterans, and career bureaucrats resentful of veterans' influence. In the spaces between them, conspiracy thinking flourished. Despite some agents' skepticism about the theories propounded by their competitors, each group remained determined to claim exclusive insight into *the* ultimate explanation of the mysterious unrest, pulling and stretching the word "conspiracy" until it acquired a transcendental quality befitting an intelligence world habitually distracted by fantasy. Indeed, in the professionals' and the veteran amateurs' eager vilification of each other's interpretations of events, what is most striking is the tenacity of the conspiracy-thinking mode. That all the dissension did not in the end discredit it is evidenced by the continued production of alarmist, speculative intelligence reports throughout the decade. The skeptics' continual protests of disbelief bespeak the indelible influence of the enthusiasts' views.

The End and Ends of Fear

Paranoia about the subversive powers of Arabia served the specific political purpose of preserving the British administration intact against all calls for reform. The General Staff summarized the "true causes" of the Iraqi rebellion as a series of triggers, beginning with the Sykes-Picot agreement and a "divergent departmental policy" and ending with Arab-Bolshevik-Turkish collaboration in a "preconceived Bolshevik plan of attack," which rendered it "idle to search for local causes." Local political failure was thus subsumed in the larger narrative of grand conspiracy, against which all efforts to mitigate local discontent would have been futile. This proleptic argument preserved the fiction of British skill in ruling "natives" and mooted any notion of recommending (expensive) policy changes—but at the cost of living in fear for the foreseeable future. The key point here is that *the series of triggers went off on their own*; agency was neither British nor Arab. Unrest stemmed from an inevitable or inexorable process. Such conspirator-less conspiracy theories emerged from the reigning idea of Arabia as a heterocosm, encoded and ordered, where cause and effect could be felt hundreds of miles away. As General Haldane put it after a tour of inspection, Iraq, "like a sheet of parchment, rises at any point where a weight [occupying troops] is lifted from its surface."[59]

As the name given to all manifestations of political discontent in the Arab world, "conspiracy" stripped them all of legitimacy. Traditionally, officials had striven to distinguish between those "against us from religious conviction," who were accorded a measure of respect, and "a common self-seeking conspirator." By attributing all motivation behind massive rebellions in India, Iraq, and other places to a handful of conspirators in Switzerland or even vaguer, more baleful agencies, British observers avoided seeing any meaning in them; they constituted no *protest* (of, say, political or economic discontent at living continuously under military occupation), only proof of geopolitical stratagem motivated solely by a malefic wish to injure the British Empire. Dickson, reporting on the Muntafiq Division, credited pro-Turkish rumors to "certain evil wishers of Government" simply because he could "only account for the phenomenon in this way." The "evil wishers" themselves remained nameless; like Bray's "force" they were an occult agency without any specific identity. Unable to conceive of dissatisfaction with British rule, agents conjured up an occult world of abstract, senseless evildoers. The "tremendous agitation" in Iraq was "a regular conspiracy...to undermine our authority." It could not simply be an *agitation*. Paranoia was in this sense a hubris-induced perversion of imagination.[60]

It also represented a colossal failure of imagination. Agents were frankly stumped by the apparent identity between their former allies and the new "extremists."[61] Paralysis drove them, as was their prerogative and habit, to look for epic meaning, which a grand conspiracy could provide—even against the backdrop of the actually epic postwar reordering of the world. While they may have felt proud of their "imaginative" divination of the hidden realities of Asian politics, in fact they could not *imagine* a multiplicity of views among "Asiatics," much less attribute to them any agency outside of blind obedience to the considerable suggestive powers of the region's collective mind.

They did not all remain in thrall to these theories. By 1926, ongoing Saudi-Hashemite hostilities and a strikingly tame conference at Mecca had begun to restore faith in the hopeless disunity of Islam. As Turkey turned "anti-religious," the Pan-Islamic bogey receded further. By 1929–1930, the Foreign Office was dismissing reports of Saudi-backed Pan-Islamism in India and elsewhere as "utopian." Its officials also grew certain that "Germany and Turkey have definitely turned their backs on Palestine, Syria and Arabia," that Italy's hands were full elsewhere, and that "the Soviet Union have far more fruitful fields for their destructive toil." The Palestine situation was admittedly "dangerous" but specifically "because of the Jew-Arab conflict"; likewise Syria, thanks to "smouldering resentment against the French." In short, there was "little substance in all this talk of an elaborate and well organised plot." Here, finally, a spark of recognition of local discontent. Colonial Office officials were still convinced (probably rightly) that the Bolsheviks were "trying to get their toes in" all over Arabia but newly satisfied that they could not of themselves cause a "row." There was the "annual danger that they *may* use the pilgrimage season to disseminate propaganda over the Moslem countries," but then the king was "bound in his own interests to resist all attempts at bolshevik penetration." As the decade wore on, British analysts also grew increasingly sanguine of the spurious nature of reports of Russian and Turkish troop amassments on the borders of the Middle Eastern empire. Reports of Ibn Saud's expansionism were likewise taken in stride by officials confident of the jejuneness of his ambitions and of the idle nature of his contacts with "Arab malcontents in the mandated territories." Thus, after a decade of apparently abortive grand conspiracies, officialdom grew more certain that they had been "domesticated," had become part of the usual oriental intrigue, ineradicable and ineffectual by definition. Officialdom had learned to "manage" paranoia.[62]

Still, not everyone was so sure. Fears of Iraqi-Syrian unity revived. At the end of the period, the specter of Pan-Islam began to haunt officials again. The term "Pan-Islamism" remained fraught, signifying, to some, an organized movement of debatable strength, and to others, a convenient catchall for the "latent energy" of anti-British movements, which, so named, acquired (rhetorical) cohesiveness and morphed into "manifestations" of a (purely notional) conspiracy. Despite relative confidence in the essentially utopian nature of Pan-Arab and Pan-Islamic ideals in a real world of intense, but comforting Hashemite-Saudi antipathy, the "pan-" bogey remained potent, as a source of potential political inspiration if not an actually realizable program. Likewise, the covert and psychological nature of the Russian and Turkish threat—propaganda, small bands, agents, and arms trafficking—prohibited official dismissal. Fear also lingered that, in the continuing absence of a significant British gesture, Ibn Saud might consort with the Bolsheviks to enhance his prestige as a "more 'independent' ruler." Despite suspicions that he deliberately stoked British fears to extort favors, many were convinced the Bolshevik danger was still "very real." The worldwide financial crisis sharpened fears of Saudi-Soviet rapprochement. Fear of extremists and Bolshevik agents gaining entry into Palestine "under the cloak of jewish immigration" also could not be conquered. There was no escape from anxiety about Arabia; the potency of the Hejaz's image as a secret center was too great and the imagined conspiracy too formless. New theories emerged about regional (Hashemite) conspiracies *against* Ibn Saud, and Hitler's rise in 1933 revived presentiments of a German attack via the Middle East. Conspiracy thinking set up a constant unthreatening threat emanating from the Middle East. Officials repeatedly concluded that there was no "immediate threat" against the Pax Britannica but also that the conspirators had not abandoned their ambitious aims. The absence of clear and present danger could not dissolve the metaphysical sort of conspiracy theories being articulated. A constant sense that the empire was under siege pervaded the decade, although never enough to warrant investment in expensive defensive infrastructure. When the IDCEU tried in 1926 to extend the SIS into Arabia—the last big gap in its organization—many departments conceded the inadequacies of the existing intelligence organization, but none was willing to spearhead increased investment in it.[63]

The very schizophrenia of this conspiracy-thinking culture helped underwrite the argument for holding onto Iraq. Cox argued that without a British presence there, they would have to reckon with "a pan-islamic combination strongly influenced from Moscow and controlling a solid block of mahommedan territory from Constantinople through...Afghanistan, whose Government will be pursuing a policy specifically designed to destroy the British position in the Middle East and India." Thus, the very existence of the British regime in the Middle East, the target of the conspirators' threat, prevented that threat from ever being consummated. Like the wartime Arab Revolt, British Iraq was a "wedge directed towards their vitals." It was the dam holding back a continental flood of subversive energy. Montagu and Curzon described the fight in Mesopotamia as a fight "for the very existence of civilization in the Middle East." Were the British driven out, "only anarchy can supervene."[64]

Like most episodes of conspiracy thinking, this one was partly symptomatic of intense social and psychological strain, produced in this case by the upheavals of war and ideological challenges to the old imperial order. But there is more to it than imperial anxiety. In the interwar period, what Gordon Wood might call the "underlying metaphysics" of British official thinking changed as it absorbed the epistemology of Arabist agents, in which a mystical reading of signs carried within it the seeds of official paranoia. Much like the new quantum theory of physics, political analysis of the Middle East rested on a belief in several possible worlds existing simultaneously. Officials and agents acted as though all scenarios were simultaneously true; they never really found out which was true and were not particularly interested in doing so—Bray could simultaneously name the Kemalists *and* Standard Oil as the mastermind behind the unrest without demur. They dealt, like the new physicists, in the cloud of probabilities produced by the ambulant nature of the objects of their scrutiny: they knew that they could never really know what was true in Arabia. In the Arabian heterocosm, conspiracy thinking was unmoored from its Enlightenment origins. British officials searched not for the hidden will of humans, or even of God, but of the region itself—it was after all, a divine region.[65]

As for the elusive "causes of the unrest," historians generally agree that the rebellion—however nationalistic or spontaneous—was an expression of protest against the enduring occupation and a crushing tax regime.[66] The intelligence world was certainly implicated in local suffering—by their own testimony. While Bell dismissed as a product of his ignorance General Haldane's obsessive claims that the rising was due "mainly to hatred of individual political officers," she confessed that in the case of Diwaniyah—where the rising began—hatred of the local political officer had "precipitated" matters if not actually caused them. Others, including Wilson and Leachman, confirmed the political officer's brutality (although Wilson protected him and others with a similar reputation from formal censure.) Bell also knew that Leachman was "deeply hated" but ended her list there. If Leachman was, in Lawrence's terms, "first and foremost a bully," Leachman's description of his colleague Major Eadie—"He has a temper almost worse than my own"—is positively chilling. With these insights, however grudging, and the evidence provided by the rash of killings of political officers (including Leachman) just before and during the rising, we can safely conclude that political officers' "operational" duties were an important factor in local resentment, above and beyond the simple fact of British rule. Some recognized the hatred, albeit through a glass darkly, as the inevitable harvest of the White Man's Burden. It was in this vein that George Buchanan's *The Tragedy of Mesopotamia* (1938) sadly affirmed that the British had become "more hated than the Turks themselves had ever been." It was, indeed, "a tragedy of heroism."[67]

In this manner, too, British officials were not entirely off the mark in their certainty that "the outbreaks are due to wider and deeper causes than...the personality of the officer administering the law." There *was* something pulling the region together, providing the infrastructure of communication and mobility as well as a common adversary: the British Empire. Hence, perhaps, General Haldane's unintentionally incriminating observation that "where British administration was most strict and, to our way of thinking, more efficient, tribal combination was most effective against us," while "in wilder districts, which were ruled with a lighter hand, such combination failed to materalise." It was the Imperial General Staff that saw Palestine, Arabia, Persia, and Mesopotamia as important links "in a chain of contiguous areas under British influence, extending from Egypt to India." Frontierlessness was what the empire fostered by incorporating ever more territory into its own singular, if still patchwork, domain. And it had devised new ways of policing that domain, ways not unrelated to the "causes of the unrest."[68]

7

Air Control

"You have to understand the Arab mind," Capt. Todd Brown, a
company commander with the Fourth Infantry Division, said as he
stood outside the gates of Abu Hishma. "The only thing they
understand is force—force, pride and saving face."
—Dexter Filkins, "Tough New Tactics by U. S.
Tighten Grip on Iraq Towns," *New York Times,*
December 7, 2003

The camp commander [at Guantanamo], Rear Adm. [Harry B.]
Harris, said he did not believe the men [three detainees]
had killed themselves out of despair. "They are smart. They
are creative, they are committed," he said. "They have no
regard for life, either ours or their own.... This was not an act
of desperation, but an act of asymmetrical warfare waged
against us."
—"Guantanamo Suicides a 'PR Move,'" BBC
News, June 11, 2006

Satan being thus confined to a vagabond, wandering, unsettled
condition, is without any certain abode; for though he has, in
consequence of his angelic nature, a kind of empire in the liquid
waste or air, yet this is certainly part of his punishment, that he is
continually hovering over this inhabited globe of earth; swelling with
the rage of envy at the felicity of his rival, man; and studying all the

means possible to injure and ruin him; but extremely limited in his
power, to his unspeakable mortification.

—Daniel Defoe, *The History of the Devil*, 1726

Against the backdrop of official paranoia, Britain devised a new surveillance
technology in Iraq known as "air control." With it, intelligence in the Middle
East became fully "operational," and the downy dream of technocratic development was turned inside out to reveal its rugged militarist lining. Air control
was an example of that "rebellion of technology" that, for Walter Benjamin in
1937, defined "imperialistic war": "Instead of draining rivers, society directs a
human stream into a bed of trenches; instead of dropping seeds from airplanes,
it drops incendiary bombs over cities." In the air control scheme, the RAF collapsed the mission of regenerating Babylonia into the more urgent task of
patrolling the country from a network of bases and coordinating information
from agents on the ground to bombard subversive villages and tribes. To be
sure, airpower was also used elsewhere in the empire in 1919, in what have
been termed "spasmodic, almost casual affairs"; it was in Iraq that the British
would rigorously practice, if never perfect, the technology of bombardment as
a permanent method of colonial administration and surveillance and there that
they would fully theorize the value of airpower as an independent arm of the
military.[1]

Air control was cheap, as many contemporaries and scholars have noted,
but reasons of cost would have applied equally elsewhere—indeed, after an
incubatory period in Iraq, modified versions of air control were exported to
other parts of the empire. The scheme's cheapness helped sell the idea to the
cabinet but cannot explain its initial formulation for Iraq. Indeed, other
European and Arab powers in the region would also have felt the need to economize, but none developed a regime as skeletally austere or dependent on total
air substitution as the British.[2] How did the British come to invent an unprecedented scheme, relying on a new technology whose uses had yet to be fully
imagined, specifically for Iraq? The explanation lies in the realm of cultural
history, in the agents' confidence that Iraq was a place peculiarly suited to aerial
surveillance and far enough beyond the pale of bourgeois "convention" to moot
concerns about inhumanity—in any case, their intimate knowledge of the
place, evidenced by this representation, would guarantee humane application
of the system. When Whitehall opened its arms to this community of agents, it
invited in their way of thinking and decision-making. The spark of innovation
that had ignited the Middle Eastern campaigns would now set the region itself
ablaze.

The Fantasy

Demobilization remained a distant dream for British troops charged with confronting the anticolonial rebellions of 1919–21. As the situation in the Middle East grew dire, British officials searched desperately for a way to avert evacuation. Arabist intelligence agents emerged fervent proponents of airpower in general and the air control scheme in particular. Lawrence dated both his interest in joining the service and his conviction that "aircraft could rule the desert" to the war. Contemporaries too numbered him "first to realize" that air control would allow control without occupation. Winston Churchill, secretary of war and air, had long been intimate with the community of Arabist agents, through common social networks and a shared sensibility besides wartime contact and close cooperation at the Peace Conference. He too wagered that airpower might be used creatively to maintain order in the Iraqi mandate after the war. Geoffrey Salmond, whom Hugh Trenchard, the chief of Air Staff, dispatched to the region to assess the efficacy of Churchill's suggestion, was at once taken with the idea of using airpower to integrate the region into an administrative whole. Lawrence, then a fellow at Oxford, assisted in the RAF's subsequent efforts to devise a workable scheme, as did Iraq's civil commissioner, Arnold Wilson. (It was partly out of gratitude that Trenchard, who was often an outcast in official circles and felt strangely at ease in the company of Bell and Lawrence, helped Lawrence secure a place in the ranks in 1922, where he remained an influential presence until his death in 1935.) All this was made easier when Churchill, as colonial secretary, inducted Lawrence, Bullard, Young, and Meinertzhagen (an old friend of Trenchard's and of the new air secretary, Frederick Guest) into his new Middle East Department.[3]

These various experts deemed Mesopotamia *peculiarly* suitable for air operations, better than Europe, for aesthetic as much as topographical reasons: its presumed flatness promised many landing grounds, little cover to insurgents, and the possibility of "radiating" British power throughout the country from a handful of fittingly spartan bases, while the reality of its varied and protean topography, when acknowledged, was held to offer ideal training for the RAF, exposing it to every sort of terrain—mountains in Kurdistan, marshes in the south, riverain territory in between, and so forth. The difficulties of communication in Iraq made "the idea of using aircraft" "extremely tempting"; they could annihilate distance in hours. Air action was deemed *in*appropriate for police action in the densely populated urban environments of Britain, Ireland, and even Palestine. It was expressly framed as an updated approach to "small wars." Lawrence insisted, "The system is *not* capable of universal application."[4]

The agents perceived a basic congruence between the liberty of action of the aircraft and the desert warrior, both operating in empty, unmapped, magical spaces. The airplane was a winged irregular. Lawrence prophesied: "What the Arabs did yesterday the Air Forces may do to-morrow. And in the same way—yet more swiftly." Both could move beyond mere concentration of force and replace it with "an intangibly ubiquitous distribution of force—pressing everywhere yet assailable nowhere." Like the equally "splendid" tanks, aircraft embodied an austere, modernist reinvention of chivalric warfare. He joined the RAF himself for this reason and for the inevitable opportunity for fresh literary inspiration. "Since I was 16 I've been...steadily getting better," he explained to Trenchard. "My last book on Arabia is nearly good. I see the sort of subject I need in the beginning of your Force." (He eventually wrote *The Mint.*) As in Arabia, now again he wanted to "shed his past and *live* the part" in the hope that the rhythm of flight, like the camel's plod, would collapse sensation into artistic insight. His views were echoed by Glubb, Philby, Bell, and others, and found greater amplification in the RAF itself. "There appears to be a sort of natural fellow-feeling between these nomad arabs and the Air Force," remarked Robert Brooke-Popham, both before and after he had served as air commander in Iraq. "Perhaps both feel that they are at times in conflict with the vast elemental forces of nature." The parallels agents had drawn between British skills at sea and in the desert were now extended to the air (indeed, as Hew Strachan notes, aircraft took war to civilians in the manner of old-fashioned maritime blockade). The "desert with all its mysterious fascination" had "an unreal atmospheric quality comparable with the sky. Perhaps," pondered a wing commander, "this is why people call it 'The Blue.'" Their quiddities were the same. Hence, perhaps, the airplane's obvious suitability to exploration of desert lands; Lawrence foresaw it opening up and rendering comprehensible the still stubbornly blank spot of the Rub al-Khali, a project he passionately (if unsuccessfully) advocated long after he had otherwise departed from the Arabian scene.[5]

Air control, like irregular warfare, was designed to work in a country "where news flies on the wings of the wind." Speed allowed aircraft to counter tribesmen's ability to anticipate, through this prolific flow of news, the arrival of ground forces. "The punishment, like the news, will fly on the wings of the wind," explained Flight Lieutenant C. J. Mackay in a prize-winning essay for the Royal United Service Institute. If it failed to, the target could simply be changed. Moreover, aircraft would turn to advantage the region's systematic exaggeration of information: where there was one plane, Arabs would spread news of dozens; a few casualties would instill fear of hundreds. Iraq's lack of natural borders would enable aircraft to use disinformation as a practical strategy (the recourse to ungentlemanly "bluff" spun as proof of the British

willingness to take risks, use new technology, and rely on "racial superiority").
Trenchard envisioned a single imperial air force dispatched like a navy, in
fleets, with Baghdad the "pivot" of an imperial air route from England to Cairo
to Karachi to Singapore, along which reinforcements could be moved economically between theaters. The "moral effect" of air control upon subversives would
derive partly from "this ocular demonstration of the linking up of the British
garrisons in their midst with forces of unknown strength outside their ken."
Power would lie off-stage, just as it did when irregulars gestured at an "unknown
quantity" of supporters in the desert fastness. The logistics of the interwar strategic doctrine of maximum projection of and minimum actual use of force
depended on a particular conception of the kind of space the new Arabian
empire was.[6]

These spatial conceptions were of special consequence in the shadow of
Whitehall's conspiracy-theory explanations of the Iraqi insurrection. Air control was designed for a population conceived of as congenitally insurgent, an
always incipient guerrilla army lacking any agency of its own but available for
exploitation by an external agent. As counterinsurgent aerial guerrillas, the
British, too, would be elusive. Air control (with the help of wireless technology)
would at once raise the apparatus of imperial rule out of reach of these "stub-
born races" and create a surveillance regime capable of coping with nomad
existence and porous desert borders: "The 'long arm' of the new weapon renders it ubiquitous...[and] makes it practicable to keep a whole country under
more or less constant surveillance." It was an ideal system for the information
problems they faced in the Middle East. Through air control, the agents could
realize in a new dimension the controversial postwar dream of a regionwide
intelligence web (see chap. 8). It was essentially a system of control by intelligence, the epitome of the new operational intelligence, with aircraft substituting for the political officer who had long combined the tasks of intelligence and
administration. Indeed, earlier brainstorming about ways to reduce the occupying garrisons in Mesopotamia had contemplated replacing them with a skeletal
network of political officers, each individually capable of projecting as much, if
not more, power than a garrison; air control was the mechanical apotheosis of
this notion, minus the Achilles' heel of susceptible health. Like intrepid Arabist
agents, aircraft would allow the British to segue into, even manage, the magical
information network. The "official version" would "get around quicker," checking the contortions of information passed "by the natives from mouth to
mouth." The Air Staff warranted, "Frequent friendly patrols, dropping leaflets
containing suitable propaganda; disseminating correct news, and preventing
the wilful misinterpretation of the orders of a political officer by intriguing
headmen, may often prevent the seeds of unrest being sown by irresponsible

agitators." Aircraft, like conspiracy thinking, provided the security of *imagined* omniscience to an empire in the throes of rebellion.[7]

It was in this paranoid atmosphere that Lawrence and Churchill obtained approval of the scheme at the Cairo Conference of 1921, attended by luminaries of the Arabia intelligence and political establishment. The RAF officially took over in Iraq in October 1922, although it had become the dominant military force during the rebellion. It commanded eight squadrons of fighters and light bombers, several thousand Iraq Levies, and four armored car units (staffed by many former Black and Tans—an empirewide counterinsurgency staff for an apparently empirewide insurgency). Like airplanes, armored cars "showed their true paces" in Iraq. (In 1919, Lawrence, who had found them critical to being "everywhere at once" in the war, had approached J. F. C. Fuller on the question of using tanks in Arabia, which the latter considered "a fairy tale...unless he could provide the magic carpet"—a condition apparently filled by the air control regime.) Army garrisons were gradually whittled back to protect only the nine RAF bases. The last British battalion left in 1927; the last Indian, in 1928. The short range of most available aircraft made advanced landing grounds and emergency fuel and bomb dumps important. Air action was used against Turkish and Najdi raiders (at a time when frontiers were very much a work in progress) as well as Kurds and Arabs within Iraq proper. Theoretically, the levies were to be the first responders to unrest, followed by an "air demonstration" and dropped messages threatening hostile action, then action against livestock, and as a last resort, against villages—but theory was not implemented in practice, as we shall see. In a single two-day operation, a squadron might drop several dozen tons of bombs and thousands of incendiaries and fire thousands of rounds of small arms ammunition.[8]

This arrival of aircraft in Iraq was, as we have seen, understood in the same romantic developmental vein as the entire conquest of Mesopotamia. But besides restoring the cradle of civilization to its rightful position on the map of global commerce and communications, aircraft themselves, as a sophisticated technology, exercised a more traditional "civilizing effect," not least by demonstrating the advanced state of British civilization. The famous "furrow" ploughed across the desert to guide pilots on the air route to Baghdad was lauded as a feat of British ingenuity. The "romance" of desert flight derived from the "demonstration of the power of modern inventions which are able to conquer vast open spaces of the world...little known to civilised man"; technology remained the handmaiden of progress. The air also afforded a lofty view from which to observe the effects of the new, loftier imperialism, to witness "adoring Asia kindle and hugely bloom," in the poetic allusion of the *Illustrated London News*. (It also fittingly revealed the otherwise invisible traces left by their ancient imperial forbears.) Aerial surveillance and disciplining fit neatly into this vision of liberal empire in the sky. Flying over the desert on behalf of the Foreign Office, Hubert Young "felt that a new era had dawned, and that with the good-will of His Majesty's Government and the powerful help of the Royal Air Force the Arabs of Iraq would undoubtedly win their independence at last." Moreover, a wing commander argued irresistibly, "the cheaper the form of control the more money for roads and development and the sooner it will be no longer necessary to use armed forces to do with explosives what should be done by policemen and sticks."[9]

Despite these hopes and the promise of omniscience, the air control regime was plagued by frequent reports of pilot disorientation, visibility problems, and instances "of quite inexplicable failures to identify such objects as columns of Armoured cars...and even whole sections of bedouin tribes on the move." It was not uncommon for aircraft to make a "demonstration" over or bomb the wrong town. It also turned out that "hostile parties" could find cover in water-courses, hillocks, and other features of the "featureless" landscape. Assessing the effect of bombing operations was "largely a matter of guesswork." However, in an infamously deceptive land, all this inaccuracy, indeed information itself, was of little consequence: Arnold Wilson dourly explained that complaints about RAF observation failures were necessarily exaggerated, as was all information in the country, not least because the mirage prevented anyone from judging the accuracy of a pilot on high. Moreover, in the end, accuracy itself was moot, since aircraft were meant to be everywhere at once, "conveying a silent warning." This "moral effect" of patrolling aircraft "which can drop Bombs whenever necessary would effectually check disturbances." Air control was intended to work like the classic panopticon, for "from the ground every inhabitant of a village is under the impression that the occupant of an aeroplane is actually looking at him...establishing the impression that all their movements are being watched and reported." Even if pilots could not be sure whether they were looking at "warlike" or "ordinary" tribes, Bedouin would behave because they could not discriminate "between bombing and reconnaissance expeditions." Thus, despite innumerable reported errors, the air control experiment was pronounced entirely successful in "this kind of turbulent country." Lord Thomson, air secretary in 1924, even spoke of bombing's "all-seeing power" in the "clear atmosphere of Iraq"; the infamous haze had apparently obliged political expedience. In its Iraqi cocoon, the RAF was safe from criticism of its accuracy, protected by the notorious fallibility of all news emerging from Arabia. Within a decade, modified air control schemes would spread to "areas where conditions are similar"—Palestine, Transjordan, Aden, and further afield—and experts would disparage as "absurd" the increasingly inconvenient contention that "some peculiar quality about the country...has enabled aircraft to achieve in Iraq what they could not achieve anywhere else."[10]

The Defense of Inhumanity

Irregular warfare, as Lawrence understood it, could be bloodless because it depended less on attack than on the "silent threat of a vast unknown desert." Likewise, proponents of air control frankly admitted that "terror" was the scheme's underlying principle—and the source of its humaneness, which some explicitly traced to Lawrence's guerrilla theory. In theory, terror inspired by occasional demonstrations of destructive power would awe tribes into submission. Alternatively, interference with its victims' daily lives, through destruction of homes, villages, fuel, crops, and livestock, would "infallibly achieve the desired result."[11] Of course, the inhumanity of the system ultimately stemmed from its inability to distinguish between combatants and noncombatants, a conflation no less iniquitous in the case of violent impoverishment of villages than in simple massacre of them. And, as early RAF statements openly acknowledged, the moral effect depended on demonstrations of exemplary violence, which could hardly be accomplished without loss of life—as even the covetous army warned, the "moral effect of a plane that mustn't bomb...is less than that of an infantry man who can at least arrest." In any case, theory aside, however diligent the RAF may have been in giving warnings by loudspeaker, leaflets, and "demonstration flights," the "pacification" of Iraq proved horrifically costly in Iraqi lives—a hundred casualties was not unusual in a single operation, not to mention those lost to starvation and the burning of villages. "Recalcitrant" tribes, which included not only those attacking British communications and personnel but also those refusing to pay taxes, ultimately had to be bombed into submission. Entire villages were bombed for "general recalcitrance"— refusal to submit to government—and for harboring wanted rebel leaders, providing the lessons of an emerging science of bombing. Attempts to reduce abuses by "cooling" impulsive requests for bombers in red tape did not curtail bombing for taxation and recalcitrance. Defenders of air control effectively allowed its moral effect to become a synecdoche for the entire regime.[12]

The antiseptic theory of moral effect in fact responded to a potent moral critique that stalked the regime even before it was fully in place, building on outrage about the Amritsar Massacre of April 1919 and quickly overtaking prosaic skepticism of the regime rooted in interservice jealousy. Besides a few local agents' concerns about the rampant bombing of villages, Churchill and other Whitehall observers were also at least momentarily aghast at the news from

Iraq. Hubert Young and his partisans criticized the Mesopotamian administration for bombing resisters of a tax that, they alleged, *was* in fact higher than the Turkish rate had been. The new war secretary offered this unsparing assessment: "If the Arab population realize that the peaceful control of Mesopotamia depends on our intention of bombing women and children, I am very doubtful if we shall gain that acquiescence of the fathers and husbands of Mesopotamia as a whole to which the Secretary of State for the Colonies looks forward." This trenchant critique was amplified in the press and Parliament, where many had looked upon the Iraqi venture as outdated imperial foolishness from the very outset (see chap. 9).[13]

All this official displeasure quickly elicited papers from the Air Ministry on the effects of bombing on "semicivilised and uncivilised tribes." Ultimately concluding, as any properly dithering bureaucracy would, that sufficient time had not elapsed to prove its effects, the ministry also reminded its colleagues that air control was not unique in eliding the distinction between combatants and civilians. "All war is not only brutal but indiscriminate in its brutality," affirmed the Air Staff, pointing to the effects on civilians of naval bombardment, shelling of a city, blockading, trampling by invading armies, or the bombing of military facilities; at least the lives of attackers were safer in air operations. The Air Staff and Air Ministry adopted the voice of the realist, presenting stark realities unblinkered by sentimentality. Some of their supporters even insisted, paradoxically, on "the great humanity of bombing," for, however "ghastly"—indeed, *because* so ghastly— the experience of "continual unending interference with their normal lives" forced the enemy to give up quickly, thereby preventing untold further losses. Churchill might have looked back with pride at his hand in developing a system based on the "minimal use of force"—a foundational moment in the evolving myth of British skill in counterinsurgency—but at the time, the violence of air control was openly acknowledged. The question is what made it acceptable.[14]

The Great War had certainly shifted notions about humanity and warfare; to many military thinkers, the moral imperative was to minimize casualties as a whole rather than civilian deaths in particular, since modern combatants were merely civilians in uniform.[15] Thus, in 1930, Air Secretary Thomson replied to Lord Cavan's criticism of air control by affecting surprise that Cavan, "who had seen so much war, should still believe that one could humanize it." Clearly, he elaborated, the most "insidious way of prolonging war as a means of settlement between nations was to endeavour to make it a gentlemanly occupation." Nevertheless, the Air Staff's defense did not really address the concerns of those who were equally offended by modern war's general brutality or of those who (rightly) considered aerial bombardment, in its all-seeing omnipotence, more lethal and terrible than older forms of barbarity. But most saliently, for my purposes, their counterexamples—naval bombardment, blockades, and the like—were all *wartime* measures. The Air Staff paper was meant to discuss bombing as a peacetime security measure, a policing technique, in "semi-civilised" areas of the world such as Iraq. What was permissible only in wartime in advanced countries turned out to be *always* permissible in Iraq. In his description of the admittedly appalling bombing in Iraq, Thomson acknowledged that there things happened "which, if they had happened before the world war, would have been undoubtedly acts of war." It was thus that the RAF alone among the armed services maintained its "war-time spirit" in this period, "particularly...in Iraq."[16]

Militarism was thus being perpetuated at precisely the moment that it had become marginalized as a political program and the myth of Britain as a uniquely peaceable kingdom had taken root.[17] How was this possible? It was not, I think, merely the result of racist conjuring—indeed, many airpower theorists based their faith in the bomber on the notion that people were the same everywhere and would respond in the same manner to its power[18]—but of the spatial packaging of the underside of British modernity, in which Arabia figured as the last bastion of the world free from bourgeois convention, a place of honor and bravery (however mindless), of manly sportsmanship and perennial conflict. Hence Lawrence's investment in guerrilla warfare as a chivalrous and individualized mode of combat suited to the region; as Glubb put it, "Life in the desert is a continuous guerilla warfare," and this meant striking hard and fast because that was the way of "Bedouin war." "Not a moderate, but a maximum weight of bombs must be dropped" to maintain the native's respect for airpower, insisted Flight Lieutenant Mackay. On his return home, General Haldane corroborated this truism about Arabs' masochistic respect for "force, and force alone," assuring audiences at the United Service Institute that though he had been "obliged to inflict a very severe lesson on the recalcitrant tribes, they bore me no resentment." To them, Glubb elaborated, war was a "romantic excitement" whose production of "tragedies, bereavements, widows and orphans" was a "normal way of life," "natural and inevitable." Their taste for war was the source of their belief that they were "elites of the human race." It would almost be a cultural offense *not* to bombard them with all the might of the empire (not least out of respect for the frequently invoked tribal principle of communal responsibility). Arnold Wilson confirmed for the Air Ministry that the problem was one of public perception, that Iraqis were used to a state of constant warfare, expected justice without kid gloves, had no patience with sentimental distinctions between combatants and noncombatants, and viewed air action as entirely "legitimate and proper." "The natives of a lot of these tribes love fighting for fighting's sake," Trenchard assured Parliament. "They have no objection to being killed." In a place long romanticized as an oasis of a prelapsarian egalitarianism and liberty, defenders of air control could rest assured that the Bedouin retained their dignity even under bombardment and were not miserable wretches deserving of a condescending pity. Mark Sykes had long before recommended rule by local agents who could "shoot and give an order and never bother natives about cant and nonsense such as the rights of man." Thus would the "natives" see them as "proper and respectable persons." The ultramechanical "knight of the air" may have brought chivalry, in the sense of honorable combat between elite warriors, back to an otherwise thoroughly grim and "vulgarised" modern warfare, but this influence, its proponents were careful to elucidate, was "quite distinct from the humanitarian one" which regarded with compassion "those whom chivalry despised." Thus, Iraqi women and children need not trouble the conscience, for, as the British commander observed, "[sheikhs]...do not seem to resent...that women and children are accidentally killed by bombs." To them, women and children were "negligible" casualties compared to those of the "really important men," Lawrence explained, conceding this was "too oriental a mood for us to feel very clearly." Frightening as such fearlessness ought to have been, it seems instead to have provoked derision, or perhaps comic relief: as air secretary, Samuel Hoare fatuously assured Parliament that bombing of flocks and herds often proved sufficient; indeed, "tribes had felt that form of local operation more severely than if they had dropped bombs on the tribes themselves. (Laughter.)"[19]

Paranoia only confirmed the view that the entire Iraqi population was a latent army easily triggered into hostile action by Britain's enemies. What was excusable as wartime excesses against the Boche would be always permissible against this population. In 1932, the high commissioner, head of the British administration in nominally independent Iraq, warned against clipping the "claws" of the RAF because "the term 'civilian population' has a very different meaning in Iraq from what it has in Europe....The whole of its male population are potential fighters as the tribes are heavily armed." This was a population at once so orientally backward and so admirably manly and phlegmatic that, to a postwar imperium increasingly in thrall to cultural relativistic notions, all principles of *ius in bello* were irrelevant. Arabia was, in British eyes, especially suited to a type of bombardment that might be morally offensive elsewhere. The austerity of tribal existence, a condition imagined to extend to all Iraqis, rendered even concern about destruction of "property" irrelevant— despite the targeting of livestock, camels, and villages. It is useful to recall here, as a counterpoint, the premise of Lawrence's guerrilla theory—that Bedouin could neither tactically nor temperamentally sustain casualties. Stereotypes of Arabs were, however, capacious enough to accommodate such contradictions, and British agents' faith in their intuitive grasp ensured that all pronouncements on Arab character were sound.[20] Only one officer, Lionel Charlton, chief of staff in Iraq in 1923, seems to have taken the softer view of tribal warfare as a more innocent, bloodless, sportlike style of retribution seriously, and he resigned in outrage against the notion that "an air bomb in Iraq was, more or less, the equivalent of a police truncheon at home."[21]

With all Iraqis transmuted into belligerents, it became easier to mute alarm about air reports by recourse to euphemism. When Churchill objected to the reporting of casualties under the "comprehensive head of 'men and women,'"[22] Trenchard, who in general shared Arabist agents' intuitive bent of mind and disinterest in statistics, insisted that in countries in which combatants and non-combatants and even the sexes could not be distinguished by visual markers, all casualties should be reported in "bulk numbers" without details as to sex or age. Air control and its indiscriminate violence were ideally suited to a place in which indiscriminate violence did not matter, as little in fact distinguished combatants from noncombatants. Casualty counts could legitimately assume that all were combatants without fear of traducing the data. Indeed, data of any kind was so notoriously difficult to find that any amount of scrupulousness in record-keeping seemed excessive. From the Middle East Department, Richard Mein-ertzhagen assured his colleagues in Iraq, "Bombs dropped on men in the open seldom have much effect beyond fright" and advised dropping the matter of results because aerial observation of casualties was "always misleading." (It is worth remembering in this connection his prewar experience using bayonets, rifles, machine guns, and fire to eliminate recalcitrant Kikuyu in East Africa.) Even political officers' failures to observe "results" on the ground were immate-rial, for, Meinertzhagen's colleague Reader Bullard assured, "news as to casual-ties will drift in from the desert gradually." This cavalier attitude rendered casualties entirely, well, casual. "If the Civil Commissioner is going on to Mosul," read a General Headquarters telegram to Wilson, "will he be so kind as to drop a bomb on Batas"—the sort of kindness he apparently never objected to. Striking at a phantom enemy and enjoying the bliss of willful ignorance at the outcome made air control sit more easily in the official mind. Only in Arabia, about which the British had long decided that nothing could ever really be known, did such fecklessness make sense and thus make air control acceptable.[23]

Air control also seemed to fit comfortably in a biblical land. In 1932, when the inhumanity of air control was of some pressing importance at the World Disarmament Conference in Geneva, the high commissioner argued that unlike the outrages inevitably committed by ground troops, "bombing from the air is regarded almost as an act of God to which there is no effective reply but immediate submission."[24] Lawrence, speaking anonymously as one "who has lived among the Arabs, one whose intimate knowledge of their ways and thoughts is universally recognized," explained the "impersonally fateful" nature of air bombing from an Arab's point of view: "It is not punishment, but a misfortune from heaven striking the community." It was the "superstition…concerning the 'god in the air'" that commanded Arabs' respect, explained a wing commander (their inevitable discovery that it was only a man in the plane making it all the more urgent that the RAF demonstrate its power "with all its might"). Arabia was a biblical place, and the people who lived there *knew* that; they expected periodic calamity and continual news of life and death. Bombardment was to them yet another kind of visitation. Air control played on Arabs' presumed fatalism, their faith in the incontrovertible "will of God." Such people could bear random acts of violence in a way that Europeans, coddled by secular notions of justice and human rights, could not. This view underwrote the frequent harping on the importance of not breeding too much familiarity with aircraft, lest the Arabs cease to view them as vehicles of divine retribution.[25]

As a biblical space, Arabia was also a place of elemental clashes between good and evil out of the realm of ordinary, mortal law. The Bedouin "world of violence, bloodshed and war" recalled, for Glubb, England's forgotten "age of chivalry"—which could itself be traced to the Arab conquest of Spain: they possessed "depths of hatred, reckless bloodshed…lust of plunder of which our lukewarm natures seem no longer capable…deeds of generosity worthy of fairy-tales and acts of treachery of extraordinary baseness." Their "love of dramatic actions" outweighed "the dictates of reason or the material needs," even, the General Staff affirmed, overcame their "inherent dislike of getting killed." In this last bastion of authentic experience, bombardment could be accommodated as yet another vitalizing experience—shared equally by airmen who were resurrecting chivalry even as its death knell was sounded (many Bristol fighters being fitted, incidentally, with Sunbeam's "Arab" engines). Dr. Miller Maguire, speaking as an "ordinary member of the public," marveled excitedly at the end of a lecture on air control at the United Service Institute that it was all familiar from Chaucer's tales about the kings of Tartary whose horses "used to ride in the air" and Milton's poems about air battles between angels and devils. Bombardment allowed bombers to at once fulfill this medieval atavism and give Arabs what they wanted. No group did more to fulfill this romantic vision of air control than Ibn Saud's puritanical avant-garde forces, who continually raided into Iraq from Najd, often eluding their patron's grasp. Gertrude Bell was fiercely proud of "our power to strike back" at the diabolical Ikhwan, who, "with their horrible fanatical appeal to a medieval faith, rouse in me the blackest hatred." All concerns about cruelty were moot among those "notorious for…cruelty and…inhuman injustices." Bloodlust made sense in heterocosmic Arabia. It was the way of the place, and, as with intelligence operations, the mantra was "When in Rome…"[26]

These clashes between good and evil transformed the "pacification" project into a series of episodes of cosmic significance. During the rebellion, Leachman, of whose unpopularity we have already read, wrote chillingly of his desire "to see...a regular slaughter of the Arabs in the disaffected areas." His adoring biographer, fellow political officer Norman Bray, describes him living in constant fear of assassination, concluding, "No wonder he...reveled in dropping bombs on Arabs concealed in a hollow." Paranoia and the transposition of real Arabia into the Arabia of myth, the consummate spy-space, made bombing palatable—even to individuals who believed they would revile it any other context. The vindication of air control grew out of long-circulating ideas about Arabia as a place somehow exempt from the this-worldliness that constrained human activity in other parts of the world. There heroes could reach the most exalted heights and villains the profoundest depths; there, as in literature, agents could find escape from the pitiful reality of human suffering into an exalted sphere in which everything possessed a cosmic significance. There, where each soul was free to work out its cosmic destiny, violence was entirely *personal*: Sheikh Dhari, Leachman's assassin—or "murderer," as he was styled in British accounts—was the single exception to the general amnesty granted after the rebellion. He was not seen as a member of that uprising, but as someone who had violated the honor between two men; the Iraqi unrest was reconfigured as an episode of medieval battle, in which the mettle of chivalric men was tested and rewarded. In this "supreme crisis," "every quality [Leachman] possessed, *even his faults*, served the cause of England."[27]

Ordering bombers was thus entirely consonant with the sensibility of the Arabist agent enchanted with notions of Arabian liberty. A journalist remarked, "It is frequently those officials who are loudest in their demand for complete independence and for the removal of the British forces and advisers who are also the first to cry out for the assistance of British aeroplanes." The agents loved Arabia for its otherworldly qualities, and it was those very qualities that made Arabia a space fit to bear the equally unearthly destruction wreaked by bombers. Britons considered the moral world of Arabia distinct from their own. From the outset, the intelligence project in Arabia had been infused with a philosophical spirit, which did not depart it at this stage.[28]

The Arabian window of acceptability opened the door to wider uses of aerial bombardment. In 1921, the Air Staff deemed it better, in view of allegations of "barbarity,"

> to preserve appearances...by still nominally confining bombardment to targets which are strictly military...to avoid emphasizing the truth that air warfare has made such restrictions obsolete and impossible.

It may be some time until another war occurs and meanwhile the
public may become educated as to the meaning of air power."

Arabia offered the Air Staff a means of selling the new warfare to the public by
exhibiting it in a famously romantic and chivalric place where, it was known,
the bourgeois rules lately exposed by the war as utterly bankrupt did not apply
anyway. (Significantly, when Iraq's former air commander, Sir John Salmond,
called the question of air control's humanity a "paradox" in a United Service
Institute lecture, the *Times* paraphrased it as "anachronism.") There, any principle not military devolved into bathos. After all, the Iraqi authorities, the Air
Staff pointed out, were among the first to concede the potentialities of aircraft.[29]
Thus, in otherworldly Arabia, bombardment became irrevocably part of this
world; eventually, British bombs fell frictionlessly all over the world, including
Europe. The gruesome relish evident in a 1924 report by the officer command-
ing Squadron 45 in Iraq is striking in this regard:

> The Arab and Kurd...now know what real bombing means, in
> casualties and damage; they now know that within 45 minutes a full
> sized village...can be practically wiped out and a third of its inhabit-
> ants killed or injured by four or five machines which offer them no
> real target, no opportunity for glory as warriors, no effective means of
> escape.

Ultimately excised, this sentence appears verbatim in early drafts of an Air
Staff report to Parliament. The officer himself later achieved distinction, and,
writes David Omissi, "in the ruins of this dying village one can dimly perceive
the horrific firestorms of Hamburg and Dresden," for the officer was Squadron
Leader Arthur Harris, head of Bomber Command in World War Two. Harris
later traced his faith in the heavy bomber as the only salvation against Germany
to his experience in the Middle East. It was in Iraq that he made the first long-
range heavy bomber by crudely converting a transport plane and developed
night bombing as a means of terrorizing Arabs into thinking airplanes could
see them even in the dark. At his side then, as during the war, were Robert
Saundby and Ralph Cochrane. Indeed, two and a half times as many British
pilots served in Iraq as elsewhere. Air control trained the RAF in bombardment; it was the only significant British experience of bombing before World
War Two. The RAF thought it was getting good training for the next war—
whatever historians' assessment of its preparation. Even the British focus on
general area bombing (as opposed to the American preoccupation with "precision")—can be traced to the emphasis on moral effect over accuracy in the Iraqi
laboratory. Tellingly, it was under Harris's wartime influence that Churchill, as

prime minister, warded off periodic pangs of conscience about bombing German cities with faith in the "higher poetic justice" that "those who have loosed these horrors upon mankind will now in their homes and persons feel the shattering stroke of retribution." It was the Ikhwan all over again, and Europe itself had become the scene of a clash between good and evil—a gradual transposition that dated to the days well before Hitler's seizure of power, when "fascist" was an epithet hurled against the Saudi government and Britons began to fear that airpower—and technological hubris more generally—would not so much secure the empire as open up the possibility of Britain's being bombed into a *desert*. The alleged prematurity with which Britons began to fear aerial bombardment in the early 1930s, before any apparent material international development, seems less remarkable when we look, as they did, beyond the European horizon of history to the distant happenings in the deserts of Arabia.[30]

The Human Face of Air Control?

Ideas about Arabia may have exonerated air control from charges of *in*humanity, but the regime's reliance on political officers on the ground, modeled on the veteran agents, was crucial to its projection of an actively humane image. Their supposed intuitive understanding of the place carried within it a claim to an empathetic style of colonial control that supposedly kept the regime from growing distant and impersonal. The theory of moral effect was intended to project a benign vision of air control, in which aircraft were explicitly modeled on the traditional political officer, merely replacing the traditional "prestige of the white man" with the prestige of a machine that took advantage of the "ignorance of the native mind." Not only were aircraft modeled on these traditional embodiments of British "moral suasion," but their continued presence on the ground provided the RAF with both scapegoats and a ready antidote, at least in theory, for all its faults of inhumanity.[31]

Initially, some feared that air control might prematurely render traditional political officers obsolete. The community of agents warned against such a development as likely to make the British as distant and hated as the late Turkish rulers of Iraq. They insisted, as seen in chapter 3, on the need for "men who are specially gifted, who have got the feeling of the Middle East in their blood." Indian officials speaking from long imperial experience likewise warned, "The *deus ex machina* is useful in his place, but is out of place in the day-to-day administration." While political officers did travel by air to reach their posts, accompany reconnaissances, and participate in bombing runs, the establishment's

gadflies had little to fear: the RAF quickly realized that it needed the cooperation of political officers on the ground to ascertain just when the desired moral
effect had been achieved and avoid unduly prolonging operations. Ground
agents were also crucial for coping with the problems of pilot disorientation and
visibility failures that continued to plague the theoretically all-seeing regime
(although they, too, often remained disoriented and requested aerial tours to
better understand the terrain). The importance of swift action without reference to a home department in a region apparently rife with conspiracies also
made a fully organized intelligence system on the ground indispensable.[32]

At first, existing political officers seemed likely to fulfill the needs of the
civil government, the army, and the air force. During the 1920 insurrection,
however, the RAF found itself somewhat constrained by the "reluctance" of
these officers "to appear to be alarmist, with the result that their reports were
too meagre and too late." Somewhat paradoxically, the regime's early excesses
were also blamed on political officers' ignorant and overly enthusiastic requests
for bombers (blindly obeyed by airmen inadequately aware of their own "semi-
political" role). These problems were remedied by the creation of an RAF
Special Service Officer (SSO) organization eventually consisting of a Central
Bureau with agents on the outside in charge of the various zones of the country. Pilots, SSOs, and administrative inspectors (as the former political officers
were now styled) worked closely together.[33]

The SSOs quickly adopted their predecessors' tactics and epistemology.
Intuitive ability and canny knowledge of local custom were deemed indispensable to acquisition of the information required for bombardment, given the
"peculiar mentality" of tribesmen, "who," Glubb explained, "deemed it a duty
to receive and to welcome a guest, although he was mapping their villages with
a view to bombing them and told them so." Immersion became a universal
principle of aircraft intelligence in theaters of irregular warfare, where selection of the correct air objective called for information materially different from
that used against a "first class power": "comprehensive and accurate knowledge
of the topography, the psychology of the enemy, his customs, characteristics,
and industries" *and* the ability to "sift the evidence very thoroughly" for truth.
The importance of constant roving, for any type of agent in the Middle East,
was etched in stone. As SSO "Akhwan Defence," Glubb, along with several others, advised pilots to heed the wisdom of their terrestrial counterparts:

> There is no golden road to the acquisition of tribal knowledge. The
> deus ex-machine [*sic*] who descends upon a miserable camp of
> frightened nomads, and shouts at them for five minutes above the
> noise of the engine, cannot expect to learn much. Only long hours,

days and weeks of intercourse will make him familiar with natives and without this familiarity, he cannot commence to understand his work.

In 1930, the Air Council formally adopted this principle. The ultimate goal for agents and pilots was, as before, to be able to think like an Arab and imitate his "magical" ability to "divine" knowledge, such as the intentions of raiders, from desert signs, even seemingly "invisible" ones. Major Jarvis marveled at Philby's prediction of approaching raiders as chief British representative in Amman: "It seems extraordinary that it remained for a British official to notice and identify a strange symbol of lines and half-circles, which to the educated Arabs conveyed nothing, and to forecast that which was shortly to occur." These agents claimed empathy with, even love for, Arabs as the source of their genius. Immersion enabled them to overcome the near impossibility, as one put it, of a man of one race ever understanding another, and to "interpret what is in [the Arabs'] mind." Air Intelligence trusted SSOs to accurately "sense impending events" (if not "dig down to the facts," a task more befitting the SIS). Successful bombardment was often attributed to SSO genius, wireless technology allowing them to communicate swiftly with aircraft—from their mouths to God's ears. They differed from prewar agents in that their work reflected the war's expansion of intelligence into the permanent nomadic warfare of peacetime, exemplified by the counter-raiding tactics of Glubb's Southern Desert Camel Corps, explicitly recalling Lawrence's wartime adventures (not to mention old-fashioned British naval policing against pirates).[34]

The security that aircraft in turn provided this ground intelligence system was lauded as the source of the regime's ultimate benevolence: air control, its defenders argued, promoted greater understanding between administrators and Iraqis by enabling political officers to roam without fear. Backed by the skeletal air regime, these men on the spot, in the eyes of the ever-nostalgic former agents in the Colonial Office, were akin to those intrepid Britons of an older, braver age who had served in frontier zones at the bidding of "an adventurous spirit." The austere air control regime was to them ideally suited to a country that had always been and would always be a sort of vast frontier zone, where one brave Briton would more than make up for the absence of troops. For all its modernity, air control strengthened the feeling that in Arabia they could be as imperialists of old.[35]

Of course, it was also political officers' untrammeled mobility that ensured the RAF received the intelligence it needed to "[pick] out the right villages and to hit when trouble comes." By this ironic logic, the RAF's successful persecution of a village testified to their *intimacy* with people on the ground, without which they would not have been able to strike it accurately. Indeed, the claim to empathy ultimately underwrote the entire air control system with its authoritative reassurances that bombardment was a tactic that would be respected and expected in this unique land. As late as 1957, RAF Marshal Sir John Slessor defended the regime by pointing to the support of SSOs, who "became so attached to their tribesmen that they sometimes almost 'went native.' " Well into the 1980s, Glubb insisted, "The basis of our desert control was not force but persuasion and love." In 1989, a military historian—much-cited, even by U.S. Air Force officers— again vindicated the regime by citing Glubb: "No European was ever closer and more sympathetic to the Arabs than Sir John Glubb." And then there are the epigraphs from the new millennium that open this chapter.[36]

At the end of the day, the claim to empathy was of course built, literally, on sand. From its Edwardian invention as an intelligence epistemology, it signaled not the recognition of a common humanity but a self-alienating strategy for coping in what was perceived as another physical and moral universe. After the war, aspiring agents, inspired partly by the legends surrounding their predecessors, continued to venture to Arabia to escape the bonds of *too much* civilization, to recover a noble, free, democratic spirit lost to "utilitarian" England. Their effort to gather intelligence in the Middle East began with the same baptismal sensations of moving in a fictional, unreal, biblical, enchanted, and uncanny space. They reached for literature and an elegiac mood to convey the "half-romantic, half-mystic feelings" the landscape aroused. Appreciation for the desert's strange beauty remained the mark of individuals *estranged* from "normal" civilization. They too found in the desert sublime a remembrance of God, a rekindling of faith far from "the cold blasts of Western doubt" and an opportunity to fulfill the nomadic instinct that was "part of the heritage of our race." Their travel in the desert was still understood as an escape into the blue, a truant fulfillment of patriotic duty. Glubb knew that "in the desert I was alone. The government was indifferent." He fashioned himself into an "enthusiastic young man" whom his superiors found "slightly unbalanced," "conceited," and often insubordinate. To enter Arabia was still to exit the *customary* world, in both senses of the word, for "the desert is a world in itself."[37]

The "extraordinary and romantic" world of the RAF in Iraq compounded the feeling of being in a world apart. Its tenuous links to "civilisation" through a miraculous wireless infrastructure, and bruits of Lawrence's presence in the ranks, only fed its Arabian mystique. If flight over the austere biblical terrain reached new heights of sublimity and divinity, an escape from "the normal things in life" to "a new mysterious world," it also produced "quite a bad effect upon one's nerves," a feeling that "the end of the world had really come," according to Brooke-Popham. Experienced agents stressed that for new pilots, this "sense of being lost at sea" was a critical "mental factor." Pilots too grew skilled at identifying "that air of quiet weariness which comes to those who have been in the desert too long." They fell prey to "a gentle, nameless terror" that made them go temporarily mad and increasingly "fey" as time passed. This was not a place for empathy but for total psychic breakdown, apparently; without some kind of bracing, Britons risked losing their minds. Emulation of Arabs was intended to enable their survival in this extraterrestrial space but did not produce compassion for the Arab victims of the surreal world of bombardment they actually created by pulling the strings of fate from the sky. Thus did Iraq actually become a place beyond the reach of secular and humanitarian law. It remained beyond the gaze of legality and society, a place agents had long used as a site for recovering an otherwise compromised *individual* sovereignty.[38]

True empathy was officially proscribed for the safety of the regime. Official indignation at the utterances and activities of the alleged "fanatics" among the veteran agents inspired efforts to prevent copycat SSOs from falling into the same pattern. Despite official encouragement of immersion, they were firmly warned against "the inclination to drift into native ways" and were expected to "maintain the standards of European life." Intelligence officers were to tour continually but strictly "without special predilections for any one of the countries." The ideal was a staff of agents like the old one, minus their eccentric passion for individual potentates and the grotesque threat of empathy with their colonial subjects. Someone perhaps like Wyndham Deedes, who was eulogized for his detachment, a "withdrawal from the world" by which he entered "the realm of contemplation in which the phenomena of daily existence are only…illusion." (Such aloofness ultimately proved unsustainable even in his case: it was partly frustration with his isolation that led him to resign as chief secretary in Palestine in 1923 to pursue the life of an ascetic and social worker in East London.) Ultimately, the air control scheme rested on terrorizing the population with an *unfamiliar* technology or, rather, with one just familiar enough to allow the effects of exemplary violence to "sink into the mind of the tribesmen"; real familiarity or, for that matter, empathy would only breed contempt. In the succinct words of one scholar, "The technique of 'empathy' remained a method of control"; it underwrote the mandate's entire dyarchical structure, a highly "exacting" form of control, as Lawrence put it, in which British advisers were entrusted with using their psychic, hypnotic influence to ensure the Iraqi government ran along lines favorable to imperial interests.[39]

Defending the Regime

In interwar Iraq, an obsession with "grand conspiracy," as in previous historical moments, was implicated in the creation of a regime founded on terror.[40]

Nevertheless, air control did little to assuage official paranoia about the Middle East. Though it owed its invention to a perception of the entanglement of outside and inside threats, its infrastructural minimalism was premised on the existence of no "outside" threats to the regime; and yet it was hurriedly installed and the exhausted army relieved before this condition had been satisfied. The Air Ministry hastily revised its estimate of the scheme's defensive powers upward and prepared to face an always imminent invasion that they knew the regime could not withstand—John Salmond later confessed that when the RAF took control in 1922, the situation on Iraq's borders was "far from that anticipated at the Cairo Conference." The air control scheme was based on bluff, on keeping the country in check by projecting untold British military power in the lonely flight of a single aircraft, and bluffs are always subject to being called, a potentiality that could only feed paranoia. Most of all, the British were painfully aware that their neighbors' "system of pin pricks and invasion by insidious methods" was being met by reliance on a scheme "which at best can be described as an experiment."[41]

While airpower became essential to Britain's ability to hold on to its new acquisitions in the Middle East, this "Land of the RAF" became equally indispensable to British preeminence in airpower. The RAF relied on its Iraqi bases in order to exist as a service. Early on, Meinertzhagen had asserted:

> If ever there was an area where AIR POWER could be exercised to its
> full extent...that area is the Middle East and all our plans for control
> and defence should be based on AIR POWER. No other country in
> the world has such a training ground, such opportunities and such a
> strangle-hold as we have in the Middle East, if we are wise.

One of the reasons for keeping the Middle East was the *space* it provided for developing Britain's aerial defenses (defenses needed primarily to keep the Middle East). Both his department and the Air Staff realized they could hardly air this factor in public. The Cairo Conference propitiously concluded that two of the scheme's major advantages—if not primary purposes—were imperial: the opportunity to train and *test* an independent air force and the creation "of an 'All Red' military and commercial air route to India." No other theater allowed combination of training "with work of the 'productive' character" going on in Iraq. The Middle East was the ideal and *only* place in which to develop the new mechanical warfare in what was increasingly seen as a postnaval age.[42]

With these imperial advantages at stake, letting go of Iraq—the proclaimed objective of the mandatory relationship—posed an awkward dilemma. Not entirely coincidentally, the theory of moral effect also made it difficult to determine when the Iraqi mandate was ready for full independence. Even apparent pacification could not license a slackening of air control, whose deterrent effect, experts argued, was the only thing keeping the country from plunging into chaos. On the eve of Iraq's admission to the League of Nations, the Air Ministry argued vigorously against withdrawal on the grounds that the RAF there protected the entire empire from collapse (not to mention preserving access to oilfields and a base for war against Russia). The ministry insisted that, despite new diplomatic agreements, Turkey, Persia, and Russia remained threatening; diminution of imperial forces would reduce "the wholesome awe" that kept these "forces of disorder" in check. This meant that intelligence arrangements also would have to remain intact—they too existed to keep tabs on Iraq's ever-precarious "external relations" and on the "precocious growth of ideas of Nationalism and Independence" likely to emerge were those relations ever settled. Such nationalism, the British foresaw, would inevitably consist in Iraqis intriguing with "different countries externally, and different parties and classes internally" to oust the British.[43]

Withdrawal would, in any case, wreck the strategic air route, force India to strengthen its reserves, and thus cost as much as continuing the regime. It was decided that the RAF should explain to the Iraqi government that if it did not think it could maintain security alone, the British government would agree, "very reluctantly," to leave the RAF in Iraq for some time on condition that Iraq would try to strengthen its forces and stand alone. A considerable advantage of this tack was that Iraq would then presumably bear the cost of maintaining the RAF, allowing the British to further ingratiate themselves by offering financial assistance. Above all, this canard would dispel "the impression...that we are anxious to keep the air force in Iraq for Imperial purposes." (To their great annoyance, the Iraqi government nevertheless greeted the offer with suspicion.) In fact, ends and means had become one; the scheme that had enabled control of frontierless Iraq now required permanent retention of Iraq for preservation of the frontierless system of colonial control. Iraq was the "key" to the imperial air route; aside from geopolitical security, it secured the empire emotionally, bringing the cherished dominions closer to "the heart of the empire." Whether it really was the pivot of the world, the arrangements based on that assumption quickly made it so.[44]

Iraq's peculiar geography was therefore pressed before the Permanent Mandates Commission, the League of Nations body in charge of supervising the mandate system, to justify the need to maintain the RAF there even after Iraq joined the league. In a besieged, frontierless country, the RAF would ensure the British could implement their alliance as per the 1930 Anglo-Iraqi treaty. (The commission observed that this would "in some way impair the independence of Iraq," an argument the British official found difficult to counter.) Technically, the RAF would remain for purposes of *external* defense only, but British officials' conviction that external enemies were always entangled with internal ones ensured they put the widest possible construction on their brief. Ambassador Sir Francis Humphrys in Baghdad affirmed that the success of postindependence Iraq would "largely depend on the moral influence which the RAF will continue to exert, on a people naturally lawless and averse to the payment of taxes." (The difficulty was that, though it was politically impossible to let it be known that aircraft might still be used to maintain internal order, not letting this fact be known might itself cause unrest, given that air control operated, in theory, largely through its moral effect.) Thus, while Iraq was launched on the path to independence, existing arrangements remained intact. Every effort was made to ensure that key elements of Iraqi defense—aircraft, wireless, armored cars, intelligence sources—were not shared with the nascent Iraqi Army. None of this was to be construed as an effort to prevent the growth of Iraqi forces; it was merely a call for a "long institutional period." In the end, the British concession of Iraqi independence in 1932 was confessedly nominal; the Air Staff made it clear that the change would be "more apparent than real." The regime's austerity allowed discreet continuity in these arrangements, for "in countries of this sort...the impersonal drone of an aeroplane...is not so obtrusive as the constant presence...of soldiers." The RAF could occupy and control the entire country without apparently doing so, simply by projecting a silent threat. Squadrons were gradually reduced, but the country was reoccupied during World War Two after Britain quashed Rashid Ali's pro-Axis government. The RAF finally departed during the Iraqi revolution of 1958.[45]

In 1960 (the year the CIA made its first attempt to assassinate the Iraqi president), John Glubb reflected on the ease with which humans justify their actions: Ibn Saud, a benign patriarch, had unleashed the massacring power of the Ikhwan to consolidate his power, all the while "breathing the benevolence and the service of God," and the United States, breathing its own lofty ideals, had dropped the atomic bomb on Hiroshima. Neither, he explains, was guilty of hypocrisy, for "the human mind is a surprising mechanism." "Hypocrisy" is indeed useless as an *explanation*, however useful it may be as a description, of the failures of avowedly enlightened regimes. I am endeavoring here to lay bare the "surprising mechanism" of the British official mind which enabled it, with mostly clear conscience on the count of hypocrisy—indeed, with confidence in a consistent paternalism—to invent and implement the world's first air control regime. The "idea of Arabia" circulated by agents over the previous twenty years provided them with a key for evading all charges of hypocrisy and brutality. Though the gulf between airmen and some of their critics may never have been bridged, enough people were convinced, indeed impressed, for the regime to remain viable for the entire interwar period.[46]

Air policing has been called "the salvation of the Royal Air Force" and "the midwife of modern Iraq"; it saved each from being swallowed into another service and country, respectively. Whatever one feels about Iraq as a nation-state or the air force as a military arm, there is, I think, a more useful reading of air control: it created a space in the air for empire at a time when imperialism was no longer at home in the world. Besides diminishing reliance on tired British and Indian troops (whose employment abroad was inciting ever louder protest in India), it allowed "control without occupation" and, as we shall see, without the approval of public opinion. Similarly, today's drawdown plans for Iraq include little-discussed plans to replace troops with airpower that could "strike everywhere—and at once," in the ominous words of a Pentagon consultant. Air control was (and is) a mechanism of control for a region and in a time in which more overt colonial rule was (and is) a political impossibility. This was the moment of covert empire, whose gossamer earthly framework we will turn to next.[47]

8

Covert Empire

At the basis of bureaucracy as a form of government...lies [the]
superstition of a possible and magic identification of man with the
forces of history. The ideal of such a political body will always be the
man behind the scenes who pulls the strings of history....The two
key figures in this system, whose very essence is aimless process, are
the bureaucrat on one side and the secret agent on the other.

—Hannah Arendt, *The Origins of
Totalitarianism*, 1951

Agents' individual acts of cunning were but a drop in an ocean of lies;
even the Arab Revolt, particularly the freedom that was its object, was
a ruse, one that troubled some agents (Lawrence's pricks of conscience
are famous), although never enough to cause them to desist from
complicity in it. They knew its aim was merely, as Sykes put it, "the
façade of an independent Arab Empire." Likewise, the Baghdad civil
administration was informed in no uncertain terms that "free" Mesopotamia was to be a British protectorate administered behind an Arab
"façade." Such were the auspicious foundations of the postwar empire
in the Middle East for which air control provided the material, if ethereal, coercive foundation. On the ground, the agents ran the show.
"The British agent-Orientalist...during and after World War I took
over both the role of expert-adventurer-eccentric...and the role of
colonial authority, whose position is in a central place next to the indigenous ruler," writes Edward Said. In fact, their position was not so

much *next* to the indigenous ruler but hovering somewhere *behind* (and above) him, and, whatever their claims to autonomy, further behind them, shrouded in obscurity, lurked all the institutional power of the British imperial state. This was a new imperial strategy of covert rule, a version of indirect rule in which professional agents operated in a hidden realm of colonial government bureaucracy. Long accustomed to working in a sphere apart from the official bureaucracy of empire and now occupying many of the administrative spaces of the new Middle Eastern empire, the community of agents took inspiration from the alleged conspiracies in the Middle East in their fostering of an intelligence organization whose enforced informality would allow covert pursuit of empire, hidden from the eyes of Middle Easterners and of critical Britons—although ultimately always suspected by both.[1]

Arranging for Covert Rule

Just as military authorities struggled to come up with creative means for holding on to the Middle Eastern empire, officials of various sorts produced a profusion of proposals for the creation of a postwar regional intelligence service. Many were prompted by the failure to anticipate the troubles of 1919–21 and by the ideal opportunity afforded by the ongoing military occupation of much of the region. More than this, however, they were inspired by conspiracy thinking, building on the anxieties unleashed by the second half of the war and the hovering surveillance network they had spawned. It was partly his precocious paranoia that had led Sykes to conclude that discontent from India to the Balkans was coordinated by enemy agents and to propose the Arab Bureau as part of an equally coordinated British response. Following the wartime trend, the postwar schemes collapsed the work of intelligence, military control, and administration together and, in the paranoid postwar context, did so explicitly, heralding an official program for a new kind of covert empire.[2]

As the war rushed to a close, Hogarth, Sykes, and Storrs, among others, prepared for the peace by proposing the creation of a central Arab Bureau in London that would extend the political influence of the institution that contained all the existing expertise on the "Arab Question." It would, of course, need to operate with a relatively free hand. "Official and regular uncomprehending routine is such an obstacle to action," noted Sykes. He pointed fulsomely to the ad hoc arrangements of the war, under which a mere "phone message, a word on a bit of paper, a mere initial has been sufficient to do the work." The system had to remain more or less in place to ensure continued efficiency after the war. Sykes died in 1919. His counsels were not heeded exactly: as part of the 1920 retrenchment, the affairs of the bureau were wound up, but the resulting exodus of agents from Cairo into Whitehall enabled the Foreign Office to temporarily seize the reins of intelligence coordination in the Middle East. Responding to requests from men on the spot, they even revived the *Bulletin*—retitled "Notes on the Middle East" to convince prying eyes that the *Bulletin* had been terminated.[3]

Even the air scheme, as we have seen, was conceived at one level as a system of rule by intelligence, the aircraft merely substituting for the political officer. In general, postwar intelligence planners hoped to hold the region with agents rather than armies. Political officers at "important centres" would serve as a kind of "Advanced Guard." The army was an impractical garrisoning force not merely because of the cost but because of the dubious loyalties of Muslim soldiers. A network of politicals was, on the other hand, ideally suited, tactically speaking, to the kind of permanent "peacetime" warfare immanent in a region seething with conspiracies. In Iraq, reasoned the General Staff, they faced

> a strange and somewhat uncomfortable situation in that, whereas Her Majesty's Government is at peace with the Soviet Union and is constrained to act accordingly, the recognised government of the Soviet Union has no doubt whatever that it is at war with the British Empire and has already achieved perceptible success through its machinations in the Middle East.

This was a proxy war that could be fought only by agents. Even the skimpy garrisons maintained to protect air bases were part of an intelligence war; serving little obvious military purpose (since they were to be withdrawn in case of external aggression), they were there, the General Staff explained to the confused Mosul garrison, "for the purpose of 'Watching.'" While agents became operational, troops became agents, their conflation ultimately sublimated in the air control regime, the epitome of operational intelligence. Arabia had, in fact, become a spy-space.[4]

In the paranoid postwar view, the whole porous region had to be considered one administrative and intelligence unit. Existing arrangements were too fragmented, intelligence circulating only "by the intersection of circumferences." In a class on intelligence, the General Staff stressed that the ubiquity of the Soviet hand meant that "it is only as a whole that the present situation in Central Asia and the Middle East can be studied." In its sprawling intelligence scheme, the War Office strove to treat distant areas "as a whole" in view of the "comparative success with which Moslem agents of all kinds can move about." Even West Africa "could no longer be considered as apart from the East." From within officialdom, Philby, Bray, Bell, Garbett, and Lawrence amplified the call to treat the region—however defined—as a single unit. Looking back, the new agent Geoffrey Wheeler noted that before 1914 a massive intelligence network in the Middle East would have been "quite impracticable and hardly necessary" but that the encircling threats of the postwar era made one "not only feasible but essential." They "posed a new problem hardly to be solved by...intelligence methods found successful in Europe." The DMO affirmed that, unlike the African colonies, the Middle East was a place where mistakes and inefficiencies in administration could not be confined to "the immediate locality," for there "we rub shoulders with the Turks in the north-west, the Russians in the north, Persians and Afghans in the East and.... The whole country is bound up with Arab and Moslem interests." Iraq was a "political sounding board"; any blow to the British "would resound...from Khartoum to Hongkong." It was the pivot of the empire, of the Islamic world, of Asia, of the globe; its centrality ensured that the effects of every local occurrence would be felt all over the continent in a kind of ripple effect, an ineluctable spilling beyond frontiers. This was a fundamental and new methodological point for intelligence-gathering.[5]

The proposals were also consciously modeled on the vision of the Middle East as a vast network of secret centers. The Arab Bureau affiliate Harold Fenton Jacob proposed a "Moslem Bureau" with branches at Gibraltar, Malta, Egypt, Constantinople, Mesopotamia, Aden, India, and Singapore functioning as "intelligence sensors" accommodating clusters of ministries, agencies, consulates, and so on. Cairo was demoted in this web; the former agents at the Foreign Office favored the more spatially attenuated Arab Bureau of 1918, foreseeing officials at Baghdad, Cairo, Beirut, Jerusalem, and Aden keeping each other informed through telegrams that would permit them to dispense altogether with a central clearinghouse. At the same time, theories of *worldwide* conspiracy originating in the Middle East drew imperial eyes closer to home. A War Office proposal created with Deedes's guidance argued that the only possible center for intelligence about the "Eastern Empire" was London, in view of the connection of Near East affairs ("Moslem countries from Kazan to Zanzibar and from Morocco to Java") with the rest of the world, and, after all, London was the capital of the world.[6]

Most striking was the proposals' shared assumption that intelligence encompassed the collection of information *and* covert administration. Counterespionage emerged as a fundamental mechanism of colonial control in a region considered so intrinsically treacherous that political control could not be wrought any other way. In the words of one intelligencer, the breakup of the Ottoman Empire had created a need and opportunity for its replacement by "a centre in the Middle East which will collect and radiate all information direct to a circumference that can include both the Governments concerned...and any of their existing agents they may still wish to maintain abroad." Intelligence would step into the vacuum left by a defunct empire. The pulsating, incorporeal, connective force that was Islam would be countered by an equally refulgent British administrative Department of Moslem Affairs. But since camouflage was essential to prevent Muslims from discovering their subjection to British rule and launching "a fanatical political campaign from East to West," in practice the department would be disguised as an "Islamic Section" of some intelligence office. The iron law of cunning in the Middle East thus produced a call for covert administration by an *intelligence* agency. The Islamic Section would be entrusted with "feeling the pulse of Islam and diagnosing accordingly," circulating its diagnoses in bulletins to various local centers of Islam. Similarly, the director of military intelligence's proposal explicitly called for using the intelligence network as "part of the mechanism of the British empire." In Cornwallis's proposal from the Foreign Office, the projected Middle East section of the Foreign Office *was* the intelligence system.[7]

In the end, all these proposals were jettisoned for a variety of reasons, including cost, uncertainty, and Indian-Egyptian infighting. For instance, the Foreign Office was initially favorable to a 1919 War Office scheme, but the undersecretary for foreign affairs, former Indian viceroy Charles Hardinge, frowned on the provision for military attachés doing the "work of spies," and Foreign Secretary Curzon, incensed at receiving the third such proposal in twenty-four hours, felt that the unsettled state of the postwar world was inappropriate for setting up "this gigantic organization, with its octopus claws scrabbling over half the universe." The deal-breaking objection to proposals couched as "Moslem" or "Islamic" bureaus was India's distaste for treating the "Islamic" world as a conceptual whole, lest such formal recognition unwittingly hasten its concretization into political reality. Conspiracy thinking proved the undoing of its own effort to combat conspiracies. The Pan-Islamist, explained Arthur Hirtzel, wanted nothing more than "to have his pretensions taken at their face value and his bogey made into something that will really make the flesh creep." On the one hand, the connectedness of the region demanded an intelligence system of equal scope; on the other, the threat was always inchoate, and the intelligence system might perversely prove the catalyst of its final consummation. Reluctance to establish a formal network stemmed ultimately from the weird, notional quality of the imagined conspiracy: Pan-Islamism was a danger, "or rather a potential danger," "a frame of mind and not a policy," explained Hirtzel, "but a frame of mind may become a policy," particularly if they helped it by creating "a special mechanism to collect Islamic information" that would make them "see everything through Islamic spectacles." While agents on the ground continued to grouse about the lack of intelligence coordination, finally, in the course of hunting for the elusive "cause" of the Iraqi rebellion of 1920, the India Office acknowledged the need for "a more highly centralised system of intelligence which will coordinate data collected in widely scattered fields"—at which point the War Office observed snidely that the India Office "apparently withdraws the objection raised" a year before to the principle behind its scheme to prevent "trouble of the nature which has now arisen." Bray, as the India Office's one-man regionwide intelligence agency in charge of considering "the whole asiatic problem from one single viewpoint," prophesied, "Rebellions may occur, dissensions arise till finally unless an organized defence is opposed to this organized advance[,] time will give the verdict to the latter." Thus, even after the immediate postwar effervescence of proposals had fizzled out, the fantasy of a Middle East archive remained potent.[8]

The fantasy endured partly because many proposals did not ask for much at all. Jacob's Moslem Bureau, for instance, was to be an agency so covert it would not have to exist. It was not to appear new, lest it arouse Muslim suspicions, nor was it to be called "Moslem Bureau" if it were staffed by Christian officials. Nor was it to give the impression of a military intelligence or espionage bureau. Nor, ultimately, did it need to be "created" per se, as the need to economize would perforce require the work to be done by existing staffs attached to the ambassador, minister, high commissioner, consul, or other such representative abroad. In London, a central bureau of "experts" would collate and publish the information. It would be a bureau smeared through space, much like the wraithlike web of 1918. Although it would be entirely undercover—for ostensibly irreproachable reasons of economy—it was definitively not to be construed as an espionage bureau. It would be a collection of *informal* contacts.

Improvisation was, of course, the agents' strong suit, and they eventually succeeded in creating a web around the region not very different from the ideal set forth in some of the proposals for a formal organization (or from its Edwardian roots), even in its informality. As the proposals were swept unceremoniously from the table, desperate agents like Bell and Philby scrambled to mend the unraveling old web, drawing on personal friendships. Responding to agents' complaints, London made fitful efforts to improvise a regionwide system, the Foreign Office, Air Ministry, India Office, and Colonial Office asking each other's officials to keep the others informed. In this informal web, intelligence and administrative functions were combined as a general rule. The region was in British hands but had to be held discreetly. The cabinet, in its determination to treat "the Middle Eastern, or rather the Arab, problem" as "one organic whole" and to avoid the thankless task of determining meaningful boundaries within it, collected even the ostensibly independent territories in the region, including the Arabian peninsula, in the new Middle East Department in the *Colonial* Office; if some of it was controlled by the British, all of it, effectively, had to be (this bureaucratic relocation only confirming Arab suspicions that mandatory rule was a fraud). One of only two formal institutions that emerged from the struggle to create a single policy and intelligence unit for the Middle East, this *administrative* department was staffed primarily by former agents whose infiltration of Whitehall depended on the social contacts formed by the long-standing overlap between intelligence, diplomacy, and administration in the Middle East. They tolerated bureaucratic life by remaining outside it, persisting in their wandering, even infecting their new, sedentary colleagues with a taste for frequent junkets to the region. Lawrence was on tour for much of his tenure at the Colonial Office—"These movements are beyond me," quipped Curzon. Even when in London, he spent little time handling routine administrative matters, serving instead as a sort of resident pontiff on Arabian questions. Indeed, even after departing the administrative world, these former agents continued to exercise an informal influence. The Colonial Office's careless handling of its ongoing relationship with Lawrence while he was pseudonymously serving in the RAF probably played a part in the discovery of his identity in 1922. Meinertzhagen, too, continued to offer his opinions, particularly to his uncle Sidney Webb, the colonial secretary in 1929. The Political Department in Iraq similarly combined colonial administration and intelligence. Bell, who as oriental secretary split her time between King Faisal, the Criminal Investigation Department (CID), and the Ministry of the Interior, wrote with obvious relish, "Isn't it strange to be part of Arab secret intelligence and to be accepted as one of themselves by the King and his head police officer!" Even in Transjordan, surveillance morphed into covert rule: Peake Pasha, who had left the Egyptian Camel Corps to form a police force for the Amman-Jerusalem road, was among a handful of Britons who, "by influence and advice, rather than by direct rule," maintained control over Arab diplomacy and politics. Because, for the entire decade, the Palestine government "did not function at all" in their part of the world, Peake and his Palestine counterpart, Major Jarvis, on the other side of the Wadi Araba, "took over, unofficially and unasked, the administration of this preserve of the outlaw and ran it as a sort of dual and quite unrecognized mandate"—earning a reputation as "a couple of twelfth-century [*sic*] Arab swashbucklers." But, Jarvis protested, "the part was forced on us!"[9]

The other formal venue for combined intelligence and administrative activity in the Middle East was the IDCEU. Formed in 1922 largely at the impetus of the zealously converted India Office, it convened after an eye-opening interdepartmental meeting on "Bolshevism as a menace to the British empire."

With Turkish and Indian nationalist organizations stretching across Europe and Asia, "no single department has at its disposal the complete evidence relating to these subjects," argued the India Office. Each was "too closely concerned...with its own particular sphere," and, "the questions...are world-wide." Hence the interdepartmental committee, which included representatives of the secret agencies. As ever, the Middle East was the region in which not only the various empires, but also the various departments of the British government collided. Lawrence sat in early IDCEU meetings for the Colonial Office; Bray, whose memorandum on Bolshevism was critical to its generation, for the India Office. A year of investigation convinced the committee that the Middle East was the most contentious spot on the globe and that "protective intelligence" was needed, especially to constrain the movement of undesirables. It assigned itself the task of ensuring coordination and dissemination of intelligence, a unique brief for a government committee. In 1926, the Committee of Imperial Defense expanded the IDCEU's mission to include consideration of *policy* and, in view of its intelligence focus, decided to solicit representatives from the fighting services as well. The IDCEU thus began to by degrees emerge as a forum for policy and the collection and analysis of intelligence about conspiracies against the British, although never entirely satisfactorily to all parties involved. It disappeared in 1927.[10]

In one of his exasperated rejections of an early intelligence proposal, Curzon predicted that an intelligence system of appropriate size and scope would eventually evolve in the region as part of the department eventually set up to deal with it. And, indeed, when the Middle East Department was formed, Meinertzhagen insisted that it should father a centralized intelligence system for the region. Still, a formal intelligence network under Colonial Office auspices remained a castle in the sky—but Curzon's forecast was not entirely misbegotten; an intelligence organization was eventually shepherded into existence by a foster parent, the RAF, which provided a distinctly new infrastructure and concrete network on which to suspend the improvised terrestrial web. Its constituents conspired to create a new intelligence community geared to entrap the nomadic, chameleon-like perpetrators of regionwide anti-British conspiracies.[11]

The Central Bureau of Air Intelligence Iraq was a major nodal point in an expanding chain of intelligence-cum-colonial authorities. Ostensibly created to guide the "pacification" effort, it also handled "secret information of Imperial rather than local Iraq interest" and was "a valuable link in the Middle East chain of Intelligence organisation." To prevent certain information from falling into the hands of Iraqi ministers, information was sent demiofficially to the head of Air Intelligence. Thus, under cover of the Iraqi intelligence organization lay a purely British one, made up of the very same advisers and SSOs, pursuing imperial interests. Air authorities in Iraq and Palestine also provided the consul in Damascus with secret service funds to pay agents, since the information gained was "almost exclusively" in their interests. In 1927, this adjunct ground intelligence establishment began to spin its own web. Pointing to sprawling Jewish-Labour conspiracy between the Middle East and Britain, Iraqi Air Intelligence urged "intelligence officers everywhere" to cooperate in a group effort that would "render the detection of increased activity or new hostile organisations...easier." Colonel Dent, chief of Air Intelligence, who already had an understanding with Persia, drew his counterpart in Beirut into a demiofficial intelligence-sharing arrangement. The lofty view of the region from Air Intelligence was advantageous, he explained, for observing border-transgressing subversive activity. The police collected "full material, sometimes too full," about individuals and organizations, but "they are not so good at putting it together or differentiating between what is important and what is not." Hence, he assured his colleague, "we are useful." This improvised organization was founded on the traditional principle that certain agents, from a privileged vantage point, possessed special insight into Arabian reality. The British liaison officer in Beirut, John Codrington, brought Cairo and Jerusalem into the ring, characteristically, through personal visits. Unsurprisingly, the ghost of the Arab Bureau hung over the discussion, but Dent doubted they could obtain government sanction for any such formal structure. Instead, their informally arranged web provided for exchange of lists and monthly summaries of communist activities and a cipher for rapid communication of the passage of suspects. Codrington offered to liaise among the various countries, as he was able to travel "more or less at will." Such arrangements allowed British authorities to create the intelligence system that they could not, officially at least, own to desire. Codrington later described this episode as an effort to "spin the beginnings of an 'anti-commintern' web." Dent, too, as he frantically searched for the secret Bolshevik center in the Middle East, stressed the need to "discover for certain the centre of the web and not feel round the circumference by chance threads."[12]

To this end, he asked the air commander to convince London to expand his reach to Moscow, Baku, and the Persian Gulf to secure warning of the departure of "bad characters and suspected agents." His proposals were circulated to the IDCEU. The committee's sudden dissolution that year was moot in terms of preventing concrete action, since, as its preliminary deliberations reveal, it felt Dent's needs would best be served by an *informal* arrangement with the high commissioners concerned (not least since his proposals were redundant with proposed extensions of and improvements of liaison with the SIS).

An intelligence organization had become literally redundant with the colonial administration—and with all the activities of Britons on the ground. Dent relentlessly but unsuccessfully pursued the matter of appointing an agent to Bushire, arguing there could be no difficulty about "cover":

> If it does not suit to make one an assistant Military attaché or the other an Air Force Liaison Officer or Imperial Airways official, surely you can work them in as assistant Consuls or assistant political residents, missionaries, doctors working out some special thesis, archeologists or concession hunters of some kind even if the APOC [Anglo-Persian Oil Company] or some other British firm cannot provide it.

The gamut of guises of prewar casual agents, once a matter of extreme official discomfort, was now forthrightly accepted as a set of expedients for circumventing official obstruction, for the Middle East was now a land in which British diplomats, technocrats, administrators, and academics were the ubiquitous minions of a covert empire; they could do as they pleased. The unofficial agents who had gathered intelligence in forbidden Arabia and rendered all British travelers suspect in local eyes furnished the models for official agents in an age that had seen the literal transformation of the region into a spy-space. Indeed, military intelligence manuals explicitly enjoined agents in irregular theaters to mimic local knowledge-gathering practices, for which they had to know the country and the language and possess courage, "cunning," a taste for exploration, and military knowledge—the qualities of the classic, amateur Arabia agent. Consuls, too, knew no scruples. The Jeddah consulate, for instance, made crafty use of royal physicians, pilgrims, and Indian pilgrimage officers to counter supposed German, Soviet, and other intrigues, ultimately encouraging Hejazi counterespionage, and, in Damascus, British officials arranged for the infiltration of the Najdi Agency to counter suspected French-Saudi intrigues.[13]

Informal expedients enabled Dent to create a web of some reach and diversity, recalling the heterogeneous crews of early times. Participating authorities included Air Staff Intelligence and the CID in Iraq; the SIS and other authorities in Constantinople; the SIS in Greece; the British military attaché in Tehran, the consul at Khuzistan, and the Anglo-Persian Oil Company in Persia; the British liaison officer in Beirut and director of Sûreté général in Syria; the CID in Palestine; and the CID, SIS, and General Staff Intelligence in Egypt. Communication was also established with India and Aden. The system was kept demiofficial to avoid dealing with the inevitably complicating "financial aspect." The Air Ministry attempted to bring some order to this makeshift "intelligence chain in the Middle East" by arranging for regular exchange of information between Iraq, the air officer commanding in Palestine, General Headquarters in Cairo, and the British liaison officer in Beirut. After some struggle, the Air Ministry also exported modified versions of the RAF's SSO organization to neighboring countries (under modified air control schemes), multiplying the anomalies in the system even while striving to regularize it. John Glubb arrived in Amman to replicate his tried-and-tested system of desert defense, which combined the tasks of intelligence and administration, at once making use of Arab assistance and keeping control of intelligence in British hands. Thus, his work in southern Iraq "affected the whole history of Arabia," in the words of a Foreign Office official. In 1928, the Air Ministry allotted the air staffs in India, Egypt, and Malta with full-time intelligence officers (to their relief) to conform to the increasingly "thorough and comprehensive system at the Air Ministry." In 1931, the Air Council formally acknowledged its responsibility for intelligence collection throughout the Arabian peninsula, except Oman and the Trucial Coast, in addition to Iraq, Syria, and Palestine. This burgeoning regional air network provided a framework for the informal arrangements on the ground as both grew in tandem, straining to fulfill the agents' holistic view of the region. At the same time, it was precisely this view that made it difficult for laggard commands to keep pace: to make their new intelligence branch effective, argued Cairo officials, they would need intelligence officers in the Sudan and Transjordan. The concerns at each headquarters quickly spilled over frontiers, making "liaison" a byword of the whole air-intelligence nexus. (Cairo got its wish.)[14]

Thus, the peculiarities of place continued to preserve anomalous improvisations. In 1930, the Jeddah post in what had become Saudi Arabia was made a legation, but Gulf officials continued to serve as primary diplomatic representatives with Ibn Saud when he was in Najd, deserts away from Jeddah. Jeddah's monthly *consular* reports were continued (legations normally submitted annual reports), a prodigious expense of labor justified on the grounds that they were "so much appreciated" by so many posts and that "Jedda is a somewhat unusual post, from the diplomatic point of view." Anomalies also endured in transmission of intelligence through private rather than formal channels. The decision to continue Iraqi fortnightly intelligence reports was based on Whitehall's concerns about being left "in the dark" by intractable agents on the spot rather than on a perception that such catalogues of disembodied information might be useful, for "it is very difficult to keep a record of the fugitive storms which sweep across the face of Iraqi...politics." Regionwide intelligence remained a work in progress. Till the end of our period, the Colonial Office resisted the Foreign Office principle of "unreserved direct exchange of information for the Middle East posts," forcing some appointees to resort to special pleading. "In this country where there are no newspapers worth the name, no telegraphic service and no nothing to keep me in touch with what happens further afield than Mecca," importuned Andrew Ryan, the first minister in Jeddah. "I am very dependent on what news I may get from [other] posts." This appeal elicited a host of reports from around the region, including quarterly reports from Amman, Glubb's intelligence, and RAF fortnightly intelligence summaries on Transjordan and Palestine.[15]

In any case, despite enduring flaws and lacunae, the half-baked intelligence mosaic was eventually deemed the most suitable to the region. So entrenched were the principles of immersion, nomadism, and intuition that no truly bureaucratic intelligence organization could gain a foothold in Arabia, even after the arrival of the professionals of the RAF. In 1926, as we know, the SIS unsuccessfully urged the government to consider expansion of its organization into Arabia. While realizing that it was "logical to suppose...that a new SIS centre situated in any one place in Arabia might be able to keep its finger upon the pulse of common internal problems," the War Office feared that in fact such a center "would require expansion to a dangerous and indeed impossible degree were it also to try and follow the ramifications of foreign policy with trails which would lead to Syria, Eritrea, Egypt, Persia, Turkey, India, etc." A gap certainly existed, "but," the office concluded, "such gaps are endemic in any machinery which revolves around the doings of autocratic rulers in the East." A sophisticated, professional intelligence bureaucracy was *futile* in Arabia, at once excessive and insufficient. Moreover, the War and Foreign offices were happy with the intelligence they got from the consulate in Jeddah: "Past experience proves that Ibn Saud is more likely to ventilate his opinions in a frank discussion with a British official who has gained his regard than in any other circumstances." The Jeddah consul affirmed his satisfaction with his ability to get "reliable and quick" information thanks to the Arab rumor mill, itself "one of the best arguments against any really organized secret service." In a place with a fully functioning magical information network, an expert individual of sufficient sympathy to the Arabs was all that was necessary and practical for intelligence-gathering. The Colonial Office was likewise sure that the Iraqi frontier, with its well-immersed SSOs and airmen who knew how to read desert signs, would remain a "pretty good thermometer" of Ibn Saud's attitude.[16]

Administration and intelligence could be one because the Middle East was the terrain of agents like Lawrence, who were "better than an office full of files." He knew everything and "carried all his knowledge in his head." The postwar decade saw the formalization of older improvisations that had redounded so gloriously to their credit during the war as to banish the thought of their replacement by more professional and bureaucratic methods. Arabia would remain the classic space of cloak-and-dagger. The official intelligence world knew it could do worse than apply for "the advice of some British merchant, bank-manager or consular official" in their work, for, as Captain Leith-Ross had reminded them at the end of the war, "many of these gentlemen have rendered valuable service to 'Intelligence'" and were "fully alive...to the need of absolute secrecy." An improvised intelligence web directed the improvised empire in the region, combining security and administration in one task.[17]

Ramifications

The veiled nature of British rule in Iraq throughout this period was what enabled Britain to preserve its control even in "independent" Iraq after 1932. Their "invisible hand" remained in place, unbeknownst to Iraqis but often suspected. Preparations for gathering intelligence in a postmandatory Iraq began as early as 1926, immediately after settlement of the Iraqi-Turkish frontier, in view of the "long period of study...over and above actual technical essentials of the work...necessary for any officer to be efficient." These plans went hand in hand with the preparations for maintaining the RAF in independent Iraq, the logic being that (1) any air action would require independent intelligence as justification and (2) external and internal affairs were always linked, not least because an imminent external threat would always be foreshadowed by "internal and tribal unrest"—the signs that would have to be expertly interpreted— or, conversely, "internal chaos would...lead to external aggression." (The Iraqi government argued in vain that, without the British leash, it would be able to establish peaceful relations with its neighbors.) And, then, of course, (3) with indigenous internal agents, the RAF could "hardly hope for a balanced and unbiased appreciation." Q.E.D.: the RAF would have to have its own internal intelligence service in independent Iraq.[18]

Needless to say, there could be no sharing of the infrastructure of intelligence with the nascent Iraqi Army any more than there could be real encouragement of an Iraqi air force. The intelligence section of the Iraqi Army General Staff would be formed under a British officer, its activities strictly limited to military lines and preparation for war, "i.e., topography, route reports, reconnaissance courses, study of military organisation of Turkish and Persian armies, personalities, and protective Intelligence as regards sedition or discontent among their own units." The Central Bureau of Air Intelligence had to remain under British direction, else when the independent Iraqi intelligence organization came under the Ministry of Defense, it would cease to form "a link in the Imperial Intelligence Chain," as Iraqi Army officers would "inevitably come in contact with that part of the organisation which is Imperial rather than local." Iraqi officers trained as SSOs "should of course know nothing of the special secret sources which do not concern them at all." The Air Ministry worked to maintain the imperial intelligence organization "under the Resident or who ever takes the place of the High commissioner...provided with S. S. funds if necessary." Air Intelligence already felt it had become distinctly more difficult "to get news of a really secret nature" after Britain had declared its intention to leave the administration to the Iraqis; their actually doing so might "create a revulsion of feeling and make news easier to get for a time," making it all the more necessary to have agents in position to gather it after 1932. The entire British intelligence organization—the very mechanism of colonial rule in Iraq—would remain in place and receive diplomatic cover. The British high commissioner (and later the ambassador) would continue to exercise a right of intervention, and the British advisory staff would pass on intelligence and, being in an "executive position," ensure that the Iraqi government conformed to British priorities (despite Iraqi expectations that the advisers would immediately retire from the scene). These arrangements were made informally by allowing a practice "to develop under [High Commissioner] Humphrys' influence," lest "foreign circles" represent it as proof that the British government, "while relinquishing the responsibilities of the mandate, will retain its advantages....We should certainly be accused of...developing a system of British intelligence officers in that administration for our own ends." Humphrys would "concentrate the sources of information and the channel of enquiry in the person of one well-placed British official"—the adviser to the Ministry of Interior (none other than Kinahan Cornwallis). The ambassador would also "receive information of increasing value from the British Consular officers who are about to be appointed in various parts of the country." The consular intelligence that the Foreign Office had scarcely deigned to admit before the war became the *less* objectionable, more routine intelligence source in the postwar covert empire. British advisers also regularly took the liberty of communicating information to London (often in private letters) without the authority or knowledge of their advisees, an arrangement the embassy and Foreign Office took pains to keep secret for their sake.[19]

As 1932 loomed near, the RAF also looked after the SSOs: presuming the SSOs would be officially required to "disappear," Air Intelligence reckoned, "One will have to have people more or less carrying out the functions of the present SSOs but normally working at Air HQ [Headquarters]" and doing "a lot of travelling about." Recruitment had to continue apace given the rare skills required for the job. Future SSOs would have to be "of a definitely higher class, and the whole machinery will need much more delicate handling." They would ideally have had experience in Iraqi intelligence. Specifically, as they would have "no chance of corroboration," they would need "a critical faculty the more highly developed." Air Intelligence estimated that about five people "of the SSO type" would be required in addition to two officers permanently at headquarters. In the event the Iraqi government refused to acquiesce in the continued presence of SSOs at "the important centers of Kerbela, Najaf, Baghdad, Hillah and Diwaniyeh," backup plans included adding an "Air Attaché" to the ambassador's staff or organizing a truly "secret intelligence service." Indeed, Iraqi suspicions of SSOs, whose euphemistic title "special service officer" Iraqis tended to "misinterpret" as "secret service officer," had already begun to vitiate the officers' ability to transmit reliable information—indeed, suspicions that SSOs were plotting a Kurdish uprising (one of them had been caught paying a Kurdish schoolmaster for information) had even held up publication of the 1930 treaty. (Refusing to accept that Iraqis actually believed this theory of British conspiracy, Brooke-Popham suspected an *Iraqi* conspiracy to forestall the treaty—or a Turkish one, since the cabinet members in question were all ex-Turkish Army officers.) When leveling with the Iraqi government about the importance of SSOs to Britain's ability to fulfill its treaty obligations failed, the agents were simply rechristened, rather blandly, as "British liaison officers" attached to each outstation headquarters. A few airfield guards with the right language qualifications were also selected to gather intelligence in the normal course of accompanying aircraft and inspecting landing grounds and during "their visits to recruiting areas." The Iraqi government would "be placed in possession of all facts concerning this organization," but, "since the main factor governing an efficient intelligence system is secrecy, the British authorities must be permitted to keep to themselves the detailed arrangements by which the information is collected." Advisers to the Iraqi government would also continue to receive intelligence reports through demiofficial channels. "Liaison officers" were soon rechristened "air liaison officers" (ALOs)—"the same individuals with new and supposedly thicker cloaks."[20]

Paranoia continued to provide rationales for an otherwise indefensible covert colonial authority. The Air Ministry defended the pre- and postmandate continuities, despite Iraqis' "strong national feelings" and widespread "suspicion of the activities of any British official," by reminding Parliament that this was "an oriental country where intrigue is rife and where the people are exceptionally susceptible to subversive or inflammatory agitation." The Air Ministry, too, had to proceed in secrecy, for "in a country in a state of such acute nationalist self-consciousness," public discussion about SSOs would only cause trouble. Paradoxically, independent intelligence was also justified on the grounds that the fractious population had *not yet* been "welded together as a national whole," making it easy for minor troubles to spread, with "wide and disastrous consequences." Privately, the Air Ministry conceded, "we really have no defence." When ministry officials worried about the agents' position under the articles on espionage in the post-1932 Iraqi Penal Code, the head of the Eastern Department of the Foreign Office argued: "It would be better for us to try to get what we want outside the law. For practical purposes, the law does not, I think, matter much." Independent intelligence became a "universal principle" and covert arm of the RAF because of its particular informational worries as an infant service in Iraq.[21]

The irony is that this tactlessly engineered, finely tuned British intelligence organization failed to predict the most epoch-making events in the region. Well after Arnold Wilson's Pollyannaish regime was rudely awakened in the summer of 1920, the view of Arabia as a land of endless raiding and exaggerating natives blinded British analysts to the seriousness of such signal events as Ibn Saud's invasion of the Hejaz in 1924, which rung the death knell on the Hashemite regime. In a decade-long delusional existence, the British satisfied themselves through the groupthink of their intelligence apparatus that their presence in the Middle East was entirely welcome and that every policy decision—from the installment of King Faisal to air control to the creation of Iraq—was what people actually wanted. Whatever its faults, the genius-dominated organization did provide exactly the intelligence that was *desired*.[22]

The agents' influence on Whitehall had a more general policy implication beyond even the basic infrastructural decisions to hold on to the new Middle Eastern colonies and rule them from the air. And that is in the *lack* of coherent policy guiding the Middle Eastern empire, which people noticed and which inspired the frequent cries for more unified control of the region; what some scholars have painted as unfortunate misguidedness or a series of mistakes was an artifact of the style of imperial rule and regime of expertise in place.[23] In 1920, Hubert Young traced Whitehall's discordant policy to the conflicting influence of two "strong personalities," Lawrence and Wilson, the former acting from pro-Arab and anti-French motives, the latter rather indelicately against them (loudly proclaiming his determination to make Mesopotamia a "wedge of British controlled territory" apart from the rest of the Arab world).[24] However divergent their political influence, both emerged from a community of individuals sharing a sense of "magic identification" with the "forces of history," as Hannah Arendt puts it in the epigraph that opens this chapter. Ultimately, the policy of the covert empire had to be incoherent; the "very essence" of the symbiotic system created by bureaucrat and spy is, Arendt explains, "aimless process," an end only abetted by an atmosphere of horizonless fear.

Arendt ultimately acquitted Britain on the count of totalitarianism, as we know, and to many this verdict was (and remains) a foregone conclusion: Orwell famously elevated Britain during World War Two:

> The whole conception of the militarized continental state, with its secret police, its censored literature and its conscript labour, is utterly different from that of the loose maritime democracy, with its slums and unemployment, its strikes and party politics. It is the difference between land power and sea power, between cruelty and inefficiency, between lying and self-deception, between the S. S.-man and the rent-collector.

Despite their sway over vast expanses of the earth, the British remained willfully blind to their status as an entrenched land power. Indeed, as we have seen, they liked to compare the deserts of Arabia to the seas they had long ruled; camel parties were like ships and aircraft—migrant patrollers of a flowing space. Such spaces required a minimal commitment of material and manpower for a maximum result of the illusion, if not the actual achievement, of total control. This piece of "self-deception," along with other soothing ideas of Arabia, are perhaps what set them and their imperial network of global surveillance apart from contemporary totalitarian regimes. The paranoia of the British imperial state found outlets abroad; indeed, British imperialism had long been predicated on various forms of authoritarian statecraft. If, under totalitarianism, "Real power begins where secrecy begins," those straining after its British echo could do worse than look to Iraq, where the secret services were in fact "wholly integrated in the administration."[25]

Contemporaries elsewhere certainly remained skeptical of Britain's political innocence. As the distinction between British intelligence and administration collapsed, various observers, unsurprisingly, grew paranoid about British activity in the region, the unreckonable potential of covert empire lending force to fears both legitimate and fantastic. The French were particularly susceptible, British officials frequently pointed out: they were principally concerned that British consuls would foment unrest in Syria, worrying especially about Philby, almost as much as the British did. And then, of course, Lawrence's specter hung over every rebellion in the world, with the Germans, Russians, Turks, Iraqis, and more or less everyone at various points identifying his hidden hand in Afghanistan, Kurdistan, Persia, Morocco, Soviet Turkestan, Tibet—wherever "trouble...could be attributed to the machiavellian designs of the imperialistic British Government," complained one official, somewhat disingenuously—reports that the *Times* invariably found newsworthy. The British remained incredulous in the face of these and other foreign allegations, typically dismissing them as propaganda planted by the truly Machiavellian Soviet government. They wrote off Turkish complaints of their intriguing around Kurdistan as "fantastic tales." The consul in Damascus tried to assure the French commander in chief that his impression of British activity was merely "part of the legend of the ubiquity and efficiency of the British intelligence organisation," to which the general replied with acuity that it was not a legend at all. Indeed, the entire thrust of the intelligence project in Arabia was shaped by the agents' ambitions to accomplish feats deserving *legendary* acclaim. The British liaison in Syria protested that the French flattered his "humble efforts to keep my superiors informed of what is happening in...the Middle East" by calling it "a thoroughly and completely organised Intelligence Service," but, as we have seen, one man's humble information-gathering could be another's covert imperial state. (In fact, besides tracking Turkish troop movements, this officer also obtained unexpurgated copies of French intelligence summaries, clearly without French authority.) He speculated that French officials in Syria had not had

> sufficient experience of life outside Europe to abstain from lending
> an all too ready ear to all sorts of fantastic reports which their agents
> and time-servers lay before them....The French Intelligence
> Service...in the Middle East, is extraordinarily badly informed. This
> I attribute to the almost complete lack of any arabic or turkish-
> speaking officers...necessitating permanent recourse to that very
> bad system—administration through native interpreters.

British officials, confident in their own immersion-induced ability to see through oriental intriguing, thus attempted to enlighten the French general about the "native agents...sowing discord between us." Paranoia answered paranoia.[26]

Unsurprisingly, Iraqis themselves were highly skeptical of British protestations of their good intentions. This topic merits its own study; here I simply want to suggest the relevance of the British side of the story to an understanding of Iraqi "paranoia" about Western imperialism as neither sui generis nor endemic to the "Arab mind." The Iraqi government constantly suspected British officials of engaging in activity of the Lawrentian sort, and ordinary Iraqis rather accurately suspected the British intelligence regime of perpetrating a gigantic fraud on the whole country by providing them with a king and "independence" while their agents continued to pull the strings behind the scene, passing a police state off as a free one. Some even thought the British were instigating the Ikhwan raids to prove that there was a significant military threat requiring continued British presence in the country. Meanwhile, in

Najd, Saudi paranoia about Philby's British loyalties rivaled the British government's anxieties over his Saudi allegiance. The Iraqi press "exposed" the imperialist activities of officers like Glubb who claimed to work in Iraq's interests:

> We see him pass from place to place in the desert penetrating into the heart of the wilderness learning the affairs of its inhabitants, mixing with all classes of the people, learning their mentality and their ways. Mr. Glubb is truly a remarkable and clever man who is well fitted to be a profitable agent for the British Government in this country. If we say that he serves British interests the wise will know the extent of his worth to Iraq: this man so strong in the methods of imperialism, this man who, up to two years ago held an important post in the British Military Intelligence Service in this country, has now been made Lord of the Earth, after having been Administrative Inspector, Diwaniyah.

He was "omnipotent in the desert," a "dictator." (Within days, another paper rose rather suspiciously to his defense, explaining that he was no spy but an employee of the Ministry of the Interior, using his "specialized knowledge" to look after the tribes while subsisting on barley and rainwater.) These are clippings from Glubb's personal papers; he knew the Iraqis didn't trust him—but, then, that was the white man's burden.[27]

But British officials did not take these allegations any more seriously than the others, in the main ascribing Iraqi suspicions to *Iraqi* paranoia: "The penetrating Iraqi eye saw through the cloak [of the air liaison officer] and discerned blackness in the heart of its wearer and it has never been possible to convince the owner of the eye that the blackness was a complete illusion!" This lament by the British ambassador in Baghdad was partly tongue-in-cheek: diagnosing the Iraqi government with "A-ell-ophobia," he nevertheless conceded that Iraqis "have never swallowed the fiction that [the ALOs] are maintained as much, more even, for their good than for ours." The blithe tone of the confession signaled the obvious inconsequence of the sin—everyone knew, it implied, that the sovereignty of countries like Iraq was merely a technical gesture not intended to interfere with the serious and universally beneficial work of "real" states and empires. Indeed, some officials evinced great relish in the knowledge of their secret power. Henry Dobbs, as high commissioner noted scornfully, "Any hint that tribesmen and others are peeping behind the arab façade and know where the real power lies drives [Faisal] wild with jealousy." The difference between British success in Iraq and French failure in Syria was not, he felt, one of degree of control but merely that "the hand has perhaps been more skillfully hidden here." (A year later, he would be assuring the Permanent

Mandates Commission that the proposed maintenance of British advisers in postmandatory Iraq would not make its independence illusory.) Covert empire was a strategy of colonial control for a people so stubbornly blind to the value of British rule and so fanatically attached to freedom (spun as anarchy) that they would not swallow control any other way. And, anyway, as we have seen, cunning was excusable, even obligatory, in Arabia—the "Court of King Feisal [was] at one with the Court of Haroun al Raschid." Leaving public service for the Anglo-Persian Oil Company in 1925, Arnold Wilson momentarily lit on the illogic of the British position: "We have been known to the world as perfide albion for a hundred years—but, like Oriental treachery—which surprises orientals on each fresh occasion, as much as us—so the British habit...surprises an Englishman on each fresh occasion." Meanwhile, the trope of needless Iraqi paranoia fed imperial delusions about good intentions, and we all know where that path leads.[28]

Concern about Iraqi suspicions did provoke some misgivings about the SSO system but never enough to shake the expert opinion and persistent fears of the RAF. In 1938, the Iraqi minister of the interior complained to his British adviser, the former political officer C. J. Edmonds, about recent "intensification" of ALO activity aimed at debauching Iraqi officers into spying on the Iraqi Army. He found this especially reprehensible given that the British Military Mission and advisers already had immediate access to information about the army. Edmonds duly asked the RAF to consider altering its arrangements, not least because ALOs were constantly watched and those who consorted with them swiftly penalized, severely limiting the ALOs' ability to obtain information of value. Echoing J. G. Lorimer decades earlier, he explained that disgruntled Iraqis used them to voice their complaints against government, and their politeness in listening encouraged the belief that they might take up the cudgels on the Iraqis' behalf. The ghost of Lawrence had not been laid to rest. Thus, for instance, an article from the Al Nahar, which the interior minister forwarded to Edmonds, talked of "hidden hands" orchestrating seditious activities, pointing specifically to the tour of an ALO accompanying one Hindle James (an Egypt-based officer whose liaison work took him all over the region) on a private visit in September 1937. In a reply that says more about the RAF's paranoia than the Iraqi government's, Air Command denied any intensification of ALO activity, *except* that occasioned by intensified political intrigue in the Iraqi Army, and suggested the minister's complaint was based on faked documentation. It stressed the danger of suppressing "the only means at present available of obtaining information in a country in which intrigue and corruption is rife, and armed rebellion is liable to break out at any moment." Now the Iraqi government was then an agreeably pro-British one (following the assassination of General Bakr Sidqi, who had instigated a coup in 1936). Some Foreign Office officials, in their surprise at *this* government raising the issue at all, conceded the currency of objections to ALOs and, bizarrely, wondered "if the Iraqis would not almost prefer a *secret* form of espionage proper, rather than the open and above board activities of the ALO's."[29]

Eventually, the RAF and the British Embassy did explore alternatives but mainly because of their own dissatisfaction with the ALOs' reports, for the other official anxiety at play in the covert empire was the reliability of the "fanatical" agents charged with maintaining it. Inveterate straining after a prophetic role had become the occupational disease of the British agent in Arabia. When the ambassador officially raised the matter of ALO activities, he complained in particular that Hindle James had "muddled up what the Embassy had told him with a great deal of tittle-tattle collected by himself, misunderstood the whole, and produced quite worthless and misleading reports." Many at the Foreign Office agreed that this "peripatetic outsider" was a "queer fish." "What right has he, as an agent of 'the British Government,'" demanded one official indignantly, "to discuss with Nuri Pasha his schemes for an Arab State Confederation and his 'inclination to hasten the inevitable revolt' in Iraq?...HMG will be suspected of being privy to this plot against the existing regime in Iraq." Nevertheless, the air commander replied that protecting imperial communications required knowledge about precisely such threats to internal order. Moreover, local etiquette prohibited junior intelligence officers from "interrupt[ing] important sheikhs while the latter were speaking." The ambassador found these arguments specious and refused to receive James at the embassy. Eventually, the Air Ministry agreed to keep him in Egypt. The difficulty was that the roguish type of the Arabist agent could not simply be replaced by, say, an uninitiated staff officer, since, "working on his own, God knows where he would get his information from. In any case God knows that he would be bound to get most things wrong and to give to what he happened to get right the traditional Royal Air Force colour that so smudges their monthly reports." In the end, reform of the system came in the shape of an air attaché appointed to the embassy in the hope that he might "induce a less bleary and jaundiced outlook on these miserable and unattractive Iraqis and their efforts to find themselves." (The first incumbent, H. H. Brookes, had until then been employed on intelligence duties at Air Headquarters, a fact that some at the Foreign Office idly if considerably worried might trouble the Iraqi government.)[30]

In the next world war, when Iraq was reoccupied, the embassy continued to make representations about the paranoid allusions of the Chief Intelligence Centre Iraq, whose widely circulated intelligence summaries had become "rather a sinister joke to British officials in this country." The problem apparently lay in the personality of Squadron Leader Dawson Shepherd, who had served in Air Intelligence before 1941 and had not "ever been able to readjust his perspective and can only look at Iraqi matters through the darkest of dark glasses." His "exaggerated and misleading" reports described an Iraqi populace fed up with its government and desiring broader British control of the country—history repeating, ad nauseam. (Skeptics assured that the situation was by no means so dire nor the existing government so incompetent.) While the SIS and Churchill's brainchild, the Special Operations Executive, joined the fray, Eric Holt-Wilson of MI5, who had been instrumental in merging General Staff Intelligence in Palestine with the Eastern Mediterranean Special Intelligence Bureau in the previous war, guided the establishment of the Political Intelligence Centre of the Middle East under Iltyd Clayton, a former political officer and the son of Gilbert Clayton. A "collecting centre," with an eye on longer-term peacetime arrangements, the Political Intelligence Centre omitted the word "Bureau" from its title to defuse fears that it was a mere resurrection of its forerunner. (An heir to the special intelligence bureau also emerged in the shape of the Security Intelligence Middle East.) After considerable debate on its ideal location, it was concealed in British military headquarters in Egypt, lest Egyptians object to it. It, like its predecessor, aroused considerable controversy in Whitehall because of its zealous staff (some hoping, for instance, to raise a *levée en masse* in Ethiopia against the Italians), its unclear brief, and its tendency to exceed its prescribed functions and geographical domain. Its most important customer was another old hand, General Wavell. In 1939, someone in MI5 had looked back at the 1909 intelligence memorandum in the files of Vernon Kell, founder of the British Security Service (forerunner of MI5), and found it "primitive but interesting," but that prewar blueprint continued to shape the British intelligence project in the Middle East.[31]

The agents were caught in the no-man's-land of covert empire, managing in willfully inventive ways their obligation to serve a state that could not speak its name. The Edwardian predicament continued to shape their work: "How were they to gather practical information and serve the British state in a region they were attracted to because of its legendary inscrutability and promise of escape from Britain?" Their adventures did not escape the notice of Iraqis and other Europeans, we know, but it continued to thrive partly because they had also caught the fancy of ordinary Britons, who provided a steady supply of willing Lawrences—until the Second World War broke the dam altogether.[32] To be sure, they were not all enthusiasts; many shared Iraqi suspicions about the schemes of British agents and their government's equally potent suspicions about the schemes of its agents. The crucial fact about this state as it traded

blindness for a panoptical illusion was that it was also an increasingly democratic one. The wider world of British society had always been culturally implicated in the intelligence project in the Middle East; postwar political changes
gave it even greater leverage on the matter. Among Dobbs's confessions was
that his fortnightly intelligence summaries, "which go to many quarters," were
deliberately imbued with an optimistic glow to preserve the fiction of the popularity and success of the British mandate. The mandate was a layering of
façades, one for Iraqi consumption, the other for British and global consumption. Indeed, officials partly justified continued covert control of the country
after 1932 as the only means of sustaining the indulgent lies about minority
rights and territorial integrity that they had told the Permanent Mandates
Commission to precipitately secure Iraq's League of Nations membership.
Having staked Britain's reputation as a successful civilizer on this prematurely
independent Iraq, the British had to uphold the fiction of its maturity "in the
eyes of the world." (They remained typically blind to the fact that the sticking
issues of minority rights and territorial integrity had themselves been shaped
by mandate policies: for instance, the postmandate plight of Iraqi Assyrians
was intimately tied to the deliberate Assyrianization of the RAF's levies.)[33] If
the imperial state in the Middle East had begun to retire from the glare of
publicity, it was partly because of the gathering constituency struggling to put
it under a harsh and unforgiving spotlight. It is to this struggle that we shall
now turn.

9

Seeing Like a Democracy

When our beneficial railways are cut, our engines and trucks seized,
and our telegraph wires torn down, it is time for us to drop the
pose of liberators.

> —"The Risings in Mesopotamia," *Times*
> (London), August 7, 1920

In civilizations without boats, dreams dry up, espionage takes the
place of adventure, and the police take the place of pirates.

> —Michel Foucault, "Of Other Spaces," 1967

Postwar hopes for redemption in the Middle East were constructed in
the mass media, but it was there also that they crumbled in the face of
growing evidence of the state's foul play. Mesopotamia was generally
agreed to have evoked more passionate discussion, both laudatory and
abusive, more quickly than any other issue in the immediate postwar
era. It was "the burning political issue of the time," according to the
Indian Secretary Lord Peel. And its register changed dramatically: "From
the days when this land of 'untapped wealth and virgin oil' was thought
to be only waiting... 'to pay the whole cost of the war', to the days of the
furious 'bag and baggage' campaign [calling for] the severance of all connection with the accursed land, might seem a far cry indeed," wrote
Richard Coke, "but the two periods were... separated by less than forty
months."[1] In a sense, the early hopes had always been tinged with a prophetic dread; Lawrence's mass popularity was double-edged, at once

stoking hopes for redemption in the desert and raising hackles at the vision of their apocalyptic fulfillment. But the turn of the tide was heralded by the Iraqi rebellion and the government's apparent abandonment of the path of imperial expiation in favor of secret pursuit of a tired old imperialism—whose secrecy was never complete. As the state vanished from public view, the British public, like the Iraqis, remained hot on its scent, ever imagining the worst.

We have long known that air control was partly designed to silence the domestic fury over extravagance in Mesopotamia at a moment calling for sober consideration of Britain's postwar recovery. But the strategy didn't work: criticism continued, for it was not, after all, only about economy. Indeed, as others have shown, public opinion remained recalcitrant enough to force continual reformulation of the mandate arrangement as Whitehall strove to appease both it and Iraqi opinion. But this obligingness was accompanied, as we have seen, by the evolution of covert empire, which allowed the British state to preserve things substantially as it liked. And this, it turns out, was the major bone of contention with the public—not cost but official secrecy surrounding the Middle East. If anything, the cheapness of air control heightened concern about such secrecy; indeed, the purpose of cost-cutting, its framers acknowledged, was not only economy but imperial autonomy—freedom from fiscal accountability to the public. It made the "taxpayer question" disappear. Emerging at the same moment as the new postwar mass democracy, the techniques of covert empire were designed to evade both the Iraqi *and* the British public.[2]

State secrecy was a pressing issue in the decade following the massive postwar expansion of the British electorate and the first interludes, at least, of Labour Party rule, in 1924 and 1929. In this increasingly self-consciously mass democracy, mindful of the follies of the recent past, faith in the paternalism and reserve that had long defined national identity *and* the British government style was on the wane.[3] And the government's Middle Eastern policy seemed to epitomize the "oriental methods" that a mass democracy could no longer tolerate. I am less interested here in the much fought over question of whether ordinary Britons knew or cared about their empire than in the interesting ways in which, at this critical juncture, various opinion-makers became exercised about public ignorance about affairs in the Middle East and went to great lengths to awaken the British public to the fact that their ignorance had been deliberately contrived by a government determined to enlighten them according to its own lights. Covert empire was partly the product of the struggle for control of foreign policy waged between the state and the cognoscenti among the British public; the critique of secrecy begat more secrecy.

Unsurprisingly, the agents figured centrally in this struggle: on the one hand, the state's efforts to "manage" the mass democratic public sphere, through secrecy, censorship, surveillance, and propaganda, was inspired by its exaggerated perception of recreant agents' powers to manipulate it; on the other, many sections of the public, building on wartime loss of faith in official news, saw in those agents' much-noted activities and cunning wielding of the pen symbolic proof of the existence of covert empire.[4]

The Press vs. the State

During the war itself, British activity in the Middle East was shrouded in a veil of secrecy, partly to avoid arousing the ire of anti-imperialists. The *Times* continually complained about the lack of information. "Why is the Persian Gulf campaign ignored?" the paper demanded; after all, it was "the most successful campaign of all" and "as much a British war as the campaign in Flanders." Even allowing for the mysteriousness of Arabia—the inaccurate reports deriving "from the bazaars of Baghdad, a home of fairy tales from immemorial times"—it was baffling that the troops' "gallant efforts...should be so sedulously veiled." Edmund Candler, who began to fill some of the gap with articles suffused with Biblical references, pointed to the intricate censorship regime produced by the need to keep Indians from knowing about the German call to jihad and to avoid offending the Arab allies (thus the term "friendly Arab" was banned because it implied the existence of unfriendly ones). Elsewhere, Allied news was generally considered reliable, affirmed Candler, but in Mesopotamia it was "nowhere believed," and "rumour flourished." His complaints were picked up in the wider press. Dunsterforce only enhanced the aura of clandestinity, which was matched farther west in the Arab Revolt. For covert operations relying on untested military tactics, concealment was de rigueur.[5]

It was the monumental failure at Kut that kept Mesopotamia from becoming a picturesque but little-known subplot of the war's grand narrative in British eyes. As the War Office seized control of the campaign, the Mesopotamia Commission exposed the Indian government's management blunders in its notorious report of June 1917. An "exposé," it set the tone of public opinion about Mesopotamia as a closeted adventure bungled by a cabal of incompetent and greedy politicians. The scandal had, in the words of one astonished contemporary, "kindled the feelings of the British public in a way that nothing else has done since the disclosures from the Crimea." Public joy over the force's fresh successes that very year did not, Arnold Wilson assures, "dull the demand for retribution" in the popular press. The *Morning Post* printed Kipling's poetic fury against the craven leadership in "Mesopotamia" (characteristically, its reproduction in Mesopotamian papers was censored). This flak was swept up on the official side in annoyance at the untimely publication of the damning report just when the force had reformed itself and was accompanied by a desperate effort to educate the public about its romantic achievements since the fall of Baghdad in March. Sincere though many Britons were in their hope for imperial redemption in the Middle East, officialdom also deliberately propagated that hope in order to strengthen morale and win public opinion over to the idea of empire in the Middle East. In a war famous for putting euphemism to such excessive and invidious use that it gave "propaganda" its unequivocally negative modern connotation, many works on Arabia, often explicitly written to official order and vetted by the War Office, insistently impressed their readers with the campaigns' worthiness and glamour. The Mesopotamia campaign's public relations appeal persuaded the pious and shrewd Prime Minister Lloyd George to make Jerusalem a "Christmas gift" to the British people—just when the Passchendaele offensive ended in costly failure. The Palestine campaign was, Eitan Bar-Yosef writes, "consciously staged by the British government as an exercise in propaganda, shaped, filtered and capitalized on in order to enhance the nation's morale." All those references to the Crusades were designed to resonate with the deepest beliefs of a long-suffering public.[6]

The euphoric reaction to the fall of Jerusalem, described in chapter 5, was in fact carefully orchestrated. And the agents were critical to the belated publicity effort. The War Office sent Harry Pirie-Gordon to write popular articles on it, and Lowell Thomas landed up at Lawrence's tent in search of that rare thing, a Great War hero, to rouse the latent militarism of the United States. He was sent by Gertrude Bell's old friend Cecil Spring-Rice, ambassador to the United States, and John Buchan, director of the Department of Information. The agents had always lived by the pen, and in the war, we know, propaganda had become a focus of their "intelligence" work, most conspicuously in Mark Sykes's vision for the Arab Bureau. Bell now composed articles for British press release for the War Office. She anonymously authored *The Arab of Mesopotamia*, a collection of historical and ethnographic essays that circulated among the troops and London literary circles to favorable reviews. Her office also issued handbooks impressing the troops with Mesopotamia's ancient role as the "main avenue for riches and the wealth of the East" and assuring that their so-called sideshow was what stood between India and the war. Likewise, the tireless Hogarth winced only at the first part of his son's description of his vocation as "imperialist propagandist." At home, Sykes, who was highly instrumental in garnering support for the Jerusalem campaign in Whitehall, urged Clayton to dispatch "popular" and "picturesque" reading for the average churchgoing Briton and "rivet the British onto the Holy Land." In the *Observer*, he described Jerusalem as a "new Light of the World" that would shine on all men and nations and bid them to "take up their lives again with hope reawakened and faith renewed." It would replace The Hague's "hypocritical conversations" among corrupt lawyers, diplomatists, and soldiers. He saw in it a means of renewing Christendom, of stimulating the flow of pilgrims to Jerusalem, of fulfilling the very dreams that had sent him to Arabia in search of personal redemption before the war. He spent hours editing propaganda put out by Buchan's department before finally setting up his own department for Middle East propaganda in the Foreign Office. He went on lecture tours spreading anti-Turkish propaganda and giving currency to the term "Middle East." His dramatic maps of Germany's "Drang Nach Osten" could be found all over Fleet Street. And then, immediately after the war, when various nations' destinies were being determined at Versailles, veterans of the Middle East earnestly hawked their tales to the hungry papers, feeding the media frenzy around its heroes. Working his contacts on Fleet Street, Lawrence submitted a series of anonymous eyewitness accounts of the revolt—based on his intelligence reports—to the *Times*, which together read like a serialized adventure story. Everything they believed in as agents—literature, epic adventure, cunning—came together in this publicity effort.[7]

This spark of excitement began to peter out under the trickle of news about unrest and unresolved tensions in the region following the armistice. Many worried that the campaigns had produced a vastly expanded empire with expensive defense needs at precisely the wrong moment from their point of view as taxpayers faced with the burden of Britain's economic recovery. Indeed, why should they be paying through the nose for the upkeep of a country "advertised since our conquest...as an Eldorado"? In the wake of the 1920 rebellion, the press began to roundly condemn the government's "insane policy in the Middle East." Some of this attack was politically motivated—Lord Rothermere's *Daily Mail* and Lord Beaverbrook's *Daily Express* fired the first salvos partly out of an effort to get rid of Lloyd George—but it soon spread to all quarters, from the *Morning Post* to the Labour benches to the *Empire Review* to the *Times* to the Liberal *Daily Chronicle* and Labour *Daily Herald*. As many commented, "that blessed word Mesopotamia," so long a synonym for instant comfort (per an old English story much cited at the time), had become instead an epithet for all bad news. In an angry series titled "The Development of Mesopotamia" in the *Times*, George Buchanan, the soured wartime conservator general of the Mesopotamian rivers, inveighed against the wild exaggerations of the country's economic possibilities and the boondoggling extravagance of the military authorities. Baghdad was a "comparatively modern and uninteresting city" unlike anything in the "Arabian Nights," disclosed a wised-up General Haldane, breaking the spell cast by a generation of unseeing fantasists. In magazines,

veterans wagered the Arab could develop his own country better left to himself;
the more self-interestedly cynical *Spectator* grew resigned that the British could
expect no material reward, "not even gratitude," from Mesopotamia. Far from
engaging in developmental investment, the government had indulged in careless "speculation." So recently treated to "rapturous prophecies" about restoring Mesopotamia, the idealistic *Guardian* found it infuriating to be told a year
later that "we must now suddenly button up our pockets and let the Arab and
his ancient glories go hang." For a brief moment, even the rabidly imperialistic
Churchill found the idea of hanging on to these "thankless deserts" at any cost
"sinister" and "gratuitous," not least because "there is no point of which [the
press] make more effective use to injure the Government." In the election of
November 1922, Andrew Bonar Law rode to victory on a promise to end super-
fluous adventures in the midst of this press campaign. "British policy in this
part of the world is continually the subject of minute scrutiny in the Press,"
observed a wartime agent by way of introduction to his tellingly titled *The Truth
about Mesopotamia, Palestine and Syria* (1923). "The matter is one about which
information is desired by all." The issue had spilled beyond the recondite world
of experts; the people wanted to know, for their hopes of redemption had been
pinned on it.[8]

They desired that information so desperately because it was desperately
difficult to come by. On his return to London, Haldane was not alone in remarking the public "ignorance about the rising." But the palpable press silence—on
details if not on demands for them—was not willful but officially contrived: the
more the British public strove to hold the government to account by ambush-
ing it in the press, the less information was made available. For when things
began to badly wrong on the ground, the administration reverted to its earlier
caginess while awkwardly attempting to preserve the appearance of regenerating Paradise. Air control and the attendant institutions of covert empire were
put in place. The British administration's censorship of news in and from
Iraq—the government published the only local newspapers—produced a com-
motion in the British press, where it was denounced as a transparent attempt
to shore up the illusion of tranquility (Beaverbrook's revenge was the *Daily
Express*'s revelation of Lawrence's presence in the RAF). Air operations grew so
covert that the RAF was stopped from decorating John Glubb for fear of parliamentary questions about the undisclosed actions for which he was being recognized. The elusiveness of statistics, frequent recourse to euphemism, and
blatant misrepresentation of what was going on all masked the regime from
public scrutiny—in its lack of provision for public surveillance of the aerial
inspectors, air control departed significantly from the classic panopticon.
Notwithstanding the growth of organized tourism, entry to the region was

strictly controlled by the RAF. Many British travelers were put off with vague excuses about unsafe conditions; Europeans and migrant Iraqis, Indians, and Persians were regarded with deep suspicion and unofficial excuses found to deter their visits. Besides nomadic peoples and pilgrims, suspicious persons included those displaced by the war and the Russian Revolution—Assyrians, Armenians, Indian laborers and soldiers, Turks, Russian-German refugees, Persian mujtahids, Kurds, Russians, and so on—whose general vagrancy threatened to spread too much information about the nature of British influence in the region. These and other policies of the unfolding covert empire remained deliberately and closely sheltered from public view. Of the creation of Transjordan at the Cairo Conference, for instance, the Middle East Department deemed, "The less we say publicly...the better." Churchill declared his general aversion to "making further public pronouncements upon matters which must inevitably arouse controversy."[9]

Arabia had again become a place that did not produce information, but this time, the explosively growing press knowingly laid blame for its coyness at the feet of its new administrators. The far from radical *Times* put itself at the head of this prototypical freedom-of-information campaign, couching its critique of the government's "huge designs in Mesopotamia" as part of an assertion of democratic control of foreign policy. Wartime concern about secret diplomacy had put even this "newspaper of record" on its guard, less stridently perhaps than the radical-liberal Union for Democratic Control—more, as we shall see, in the populist (but ever dignified) vein of a guardian of English common sense and constitutionalism. From the outset, it argued that Britain was too overextended to remain in Iraq, whatever its obligations to territories it had liberated, but, more importantly, that "the time is past when *any Government* could commit the nation to the acquisition of a considerable new Empire...without first making an exhaustive public statement of their intentions." This was a critique of the state more than of a particular party. Concern over expenditure was not separate from but the starting point of a halting critique of government secrecy about the Middle East. In the Commons, a frustrated Liberal among the many elected in 1922 on the pledge to reduce expenditure in Mesopotamia, asked, "If £137,000 had been spent on a residency in Mesopotamia without any home department knowing anything about the project till the work was well advanced, how was the House to feel assured that this £800,000 would not be spent in the same manner?" If the "average citizen" who had been kept ignorant of "what we have been doing there" had at least been apprised of "what it has cost him," he might have complained even more loudly, reckoned the *Spectator*. The public required immediate "enlightenment" on Mesopotamia because it was not merely a matter of "foreign politics," concurred the *Guardian*, but "bread-and-butter politics." The press framed the conflict as a contest between the public—for which it spoke—and the government: when, goaded by the *Times*, Herbert Asquith beat Churchill with the economy stick in the Commons, the government responded by tartly advising skeptics like him to "assume most of the statements in *The Times* are wrong," to riotous laughter. Among those involved in the debate was the dissident ex-agent and Conservative member of Parliament (MP) Aubrey Herbert, who wrote to the *Times* amplifying his disapproval of profligate expenditure on the defense of a "land without frontiers": "Honesty and openness remain the best and the cheapest policy," he advised, reckoning heavy taxation as the price of "secrecy and the repudiation of our pledges."[10]

If ruinous financial extravagance did not provide sufficient evidence of the poor judgment exercised in the exalted corridors of government, the continuing commitment to military action at a time when the rest of the country hungered for peace provided indisputable proof. Of particular concern was the news that after the killing of British officers in Kurdish Iraq, "straightaway, without the knowledge of the public at home, tiny punitive columns were mobilized." If the British government worried about secret Russian or Turkish incursions in their Middle Eastern empire, the British public was equally concerned about *its own government's* covert operations in the region. The frontier-like Middle East offered vastly enlarged scope for the secret warfare until then safely (and relatively cheaply) confined to the small corner of the North West Frontier. In Mesopotamia, they had a "new infinitely bigger frontier problem on our hands"—which also meant *bigger* secret operations. The *Times* believed operations in Kurdistan since the armistice had been "far more considerable than the public have been allowed to know." The daily editorial onslaught grew increasingly shrill, and the paper warned Churchill to heed the fact that, "as on the Indian frontier, so in Mesopotamia and Persia, the concealment of unfavourable news will no longer be tolerated. There has been far too much secrecy about the military operations in Mesopotamia." "The nation" had to have information in order to judge for itself the wisdom and practicality of the Mesopotamian venture. (The *Guardian* echoed these sentiments, if somewhat more deferentially.) Belated news of the extent of the uprising in August 1920, drawn from the dispatch of the Tehran correspondent, fueled this fire. Before the war, such incidents would have kept the country ringing with news, the editors pointed out wistfully, insisting that public perception of their seriousness had not been lessened by the "altered conceptions of casualty lists" of the last four years. It was not the public, but the state, that had become numb to violence; its covert prosecution of violent small wars confessed its distance from a public that had exorcised the demon of militarism during the war.[11]

In these concerns about costs and continuous small wars, official mendacity was as much at issue as secrecy. The *Times* knew they would have to "probe much more deeply before we learn the whole truth about the Government's mysterious, costly, and questionable policy in the Middle East," since official statements on the matter had long been "vitiated by evasions, concealments, and half-truths." The paper's hunger for information grew increasingly ferocious as 1920 unfolded, and it damned the series of "evasions, of subterfuges, of concealments, and of positive mis-statements" that continued to issue from the government. Other papers echoed the "mistrust [of] all official figures from Mesopotamia." The *Times* questioned sharply official conspiracy theories of Turkish and Bolshevist promptings behind the rising, favoring the more local and obvious mainspring of the British presence. They and the *Guardian* agreed that the big mystery about the rising was not so much its origins but the government's reluctance to submit to the public the actual extent of the problem and what it intended to do about it. The *Spectator* was more sympathetic to the possibility of real conspiracy but remained baffled at the government's refusal to exploit its most obvious antidote: publicity. Even the relief afforded by the 1922 announcement of military and financial reductions in the wake of the air control scheme did not muzzle antagonism of the government on these points. The government's actions looked as conspiratorial and sinister as anything emanating from the Middle East: the *Times* accused the War Office and the India Office of "combining" to conceal the gravity of the situation in Mesopotamia. The official renaming of the mandate from Mesopotamia to "Irak" (or "Iraq"), apparently a product of Churchill's "durbar in Cairo," was deemed a mere ploy to divert taxpayers' from "a name of evil omen," an accusation so frequent in the "more popular newspapers" that officials were compelled to noisily protest its greater semantic accuracy.[12]

As the snide reference to Churchill's "durbar" intimates, just as the state feared agents' overly zealous conversion to Arab ways, so the press feared that the state—perhaps through those agents—had lost its bearings and gone wildly native. Churchill's appointment to the Colonial Office in 1921 provoked qualms that he would "rule on an Oriental scale" in the Middle East. His special imaginative gifts made him all the more susceptible to "the seductions of the Orient," warned the *Times*. After the Cairo Conference, the press challenged the government to "come out from behind the veil" and submit the issues to Parliament. Even once the *Times* had expressed its support for air control as an efficient means of colonial control, it continued to nag the government for falling short of full public disclosure, for instance, during the hushed visit of the colonial and air secretaries to Iraq in 1925. Rhetorically absorbing official secrecy into the esoteric nature of the country, the paper could only muse on the undisclosed matters "mixed up with the tangled ethnography, history, and religions of this very remote corner of one of the oldest countries of the world." What was more, the government seemed also to have adopted "oriental meth-ods" in military practice—so that, for instance, the general commanding in Mesopotamia was also the commander in northwest Persia.[13]

Living with this oriental government, the press now developed a sympathy for its subjects in the Orient. Iraqi suspicions of British motives were fully war-ranted, the *Times* and the *Guardian* reminded readers, for this was the genera-tion of Iraqis that had endured Great Power intrigue before the war and seen its postwar hopes crushed by "Western imperial aims." And now Britons, they pronounced, had become victims of the same arrogant and unaccountable sys-tem of government. The *Times* likened unchecked ministerial power at home, produced by wartime expansion, to Arnold Wilson's "uncontrolled power" in Baghdad (which, they noted charily, had triggered insurgency there). Iraqis and Britons were linked in a common yoke of oppressive taxation. Lack of oversight had allowed "ambitious" officials in Iraq to inflict on the local population "taxa-tion…beyond their capacity" while simultaneously "imposing upon the tax-payers of this country charges for Mesopotamia alone which seem likely this year to reach a total equal to half the pre-war Budget of 1913." The claim to empathy at the heart of the air control regime may have been something of an empty phrase, but empathy was critical in the articulation of anti-imperial sen-timent with respect to the Middle East, not so much in the sense of conscious-ness of a shared humanity but in the more particular feeling of shared misery under an autocratic state. And it was a piquant empathy, revealing how low British democracy had been brought—low enough to create common experi-ence with an oriental people, part of that swath of humanity famous for having known nothing but despotism. It was less the state's imperialism than its impe-riousness that stung. Indeed, many critics of Britain's Middle East policy pro-tested their enduring faith in the justice and decency of the empire, pointing their swords punctiliously at the government's recent waywardness, its sudden reliance on "subterfuges and euphemisms."[14]

In this regard, the significance of the wartime rise of a particular regime of expertise and influence over Middle Eastern affairs (echoed on an imperial scale with the rise of proconsuls such as Curzon and Alfred Milner in the war government) was not lost on the lay public. We have long known that Socialists took to warning the democracy about "experts" too interested in their own expertise to do right by the nation.[15] But this critique had a particular currency with respect to Middle Eastern policy, whose concentration in the hands of "experts from outside" the *Times* repeatedly berated. With "every department a law to itself," the experts at the helm of the "autocratic machinery" could "embark...at their own will, often at their own whim, upon every kind of costly adventure, both at home and abroad," railed Asquith in a campaign on the Isle of Wight, singling out Mesopotamia as a particular instance of this type of covert government. "Nobody knows" what they were doing there, he insisted, "and no responsible minister can tell us." How was responsibility for Middle Eastern policy allocated? the *Times* asked pointedly. Was it under Curzon, Haldane, Churchill, Montagu? Everyone denied responsibility, but who, after all, did Cox report to? Watchful members of the public amplified these queries, while Lawrence, speaking as a "renegade from the enemy cause," to borrow Richard Hofstadter's term, condemned the Arab Revolt as a "conspiracy to trick the Arabs into fighting for self-government" and twitched back the curtain in the *Sunday Times* to reveal that the Mesopotamian insurrection was the result of the British civil authorities being "controlled from no Department of State, but from the empty space which divides the Foreign Office from the India Office." (He would soon patch things up with the government, graciously joining the Colonial Office (whose invitation was partly strategic) to help sort out the mess.) A gripping human-interest angle on this cause of the unrest was provided by the captivity story of a British administrator's wife, Zetton Buchanan, which reached the British public through the *Times*' publication of her letters to her sister, and then, by arrangement with the publisher of her inevitable book, a serialized rendition of her "adventures." Her sense that "all the glamour" of Iraq, its "Arabian Nightish romance," had departed was accompanied by a loss of faith in her government, which she saw "with very different eyes." She wondered about the reasons for her bungled rescue in a by now familiar refrain: "Nobody could say, and there seemed no one responsible. Every difficulty was put in the way of my finding things out." It was in the midst of this discussion about the lack of official accountability about Iraq that the People's Union for Economy formed to push for cleanup of the wartime explosion of the state, which had made covert empire possible by camouflaging dark corners of government in thickets of untamed bureaucracy. Churchill's creation of the Middle East Department in 1921 seemed alarmingly to suggest that, far from retrenching, the reign of experts was to be a permanent feature of peacetime government. The *Guardian* protested the wide berth and sweeping powers given to him in the months that he served simultaneously as colonial *and* air secretary. When Ibn Saud ousted Sherif Hussein from the Hejaz in 1924, Arnold Wilson wrote to the *Times* urging transfer of the department to the Foreign Office, since the "purely personal considerations" that had ensconced it in the Colonial Office had passed. The *Guardian* similarly seized that moment to point out again the damaging influence on Britain's Arabian policy of "enthusiastic experts...scattered" among government departments. Concern about Middle East policy was bound up with concern about *who* was framing it, about the distortions the war had wrought on the state just when the public had steeled itself to assert a democratic check on it.[16]

The press did not consider their demands for ministerial accountability radical, merely calls for proper implementation of the constitution. In June 1920, news of the government's decision to assume a mandate for Mesopotamia elicited indignant complaints in the *Times* that it had done so "without obtaining the sanction of Parliament, or even of going through the pretence of seeking Parliamentary approval." The existing democratic check of Parliament was especially vital, the paper urged, given the weight of the burden on the taxpayer and the obvious obliviousness to that condition of officials blissfully searching for sites to build airfields. The state was out of touch with common sense—the sense of ordinary Britons. Ministerial aloofness was particular disquieting now that ministers could wield their power in the remote venue of the League of Nations. The press maintained a tenacious watch over transgressions of parliamentary procedure in the name of the league, frequently calling British officials to order for making important announcements in Geneva before they had addressed their home public. (Baldwin's government certainly used the excuse of matters being "sub judice" at the league to evade uncomfortable questions about when, exactly, the British would be leaving Iraq.) For instance, echoing a fiery letter from the radical Liberal MP Joseph Kenworthy, the *Times* denounced as a "mockery" of popular and representative government the cabinet's failure to obtain parliamentary approval of the terms of the mandate before submitting them to the league; even the pro–League of Nations *Guardian* denounced this "despotism by the Executive." The point was less that the nation did not want to hold on to a land that had always been "the grave of empires," Kenworthy explained, more that this was the greatest departure from parliamentary oversight "since the days of the Stuart Kings." It was a matter of constitutional rights, the *Times* seconded; Churchill would soon be gathering with his "array of experts" at Cairo to create a Middle Eastern empire without so much as a by-your-leave. The old "Crown vs. Parliament" conflict had revived in the guise of the "executive vs. the nation," the paper declared. A gaggle of readers responded in enthusiastic accord. Similarly, in 1926 a Labour MP pointed to the diplomatic settlement of Iraq's frontiers as an example of the country's drift "towards government by individual Ministers, who appeared to take on themselves the settlement of great issues assured that they need only report their decisions to the House of Commons in order to get them ratified." Such high-handedness betokened a dangerous reversion to "bad old ways" that would again risk "catastrophe," intoned the *Guardian*.[17]

Middle Eastern policy was thus central in heretofore unrecognized ways to the movement for democratic control of foreign policy. It was in this political climate, indeed in the midst of Labour questions about the secret diplomacy at Lausanne, where in 1922–1923 the Allies were attempting to arrive at a fresh agreement with Turkey, that E. D. Morel, having ousted Churchill from his Dundee seat, proclaimed foreign and domestic affairs "inextricably inter-twined" and Labour's opposition to their being carried on "under a veil of secrecy." His party, he announced, would "press relentlessly for full democratic control over foreign affairs." (It is another matter that when Labour took office in 1924, Ramsay Macdonald famously brushed aside Morel's claim to the for-eign ministry, abandoning the vision of democratic diplomacy to realpolitik.) The secret wartime correspondence with Sherif Hussein was another thorn in the side of radical Liberal and Labour MPs committed to democratic control of foreign policy. (Lloyd George's pose of indignation prompted Asquith's face-tious reminder of his usurper's own failure to publish it.) And it was in particu-lar the Middle Eastern mandates, whose idealistic framework practically cried out for betrayal by the powers that be, that made the League of Nations central to radical Liberal and Labour concerns about secret diplomacy.[18]

Diplomacy was the "last redoubt" of the aristocracy, and this made dimin-ishing sense, critics argued, in an era of total war in which the masses suffered the consequences of diplomacy. But alongside this apprehension about the state's social and physical distance from the people emerged complaints of the more sinister abuse of power in the service of private interests, oligarchy add-ing insult to the injury of autocracy. The government's actions made sense, the *Times* explained in somewhat paranoid accents (if not unjustifiably), when one recalled that "in the background, and very audible though only dimly visible, are the gentlemen representing various conflicting oil interests, all hammering on the doors of Ministerial offices." The bureaucratic disorganization fostered by wartime autocracy had multiplied the shadowy spaces in which private inter-ests could corrupt the government, nowhere more so than in the informally organized world of the Middle Eastern covert empire. The War Office claimed to be sick of the whole Mesopotamian adventure, reported the *Times*, but, "Who, then, is responsible for its continuance? We can only surmise that some-where in the background there are traces of the influence of oil." They and the *Guardian* repeatedly claimed to articulate a generally prevailing fear of govern-ment consorting with private interests, from oil to carpet factories, at public expense (and in contravention of mandatory rules), evidence for which they found in the frequent reappearance on the scene of former public officials and experts in new private guises—the press had learned to recognize the ways of covert empire. Audiences were clearly receptive to this line of argument: in a campaign speech, Asquith's rhetorical questions about the meaning of British Middle Eastern policy elicited spontaneous heckles of "oil." At Lausanne, too, Labour spied a "hidden hand...behind the scenes"—oil interests "pulling wires" in every hotel lobby—although its accusations merely elicited the government's patronizing diagnosis that the opposition was unreasonably obsessed by the notion of "the hidden hand." But then, the *Guardian* pointed out, the government claim of "sincerity, subjected to the ordeal of oil, comes out badly." (Touché.) Rumors that the oil proposition was weaker than initially presumed only made the government more despicably venal in the *Times'* eyes for not only pursuing a private interest, but an unprofitable one at that. By 1923, the Panglossian *Guardian* had grown more dismissive of arguments that it was "all about oil," doubting "a motive so paltry and so sordid" could have determined critical policies, but finding the government's continued equivocation on the matter an embarrassing liability as they affirmed its good faith. Echoes of the Union for Democratic Control's critique of the arms industry's corruption of government could also be heard in parliamentary questions about Britain knavishly subsidizing both the Sherifians and their enemy, Ibn Saud. Suspicion of a stealthy autocracy, crafty oligarchy, and other nefarious sorts of corruption of democracy via the Middle East remained a staple of radical-liberal critique in the Commons.[19]

Without wanting to equate them—some conspiracy theories have more merit than others (there was, after all, a covert empire in the making)—I do want to point out the important political-cultural fact of the shared taste for conspiracy thinking between postwar critics of empire and British officialdom, especially when it came to affairs in the Middle East. To be sure, British anti-imperialism had always possessed a conspiracy-theorist dimension. Drawing on theories of Jewish conspiracy, J. A. Hobson had interpreted mass consciousness as essentially irrational and vulnerable to the machinations of a jingoistic class. The Union of Democratic Control and the Independent Labour Party also pointed to the operation of a "herd instinct" in mass democracy, evident in its easy duping during the war. In this moment, Hobson's 1902 *Imperialism* received greater attention than ever before, but the masses' deception was blamed less on themselves and the jingoistic class than on a state that had betrayed its paternalistic duty to them—by allowing itself to be captured by that jingoistic class. The press—even the sensationalist dailies that Hobson had upbraided—now assigned itself the investigative task of unmasking the state's true identity and purposes. The jaded *Times* scoffed at "innocent imperialists" rabbiting away about the civilizing mission, the defense of India, and so on, without an inkling that the government was fraternizing with oilmen "behind the scenes" on the assumption that the British taxpayer "inoculated with imperial enthusiasm" would be duped into paying for a permanent garrison to protect their interests. As in Whitehall, this popular conspiracy thinking traded on the trope of Arabian mysteriousness: only in a land so conveniently full of veils could hidden hands operate so freely. And it, too, found its enthusiastic adherents among the agents, among the smaller subset lost to officialdom. If, on the one side, Norman Bray and Mark Sykes appeared unhinged in their intense belief in conspiracy against the empire, on the other side was St. John Philby, exiled to Jeddah after his falling-out with the government in 1924, where a journalist colleague found him "slightly deranged" and obsessed with the idea that "British imperialism is at the bottom of everything." Covert empire, itself grounded in political paranoia, necessarily (and often rightly) produced such limitless suspicion, as some keen-eyed observers, at home and abroad, deduced that the tranquil façade of mandatory government concealed a hidden reality but knew not how far to let their imaginations run.[20]

And the biggest provocation to their imagination was air control, whose establishment—in the teeth of considerable press skepticism[21]—certainly took some of the wind out of criticism of the costs of the Mesopotamian venture, momentarily resuscitating visions of a prosperous Iraq emerging from British tutelage (see chap. 5), but only amplified remonstrations about secrecy, this time about state-authored violence. Early on, concern about official secrecy surrounding Middle Eastern affairs was deepened by fears that it existed to hide embarrassingly un-British atrocities at the hands of the British occupiers. Why, asked the *Guardian*, did they need to send "all this machinery, all these forces, all these punitive expeditions... if we were establishing a political system on the basis of popular consent"? Suggestions of excessive force first surfaced during the rising, which some erstwhile promoters of the Middle East campaigns saw as the first proof of Britain's betrayal of its promises to the Arabs and the domestic public, emerging as part of the writing public taking up the cudgels against the postwar regime and incidentally (or perhaps not so incidentally) feeding their own heroic images in the media. Depressed in sudden political isolation at All Souls' and absorbed, significantly, in Doughty's "Adam Cast Forth," Lawrence threw down the gauntlet in the *Sunday Times* (at the paper's request):

The people of England have been led in Mesopotamia into a trap...
tricked into it by a steady withholding of information.... Our administration [has been] more bloody and inefficient than the public
knows.... How long will we permit millions of pounds, thousands of
Imperial troops and tens of thousands of Arabs to be sacrificed on
behalf of a form of Colonial administration which can benefit nobody
but its administrators?

Glimmers of the true extent of the rising emerged in his graphic and sarcastic denunciations of the violent counterinsurgency: "It is odd we do not use poison gas," he wrote in the *Observer*. "By gas attacks the whole population of offending districts could be wiped out neatly; and as a method of government it would be no more immoral than the present system [of burning villages]." He received letters of support from Wilfred Blunt, George Lloyd, Doughty, and the endlessly outraged Philby, whose jeremiads against British perfidy in Arabia found an eager audience through the mass media and prestigious lecture venues, including *Nineteenth Century*, the *Nation*, the *Daily Herald*, the *Westminster Gazette*, the Central Asian Society, the Anglo-Turkish Society, the Near and Middle East Association, the No More War Association, and the Summer School of the Fabian Society. People flocked to him as a famous authority on a place whose guilty possession had begun to produce a general sense of unease. Other disgruntled agents and officials, such as George Buchanan and Aubrey Herbert, also denounced the unreformed military administration of the mandates. Philip Graves, as the *Times'* correspondent in Jerusalem, wrote authoritatively on the fundamental incompatibility of Arabs' love for freedom with any highly bureaucratic form of government. The *Guardian* quoted Lawrence and Herbert at length to express its worst fears about the uses of airpower in tax collection.[22]

With the memory of these early events in mind as the air control regime was consolidated after the rising, many remained skeptical of official abjurations of cruel uses of airpower, such as for tax collection. Fears that frontier-style operations could occur in this vast, frontierlike region without public knowledge were doubled by the fear that those operations risked becoming extraordinarily violent without public oversight. The secrecy had to be covering *something*: what transpired behind the closed doors of the mysterious place known as Iraq must, they thought, be simply too grisly to bear the light of day. Neither was the government's sanitized language lost on them—the *Guardian* knew that "what the Colonial Office describes temperately as 'air action'" was "commonly known as bombing" (and used not as a "last resort"), surmising that had two British airmen not been killed in the incident at hand, the public would have heard nothing of it. The British press knew it shared not only Iraqis' fiscal enslavement but also their ignorance about the violence done to their country, but here again empathy was undercut by the presumption that the source of the air force's corruption, like the government's, was the Middle East itself. If the RAF used the bomber as "a regular instrument of our administration" for, say, collection of taxes, warned the *Round Table*, "our rule will have become Oriental and its end will be near." The *Guardian* similarly brooded that propping up an Arab government had put Britain in the position of using "methods discreditable to any civilised Power."[23]

They urged the House of Commons to extract full information from the government. And, indeed, in Parliament, too, the secrecy debate shifted from a focus on economy to humanity. It, too, was "a question of the Press vs the Administration," declared the radical Colonel Wedgwood. Labour Party questions about Iraqi casualties invariably met with the bald assertion that, although no numbers were available, air operations had certainly resulted in fewer deaths than would have been produced by ground operations, usually prompting a vituperative rhetorical flourish from Labour on the lines of: "Don't you think the time has come to stop this hunnish, barbarous method of warfare against unarmed men?" But then the tables were, of course, turned when Labour took office in 1924. The radical Kenworthy continued to raise the issue of government reticence on air operations in Iraq, demanding clarification of obscure descriptions of "slight air action" at Sulimaniyeh. The undersecretary of state for air, William Leach, admitted he could not say whether the phrase indicated that any bombing or casualties had occurred. The debate ended with the usual burst of outrage, in this instance from the rebellious Labour backbencher George Lansbury, who asked, "Does the hon. gentleman think that by those operations we are teaching the natives...the blessings of the Sermon on the Mount? That is what the Germans did to us." The debate was drowned out in raucous laughter. A few days later, Leach was again cross-examined on recent casualties and operations. Neatly skirting the issue, he strove to explain the different meaning of air action "in areas where violence is habitual": his ostensibly reassuring example was an operation in which the RAF had killed all the men *and boys* in a raiding party that had allegedly killed nearly three hundred Iraqis. Such simpering obfuscations triggered Lansbury's demand for "a White Paper giving particulars of where and why these bombardments have taken place...together with the fact that no one but the airmen concerned is ever present to know whether inhabitants have been killed?" Within weeks, the Air Ministry issued a White Paper on the "Method of Employment of the Air Arm in Iraq," in which, as we have seen in chapter 7, the defense of air control's humanity was formally laid out, centering on the argument that the "terror of the Air," coupled with empathetic agents on the ground, saved lives through its "moral effect." The argument about air control's humanity had been subsumed in an insistent demand for full disclosure—let the public judge, and control, it. The rationales for the slaughter had always been necessary for the conscience of the few in the know; now they became part of a politically more pressing— although entirely bipartisan—defense of air control as its lurid details trickled into the light of day.[24]

The silence about aerial operations in Iraq enforced a more general silence on the uses of the RAF, inspiring wise speculations that they were simply too grim for public consumption. In the 1926 debate on the budget for air defenses, a frustrated young Clement Atlee confessed that his ignorance about the purpose of a separate air service remained undiminished if its primary function, as far as they were given to know, was merely to support the navy and the army. Was there some other secret purpose to which it would be put? Was it, he asked, pointing to Iraq, to be held "*in terrorem* over civilian populations?" Would it be used to destroy the "*moral*" of an enemy country? Critics continued to accuse the government of evasiveness about the "real meaning" of the air force, made easy by the alleged elusiveness of "results" in "remote parts of the world."[25]

In a 1939 work titled *Imperial Policing*, Major General Sir Charles W. Gwynn was still marveling that "many sections of public opinion have drawn the conclusion that military control involves ruthlessness and reprisals to an extent which brings all action inspired by military authority under suspicion." The more the state protested its mildness, the more the public suspected it protested too much. From the early speculations about Iraq, exposing the hidden brutalities of their empire became the obsession of liberal critics who came to shrewdly equate empire with militarism. A misty-eyed (and now fully blind) Aubrey Herbert recalled his prewar anticipation of British rule in the Middle East, explaining that that was a time when they ruled well and fairly, without kicking, cajoling, or exploiting. Such jerry-built nostalgia was supplemented by a more iconoclastic reconsideration of British imperialism. It was not only the Amritsar Massacre but the unending outcry over Mesopotamia that inspired Edward Thompson to interrupt his decade-long effort to render his Middle Eastern experiences with a revisionist account of the Indian "mutiny," *The Other Side of the Medal* (1925). The *New Statesman* praised him for uncovering "the policy of terrorisation" behind that event. Two years later, his novel about the Mesopotamian campaign, *These Men, They Friends*, again strove to explain why the British had become so hated by other races. In 1931, on his way to India, he met another Mesopotamia veteran, Geoffrey Garratt, with whom he wrote *Rise and Fulfilment of British Rule in India* (1934).[26]

The State Strikes Back

Thompson was not only critical of secrecy about government brutality; he was also incensed by government "propaganda"; the equation of imperialism with militarism rested on the assumption "that virtue was only paraded in order to conceal vice," to borrow the words of A. P. Thornton. It was the sense of a contest over truth about imperial affairs that determined Thompson to write his books. He was echoed by a legion of somewhat less prolific skeptics. In 1928, critics seized on a press report about the detention of press telegrams in Baghdad. In answer to parliamentary questions, Colonial Secretary Leo Amery denied the allegation of censorship and cited a report from the high commissioner describing a long-standing arrangement by which press telegrams appearing to give "exaggerated or misleading" news were delayed so that his office could provide the journalist with the "true facts"—the difficulties posed by the Arabian information network providing a convenient, if sincere, excuse for censorship. But to Kenworthy and Wedgwood, this explanation merely added insult to injury; the system amounted to "government control of information sent by private Press correspondents in Mesopotamia," in a word, "government 'dope.'" Critics of covert empire were equally alive to the smoke and mirrors of the local authorities: "The civil authorities in Mesopotamia are unusually gifted in the practice of the arts of publicity," the *Times* sneered, "but they tell us effusively the things we are not eager to know." These detractors doubted the existence of a true democracy. "Propaganda," they knew, was "the executive arm of the invisible government."[27]

Indeed, besides Colonial Office and Air Ministry requests to local officials for statements on bombing policy, the attack on air control had provoked other kinds of public relations activity that built on the marketing lessons learned during the war. The Air Ministry mounted a series of air demonstrations and pageants to awe the British public and make it more "air-minded." In 1920 and 1921, the demonstrations drew inspiration from the war, but from 1922 to 1930 they mimicked imperial policing in desert zones, invariably eliciting references to Iraq. On the eve of the 1923 Hendon display, the *Times* anticipated a "thrilling rescue...based on an actual occurrence in Iraq last year." The paper hailed the 1927 display as a new departure for the crowd pleaser. Under Air Marshal Sir John Salmond's guidance, the stunning set pieces provided a "definite lesson," depicting the rescue of a white population from the fury of a "barbarian mob" in a manner, again, recalling an incident in Iraq. Nor was there anything "artificial" about the 1930 exhibition, congratulated the paper; it recalled precisely the conditions in southern Iraq. These spectacular and fashionable events, which were copied in Fascist Italy, drew the highest social ranks among the hundreds of thousands who paid admission; innumerable others crowded together at nearby vantage points for a free glimpse. The presence of children was somewhat controversial, but they, too, attended in tens of thousands. Aside from the displays, RAF personnel such as Trenchard used recruitment tours around the country to expound on the humanity of air policing. Iraq's importance as a training ground for the RAF and a link in imperial air communications became part of this hard sell after Amery's 1925 visit to Iraq convinced him of the need to postpone the British departure well beyond the four years then under consideration and thus to devise a fresh, nationalistic propaganda angle recasting Britain's role there.[28]

The 1924 and 1929 Labour governments' commitment to this publicity blitz was especially intense, for the party had to defend its continuance of Conservative policy to a confused constituency. In public lectures and press statements, Air Secretary Lord Thomson and Undersecretary Leach combined protestations of their pacifism and helplessness in the face of the previous government's binding legacies with affirmations of air control's many advantages. Thomson published *Air Facts and Problems* (1927), and Montagu, his successor in 1929, praised the RAF's humane work in Iraq in Parliament (pushing the Independent Labour Party and many Labour intellectuals toward a sharply critical stance on the party's colonial policy).[29] Even Lionel Charlton, who had resigned from RAF service in Iraq in disgust at its violence, eventually paid his dues with his 1940 book, *Deeds That Held the Empire, by Air*, which, bafflingly, cites air policing in Iraq as an example of aviation as "an art of peace."[30]

In the free cultural space outside the world of government propaganda—although perhaps also inspired by it—poets, pulp fiction, and films also glorified aviation, especially the war's flying aces. The mania for airpower, especially airpower in conjunction with imperial adventure, ensured that the Edwardian "pleasure culture of war," in Michael Paris's phrase, remained in full force despite the revulsion against warfare that the Great War is presumed to have produced. It was thus that, in his 1936 edition of the *Oxford Book of Modern Verse*, Yeats included his own "An Irish Airman Foresees His Death" (1919) but notoriously ignored the war poets as too self-absorbed and too lacking in the operatic elements that were the backbone of soldiers' ballads. Airmen were not such ordinary soldiers; they were elites signifying a new military order, and if imperial conquest no longer seemed viable—or possible, given levels of global saturation—the task of maintaining peace in the Middle East from the air provided ample terrain for glorious adventure.[31]

Supplementing this romantic vision of the aerial empire was a more diversified effort to airbrush the overall image of the British Middle East, to which many agents who had long since staked their careers on the endurance of imperial romance rallied, as they had during the war. Desperate that the public be told something of what the British were "really doing" in Iraq, Bell sent the Colonial Office articles and photographs for press publication and urged film be used to reach an even wider audience, especially given Faisal's obvious draw in such a medium. It was not intended that pictures be shown "*as* propaganda," explained her Colonial Office spokesman, Reader Bullard, only that "some good subjects which would be of interest to the public, could be found in Iraq and that they would at the same time serve as propaganda." By that time, the Middle East Department had hired a publicity agent responsible for serving up to the press whatever suitable material the department gave him. The agents' slippery status within the bureaucracy gave them exceptional latitude, and their long romance with the pen and with the notion of Arabia's suitability to literary representation helped blur the moment when their writings shaded from literary into propaganda pieces. Traditional constraints on government officials were abrogated for them: regulations stipulated that officials could not contribute even anonymously to periodicals on political or administrative issues, but in the case of Bell's "political" articles in the *Round Table*, which relied on official information, the Colonial Office ruled, "Miss Bell is by no means an ordinary 'public officer.'" She was a long recognized authority on Arab affairs with an appointment of an "entirely exceptional character"; hence, "the letter of the law" need not be applied "too strictly." At home, a book written at her instigation strove to communicate "the difficulties which face the young administration in Iraq, the prejudices and conflicting tendencies with which she is gallantly and successfully attempting to deal." Paintings of "Five Months in Baghdad" by Edith Cheesman, wife of R. E. Cheesman, the naturalist and wartime secretary to Cox, were exhibited at a gallery in New Bond Street explicitly to help correct impressions of Mesopotamia as "a far-off and unprofitable venture." The *Round Table* published an obviously inspired piece by "a correspondent with intimate knowledge of conditions in Mesopotamia," aimed at correcting public misperceptions about the government's selfish interests in the region, the "fatal financial hemorrhage" they were causing, the inhumanity of air policing, and the feasibility of real development. John Buchan too entered the fray, writing turgidly in the *Spectator* about the "Liberties" secured by air policing and the Arab love of "fighting for its own sake." The *Times* ran articles by an unnamed correspondent promoting Emir Faisal as a "modern Saladin" lest the public indulge suspicions that he was a mere puppet in an "insidious scheme to spread British influence." Such speculations had "hidden the real Feisal from the public eye." In *Blackwood's*, this sketch turned treacly as another veteran invoked comparisons to "Drake or Raleigh." This effort continued into the late 1920s with the Baghdad correspondent's salute to the difficult work of British advisers in Iraq and Cox's defense of the fruits of the campaign when exposure of the War Graves' Commission's failure to locate all the bodies of British soldiers threatened to confirm the growing suspicion that they had died in vain.[32]

The very accusation of secrecy itself had to be answered. Clippings of press complaints about official secrecy can be found in the files of the India Office's Political and Secret Department, where they fueled a growing desperation to talk back to the public. In due course, a special *Times* correspondent in Tehran, the much-traveled Arthur Moore (from whose conclusions the editors tellingly distanced themselves) chimed in with the assurance that "if there is official secrecy [with regard to the Mesopotamian administration] it is in London that the pall hangs. Here there is none at all." Produced in war conditions, the civil administration was naturally undemocratic, Moore wrote indulgently, but it was "at least democratically minded," since "publicity is the best substitute for democracy." Indeed, it produced such a wealth of information, he insisted, that "in selection from it lies the principle difficulty of presentment to a public at home hitherto provided with little or none." With this spin, the British state in Mesopotamia was quintessentially English, a comfortably paternalistic "people's" government with nostalgic appeal for those perhaps discomfited by the increasingly assertive democracy at home. In Parliament, following former agent and Conservative MP William Ormsby-Gore's spirited defense of Mesopotamia policy, another veteran and Conservative, Earl Winterton, turned the tables on the secrecy debate, assuring his colleagues, as one who had fought with the Arabs, that England would know just how trustworthy Faisal was but for the government's "usual practice of secrecy."[33]

Those in the know also made a case for government management of information on the grounds that unmediated information from Arabia produced confusion, to the detriment of Britain's good relations in the region. In 1928, when questions arose about sensational reports in the "cheaper newspapers" of imminent Wahhabi holy war, a *Times* correspondent conveyed High Commissioner Dobbs's confidence that such rumors were "a fairy tale brought to Basra by some untutored Beduin. Such stories in Arabia passed rapidly from mouth to mouth, and were invariably improved in the telling." By way of bulletproof reassurance, he added, "British intelligence officers...obtaining information from the interior of Arabia, had been unable to find foundation for the alarmist reports." When the raids had passed, Dobbs chastised the press for having irresponsibly frightened European investors. In 1932, Philby similarly reprimanded the press. In a letter to the *Times* (which he excepted from his complaints), he explained that the reported "raids" were part of the usual tribal fighting, if perhaps exacerbated by the global Depression. Such news might momentarily delight the press, but their sensationalism, he warned, served Ibn Saud's cunning enemies (neighboring British protégés) by unwittingly propagandizing the view that his empire was seriously threatened, thereby also embittering Saudis against Britain, since in Arabia, he patiently elaborated, the tendency was to "regard the Press of a country as a mirror of its public and official sentiments." To this list of unintended consequences of uncensored reporting on Arabia he added the suffering of the Hejazi economy from pilgrim fright. His own practice, he condescended to explain, was to disregard as untrue any report about the peninsula emanating from such distant and ill-served sources as Basra, Baghdad, Amman, Jerusalem, and Cairo—all *"prima facie* tainted by prejudice." Since the general public could not be expected to exercise such judiciousness, he urged the corrective of government communiqués, especially for the benefit of the empire's Muslim subjects. So the expert explained to the lay public why the peculiarities of news flow and arcana of intrigue in Arabia made official management of information necessary. Other officials back from the Middle East, where they had grown accustomed to receiving "revelations" from Arnold Wilson and other prophets "of what was going on beneath the surface," also resolved to "doubt the complete accuracy of the occasional news of Mespot that comes out in the papers," written by "men who have not been on the spot." Suspend belief in published news from Arabia, was the experts' wise instruction.[34]

The scholarly societies provided an important liminal space through which the state's supporters could attempt to manage public opinion about Middle East policy. At Robert Brooke-Popham's 1919 lecture at the Royal United Services Institute, Chairman Major General R. M. Ruck affirmed the institute's role as "a halfway house between the authorities and the public" that could leaven the meager information available from "the usual official channels" with its own expertise. ("Authorities" included Nesta Webster, whose pablum on Bolshevism and secret societies the group swallowed whole.) The overlap between state representatives and society members, between government experts and scholars, ensured that the societies soon shared the state's outrage against the vicious "propaganda" and "orgy of ill-informed criticism" against Middle East policy after the rising. Following General Haldane's attempt to enlighten public opinion about it three years later, General Sir Edmund Barrow, wartime military secretary to the India Office, excoriated the "unfortunate pressure exerted on military policy by an ill-informed Press, backed by ignorant public opinion." "It is, I fear, one of the penalties we have to pay for 'democratic control,'" he concluded, launching into a vainglorious description of the mayhem that would follow fulfillment of untutored calls for evacuation of Mesopotamia. The chairman, Viscount Peel, then also secretary of state for India, gently tut-tutted Barrow for violating society rules against discussing politics, but, when chairing the Central Asian Society a few years later, found himself echoing these very sentiments: the ills of the press's "open diplomacy" were as bad if not worse than "the evils of secret diplomacy," he affirmed. To form a "just judgment" on the knotty issues of the day, the public needed guidance, "inspiration from wells of mature information and of ripened judgment," which service a society like theirs, "the fountain-head of knowledge of Central Asia," could provide. When it came to topics like airpower in the Middle East, its views, "carrying the weight our members do," could exercise a salutary "effect on public opinion." Besides these avowedly open forums, at the new, "rather exclusive" and "secret" British Institute of International Affairs (Chatham House), Bertram Thomas, David Hogarth, Percy Cox, Arnold Wilson, Ormsby-Gore, and others delivered "public" lectures on various Arabian topics. The Foreign Office supported the societies' arrogation of this paternalistic role; hence its relief that the Saudi representative in London had been persuaded to "to give up his first fantastic idea of giving a public lecture [on Wahhabism] in the Albert Hall!" in favor of the more disciplined environment of the Central Asian Society, where a Foreign Office official was deputed to observe the proceedings. The Colonial Office also vetted society lectures. Under cover of an anonymous member of the public, the state also used unattributed articles in society journals to cultivate progovernment opinion. Just when, in Chicago, Walter Lippmann was arriving at his gloomy conclusions about opinion makers' stranglehold on public opinion (in *Public Opinion* [1922]), the British state was doing its utmost to prove him right.[35]

Their efforts clearly met with considerable success. A notably violent description of "the use of aircraft in small wars" at the United Service Institute concluded with a few photographs nodding to aircraft's peaceful uses in activities such as archaeology, prompting this homily by a thrilled physician in the audience:

> I have never been in Mesopotamia, but I have been reading about it
> since I was a child....I have longed to see the Tower of Babel, but
> I never thought I would do so....Could I ever stand where Moses stood
> and have a Pisgah view...and here we have a lecturer to-day who has
> actually photographed not only where Moses stood but other places of
> importance in the Holy Land, and he has shown us on a screen in the
> centre of London Pisgah views, including the Jordan itself!

The progovernment side got considerable mileage simply from the romance surrounding the places at the heart of its speakers' lectures and from the heroic aura around the speakers themselves. Similarly, through puff pieces on topics such as "the Arab soldier," society journals could "educate" their readership on the "born fighters" of the besieged states of Iraq and the Hejaz, who lacked only experience of modern military organization, which British assistance could remedy. A winking reference to Lawrence sealed the charm of the proposition: "There is at least one officer whose knowledge of the Arab's character and...customs as well as his military talents make him a fit person to be entrusted with the task of raising and organising a military force for...the newly crowned King of Irak."[36]

Both critics and supporters of the government thus claimed to have come far from their jejune prewar views to arrive at a sophisticated understanding of government. The government's side in this contest for control of foreign policy played on the fact that public skepticism about official pronouncements was, if anything, exceeded by suspicion of the press, especially atrocity stories.[37] Before the war, the press had been blamed for fanning jingoist fever among the masses; after the war, when the press had come to be universally doubted and took a position *against* empire in the Middle East, imperialists blamed it for encouraging political cowardice. But the agents in officialdom also tried to win it back to their corner by informing the public about Asiatic conspiracies, reasoning that an accurate perception of the dangers surrounding the Middle East would curb criticism of both secrecy and air control. In 1920, as he presented his picture of gathering threats to the India Office, Norman Bray recommended taking "certain sections of the Press...into our confidence." His frightful memos prompted other official urgings that the public be informed of the existence of "this danger and HMG's recognition of the fact." He submitted a version of at least one of his reports to Reuters as "counter propaganda." The effort to protect the occupying army from criticism, which had partly inspired his investigations, also made the India Office and Cox eager to issue a public statement based on them, in not as crude a form as an official communiqué but handed "unofficially" to a Reuters representative for wider distribution without disclosure of its "official origin." The press statement released so conspiratorially revealed that the impression then current of Soviet efforts to revert to peaceful coexistence with its neighbors was a carefully contrived illusion; in fact, a "combination of wire-pullers and conspirators" were at work in Europe, Turkey, Syria, and Russia, and "Mesopotamia was to receive the full brunt of bolshevik Turkish nationalist and Arab nationalist intrigue." War Office communiqués were also instrumental in framing the meager press coverage of the rising around the notion of conspiracy, hemmed in by news of "conspiracy" in contexts as varied as Canada, Russia, and India. Similar fare was on offer elsewhere, building obliquely on the popular, fictional foundations of Buchan's *Greenmantle*. In a public lecture, Valentine Chirol conjured a reawakened Orient in which surged "many Old World forces...tending more and more to combine together against the common menace of the Occident." However much Mesopotamia stank "in the nostrils of the British taxpayer," positioned at the heart of Islam and historically anarchic, it would, if left to itself, become "a Middle East-Bolshevist Power, the nucleus and focus of all the evil forces in the world," in the apocalyptic vision published by an Iraq-returned officer. The duke of Northumberland's much-discussed pamphlets and lectures propounding theories of Bolshevik and Jewish conspiracy behind labor unrest (generously incorporating global secret societies, Sinn Fein, the Germans, Indian national-ists, and so forth) were part of this textual mix. So, too, were Churchill's inflam-matory speeches on worldwide conspiracy against the empire. Paralleling official geographic imaginaries, postwar fiction seized on Russia's "Asiatic fea-tures," depicting the Red Army as the refuge of coolies, Afghans, and Hindus led by Germans and Turks. Expressing its skepticism about Churchill's mercu-rial Army Estimates for the Middle East, even the *Times* momentarily suc-cumbed, directing readers to a letter by one "S" describing from "authoritative sources" the close connection between the Nationalist Turks and the Bolshevists—the usual "drama of conspiracy" about Turks of various political stripes spreading Pan-Islamic propaganda for the Bolsheviks with backing from Berlin and organized Jewry, and targeting Mesopotamia in particular. Still, the irreverent *Times* used this theory to *criticize* the government, as evi-dence of the impossibility of its ever keeping its commitment to limiting British responsibilities in the region.[38]

Commenting on all this in 1920, H. G. Wells remarked England's "peculiar style of thinking," its reflexive falling back "upon the notion of conspiracy" as a form of explanation. Indeed, conspiracy thinking about the Middle East was geographically—and figuratively—at the heart of a wider postwar preoccupation deliberately encouraged by the state. And this helps us make better sense of those weird postwar cultural phenomena: the *Morning Post* series on world unrest, which appeared in July 1920 in the midst of the raging debates on Mesopotamia in the press and Parliament, and the fall publication of Victor Marsden's translation of the *Protocols of the Elders of Zion* (a private edition had appeared earlier that year). The *Post*'s very notion of searching for "Causes of the World Unrest" echoed the frantic contemporary search for causes of the Mesopotamian unrest. Nesta Webster, a great sympathizer of the duke of Northumberland, contributed to this series about a secret organization behind unrest in Russia, Turkey, Portugal, Germany, and elsewhere. The fifth article was likely based on Bray's memo on "Events in Asia." Titled "The Cause of the World Unrest," it described a "vast and cunning organisation," "spread through-out the Orient" and known to "anyone who is well acquainted with the East," particularly those who had made "a long and careful study of the tortuous poli-tics and secret tendencies of Asia." The notion of world conspiracy against law and order and Christian civilization would have seemed absurd before the war, the article conceded, but the war had produced a "complete change of mental-ity," providing "concrete proof" of the close connection between "rebellion in Ireland, trouble in Egypt, disaffection in India, revolution in Russia." Behind Germany was a "Formidable Sect," a Jewish organization, which endured after German defeat and operated through "zones of influence" and "centers" of subversion radiating throughout Asia, plying propaganda strikingly similar to the "programme of violence and hypocrisy" advocated by the *Protocols*. Asians were not themselves agents of a secular, anti-imperialist ideology but the passive objects of "missionaries of discontent" dispatched by a "single secret agency." The *Morning Post* thus inserted the "Eastern Unrest" into a wider tale of world unrest. The *Post* series and the popularity of the yet more scandalous *Protocols of the Elders of Zion* were part of a wider postwar ideological and epistemological trend that identified a shadowy Middle East—encompassing Jews, secret societies, and an open road to Russia—as the pivot of all grand conspiracy. Usually dismissed as a crank fringe of British fascists, adherents of these theories were, in my view, merely the crankiest among a wider public fascinated by the idea of conspiracy against the empire via the roiling Middle East.[39]

None of this is to diminish the importance of the specifically anti-Semitic roots of the *Protocols'* appeal but to place it within a wider culture of conspiracy thinking. However "Western" their knowledge, Jews remained an "Eastern people," fundamentally similar to the Arabs, the very antinomy that had made their presence in Palestine a comfort, as a "vital bridge between Arabs and Europeans," in early discourses on development, now cogitated in more alarming terms. Just as their apparent internationalism made them a threat in the eyes of scaremongering sections of the British public, so too did the rampant border-crossing of all Middle Easterners. Iraq was susceptible to subversion by international intrigue because of its "eternal magnetism...as the road to India and the open sea," "central position among the Moslem States," and "geographical position...which renders the philandering of Pan-Islamism with Bolshevism a matter of grave importance," in the words of the *Daily Telegraph*. The two most prominent Jewish politicians in Britain—the Zionist Herbert Samuel and anti-Zionist Edwin Montagu—had both been appointed, not accidentally, to the Eastern empire, and both were vilified by the Right as "Orientals" who would usher in anarchy. That the *Protocols* affair was part of this swirl of official and public debate on disorder, Jews, and the Middle East is perhaps most evidenced by the fact that it was Philip Graves, then *Times* correspondent in Constantinople, who unmasked the forgery in 1921, for which he was attacked as a philo-Semite, partly because of his past association with Palestine.[40]

Popular conspiracy thinking of this period was thus deliberately generated as part of an effort to win over public opinion on the mandates. When Thomas Lyell, an officer back from Iraq, argued in his book that the Mesopotamian policy looked "wantonly extravagant" when considered in isolation but appeared entirely justified as part of the "immense problem of empire—as the key to the future of our dominions," he was speaking to an audience familiar with the conspiracy fears of the government. The dawning recognition of the military lessons of the Mesopotamia campaign was also partly a result of this effort to train eyes on the Middle East as the future testing ground of world peace. A *Times* "special correspondent"—a designation that, in reports on this region, often seems to signal official inspiration—reported the Quetta Staff College's tour of Iraq's battlefields in 1923, when it was "beginning to be realized that the Mesopotamian operations, subsidiary though they were at the time, have a special value in the study of military science," despite their having been fought out "in a peculiar country" calling for "very special measures." Crucially, the theater was "typical of the Middle East…in which great wars of the future may quite possibly have to be decided." The feature described the college's reenactment of the wartime voyage upriver on war-era boats. (The author noted archly that local opinion suspected the group of spying out a new air route from Quetta "for some unknown plot!") In Baghdad, they left the "battles of the past…and looked at the future in the air" through a social and educational program generously assembled by the RAF. The unique tactics of the Mesopotamian theater may have merited study on their own account, but it was the particular obsessions of the postwar political climate and the RAF's ever-ready propaganda machine that sealed its canonical status in the annals of military science.[41]

This was the political culture that inspired Leonard Woolf's 1925 essay "Fear and Politics," but, to those responsible for it, it was merely an effort to enlighten public opinion in the new mass democracy (even if the public's ignorance was the product of official censorship).[42] And it worked, substantially, keeping control of air policy beyond the reach of public criticism, as we have seen in chapter 7. The new awareness of danger cross-cut the image of bombs civilizing the Arabian deserts with more disturbing images of Britain bombed into a desert, the hypothetical scenario on which fear traded. According to this logic, air control in the Middle East checked the destruction of Britain and civilization itself. Perhaps most famously, Cicely Hamilton's much-reprinted *Theodore Savage* (1922), tellingly subtitled *A Story of the Past or the Future*, told of the apocalyptic fallout of the League Court's decision against a small Eastern country that was being "encouraged to make trouble" by some force as part of a general anarchic program. Recounting the nomadic survival of one civil servant after bombardment had razed British civilization, it describes a world in which rumor flourishes as "the outside world…veiled itself in silence," society relapsed into tribal disorder, and the lost old world is remembered as the Garden of Eden. Such imagery periodically swayed even the fastidious *Times*, for instance, in 1923 when the paper admired Air Secretary Hoare for "at last awakening" the public "to the reality of the danger" in a "clear and straightforward account" that "fully justified" the Iraqi air regime "on the two grounds of economy and humanity." The excitements of the 1930 Hendon display induced further concessions of the soundness of air control. The public was grasping, in fits and starts, that there was too much at stake to contemplate a loosening of Britain's grip on the Middle East.[43]

Indeed, so successful was the spin-doctoring that in the distant context of a Commons debate about striking coal miners in the dark year of 1926, a Conservative likened trade unionist talk of "liberty" to the "Arab chief in Iraq who, when he was prevented from carrying out a punitive expedition, which included ravaging and burning villages, exclaimed, 'We have always done this. Why do you interfere with us now? Where is your boosted British liberty?'" As Nicholas Dirks might have it, the scandals and scandal of air policing had migrated from the scheme itself to its victims. Affirmations of aerial progressivism had sunk deep roots; England's militarist and technophile culture had been disguised by what David Edgerton aptly calls "the cuteness of the English aeroplane," a central feature of what Jon Lawrence terms the myth of the "peaceable kingdom." Edgerton traces this myth to George Orwell, but by 1944 even he was wondering at the "automatic way in which people go on repeating certain phrases...[such as] 'the aeroplane and the radio have abolished distance' and 'all parts of the world are now interdependent.'" "Actually," he retorted wearily in the midst of yet another world war, "the effect of modern inventions has been to increase nationalism, to make travel enormously more difficult, to cut down the means of communication between one country and another."[44]

The secret to the "automatic" association of the airplane not only with peace but with internationalism lay in the corollary to the state's rhetorical focus on the dangers circling the Middle East: the silver bullet of development. This dazzling goal, however miragelike, remained relatively unbesmirched among dreams of Middle Eastern empire, as we have seen in chapter 5, and sealed the argument for the benevolence of official secrecy. In 1924, the Times' Baghdad correspondent continued to believe that the dispatch of irrigating experts and the like would give Britain a chance to prove its good faith toward the understandably doubtful Iraqis; Baldwin's 1925 government, the paper believed, was committed to a constructive policy in Iraq, for the sake of national honor, not oil. While continuing to chide the regime for its dependence on the bomb, the Guardian was relieved when criticism dissipated enough to allow it to proceed with its real, developmental work. Faith in the development trope ensured that when it came to the matter of departure dates, the Times spoke as sympathetically of the "natural caution of the mandatory power" as it had of Iraqi fears that the British intended to remain in their country forever. It even professed bewilderment at Labour complaints that the government used the League of Nations as a venue for autocratic decision-making (while continuing

to press for a more open Permanent Mandates Commission). The development antidote helped extrude the *Times'* poisoned view of the state, subtly
reshaping the villain behind the trampling of English constitutional rights
from a willfully negligent government to an unfortunately flawed League of
Nations structure. Voicing his concerns about official honesty, Richard Coke
also found redemption in the commitment to development. "Material rewards"
aside, he admired the "power and vision which sees the British Empire as a vast
army of many nations and cultures sweeping up the varied civilisations of the
past in the march forward to that ideal world of brothers." This vision of developmental empire, he felt, offered a convincing rejoinder to the press's wholly
cynical view of the Middle Eastern empire *and* recuperated state secrecy as stupid but well intentioned: a democratically controlled foreign policy would necessarily prove too short-sighted to implement such a vision, he explained, given
British taxpayers' limited notion of their "collective interests" and the obvious
objection that "there was plenty of scope for [charity] nearer home." Democracy
was too selfish to finance developmental imperialism; the crime of the secretive
government was unchecked generosity.[45]

All the same, public opinion remained skeptical of a too obviously militarist policy in Iraq, as a Conservative survey discovered in 1927. The Conservatives'
refusal to reduce commitments in Iraq was among the factors that cost them
the election in 1929, and Labour's greater willingness to heed British and Iraqi
public opinion (the latter conveyed through the wise counsels of High
Commissioner Gilbert Clayton on the eve of his death) eventually resulted in
the treaty of 1930—and the full submergence of empire into the covert realm.[46]
Officialdom discovered by accident, through the investigations of Hubert
Young in the Foreign Office, that its public advertisement of the new atmosphere of trust in Iraq in 1930 was based entirely on a *Times* article, which, it
turned out, was merely a press message provided by the government. Periodic
intercession of this kind perhaps explains why the *Times* remained so exasper-
atingly mercurial on Iraq. When the League of Nations deliberated on the Iraqi
application for admission, the paper aired its concern about the possible mis-
use of the RAF by an independent Iraqi government bent on settling old scores.
Perhaps contemplating an RAF unleashed from prudent British control, and
perhaps in the shadow of the disarmament conference that year, the paper
reverted to its skeptical posture on the humanity of air policing, arguing that a
government that supported restriction of bombing in regular operations should
not tolerate it in irregular ones—instantly provoking a rebuke from High
Commissioner Dobbs.[47]

The impossibility of ever settling the matter was partly due to the unresolved view of the community that functioned at once as key opinion makers

and representatives of the state's covert power. It would not do to indict the government alone on the count of misinforming the public, argued Richard Coke in *The Arab's Place in the Sun* (1929); the "highbrow," "arabized" experts of the scholarly societies and "lowbrow," "romantic" publicists and Hollywood had done equal damage. Trapped between hell and high water, the public needed to cultivate its own knowledge and wrest responsibility for Middle East policy from officials and experts.[48] The state may have leached into the public sphere to manage public opinion, but the loyalties of the experts representing it there were by no means clear; their shadowy figures became the focus of the state's and the public's implacable suspicions in their irresolvable struggle over control of foreign policy.

Slouching between the State and the People

Early in 1929, suspicion that the RAF was being used as a means to covertly pursue empire surfaced in Labour MP Ernest Thurtle's questions about the use of British airplanes in the rescue of former King Inayatullah from Kabul during the Afghani civil war. Others echoed his demand for official comment on rumors of British interference in Afghanistan. The government demurred, but the next item on the Commons' agenda was the significance of the Najdi-Iraqi border raiding, followed by a debate on "Colonel Lawrence," in which Thurtle took the offensive again, inquiring how long and for what purpose the colonel, under the false name Aircraftman Shaw, had been stationed on the Indian frontier near Afghanistan. (Lord Winterton, now undersecretary for India, replied lamely that to his knowledge people often enlisted under names other than their own.)[49] The tumbling of these topics one over the other—in parliamentary discussion and reporting on it—testifies to the strength of the conviction that these events—the tensions in Afghanistan and Iraq, the RAF, Lawrence—added up to more than met the eye in this intricately connected region. In the government's calculus, the common denominator was the Bolshevik hand, but to many among the British public, it was their own government interfering where it dared not admit to—and Lawrence's presence on the Indian frontier was their proof.

For its part, many in the government saw in the intemperate Arabist "enthusiasts" proof of the need for special discretion about British activity in the Middle East. In an article that the *Times* editors expressed reservations about in 1920, their pro–civil administration correspondent, Arthur Moore, invoked the usual cocktail of Bolshevist, Turkish, Syrian, and other foreign conspiracies behind the Mesopotamian unrest, urging the public to temper the "storm of home criticism" and support the government in a conflict that was as big as the South African War. In particular, such discipline and constancy would require curtailment of the activities of "our official pan-arabs," whose wartime profligacy and enthusiasm had, he claimed, caused the present waste of lives and money. The scales soon fell from Moore's eyes when he discovered that the civil administration in which he had placed such faith had betrayed its commitment to representative government in favor of a monarchical solution. The next year he submitted a much-hyped three-part series called "Mesopotamian Mystery," in which, far from urging public docility, he lambasted official secrecy about Middle East policy as the work of the same "Arab enthusiasts." The "mystery" in his title linked Mesopotamia's oriental qualities with the secret history of the conspiratorial rise of these enthusiasts in the halls of government as he explained how, with a wave of the wand in Cairo, "a few men working in the dark," far from the eyes of the public, had recklessly produced an Iraqi king on the eve of the promulgation of an Iraqi electoral law. He demanded immediate evacuation of Mesopotamia and public scrutiny of every line of the new treaty with Faisal, "for we may be sure that the Pan-Arabs are at work upon it." If he saw the hand of the Arab enthusiast behind both the public's *and* the state's serial betrayal of a righteous Middle Eastern policy, officialdom saw a similar hand behind Moore's apparent volte-face (more or less missing his [and the *Times*'] point about genuine Arab government). The "Mesopotamian Mystery" series was much studied at the Colonial Office where Churchill had his Arabist experts, Lawrence and Bullard, annotate it in order to get "truth separated from fiction." Bullard identified the author as Moore, "a rather violent Irishman" who, he deduced, had "imbibed a lot of hot air from Philby."[50]

Official propagation of conspiracy theories was partly designed—and defended—as a response to such "hot air," as a weapon for combating criticism that many of the ex-agents in Whitehall saw as the mark of *other* agents' interventions in the public sphere. They, too, had little faith that public opinion actually existed; the herd had to have been duped by someone. Before Lawrence joined the government, Whitehall considered the negative press about Iraq all his doing. In 1919, the Foreign Office blamed him for *all* recent articles on the Syrian question, including twelve in the *Times*. The India Office's search for the true causes of the unrest was predicated on its determination to thwart a press campaign it attributed entirely to Lawrence and to which it traced the prevailing misconception "that we are fighting against Nationalists who are demanding only a form of government that shall be reasonably independent and British-advised." The Colonial Office appointment seemed momentarily to tame Lawrence (although at the cost of invigorating popular suspicions about his work), and, as Bullard's contumacious dismissal of Moore suggests, the benighted Philby emerged as the most frequently suspected fountainhead of any markedly vehement invective against Whitehall policy. To the government, the press debate was as an intraofficial dispute dragged into the public by tergiversatory "enthusiasts" among the agents. The government's own skillful and conspiratorial use of the literary talents of the agents at *their* disposal, such as Bray and Bell, made it easy for them to impute such prolific powers to rogue agents. It was part of the conspiracy-thinking mode that gripped Whitehall. With its exaggerated sense of the agents' powers of influence and of the mind-bending required to grasp the Arab perspective, officialdom put public criticism of its policies down to their machinations.[51]

Loyalty was rewarded—the political officer James Mann's protest against the *Nation*'s criticisms of the Mesopotamian administration earned him consideration for "special work"—but more pertinently, reprobates were disliked, disciplined, and watched. Lawrence was much hated by "most government officials, regular soldiers, old-fashioned political experts and such like," according to Robert Graves, for he was a "disturbing element in their ordered scheme of things, a mystery and a nuisance." Even as an RAF mechanic he seemed liable to engage in "some diabolic trick for raising mutiny or revolt." (Graves's reviewer in the *Times* noted that Graves had apparently inherited "a certain cocksureness...from some of the more ardent experts on Arab affairs.") Indeed, Lawrence was enough of a security concern that in 1929 Trenchard banned him from leaving the United Kingdom and speaking to any of the "great," particularly Opposition politicians such as Churchill and Lady Astor. (Nevertheless, he continued to meet with Philip Sassoon, George Lloyd, and others.) The bit of public sphere comprising his friendships was deemed worthy of government surveillance. As Philby stole the mantle of alpha-defector, he and his sometime travel partner Rosita Forbes attracted intense official and media attention (news clippings by and about him were painstakingly collected in Whitehall). Basil Thomson's Home Office spooks also closely watched left-leaning British "Pro-Turks," especially the notorious Muslim convert and novelist Marmaduke Pickthall. Academic societies, as mentioned earlier, were subjected to surveillance, especially for the utterances of wayward agents who remained welcome by virtue of their status as "experts." Even the distinguished Sir William Willcocks found himself on trial for sedition when his suggestions for improving the Aswan Dam were taken up by Egyptian nationalists. (He was spared imprisonment and returned to his native Bengal.)[52]

This vigilance was part of the rapid growth of "security consciousness and political surveillance" produced by the war. With official conspiracy theories homing in on Britain itself as a center of anti-imperial subversion, the focus on Lawrence, Philby, and so forth was the domestic counterpart of the air

surveillance and covert empire (the British hidden hand) in the Middle East—
not much of a stretch given that Trenchard retired from the RAF in 1929 to
head the Metropolitan Police. Just as fears of Russian subversion were absorbed
into official conspiracy thinking about unrest in the Middle East, so the Middle
Eastern connection was absorbed into the effort to identify the Russian hand
behind left-wing and other forms of domestic subversion. A new history of the
French Revolution elicited one reviewer's call for the arrest of all the Bolshevik-
backed "polyglot rascals" in the country, lest it witness "the degraded spectacle
of honest Englishmen murdered by the worst Chinamen and the worst niggers
whom brutality can control." That illustrious visitors to the Soviet Union, such
as the Webbs, Lady Astor, and Bernard Shaw, were closely linked to Lawrence
and Meinertzhagen certainly did not help compartmentalize Communist- and
Middle Eastern–inspired dissent. (Indeed, Meinertzhagen was in Moscow at
the same time as his uncle Sidney and, typically, tried without success to
instruct him in seeing the "real Russia" hidden by Russian officials.)[53]

The agents' earlier peccadillos were as nothing before the colossal postwar
concern with their fundamental "loyalties" (the title of Wilson's memoir), with
the possibility of their succumbing to their chief occupational hazard and shifting their loyalties to their Arab advisees. The 1923 protocol that reshaped Iraq's
British governors into "administrative inspectors" overseeing Iraqi governors
responded partly to the reproach that British agents were becoming "more
native than the native himself." Indeed, a political agent at Bahrein returned
from a mission to Ibn Saud announcing he would thenceforth serve as *Ibn
Saud's* private agent in London. And, most famously, after being shunted
between displeased administrations, the obstreperous Philby defected to Saudi
Arabia (and Islam), where he remained a perennial nuisance to officials anxious over his potentially subversive influence on the sultan. A Saudi legation in
London remained elusive as long as officials remained captive to the fear that it
would merely provide "the mischievous Mr. Philby" an "extra 'sounding board'
or 'loud-speaker' for propaganding philby-esque and anti-HMG doctrines!" (By
1928, unable to arrest his movements or his pen, which prosecution in any
case threatened only to amplify, officialdom adopted the "Philby policy" of
ignoring him.) Similarly, the Colonial Office obstructed all attempts to appoint
a British representative to Ibn Saud's government for the entire decade. While
Bertram Thomas, Dickson, and others passionately entreated consideration for
the position, the Colonial Office cautioned shrewdly: "We all know what happens when British officers get themselves attached to remote Arab courts. The
local atmosphere is too much for them. They become *plus royalist que le roi* and
encourage their pet potentate to raise all kinds of unnecessary questions and
put forward every sort of embarrassing claim. We have suffered enough in the

past. Do not let us make this mistake again." In two years, this opinion had desiccated into a theorem: a representative with Ibn Saud was impossible because "very close association with an Arab potentate or an Arab regime does, in practice, make nearly all European officers very unreliable agents of their own Governments." They became "more arab than the arabs"—the stigma of the dangerously empathetic. Implicit in this reading of corruption in Arabia was a belief in the region's cabalistic power to sway minds—the more natively Arab, the more susceptible. Thus paranoid, officialdom traced the political recalcitrance of rogue agents to an effect of the place itself; their criticism of British policies and intentions was merely proof of their having been "got at." By the mid-1920s, agents attempting to prove their bona fides knew to distance themselves from this recognizable "type." In his application for the Najd posting, Thomas took care to press his experience of Arabia from "more angles than any other British officer," which "perhaps has saved me from succumbing to one or other of the 'crank' schools, of which Arabia is a hotbed, of course." The early romantics, drawn to Arabia as the place for authentically free, individualistic, manly men, had been exposed as veritable nuisances. This sort of agent would not cease bucking against an imperial bureaucracy bent on constraining the liberty of Arabia—or more properly, *their liberty* in and on Arabia. This is not to say Lawrence and Philby were not imperialists but to point to a shift in official culture. The longer history of agents' intelligence-gathering efforts in Arabia betrays a sort of willful irrationalism, useful and harmless as the mark of genius in the halcyon days when deliverance of the Arab lands from Ottoman tyranny was a visionary scheme with broad appeal. After the war, when the British themselves had stepped into those Ottoman shoes, it was denigrated as blind and highly un-English fanaticism "of no practical use." To officialdom, the Arab was treacherous by definition, but several British agents, formerly proud representatives of their empire, had allowed themselves to become complicit in oriental intrigue. To those on the other side of the rift, "certain British officers" with intimate knowledge of Arabs had simply lost all reason and, in an orgy of sentimentality, begun to promote the cause of Arab nationalism, among other sorts of skullduggery. They had become the enemy within, the greatest betrayal of all and the greatest source of paranoia.[54]

But as Thurtle's interpellation on Lawrence underscores, while the state grew paranoid about delinquent agents, many Britons seized on the very same rogue elements as proof that the state could covertly pursue imperialist ends, whatever its proclamations to the contrary or pretended efforts to end secret diplomacy. The agents' heroism had always encompassed the queer mix of honor and dishonor long since embodied in the figure of the spy and the imperial martyr. Bray tellingly glorified every dead political officer as "another

Gordon upholding the honour of England," and Meinertzhagen similarly called Noel "one of the General Gordon type, a fanatical enthusiast, who is capable of leading the Empire to disaster in order to fulfil his own dreams." Such megalo-maniacal "dreamers of empire," "the legion of the Damned," "non-conforming, therefore anarchic," were much on the mind of interwar Britons nostalgic for a more visionary age, however ill-starred its visions. Thus, agents who broke with the government earned even more celebrity, their antiestablishment pro-nouncements serving as a badge of their eccentricity, Englishness, heroism—at once convincing the government of their sway over popular opinion, attracting the public's wary, if also admiring, eyes, and fueling their own delusions of grandeur. Philby pointed self-servingly to the

> curious fact that most of the giants of Arabian adventure ... have
> displayed a tendency to fall foul of their own folk. ... Sir Richard
> Burton ... was never comfortable in official harness, but was none the
> less great for his failure to achieve high office. ... Blunt ... had a
> perpetual feud with the British Government in his fight for the rights
> of Arabs and Irishmen. ... Lawrence himself was a declared
> rebel. ... Bell was never popular, and was regarded rather as a
> nuisance than an asset in British official circles. ... My own case was
> similar.

If the agents' initial postwar appeal stemmed from their affiliation with the heroic and redemptive project in the Middle East, their rage against its betrayal kept them in the public eye as precious honorers of liberty—the *Spectator* opposed Lawrence's "blunt and honest rashness" to the "tortured and timid tergiversations of the ... politician"—but also as rogues, inconstant and ever inscrutable. The trope of agent fickleness became potent enough to threaten their heroism, forcing biographers to explicitly exempt their individual idols from the inglorious company of those who learned to "see things from the Beduin standpoint" only to lose "their English outlook ... and ... the British character." The perceived overlap of Arab and Irish sympathies was central to the construction of the Arabia agent as agent of anarchy. Philby, "as an Irishman ... was 'agin' the Government, or indeed *any* Government, on princi-ple," explained Stirling (though in fact Philby was not Irish at all). The Arab-Irish overlap shared by Lawrence (who was planning a sympathetic biography of Roger Casement), Erskine Childers (who had become involved in gun-running in Ireland and would later write pro-Arab political works), Blunt, Moore, Glubb, and others painted them as distillations of a catholic anti-establishment fervor. By 1922, what George Bernard Shaw called "the English Turk pro the Irish Arabian" was a recognizable type. Moreover, their playground was a slippery one, "debatable," as Hogarth had termed it, under the sway of Islam, a religion at once heretic and familiar, mysterious and sinister. Arabia's deserts were threatening as much as recuperative, promising redemption and apocalypse by turns.[55]

Contemporary literature attempted to capture this collapsed vision of hope and dread, perhaps none so vividly or famously as Yeats's "Second Coming," whose nightmarish vision of "anarchy loosed upon the world" and the drowning of innocence reflected his preoccupation with the state of the world in 1920. That was the year in which Britain's sleep was certainly "vexed to nightmare by a rocking cradle"—the cradle of civilization. Many feared the center would not hold, and things did indeed fall apart. Drawing heavily on Doughty, Yeats looked to the desert for signs of imminent apocalypse and redemption: "Surely some revelation is at hand." But the image out of *spiritus mundi* was a troubling one: "A shape with lion body and the head of a man" emerging from the desert with "a gaze blank and pitiless as the sun." This image of a terrible redeemer symbolized perhaps the monstrous machine of imperial government bent on delivering this region; in 1936, he described the poem as the first in a series intended to express his growing "horror at the cruelty of governments." In 1920, the problem lay in the personnel available: "The best lack all convictions, while the worst/ Are full of passionate intensity." Yeats thought he was the inspiration for his antiheroic fictional contemporary: the significantly named Medina of John Buchan's *The Three Hostages* (1924). Richard Hannay's antagonist, Medina conceals behind his façade of respectability as an explorer and MP "a demon who is determined to annihilate the world of ordinary moral standards." He has learned from the East the art of dominating men "through their souls" but is in fact an Irish poet of Spanish extraction (his mix of exoticism and Englishness ultimately signaling his Jewishness), a genealogy winding together the Celtic/Arab affinity long assumed by British Arabists: Robert Graves (himself half Anglo-Irish) speculated that Lawrence's peculiar qualities, including his love of poverty and failure, had either been absorbed from the desert or were "latent in his blood, of which the Spanish strain—and Spanish is half-Arab—shows in the severity of his jaw." (Graves himself decamped to Spain after his stint in Cairo and just after producing his Lawrence biography and his war memoir.) The protagonist of the popular film *The Sheik* is similarly revealed to be the son of an English earl and a Spanish noblewoman.[56]

Mistrust of the man on the spot in the Middle East was thus cultural as much as political, extending beyond what we know about Socialists' suspicions that imperialists of the Right were addicted to conflict. The dual image of heroic Arabist agents, coupled with the memory, embellished by the media, of their demonstration in wartime that empire, or any other covert agenda, could be pursued by means of a special force or even a single Lawrentian agent, was the smoking gun in the case that some sections of the public built to prove the existence of an "invisible arm" of government behind the democratically accountable façade. Sensationalist contentions ("Why do we stay in Mesopotamia—Cherchez la femme...Miss Gertrude Bell..."the Diana of the Desert") made sense to this public. It was as "the Mystery Woman of the East, the uncrowned Queen, the Diana of the Desert," that Bell became a "legendary personality...in the imagination of the general public," her stepmother attests. Lawrence the press regarded as an even more enigmatic figure. Other nations' obsessive tracking of his suspicious whereabouts, described in chapter 8, fed the even more intense British coverage of his checkered career. The front-page story about his pseudonymous presence in the RAF fed the conviction that he was the top agent of the secret imperial state. His motives and influence were open to endless speculation, his social world becoming as central to lay efforts to understand his covert official life as it was to the state's attempts to keep tabs on him. Even casual acquaintances found an eager market for "revealing" articles. Parliamentary questions were posed about his alleged complicity in various imperialistic plots, including a plan to overthrow the Soviet government per statements in Soviet show trials of 1927 and 1930. His RAF posting near the Afghan border in 1929 inspired not only parliamentary debate but a public outcry against this "most mysterious man in the empire," the "ultimate proconsul of Britain in the East." The *Daily Herald* broke this story of "the arch spy of the world." Socialists rioted and burned him in effigy at Tower Hill. The inept and miscalculated secret operation to bring him home in the face of such "deliberate misrepresentations" in "certain newspapers" only stoked suspicions about his "real" role in the RAF, as millions watched the homecoming on cinema newsreels. While the autocratic Indian government cracked down on the press there, in Britain the fiery Indian Communist Shapurji Saklatvala informed Parliament that the "mysterious way" in which Lawrence had been whisked away had given currency to a further report that "the real Col. Lawrence was still there and that someone else had been brought here." Even exiled to technical craft, he remained dogged by suspicion. The *Sunday Chronicle* pointed to his work on RAF speedboats as "the real secret reason" for his presence in the ranks: the "uncrowned king of Arabia, now uncrowned king of speed." He was the man "to whose steely brain the most abstruse problems of speed, in air or water, are referred...the ultimate government testing shop." (Protests at the Air Ministry resulted in his reassignment to normal duties at Plymouth.) The following year saw Edward Thompson correcting an American author's statements that Lawrence was in command at Baghdad. Indeed, Lawrence and the Arab Revolt became such celebrated yet sensitive subjects that Alexander

Korda's persistent efforts to make a film about them in the 1930s failed primarily because of the government's insistence on shaping—censoring—the screenplay. Philby's shifting status posed an equal problem. When he attempted to go to Najd to mediate between Ibn Saud and Hussein *as a private individual* just after leaving government service in 1924, the Middle East Department could only futilely contradict press statements that he was going as a government agent, for precisely such private and unofficial relationships had been the mainstay of official interactions with Arabian potentates in the past. Their démentis were considered newsworthy only in the *Guardian*. Misgivings about oil interests were likewise bound up with concern about unchecked agents. Besides raising questions about Lawrence, Thurtle voiced the suspicion that the "real reason" behind the government's insistence on including Mosul in Iraq was oil, given that the province was conquered only *after* the armistice, at Arnold Wilson's special insistence. "There is some kind of connection between these things," he deduced, especially since, after his retirement, Wilson became "General Manager of the A. P. O. C. [Anglo-Persian Oil Company] for the Persia and Mesopotamia area." The old trust in public servants crumbled as the legends around the agents produced the image of a new type of public servant, more heroic but also practiced in deception. The Mesopotamia veteran and critic of empire Geoffrey Garratt wrote to the *Times* amplifying that paper's concerns about Wilson's unseemly employment.[57]

In short, the long tradition of mixing administration and intelligence-gathering in the region made it impossible to rule out their mixing wherever the agents went. Even official denials were suspected as the agents' handiwork; awareness of their sway extended to an awareness that, for instance, "many officers [from Iraq] write letters to the newspapers trying to prove that Mesopotamia is indeed a blessed word." This conviction was central to doubts about the practicality of a project of enlightened public opinion.[58] With the help of such ne'er-do-wells (plus equally unaccountable aircraft), some postwar citizens protesting their new, sophisticated immunity from the jingoistic propaganda of the past feared the state might disregard their competing vision of Britain's real interests and continue hell-bent on its scheme to reap the benefits of a Middle Eastern empire.

Despite the shadow their skeptical state and many of its trepidatious citizens cast over their work, most agents unflappably continued to see their work as the unimpeachable discharge of the obligations of a mandatory power, unsullied either by its covert nature or by the subtle merging of imperial interests with the obligations to the mandate. Jarvis, who, as I mentioned, together with Peake, ran the region between Beersheba and Akaba as a "quite unrecognized mandate," found it "amusing" that whenever British troops were compelled to step in to maintain order in the Middle East, the three constituencies at stake—"all the inhabitants of the State in question...all foreign governments, and...the British public"—immediately jumped to the conclusion "that the British Representative on the spot has connived at and instigated the move."[59] Whitehall's incredulity in the face of foreign and Iraqi paranoia about British activity in the region was replicated on the ground by agents' almost disarming bafflement at their persecution by the people, the state, and the enemy.

The memoirs of the Great War—from Lawrence to Sassoon—tell a collective story of disillusionment and betrayal, we know; they construct the war as an avoidable folly caused by the blindness of statesmen and the stupidity of generals.[60] After the war, the Mesopotamian rebellion not only renewed this sense of disillusionment but stoked suspicions that the statesmen and generals were not so much blind and stupid as incorrigibly imperialist. The assumption of a hidden reality behind the façade of democratic government was a feature of the public's efforts to understand the state's activities in the Middle East and a reality produced by the state's effort to understand and hold the Middle East. The public's assertion of "knowingness" about the state's secret activities and agenda were part of the new self-consciousness (and skepticism) about democratic politics after the war revealed, and considerably swelled, the leviathan power of that state. The covert empire was found out but was, after all, covert enough—and the press mistrusted enough—that no one could build an *accurate* case against it. As the newly broadened public sphere attempted to surveil the state, it too became subject to state invigilation. Middle Eastern conspiracy did, in this sense, spill over into Britain.

Skepticism about official news and the press, which Paul Fussell has so memorably described, certainly had roots older than the war, but this epistemological tendency, grounded in a more malevolent vision of the state than ever before, found especially rigorous favor when the Great War drove the word "improbable" from "our vocabulary," as John Buchan wrote at the start of *Greenmantle*. Unimaginable things happened daily, and "coincidence... stretches a hundred long arms hourly across the earth." Among the unimaginable things most on Buchan's mind were the events and characters surrounding the Middle Eastern campaigns—part of the "revolt against reality" that disfigured interwar Europe. The possibilities revealed by those storied wars continued to haunt postwar Britons attempting to come to grips with their new democracy; whether on the Right or the Left, they could never again be sure that things were as they seemed, and in their vicissitudinous imaginations, Semites and Arabia more generally figured both positively and negatively. If the campaigns safeguarded the British culture of adventure, that culture's survival was something like what Adorno and Horkheimer would soon call a translation of myth into a novel, a process that swept myth into time, "conceal-ing the abyss that separates it from homeland and expiation." Redemption and unease mingled together in the cultural legacy of the British wars in and occu-pation of the Middle East. If Britons went to the Middle East to soothe the mod-ern homesickness for nomadic life, they were ultimately there as invaders and conquerors; even if they had found utopia, they could never feel at home.[61]

Conclusion

Official Secrecy is not a way of denying us honest information. It is a way of selling us pre-packaged decisions.

—E. P. Thompson, 1979

All Members of this House and all the people of this country have a shared interest in building trust in our democracy. And it is my hope that, by working together for change...we can agree a new British constitutional settlement that entrusts more power to Parliament and the British people.... On the grave issue of peace and war it is ultimately this House of Commons that will make the decision.... We must give new life to the very idea of citizenship itself.

—Prime Minister Gordon Brown, House of Commons, July 3, 2007

Stanley Baldwin famously called the devaluation of the pound in 1931 the "acid test of democracy." Then too fearmongers deftly conjured an atmosphere of impending crisis to shore up the government, in that case the democratically elected National Government asking for a "blank cheque" to pursue antidemocratic measures—triggering a fresh tide of public speculation about government and bank conspiracies.[1] Notwithstanding Baldwin's assessment of the moment, in fact the postwar democracy had been more or less under audit since its inception, as many Britons grappled for evidence that they could in fact exert some control over what their government did, cutting their teeth on the matter of the Middle Eastern mandates.

If we were to think, for a moment, like political scientists, the story of that struggle might at first seem to deliver a rather dismal verdict on the potential for true democracy. However, leaving aside even the historian's protest that this is the story of a particular democracy at a particular moment in its historical evolution, in fact it can be read simply as a cautionary tale about the true meaning of democratic oversight of the state. If the uncouth masses scrambling all over the British state's private domain, rifling through its papers, poking their noses where they had no business, inspired interwar state officials and ministers to sweep ever more secrets under the magic carpet of aerial control, they also continued to force those officials to account. Indeed, in the 1930s they seemed to be acquitting themselves credibly enough, compared to the squalid fascist democracies on the Continent, to earn the regard of the elitist British Left, who began to experiment with new ways of documenting and educating public opinion—the recuperative project to which we owe much of our forgetfulness about British militarism.[2] Despite British democracy's failure to check the state's activity in the Middle East (and we must be clear on its objective—it was against secret, excessively brutal and costly empire, not against empire itself, even though the cheap and peaceful empire of its fantasy was, in fact, fantasy), British democracy was not a sham so much as a constant work in progress, as perhaps democracy must be—ever on its guard, ever vigilant, ever straining after that elusive goal of "enlightened public opinion," lest it lapse into a populist rubber stamp for the state's misadventures. It is not a set of institutions whose well-oiled machinery of checks and balances, once in place, eternally guarantees the voice of the people is heard. It is an active, embattled, *investigative* cultural and political posture. Perhaps its muscularity, its articulateness, even its ability to see, are more secure when it takes to the streets.

I certainly should not be one to say: as the author of this book, I am stuck in the moment inaugurated by Edward Thompson, whose postwar disillusionment produced his passionate faith in the historian's craft as the most effective means of truth-telling against the government. Thompson's son Frank died while serving in Middle Eastern intelligence in World War Two, but his ideas certainly shaped the career of his other son, Edward P. Thompson, who served in North Africa and grew up, as he later recalled, "expecting governments to be mendacious and imperialist and expecting that one's stance ought to be hostile to government." It was in this mood that he began to build on early-twentieth-century social investigatory practices to open up history's narrow prospect of the state and the Great and reveal the unwashed masses on the horizon in their full human complexity. Indeed, he wrote *The Making of the English Working*

Class (1963) while helping to launch the Campaign for Nuclear Disarmament (1958–1963) which protested the autocratic decision-making about nuclear armament as much as the weapons themselves. As his writings during the revived campaign of 1979–1981 make clear, he saw the historic libertarian tradition of radical and working-class groups as the only force capable of checking the excesses of the "secret state" that had emerged in twentieth-century Britain and, at the same time, as the ironic source of that state's peculiar invisibility and lack of accountability: their very unpopularity had forced security and policing agencies into the "lowest possible visibility" and encouraged them to develop "techniques of invisible influence and control." They had adapted, he explained, by drawing on the corrosive ideology and experiences of those who had invigilated subversives and engaged in measures of "pacification" in the "external empire," thanks to the intense "inter-recruitment, cross-postings and exchange" between the realms of imperial and domestic policing. This was "the world of a John Buchan novel."[3] If E. P. Thompson looked for redemption in the lost voices of stockingers, weavers, and artisans, this book, alas, is not so heroic in its aspirations. Its characters are largely the personnel of the state, although I have tried to embed them fully in the social and cultural world with which they—and, through them, the state—remained integrated. It is a new kind of history of an old historical subject. Then too, long as the shadow of the elder Thompson is, we have come to realize history's own shortcomings as a means of truth-telling and the inadequacy of the very notion of objective truth. The truth, as far as the historian's craft is concerned, is something of a mirage; the work of history, a fictional account of facts, facts gathered carefully from the inscrutable mess of the past and handwoven into an intelligible story, not neutrally, of course; the warp of facts is made whole by the weft of politics. Dare I say it: a small knowledge in harmony with itself.

I chose to assemble a small knowledge about the British Middle East because it seemed to me a gaping hole at the heart of our understanding of the British Empire in the twentieth century. But to interwar Britons, its importance was, as we have seen, painfully obvious. It is no surprise that they made it the testing ground of the authenticity of their democracy; it was already the testing ground of empire against empire, of the RAF against colonial insurgency, of faith against reason, of language against the sublime, of man against nature, of intuition against the inscrutable, of the imagination against the void, of myth against reality. It was the natural site for pitting the fantasy of carefree covert empire against the reality of imperial conscience. Perhaps historians' neglect of the Middle Eastern empire is largely a function of the fact that it is simply harder to write about—and grasp the importance of—covert empire. Indeed, we are still endlessly proving the importance of *formal* empire to Britain's history and even whether empire is such a bad thing. These self-servingly mis-placed debates betray our enduring preoccupation with soothing Britain's conscience rather than with addressing the political, economic, institutional, social, and cultural distortions and iniquities that modern empire produced in the world, however good its intentions or glancing its economic and mass cultural impact at home in some minds.[4]

My discovery of the dilemmas of the unseeing state provided me with the key to understanding the origins of unseen empire, whose titanium sinews may not have registered by weight next to the full complement of traditional mechanisms of colonial control but which exerted as much if not greater force. The unseeing state was a state captive as much to the spiritual and cultural as the geopolitical imagination about the Middle East; its myopia and the compensatory practices it evolved were shaped by that imagination. So it happened that in wartime politically and militarily useful knowledge had to be extracted from an intelligence community committed to a mode of intelligence-gathering that prioritized intuition over evidence and romantic, quasi-military action over office work. Though the war in the Middle East seemed for a moment to fulfill all the striving after spiritual, cultural, and imperial redemption, those hopes quickly turned sour during the peace, as the Middle Eastern colonies turned against their would-be deliverers. Shaped by the agents' imagination and the public's gnawing curiosity about the land the agents had made famous, a new covert, brutal, and paranoid postwar imperial state emerged in the region, centered on the world's first regime of aerial surveillance and bombardment. The domain of cultural practices is indispensable to understanding its emergence, and the history of the intelligence and imperial project in the Middle East is equally critical to making sense of early-twentieth-century British literary, military, and political culture.

Many of the key intelligence agents in this story died during the period in question: Shakespear in cross-fire in 1915; Sykes from the Spanish flu in 1919; Bury from pulmonary trouble in 1920; Leachman and Mann in the rising of 1920; Soane of consumption in 1923; Herbert of blood poisoning the same year; Bell of a suicidal overdose in 1926; Hogarth of old age in 1927; likewise Clayton in 1929; and Lawrence, most famously and typically dramatically, in a motorcycle accident in 1935. The death knell was also eventually rung on the hope for development of Iraq. With no railway or irrigation project completed nearly a decade after the wartime occupation, "the brilliant chance which the British had of restoring an ancient country and opening up for the world a new agricultural belt would now appear to have been completely lost," wrote the theretofore patiently supportive Richard Coke. *The Tragedy of Mesopotamia* (1938), George Buchanan's bitter book-length amplification of his series in the

Times years before, encapsulated the idea of hopes and promises betrayed, "a tragedy of heroism, suffering, wasted lives, and wasted effort."[5]

And thus our story comes to an end, or at least at first glance, for many members of this ensemble cast remained on the scene through World War Two, including Arnold Wilson, Stirling, Meinertzhagen, Iltyd Clayton, Dickson, and others. (Certainly, not everyone was fully reinstated: Philby was imprisoned as a Nazi sympathizer (only briefly, thanks to the intercession of George Lloyd), and the toxic Bray was refused permission to join Middle Eastern intelligence). We have already seen the continuities in Middle East intelligence-gathering in chapter 8. But more than this, the romance of the Middle East campaigns of World War One profoundly influenced the aerial, desert, partisan, and deception operations of World War Two, and the outlook of the generation that fought it. Graham Dawson writes, "After 1918—and especially after 1940—the imaginative resonance of the colonial periphery becomes condensed with that of the occupied territory.... A direct line runs from Lawrence to the Second World War." For at least one British boy, a chance encounter with the relatively modest figure of "Stirling the Wise" en route to the Balkans on "highly clandestine matters" virtually defined the war. Just as the legitimizing discourses about air control were reproduced during the bombardment of Germany, the "specific psychic charge" of adventure located in colonial imaginative geography "was displaced into the universal struggle for Good against Evil in the war against Nazism and Fascism." In the "People's War," being amateur was a source of pride; Special Operations Executive (SOE) recruits found in John Buchan's heroes and Lawrence a model for what they might become (indeed, some were direct descendants of the first generation, including Orde Wingate of Burma fame, who had earlier achieved renown for his invention of the Special Night Squads in 1937 in Palestine, and Ronald Wingate, himself formerly of the Mesopotamia Political Department, who helped coordinate worldwide deception operations from London). And, as ever, such agents aroused fears of covert imperial designs, for the resistance groups they helped also saw "the average SOE officer as a would-be Lawrence of Arabia," that is, " 'the perfidious arrogant champion of an Empire,' " in the words of the Yugoslavian Partisan and dissident Milovan Djilas. The legends surrounding such agents shaped what one scholar calls "the Great Game element of SIS mythology," the British spy's awkward combination of adventurous action with discreet information-gathering. That spies exist may be inevitable, but the modern British spy did not have to emerge the way he did; his style and mode of operation are historically contingent, and the Edwardian moment in which he discovered Arabia was crucial to his subsequent evolution.[6]

Indeed, if the British were long in leaving the Middle East (chapters 7 and 8), the fascination with Arabia was even longer in leaving Britain. In the 1950s, travelers such as Wilfred Thesiger continued, if more self-consciously, to venture to the region in search of escape into a mythical place untouched by motorcars, aircraft, and the bureaucratic state (without, it seems, noting the irony).[7] But the agents' representativeness as "spy's spies" is perhaps most evident in the, at first sight, uncanny connections between them and the Cambridge Five of the Cold War: Philby's son Kim I have already mentioned. The Soviets recruited him just when his father was brokering the negotiations that led to the Saudi concession to Standard Oil in 1933; they hired him partly to keep tabs on the elder Philby who they continued to believe was a powerful British secret agent (despite his travailed relations with his government—after all, he *was* powerful enough to abet America's rise in the peninsula). It was an old member of the Middle East intelligence community, Colonel Vivian, who, as the head of MI6's counterespionage unit during World War Two, first approached Kim for recruitment to that organization. Naturally, he did so by arranging a luncheon with his old friend St. John Philby just after the latter was released from detention. Of course, Kim himself had passed much of his childhood in the Middle East and would serve there as well. In 1956, after he had already fallen under suspicion as a double agent and in the midst of the events that would precipitate the infamous Suez Crisis, he was sent under cover as a journalist in Lebanon, living with his father, who had been exiled from Saudi Arabia after quarreling with the new king. (By then, like his son, he too had fully embraced Soviet communism, but openly.) It was largely as his father's son that his expertise was sought out during the critical circumstances surrounding the U. S. intervention in Lebanon and the Iraqi revolution of 1958. After St. John Philby's death in 1960, the bereft Kim spiraled into a life of heavy drinking and increasingly erratic behavior until his flight from Beirut to Moscow in 1963.[8] But besides Kim Philby's obvious links to the older Middle East intelligence community, there was also Anthony Blunt, a cousin of Sir Wilfrid, and John Cairncross, who is likely a descendant of the wartime spy in Mesopotamia of the same name—his autobiography at least traces his adult tastes to a childhood fascination with the *Arabian Nights*. Now, among the spies whose careers Kim Philby destroyed was David Cornwell, who then poured his imaginative energy into his career as spy novelist John Le Carré, famous for a brisk style disciplined by years of field reporting (the Foreign Office's aesthetic had apparently evolved). Kim Philby, whose very name and life were inspired by fiction, provided the model for his most famous fictional mole, Bill Haydon of *Tinker, Tailor, Soldier, Spy* (1974), a "latter-day Lawrence of Arabia" whose favorite prewar "stamping-ground" had been the Middle East. As an Oxford student, Haydon had had a taste for eavesdropping, or, as he puts it, liked "now and then to put on Arab costume and go down to the bazaars." During the war his methods had been "unorthodox and occasionally outrageous" and, Le Carré's phlegmatic protagonist George Smiley concedes, "probably heroic." He is besides an amateur artist, whose subjects include deserts and Damascus. Ultimately, his betrayal stems from his perception of a glorious Englishness betrayed and his hatred for the materialism and greed of the West. To Le Carré too, then, the transgressions of Cold War moles seemed to do as much with nostalgia for the unorthodox atmosphere of Arabia intelligence as with sympathy for the Soviet Union (which in any case, as we have seen, tended to shade into the Middle East), particularly after the geographical transpositions inaugurated by World War Two had reinscribed the fight between Good and Evil as the Cold War between East and West.[9]

Indeed, perhaps the story has no end, as I suggested at the start of this book; a feature of covert empire is its capacity to go on right under our very noses. The pressures of the Edwardian moment—both cultural and geopolitical—generated ideologies and practices that continue to shape the modern world. The story is cosmopolitan in its unending fallout. The Marines in charge of the U.S. occupation of Haiti in the very period covered by this book were also inspired by legends of Lawrence. The memoir of one captain, John Houston Craige, was, significantly, titled *Black Bagdad*.[10] Lawrence's legend also influenced the use of commando forces by the Abwehr, the German intelligence organization from the 1920s through the war; and his legend and the practical work of other British agents have furthered the United States' increasing domination of the Middle East. As Standard Oil's power grew in Saudi Arabia, so too did St. John Philby's usefulness to it, as one of the few sources the company and the CIA could turn to for authoritative knowledge about the region, obligingly tailored to their tastes. The CIA's Middle East section would eventually depend heavily on the American "Kim," Kermit Roosevelt Jr., son of another famous Mesopotamia veteran and grandson of Theodore Roosevelt. The elder Kermit's reckless heroism as a British Army captain in Mesopotamia fetched a typically wretched end in alcoholism and, ultimately, suicide in Alaska during World War Two, but "Kim" Roosevelt went on to mastermind the CIA's postwar pièce de resistance, the joint British-American Operation Ajax against Iranian Prime Minister Mohammed Mossadegh in 1953. Through such ties and collaboration, the CIA quickly learned the business of shaping the production of cultural knowledge about the Middle East as it embarked on unending covert activity in the region—following close on the heels of the RAF when it departed Iraq in 1958. The RAF departure was part of the Iraqi revolution against the ever-compromised Iraqi monarchy and premiership of Nuri al-Said; two years later the CIA made its first attempt to assassinate the new republic's president, Abd al-Karim Qasim, succeeding in bringing him down in 1963 by assisting a Baathist coup. Lawrence's work remains part of the curriculum at the Special Warfare Center in Fort Bragg where it is seen as critical instruction for American Special Forces' relations with "native" guerrillas. Today, his book and Callwell's *Small Wars* are daily consulted by British and American counterinsurgency operations in Iraq (excerpts are even e-mailed directly to officers in the field), and the difficulties of counterinsurgency are enunciated in terms of peculiarities of the place—the lack of addresses, maps, street names, the consequent importance of immersion and disguise and meeting cunning with cunning, and the dovetailing between all intelligence work and special operations.[11] Fittingly, 2005 saw the issue of the original, 1922 version of *Seven Pillars of Wisdom*. Besides the nomad's continued challenge to imperial states, conceptually too his defiance and state appropriation of "nomad science" remain central to our understanding of the modern state via the work of Bergson's philosophical heirs, Gilles Deleuze and Felix Guattari.[12] And then, of course, there is the discipline of history itself.

The interwar agents' fractious relationship to their state is echoed in our contemplations about true patriotism in the midst of the latest attempt to "liberate" Iraq. In the listless post–Cold War intelligence world of Le Carré's recent *Absolute Friends* (2003), the shared anti-imperialism of two renegade spies incites the wrath of the United States. Both spies are cut from a familiar cloth: Ted Mundy, born in the field of the Great Game (newly christened Pakistan), imagines his MI6 "family" as "descendants of the classic school of Arabian explorer, crossing the Empty Quarter by camel with nothing but the stars"; and Sasha, his Eastern European comrade, learns how to be a double agent during long wanderings through the Middle East and extended reveries about guerrilla tactics.[13] As their tale exemplifies, the Middle East has reemerged as the site of the confrontation between Good and Evil, and real-life commentators now borrow liberally from a World War Two and Cold War vocabulary of gulags, fascism, and totalitarianism, just as Saddam Hussein, if not Osama bin Laden and Mullah Omar, borrowed practices.[14] The romance with Arabia that colors the history and historiography of British intelligence in the Middle East is also easily identifiable in much that passes for critical commentary today.[15] The Middle East remains the special terrain for battling agents, as much for Westerners as for Middle Easterners who have lived through decades of special operations and proxy warfare. In his recent memoir, the CIA agent Robert Baer describes with an air of exasperation the "Iraqi belief that dark, unseen forces ran the world and history could be reduced to a series of conspiracies, interconnected by an overarching design known to only a few.... Imperialism couldn't work any other way." A few pages above, however, he writes in the course of describing his (unauthorized) mission to Lebanon during the 1984 hostage crisis: "Everything in the Middle East is interconnected. Pull on one thread and a dozen more will come up." Understanding this region, he urges, requires investment in traditional human intelligence, "people on the ground...a network of traitors, and a case officer willing and able to work it." Bafflement at Iraqi paranoia is, well, baffling, in the face of all this. The wages of covert empire.[16]

Indeed, as I write, the United States, self-consciously repeating British debates from the years after the Great War, is reconfiguring its own imperial identity in the wake of conquest of Iraq, while many Britons are seized by the sense that we have been here before and that they must make their experience—both historical and military, spun both positively and negatively—available to the new, somewhat unsophisticated, swashbuckling imperial power in the region. Intimations of the pride that comes before the fall draw in equal measure from Kipling and the example of ancient Mesopotamia.[17] Here and in Britain, fear of global conspiracy has resulted in paranoia and surveillance at home and renewed suspicion about the covert activity of the state. When Marx said, "History repeats itself, first as tragedy, then as farce," he was underscoring the notion that history cannot in fact repeat itself, that it is always developing, dialectically. The United States is not repeating, coincidentally or unwittingly, what Britain did in Iraq decades ago; those events produced what Foucault might call the episteme, the conditions of possibility—the moral geography?—for what is happening today. To this Marx might offer the correction, and I would agree, that those conditions of possibility were material as much as epistemological.

Notes

ABBREVIATIONS

BL   British Library, London
IOR   India Office Records
JCAS   *Journal of the Central Asian Society*
JRUSI   *Journal of the Royal United Service Institute*
LHCMA   Liddell Hart Centre for Military Archives, King's College,
          London
LCLUL   Liddle Collection, Leeds University Library
MECA   Middle East Centre Archive, St. Antony's College, Oxford
          University
NAM   National Army Museum, London
TLS   *Times Literary Supplement*

INTRODUCTION

1. On modern states' knowledge-gathering practices, see James Scott, *Seeing Like a State*. On Burke's complex universalism, see Nicholas Dirks, *Scandal of Empire*.

2. Existing literature, which is generally anecdotal (and deeply error-ridden) suffers from this fascination. See H. V. F. Winstone, *The Illicit Adventure: The Story of Political and Military Intelligence in the Middle East from 1898 to 1926*; Peter Morris, "Intelligence and its Interpretation: Mesopotamia 1914–16," 77–79; Richard Popplewell, "British Intelligence in Mesopotamia, 1914–1916," 141; Bruce Westrate, *The Arab Bureau: British Policy in the Middle East, 1916–1920*; and a bevy of biographies of individual agents cited throughout. Their intellectual continuity with the cultural

products of the period itself is perhaps most evident from the fact that Winstone co-edited a book (*The Road to Kabul: An Anthology*) with one of the more prolific special service officers in Iraq, Gerald de Gaury. The one exception to this trend is Yigal Sheffy's highly precise *British Military Intelligence in the Palestine Campaign, 1914–1918*.

3. The important role of non-Britons, such as Arab and Turkish officials and elites, Muslim vice-consuls and pilgrims, "native agents," and Arab guides, in this information order must be left to a future scholar.

4. The actual experiences of Arabs caught in this web of surveillance have not, to my knowledge, been described at any length and seem a pressing topic for examination by a Middle East historian.

5. This argument differs from Kathryn Tidrick's interesting argument, grounded in the nineteenth century, that Britons felt that a suppressed racial affinity or intrinsic similarity endowed them with miraculous insight into Arab affairs. Tidrick sees this confidence as the foundation of the British ability to *refrain* from violence in the region (*Heart-Beguiling Araby*, 208). The importance of intuition in the period I am talking about also raises interesting questions about gender—Lawrence's "virility," for instance, was said to be mingled with a "woman's sensibility" (H. St. John Philby, quoted in Robert Kaplan, *The Arabists: The Romance of an American Elite*, 51). However, his amply dissected and complex sexuality did not necessarily detract from the type of imperial heroic masculinity he seemed to embody or from the fascination with the desert as a space for manly men. See biographies cited throughout and Graham Dawson, *Soldier Heroes: British Adventure, Empire, and the Imagining of Masculinities*. The key female member of this intelligence community, Gertrude Bell, followed in a line of aristocratic women travelers in the desert, explicitly bucking bourgeois, Victorian gender stereotypes. See Billie Melman, *Women's Orients: English Women and the Middle East, 1718–1918*, which, however, excludes Bell as an already well-studied figure (21).

6. J. Scott, *Seeing Like a State*. This regime, particularly its interest in cultivating local knowledge, was shaped by the very cultural moment that saw the emergence of the critique of universalist rationalism at the heart of Scott's work.

7. In the Foreign Office papers, intelligence files on the Middle East were filed under different headings from similar files on Europe and elsewhere. On British empiricism in other areas, see Nicholas Dirks, *Castes of Mind: Colonialism and the Making of Modern India*, 44; Roslynn Haynes, *Seeking the Centre: The Australian Desert in Literature, Art and Film*, 60–61, 70; Johannes Fabian, *Out of Our Minds: Reason and Madness in the Exploration of Central Africa*; and G. E. Fogg, *A History of Antarctic Science* (I thank Peder Roberts for the last). Of these, Fabian's mad explorers were perhaps most akin to the agents in this book; however, their state of "ecstasis" was neither nonrational nor escapist and did not interfere with their commitment to empiricism, however meager their actual accomplishments (8, 181–89). (I am also skeptical about Fabian's claims about the understanding and nonviolent state power produced by this mode.)

8. KV 1/4: "Intelligence Methods in Peace Time," 1909.

9. Lawrence to Sykes, 1917, quoted in Jeremy Wilson, *Lawrence of Arabia: The Authorised Biography of T. E. Lawrence*, 443; Westrate, *Arab Bureau*, 76; Edward Said,

Orientalism, 225. The French presence in the period between the Entente and the war was also small compared to the others. The spies at the center of Michael Miller, *Shanghai on the Métro: Spies, Intrigue, and the French between the Wars* were in the Far East.

10. See, for instance, the following surveys of the literature in the *Oxford History of the British Empire*: Peter Sluglett, "Formal and Informal Empire in the Middle East"; Francis Robinson, "The Muslim World and the British Empire," 407; Glen Balfour-Paul, "Britain's Informal Empire in the Middle East." The qualities that set the Middle Eastern empire apart from the paradigmatic sites of indirect rule—sub-Saharan Africa and princely India—have not been much considered. See, for instance, John Cell, "Colonial Rule," and Ronald Hyam, "Bureaucracy and 'Trusteeship' in Colonial Empire."

11. This is the argument recently put forward in Toby Dodge, *Inventing Iraq: The Failure of Nation Building and a History Denied*, 1–2. The Great War alone prevented such easy continuity, although, curiously, Dodge does not connect his story to that event. Even more curiously, after recounting the history of misguided liberal empire in Iraq, he urges greater and longer-term American control of the country, equating this with "international oversight" (170). Sadly, D. K. Fieldhouse, after assessing the selfish motives and failures of Britain's rule in Iraq, similarly concludes that Iraqis were victims of too little imperialism—if only Britain had committed to having "something like the impact [they] had...in British India or Ceylon" (*Western Imperialism in the Middle East, 1914–1958*, 115).

12. On the cultural legacy of the war, see paradigmatically Paul Fussell, *The Great War and Modern Memory*. Others have argued that other fronts have simply not entered the "myth" of the war in the same way as they did in the Second World War (Samuel Hynes, *A Soldier's Tale: Bearing Witness to Modern War*, 116; Eitan Bar-Yosef, "The Last Crusade? British Propaganda and the Palestine Campaign, 1917–18," 108). This singularity of myth is, I think, more ours than postwar Britons': witness the entwining of the Lawrence and Western front myths in Robert Graves's *Good-bye to All That* (1929) and the centrality of the myth of the air and desert wars in the prosecution of World War Two, cited by Hynes himself. On the limits of the cultural rupture posited by Fussell, see also Jay Winter, *Sites of Memory, Sites of Mourning: The Great War in European Cultural History*, 2–5; Michael Paris, *Warrior Nation: Images of War in British Popular Culture, 1850–2000*, 151–85; John Mackenzie, *Propaganda and Empire: The Manipulation of Public Opinion, 1880–1960*, 256; and Janet S. K. Watson, *Fighting Different Wars: Experience, Memory, and the First World War in Britain*. Paris points particularly to the role of imagery of the air and Middle Eastern wars in preserving the romantic image of war. On the "intellectually arid" diplomatic preoccupations of historiography on twentieth-century British imperialism in the Middle East, see Sluglett, "Formal and Informal Empire," 422.

13. Steven Pierce, *Farmers and the State in Colonial Kano*, 7.

14. Existing literature dates the developmental turn to World War Two (and primarily in sub-Saharan Africa). See Frederick Cooper, "Modernizing Bureaucrats, Backward Africans, and the Development Concept," 70; Frederick Cooper and Randall Packard, introduction to *International Development and the Social Sciences*, 7; Stephen

Constantine, *The Making of British Colonial Development Policy, 1914–1940*, 303–04; Timothy Mitchell, *Rule of Experts: Egypt, Techno-Politics, Modernity*, 82–83.

15. The one acknowledged exception being the infamous "Protocols of the Elders of Zion," which Richard Thurlow puts down to "continental influences" ("The Powers of Darkness: Conspiracy Belief and Political Strategy," 2). I will have more to say about this apparent exception in chapter 9.

16. The meager historiography on British conspiracy thinking about the "Eastern Unrest" is narrow in scope and strictly expository in nature. See John Fisher, "The Defence of Britain's Eastern Empire after World War One: The Role of the Interdepartmental Committee on Eastern Unrest, 1922–1927," and "The Interdepartmental Committee on Eastern Unrest and British Responses to Bolshevik and Other Intrigues against the Empire during the 1920s"; A. L. Macfie, "British Intelligence and the Causes of Unrest in Mesopotamia, 1919–21"; and Aaron Klieman, *Foundations of British Policy in the Arab World: The Cairo Conference of 1921*, 57–58. Other secondary works take the conspiracies and conspiracy theories for granted: see, for instance, Winstone, *Illicit Adventure*; Peter Morris, "Intelligence and Its Interpretation," 89; David Fromkin, *A Peace to End All Peace: Creating the Modern Middle East, 1914–1922*, 416 passim. Like Macfie, John Ferris claims conspiracy thinking was overwhelmingly without practical effect and ended in 1922 (*The Evolution of British Strategic Policy, 1919–26*, 41–43).

17. See David Vincent, *The Culture of Secrecy: Britain, 1832–1998*; Richard Thurlow, *The Secret State: British Internal Security in the Twentieth Century*; and Bernard Porter, *Plots and Paranoia: A History of Political Espionage in Britain, 1790–1988*. On working-class suspicions of the state, see Patrick Joyce, *Visions of the People: Industrial England and the Question of Class, 1848–1914*, 71–76. Such a view can be traced even earlier, as, for instance, in Peter Lake, "Buckingham Does the Globe: Shakespeare's Henry VIII and the Origins of the Personal Rule," lecture at Stanford University, 12 April 2007. I am arguing here for the entanglement of colonial and metropolitan history, but I am not invested in the idea that British history was always written abroad, in the empire: for instance, I do not argue that the covert empire in the Middle East alone inspired the critique of state secrecy but that we can understand better the context and significance of that critique by attending to the way the Middle East figured in it.

18. On the struggle for democratic control of foreign policy, see Gordon Craig and Felix Gilbert, "Introduction," in *The Diplomats: Volume 1: The Twenties*, 5–6. The emergence of a broader critique of state secrecy as part of this movement has not been much noted—David Vincent briefly mentions such a critique, albeit one focused narrowly on secret diplomacy (*Culture of Secrecy*, 177–80), but the phrase does not even appear in standard histories of anti-imperialism, including Nicholas Owen, "Critics of Empire in Britain"; A. P. Thornton, *The Imperial Idea and Its Enemies*; Stephen Howe, *Anticolonialism in British Politics*, chap. 2; and Paul Rich, *Race and Empire in British Politics*, chap. 4.

19. Cultural history of military institutions of the imperial state (if not intelligence practices) is of course not new—see, for instance, the rich work on "martial race" theory and the Indian Army, including, most recently, Gavin Rand,

"Martial Races and Imperial Subjects: Violence and Governance in Colonial India 1857–1914"; and Heather Streets, *Martial Races: The Military, Race, and Masculinity in British Imperial Culture, 1857–1914.*

20. Said, *Orientalism*, 273. For a similar view of culture and violence, see Mary Renda, *Taking Haiti: Military Occupation and the Culture of U. S. Imperialism, 1915–1940.* My approach differs from C. A. Bayly's in *Empire and Information: Intelligence Gathering and Social Communication in India, 1780–1870,* which does not allot the orientalist vision a productive role in the elaboration of state intelligence practices, taking knowledge as something objective and neutral rather than culturally constructed. For a good discussion of the divergences between Bayly's and Said's work, see Dirks, *Castes of Mind*, 303–15. Existing literature on the air control regime in Iraq is primarily concerned with its efficacy as a policing technique and an incubus for the fledgling RAF. See David Omissi, *Air Power and Colonial Control*; Elmer B. Scovill, "The RAF and the Desert Frontiers of Iraq, 1919–1930"; and Jafna Cox, "'A Splendid Training Ground': The Importance to the Royal Air Force of Its Role in Iraq, 1919–32." Works that examine air control's darker side: Charles Townshend, "Civilization and 'Frightfulness': Air Control in the Middle East between the Wars"; Sven Lindqvist, *A History of Bombing*, 42–43; and Dodge, *Inventing Iraq*, chap. 7.

21. Mark Mazower, "Violence and the State in the Twentieth Century"; Hew Strachan, "Total War in the Twentieth Century"; Isabel Hull, *Absolute Destruction: Military Culture and the Practices of War in Imperial Germany*; Caroline Elkins, *Imperial Reckoning: The Untold Story of Britain's Gulag in Kenya*; and A. Dirk Moses, "Conceptual Blockages and Definitional Dilemmas in the 'Racial Century': Genocides of Indigenous Peoples and the Holocaust."

22. Hannah Arendt, *Imperialism: Part Two of "The Origins of Totalitarianism,"* 101.

23. See, for instance, many of the academic reviews of Elkins, *Imperial Reckoning.*

24. See Richard Price, "Is Bernard Porter's *Absent-Minded Imperialists* Useful for the Study of Empire and British National Culture?"; Dirks, *Scandal of Empire*; T. Mitchell, *Rule of Experts*, chap. 2. More generally, on the rule of law and the colonial state, see the debate launched in E. P. Thompson, *Whigs and Hunters: The Origins of the Black Act,* epilogue; and Ranajit Guha, *Dominance without Hegemony: History and Power in Colonial India,* esp. 66–69. For a recent analysis of this debate, see also Lauren Benton, *Law and Colonial Cultures: Legal Regimes in World History, 1400–1900,* chap. 7.

25. David Edgerton, *Warfare State*, esp. 210, 276, 304; Jon Lawrence, "Forging a Peaceable Kingdom: War, Violence, and Fear of Brutalization in Post–First World War Britain." For an exemplar of the endurance of the myth of special British skill in counterinsurgency, see Thomas Mockaitis, *British Counterinsurgency, 1919–60.* See also the writings of Niall Ferguson, which schizophrenically praise both the Pax Britannica *and* British imperialists' willingness to use force unsqueamishly.

26. T. E. Lawrence, *The Seven Pillars of Wisdom*, 23. Much scholarly ink has been spilt in determining how much credit for the Arab Revolt is really due him and how much he seized by a clever wielding of his own pen. See John Mack, *A Prince of Our Disorder: The Life of T. E. Lawrence*, 177–86. See Lt.-Col. W. F. Stirling, *Safety Last*, 84–85, for a contemporary response to Lawrence's detractors.

27. Yigal Sheffy, "British Intelligence in the Middle East, 1900–1918: How Much Do We Know?" Sheffy argues that the situation changed radically when formal agencies were created during the war, but one of my arguments is that even they functioned in a strikingly ad hoc manner, leaving an equally patchy paper trail. See also, in general, Wesley Wark, "In Never-Never Land? The British Archives on Intelligence."

28. On the contingency (if not the historical evolution) of the "secrecy" of intelligence work and the activities it comprises, see Len Scott, "Secret Intelligence, Covert Action, and Clandestine Diplomacy."

29. FO 371/353: 22035: General Staff, "Notes on Arabia," June 1907; Robert Graves, *Lawrence and the Arabs*, 59–60; CO 732/6: 22018: Anglo-Ottoman Society to David Lloyd George, 12 April 1922; Edmund Candler, *The Long Road to Baghdad*, 2:198; FO 371/2486: 188109: Mark Sykes to DMO, 15 Nov. 1915; Lawrence to Mrs. Rieder, March 1916, in *T. E. Lawrence: The Selected Letters*, 80; IOR: L/PS/10/586: Arabian Report, 1 March 1916; Mark Sykes, *The Caliph's Last Heritage: A Short History of the Turkish Empire*, 436; Aubrey Herbert, *Ben Kendim: A Record of Eastern Travel*, xiv; Keast Burke, ed., *With Horse and Morse in Mesopotamia: The Story of ANZACs in Asia*, 49; IOR: L/PS/20/E84/1: *A Handbook of Arabia*, Vol. 1, *General*, 9; David Hogarth, *Arabia*, 1; FO 882: Hogarth, "The Arab Bulletin," *Arab Bulletin* 100 (Aug. 1918), 275–77; Lawrence to his mother, 12 Feb. 1917, in *Selected Letters*, 105.

30. Tidrick, *Heart-Beguiling Araby*, 36–37. Certainly, much of what I argue about Iraq in the later sections can easily be extended to Egypt and Palestine through the early 1930s, but my focus is on the invention of certain surveillance strategies first applied in mandatory Iraq and their relationship to British ideas about "Arabia," an imaginary in which Egypt and Palestine—in the minds of Egyptians and Palestinians as much as Britons—were often marginal. Indeed, most Egyptian elites in the period under review did not consider their country Arab. See Israel Gershoni and James Jankowski, eds., *Rethinking Nationalism in the Arab Middle East*. I thank Joel Beinin for this reference.

31. Valentine Chirol, *The Middle Eastern Question, Or Some Political Problems of Indian Defence*, viii, 5. Mahan's coinage is disputed: a British intelligence officer in Persia, General T. E. Gordon, used the term in a similar sense in "The Problem of the Middle East," *Nineteenth Century* 47 (1900).

32. Angus Hamilton, *Problems of the Middle East*, xiii; Winston Churchill, *The Story of the Malakand Field Force*, 303; Gertrude Bell, Feb. 1905, quoted in Elizabeth Burgoyne, *Gertrude Bell: From Her Personal Papers*, 1:204; Sykes, 12 Aug. 1913, quoted in Shane Leslie, *Mark Sykes: His Life and Letters*, 202; David Hogarth, *The Nearer East*, 280–81. See also A. J. Plotke, *Imperial Spies Invade Russia: The British Intelligence Interventions, 1918*, 52.

33. On these changes, see Thomas Fergusson, *British Military Intelligence, 1870–1914*; Jock Haswell, *British Military Intelligence*, 61; B. A. H. Parritt, *The Intelligencers: The Story of British Military Intelligence up to 1914*, 189–221; Peter Gudgin, *Military Intelligence: The British Story*, 37; and John Ferris, "Before 'Room 40': The British Empire and Signals Intelligence, 1898–1914."

34. H. J. Mackinder, "The Geographical Pivot of History." On the lull in the Great Game, see Gerald Morgan, "Myth and Reality in the Great Game," 61.

35. General Staff, "Notes on Arabia"; IOR: L/PS/3/413: Townley to Landsowne, 14 Dec. 1904; FO 371/1008: 12174: J. G. Lorimer, Report on Events in February 1910 and 1909: Lorimer, Tour Journal no. 1 of 1910, 11 Feb. 1910. On Britain's secret diplomacy in the Gulf, see Frederick Anscombe, *The Ottoman Gulf: The Creation of Kuwait, Saudi Arabia, and Qatar, 1870–1914*. On the Taba affair, see Sheffy, *British Military Intelligence*, 12, 27. Historians now argue that the Ottoman Empire was in fact reconstructing itself in the Arab lands on the eve of the war. See, for instance, Fieldhouse, *Western Imperialism*, 19–20, 34.

36. David Hogarth, *The Penetration of Arabia: A Record of the Development of Western Knowledge concerning the Arabian Peninsula*, v–vi; Douglas Carruthers, *Arabian Adventure: To the Great Nafud in Quest of the Oryx*, 6–7. On the early, failed proposals, see IOR: L/PS/20/C91/1: J. G. Lorimer, ed., *Gazetteer of the Persian Gulf, Oman, and Central Arabia*, Vol. 1, *Historical*, 1157; FO 78/5488: Gaskin to Kemball, 7 Nov. 1903, Russell to Kemball, 6 Jan. 1904, IO to Government of India, draft telegram, 1904, and O'Conor to Landsowne, 26 Feb. 1904; FO 371/156: 37869: IO to Government of India, 9 Nov. 1906. Others remarking the lack of intelligence on the region: A. J. B. Wavell, *A Modern Pilgrim in Mecca and a Siege in Sanaa*, v–vi, 2; G. Wyman Bury, *The Land of Uz*, ix; "Turkey in Arabia," *Times*, 20 Aug. 1913; "The Situation in Arabia," *Times*, 2 Feb. 1912; IOR: L/PS/10/135: Edgerley to Secretary to Government of India in the Foreign Department, 9 March 1904, and Bury to Ritchie, 22 Nov. 09. See also Stuart Cohen, *British Policy in Mesopotamia, 1903–1914*, 68; H. V. F. Winstone, *Captain Shakespear*, 66.

37. Judith Walkowitz, *City of Dreadful Delight: Narratives of Sexual Danger in Late-Victorian London*, 20; Seth Koven, *Slumming: Sexual and Social Politics in Victorian London*, esp. 19, 61. On the entwined histories of the spy novel and the spy, see Christopher Andrew, *Her Majesty's Secret Service: The Making of the British Intelligence Community*, 34–58.

38. Walkowitz, *City of Dreadful Delight*, 33, 39. On Booth's (and subsequently Rowntree's) actual impressionism, see E. P. Hennock, "The Measurement of Urban Poverty: From the Metropolis to the Nation, 1880–1920." See also Raymond Kent, *A History of British Empirical Sociology*.

39. Sluglett, "Formal and Informal Empire," 419–20; A. T. Wilson, "Mesopotamia, 1914–1921," *JCAS* 8 (1921), 151. See also Keith Jeffrey, *The British Army and the Crisis of Empire, 1918–22*, 35; Daniel Yergin, *Prize: The Epic Quest for Oil, Money, and Power*; David Gillard, *The Struggle for Asia, 1828–1914: A Study in British and Russian Imperialism*; Marian Kent, *Oil and Empire: British Policy and Mesopotamian Oil, 1900–1920* and *Moguls and Mandarins: Oil, Imperialism and the Middle East in British Foreign Policy, 1900–1940*; Cohen, *Policy in Mesopotamia*, 253; Helmut Mejcher, *Imperial Quest for Oil: Iraq 1910–1928*; George E. Gruen, "The Oil Resources of Iraq: Their Role in the Policies of the Great Powers." Postwar oil prospecting in Iraq is largely a story of opportunities botched by corporate infighting. The Turkish Petroleum Company (a consortium of various European companies trying to submerge their rivalries in a single entity) finally obtained a concession based on prewar Turkish promises in 1925. Oil was discovered in Mosul in 1927 but was not developed until the 1930s because of conflicts between the consortium members

(renamed the Iraq Petroleum Company). Some postwar agents did report on illicit oil prospecting by Standard Oil and stray fortune hunters but do not seem to have engaged in prospecting themselves (except perhaps H. St. John Philby who defected from Britain altogether and, by the end of our period, directed the trading company Sharquieh in Saudi Arabia).

CHAPTER I

1. Andrew's *Her Majesty's Secret Service* does not address Middle Eastern intelligence but provides the sociological framework of this book. By positing the existence of a unified community, I do not want to minimize the discord between the Indian and London establishments on policy matters but to argue that there was, nevertheless, fundamental agreement on the need to collect more intelligence on the region.

2. This was the result of the westward spread of the old East India Company's consular establishments into Iraq, Persia, and the Persian Gulf and the eastward expansion of the Levant Company's consular establishments, which had passed to the Crown in 1825. Officers were generally appointed by the Indian government and the cost shared by both governments. "Residents" were the main administrative and diplomatic representatives of the Indian government in regions surrounding India. Staffed by the Indian Political Service, residents had responsibilities that could verge on executive control even in ostensibly sovereign regions (e.g., the Persian Gulf Residency [and consulate] at Bushire). "Political agents" were Indian political officers in Ottoman provinces that possessed some autonomy, such as the Hejaz and Kuwait. The Levant Consular Service (like the Far Eastern and General Consular Services) reported to the Foreign Office. The overlap meant, for instance, that the Jeddah consulate dealt most often with British Indian pilgrims and was also in close touch with the Aden Residency for intelligence questions.

3. [J. H. Longford], "The Consular Service and Its Wrongs," *Quarterly Review* 197 (1903), 610; C. M. Kennedy, 1871, quoted in D. C. M. Platt, *The Cinderella Service: British Consuls since 1825*, 127; East India House to Harford James, 5 July 1798, Annexure II in Lorimer, *Gazetteer*, 1:1620-21; FO 371/1845: 42138: Lorimer, Baghdad Summary for July 1913. See also MECA: Geoffrey Wheeler Papers: File 1: Wheeler, memoirs, "Fifty Years of Asia," chap. 7; Sheffy, *British Military Intelligence*, 8, 12. Dating from the sixteenth to eighteenth centuries, the Capitulations granted European countries extraterritorial jurisdiction over their own nationals and coreligionists in Ottoman territory.

4. FO 371/1510: 38625: Marling to Maxwell, 11 Sept. 1912; FO 371/1493: 13620: Lowther to Grey, 24 April 1912, and minutes thereon.

5. FO 371/155: 35658: Barclay to Hardinge, 15 Oct. 1906; FO 371/154: 29027: O'Conor to Grey, 21 Aug. 1906; Wilkie-Young to Drummond-Hay, 23 March 1904, in A. L. P. Burdett, ed., *Records of the Hijaz: 1798-1925*, 6:467; FO 371/2135: 29829: Erskine, Residency Summary, 12 May 1914; Lorimer, Irak Report for Feb. 1912; FO 371/1263: 43730: Extract from private letter quoted in H. E. W. Young to Lowther,

24 Oct. 1911; FO 371/156: 40123: Ramsay to Dane, Secretary to the Government of India in the Foreign Department, 29 Sept. 1906.

6. FO 78/5488: Gaskin to Kemball, 7 Nov. 1903 and Kemball to Secretary to the Government of India in the Foreign Department, 5 Feb. 1904; FO 371/1799: 11950: Crow to Lowther, 31 May 1913. See also FO: 371/1490: 3020: Scott, report, 4 Dec. 1911; A. J. B. Wavell, *Modern Pilgrim*, 182.

7. FO 371/1799: 11950: Crow to Lowther, 15 March 1913; FO 371/1008: 17336: Lorimer, Summary for March 1910; Lorimer, *Gazetteer*, 1:1615; Ramsay to Dane, 29 Sept. 1906; Lorimer, Tour journal no. 1 of 1910.

8. FO 371/1811: 16626: FO minutes on Messrs. Stephen Lynch and Co. to the FO, 3 March 1913; FO minute on Marling to Maxwell, 11 Sept. 1912; FO 371/1510: 38625: Lowther to Maxwell, 24 Oct. 1912, and Hony to Marling, 16 Aug. 1912.

9. Quoted in Winstone, *Illicit Adventure*, 59. See also FO 371/1013: 29805: Shakespear to Cox, 4 April 1910.

10. FO 371/153: 24676: Cox to Dane, 28 Feb. 1906; IOR: L/PS/20/C91/4: Lorimer, *Gazetteer*, Vol. 2: *Geographical and Statistical*, 2:759–61n; Winstone, *Illicit Adventure*, 58–59; IOR: L/PS/10/259: correspondence about Hunter, Feb.–April 1910; IOR: R/15/2/45: Lorimer to Cox, 28 Aug. 1906. Volume 2 of the *Gazetteer* was published first, in 1908. Lorimer had all but completed Volume 1 when he died in 1914. L. Birdwood, later Cox's assistant, finished it in 1915. The *Gazetteer* remained on the "Secret" list until 1930, when it was marked "for official use only." It is now held up as a key artifact of the historiography of the peninsula. See J. E. Peterson, "The Arabian Peninsula in Modern Times: A Historiographical Survey."

11. Fergusson, *British Military Intelligence*, 169–85, 212–13; Alfred Vagts, *The Military Attaché*, 33; Sheffy, *British Military Intelligence*, 12–13; Lowther to Maxwell, 24 Oct. 1912. A standing intelligence corps of the Indian Army did operate on the North West Frontier.

12. DMO to Haldane, quoted in Winstone, *Illicit Adventure*, 31. On the Survey of Egypt and Egyptian intelligence, see *Illicit Adventure*, 6–7, and *Leachman: "OC Desert,"* 74; Sheffy, *British Military Intelligence*, 5–6. On the PEF's relationship to the War Office, see Rashid Khalidi, *British Policy towards Syria and Palestine, 1906–1914*, 332–33; Neil Asher Silberman, *Digging for God and Country: Exploration, Archaeology, and the Secret Struggle for the Holy Land, 1799–1917*; Sheffy, *British Military Intelligence*, 21–22. On amateur intelligence elsewhere, see Andrew, *Her Majesty's Secret Service*, 33, 78–85.

13. Military Operations Directorate, Instructions Regarding the Conduct of Work, 1909, quoted in John Fisher, "On the Baghdad Road: On the Trail of W. J. Childs," 54; Bury, *Land of Uz*, 123; IOR: L/PS/10/135: 3509: Bury to Lamington, 12 Aug. 1910.

14. FO 371/354: 28053: FO minutes on Sykes, report, 14 Aug. 1908; IOR: L/PS/10/259: 446: IO to FO, 22 March 1910; FO 371/1009: 13041: Lowther to Grey, 4 April 1910 and enclosed letter, Tyrell to Lowther, 29 March 1910; Lorimer, report on events in Feb. 1910; FO 371/1490: 3025: Lorimer, Summary, 6 May 1912. See also FO 371/1819: 20903: Greenway to IO, 11 Sept. 1912; FO 371/1447: 38642: correspondence regarding proposed journey of Lt. C. W. Wallace, Sept. 1912; FO 371/1819: 20903: Grey to IO, 8 May 1913; FO 371/1496: 27562: IO to FO, 28 June 1912; L/PS/10/259: 3163: Lowther to Grey, 15 Feb. 1910, 3263: IO to Capt. Hunter,

25 April 1910, and 3318: correspondence on "withholding... permission... to make journeys in Mesopotamia," 1910.

15. Winstone, *Captain Shakespear*, 129; Leachman, letter, 24 Aug. 1911, quoted in N. N. E. Bray, *A Paladin of Arabia*, 216; FO 371/2124: 1990: Shakespear to Hirtzel, 26 June 1914. On Meinertzhagen's manipulations, see Mark Cocker, *Richard Meinertzhagen: Soldier, Scientist, and Spy*, 73; Winstone, *Illicit Adventure*, 220; Richard Meinertzhagen, *Army Diary, 1899–1926*, 54–58.

16. Crow, quoted in Winstone, *Leachman*, 95; Hubert Young, *The Independent Arab*, 28, 33; FO 371/1006: 8742: Lorimer, Tour Diary no. 1 of 1909, 6 Feb. 1910; Herbert, *Ben Kendim*, 114–15; FO 371/1008: 12174: Lorimer, summary, 6 June 1910; Lorimer, report on events in Feb. 1910; Winstone, *Leachman*, 104; Leachman to Lorimer, 22 Feb. 1910 in Lorimer, summary for March 1910; Lorimer, Tour Journal no. 1 of 1910; IOR: L/PS/7/253: Lorimer, summary, 2 Oct. 1911; Lorimer, summary, 6 May 1912.

17. Holderness, IO to Mallet, quoted in Winstone, *Illicit Adventure*, 112; see also 91.

18. FO 371/1008: 12038: FO minutes on WO to FO, 13 April 1910; IOR: L/PS/10/135: 3216: Ritchie to Undersecretary of State, IO, 12 Jan. 1909; IOR: L/PS/3/413: FO and IO correspondence for 10–21 Jan. 1905. See also David French, "Spy Fever in Britain, 1900–1915," 362; Keith Neilson, "'Joy Rides'?: British Intelligence and Propaganda in Russia, 1914–17," 885.

19. Lowther to Grey, 4 April 1910 and minutes thereon; Winstone, *Captain Shakespear*, 189; Meinertzhagen, 1 Nov. 1913, in *Army Diary*, 58; Lorimer, summary, 6 May 1912.

20. FO 371/1819: 20903: Duff to FO, 16 July 1913; FO 371/2131: 17932: Viceroy to IO, 20 April 1914 and Crowe, FO to IO, 27 April 1914; FO 371/1848: 57883: IO to FO, 23 Dec. 1913.

21. IOR: R/15/2/45: Stewart, Criminal Intelligence, Simla to Bill, Bushire, Circular memo no. 3852, 9 Aug. 1906; J. Wilson, *Lawrence of Arabia*, 112–15. See chapter 3 on Britons' furtive modus operandi in the region.

22. See, for instance, FO 371/354: 28053: Sykes to Grey, 14 Aug. 1907; FO 371/542: 13719: Sykes, report, c. April 1908.

23. FO 371/535: 1629: Fraser to Gleichen, 14 Dec. 1907; FO 371/154: 30424: Grey, minute on Maclean to FO, 7 Sept. 1906; FO 371/355: 34641: Harris to Grey, 17 Oct. 1907; FO 371/1490: 3025: Baghdad Resident, Irak report, 4 Dec. 1911; FO 371/155: 32383: Niege to JCA, 9 July 1906 and 34559: 5 Aug. 1906. See also General Staff, "Notes on Arabia"; IOR: L/PS/20A/G49: "Record of Some Travellers... Whose Works Have Been of Interest to the Government of India Commencing from 1875," official handbook, Simla, 1910.

24. Among those suspecting the archaeologists of more: Winstone, *Illicit Adventure*, 79; Fergusson, *British Military Intelligence*, 235; C. Ernest Dawn, "The Influence of T. E. Lawrence on the Middle East," 62. For refutations, see J. Wilson, *Lawrence of Arabia*, 98, 100; Mack, *Prince of Our Disorder*, 102.

25. FO 371/146: 5091: O'Conor to Grey, 3 Feb. 1906; FO 371/1490: 3025: Lorimer, summary, 4 June 1912; David Hogarth, *A Wandering Scholar in the Levant*, 6.

26. Lawrence to his family, 4 Jan. 1914, in M. R. Lawrence, ed., *The Home Letters of T. E. Lawrence and His Brothers*, 279–80; Lawrence, quoted in Sir Basil Henry Liddell Hart, *"T. E. Lawrence": In Arabia and After*, 94; Exodus (18:20), as quoted on dedicatory page of Leonard Woolley and T. E. Lawrence, *The Wilderness of Zin*. See also J. Wilson, *Lawrence of Arabia*, 136–45; Leonard Woolley, *As I Seem to Remember*, 88–93.

27. Bell to Hugh Bell, 18 March 1911, in *The Letters of Gertrude Bell*, 1:292; IOR: L/PS/10/576: [Arthur Hirtzel?], marginal note on minutes on FO to IO, 20 Jan. 1917; FO 371/1848: 56311: minute on Mallet to Grey, 14 Dec. 1913; FO 371/2127: 3538: Mallet to Grey, 20 May 1914. See also Rosemary O'Brien, ed., *Gertrude Bell: The Arabian Diaries, 1913–1914*, 11.

28. IOR: L/PS/8/9: correspondence, June 1902; BL: Add. MSS: 55133: Macmillan Papers: Hogarth to Macmillan, 31 May 1911.

29. Before 1904, Levant consular students studied at the Bosphorous, but the curriculum was shifted to England as they were getting too "debauched," explains Sir Laurence Grafftey-Smith in *Bright Levant*, 3.

30. Quoted in Margaret Fitzherbert, *The Man Who Was Greenmantle: A Biography of Aubrey Herbert*, 93–94.

31. Lawrence to Doughty, 30 Nov. 1909, in *The Letters of T. E. Lawrence*, 82–83; Pres. Leonard Darwin, commenting on Captain S. S. Butler, "Baghdad to Damascus via El Jauf, Northern Arabia," lecture, 22 Feb. 1909, *Geographical Journal* 33 (1909), 535. This was a DMO-sponsored journey.

32. Bell to her stepmother, 29 Dec. 1902, quoted in Burgoyne, *Gertrude Bell*, 1:138–39; N. N. E. Bray, *Shifting Sands*, 15; J. Wilson, *Lawrence of Arabia*, 38.

33. John Mackenzie, "T. E. Lawrence: The Myth and the Message," 156; Bell to Florence Bell, 13 Aug. 1902, in *Letters of Gertrude Bell*, 1:150.

34. Lorimer, summary for March 1910; Winstone, *Illicit Adventure*, 8, 12, 48, 77; Gideon Gera, "T. E. Lawrence: Intelligence Officer," 206; Peter Morris, "Intelligence and Its Interpretation," 82; IOR: L/PS/3/420: Commander Somerville to C-in-C, East Indies Station, report, 24 Nov. 1905; FO 371/1799: 11950: Commander Wood, Basra report no. 2, 17 May 1913; FO 371/154: 29543: Gabriel, Simla, memorandum, 1 July 1906; FO 371/355: 31953: Holland, Simla, memorandum, 1 Aug. 1907; Lorimer, *Gazetteer*, 2:759–61 n. For other composite reports, see Cohen, *Policy in Mesopotamia*, 69.

35. On the campaigns, see Fromkin, *Peace to End All Peace*; J. Wilson, *Lawrence of Arabia*; Matthew Hughes, *Allenby and British Strategy in the Middle East, 1917–1919*; M. E. Yapp, *Making of the Modern Near East, 1792–1923*; A. J. Barker, *The Bastard War: The Mesopotamian Campaign of 1914–1918*; Albert Hourani, *Emergence of the Modern Middle East*; John Fisher, *Curzon and British Imperialism in the Middle East: 1916–19*; Elie Kedourie, *England and the Middle East: The Destruction of the Ottoman Empire, 1914–1921*.

36. Roger Adelson, *Mark Sykes: Portrait of an Amateur*, 123; FO 882: "Archaeologist Enemy Agents," *Arab Bulletin* 92 (June 1918), 194–95; FO 371/2141: 46925: Oliphant, minute endorsing Bell to Deedes, 5 Sept. 1914; FO 371/2201: 44488: Woolley to FO, c. Aug. 1914; Woolley, *As I Seem to Remember*, 93. Woolley had not

overestimated his reputation—see 44488: FO to Secretary to the Army Council, 2 Sept. 1914.

37. Robert W. Graves, *Storm Centres of the Near East: Personal Memories, 1879–1929*, 297.

38. Col. W. H. Beach, "Note on Military Intelligence in the Mesopotamia Campaign," 25 Feb. 1924, appendix 30 of F. J. Moberly, *The Campaign in Mesopotamia 1914–1918*, 2:537–38; NAM: ARC 1983-12-69-10: Leith-Ross Papers, Leith-Ross, "The Strategical Side of I(a)," n.d., 9, and "The Tactical Side of I(a)," n.d.; Young, *Independent Arab*, 38–39, 79; Reader Bullard, *The Camels Must Go: An Autobiography*, 85; MECA: H. R. P. Dickson Papers: Box 1: File 3A: Dickson to his mother, 10 Nov. 1914; Arnold T. Wilson, *Loyalties: Mesopotamia, 1914–1917*, 78. Leachman was initially to replace Shakespear after the latter's death in cross-fire, but Ibn Saud's increasing wariness mooted the mission. Strictly speaking, Philby had minimal knowledge of Arabic on arrival in Basra but was fluent in a year; nor had he traveled in "Arabia" before the war. For more on staff members' prewar antecedents, see Philip Graves, *The Life of Sir Percy Cox*, 185.

39. A. T. Wilson, quoted in John Marlowe, *Late Victorian: The Life of Sir Arnold Talbot Wilson*, 100; Dickson Papers: Box 1: File 4: Dickson to his mother, 21 Nov. 1915; Candler, *Long Road*, 1:277; Dickson Papers: Box 1: 3rd booklet: Dickson to Gwenlian Greene, 4 Aug. 1915; Box 2: File 1: Dickson to his mother, 3 Jan. 1916, Box 1: File 4: 26 Sept. 1916 and File 3A: 29 Dec. 1914; Beach, "Note on Military Intelligence"; Michael Occleshaw, *Armour against Fate: British Military Intelligence in the First World War*, 201; Neilson, "'Joy Rides,'" 903; FO 882/II: AP/15/8: Parker to DMO, 21 Nov. 1915; MECA: Cecil J. Edmonds Papers: Box 26: Edmonds, Diary 1915–1924, 10 Nov. 1915; Leachman to his family, [early 1916], quoted in Bray, *Paladin of Arabia*, 282–83.

40. A difficult task given that the Turks had retreated with their records in tow. Political officers took the place of Turkish administrators. They, too, were addressed as *kaimakam* and preserved the Turkish system of revenue assessment and collection through tribal chiefs.

41. The administration earned roughly £30,000 in 1915–1916 and £3 million in 1919–1920 when the whole country was occupied. George Buchanan, *The Tragedy of Mesopotamia*, 268.

42. Dickson Papers: Box 1: 3rd booklet: Dickson to Greene, 17 Sept. 1915; Young, *Independent Arab*, 52; FO 371/2779: 152059: Dobbs, appendix A in Arabian Report no. 8 (new series), [late 1916]; Buchanan, *Tragedy of Mesopotamia*, 139–45; Cox to Hirtzel, 23 July 1916, quoted in P. Graves, *Percy Cox*, 207–09; Lawrence, Report on Intelligence of IEF "D," May 1916, in appendix 3, J. Wilson, *Lawrence of Arabia*, 949–52.

43. By 1915, political responsibilities were divided between Basra and Cairo on lines analogous to but even vaguer than the military division. The operational area of the Egyptian Army, including Hejaz and an undefined "Syria," fell under the Foreign Office's high commissioner, who was independent of the army; eastern Arabia and Mesopotamia fell to the Government of India, through Cox in his capacity as Gulf resident for nonoperational areas and through Force D, whose chief political officer was also Cox, for an undefined "Mesopotamia."

44. Popplewell, "Intelligence in Mesopotamia," 139; Candler, *Long Road*, 1:212. No other British army had surrendered with its colors since Yorktown, and none would again until Singapore fell in 1942.

45. FO 371/2491: 148549: Sykes to Lloyd, 4 Sept. 1915; Sykes in Parliament, mid-Feb. 1916, and Sykes to Cecil, 4 Oct. 1915, quoted in Adelson, *Mark Sykes*, 203, 192; FO 882: MES/16/2: Bell to Lawrence, 18 March 1916; FO 371/2491: 158561: Sykes to Callwell, 9 Oct. 1915 and FO 371/2486: 158561: 15 Nov. 1915; FO 882/II: ARB/15/3: Sykes, memorandum, 23 Dec. 1915. Bell had earlier made a similar recommendation to Hall—noted in FO 882/XIII: MES/16/3: Bell to Lawrence, 25 March 1916.

46. Ernest Main, *Iraq: From Mandate to Independence*, 58. On political wranglings over the bureau, see Westrate, *Arab Bureau*; and Adelson, *Mark Sykes*, 198. At India's insistence, bureau propaganda would stop at the Indian frontier, and policy would remain subordinate to that pursued by the commander in Mesopotamia. Its Basra branch would be in Cox's office. Geographically, the bureau covered Africa, Greece, the Balkans, "Arabia," Persia, the Caucasus, Central Asia, Turkey, and India, as well as Turkish and Arab activities in central Europe.

47. FO 882/II: ARB/15/4: Sykes to Clayton, 28 Dec. 1915; FO 371/8954: W. J. Childs, memorandum on the Arab Bureau, 19 April 1923.

48. FO 371/2771: 18845: Hogarth, Arab Bureau, First Report [10 May 1916]; Bell to Hugh Bell, 6 Jan. 1916, 24 Jan. 1916, and 18 Feb. 1916, in *Letters of Gertrude Bell*, 1:363–67; Bell to Lawrence, 18 March 1916; FO 882/IV: HRG/16/8: Lloyd to [Clayton?], 27 May 1916; FO 882/II: ARB/16/16: French to Clayton, 13 July 1916; Parker, report, 5 Oct. 1916, quoted in H. V. F. Winstone, *The Diaries of Parker Pasha*, 138; FO 882/II: ARB/16/17: Clayton to French, 27 July 1916; FO 882/XIII: MES/16/16: Bell to Hogarth, 20 May 1916; IOR: L/PS/10/576: Cox, memorandum, 15 July 1916.

49. FO 371/2781: 188311: Cornwallis, report, 10 Sept. 1916; Hogarth to his family, 12 May 1917, quoted in Westrate, *Arab Bureau*, 189; MECA: D. G. Hogarth Papers: File 3: Hogarth to his mother, 20 Sept. 1918, and to his wife, 10 April 1918; Westrate, *Arab Bureau*, 201.

50. FO 371/2779: 152059: Wilson, report, 7 July 1916, appendix to Arabian Report no. 3 (new series); FO 882/IV: HRG/17/6: Wilson to Newcombe, 15 Jan. 1917; FO 882/IV: HRG/16/95: Lawrence to Clayton, Dec. 1916; Westrate, *Arab Bureau*, 188; Young, *Independent Arab*, 143–46; Lawrence to his mother, 27 Aug. 1917, in *Selected Letters*, 116.

51. KV 1/17: The Organization of the Eastern Mediterranean Special Intelligence Bureau, 1921; KV 1/19: MI5 "D" Branch Report, 1921; Lawrence to Hogarth, 20 April 1915, in *Letters of T. E. Lawrence*, 196; FO 882/II: ARB/16/8: McMahon to Sir Arthur Nicolson (private), 2 Feb. 1916; Compton Mackenzie, *Greek Memories*, 10–11, 33. This paragraph is based on diverse official and unofficial sources, cited throughout, but see, in particular, the memoirs of Compton Mackenzie, Robert W. Graves, Alec Kirkbride, and L. F. B. Weldon. See also Sheffy, *British Military Intelligence*, 83–88.

52. Ernest M. Dowson, "Mapwork and Printing in the Near East," in *T. E. Lawrence, by His Friends*, ed. A. W. Lawrence, 110–23. On Indian paranoia about the bureau's incursions into Mesopotamia, see Westrate, *Arab Bureau*, 86–88.

53. Lloyd to [Clayton?], 27 May 1916; Lawrence, Report on Intelligence. Emphasis added.

54. Bell to her family, 4 May 1916, quoted in Burgoyne, *Gertrude Bell*, 2:38; Bell to Hogarth, 20 May 1919; Lawrence to his family, 18 Nov. 1916, in *Home Letters*, 332; Cox to Hirtzel, 23 July 1916; Lawrence, *Seven Pillars*, 556; Bell to Hugh Bell, 24 March 1916, and Bell to Maurice, 8 Dec. 1916, in *The Gertrude Bell Papers*, available at http://www.gerty.ncl.ac.uk [23 Jan. 2007]; Plotke, *Imperial Spies*, 132.

55. FO 882/XIII: MES/16/18: Bell to Hogarth, 15 June 1916; P. Graves, *Percy Cox*, 204; Bell to Chirol, 13 Sept. 1917, quoted in Burgoyne, *Gertrude Bell*, 2:64.

56. Bell to Hugh Bell, 19 Aug. 1916, in *Letters of Gertrude Bell*, 1:385; Lawrence to his family, 1 July 1916, in *Home Letters*, 327; FO 371/2781: 201201: Sykes, appreciations of Arabian Reports no. 14, [Aug. 1916]; no. 15, [Sept. 1916]; and no. 13, [Oct. 1916].

57. FO 371/3057: 103481: Bray, note, 25 March 1917 (and synopsis thereof); FO 686/6/Pt.1: Lloyd, Report on the Hejaz, 22 Dec. 1916. On the Silk Letter Plot, see FO 686/149: Cleveland to fforde, notes, 22 Sept. 1916, and minutes thereon; IOR: L/PS/10/576: Vivian to C. E. Wilson, 7 Dec. 1916. See also Yuvaraj Deva Prasad, "The Silk Letter Plot: An Anti-British Conspiracy in World War I." On the von Stotzingen mission, see FO 882: "Arabia," *Arab Bulletin* 22 (Sept. 1916), 272; FO 882/IV: HRG/16/25: Part II, Record of the Rising, January to June 1916, [July 1916], ff. 169–72. Other events were similarly inserted retroactively into a narrative of narrowly averted apocalypse. See "Note by Cairo," *Arab Bulletin* 25 (Oct. 1916), 338; FO 882/IV: HRG/18/15: General Staff, appendix F, in Summary of the Hejaz Revolt, 30 Sept. 1918, 21; "Enemy Intelligence on the Euphrates," *Arab Bulletin* 98 (July 1918), 257–59.

58. FO 882/VIII: IS/17/1: Cox to Arbur, 12 Jan. 1917; Sykes, minute, 28 Aug. 1916, on Cox, memorandum, 15 July 1916.

59. FO 686/6/Pt.1: Lloyd, report, 22 Dec. 1916; Westrate, *Arab Bureau*, 57; Hogarth to his wife, 10 April 1918 (my italics); Alec Kirkbride, *An Awakening: The Arab Campaign, 1917–1918*, 33, 45; FO 686/6/Pt.1: Joyce, intelligence summary, 25–28 Jan. 1917; Parker to Cornwallis, 26 Oct. 1916, quoted in Winstone, *Illicit Adventure*, 284; FO 686/6/Pt.1: Joyce, intelligence report, 14 March 1917; Parker to Arbur, 7 Oct. 1916, quoted in Winstone, *Diaries of Parker*, 141; FO 882/VI: HRG/17/19: [illegible] to Sir W. Robertson, 19 March 1917; FO 882/XII: IND/16/4: Arbur minute, 1 Nov. 1916; IND/17/1: Wilson to Arbur Director, 12 Jan. 1917; IND/17/5 13 Sept. 1917; IND/17/6: Cornwallis to Symes, 26 Sept. 1917, minute; FO 882/XV: PNI/17/1: Wilson to Cleveland, March 1917; FO 882/XVI: SP/17/1: Sykes, memo, 2 Feb. 1917; FO 882: "Arab Bureau, Jerusalem," *Arab Bulletin* 91 (June 1918), 176 (my italics); Ferdinand Tuohy, *The Secret Corps: A Tale of 'Intelligence' on All Fronts*, 183, 193; FO 371/3047: 15354: Arab Bureau Report, Jan. 1917; MI5, "Organization of the EMSIB." See chapter 2 for more on the view of nomadic Arabia as a spy-space in essence.

60. [Gertrude Bell], *The Arab of Mesopotamia*, 31; Leith-Ross Papers: Leith-Ross, "Secret Service or Intelligence, Sub-Section (B), GHQ," n.d., 1; MECA: H. St. John Philby Papers: Box 4: File 4: Political Diary for 16 Feb. to 11 May 1917; Dickson Papers: Box 1: 3rd booklet: Dickson to Greene, 10 Sept. 1915; Cox to Hirtzel, 23 July 1916; Bell to Hirtzel, 15 June 1917, quoted in P. Graves, *Percy Cox*, 226 passim; Leith-Ross, "Tactical Side," 29, 32; Tuohy, *Secret Corps*, 183, 193.

61. Adelson, *Mark Sykes*, 217–18; FO 882/XVI: SP/17/4: W. Robertson to GOC-in-C, EEF, 21 Feb. 1917; FO 371/4363: PID/116/18: memo, "German and Turkish Activities in the Middle East...," 8 May 1918. On France's claim to Syria, see Fieldhouse, *Western Imperialism*, 45–52.

62. Young, *Independent Arab*, 142, 169 passim; Kirkbride, *Awakening*, 20–21, 36–38; Leith-Ross, "Tactical Side," 15–19. The information in this paragraph is, again, culled from sources cited throughout.

CHAPTER 2

1. Simon Ryan, *The Cartographic Eye: How Explorers Saw Australia*, 117. On imperialist exploration and the cultural production of places, see also Mary Louise Pratt, *Imperial Eyes: Travel Writing and Transculturation*, 5.

2. Review of *By Desert Ways to Baghdad*, by Louisa Jebb, *Nation* 4 (Oct. 1908), 57–58; Haynes, *Seeking the Centre*, 25, 30; [Gertrude Bell], review of *Wanderings in Arabia*, abridgement of Doughty's *Travels in Arabia Deserta*, ed. Edward Garnett, and of Alexander Kinglake's *Eothen* (1844), ed. D. G. Hogarth, *TLS*, 13 Feb. 1908, 52. On Arabia in early British cinema, see Sari Nasir, *The Arabs and the English*, 142–46.

3. Lawrence to his family, 22 Oct. 1912, in *Home Letters*, 239. By contrast, the self-consciousness of Canada's explorers made published accounts confirm the ideologies of the home culture. See Ian MacLaren, "Exploration/Travel Literature and the Evolution of the Author."

4. [David Hogarth], "Two Girls in Turkey," review of *By Desert Ways to Baghdad*, by Louisa Jebb, *TLS*, 17 Sept. 1908, 301; Mark Sykes, *Dar-ul-Islam: A Record of a Journey through Ten of the Asiatic Provinces of Turkey*, 1. This paragraph is based on contemporary assessments expressed in periodicals and memoirs as well as the historical judgments of biographers cited throughout. On the literary uses of the "mythology of the heroic explorer," see also S. Ryan, *Cartographic Eye*, 48–49, 53; Felix Driver, *Geography Militant: Cultures of Exploration and Empire*, 8, 10.

5. Wells to Sykes, 7 May 1904 and Kipling to Sykes, 6 May 1904, quoted in Leslie, *Mark Sykes*, 99; Richard Meinertzhagen, *Diary of a Black Sheep*, xv.

6. Woolf to Emma Vaughan, 17 June 1900, in *The Letters of Virginia Woolf*, Vol. 1: *1888–1912*, 34; FO 371/1819: 20903: Young to Military Secretary, IO, 28 May 1913.

7. BL: Add. MSS: Wentworth Bequest: 54107: Wilfrid to Anne Blunt, 11 June 1902; Add. MSS G. B. Shaw Papers: 50515: Blunt to Shaw, 24 Jan. 1907; Tidrick, *Heart-Beguiling Araby*, 157. On Churchill's fascinations, see David Stafford, *Churchill and Secret Service*.

8. See Wesley Wark, "Introduction: Fictions of History," *Intelligence and National Security* 5 (1990), 1–3; Anthony Masters, *Literary Agents: The Novelist as Spy*, 1; Thomas Price, "Spy Stories, Espionage and the Public in the Twentieth Century." Early novelist-spies were recruited *because* they were novelists, while Cold War spy novelists drew on their experience as spies to become writers.

9. Peter Brent, *Far Arabia: Explorers of the Myth* (London, 1977), 168 ; [Hogarth], review of *The Short Cut to India*, by David Fraser, *Spectator*, 13 March 1909, 423–24; [Hogarth], "Two Girls in Turkey"; [Halford John Mackinder], "Unknown Arabia,"

review of *The Penetration of Arabia*, by Hogarth, *TLS*, 10 June 1904, 178. These works were, however, clearly different from nineteenth-century travel narratives on Arabia, authored by confident agents of an established imperial power, rather than tentative explorers in hostile territory. On the popularity of adventure-quest narratives in this period, see Dawson, *Soldier Heroes*, chap. 3.

10. Janet Hogarth, describing Bell and Lawrence, quoted in Burgoyne, *Gertrude Bell*, 1:2; Doughty to Hogarth, 1902, quoted in David Hogarth, *The Life of Charles M. Doughty*, 114. On the Romantics, see Tidrick, *Heart-Beguiling Araby*, 34–35, 152; Eira Patnaik, "Europe's Middle East: History or Invention?" 350. For nineteenth-century reconstructions, see, for instance, H. Swainson Cowper, *Through Turkish Arabia*; and Lady Anne Blunt, *A Pilgrimage to Nejd* and *Bedouin Tribes of the Euphrates*. On Doughty and the emergence of a genre of Arabian-English prose, see Stephen Tabachnick, "Art and Science in *Travels in Arabia Deserta*," 30.

11. Louisa Jebb, *By Desert Ways to Baghdad*, 63, 260; Candler, *Long Road*, 1:120; Gertrude Bell, *The Desert and the Sown*, 50, 60–61; Patrick Brantlinger, *Rule of Darkness: British Literature and Imperialism, 1830–1914*, 232. By comparison, the style of contemporary Australian explorer-authors was distinctly unliterary; they were particularly inimical to modernist fashions and any attempt to romanticize the desert as anything but an embarrassment to their new, modern nation. This changed in the late 1930s, largely under the influence of Arabian travel writing. See Haynes, *Seeking the Centre*, 60–61, 140, 149. On Edwardian fascination with the "void," see Stephen Kern, *The Culture of Time and Space: 1880–1918*, 166–70; Richard Bevis, "Desert Places: The Aesthetics of *Arabia Deserta*," 62–63.

12. Sykes, *Dar-ul-Islam*, 12 n; *Caliph's Last Heritage*, 302–303; Sykes to Baden-Powell, 28 Dec. 1911, quoted in Leslie, *Mark Sykes*, 194; Lawrence to M. R. Lawrence, 12 Sept. 1912 and to his family, 11 April 1912, in *Home Letters*, 207, 230.

13. Tabachnick, "Art and Science," 8; Bevis, "Desert Places," 66–75. On Sykes's literary tastes, see Adelson, *Mark Sykes*, 83–84; on Lawrence's, see Mack, *Prince of Our Disorder*, 41–47.

14. Flecker to [Frank Savery], 10 Jan. 1912, in *Some Letters from Abroad of James Elroy Flecker*, 64; Henry Liebersohn, "Recent Works on Travel Writing," 621; Virginia Woolf, *The Voyage Out*, 8, 34–35, 161–66, 246; Vita Sackville-West, "Morning in Constantinople," in *Poems of West and East*, 40; James Joyce, "Araby" and "The Sisters" in *Dubliners*; Joseph Conrad, *Lord Jim*, 251; [George Street], review of *The Garden of Allah*, by Robert Hichens, *TLS*, 14 Oct. 1904, 311–12. Hichens's book was in its sixteenth edition by 1907. Among "popular" novels, see also Nevill Myers Meakin, *The Assassins: A Romance of the Crusades* (1902) and Marmaduke Pickthall, *The House of Islam* (1906) (reviewed in the *TLS*, 21 Sept. 1906, 322).

15. [Hogarth], "The Desert," review of *In the Desert*, by L. March Phillips, *TLS*, 3 Nov. 1905, 368; [Stanley Edward Lane-Poole], review of *The Desert and the Sown*, by Bell, *TLS*, 25 Jan. 1907, 28. (Lane-Poole was an Arabist and historian who edited *The Thousand and One Nights* in 1906.)

16. John Buchan, quoted in introduction to Buchan's *Greenmantle*, by Kate Macdonald, x; Buchan, *The Thirty-Nine Steps*, 1, 24; Buchan, quoted in Alan Judd, *The Quest for C: Sir Mansfield Cumming and the Founding of the British Secret Service*, 37;

Erskine Childers, *The Riddle of the Sands*, 66, 79; Liddell Hart, "T. E. Lawrence," 34; Capt. L. F. B. Weldon, *"Hard Lying": Eastern Mediterranean, 1914–1919*, 117. On Childers's novel, see also Thomas Richards, *The Imperial Archive: Knowledge and the Fantasy of Empire*, 134; Deak Nabers, "Spies Like Us: John Buchan and the Great War Spy Craze," 4. Incidentally, Thomas Mann similarly romanticized the North Sea sands in *The Magic Mountain* (1924).

17. James Elroy Flecker, *Hassan: The Story of Hassan of Bagdad and How He Came to Make the Golden Journey to Samarkand*, 86; Sackville-West, "Nomads," in *Poems of West and East*, 24–25. On the spy novel and imperial anxiety, see David Stafford, "Spies and Gentlemen: The Birth of the British Spy Novel, 1893–1914" and "John Buchan's Tales of Espionage: A Popular Archive of British History"; Price, "Spy Stories, Espionage," 81; John Cawelti and Bruce Rosenberg, *The Spy Story*; David Trotter, "The Politics of Adventure in the Early British Spy Novel," 32.

18. Said, *Orientalism*, 230–31; Meredith Townsend, *Asia and Europe*, 305–06; Mark Sykes, "Journeys in North Mesopotamia," *Geographical Journal* 30 (1907), 247. Even the baldly racist Doughty said he *preferred* the minimalist life of nomads (Bevis, "Desert Places," 75). Townsend's book collected his *Spectator* articles on Asia; on the influence of its much-reprinted, "prophetic pages," see John St. Loe Strachey, *The Adventure of Living: A Subjective Autobiography*, 231.

19. John A. McClure, *Late Imperial Romance*, 1–28; Andrew Lang, "The Supernatural in Fiction" (1905), quoted in Brantlinger, *Rule of Darkness*, 240; Ali Behdad, *Belated Travelers: Orientalism in the Age of Colonial Dissolution*, 93; Driver, *Geography Militant*, 199, 205; Stirling, *Safety First*, 29; "Turkey in Arabia," *Times*, 20 Aug. 1913, 7; D. G. Hogarth, "Problems in Exploration I. Western Asia," *Geographical Journal* 32 (1908), 549–50; "New and Projected Exploring Expeditions," *Times*, 18 Jan. 1909, 10; [Bell], "Arabia and the Levant"; Hogarth, *Penetration of Arabia*, 64; A. J. B. Wavell, *Modern Pilgrim*, 27. See also "The Situation in Arabia," *Times*, 8 Feb. 1912, 5. Certainly, Arabia's forbiddenness had fascinated earlier generations, but Peter Brent points out that this fascination was superseded by nineteenth-century Darwinian ideas about the desert as a testing ground for manhood (*Far Arabia*, 21–24). While the Poles were also being explored for this first time, Arabia was the last inhabited area where Europe could still dream of shining the light of civilization and progress. Tibet also fascinated Edwardians but had been sufficiently mapped by 1907 (when an accord was struck with the Russians) to rank lower than Arabia in the list of the "Still Unknown." Thomas Richards dates its emergence as a utopian site in the British imagination to the 1930s (*Imperial Archive*, 32).

20. Meinertzhagen, *Black Sheep*, 149–213; Hogarth, "Problems in Exploration," 554; A. J. B. Wavell, preface, in *Modern Pilgrim*, v–vi; "The Late Major Soane," *Times*, 17 March 1923, 12; Bell to Hugo Bell, 30 March 1902, in *Letters of Gertrude Bell*, 1:133; MECA: Sir Hubert Young Papers: typed memoir of prewar journey, n.d.; Haynes, *Seeking the Centre*, 52.

21. Bury, *Land of Uz*, xxi; Lawrence's brother, quoted in Mack, *Prince of Our Disorder*, 41. On the Romantics, see Said, *Orientalism*, 115. Certainly, medievalism had underpinned British fascination with other places, for instance, princely India (Thomas Metcalf, *Ideologies of the Raj*, 72–80), but there it impinged on the style and

form of an already existing colonial rule rather than on the formation of a new intelligence community.

22. See Melman, *Women's Orients*.

23. Bury to Ritchie, 22 Nov. 1909; Hogarth, comment on Douglas Carruthers, "A Journey in North-Western Arabia," *Geographical Journal* 35 (1910), 245; D. Carruthers, *Arabian Adventure*, 240; Sykes to Edith Gorst, 8 Aug. 1900, quoted in Leslie, *Mark Sykes*, 71; Brent, *Far Arabia*, 26. See also Tidrick, *Heart-Beguiling Araby*, 124.

24. Brent, *Far Arabia*, 133; Sykes, *Caliph's Last Heritage*, 5, 118; *Dar-ul-Islam*, 13; "The Late Major Soane," *Times*; D. Carruthers, *Arabian Adventure*, 32. Some even posited a common racial background between the ancient clans of Britain and the tribes of the Middle East. See Sir Thomas Holdich, "The Geography of the North-West Frontier," *Geographical Journal* 17 (1901), 461; E. B. Soane, *To Mesopotamia and Kurdistan in Disguise*, 399; Edwyn Bevan, *The Land of the Two Rivers*, 35. On the nineteenth-century roots of this perception, see Tidrick, *Heart-Beguiling Araby*, 31, 41. It rendered the orientalist interaction with Arabia quite different from, say, that with Africa or India.

25. MECA: Gertrude Bell Papers: Bell, Diary of a Journey to Hayyil, 16 Jan. 1914; Gertrude Bell, *Amurath to Amurath*, 159, 167; FO 371/1013: 29805: Shakespear, tour diary 1910, 2 Feb. 1910; Bell to her family, 8 Feb. 1905, in *Letters of Gertrude Bell*, 1:182; D. Carruthers, *Arabian Adventure*, 10, 22, 42, 84, 120; Bell to Florence Bell, 20 Dec. 1913, in *Letters of Gertrude Bell*, 1:313–14; R. Graves, *Lawrence and the Arabs*, 159; Buchan to a friend, 1923 (at Herbert's death), quoted in Fitzherbert, *Man Who Was Greenmantle*, 1.

26. Vyvyan Richards to Robert Graves, quoted in R. Graves, *Lawrence and the Arabs*, 15; Lawrence, quoted in Mack, *Prince of Our Disorder*, 57; E. F. Hall, quoted in *Prince of Our Disorder*, 58; Mack, *Prince of Our Disorder*, 74; John Presland [Gladys Skelton], *Deedes Bey* (London, 1942), 131, 238–40; Compton Mackenzie, *Gallipoli Memories*, 62; Buchan, *Greenmantle*, 225; Grafftey-Smith, *Bright Levant*, 9, 12, 15; Tidrick, *Heart-Beguiling Araby*, 132; Helen Carr, "Imagism and Empire," 85–86. The dinner was reported in the *Times*, 20 Jan. 1914, 5.

27. D. Carruthers, *Arabian Adventure*, 2; M. E. Hume-Griffith, *Behind the Veil in Persia and Turkish Arabia*, 130; Jebb, *By Desert Ways*, 260–63; Bell, 24 Jan. 1914, quoted in Burgoyne, *Gertrude Bell*, 1:291; C. Mackenzie, *Gallipoli Memories*, 99–100; Meinertzhagen, 3 Jan. 1918, in *Army Diary*, 226; Bray, *Paladin of Arabia*, 303; P. Graves, *Percy Cox*, 339; Kirkbride, *Awakening*, 86; Stirling, *Safety Last*, 49; "Obituary: Sir Reader Bullard," *Times*, 27 May 1976, 18; Presland, *Deedes Bey*, 131; Hogarth, *Penetration of Arabia*, 5–6; [George Frederick Abbott], "A Wandering Scholar," review of *Accidents of an Antiquary's Life*, by Hogarth, *TLS*, 7 April 1910, 121; Winstone, *Illicit Adventure*, 46. Abbott wrote on "Eastern subjects" and joined Turco-Arab forces in 1911–12 in North Africa. On the nineteenth-century roots of the "pilgrimage" metaphor, see Said, *Orientalism*, 168.

28. F. R. Maunsell, comment on Hogarth, "Problems in Exploration," 566; J. A. Mangan, *Athleticism in the Victorian and Edwardian Public School*; "Intelligence Methods in Peace Time." On Arabia's explorers as imperial hangovers, see also Brent, *Far Arabia*, 167. On *Kim* and colonial knowledge, see Jon Thompson, *Fiction, Crime, and Empire*, 92; T. Richards, *Imperial Archive*, 22. Of course, Victorian explorers had

not been as freelance as the Edwardian myth imagined—Burton was, after all, in government service some of the time. (In an interesting twist, it has been said that Creighton, Kim, Lurgan Sahib, et al. were all based in varying degrees on Burton. See Kaplan, *The Arabists*, 47.) On Edwardian views of the spy and the gentleman, see Stafford, "Spies and Gentlemen"; Robert Colls, "The Constitution of the English," 104; Joseph Kestner, *The Edwardian Detective, 1901–1915*.

29. Morgan, "Myth and Reality in the Great Game," 197; Michael Silvestri, "The Thrill of 'Simply Dressing Up': The Indian Police, Disguise, and Intelligence Work in Colonial India," para. 13, available at http://muse.jhu.edu/journals/journal_of_colonialism_and_colonial_history/v002/2.2silvestri.html [2 Feb. 2007]; C. A. Bayly, "'Knowing the Country': Empire and Information in India," 36.

30. "Intelligence Methods in Peace Time"; Hogarth, comment on D. Carruthers, "Journey in North-Western Arabia," 245; A. Hamilton, *Problems of the Middle East*, xiii; FO 371/1015: 34750: Lorimer to Government of India, 20 Aug. 1910; Churchill, *Malakand Field Force*, 38–39. Kim himself was "hand in glove with men who had led lives stranger than anything Haroun al Raschid dreamed of" (Rudyard Kipling, *Kim*, 51). Hannah Arendt also points to *Kim* as the foundational legend of the British secret agent (*Imperialism*, 97). On Shia Indian-Iraqi connections, see Juan Cole, *Roots of North Indian Shi'ism in Iran and Iraq*; and Meir Litvak, "Money, Religion, and Politics: The Oudh Bequest in Najaf and Karbala, 1850–1903" and "A Failed Manipulation: The British, the Oudh Bequest and the Sh i Ulama of Najaf and Karbala." The bequest originated in a loan the East India Company extracted from the king of Awadh in 1825 to finance war in Nepal. The principal was never repaid; the interest was to be applied in perpetuity to specific purposes, particularly support of religious education at Najaf and Karbala. Mujtahids withdrew the accumulating funds from the East India Company treasury through the good offices of the British resident at Baghdad, who gradually tightened his control in order to ensure they were used properly—partly to assuage Ottoman concerns. British officials also found the fund useful for influencing ulema in Iran and Iraq and earning the goodwill of Indian Shias.

31. A. J. B. Wavell, *Modern Pilgrim*, 191, 240. See also Bell, diary, 21 May 1905, quoted in Burgoyne, *Gertrude Bell*, 1:223, 225; Bury, *Land of Uz*, 17; D. Carruthers, *Arabian Adventure*, 88; Sykes, *Caliph's Last Heritage*, 508; "Constantinople: A Reminiscence," *Blackwood's Magazine* 180 (Oct. 1906): 485–501. Many pointed to the sultan's own obsessive spying on his subjects. In fact, Abdul Hamid's preoccupation with surveillance was rooted in his personal paranoia and fascination with detective fiction; and, rather than provide useful intelligence, his officials used spy reports as a means of expressing loyalty to him. M. Şükrü Hanioglu, "Invention of Traditions: Pan-Islamism and Espionage," lecture, 15 Oct. 2000, Princeton University.

32. Brent, *Far Arabia*, 163–64; Sykes, *Caliph's Last Heritage*, 533; David Fraser, *The Short Cut to India*, 234; Bell, reported in Hogarth Papers: File 2: Hogarth to Billy, 19 Feb. 1917; D. Carruthers, *Arabian Adventure*, 4, 62–63. On the Romantics, see Said, *Orientalism*, 100–01.

33. Captain John Hugh Smith, "Diary of a Journey from Aleppo to Urfa," appendix to Sykes, *Dar-ul-Islam*, 282; Sykes, *Caliph's Last Heritage*, 302, 450; Bell to Doughty-Wylie, 17 April 1914, quoted in O'Brien, *Gertrude Bell*, 116.

34. Bell, *Desert and the Sown*, 15, 236. "This is the English, not the Turkish court;/ Not Amurath an Amurath succeeds,/ But Harry Harry…" (*Henry IV, Part II*, act 5, scene 2).

35. Bell, 4 Feb. 1914, quoted in Burgoyne, *Gertrude Bell*, 1:294; Shakespear, tour diary 1910, 4 Feb. 1910; Jebb, *By Desert Ways*, 218; Bell, 17 Feb. 1914, quoted in Burgoyne, *Gertrude Bell*, 1:297; Sykes, *Dar-ul-Islam*, 177; D. Carruthers, *Arabian Adventure*, 19; Bell, Diary of a Journey to Hayyil, 24 Feb. 1914, 38; Winstone, *Captain Shakespear*, 56.

36. LCLUL: RNMN/MILWARD: Milward to his mother, 14 Dec. 1914; FO 882/XIII: MES/16/17: Bell to Hogarth, 27 May 1917; Candler, *Long Road*, 2:85–87; Edward J. Thompson, *The Leicestershires beyond Baghdad*, 78; Hogarth Papers: File 1: Hogarth to Doughty, 6 Dec. 1915; *Handbook of Arabia*, 1:19; Lawrence, foreword to reissue of *Arabia Deserta*, quoted in Mack, *Prince of Our Disorder*, 295; Presland, *Deedes Bey*, 288; Sir Hubert Easton, quoted in A. F. Wavell, *Allenby: Soldier and Statesman*, 162; Vivian Gilbert, *The Romance of the Last Crusade: With Allenby to Jerusalem*, 180–86.

37. On the Western front, see Fussell, *Great War*, 135–44, 154–55.

38. C. Mackenzie, *Gallipoli Memories*, 99, and *Aegean Memories*, 401. See also J. E. Tennant, *In the Clouds above Baghdad, Being the Records of an Air Commander*, 27 passim; Marlowe, *Late Victorian*, 105.

39. Lawrence to Clayton, 18 Oct. 1916, in *Selected Letters*, 90; Lloyd, quoted in Colin Forbes Adam, *The Life of Lord Lloyd*, 88; Dickson Papers: Box 2, File 1: Dickson to his mother, 26 Aug. 1915, 10 Aug. 1915, 14 Feb. 1917, 8 Nov. 1915, and 21 Feb. 1916; Box 1: 3rd booklet: Dickson to Greene, 25 Oct. 1915, 14 Aug. 1915, and 8 Nov. 1915. On Lawrence, see also Dawson, *Soldier Heroes*, 167–230.

40. Lawrence to Hogarth, 2 Feb. 1915, in *Letters of T. E. Lawrence*, 192; C. Mackenzie, *Greek Memories*, 72; *The Memoirs of Sir Ronald Storrs*, 4 and 19 June 1917, 256, 264; John de vere Loder to his mother, 3 Dec. 1916, in *Tales of Empire: The British in the Middle East, 1880–1952*, ed. Derek Hopwood, 91; Compton Mackenzie, *First Athenian Memories*, 255; Bell to Florence Bell, 9 April 1916, in *Letters of Gertrude Bell*, 1:372; Dickson Papers: Box 2: File 1: Dickson to his mother, 1 Sept. 1918.

41. Tidrick, *Heart-Beguiling Araby*, 178, 181; T. E. Lawrence, *Seven Pillars*, 327 (my italics); Albert Hourani, "The Myth of T. E. Lawrence," 23; Vyvyan Richards, *Portrait of T. E. Lawrence*, 208; Lawrence to his family, 1 July 1916, in *Home Letters*, 327; Mack, *Prince of Our Disorder*, 37, 192–93; T. E. Lawrence, *Seven Pillars*, 24, 549, 661; Lawrence to Vyvyan Richards, 15 July 1918, in *Letters of T. E. Lawrence*, 244; Lawrence to Manning, May 1930, quoted in Mack, *Prince of Our Disorder*, 383.

42. Candler, *Long Road*, 2:198.

43. J. Thompson, *Fiction, Crime, and Empire*, 87; Bevan, *Land of the Two Rivers*, 14; Kern, *Time and Space*, 38. On this mentality, see also, paradigmatically, Samuel Hynes, *The Edwardian Turn of Mind*, 134–39.

44. Alex Owen, *The Place of Enchantment: British Occultism and the Culture of the Modern*, 3–31; Hynes, *Edwardian Turn of Mind*, 139.

45. Demetres Tryphonopoulos, "The History of the Occult Movement," 45; G. R. S. Mead, *Fragments of a Faith Forgotten* (1912), quoted in "History of the Occult Movement," 23; Bell, *Desert and the Sown*, 123.

46. [Reginald Campbell-Thompson], review of *Mesopotamian Archaeology*, by Percy S. P. Handcock, *TLS*, 27 June 1912, 266; Townsend, *Asia and Europe*, 307; Leon Surette, preface to *Modernism and the Occult*, xvi; Elleke Boehmer, " 'Immeasurable Strangeness' in Imperial Times: Leonard Woolf and W. B. Yeats," 93, 99; Hulme, quoted in Carr, "Imagism and Empire," 80. See also Kern, *Time and Space*, 60, 166–79.

47. Hynes, *Edwardian Turn of Mind*, 146; Hogarth, *Wandering Scholar*, 153–54. On the Romantics, see Tidrick, *Heart-Beguiling Araby*, 33–35. On our under-appreciation of occultism's influence on modernism, see Surette, preface to *Modernism and the Occult*, xiv.

48. John Buchan, *Memory Hold the Door*, 194–95; *Greenmantle*, 182–83; Liddell Hart, "T. E. Lawrence," 98–99.

49. S. B. Bushrui, "Yeats's Arabic Interests," 280–81, 290, 292–93; Philip Rahv, quoted in Timothy Materer, "The Alchemy of Myth in Ted Hughes's *Cave Birds*," 176; *The Autobiography of William Butler Yeats*, 285; James Lovic Allen, "The Road to Byzantium: Archetypal Criticism and Yeats," 61; W. B. Yeats, "Swedenborg, Mediums, and the Desolate Places," 1914, in *If I Were Four-and-Twenty*; "Magic," in *Ideas of Good and Evil* (1896–1903), in *Essays by W. B. Yeats*, 50; Yeats, quoted in Bernard Levine, *The Dissolving Image: The Spiritual-Esthetic Development of W. B. Yeats*, 18; *Where There Is Nothing* (1903), in *The Variorum Edition of the Plays of W. B. Yeats*, 1064–65; "Anima Mundi," in *Per Amica Silentia Lunae* (1916–17), in *Essays by W. B. Yeats*, 508, 530; Carr, "Imagism and Empire," 74–78; Buchan, *Greenmantle*, 24, and *Memory Hold the Door*, 22; Alec Kirkbride, *A Crackle of Thorns: Experiences in the Middle East*, 62. On occultists' fascination with primitivism, see also Brantlinger, *Rule of Darkness*, 232. On Yeats and Leo Africanus, see also R. F. Foster's recent two-volume biography of Yeats; B. Lindsley, "W. B. Yeats's Encounters with His Daimon, Leo Africanus: The Daimon and Anti-Self Concepts in *Per Amica Silentia Lunae*" (1995), available at http://www. csun.edu/~hceng029/yeats/lindsley.html; and Yeats, entry 244, July 1913, in *Memoirs: Autobiography—First Draft; Journal*, ed. Denis Donoghue, 269. Yeats left an unpublished manuscript, "Leo Africanus," consisting of epistolary exchanges with the spirit. Current Western interest in the Muslim world has again led to rediscovery of Leo Africanus: see Natalie Zemon Davis, *Trickster Travels: A Sixteenth-Century Muslim between Worlds* (2006). The Arabian fascinations of Edwardian occultists have not been much noted; Alex Owen focuses on their Indian passions in *The Place of Enchantment*. On occultists' Celtic interests, see also Owen, *Place of Enchantment*, 68–69. Gilles Deleuze and Félix Guattari refer to an unpublished work, *Intellectual Nomadism*, by the Scottish poet and heir to the Yeatsian strain of mystical modernism, Kenneth White, observing that "the marriage of the Celt and the Orient, inspires a properly nomad thought that sweeps up English literature and constitutes American literature" (*A Thousand Plateaus*, 379). See also chapter 9.

50. Woolf, *Voyage Out*, 205; Woolf to Lytton Strachey, 1916, quoted in Peter Stansky, *On or About December 1910*, 67; Nigel Nicolson, preface to *Letters of Virginia Woolf*, 1:xxi.

51. Sykes, *Dar-ul-Islam*, 219; D. Carruthers, *Arabian Adventure*, 4, 15; Fraser, *Short Cut to India*, 135, 137, 217; Soane, *To Mesopotamia*, 90; Bell to Florence Bell, 5 March

1911, in *Letters of Gertrude Bell*, 1:288; Lawrence to his mother, 2 Aug. 1909, in *Letters of T. E. Lawrence*, 71; Sykes, "Journeys in North Mesopotamia," 238; Herbert, *Ben Kendim*, 58–59, 115. On the progressivism of occultists, see Owen, *Place of Enchantment*, 26. On European travel's secularization of time, see Johannes Fabian, *Time and the Other*, 6–13; Said, *Orientalism*, 122; Pratt, *Imperial Eyes*, 27.

52. A. J. B. Wavell, *Modern Pilgrim*, 126, 130–31; Bray, *Shifting Sands*, 23; Bell, *Amurath to Amurath*, 160; Walter Benjamin, "The Work of Art in the Age of Mechanical Reproduction." To be sure, despite, or perhaps because of, industrialization, parts of England were also still hallowed by their past. See John Taylor, *A Dream of England: Landscape, Photography, and the Tourist's Imagination*, 27, 81, 107. The Irish, Scottish, and Welsh landscapes were also highly romanticized, but none of these had quite the feel of the truly antique and sacred land, especially given the recent geological and archaeological discoveries about the Middle East. Moreover, the aura perceived by an intelligence agent on the job matters quite differently from that perceived by a weekend tramper.

53. Tidrick, *Heart-Beguiling Araby*, 35–36; Leonard Woolley, *Dead Towns and Living Men: Being Pages from an Antiquary's Notebook*, 108–09; A. J. B. Wavell, *Modern Pilgrim*, 56–57, 105; Sykes to Wyndham, 25 March 1908, quoted in Leslie, *Mark Sykes*, 94; D. Carruthers, *Arabian Adventure*, 62; F. R. Maunsell, "The Hejaz Railway," *Geographical Journal* 32 (1908), 570; Bury, *Land of Uz*, xxviii; *Arabian Adventure*, 68; Bell, *Amurath to Amurath*, 124, 268–69; Philip Baldensperger, *The Immovable East: Studies of the People and Customs of Palestine*, xiii; T. E. Lawrence, *Seven Pillars*, 414; Kirkbride, *Awakening*, 45; Hogarth Papers: File 3: Hogarth to Mary, 19 Jan. 1918; Candler, *Long Road*, 2:105; FO 882/XIV: MIS/16/14: W. Ormsby-Gore, draft memo, Oct. 1916. My italics.

54. D. Carruthers, *Arabian Adventure*, 14, 16, 68; Jebb, *By Desert Ways*, 28; LCLUL: MES 043: Prof. G. B. Harrison, 2nd Lt., "My First War," TS, n.d.; Bell to Florence Bell, 27 Aug. 1916, in *Letters of Gertrude Bell*, 1:386; Dickson to his mother, 10 Aug. 1915; Owen, *Place of Enchantment*, esp. 159.

55. Bell, *Amurath to Amurath*, 193, 197; Sykes, *Caliph's Last Heritage*, 1, and *Dar-ul-Islam*, 52.

56. Bell, *Amurath to Amurath*, vii; Bell, 28 Jan. 1914, quoted in Burgoyne, *Gertrude Bell*, 1:292; Jebb, *By Desert Ways*, 15, 185, 203, 260–63, 305–06; Hogarth, *Penetration of Arabia*, 5; Soane, *To Mesopotamia*, 54; Sykes, *Caliph's Last Heritage*, 4, 57, 396, 468; Hume-Griffith, *Behind the Veil*, 131, 257–60; Lawrence, quoted in Jean M. E. Béraud-Villars, *T. E. Lawrence; Or, The Search for the Absolute*, 207; Bell to Florence Bell, 26 May 1916, in *Letters of Gertrude Bell*, 1:378; LCLUL: MES 043: Harrison, handwritten document, Dec. 1915; Said, *Orientalism*, 120–22; Kinglake, 1844, quoted in *Orientalism*, 193.

57. Bell, quoted in Janet Wallach, *Desert Queen: The Extraordinary Life of Gertrude Bell*, 90; Hogarth, *Wandering Scholar*, 1–2; Bell, *Amurath to Amurath*, 116; Jebb, *By Desert Ways*, 185–86. The geologist Doughty had inaugurated this trend. Tidrick, *Heart-Beguiling Araby*, 143–55.

58. Bell to Chirol, 5 April 1914, quoted in Burgoyne, *Gertrude Bell*, 1:304; Walter de la Mare, "Arabia" (1912), available at http://www.theotherpages.org/poems/

delamar1.html [8 Feb. 2007]. The permanence of this change set Edwardians apart from their predecessors—see Tidrick, *Heart-Beguiling Araby*, 160; Rana Kabbani, *Europe's Myths about the Orient*, 93. In *Asia and Europe*, Townsend quotes a poem by Wilfrid Blunt embodying a similar sentiment: "Yours…the way/ Of an old wisdom by our world forgot,/ The courage of a day which knew not death./ Well may we sons of Japhet in dismay/ Pause in our vain mad fight for life and breath,/ Beholding you. I bow and reason not" (301).

59. Bell, "A Post-Road through the Syrian Desert, Part I," *Blackwood's Magazine* 194 (1913), 584; [Bell], review of *Land of Uz*, by Bury, *TLS*, 4 Jan. 1913, 4; [Abbott], "A Wandering Scholar"; Hogarth, quoted in H. V. F. Winstone, *Gertrude Bell*, 119; [Bell], review of *The Immovable East*, by Baldensperger, *TLS*, 1 May 1913, 182; Jebb, *By Desert Ways*, 111; William Willcocks, "Mesopotamia: Past, Present, and Future," *Geographical Journal* 35 (1910), 1.

60. Keith Neilson, "Tsars and Commissars: W. Somerset Maugham, *Ashenden* and Images of Russia in British Adventure Fiction, 1890–1930," 481–87.

61. Boehmer, "'Immeasurable Strangeness,'" 100–02.

CHAPTER 3

1. Beach, "Note on Military Intelligence"; J. Scott, *Seeing Like a State*, 54; Marlowe, *Late Victorian*, 152. See also Winstone, *Illicit Adventure*, 181.

2. The incomplete success of the Arab Revolt has been put down to exaggerated reports about the strength of the Arab Party, and the Kut disaster has been put down to generals' whimsical attitude toward intelligence that they presumed to be inherently unreliable. See Fromkin, *Peace to End All Peace*, 186; Popplewell, "Intelligence in Mesopotamia," 157, 159; Peter Morris, "Intelligence and Its Interpretation," 97; P. Graves, *Percy Cox*, 195; W. D. Bird, *A Chapter of Misfortunes: The Battles…in Mesopotamia*, 30, 35; Moberly, *Campaign in Mesopotamia*, 2:51–57; G. M. Chesney, "The Mesopotamian Breakdown," *Fortnightly Review* 108 (1917), 251.

3. Bell, 1928, quoted in O'Brien, *Gertrude Bell*, 9–10. Fromkin mentions in passing the intelligence community's tendency to accept information without checking it, relying instead on an "intuitive ability…the gift of being able to divine the extent to which any native is telling the truth" (*Peace to End All Peace*, 93). Dodge puts the British failure to attempt extensive surveying or census-taking in occupied Iraq down to costs, local antipathy, and loss of confidence in such methods in the changing international context (*Inventing Iraq*, 63, 73–75).

4. Colonel C. E. Callwell, *Small Wars: Their Principles and Practice*, 49–50; Lorimer, Tour Diary no. 1 of 1909; Leachman, quoted in Bray, *Paladin of Arabia*, 171; Consul Monahan to Lowther, 2 Dec. 1908, in *Records of the Hijaz*, 6:559; Lorimer, summary, 4 June 1912; Bell, quoted in Fromkin, *Peace to End All Peace*, 9; A. J. B. Wavell, *Modern Pilgrim*, 147–48, 191, 309. Callwell's text was based on his experiences in the Second Afghan War and the First Boer War. The work, which became the official textbook on the subject, began as an essay that won the Royal United Service Institute gold medal in 1885 but appeared as a book in 1896 after he had also served in Middle Eastern intelligence.

5. Bray, *Paladin of Arabia*, 137, 146; Churchill, *Malakand Field Force*, 43; FO 371/153: 24676: Knox to Cox, tour notes, 28 March 1906; Leachman, "A Journey in North-Eastern Arabia," *Geographical Journal* 37 (1911), 266; Consul Jeddah to O'Conor, 15 Jan. 1903, in *Records of the Hijaz*, 6:259; Bell, *Amurath to Amurath*, 196; D. Carruthers, *Arabian Adventure*, 88; IOR: L/PS/10/135: Darwin to IO, 11 Feb. 1909; Callwell, *Small Wars*, 53–54 (my emphasis); Lorimer, Tour Diary no. 1 of 1909; Consul, "Report on…Hejaz Vilayet," 12 Feb. 1905, in *Records of the Hijaz*, 6:363–71; A. J. B. Wavell, *Modern Pilgrim*, 147–48; Bray, *Shifting Sands*, 184–85.

6. Bell to Hugh Bell, 27 July 1917, quoted in Burgoyne, *Gertrude Bell*, 2:62; Aubrey Herbert, *Mons, ANZAC, and Kut*, 62; FO 371/3393: 93384: PO Hamilton, memo on Koweit, 2 April 1918; Black Tab [pseud.], *On the Road to Kut; A Soldier's Story of the Mesopotamian Campaign*, 286. Further examples abound; see, for instance, Edmonds Papers: Edmonds to "Chick," 24 April 1916; FO 371/2781: 201201: Arabian Report no. 21, n.d.; FO 371/3058: 128482: Small to CPO Baghdad, Intelligence Report, 5 April 1917; Parker, reports to Arab Bureau, 7 Oct. 1916 and end-Oct. 1916, quoted in Winstone, *Diaries of Parker*, 141, 167; FO 882: T. E. Lawrence, "Diary of a Second Journey," *Arab Bulletin* 36 (Dec. 1916); "Record of the Rising"; Clayton to Wingate, 13 Nov. 1916, quoted in J. Wilson, *Lawrence of Arabia*, 323; FO 371/2140: 46261: Consul Jeddah to Mallet, 12 Sept. 1914; FO 371/2144: 69321: Knox to Foreign Department, Simla, 30 Sept. 1914; Leith-Ross, "Secret Service or Intelligence," 8, and "Character and Qualifications of Intelligence Personnel," n.d., 8; FO 882/XV: RS/16/18: Wemyss, notes, 31 March 1916; FO 882/XII: IND/17/6: fforde, 26 Sept. 1917; FO 686/6/Pt.2: Newcombe to Wilson, 3 April 1917; FO 686/6/Pt.1: Garland, report, 6 March 1917; LCLUL: EP 066: A. T. P. Robertson, "Experiences of a Brigade Intelligence Officer: Palestine, 1917–18"; WO 106/6055: W. H. Gribbon, MI2b, 18 March 1918; FO 686/6/Pt.1: [Lloyd or Lawrence], Report on Sherif's visit to Jedda, Jan. 1917; FO 371/2775: 178900: Storrs, report on Jeddah, 10 June 1916; FO 686/6/Pt.2: Joyce to Director, Arbur, 9 April 1917.

7. Said, *Orientalism*, 216; Callwell, *Small Wars*, 44; IOR: L/PS/10/259: 3263: Hunter to Assistant Surveyor-General, 6 April 1910 and 5125: Shakespear's correspondence; IOR: L/PS/10/135: 3216: Bury to Ritchie, 15 Nov. 1909; A. J. B. Wavell, *Modern Pilgrim*, 181.

8. S. Ryan, *Cartographic Eye*, 24; Hogarth, *Penetration of Arabia*, v, 323; Hugh Robert Mill, "The Present Problems of Geography," *Geographical Journal* 25 (1905), 7; E. A. Reeves, "Notes and Suggestions on Geographical Surveying," *Geographical Journal* 23 (1904), 100, 103; Malcolm Fergusson, "Appendix: Methods Used in Surveying," *Geographical Journal* 17 (1901), 37; appendix I "Difficulties of Penetrating Arabia," in General Staff, "Notes on Arabia"; Crowe to Wavell, 16 Jan. 1912, in A. J. B. Wavell, *Modern Pilgrim*, 340; Bell, *Amurath to Amurath*, 131, 167, 201; Sykes, *Caliph's Last Heritage*, 436; D. Carruthers, "Journey in North-Western Arabia," 234; Shakespear, 2 Feb. 1910, tour diary 1910; Bell to her family, 5 March 1911, and to Florence Bell, 20 Dec. 1913, in *Letters of Gertrude Bell*, 1:288, 313–14; Bell to her father, 30 Jan. 1900, quoted in Burgoyne, *Gertrude Bell*, 1:87; Sykes, "Journeys in North Mesopotamia," 242; D. Carruthers, *Arabian Adventure*, 120; Jebb, *By Desert Ways*, 224–25; Brent, *Far Arabia*, 145. On the mirage's resistance to imperial scrutiny, see *Cartographic Eye*, 86;

on vision and exploration, see also Pratt, *Imperial Eyes*, 204; Matthew Edney, *Mapping an Empire*, chaps. 2 and 3.

9. D. Carruthers, *Arabian Adventure*, 51; Jebb, *By Desert Ways*, 63, 260–65; Bell to her family, 17 Feb. 1911, in *Letters of Gertrude Bell*, 1:276.

10. "Across Arabia in a Motor-Car," *Times*, 10 May 1909, 7; FO 882/XIII: MES/16/3: Bell to Hogarth, April 1916; Lawrence to Hogarth, 20 April 1915; Lawrence to Clayton, Dec. 1916; Dickson to his mother, 26 Aug. 1915; WO 287/20: Indian General Staff, *Handbook on Routes in Arabia: 1916* (Simla, 1915); LCLUL: GS 1276: Box 3: Capt. C. R. S. Pitman to his family, 17 Feb. 1916; FO 882/XVI: SY/16/1: Lawrence, "The Conquest of Syria," 1916; Leith-Ross Papers: Leith-Ross, "Report on Surveys, Mesopotamian Expeditionary Force," n.d., 1; Popplewell, "Intelligence in Mesopotamia," 152; Captain H. Birch Reynardson, *Mesopotamia, 1914–15: Extracts from a Regimental Officer's Diary*, 214; Martin Swayne, *In Mesopotamia*, 7, 66–67, 119; A. G. Wauchope, chap. 7, in *With a Highland Regiment in Mesopotamia: 1916–1917*, by One of Its Officers, 70–71 (originally in *Blackwood's* [Aug. 1917]); LCLUL: GS 1276: Box 3: Pitman to his family, 29 Sept. 1916; Bell to Hugh Bell, 23 Nov. 1916, in *Letters of Gertrude Bell*, 1:389; Milward to his mother, 14 Dec. 1914; FO 882/VI: HRG/17/19: [illegible] to CIGS, 19 March 1917; DMO to War Cabinet, late 1917, described in Hughes, *Allenby and British Strategy*, 62; Kirkbride, *Awakening*, 53; Wireless officer, reported in Swayne, *In Mesopotamia*, 66–68 (my italics); Leith-Ross Papers: Leith-Ross, "The Physical and Climatic Difficulties of the Mesopotamian Theatre of War," 14 Aug. 1916; Edmund Dane, *British Campaigns in the Nearer East, 1914–1918*, 1:288; Candler, *Long Road*, 1:111, 117; Tab, *Road to Kut*, 220, 232, 282–83; WO 32/5225: General Staff, appendix 1 in Cabinet Paper on Mesopotamia, 12 Nov. 1919; Herbert, 10 March 1916, quoted in *Mons, ANZAC, and Kut*, 194; Leith-Ross, "Tactical Side," 12; "Report on Surveys," 1. Further examples abound: for instance, MECA: J. D. Crowdy Papers: diary of letters to his wife, book 4, 13 Feb. 1916, f. 24; MECA: Sir Harold Frederick Downie Papers: diary of Jan.–June 1916; LCLUL: MES 092: Capt. Ernest Charles Rycroft, diary, 8 Feb. 1918; LCLUL: GALL (REC) 206/1: Brigadier R. B. Rathbone, recollections; LCLUL: MES 007: Brigadier Captain E. V. R. Bellers to his mother, 24 Feb. 1917; IOR: Eur MSS: F177/87: Emily Lorimer, "The Land of the Lost," *Basrah Times*, 1916.

11. Lorimer, *Gazetteer*, 2:767; Butler, "Baghdad to Damascus," 520; D. Carruthers, "Journey in North-Western Arabia," 240; Jebb, *By Desert Ways*, 185–86; *Handbook of Arabia*, 1:18; FO 882: Lawrence, "Syria: The Raw Material," *Arab Bulletin* 44 (March 1917), 107–14; Parker, 15 Nov. 1916, in Winstone, *Diaries of Parker*, 175; Bray, Arabian Report no. 18, 20 Nov. 1916, in *Records of the Hijaz*, 7:443; H. Young Papers: File 3: Notes for Lecture at Staff College, TS, [early 1920s]. On explorers' treatment of Australia's aborigines, see S. Ryan, *Cartographic Eye*, 124. The continually reorganized Turkish Order of Battle made it a difficult intelligence target, convincing Popplewell that Kut was not the fault of Britain's poor intelligence-gathering; the changeling Turkish Army was beyond reasonable assessment ("Intelligence in Mesopotamia," 148–49, 166; also Sheffy, *British Military Intelligence*, 326–27; Anthony Clayton, *Forearmed: A History of the Intelligence Corps*, 47). But idiosyncratic military organization was hardly an "oriental" peculiarity: Leith-Ross attests: "The nomenclature of our units was a constant source of trouble to the enemy, whose own units are numbered.... Our

many abbreviations, crests and distinguishing badges of formations also puzzled the enemy badly" ("Secret Service or Intelligence," 8).

12. Colonel T. H. Holdich, review of *Topographical Surveying,* by H. M. Wilson, *Geographical Journal* 19 (1902), 75; Wahab, quoted in Hogarth, "Problems in Exploration," 565; "Problems in Exploration," 551, 553; Maunsell, "Notes to Accompany Lt-Col. Maunsell's Map of Eastern Turkey in Asia," *Geographical Journal* 28 (1906), 163. The viewer's external position is essential to Western cartography, as is his implied position at the mapped area's center (S. Ryan, *Cartographic Eye,* 101).

13. Hogarth, comment on Butler, "Baghdad to Damascus," 533–34; Butler, "Baghdad to Damascus," 517–26; D. Carruthers, "Journey in North-Western Arabia," 225–46; Bell, "The East Bank of the Euphrates from Tel Ahmar to Hit," *Geographical Journal* 36 (1910), 513; Leachman, "A Journey in North-Eastern Arabia," *Geographical Journal* 37 (1911), 265; Hogarth, review of Bell's *Amurath to Amurath, Geographical Journal* 37 (1911), 435; Lt.-Col. F. Fraser Hunter, "Reminiscences of the Map of Arabia and the Persian Gulf," *Geographical Journal* 54 (1919), 356.

14. Hogarth, "Problems in Exploration," 549–50, 562–63; A. J. B. Wavell, *Modern Pilgrim,* 203; Bell to Chirol, May 1907, quoted in Burgoyne, *Gertrude Bell,* 1:245; Bell, Diary of a Journey to Hayyil, 16 Feb. 1914, 33; Jebb, *By Desert Ways,* 16; Holdich, *Tibet the Mysterious* (1906), quoted in T. Richards, *Imperial Archive,* 21–22; Adelson, *Mark Sykes,* 123. Certainly, maps did improve, but the top-rated maps were not those based on direct observation and mathematical survey but on compilations of classical descriptive works (Lorimer, *Gazetteer,* 2:658, 1313). In short, the mapping process was nothing like either the earlier, epic surveying of India or the fanatically scientific Ordnance Surveys of Britain. When maps eventually were produced and Mesopotamia triangulated during the war, it was by adopting special rules and procedures to accommodate the "peculiarities" of the landscape. Leith-Ross Papers: Leith-Ross, appendix 4, "Notes on the special topographical features and information peculiar to Mesopotamia required on a military map," 21–22; Lawrence, Report on Intelligence; F. W. Pirrie, "War Surveys in Mesopotamia," *Geographical Journal* 52 (1918); G. A. Beazeley, "Surveys in Mesopotamia during the War," *Geographical Journal* 55 (1920).

15. Bell to Hugo Bell, 16 May 1900, in *Letters of Gertrude Bell,* 1:104. Sykes, *Caliph's Last Heritage,* 307, 395–96, 533; D. Carruthers, *Arabian Adventure,* 122–23; Capt. A. F. Townshend, *A Military Consul in Turkey,* 61; Bell, Diary of Journey to Hayyil, 23 Jan. 1913, 11; A. J. B. Wavell, *Modern Pilgrim,* 158; FO 371/152: 22155: Sykes, report, 24 June 1906; Swayne, *In Mesopotamia,* 51; Lawrence to his family, 18 May 1916, in *Home Letters,* 321; Crowdy, diary of letters, book 3, 29 Jan. 1916, f. 22; Dickson Papers: Box 1: 3rd booklet: Dickson to Greene, 15 Nov. 1915; Candler, *Long Road,* 1:85; Tennant, *In the Clouds,* 11, 281; Sykes, *Dar-ul-Islam,* 290; Hume-Griffith, *Behind the Veil,* preface, 328. On Australia, see S. Ryan, *Cartographic Eye,* 86. On the end of the Arctic, Alpine, and English sublimes, see Chauncey C. Loomis, "The Arctic Sublime"; David Robertson, "Mid-Victorians amongst the Alps," 112; George Levine, "Ruskin and the Novelists," 133–34, 142; J. Taylor, *Dream of England,* 36. On the desert sublime, see Bevis, "Desert Places," 62–64. On silence and the void, see Kern, *Time and Space,* 170.

16. See reports cited throughout. On realism and fiction in exploration reports, see S. Ryan, *Cartographic Eye,* 42.

17. Knox to Cox, 28 March 1906; IOR: L/PS/7/253: Lorimer, summary for September 1911, 2 Oct. 1911; Shakespear, tour diary, 13 Feb. 1910; Sykes, report, c. April 1908; Capt. J. H. Smith, "Diary of a Journey," 272; Sykes, report, 24 June 1906, and FO minute, 7 July 1906 thereon. Adelson's conclusion that Sykes's reports "lacked the form and objectivity necessary to be taken seriously in Whitehall" discounts Whitehall's own taste for the fantastic (*Mark Sykes*, 118, 123).

18. Churchill, *Malakand Field Force*, 43; Woolley, *Dead Towns*, 108–09.

19. Candler, *Long Road*, 1:117; Lloyd to [Clayton?], 27 May 1916; FO 371/2486: 34982: Sykes to DMO, 2 Aug. 1915 (my italics); FO 686/6/Pt.2: McMahon to Grey, 10 May 1916; Bell to her parents, 9 May 1918, quoted in Burgoyne, *Gertrude Bell*, 2:85; Weldon, *"Hard Lying,"* 154; Bell to Hugh Bell, 18 May, 2 March, and 29 Dec. 1917, in *Letters of Gertrude Bell*, 1:399, 2:410–11, 437–38; FO 882/XIII: MES/16/15: Bell to Hogarth, 14 May 1916 and MES/16/13: April 1916; Hogarth, "Arab Bulletin"; Malcolm Brown, introduction to T. E. Lawrence, *Secret Despatches from Arabia*, 16–17, 22; Lawrence to C. E. Wilson, 2 Sept. 1917, in *Selected Letters*, 121; Lawrence to Richards, 15 July 1918; Hamilton, memo on Koweit; T. E. Lawrence, "The Howeitat and Their Chiefs," *Arab Bulletin* 57 (July 1917); "Syria: The Raw Material." Examples of others' reports: FO 882/VII: HRG/18/27: Garland, "A Day at El Jafr," Dec. 1918; Philby, report, *Arab Bulletin* 84 (April 1918), 106; FO 371/2782: 205732: Storrs, diary...Jeddah, 27 Sept. 1916, minuted as "entertaining reading"; FO 371/3046: 12686: Bell, "A Ruler of the Desert," 27 Nov. 1916; FO 371/3390: 204149: Hamilton, diary...Nejd, 1 Feb. 1918. Peter Morris has also remarked these agents' oddly "impressionistic" and "highly-coloured" reporting ("Intelligence and Its Interpretation," 85). The bureau became an impromptu archive. Old reports and travelogues were hastily shipped there. Much material was transferred from the Egyptian War Office library and the Khedivial library on loan; some brought from Khartoum. A shopping list was submitted to the Admiralty. Eventually it housed more than three hundred volumes.

20. Winstone, *Gertrude Bell*, 196–96; Wallach, *Desert Queen*, 207; IOR: L/PS/10/586: Hirtzel, minute, 22 Jan. 1917, on Arabian reports no. 25 and 26; Westrate, *Arab Bureau*, 104–05; Brown, "Lawrence of *Secret Despatches*," 12; Connell, quoted in Winstone, *Illicit Adventure*, 361; Meinertzhagen, 10 Dec. 1917, in *Middle East Diary: 1917–1956*, 28. See also Bar-Yosef, "Last Crusade?" 108–09.

21. Sykes, *Caliph's Last Heritage*, 475; Isaiah Berlin, *Historical Inevitability*, 1955, quoted in Said, *Orientalism*, 70; D. Carruthers, *Arabian Adventure*, 35; "Journey in North-Western Arabia," 230; Sykes, "Journeys in North Mesopotamia," 242, and *Dar-ul-Islam*, 52. See S. Ryan, *Cartographic Eye*, 122, 126, on Australia.

22. Said, *Orientalism*, 70; A. J. B. Wavell, *Modern Pilgrim*, 40–45; "Intelligence Methods in Peace Time."

23. Frederic Lees, introduction to Baldensperger, *Immovable East*, vii; Liddell Hart, "T. E. Lawrence," 23–24; Hogarth, quoted in Nasir, *Arabs and the English*, 125; Dobbs, report on Bell to the CO [postwar], quoted in "Gertrude Bell's Letters," *Times*, 23 Aug. 1927, 11; Bell, *Desert and the Sown*, 260; Kemball to Secretary to the Government of India in the Foreign Department, 5 Feb. 1904; FO 685/3: Vice Consul Hodeidah to Jeddah Consul, 6 May 1904; "Intelligence Methods in Peace Time"; A. J. B. Wavell,

Modern Pilgrim, 28, 40–41, 204; D. Carruthers, "Journey in North-Western Arabia," 228. Emphasis added. Mack writes that Lawrence was not actually poor but lived *"as if he were* a poor native" to enter local life, in a manner recalling Kim (*Prince of Our Disorder*, 92).

24. FO 882: Lawrence, "Twenty-Seven Articles," *Arab Bulletin* 60 (Aug. 1917), 347–53; Joyce to Clayton, 25 Sept. 1917, quoted in J. Wilson, *Lawrence of Arabia*, 448; Liddell Hart, in *T. E. Lawrence, by His Friends*, ed. A. W. Lawrence, 150; H. St. John B. Philby, *Arabian Days: An Autobiography*, 96, 113; Philby Papers: Philby, "Mesopotage," chap. 5, MS, [1930s]; Tennant, *In the Clouds*, 27; Presland, *Deedes Bey*, 266–67 (my italics).

25. A. Blunt, *Pilgrimage to Nejd*, 1:xvii, and *Bedouin Tribes*, 7. Nasir, *Arabs and the English*, 122; Liddell Hart, "*T. E. Lawrence*," 24; Will Lawrence to a friend, 14 Oct. 1913, quoted in *Letters of T. E. Lawrence*, 158; Soane, *To Mesopotamia*, 317; D. Carruthers, *Arabian Adventure*, 28; Lawrence to Mrs. Reider, 12 Sept. 1912, in *Letters of T. E. Lawrence*, 149; A. J. B. Wavell, *Modern Pilgrim*, 206. My italics.

26. Macmillan Papers: Hogarth to Macmillan, 31 May 1911; FO 371/2135: 24783: Erskine, summary, 19 June 1914; Sykes, *Dar-ul-Islam*, 171; Soane, *To Mesopotamia*, 365–66; IOR: L/PS/10/135: 801: Bury to the Government of Bombay, 7 Nov. 1905, and Maitland to the Government of Bombay, 10 May 1901; Bray, *Paladin of Arabia*, 255–56; Sir Edwin Pears, *Forty Years in Constantinople*, 138; Philip Graves, *Briton and Turk*, 158; Silvestri, "Thrill of 'Simply Dressing Up'," par. 6–7. Their colonial backgrounds quickly convinced commissioners of the Metropolitan Police of the acceptability of disguise in their work too. See Stefan Petrow, "The Rise of the Detective in London, 1869–1914." On espionage and gentlemanliness, see also chapter 2, note 28.

27. Kabbani, *Europe's Myths*, 91; Said, *Orientalism*, 195–97; T. Richards, *Imperial Archive*, 25; Winstone, *Captain Shakespear*, 73; Andrew, *Her Majesty's Secret Service*, 26; Bell to her family, 5 March 1911, in *Letters of Gertrude Bell*, 1:289; Crow to Lowther, 15 March 1913; Bayly, *Empire and Information*, 55, 179; A. J. B. Wavell, *Modern Pilgrim*, 40–41; Lawrence, quoted in Liddell Hart, "*T. E. Lawrence*," 24.

28. Lawrence to Richards, 15 July 1918; H. St. John Philby, *The Heart of Arabia: A Record of Travel and Exploration*, 1:86–87; Buxton to his family, 4 Aug. 1918, quoted in R. Graves, *Lawrence and the Arabs*, 337; Sykes to DMO, 15 Nov. 1915; Philby, *Arabian Days*, 148; Young, *Independent Arab*, 156; FO 686/6/Pt.2: Garland to Director, Arab Bureau, and Wilson, 31 Aug. 1917; FO 686/6/Pt.1: Newcombe, report, 6 March 1917; Lawrence, "Twenty-Seven Articles"; Bray, *Paladin of Arabia*, 303–04; Lawrence to Liddell Hart, quoted in Mack, *Prince of Our Disorder*, 162. Early in the war, Lawrence did pose as a Syrian officer in the Hejaz. Some insisted that Leachman never tried to pass as an Arab among his Arab friends—C. F. M., "Lieut.-Col. G. E. Leachman...," *JCAS* 8 (1921).

29. FO 371/350: 15856: Maunsell to Gleichen, 16 April 1907; "Difficulties of Penetrating Arabia by Travellers," in General Staff, "Notes on Arabia"; Sykes, *Caliph's Last Heritage*, 4; D. Carruthers, "Journey in North-Western Arabia," 234; FO 371/1015: 34750: Lorimer to Government of India, 20 Aug. 1910; Lorimer, Tour Diary no. 1 of 1909, appendix; Bray, *Paladin of Arabia*, 184; Chirol, *Middle Eastern Question*, 299–301; FO 371/1820: 22076: IO to FO, 9 July 1913; A. F. Townshend, *Military*

Consul, 220; Monahan to Chargé d'Affaires, Constantinople, 14 April 1908, in *Records of the Hijaz*, 6:601; Lorimer, summary, 6 May 1912; Bell, *Desert and the Sown*, ix, 227; Sykes to Grey, 14 Aug. 1907. (In *The Caliph's Last Heritage*, he cites 7,500 miles of riding [553].)

30. *Memoirs of Sir Ronald Storrs*, 180; FO 882: *Arab Bulletin* 95, 96, 98 (July 1918), 227, 235, 264; Elizabeth Monroe, *Philby of Arabia*, 78; FO 882/VII: HRG/17/55: Clayton to CIGS, 11 July 1917; Bell to her parents, 16 March 1918, quoted in Burgoyne, *Gertrude Bell*, 2:73; Philby, *Arabian Days*, 145, 167, 353–54; *Heart of Arabia*, 1:234. This paragraph is also based on Young's, Lawrence's, Kirkbride's, Philby's, Newcombe's, Edmonds's, and Bell's wartime papers and reports. For reports on some political officers' tours, see FO 371/3400; FO 882/VII: HRG/17/93: Joyce to Clayton, 4 Nov. 1917; Bray, note, 27 Sept. 1917. See chapter 1 for more on agents' wartime freedom.

31. *Oxford English Dictionary*, 3rd ed., s.v. "Intuition"; Bell, *Desert and the Sown*, ix, 227, and *Amurath to Amurath*, 321; Aylmer Haldane, *The Insurrection in Mesopotamia, 1920*, 314; Townsend, *Asia and Europe*, 167; FO 371/156: 40660: Sykes, report, 3 Dec. 1906; Churchill, *Malakand Field Force*, 39; Lawrence, *Seven Pillars*, 600; Wireless officer, reported in Swayne, *In Mesopotamia*, 66–68; Dickson Papers: Box 2: File 1: Dickson to his mother, n.d.; Candler, *Long Road*, 2:84–85. All this calls into question historians' uncritical reproduction of contemporary descriptions of obstacles to intelligence collection (Barker, *Bastard War*, 28, 404–05; Popplewell, "Intelligence in Mesopotamia," 149–52). Deleuze and Guattari describe "smooth space" as a place not strictly measurable, where one must listen and feel direction as much as see it. "Immersion in nomadic smooth space," they explain, "is immersion in something more vast than any psyche can provide.... The desert or the sea ... is limitless in the arc of its vanishing" (*Thousand Plateaus*, 389). See also Edward Casey, *The Fate of Place*, 305–07.

32. Jebb, *By Desert Ways*, 16–17; Bell to her family, 16 May 1900, in *Letters of Gertrude Bell*, 1:103; Fraser, *Short Cut to India*, 301; Sykes, *Caliph's Last Heritage*, 4–5; Bell, *Amurath to Amurath*, 303; LCLUL: MES 074: K. K. O'Connor to his sister, 10 March 1917; LCLUL: MES 090: P. J. Rolt to Liddle, 20 Dec. 1972; LCLUL: GS 1144: Box 2: 2nd Lt. R. C. Morton, "Diary of an eastern excursion...," 29 May 1917; Candler, *Long Road*, 1:144; 2:97; Reynardson, *Mesopotamia*, 234; Lawrence, *Seven Pillars*, 439, 563; Edmonds Papers: Edmonds to his mother, 24 April 1916; Philby, *Heart of Arabia*, 2:257; Dickson Papers: Box 1: File 3A: Dickson to his mother, n.d. [c. 1914–15]; Swayne, *In Mesopotamia*, 76, 160–61.

33. Sykes, *Caliph's Last Heritage*, 303; Liddell Hart, "T. E. Lawrence," 24–25.

34. D. Carruthers, *Arabian Adventure*, 16, 25, 51; Sykes, report, 24 June 1906; *Handbook of Arabia*, 1:20–22; Bury, *Land of Uz*, 151; Bell to her family, 8 Feb. 1905, and 20 May 1900, in *Letters of Gertrude Bell*, 1:106, 182; Sykes, *Caliph's Last Heritage*, 307; Bell, *Desert and the Sown*, 48–49, 60; Bray, *Shifting Sands*, 14. My italics.

35. Bury, *Land of Uz*, 252; Bell, *Desert and the Sown*, 116; Sykes, *Dar-ul-Islam*, 59; Liddell Hart, "T. E. Lawrence," 26; Philby, *Heart of Arabia*, 2:215 (my italics); D. Carruthers, "Journey in North-Western Arabia," 234, 237–38; FO 371/153: 24676: Knox to Cox, 7 Feb. 1906 and enclosed report by Shakespear; Shakespear to Cox, 4 April 1910; Owen, *Place of Enchantment*, 239. Interestingly, Wilfrid Blunt had tried to

disabuse contemporaries of their belief in Bedouins' "wonderful faculties of sight and hearing" and navigational genius by pointing to their inveterate zigzagging (appendix, in A. Blunt, *Bedouin Tribes*, 389). Under Herbert Spencer's empiricist influence, Meinertzhagen perhaps alone recognized that he saw life where others saw emptiness not because of "better vision but of better eye-training" (*Black Sheep*, 274).

36. Liddell Hart, "*T. E. Lawrence*," 61; Maitland to Government of Bombay, 10 May 1901; Leslie, *Mark Sykes*, 57; Flecker to Frank Savery, July 1913, in *Letters from Abroad*, 98; Lorimer, Tour Journal no. 1 of 1910; *Gazetteer*, 2:iii, 1352; Shakespear to Cox, 4 April 1910; Sykes to Grey, 14 Aug. 1907; FO 371/1799: 11950: Crow to Lowther, 9 and 31 May 1913; FO 371/156: 40123: Knox, report, 26 Sept. 1906; G. W. Steevens, *With Kitchener to Khartum* (1900), quoted in Fromkin, *Peace to End All Peace*, 90; FO 371/1799: 11950: Commander Wood, report no. 9, 28 June 1913.

37. FO 882/VI: HRG/17/16: Clayton to Pearson, 2 March 1917; FO 882/XVI: SP/17/39: Clayton to Sykes, 22 July 1917; Stirling, *Safety Last*, 80, 128; Lawrence, *Seven Pillars*, 314; S. C. Rolls, *Steel Chariots in the Desert*, 238; Bell to Hugh Bell, 14 May 1916, in *Letters of Gertrude Bell*, 1:375; Dobbs, report on Bell to the CO [postwar]; Brigadier-General G. S. Clive, confidential report on Meinertzhagen, 1918, quoted in Occleshaw, *Armour Against Fate*, 97; IOR: L/PS/10/576: [Hirtzel?], minute on FO to IO, 20 Jan. 1917; FO 882/XV: PNA/16/2: Lawrence to Intrusive, 8 April 1916; Bray, *Paladin of Arabia*, 362; Presland, *Deedes Bey*, 168; "A fellow officer," obituary for Leachman, *Daily Telegraph*, 21 Aug. 1920; Tuohy, *Secret Corps*, 172–73; W. Ormsby Gore, "The Organization of British Responsibilities in the Middle East," *JCAS* 7 (1920), 95–96; Major C. S. Jarvis, *Arab Command: The Biography of Lieutenant-Colonel F. G. Peake Pasha*, 4th ed., 127. See also the obituary for Parker, *Times*, 3 Jan. 1936, 17; MECA: J. W. A. Young Papers: "A Little to the East," memoir, [c. 1940s], 141, on Lloyd and Lawrence.

38. Lawrence, *Seven Pillars*, 214; "Twenty-Seven Articles"; Lawrence to his family, 8 March 1918, in *Home Letters*, 348; Albert Cook, "*Seven Pillars of Wisdom*: Turns and Counter-Turns," 98; Bray, *Paladin of Arabia*, 190; Candler, *Long Road*, 2:210; Lawrence, Report on Intelligence; Leith-Ross Papers: "NOTES on the INTELLIGENCE COURSE held in BAGHDAD in October 1918," n.d.; WO 106/6055: Alexandria, telegram, 13 Aug. 1916; A. T. Wilson, *Loyalties*, 92; Bray, *Paladin of Arabia*, 361.

39. Bell to Hogarth, 20 May 1916; Meinertzhagen, *Army Diary*, 127; FO 882/XV: PNI/17/2: Bray to Wilson, 27 March 1917; FO 882/XII: KH/17/17: Lawrence to Wilson, 28 July 1917; FO 882/XV: PNI/17/1: Wilson to Cleveland, March 1917; FO 371/2781: 201201: Bray, 8 Nov. 1916, in Arabian Report no. 18, n.d.; FO 371/3403: 53608: Sykes, minute, 25 March 1918; FO 371/2140: 46261: Cairo to Military, India, 21 Sept. 1914; FO 371/2144: 69321: Knox to Foreign and Political Department, Simla, 30 Sept. 1914; IOR: L/PS/11/129: H. Whittall, intelligence on Mesopotamia, 7 Aug. 1917; C. Mackenzie, *Gallipoli Memories*, 99, and *My Life and Times: Octave Five, 1915–1923*, 89; Lawrence to his family, 14 Dec. 1917, in *Home Letters*, 344; Bertram Thomas, *Alarms and Excursions in Arabia*, 26; *Memoirs of Sir Ronald Storrs*, 204; R. Graves, *Lawrence and the Arabs*, 24; Philby, *Arabian Days*, 93; L. C. Dunsterville, *Stalky's Reminiscences*, 280; Raymond Savage, *Allenby of Armageddon*, 276, 309; "A fellow officer," obituary for Leachman; C. Mackenzie, *Greek Memories*, 29; Chesney, "Mesopotamian Breakdown," 251.

40. Stirling, *Safety Last*, 83–84; Tennant, *In the Clouds*, 27–28; Bray, *Paladin of Arabia*, 276, 303; Jarvis, *Arab Command*, 48; Rolls, *Steel Chariots*, 211; Ferdinand Tuohy, *The Crater of Mars*, 174–75; Lawrence, "Twenty-Seven Articles." On Dickson's and Soane's similar powers, see Dickson Papers: Box 2: File 1: Dickson to his mother, 14 Feb. 1917, and Box 1: File 4: 23 Jan. 1916; P. Graves, *Percy Cox*, 235. On Storrs's vain efforts, see Winstone, *Illicit Adventure*, 186.

41. Young, *Independent Arab*, 10, and Notes for Lecture at Staff College, 7–9; FO 371/2480: 88183: Bray to FO, 30 June 1915; FO 882/XIV: MIS/14/1: Intelligence Department, Cairo, "Appreciation of Situation in Arabia," 6 June 1914; FO 882/XX: AP/14/3: FO, telegram, quoted in Clayton to Wingate, 21 Nov. 1914; IOR: L/PS/10/523/Pt.1: Holderness to Chamberlain, 6 Nov. 1915; FO 882/II: AP/15/8: Parker to DMO, 21 Oct. 1915; IOR: L/PS/10/586: Hirtzel, minute, 29 Aug. 1916, on Arabian Report no. VI. For more, see Fromkin, *Peace to End All Peace*. Although Force D had initially been deployed partly with the idea of encouraging an Arab uprising in Mesopotamia, agents ultimately intuited that the Arab movement did not exist substantially there (FO 882/XII: KH/17/16: Clayton to Wilson, 28 April 1917; Lawrence to Clayton, 9 April 1916, quoted in J. Wilson, *Lawrence of Arabia*, 267; Lawrence, Report on Intelligence). A few efforts to reach out to Basra nationalists aside, British and, especially, British Indian ambitions in the area precluded a thorough exploration of the potential for an Arab revolt. Instead, Lawrence prescribed developmental projects to discipline the anarchic tribes: occupation rather than liberation.

42. FO 371/2486: 97255: Grey to Gulf resident, 9 June 1915; FO 882/XVII: SY/18/12: Walrond to Clayton, 17 July 1918 and SY/18/15, July 1918, and memo, SY/18/8: May 1918; Lawrence to E. T. Leeds, 16 Nov. 1914, in *Selected Letters*, 66–67. Walrond's notes formed the basis of the *Bulletin's* retrospective coverage of these organizations (90 [May 1918], 165–67), and of scholarship on the subject (Eliezer Tauber, "Secrecy in Early Arab Nationalist Organizations"). On this historiography, see Ghassan Atiyyah, *Iraq, 1908–1921*, chap. 2; Fieldhouse, *Western Imperialism*, 21–35 (which concludes the Arab movement was in its infancy in 1914). On the Declaration to the Seven, see Elizabeth Monroe, *Britain's Moment in the Middle East, 1914–1956*, 48.

43. Compton Mackenzie, quoted in Presland, *Deedes Bey*, 190–91; *Deedes Bey*, 238–39; Philby, *Arabian Days*, 113; Adelson, *Mark Sykes*, 186; FO 371/2379: 10096: Rodd to Grey, 19 July 1915, and G. R. C., minute thereon.

44. Lawrence, *Seven Pillars*, 468. On Lawrence's (often self-contradictory) monism, see Stephen Tabachnick, "A Fragmentation Artist," 17.

45. Edward Carpenter, *The Drama of Love and Death* (1912), quoted in Hynes, *Edwardian Turn of Mind*, 137. See also Sanford Schwartz, *The Matrix of Modernism*, 4–6; "The Mystical Revival," *TLS*, 20 March 1913, 117–18; review of *Man and Universe*, by Oliver Lodge, *TLS*, 15 Oct. 1908, 344.

46. See Mary Ann Gillies, *Henri Bergson and British Modernism*, 25–33, 41; Mark Antliff, *Inventing Bergson*, 10; Schwartz, *Matrix of Modernism*, 6.

47. Henri Bergson, *Creative Evolution* (1907), quoted in Gillies, *Henri Bergson*, 19; *Henri Bergson*, 37; Antliff, *Inventing Bergson*, 11; Schwartz, *Matrix of Modernism*, 27; Martin Jay, *Downcast Eyes: The Denigration of Vision in Twentieth-Century French*

Thought, 186, 196, 201. Jay writes that Arendt considered Bergson the first philosopher to dispute the nobility of sight. This was part of a broader revolution in spatial theory—the end of the Euclidean monopoly—partly resulting from study of tribal societies. Kern, *Time and Space,* 133–39; Schwartz, *Matrix of Modernism,* 16–17.

48. Schwartz, *Matrix of Modernism,* 12, 31; Ann Banfield, *The Phantom Table: Woolf, Fry, Russell, and the Epistemology of Modernism,* 6, 48; Bertrand Russell, "The Relation of Sense-Data to Physics," 1914, quoted in *Phantom Table,* 6.

49. Banfield, *Phantom Table,* 363; Bertrand Russell, *Our Knowledge of the External World* and *Problems of Philosophy* (1912) and *Problems of Philosophy* (1912), quoted in *Phantom Table,* 204.

50. *Uncle Hilary,* quoted in John Harwood, *Olivia Shakespear and W. B. Yeats,* 125–27; Flecker, *Hassan,* 6; J. Thompson, *Fiction, Crime, and Empire,* 111. See also Michael Levenson, *The Genealogy of Modernism: A Study of English Literary Doctrine, 1908–1922,* 211.

51. T. Richards, *Imperial Archive;* Buchan, *Greenmantle,* 13, 24, 26, 233, *Thirty-Nine Steps,* 83, and "Space," in *The Moon Endureth: Tales and Fancies,* 101–09, 116 (first appeared in *Blackwood's* 189 [May 1911], 600–613); Herbert, *Ben Kendim,* xv. Italics mine.

52. G. K. Chesterton, *The Man Who Was Thursday: A Nightmare,* in *The Essential G.K. Chesterton,* 195; T. Richards, *Imperial Archive,* 131–37; Fromkin, *Peace to End All Peace,* 93. See also Elmar Schenkel, "Visions from the Verge: Terror and Play in G. K. Chesterton's Imagination," 35.

53. Owen, *Place of Enchantment,* 21; Mead, quoted in Tryphonopoulos, "History of the Occult Movement," 19, 20; Sackville-West, "Nomads"; Mead, "The Rising Psychic Tide," *Quest* 3 (1911–12), 420, quoted in "History of the Occult Movement," 22; "The Secrets of Central Asia," *Spectator,* 13 March 1909, 413–14. On modernists' views of the artist, see James Joyce, *A Portrait of the Artist as a Young Man,* 319; Schwartz, *Matrix of Modernism,* 134. On Bergsonists as artists, see Gillies, *Henri Bergson,* 20. Bergson himself was not an occultist.

54. [Lane-Poole], review of *Desert and the Sown;* [R. G. Corbet], review of *The Witness of the Wilderness,* by G. Robinson Lees, *TLS,* 8 April 1909, 134 (Corbet had authored *Mohammedanism and the British Empire* [1901]); [Bell], review of *To Mesopotamia,* by Soane, *TLS,* 7 Nov. 1912, 490.

55. Said recognizes such a shift as well but dates it to the postwar period when orientalists began to advise Arab governments (*Orientalism,* 221–23).

CHAPTER 4

1. FO 882: [Lawrence?], "Mesopotamia: Note on the Supply of Labour in the Occupied Territories," *Arab Bulletin* 18 (Sept. 1916), 206; Lawrence, "Twenty-Seven Articles," and *Seven Pillars,* 346; Young, *Independent Arab,* 170; Rolls, *Steel Chariots,* 164–65; Bray, *Paladin of Arabia,* 272–73; Dickson Papers: Box 2: File 1: Dickson to his mother, 16 Dec. 1917 and File 2: 6 April 1918, 1 Sept. 1918; Bell to Hogarth, 20 May 1916.

2. Leith-Ross Papers: Leith-Ross, "Tactical Side," 33–34; "The control and safeguarding of codes and ciphers"; "Leakage of information through prisoners of war, September 1918"; "Secret Service or Intelligence," 1–2, 5–6.

3. Bell to Hogarth, 27 May 1916; MES/1/4: Sykes, memo, 28 Oct. 1915; FO 371/2771: 18845: Sykes to George [Lloyd?], n.d.

4. Dickson Papers: Box 1: File 3A: Dickson to his mother, 17 Feb. 1915; File 4: 13 March 1916; Box 2: File 1: 14 Feb. 1916; Philby, "Mesopotage," chap. 5; Obituary for Parker, *Times*, 3 Jan. 1936; "eye-witnesses," quoted in Liddell Hart, "*T. E. Lawrence,*" 296; Obituary for Leachman, *Daily Telegraph*; Meinertzhagen, 24 Dec. 1921, in *Middle East Diary*, 34, 86; Lawrence, Report on Intelligence (also for subsequent paragraph). On the controversy surrounding Meinertzhagen's diary entries on Lawrence, see J. N. Lockman, *Meinertzhagen's Diary Ruse.*

5. Tuohy, *Crater of Mars*, 173; Dickson Papers: Dickson to his mother, 10 Aug. 1915, 26 Sept 1916, and Box 1: File 4: 8 Jan. 1916; Tuohy, *Secret Corps*, 172.

6. FO 882/VIII: IR/18/9: Philby to Hogarth, 11 July 1918; FO 371/2140: 46261: Mallet to Grey, 28 Oct. 1914; J. Wilson, *Lawrence of Arabia*, 239; Leslie, *Mark Sykes*, 249; Tidrick, *Heart-Beguiling Araby*, 173; Arendt, *Imperialism*, 100; A. T. Wilson, *Loyalties*, 303.

7. Lawrence, *Seven Pillars*, 615; Candler, *Long Road*, 2:80; Brian Gardner, *Allenby*, 126; Tuohy, *Crater of Mars*, 210.

8. A. F. Wavell, *Allenby: Soldier and Statesman*, 195; Bruce Watson, *Desert Battle*, 106–08; Cox to IO and Government of India, 25 May 1918, quoted in P. Graves, *Percy Cox*, 223; Brevet-Major F. V. B. Witts, "The Passage of the Tigris at Shumran, 23rd February, 1917," *JRUSI* 68 (1923), 441.

9. Allenby to his wife, 17 Dec. 1917, quoted in Gardner, *Allenby*, 163; A. F. Wavell, *Allenby: Soldier and Statesman*, 235; Smith, quoted in A. F. Wavell, *Allenby: Soldier and Statesman*, 187; Meinertzhagen, *Army Diary*, 225; Savage, *Allenby of Armageddon*, 198. Allenby also drew on certain aspects of the relief of Kimberley in the Boer War. British entry into Jerusalem, anticipated by the construction of a water pipeline from Egypt, was held to signal the fulfillment of local prophecy about a Western prophet liberating Jerusalem when the Nile flowed into Palestine. Many remarked that "Allenby," transliterated as "Al Nebi," was "prophet" and backwards was "Ibn Allah," or "The Son of God."

10. Candler, *Long Road*, 1:111; Dickson to his mother, 29 Dec. 1914; E. Thompson, *Leicestershires beyond Baghdad*, 75; Tuohy, *Crater of Mars*, 165–66.

11. Swayne, *In Mesopotamia*, 68; Candler, *Long Road*, 1:110–11; Tab, *Road to Kut*, 57l; Dickson Papers: Box 1: File 3A: Dickson to his sister, 12 March 1915 and to his mother, 6 March 1915; 2nd booklet: Dickson to Greene, 10 March 1915; Dane, *British Campaigns*, 2:153, 1:v; Rolls, *Steel Chariots*, 170.

12. Dickson to Greene, 10 March 1915; FO 882: Lawrence to Wilson, 8 Jan. 1917, *Arab Bulletin* 42 (15 Feb. 1917), 77; Rolls, *Steel Chariots*, 170.

13. Dickson Papers: Box 1: 1st booklet: Dickson to Greene, 7 Feb. 1915; Liddell Hart, "*T. E. Lawrence,*" 245; Presland, *Deedes Bey*, 275; Leith-Ross, "Tactical Side," 4–7.

14. FO 882: Lawrence, "The Occupation of Akaba," *Arab Bulletin* 59 (Aug. 1917), 231–32, and *Seven Pillars*, 385; Leith-Ross, "Secret Service or Intelligence," 11 (emphasis added); WO 287/228: War Office, *Manual of Military Intelligence in the Field* (London, 1922), which draws much of its material from Callwell, *Small Wars*. Certainly, Lawrence and Faisal also kept their real intentions secret from their men in order to prohibit broadcast of their plans, as did Allenby before Megiddo.

15. Cocker, *Richard Meinertzhagen*, 105 (my italics); Liddell Hart, "*T. E. Lawrence*," 237, 341; C. Mackenzie, *Gallipoli Memories*, 96–97; Sheffy, "Institutionalized Deception," 211; Tuohy, *Crater of Mars*, 210–11; Meinertzhagen, 30 Sept. 1918, in *Army Diary*, 243. Meinertzhagen drew partly on ruses he had invented (also against Arabs) in East Africa.

16. Tuohy, *Crater of Mars*, 210–11. On the actual improvements in British intelligence before "Z-Day" for Gaza, see Sheffy, "Institutionalized Deception," 218–19.

17. Dickson to his mother, 6 March 1915; Candler, *Long Road*, 1:112, 2:25.

18. Candler, *Long Road*, 1:111; FO 882: Lawrence, "Military Notes," *Arab Bulletin* 32 (Nov. 1916), 480; "Twenty-Seven Articles."

19. Lawrence, "The Evolution of a Revolt," *Army Quarterly*, Oct. 1920, reprinted in *Oriental Assembly*, 112–15, 133–34; note for inclusion in a biography, quoted in J. Wilson, *Lawrence of Arabia*, 629. Much of Lawrence's article reappeared in *Seven Pillars*.

20. Lawrence, "Evolution of a Revolt," 112–13, 116, 122; *Seven Pillars*, 192, 196; Lawrence to his family, 12 Feb. 1917, in *Home Letters*, 335; Lawrence to Clayton, 27 Aug. 1917, in *Selected Letters*, 120; Liddell Hart, "*T. E. Lawrence*," 375.

21. Lawrence, *Seven Pillars*, 195, 339, 381, and "Twenty-Seven articles." See also his "Military Notes" and FO 371/3044: 1256: Sykes, appreciation of Arabian Report no. 22, n.d.

22. Meinertzhagen, 10 Jan. 1938, in *Middle East Diary*, 41; Lawrence, "Evolution of a Revolt," 123, 128–31; *Seven Pillars*, 340; Rolls, *Steel Chariots*, 158; LCLUL: MES 020: Robert Stewart Campbell to his family, 10 Jan. 1916; Plotke, *Imperial Spies*, 185; Basil Liddell Hart, *The British Way in Warfare*; Hynes, *Soldier's Tale*, 121–22; Hew Strachan, "The British Way in Warfare Revisited." Liddell Hart's entry on guerrilla warfare in the *Encyclopaedia Britannica* was based on Lawrence's essay. Of course, Lawrence did not actually "invent" guerrilla warfare; indeed, Callwell's *Small Wars* might be considered the first codification of irregular warfare in colonial theaters. For other military innovations credited to Lawrence, see Liddell Hart, "*T. E. Lawrence*," 261–67.

23. Lawrence, "Evolution of a Revolt," 108–09, 111, 121; Stirling, *Safety Last*, 84 (my italics); Kirkbride to Liddell Hart, [post-1962], quoted in Mack, *Prince of Our Disorder*, 239; Lawrence, "The Suppressed Introductory Chapter for *Seven Pillars of Wisdom*," in *Oriental Assembly*, 144; Lawrence to Stirling, 25 Sept. 1918, quoted in J. Wilson, *Lawrence of Arabia*, 447; Lawrence to E. T. Leeds, 24 Sept. 1917, in *Selected Letters*, 124; Lawrence to Archibald Becke, 28 Dec. 1929, in *Selected Letters*, 433–34.

24. Lawrence to Richards, 15 July 1918; Lawrence to Newcombe, 17 Jan. 1917, quoted in J. Wilson, *Lawrence of Arabia*, 351 (my italics); Lawrence, "Military Notes."

25. Bray, 8 Nov. 1916, in Arabian Report no. 18; Storrs, c. Dec. 1916, quoted in J. Wilson, *Lawrence of Arabia*, 342; FO 686/6/Pt.1: Intelligence report, 28 Dec. 1916; Candler, *Long Road*, 1:111; Presland, *Deedes Bey*, 179; Young, *Independent Arab*, 162.

26. Lawrence, "Twenty-Seven Articles"; LHCMA: Pierce Joyce Papers: Joyce, "Notes on Arab Tactics," c. Feb. 1917; Lawrence, "Evolution of a Revolt," 123.

27. WO 158/603: Wingate to Arbur, 7 Nov. 1916; Leachman, quoted in Winstone, *Illicit Adventure*, 299; Lawrence to his family, 31 Jan. 1917, in *Home Letters*, 334;

McMahon to Murray, 20 June 1916, in *Records of the Hijaz*, 7:269–70; Hogarth to Leeds, 23 Jan. 1917, quoted in J. Wilson, *Lawrence of Arabia*, 350; Liddell Hart, "T. E. Lawrence," 164; Q. L., "With the 13th Indian Cavalry Brigade in Palestine," *JRUSI* 64 (1919), 245; A. F. Wavell, *Allenby: Soldier and Statesman*, 245–46.

28. Lawrence, "Evolution of a Revolt," 115, 117; Lawrence to Liddell Hart, 1933, in *Letters of T. E. Lawrence*, 323; Lawrence, *Seven Pillars*, 322, 507; R. Graves, *Lawrence and the Arabs*, 217; J. F. C. Fuller, "Moral, Instruction, and Leadership," *JRUSI* 65 (1920), 669; "The Application of Recent Developments in Mechanics and Other Scientific Knowledge to Preparation and Training for Future War on Land," *JRUSI* 65 (1920), 254, 259–60.

29. Stuart Cohen, "The Genesis of the British Campaign in Mesopotamia, 1914"; FO 882/XIII: MES/16/5: London to Intrusive, 29 March 1916; FO 882/XVIII: TU/16/2: Intelligence Section, Cairo to Buckley, 28 March 1916; FO 882/XV: PNA/16/1: [unsigned] to Lawrence, 26 March 1916; FO 882/VII: HRG/17/61: Wingate to Cox, 24 July 1917; AIR 20/504: Maude to Chief London and CGS India, 24 June 1917; Arnold T. Wilson, *Mesopotamia, 1917–1920: A Clash of Loyalties*, 3–4.

30. Candler, *Long Road*, 2:211; Plotke, *Imperial Spies*, 41, 171.

31. Plotke, *Imperial Spies*, 37; Burke, *With Horse and Morse*, 104; Candler, *Long Road*, 2:285–86; Tennant, *In the Clouds*, 255; LCLUL: GS 1429: Sir Reginald Savory, recollections, TS, n.d.; L. C. Dunsterville, *The Adventures of Dunsterforce*, 3, 68–69.

32. AIR 1/426/15/260/3: Air Staff, "On the Power of the Air Force and the Application of that Power to Hold and Police Mesopotamia," March 1920. For a general narrative of the Royal Flying Corps' work in the Middle East, see H. A. Jones, *The War in the Air*, Vol. 5, chaps. 3–5; and vol. 6, chaps. 5–6.

33. Dickson to Greene, 7 Feb. 1915; Wilfred Nunn, *Tigris Gunboats*, 90; AIR 1/140/15/40/306: General, Force "D" to WO, 5 Feb. 1916; AIR 2/940: Tennant, Resume of operations, 30 March 1917; Wauchope, chap. 7, 70; Tennant, *In the Clouds*, 35, 38–39, 141; FO 686/6/Pt.1: Joyce to Wilson, 24 March 1917. The first aircraft arrived in 1915 in poor condition, without repairmen, photographic equipment, spares, sufficient pilots, and so on. In August, two newer machines arrived, the germ of Squadron 30. Only after transfer of command to the War Office did new planes and the latest photographic equipment arrive. Late in 1916, these squadrons joined the Middle East Brigade under W. G. H. Salmond.

34. AIR 10/1001: RAF, Preface of "Notes on Aerial Photography, Part II, The Interpretation of Aeroplane Photographs in Mesopotamia," 1918; Occleshaw, *Armour against Fate*, 61–62. On the agents' development of aerial photography in Egypt, see J. Wilson, *Lawrence of Arabia*, 189, 198 n. 77.

35. Tennant, *In the Clouds*, 38, 60–61; WO 158/626: Salmond to CGS EEF, 12 Nov. 1916, and Note in Egyptforce to Wingate, 14 Nov. 1916; Lawrence to GOC, Egypt and DMI, 17 Nov. 1916, in Arabian Report no. 18; AIR 1/2399/280/1: Squadron Leader L. G. S. Payne, "The Use of Aircraft in Connection with Espionage," 7 Nov. 1924.

36. Philby, "Mesopotage," chap. 7, and *Arabian Days*, 129; Leith-Ross, "Tactical Side," 3, 7, 8; Lawrence to C. E. Wilson, 6 Dec. 1916, in *Letters of T. E. Lawrence*, 211–12; Marlowe, *Late Victorian*, 129; BL: Add. MSS: Sir A. T. Wilson Papers: 52455C: Wilson to Hirtzel, 22 May 1918.

37. FO 371/3044: 1256: Sykes, appreciation of Arabian Report no. 27, 25 Jan. 1917; R. M. P. Preston, *The Desert Mounted Corps*, 5–6; Lawrence, *Seven Pillars*, 615; various documents on aerial signalling and cooperation in AIR 2/940; AIR 1/1661/204/97/14: Genstaff (operations) EEF to GOC, 3 Aug. 1916; RAF, "Notes on Aerial Photography"; Leith-Ross, "Tactical Side," 10.

38. AIR 2/940: Tennant to GOC RFC Egypt, 30 Dec. 1916; FO 882/VI: HRG/17/15: Pearson to Wingate, late Feb. 1917; Dov Gavish, "Wadi Fari'a—The 'Valley of Death' in the Great War," 362–65; Lionel Charlton, *Deeds That Held the Empire, by Air*, 82–88; AIR 1/725/115/1: Salmond to General, n.d. (36 hours after the battle). See also H. R. Brooke-Popham, lecture, 3 Dec. 1919, in *JRUSI* 65 (1920), 57; Flight Lieutenant C. J. Mackay, "The Influence in the Future of Aircraft upon Problems of Imperial Defence," *JRUSI* 67 (1922), 302. The first airlift in history also occurred in Mesopotamia, during the siege of Kut.

39. Group Captain Amyas Borton, "The Use of Aircraft in Small Wars," 25 Feb. 1920, in *JRUSI* 65 (1920), 310–19; Leith-Ross, "Tactical Side," 8–9; Tennant, *In the Clouds*, 163.

40. Lawrence, *Seven Pillars*, 550 (see also 308, 633); Bray, 8 Nov. 1916, in Arabian Report no. 18. Lawrence frequently invoked Coleridge's "The Rime of the Ancient Mariner" to describe man's conquest of the air, "as lords that are expected." On the perceived chivalry of aircraft, see especially David Edgerton, *England and the Aeroplane*, 43–58; M. Paris, *Warrior Nation*, 156–58; J. M. Spaight, *Air Power and War Rights*, 23–24, 102–06.

41. Candler, *Long Road*, 2:154; Bray, *Paladin of Arabia*, 347–48; Tuohy, *Secret Corps*, 213–14.

CHAPTER 5

1. On the myth of an antitechnocratic England, see Edgerton, *England and the Aeroplane*.

2. LCLUL: GS 0089: File 2: F. S. G. Barnett to his mother, 10 March 1917; Reynardson, *Mesopotamia*, 14–15; Army YMCA of India, *The Land of Two Rivers*, much reprinted pamphlet, found among the papers of soldiers in Mesopotamia, e.g. LCLUL: GS 1144: Papers of R. C. Morton, Box 4; Sir Arthur Lawley, *A Message from Mesopotamia*, 11, 34, 91, 92; Arthur Tillotson Clark, *To Bagdad with the British*, 2; LCLUL: MES 082: Box 1: W. W. A. Phillips correspondence with his mother, April 1915; "L.M.H.," "An Arabian Night," *Blackwood's* (1918), 379; LCLUL: EP 098: Captain John Stevenson's letters to his mother, 1917; Mann to his mother, 15 March 1920, in *Administrator in the Making: James Saumarez Mann, 1893–1920*, 234; IOR: Eur MSS: F177/21: Emily Lorimer to her mother, 31 March 1917; LCLUL: GS 1162: Joseph Napier to his mother, 9 and 18 March 1917; LCLUL: MES 071: Lt. L. R. Missen, essay, "Written for the 'Pelican,' the Perse School Magazine and passed by the editor to my mother, 19 Apr. 1917"; Hogarth to Billy, 19 Feb. 1917; review of *Loyalties: Mesopotamia, 1914–17*, by Arnold T. Wilson, *Times*, 11 Dec. 1930, 10; Edward Thompson, *These Men, Thy Friends*, 211, 244.

3. Peter Morris, "Intelligence and Its Interpretation," 90; LCLUL: GS 0993: Lt. Col. L. A. Lynden-Bell, interview with Peter Liddle, TS, Oct. 1977; Reynardson,

Mesopotamia, 240–42; Savory, recollections; LCLUL: MES 094: Army YMCA of India, "Baghdad: The City of the Caliphs," June 1918, Baghdad. Cf. Hynes, *Soldier's Tale*, 76–81. On the early decisions about the scope of the campaign, see John S. Galbraith, "No Man's Child: The Campaign in Mesopotamia, 1914–1916"; Cohen, "Genesis of the British Campaign"; Paul K. Davis, *Ends and Means: The British Mesopotamian Campaign and Commission*; Briton Busch, *Britain, India, and the Arabs, 1914–1921*, 3–55; Report of the Mesopotamia Commission (hereafter MCR), Cd. 8610, *Parliamentary Papers* (*PP*), 1917–18, 16:20–28.

4. Savage, *Allenby of Armageddon*, 198; Owen Tweedy, *Gathering Moss*, 65–66; Jarvis, *Arab Command*, 50; review of *Lawrence and the Arabs*, by Robert Graves, *Times*, 18 Nov. 1917, 9; Fussell, *Great War*, 135–44, 154; Candler, *Long Road*, 2:198, 298. For more on the "crusade" propaganda, see Bar-Yosef, "Last Crusade?"

5. Bar-Yosef, "Last Crusade?," 89, 94–99; MECA: Edward Kinch Papers: File 1/2: autobiographical notes, MS, n.d., 27; Eleanor Franklin Egan, *The War in the Cradle of the World: Mesopotamia*, 74–76, 232, 242; Conrad Cato, *The Navy in Mesopotamia 1914 to 1917*, 17; V. Gilbert, *Romance of the Last Crusade*, 111–22, 235; Savory, recollections (my italics); "Allenby's Crowning Mercy," *Times*, 31 Dec. 1918, 9; FO 882: Lawrence, "Wejh to Wadi Ais," *Arab Bulletin* 51 (23 May 1917), 240. The American correspondent Egan entered Mesopotamia by the good offices of Bell's friend in Washington, Cecil Spring-Rice. Much of her book appeared in the *Saturday Evening Post* and smacks of propaganda. One presumes Spring-Rice sent her in much the same spirit as he sent Lowell Thomas to Palestine.

6. *Times* cutting, enclosed in LCLUL: AIR 032: Robert Blucke to his father, 25 June 1917; Clark, *To Baghdad*, 47–49; Rolt to Liddle, 20 Dec. 1972; Swayne, *In Mesopotamia*, 51. See also Dawson, *Soldier Heroes*, 151, 171, 174, although Dawson sees the campaign as an *escape* from modernity. Historians have generally argued that the war ended traditional notions of heroism: see Fussell, *Great War*; Stephane Audoin-Rouzeau and Annette Becker, *14–18: Understanding the Great War*, 28.

7. Candler, *Long Road*, 1:47, 51, 111–20, 132,164, 2:223–24; MCR, 37–38, 105; Charles Munro, quoted in G. Buchanan, *Tragedy of Mesopotamia*, 129; Nunn, *Tigris Gunboats*, 168; LCLUL: GS 1162: Joseph Napier to Department of War Studies, Sandhurst, 1976, and to his mother, 28 Feb. 1917; Dane, *British Campaigns*, 2:226–27; V. Gilbert, *Romance of the Last Crusade*, 186. Recent defense cuts had prevented the Indian government from equipping the force for anything more than frontier warfare.

8. Candler, *Long Road*, 1:47; V. Gilbert, *Romance of the Last Crusade*, 222; Charles Vere Ferrers Townshend, *My Campaign*, 1:1–36; "Mesopotamia To-Day," *Times*, 11 July 1917, 7; J. T. Parfit, *Serbia to Kut: An Account of the War in the Bible Lands*, 45; LCLUL: MES 053: Captain L. W. Jardine to Colin [brother?], 18 March 1917; "Dalil," "The Campaign in Mesopotamia—The First Phase," *JRUSI* 69 (1924), 510–11; Col. H. Rowan Robinson, "The Relations of Mobility and Power," *JRUSI* 65 (1920), 579. On Haig's commitment to mobile modern warfare, see Timothy Travers, *The Killing Ground: The British Army, the Western Front, and the Emergence of Modern Warfare, 1900–1918*, 72, 87–88, 95.

9. Montagu, quoted in the *Times*, 7 Aug. 1918, 8; Swayne, *In Mesopotamia*, 17, 51; Nunn, *Tigris Gunboats*, 10; Candler, *Long Road*, 1:72. For more on this, see my

"Developing Iraq: Britain, India, and the Redemption of Empire and Technology in World War I." Like Chamberlain's vision, but unlike later formulations, in practice development of Mesopotamia was limited to activities, such as the settlement of tribes and provision of transportation, that would make it a supplier of raw materials for industrial Britain rather than an industrial nation in its own right. See also Dodge, *Inventing Iraq*, on how the British Iraqi state's modernizing imperatives articulated with an orientalist perspective of Iraqi society to produce a regime that preserved the semifeudal power of tribal chiefs.

10. Constantine, *British Colonial Development*; Cooper, "Modernizing Bureaucrats"; David Matless, *Landscape and Englishness*, 29–30.

11. Review of *Four Centuries of Modern Iraq*, by Stephen Longrigg, *Times*, 22 Jan. 1926, 17; review of *By Tigris and Euphrates*, by E. S. Stevens, *Times*, 14 Dec. 1923, 8; Richard Coke, *The Arab's Place in the Sun*, 11–12; FO 371/6342: E5373: "Britain and Mesopotamia," *Daily Telegraph*, 10 May 1921; Captain R. J. Wilkinson, "The Geographical Importance of Iraq," *JRUSI* 67 (1922), 663; Edgerton, *Warfare State*, 284, 312, 317. On development and empire, see T. Mitchell, *Rule of Experts*, 78, 230; J. Scott, *Seeing Like a State*; Jonathan Crush, "Imagining Development," in his *Power of Development*, 2, 15. On the Indian contrast, see Meeta Sinha, "'Where Electricity Dispels the Illusion [of the *Arabian Nights*]': The British and the Modern in Interwar India."

12. Reynardson, *Mesopotamia*, 272; Barker, *Bastard War*, 42; Bell to her family, 5 Dec. 1918, quoted in Burgoyne, *Gertrude Bell*, 2:101; Cato, *Navy in Mesopotamia*, 106, 117; Richard Coke, *The Heart of the Middle East*, chap. 20; Wilkinson, "Geographical Importance of Iraq," 665; Bevan, *Land of the Two Rivers*, 10–11, 112, 124–26; [Bell], *Arab of Mesopotamia*, 117; Cecil, reported in *Times*, 24 July 1918, 10; Egan, *War in the Cradle*, 252.

13. Candler, *Long Road*, 1:176; Wauchope, "The Battle That Won Samarrah," chap. 8 in *With a Highland Regiment*, 85; [Lawrence], "The Changing East," *Round Table* 40 (Sept. 1920), in *Oriental Assembly*, 87; FO 882/XIV: MIS/15/9: Wingate, note, 26 Aug. 1915.

14. Bevan, *Land of the Two Rivers*, 124–26; "A New Mesopotamia," *Guardian*, 31 Dec. 1919, 12; Clark, *To Baghdad*, 208, 239; Wauchope, chap. 7, 65 (my italics); Candler, *Long Road*, 2:97; Savory, recollections; Bell to Florence Bell, 22 Nov. 1917, in *Letters of Gertrude Bell*, 2:432–33; A. T. Wilson, *Loyalties*, 278; Philby, *Arabian Days*, 127; clipping in LCLUL: GS 1276: Pitman to his parents, 3 April 1917; Tab, *On the Road to Kut*, 111. On William Willcocks's prewar calls for imitation of the ancient empires' mastery of irrigation in Mesopotamia, see David Gilmartin, "Imperial Rivers: Irrigation and British Visions of Empire," in *Decentring Empire*.

15. Reynardson, *Mesopotamia*, 50, 172; MECA: Sykes Papers: Box 2: File 7: Doc 78: "Political Note on Our Advance in Irak," 17 Sept. 1917; Bell to Hugh Bell, 10 Nov. 1922, and to Hugh and Florence Bell, 31 Jan. 1918, in *Letters of Gertrude Bell*, 2:441–44, 657; Montagu, reported in *Times*, 7 Aug. 1918, 8; Hogarth Papers: File 3: Hogarth to Billy, 30 May 1918; Curzon at CAS, reported in *Spectator*, 16 Oct. 1920, 487; Candler, *Long Road*, 2:188; AIR 5/1298: "Lest We Forget," *Times of Mesopotamia*, 3 May 1924; "The League of Nations and Mosul," *Spectator*, 12 Sept. 1925, 398; *Economist*, 10 May 1924, 955; LCLUL: GS 0089: Barnett to his mother, 6 Oct. 1916; Cabinet Paper on

Mesopotamia, 12 Nov. 1919; East India (Military), Cd. 7624, *PP*, 1914–16, 49:15; *Times Trade Supplement*, 2 Dec. 1918, 206b; Sir Nigel Davidson, "Iraq: The New State," *JCAS* 19 (1932), 212–16. The vision of Iraq as an imperial granary was not the basis of the decision to go for Baghdad but was adduced to persuade others to agree to it (Yapp, *Modern Near East*, 332).

16. J. T. Parfit, *Mesopotamia: The Key to the Future*, 1; [Bell], "Turkish Provinces—the Anatolian Coast," and "Arab Provinces-Baghdad," in *Arab of Mesopotamia*, 131, 201–02; Bell to Hugh Bell, 18 May 1917, and to Florence Bell, 15 Nov. 1917, in *Letters of Gertrude Bell*, 2:410–11, 431–32; Candler, *Long Road*, 2:183; "A New Mesopotamia," *Guardian*, 13 Dec. 1919, 12; Major quoted in Swayne, *In Mesopotamia*, 166; "The Palestine Mandate," *Guardian*, 23 June 1922, 6; Amery, Leeds Luncheon Club, quoted in *Times*, 9 Feb. 1926, 11; J. Lawrence, "Forging a Peaceable Kingdom"; J. Mackenzie, *Propaganda and Empire*, 256.

17. Colls, "Constitution of the English," 105; Roger Casey, *Baghdad and Points East*, vii–viii, 98; George Orwell, "The Lion and the Unicorn: Socialism and the English Genius," Part 4; Vita Sackville-West, *Passenger to Teheran*, 60; John Glubb, *Story of the Arab Legion*, 19; Mann to his mother, 25 Jan. 1920, in *Administrator in the Making*, 206; Jeffrey Richards, *Films and British National Identity*, 33. See also applications in IOR: L/PS/10/676.

18. Busch, *Britain, India, and the Arabs*, 158, 190, 275; Owen, "Critics of Empire," 193. For postwar accounts of wartime achievement, see, for instance, Richard Coke, *Baghdad: The City of Peace*; G. Buchanan, *Tragedy of Mesopotamia*; "A New Mesopotamia," *Guardian*, 31 Dec. 1919, 12.

19. Dawn, "Influence of T. E. Lawrence," 80; Meinertzhagen, 24 Dec. 1921, in *Middle East Diary*, 33; Philby, quoted in Wallach, *Desert Queen*, 291; A. T. Wilson, "The Annual Dinner," *JCAS* 19 (1932), 644.

20. Wavell, in *Lawrence, by His Friends*, 128; Stirling, *Safety Last*, 83–84.

21. Dawson, *Soldier Heroes*, 194.

22. Dawson, *Soldier Heroes*, 167–83; J. Mackenzie, *Propaganda and Empire*, chap. 3; M. Paris, *Warrior Nation*, 151, 171; IOR: Eur. Mss: C874: Ilay Ferrier, "The Trans-Desert Route," TS, 1926; Billie Melman, *Women and the Popular Imagination in the Twenties: Flappers and Nymphs*, 91; Virginia Woolf, *Night and Day*, 83; R. Graves, *Lawrence and the Arabs*, 57; Percy Cox, review of *Revolt in the Desert*, by Lawrence, *Geographical Journal* 69 (1927), 581–82. On Arab-themed films, see Nasir, *Arabs and the English*, 125, 146–48.

23. Advertisement, *Times*, 9 March 1928, 12; Winstone, *Woolley of Ur*, 140; Kenneth Hudson, *A Social History of Archaeology: The British Experience*, 92–94; "Travellers' Tales," *Times*, 29 Sept. 1922, 15; "Books of the Day," *Times*, 11 Dec. 1928, 22; review of *Arabia of the Wahabis*, in *Times*, 24 Oct. 1930, 8; Percy Cox, review of *Arabia Felix*, by Bertram Thomas, *JCAS* 19 (1932), 321; "Ninety Days in the Desert," *Times*, 29 June 1932, 13; Woolf, quoted in J. Wilson, *Lawrence of Arabia*, 785.

24. Wilson Papers: 52456A: Stephenson to Wilson, 26 May 1920; introduction to Bertram Thomas, "Across the Rub Al Khali," *JCAS* 18 (1931), 489; H. St. John Philby, "A Survey of Wahhabi Arabia, 1929," *JCAS* 16 (1929), 468; "List of Members of the CAS," *JCAS* 15 (1928), 3–39; T. E. Lawrence, foreword to Bertram Thomas, *Arabia Felix*, vii–viii; D. G. Hogarth, Address at the Anniversary General Meeting, 21 June 1926,

Geographical Journal 68 (1926), 100; H. St. John Philby, *Arabia of the Wahabis*, vii; A. C. Yate, discussion on F. W. Barron, "The New Responsibilities of the British Empire Created by the Assumption of Mandates in the Middle East...," 8 March 1922, in *JRUSI* 67 (1922), 269.

25. Rolls, *Steel Chariots*, 13. See works cited in this chapter and bibliography.

26. James Ferrier, preliminary note (1999), on Ferrier, "Trans-Desert Route"; "Trans-Desert Route"; Bell to Hugh Bell, 11 March 1925, in *Letters of Gertrude Bell*, 2:725; review of *The Arab at Home*, by Paul W. Harrison, *JCAS* 13 (1926), 279; A. T. Wilson, comment on Bertram Thomas, "Across the Rub Al Khali," *JCAS* 18 (1931), 502–03; Jarvis, *Arab Command*, 141–42; Liddell Hart, "T. E. Lawrence," 98–99. See also the works listed throughout this chapter and in the bibliography.

27. Yeats, *A Vision*, 41; V. M. Yeates, "Winged Victory," 25, 30, 145, 213. This paragraph draws heavily on Stanley Weintraub, "Lawrence of Arabia: The Portraits from Imagination," 270–72; Bushrui, "Yeats' Arabic Interests," 294. The Sopwith Camel was the war's highest scoring fighter, known for its liability to spin out of control. Many pilots died in training.

28. Mack, *Prince of Our Disorder*, 365.

29. Bruce Rogers, Dec. 1927, quoted in Mack, *Prince of Our Disorder*, 373; Tomlinson to Lawrence, 13 May 1930, in *Letters to T. E. Lawrence*, ed. A. W. Lawrence, 193–95; Lawrence to Doughty, 7 May 1920, in *Letters of T. E. Lawrence*, 303; J. Wilson, *Lawrence of Arabia*, 675; Charles Grosvenor, "The Subscribers' *Seven Pillars of Wisdom*: The Visual Aspect."

30. R. Graves, quoted in Fussell, *Great War*, 205; Lawrence to R. Graves, 21 April 1931, and Brown's note thereon, in *Selected Letters*, 452–53; Yeats to Lawrence, 26 Sept. 1932 and to Charlotte Shaw, 22 Sept. 1932, in *Letters to T. E. Lawrence*, 213–14; Lawrence, quoted in Mack, *Prince of Our Disorder*, 335; D. Stewart, *T. E. Lawrence* (Paladin Grafton, 1979), 233, quoted in Dawson, *Soldier Heroes*, 205; Buchan to Lawrence, 13 July 1927, in *Letters to T. E. Lawrence*, 20–21; Buchan, *Memory Hold the Door*, 218; Meinertzhagen, 19 June 1935, in *Middle East Diary*, 36. Lawrence was not Irish by "blood"; his father had been an Anglo-Irish baronet before abandoning his wife, changing his name, and setting up house in England with his daughters' governess (they never married). Lawrence was one of their five sons.

31. See also Hynes, *Soldier's Tale*, 79–80; Dawson, *Soldier Heroes*, 173–228. On Lawrence's awe of artists, see Lawrence to Forster, 20 Feb. 1924, in *Letters of T. E. Lawrence*, 455.

32. Lawrence to Graves, quoted in J. Wilson, *Lawrence of Arabia*, 668; Garnett to Lawrence, Guy Fawkes Day, 1927, and Sassoon to Lawrence, 6 Dec. 1923, in *Letters to T. E. Lawrence*, 76–78, 155; R. Graves, *Lawrence and the Arabs*, 417; Tomlinson to Lawrence, 19 March 1930 and 5 Dec. 1928, in *Letters to T. E. Lawrence*, 189–93. On the last point, see also Dawson, *Soldier Heroes*, 176. On literary taboos of the war, see Audoin-Rouzeau and Becker, *14–18: Understanding the Great War*, 37–44.

33. Lawrence, May 1926, quoted in J. Wilson, *Lawrence of Arabia*, 770.

34. Sackville-West, *Passenger to Teheran*, 57–61; Woolf to Sackville-West, 26 Jan., 31 Jan., 1 March, and 16 March 1926, *Letters of Virginia Woolf*, 3:231–48; Leonard Woolf, "A Tale Told by Midnight," *Stories of the East*, 28.

35. Hynes, *Soldier's Tale*, 92; Eugene Goodheart, "A Contest of Motives: T. E. Lawrence in *Seven Pillars of Wisdom*," 122; BL: Add. MSS: Lawrence Papers: 45903: Lawrence to Charlotte Shaw, 16 July 1927; Edward Garnett to Lawrence, 9 Sept. 1922, and Manning to T. E. Shaw, 9 May 1930, in *Letters to T. E. Lawrence*, 87–89, 134–37; R. Graves, *Lawrence and the Arabs*, 24; Callisthenes, "Knowledge Which Is In Harmony," *Times*, 7 Dec. 1927, 12; Kern, *Time and Space*, 26–27.

36. Ernst Bloch, "A Philosophical View of the Detective Novel," 251; Yeats, note appended to *Later Poems* (1922), cited in review of *The Vision*, in *The New Statesman*, 27 March 1926, 749–50; Brantlinger, *Rule of Darkness*, 251–52; Virginia Woolf, *To the Lighthouse*, 73; Cook, "*Seven Pillars*," 100. See also Banfield, *Phantom Table*, 85, 149, 204, 207; Gillian Beer, "The Island and the Aeroplane: The Case of Virginia Woolf"; Peter Liebregts, "'Between that staring fury and the blind lush leaf': William Butler Yeats and the Occult," 69; Bushrui, "Yeats' Arabic Interests," 280, 311–13.

37. Liddell Hart and Baker, in *Lawrence, by His Friends*, 149, 205; Buchan, *Greenmantle*, 179; Liddell Hart, "*T. E. Lawrence*," 447 (last page).

38. MECA: William Rupert Hay Papers: Box 2: File 2/3: Hay, 7 March 1919, in diary; Philby, *Arabian Days*, 2–5. See also Cook, "*Seven Pillars*," 100; William M. Chace, "T. E. Lawrence: The Uses of Heroism," 132; Dawson, *Soldier Heroes*, 177–78, 183–88.

39. Meinertzhagen, memo, Peace Conference, 9 April 1919, quoted in Cocker, *Richard Meinertzhagen*, 129; FO 371/16878: 3999: Warner, minute, 25 July 1933; Richard Thurlow, "The Return of Jeremiah: The Rejected Knowledge of Sir Oswald Mosley in the 1930s."

40. Wells to Lawrence, 17 May 1927, in *Letters to T. E. Lawrence*, 212.

41. Liddell Hart, "*T. E. Lawrence*," 386; Buchan, *Memory Hold the Door*, 212; Lawrence, *Seven Pillars*, 259; Winterton, quoted in Tidrick, *Heart-Beguiling Araby*, 211; Coke, *Arab's Place*, 12, 289; Philby, "Why I Turned Wahhabi," *Daily Herald*, 8 Sept. 1930; MECA: Glubb Papers: Iraq S. Desert (2): "On Bedu Dialect," draft, 1926; R. Graves, *Lawrence and the Arabs*, 57; *Daily News*, quoted in J. Wilson, *Lawrence of Arabia*, 783. See also Dawson, *Soldier Heroes*, 170.

42. Brent, *Far Arabia*, 197; T. E. Lawrence, foreword to *Arabia Felix*, vii–viii; Philby, review of *The Life of Charles M. Doughty*, by Hogarth, *JCAS* 16 (1929), 398; Said, *Orientalism*, 246; M. Paris, *Warrior Nation*, 185; Cawelti and Rosenberg, *Spy Story*, 32; Colls, "Constitution of the English," 109.

43. Alison Light, *Forever England*, 1–19; Miles Taylor, "Patriotism, History and the Left in Twentieth-Century Britain"; Lawrence to Ralph Isham, 10 Aug. 1927, to Ezra Pound, 7 Dec. 1934, to Charlotte Shaw, 14 Oct. 1931, and to Robin Buxton, 4 March 1927, in *Selected Letters*, 319, 343, 459, 507.

44. "The Outlook in the Middle East," *Round Table* 37 (Dec. 1919), 97 (my italics); *Spectator*, 19 June 1920, 813.

CHAPTER 6

1. For a contemporary account, see Haldane, *Insurrection in Mesopotamia*.

2. See Peter Sluglett, *Britain in Iraq, 1914–1932*; Dodge, *Inventing Iraq*, 1–41, and "International Obligation, Domestic Pressure, and Colonial Nationalism: The Birth of

the Iraqi State under the Mandate System." More generally, see Aaron Klieman, *Foundations of British Policy*; Roger Adelson, *London and the Invention of the Middle East*; John Darwin, *Britain, Egypt and the Middle East: Imperial Policy in the Aftermath of War 1918–1922*; Uriel Dann, ed., *The Great Powers in the Middle East 1919–1939*; Clive Leatherdale, *Britain and Saudi Arabia, 1925–1939*; Fromkin, *Peace to End All Peace*; John Wilkinson, *Arabia's Frontiers*.

3. See also Macfie, "British Intelligence"; Jeffrey, *British Army and the Crisis*, 48; Atiyyah, *Iraq*, 357.

4. T. Richards, *Imperial Archive*, 109; Richard Hofstadter, *The Paranoid Style in American Politics*, 37.

5. FO 371/1012: 15856: Maunsell to Gleichen, 7 April 1907; IOR: L/PS/7/253: Lorimer, Summary, 26 Oct. 1911; General Staff, "Notes on Arabia"; A. F. Townshend, *Military Consul*, 189; Bell, *Desert and the Sown*, 58, 140, 227–28; minutes on FO 371/2124: 1990: Shakespear to Hirtzel, 26 June 1914; FO 371/152: 22155: Sykes to O'Conor, 3 June 1905; A. J. B. Wavell, *Modern Pilgrim*, 45, 74–75; 240; "Turkey in Arabia," *Times*, 20 Aug. 1913, 7; Lorimer, summary, 4 June 1912; Sykes, report, 3 Dec. 1906; A. Hamilton, *Problems of the Middle East*, 275; IOR: R/15/2/45: [A. Hule?] to PA Bahrein, 4 Dec. 1906; FO 602/52: Marling to Crow, 24 Dec. 1910; Stewart to Bill, 9 Aug. 1906; FO 371/126: 21703: documents on Pan-Islamist agents, 1906; FO 371/354: 31310: Government of India to IO, 4 and 11 July 1907; FO 371/451: "D," report, 1908; FO 371/505: 22144: Cox to Marling, 27 March 1908; Lorimer, Events for April and May 1910; FO 371/1008: 12174: Lorimer, summary for March 1910; Lorimer, Tour Diary no. 1 of 1909; FO 371/1490: 3025: Scott, report, 4 Dec. 1911; Bray, *Shifting Sands*, 184; G. Wyman Bury, *Pan-Islam*, 16; FO 371/1490: 3025: Consul Baghdad, report, 3 Jan. 1912; FO 371/2135: 24783: Erskine, summary, 12 May 1914; FO 371/159: 8560: Cromer to Grey, 28 Feb. 1906; FO 371/452: 8560: Minutes on de Salis to Grey, 8 July 1908.

6. FO 371/1010: 20761: Lowther to Marling, report, 29 June and 29 May 1910; FO 371/992: 177: Marling to Grey, 27 Dec. 1909; Fromkin, *Peace to End All Peace*, 41; Kenneth Lunn, "Political Antisemitism before 1914."

7. FO 371/2486: 34982: Clayton, memo, c. Oct. 1915; IOR: L/PS/10/586: Arabian Report, 1 March 1916; Sykes Papers: Box 1: File 1: Doc 24: Summary, 30 Aug. 1916; Bury, *Pan-Islam*, 80–81, 109; Ronald Wingate, *Wingate of the Sudan: The Life and Times of General Sir Reginald Wingate*, 176–77; Cleveland to fforde, 14 Sept. 1916; FO 371/2771: 30673: Director of Intelligence [Bell? Hogarth?], memo, [c. Feb. 1916]; Sykes, quoted in Plotke, *Imperial Spies*, 44 n; FO 882: D. G. Hogarth, "Pan-Turan and the Arabs," *Arab Bulletin* 74 (Dec. 1917); HRG/18/15: General Staff, appendix F, 21.

8. FO 882/XIII: KH/17/16: Clayton to C. E. Wilson, 28 April 1919; Lawrence Papers: 45904: Lawrence to [Charlotte Shaw?], Dec. 1934.

9. FO 371/5229: 2719: [Wilson], telegram, 3 Feb. 1920, quoted in Montagu, note, [c. 25 Aug. 1920]; FO 371/5228: 2719: Extract from Pulley, 14 July 1920, quoted in Wilson to IO, 6 Aug. 1920; Wilson Papers: 52459A: Wilson to S/S IO, 16 Aug. 1920, and GHQ Baghdad to Troopers, 15 July 1920; Mann to his parents, 30 May and 17 June 1920, in *Administrator in the Making*, 277–78, 284; Bell to her mother, 16 Nov. 1920, quoted in Burgoyne, *Gertrude Bell*, 2:183.

10. Wilson Papers: 52456A: Stephenson to Wilson, 5 Aug. 1920; Montagu, note [c. 25 Aug. 1920]; FO 371/5255: 5114: Bray, memo, [May 1920]; FO 371/5230: 2719: S/S to C. C. Baghdad, 23 Sept. 1920; FO 882/XIII: MI/19/8: Supplement to GHQ Intelligence Summary, EEF, 26 April 1919; WO 106/196: GHQ Intelligence Summary, EEF, 9 April 1920; FO 371/10110: 2029: IDCEU report in IO to FO, 30 April 1924. Samples of other theories: FO 371/4241: 167691: C-in-C India to CIGS, 1 Jan. 1920; FO 371/3718: 98498: Thomson to Graham, 4 July 1919; WO 106/201: General Staff, Situation in Turkey, 2 Nov. 1920; FO 371/5228: 9849: Minutes, 14 Aug. 1920; FO 371/6345: 13886: Weakley, memo (and enclosures), 17 Dec. 1921; FO 686/26: British Agency, Jeddah to Arbur, 11 Sept. 1919; AIR 5/485: The Khilafat—Summary, for the CID [Committee of Imperial Defence], 28 May 1926; WO 32/3514: Genstaff, memo, 8 Oct. 1919.

11. FO 371/7771: 4828: Iraq Intelligence Report no. 8, 15 April 1922; FO 371/6345: 13559: IO to FO, 9 Dec. 1921; AIR 5/485: Turco-Russian Policy in…Arabia, 23 June 1927, EU 14, draft; FO 371/7790: 14032: IDCEU, report, [Dec. 1922]; KV 1/19: History of the D Branch of MI5, 1921; AIR 5/485: IDCEU, report, EU 12, draft, in Smith, note, 18 May 1927.

12. FO 371/5255: E5114: Tilley and Patrick, minutes, 27 May 1920; FO 371/5220: E6024: Tilley and Young, minutes, 9 June 1920; Patrick, minute, 16 Aug. 1920, on Montagu, note, [c. 25 Aug. 1920]; FO 686/26: Political Report, 1 to 12 June 1920; CO 732/3: 53115: Clauson and Bullard, minutes, 26 Oct. 1921; CO 732/6: 465: Meinertzhagen, minute, 5 Jan. 1922; FO 371/10110: E3134: Osborne, minute, 8 July 1927.

13. FO 800/261 and FO 371/12407: F6452: Chamberlain to [fellow Cabinet member], 14 July 1927 and 12 Aug. 1927; FO 371/5229: E10923: Tilley, minute, 30 Aug. 1920; FO 371/5230: E12339: Young, minute, 12 Oct. 1920, on Bray, report, 14 Sept. 1920. See also the work of John Fisher.

14. Young, minute, 12 Oct. 1920 (paraphrasing Cornwallis) (my italics); H. Young Papers: File 3: Young to Deedes, 15 Oct. 1920; FO 371/5231: E12966: Cornwallis, minute, 22 Oct. 1920, on Bray, report, [Oct. 1920]; Cornwallis, Remarks, 12 Oct. 1920, on Bray, report, 14 Sept. 1920; [unreadable], minute, 26 Aug. 1920, on Montagu, note, [c. 25 Aug. 1920].

15. Hanna Batatu, *The Old Social Classes and the Revolutionary Movements of Iraq*, 389–404; Eliezer Tauber, *The Formation of Modern Syria and Iraq*; Jacob Landau, *The Politics of Pan-Islam*; John Baldry, "Soviet Relations with Saudi Arabia and the Yemen, 1917–1938"; B. Gokay, *A Clash of Empires: Turkey between Russian Bolshevism and British Imperialism, 1918–1923*; Peter Hopkirk, *Setting the East Ablaze: Lenin's Dream of an Empire in Asia*. On Indian Ocean ties more generally, see Sugata Bose, *A Hundred Horizons: The Indian Ocean in the Age of Global Empire*.

16. See also Macfie, "Causes of the Unrest"; Howe, *Anticolonialism in British Politics*, 62.

17. See, for instance, WO 106/200: IO to DMI, 27 Oct. 1920.

18. FO 882/XXIV: SY/19/10: Bell, "Syria in October 1919," 15 Nov. 1919; Lawrence to Curzon, 25 Sept. 1919, quoted in Mack, *Prince of Our Disorder*, 280; FO 882/XXIII: MES/20/1: Wilson to S/S India, 25 March 1920; Wilson, 9 June 1920, and

memo, 19 Jan. 1921, quoted in Marlowe, *Late Victorian*, 195, 233; FO 373/5/2: Historical Section, *Mesopotamia* [handbook], Feb. 1919; AIR 23/9: Glubb, Part III, in Report, 16 April 1925; Bell, 4 Nov. 1920, quoted in Burgoyne, *Gertrude Bell*, 2:181; FO 371/9016: E11170: Smart to Curzon, 30 Oct. 1923; FO 371/5228: E8483: Young, memo, 18 June 1920; AIR 23/2: GSI, Iraq to WO, Situation wire, 30 Sept. 1922; AIR 5/202: Viceroy to S/S IO, 2 Dec. 1922; AIR 1/432/15/260/23 (A-B): Intelligence reports from 17th Division, 12 June and 3 July 1921, and from 18th Division, 1 July 1921; AIR 23/383: SSO Basra to Air Staff Intelligence, 10 May 1932; FO 686/139: correspondence of BA Jeddah and Vice Consul Suez from 30 Jan. 1925.

19. A. T. Wilson at the Central Asian Society, 18 Jan. 1926, quoted in Marlowe, *Late Victorian*, 248; WO 32/5916: CIGS, 26 Feb. 1927; CO 730/1: 11341: Bullard, minute, 16 March 1921; IOR: L/PS/11/141: Toynbee, memo, 10 Jan. 1918, 5; FO 371/13027: E1668: Irak Intelligence Report, 14 March 1928; CO 727/3: 10766: Dickson, report, 12 Aug. 1920; FO 371/14483: E4309: Warner, minute, 12 Aug. 1930; FO 967/26: Bond to Rendel, 19 Nov. 1929; CO 732/53/3: minute on FO to Simon, 26 Nov. 1931, and Baxter to FO, 30 Dec. 1931; Keith Neilson, " 'Pursued by a Bear': British Estimates of Soviet Military Strength and Anglo-Soviet Relations, 1922–1939"; Bray, note, 27 Sept. 1917.

20. AIR 23/437: DCAS, minute to CAS, and reply, 26 Jan. 1923, and [unreadable] to CSO, [26 Jan. 1923]; FO 371/7844: E14290: Loraine, telegram, 20 Dec. 1922; H. A. Jones, *Over the Balkans and South Russia: Being the History of No. 47 Squadron Royal Air Force*, 155; WO 32/5843: GSI, Iraq to WO, 14 Feb. 1922; CO 730/47: E. A. S., minute, 4 Jan. 1923, on FO to CO, 3 Jan. 1923.

21. Toynbee, memo, 10 Jan. 1918; Bray, note, 27 Sept. 1917; FO 371/4020: 80440: [counterespionage section, Constantinople], memo, 2 May 1919 (and Young's minute).

22. FO 967/22: Lloyd to Chamberlain, 5 June 1929; FO 371/4144: 4370: Peterston, minute, 11 Jan. 1919; FO 371/4237: 132835: minutes, Sept. 1919; FO 371/4236: 129405: Lawrence, note, [20 Sept. 1919].

23. Fromkin, *Peace to End All Peace*, 247; AIR 23/433: Codrington to Dent, 5 Jan. 1928 and Dent to AOC, 10 Jan. 1928.

24. Bullard, minute, 16 March 1921; AIR 5/338: "The use of air force in Iraq," [late 1923].

25. Parker to DMO, note, 21 Nov. 1915; IOR: L/MIL/17/15/74: Office of the CPO, IEF D, *A Sketch of the Political History of Persia, Iraq and Arabia, with Special Reference to the Present Campaign* (Calcutta: Government Press, 1917), chap. 1; Candler, *Long Road*, 1:3, 2:279; Parfit, *Serbia to Kut*, 1; FO 882: Hogarth, "Arabs and Turks," *Arab Bulletin* 48 (April 1917), 174; Bell to Hall, 1 March 1916, quoted in Winstone, *Gertrude Bell*, 155; Lawrence, "Syria: The Raw Material."

26. Sykes to Clayton, 28 Dec. 1915; FO 882/XII: ARB/16/5: Clayton to Hall, 13 Jan. 1916; FO 371/2486: 34982: Sykes to DMO, 23 July 1915; FO 882/II: AP/15/14: Clayton to Parker, 10 Dec. 1915; Presland, *Deedes Bey*, 241.

27. Dickson to his mother, 21 Nov. 1915, 10 Aug. 1915; Candler, *Long Road*, 1:17, 2:209–10; Young, Notes for Lecture at Staff College; FO 882: "Note by Cairo," *Arab Bulletin* 1 (June 1916), 6; Bell to Hogarth, 20 May 1916; FO 882/VI: HRG/17/4: Hogarth, memo, 10 Jan. 1917; FO 882/XV: PIL/14/1: Sudan Agency to Acting HC,

Cairo, 24 Dec. 1914; FO 371/2781: 201201: Sykes, appreciation of Arabian Report no. 16, Oct. 1916.

28. AIR 20/516: General Baghdad to Troopers, London, 6 May 1929; WO 32/5230: General Staff memo, 10 May 1920; Bray, *Shifting Sands*, 184; FO 371/9002: E6911: Bolshevik intrigue in Persia, for IDCEU, 10 June 1923; AIR 23/433: AOC Iraq to Air Ministry, 9 June 1927; [counterespionage section, Constantinople], memo, 2 May 1919; FO 371/4161: 174130: Ryan, memorandum, 29 Dec. 1919; FO 882/XVIII: TU/17/8: "The Turanian Movement," memo, 6 Nov. 1917; Lloyd to Chamberlain, 5 June 1929; FO 371/7771: E4828: Iraq Intelligence Report no. 8, 15 April 1922; WO 106/191: [unsigned] to Buckley, MI, [mid-1919]; Thomas Lyell, *The Ins and Outs of Mesopotamia*, 17, 21; Young, Notes for Lecture at Staff College. On Deleuze and Guattari, see chapter 3, note 31.

29. Bury, *Pan-Islam*, 16, 84; FO 967/22: Petrie, IB, Delhi to Stonehewer-Bird, 2 April 1929; FO 371/11446: E7047: Mayers to Petrie, 28 Nov. 1926; FO 686/145: FO to CO, 30 April 1925; CO 727/10: 21766: Jeddah report no. 31, 20 March to 11 April 1925; FO 371/13008: E765: Rogers to Naval C-in-C, East Indies Squadron, 27 Dec. 1927; FO 371/11446: E1426: Lloyd to Chamberlain, 20 Feb. 1926; FO 967/22: Extract, 4 July 1929, in Intelligence Bureau, Simla to Jedda agent, 5 Sept. 1929; FO 967/22: Bond to Champion, 6 Aug. 1929; AIR 4/485: Chair Seton, minutes of 4th Meeting of subcommittee on SIS in Arabia, 5 Oct. 1926; FO 967/22: Mayers to FO, 18 March 1927.

30. Bray, memo, [May 1920]; IOR: L/PS/11/154: minute, 5 Feb. 1920.

31. FO 882/XXIII: MI/19/9: Whittall, Intelligence Report, [7?] May 1919; AIR 23/433: Dent to Carmichael, 24 Aug. 1927 and Codrington to Dent, 5 March 1928; FO 371/3718: 104620: Thomson, Special Report no. 3, [1919]; FO 371/4233: 141286: Kideston, minute, 27 Oct. 1919.

32. Bell to Chirol, 5 Dec. 1913, quoted in Burgoyne, *Gertrude Bell*, 1:284; Bray, note, [c. 25 Aug. 1920]; General Staff memo, 10 May 1920; WO 32/5806: WO, Statement shewing our potential enemies…, [April 1920]; General Baghdad to Troopers London, 6 May 1929; WO 32/5897: DMO, minute to DCIGS, 18 Feb. 1921.

33. Bray, memo, [May 1920] and IO minute, 5 Feb. 1920.

34. FO 371/5230: E12038: Thomas to C. C. Baghdad, [c. mid-1920] and FO 371/5231: E12721: 27 Aug. 1920; Jarvis, *Arab Command*, 83; Bray, note, 25 March 1917 and covering letter to Wilson, 27 Sept. 1917; *Shifting Sands*, 7.

35. CO 730/12: 28827: C. C. Baghdad, telegram, 17 June 1920; IOR: L/PS/10/556: 5068: minutes of Garbett, 7 Aug. 1920, Wakely, 3 July 1920, Shuckburgh, 8 July 1920; FO 371/6360: E2276: Weakley, memo and enclosures, 25 Jan. 1921 and Oliphant to Secretary of the Army Council, 1 March 1921; CO 730/12: Bullard, minute, 15 March 1921; Oliphant and Osborne, minutes on Rogers, report; IOR: L/PS/10/839: [unreadable], 14 Dec. 1920, minute on Police Report, Baghdad, 29 Oct. 1920; General Staff, Situation in Turkey, 2 Nov. 1920; FO 882/XXIV: SY/20/12: Director, Arab Bureau to Courtney, 11 May 1920; FO 371/7790: E5336: Cox to S/S CO, 21 Nov., 11 Oct., and 25 Nov. 1921, in Interim Report of IDCEU, [May 1922] and Garbett, statement [revised and not "verbatim"], 24 Feb. 1922, in appendix; FO 371/16027: E4105: Glubb, monthly report, 2 July 1932; FO 371/7794: E7265: Philby to HC Jerusalem, 12 May 1922; FO 686/71: Acting Consul, Damascus to FO, 18 Dec. 1924.

36. WO 33/969: General Staff, "An Examination of…Factors Underlying the Disturbed State of the Whole Middle East," Oct. 1920; Interim report of IDCEU; Wilson Papers: 52455C: Wilson to Hirtzel, n.d. [late July 1920]. See also IOR: L/PS/11/154: Bray, Note, 28 July 1919; AIR 23/429: Extract from Squadron Leader Buss, letter, 5 Feb. 1927.

37. IOR: L/PS/10/866/Part 2: Minute to S/S, 7 March 1921; FO 371/5266: E10646: Shuckburgh, IO to Bray, 28 Aug. 1920. For the positive response to Bray's work, see Cecil, handwritten note atop synopsis of Bray, note, 25 March 1917 and Wilson to Wingate, 29 March 1917; FO 882/XII: KH/17/12: Clayton to Wilson, 18 April 1917; Hogarth, handwritten notes on Bray, note, 27 Sept. 1917.

38. Philby, *Arabian Days*, 191; FO 371/5064: E12043: Scott, telegram, 30 Sept. 1920; FO 686/26: J. N. Clayton, Damascus, report, 29 Sept. 1919; FO 371/6253: E2440: Hutchinson, HMS Clematis, report, 17 Dec. 1920; CO 730/10: 55272: Hall, minute, 9 Nov. 1921; CO 727/3: Dickson, memo, 12 Aug. 1920; FO 371/6347: E12875: Genstaff, memo, CP 3494, 21 Nov. 1921; IOR: L/PS/10/556: Wilson to S/S, 3 Aug. 1920; FO 686/26: Clayton, 15 Oct. 1919; IOR: L/PS/10/619: SSO Mosul to Intelligence, GHQ, 23 Jan. 1919; WO 106/191: MI2b document, 11 May 1919; FO 371/4141: 71: Rumbold to Curzon, 3 April 1919; FO 686/26: Jeddah report of 20–30 Sept. 1920; FO 371/4186: 163275: Clayton, report no. 37, 15 Oct. 1919; FO 371/7847: E5338: Palmer, 12 May 1922; FO 371/7797: E2015: Palmer, 2 Feb. 1922.

39. FO 371/10092: E9793: Salisbury Jones to GHQ Palestine, 29 Oct. 1924 (my italics) and minutes thereon; Mann to his mother, 30 May 1920; IOR: L/PS/10/839: Garbett, minute, 18 March 1920, and Wilson to S/S, 1 Feb. 1920.

40. FO 967/22: Mayers to FO, 18 March 1927; FO 371/7770: E4033: Cox to CO, 15 April 1922; WO 32/5843: GHQ Iraq to DMI, 28 April 1922.

41. WO 106/200: S/S to HC Mesopotamia, 23 Oct. 1920; AIR 23/433: Extract from Dent to Saunders, 1 Sept. 1927; Bell to her mother, 16 Nov. 1920, quoted in Burgoyne, *Gertrude Bell*, 2:183; FO 371/10013: E5968: Rodd, minute, 10 July 1924; LHCMA: Lt.-Col. John Alfred Codrington Papers: "Gathering Moss, 1898–1944," TS, 1947, 248, 281 (crossed-out paragraph). For official characterizations of the Arabian spy-space, see, for instance, WO 33/1024: General Staff, *Supplement I to Manual on Military Intelligence in the Field* (London, 1923); Dickson Papers: Box 2A: File 5A: Dickson to C. C. Baghdad, 19 Feb. 1920; File 4: Dickson, Political Diary…October 9th 1922; FO 882/XXI: IS/19/37: Philby, Note, c. July 1919; FO 686/26: Jeddah report of 21 Feb. to 2 March 1920; CO 727/8: 32041: Bullard, Jeddah Report, 3 July 1924.

42. FO 371/13728: E3449: Steel, minute, 9 Aug. 1929; General Staff, "An Examination of…Whole Middle East," Oct. 1920; Cornwallis, remarks, 12 Oct. 1920. Some literary intelligence reports: FO 371/13010: E6113: Jakins, Jedda Report of 1–31 Nov. 1928 and E484: Bird, Jeddah Report, 1 Feb. 1928; CO 727/14: Mayers, Jeddah, report for 1–31 Oct. 1926; CO 730/19: Irak Intelligence Reports for 1924; FO 371/5195: E3958: Notes on the Middle East, no. 3; CO 727/6: Bullard, Jeddah report, 1923; FO 686/26: British Agent, Jeddah, report, 26 Oct. to 21 Nov. 1919 and to Arbur, n.d.; FO 882/XXI: IS/20/1: Dickson, Bahrein, diary, Feb. 1920; FO 371/16023: E2055: Hope-Gill to Warner, 8 April 1932; AIR 5/219: Captain F. E. Carver, *Syrian Desert Reconnaissance, May 1921* (Baghdad: Government Press, 1921). For Whitehall's taste for this literary quality, see minutes on these and other reports from Jedda and Iraq.

43. Dickson, memo, 12 Aug. 1920; FO 371/16015: E3676: Ryan, report, 29 June 1932; AIR 20/523: External Intelligence Report no. 4, 20 Sept. 1921.

44. FO 882/XXIV: PNI/20/2: Vivian to Courtney, Cairo, 26 March 1920.

45. Bray, note, 25 March 1917; *Shifting Sands*, 11; report, 14 Sept. 1920. Usually, the "paranoid style" presumes "a world of autonomous, freely acting individuals who are capable of directly and deliberately bringing about events through their decisions and actions." Gordon Wood, "Conspiracy and the Paranoid Style: Causality and Deceit in the Eighteenth Century," 409. On theories of "Eastern" conspiracy, see also Derek Sayer, "British Reaction to the Amritsar Massacre, 1919–1920."

46. FO 371/4141: 71: [Kidston], minute, 9 April 1919; Churchill, 4 Nov. 1920, quoted in Martin Gilbert, *Winston S. Churchill*, Vol. 4: *1916–1922* (London, 1975), 912–13.

47. FO 882/XXIII: MI/19/2: [Clark?], GSI to Courtney, IB, 10 Feb. 1919; FO 882/XXIV: PNI/20/1: GSI, Constantinople, "Pan-Islamism," 8 Jan. 1920; FO 371/10110: E3657: IDCEU, "Pan-Islamism and the Caliphate," in IO to FO, 30 April 1924; Bray, note, 25 March 1917.

48. WO 32/5806: "Invasion of Mesopotamia," n.d.; IOR: L/PS/10/866 Part 2: Bray to Wakely, 3 March 1921; Bray, report, [Oct. 1920]; FO 371/14482: E5169: Ryan, minute, 30 Sept. 1930; FO 371/5230: E12545: S/S [summarizing Bray's report] to C. C. Baghdad, 7 Oct. 1920; Wilson Papers: 52459B: Extract from speech, 20 Sept. 1920.

49. IOR: L/PS/11/154: Garbett, minute, 26 Aug. 1919; FO 882/XXIII: PA/20/1: Courtney to MI5, 24 June 1920; Whittall, Intelligence report, [7?] May 1919.

50. AIR 23/542: J. M. Salmond, report, [c. April 1924]; AIR 23/800: C. W. Jacob, CGS, memo, 12 May 1920.

51. Bury, *Pan-Islam*, 103–04; Aylmer Haldane, *A Soldier's Saga* (London, 1948), 374–75, quoted in Klieman, *Foundations of British Policy*, 55–56; Young, memo, 18 June 1920; Bell to her parents, 1 Nov. 1920, in the Papers of Gertrude Bell [Online]. Emphasis added.

52. WO 106/206: Palmer to S/S FO, 18 Feb. 1921; CO 732/6: 1702: Lawrence, minute, 12 Jan. 1922; CO 730/29: 39693: Mills, minute, 14 Aug. 1922 and 42064: Palmer, report, 26 July 1922.

53. CO 730/21: 21941: Cox to Shuckburgh, 28 April 1922; CO 837/859: Young to Clayton, 14 Sept. 1923, and reply, 5 Oct. 1923 and minutes thereon; "Britain and Iraq," *Times*, 21 Sept. 1929, 11.

54. Wheeler, "50 Years of Asia," chaps. 6, 7; LHCMA: Robert Brooke-Popham Papers: File 2/1: Brooke-Popham to [Trenchard], 5 Dec. 1929 and to Salmond, 11 Jan. 1930.

55. FO 371/2771: 18845: McMahon to Grey, 25 Jan. 1916; FO 371/6239: E4035: R. C. L., minute, 4 April 1921; Churchill to his wife, quoted in J. Wilson, *Lawrence of Arabia*, 645; Masterton-Smith to Churchill, 14 Feb. 1921, in Martin Gilbert, *Winston S. Churchill: Companion Volume 4, Part 2: Documents July 1919–March 1921*, 1348–49; FO 371/6347: E14134: minute on Middle East Department, CP 3566, 13 Dec. 1921; Helm, minute, 17 Aug. 1932, on Glubb, report, 2 July 1932; Wilson Papers: 52458B: Wilson to Leachman, 22 Aug. 1919, 52456A: Wilson to Stephenson, 12 Dec. 1919, 7 Feb. 1920, 24 April 1920, 52456B: Shuckburgh to Wilson, 1 Feb. 1920 and Wilson to Shuckburgh, 5 Dec. 1919; A. T. Wilson, *Mesopotamia*, 275–76.

56. A. T. Wilson to Stephenson, 1919, quoted in Marlowe, *Late Victorian*, 171; FO 371/4236: 129405: Young, minute, 16 Sept. 1919; Meinertzhagen, 13 Nov. 1922, in *Middle East Diary*, 126; FO 371/13714: E809: Rendel, minute, 20 Feb. 1929; Meinertzhagen, *Black Sheep*, 72; FO 371/13734: E2404: Rendel, minute, 21 May 1929; FO 371/13731: E3061: J. Murray, minute, 29 June 1929; correspondence in FO 800/261; Dickson Papers: Box 2: File 4: Dickson to Philby, 31 July 1923; FO 371/13741: E5405: Lindsay to Hohler, 11 June 1929 and E4528: Laithwaite to Nevile Butler, 26 Sept. 1920; Childs, quoted in John Fisher, *Gentleman Spies*, 126; FO 371/13728: E4453: Hohler to Lindsay, 29 Aug. 1929; Tweedy, 26 April 1927, in *Gathering Moss*, 135; CO 537/822: Cox to S/S, 6 July 1921; FO 371/10017: E8869: correspondence, Oct. 1924; CO 727/4: minutes, Dec. 1922, on Jeddah report for 11–30 Aug. 1922.

57. FO 371/13729: E200: Butler, minute, 24 Sept. 1929; FO 371/14476: E4633: Ryan to Humphreys, 2 July 1930; FO 371/16018: E2303: Hope Gill, 27 April 1932, and minutes thereon; WO 181/3: [unreadable] to Peake, 10 June 1932 and Newcombe to Macleod, 30 May 1932; minutes on Glubb, report, 2 July 1932; FO 371/13741: E4528: Stonehewer-Bird, minute, 17 Sept. 1929 on Bray to Henderson, 3 Sept. 1929, Hohler to Lindsay, 21 Feb. 1929, and E5405: Bray to Jebb, 19 Oct. 1928.

58. FO 371/13729: E5102: Rendel, minute, 5 Oct. 1929; minutes on Bray to Henderson, 3 Sept. 1929; Dickson Papers: Box 2: File 4: Philby to Dickson, 26 Dec. 1923 and Thomas to Dickson, n.d.; File 3: Thomas to Dickson, 9 July 1920; Glubb Papers: Box 1 Iraq: File S. Desert (1), 1927–1928: Philby to Glubb, 8 Nov. 1925.

59. AIR 5/1253: 5330: Haldane, Operations, summer of 1920, in *London Gazette*, by MacMunn, 1 July 1921.

60. FO 882/XII: IND/17/2: Arbur, notes on leading conspirators, 31 Jan. 1917; War Cabinet 615, FO 371/4234: 114598: Draft minutes of meeting, 15 Aug. 1918; IOR: L/PS/10/619: Dickson, report, 30 Nov. 1918.

61. Bell to her mother, 12 Jan. 1920 and to Chirol, 12 Feb. 1920, quoted in Burgoyne, *Gertrude Bell*, 2:125–28.

62. FO 371/11433: E4677: Osborne, minute, 11 Aug. 1926, and Mallet, minute, 10 Aug. 1926; FO 371/11449: E6801: Rendel, minute, 13 Dec. 1926; AIR 23/405: "Notes on Pan-Islam and Pan-Arabianism," 7 Nov. 1931, passim; FO 371/15285: E3099: Rendel, minute, 15 June 1931; CO 732/41/1: Clauson, minute, 8 Aug. 1929; FO 967/22: Viceroy to S/S IO, 20 Aug. 1929; FO 371/13012: E3247: Rendel, minute, 29 June 1928; AIR 5/1257: periodic appreciations by MI2 and AI, 1923–26; FO 371/14461: E6760: Warner, minute, 22 Dec. 1930.

63. FO 371/16009, 16086, 16884; AIR 23/4305: Deputy Commandant (CID) to Chief Secretary (Palestine), 18 Feb. 1931, Extract from Palestine Weekly Summary for 21 March 1931, Percy to Oliphant, 12 June 1931, and HC Cairo to Henderson, 27 Feb. 1931; FO 371/15282: E1205: Rendel, minute, 23 March 1931; AIR 23/405: HC Iraq to Reed, note, 14 Nov. 1931; FO 371/14459: E5157: Ryan to Rendel, 22 Sept. 1930; AIR 4/485: IDCEU report no. 8, 12 April 1927; FO 371/13731: E2631: Jebb, memo, 23 May 1929; FO 371/13008: E612: Osborne and Oliphant, minutes, 9 Feb. 1928, E1672: Bird to Oliphant, 6 March 1928, and E2263: Bird to Chamberlain, 9 April 1928; FO 371/13008: E2682: Bird to CBR Amman, 3 May 1928; FO 371/13731: E3061: minutes on Jebb, memo, 23 May 1929 and Jebb, minute, 27 June 1929; FO 371/16027: E4002: Ryan,

28 July 1932; CO 732/41/1: Shuckburgh, minute, 14 Aug. 1929; FO 371/16014, 16015, 16004, 16017, 16016, 16726, Reader Bullard, *Britain and the Middle East*, 89; AIR 5/485: IDCEU to CID [Committee of Imperial Defence], Note, Nov. 1926; minutes of 4th Meeting on SIS in Arabia, 5 Oct. 1926.

64. AIR 8/57: Cox to Cabinet Committee on Iraq, Feb. 1923; Montagu, note, [c. 25 Aug. 1920]; Curzon in House of Lords, quoted in *Spectator*, 3 July 1920, 2.

65. Wood, "Conspiracy and the Paranoid Style," 407; WO 32/5897: Shuckburgh, Minutes of 1st meeting of Middle East Committee, 5 May 1921. See also Timothy Tackett, "Conspiracy Obsession in a Time of Revolution: French Elites and the Origins of the Terror, 1789–1792." (Tackett and Wood differ on the relationship between conspiracy thinking and the Enlightenment.) There remains the issue of Arab contribution to British conspiracy thinking—a topic certainly meriting its own study. According to materials in the British archives, several elites, including Faisal, Ibn Saud, and Hussein, either confirmed British suspicions of an all-embracing plot behind local unrest or used that suspicion to their material advantage. Other Muslims, including British Indian agents in Mecca, also fed British fears.

66. See, for instance, Dodge, *Inventing Iraq*, 8; Atiyyah, *Iraq*, chaps. 7, 8; Klieman, *Foundations of British Policy*, 59. Arnold Wilson privately admitted that the continued conditions of military occupation were a considerable motivating factor. Wilson Papers: 52459A: Wilson to [Hotart?], 22 June 1920; 52455C: Wilson to Hirtzel, 24 May 1920; 52458B: A. S. Meek to Wilson, 18 May 1919. See also Bell's (skeptical) report on Mesopotamian grievances in "Syria in October 1919."

67. Bell to her father, 12 Sept. 1920, quoted in Burgoyne, *Gertrude Bell*, 2:163; Wilson Papers; 52459A: Wilson to Daly, 14 July 1920; 52459B: Wilson to Daly, 5 Oct. 1920; 52456A: Wilson to Stephenson, 24 April 1920 and 26 July 1920; Lawrence, 1925, and Leachman, 1920, quoted in Winstone, *Leachman*, 180, 216; G. Buchanan, *Tragedy of Mesopotamia*, 278, 285.

68. Wilson Papers: 52459B: Wilson to [Frewen?], copy of extract of speech, 15 Sept. 1920; Haldane, *Insurrection in Mesopotamia*, 220; General Staff, appendix I, in Cabinet Paper on Mesopotamia, 12 Nov. 1919.

CHAPTER 7

1. Benjamin, "Work of Art," 242; John Laffin, *Swifter Than Eagles: The Biography of Marshal of the Royal Air Force Sir John Maitland Salmond*, 192. On the 1919 use of airpower in Egypt, Punjab, Somaliland, South Russia, Afghanistan, and the North West Frontier, see Omissi, *Air Power*, 11; Lindqvist, *History of Bombing*, 42–43. Earlier imaginings about the uses of airpower had focused on its general suitability for tribal areas. See Michael Paris, *Winged Warfare*, esp. 241–54; Robert Wohl, *A Passion for Wings: Aviation and the Western Imagination, 1908–1918*.

2. See Omissi, *Air Power*, 184–209; Philip Anthony Towle, *Pilots and Rebels: The Use of Aircraft in Unconventional Warfare*, 11–12; James S. Corum, "The Myth of Air Control: Reassessing the History," 69–70; AIR 5/269: Macneece, Air Staff, Baghdad, report on visit to the French Army of the Levant, 8 Feb. 1923; CO 730/46: 52469: Air Staff, Remarks on Iraq Intelligence Summaries, [late Oct. 1923]; Robert J. Young,

"The Strategic Dream: French Air Doctrine in the Inter-War Period, 1919–39," *Journal of Contemporary History* 9 (1974); Pascal Vennesson, "Institution and Airpower: The Making of the French Air Force," 54–55.

3. Lawrence to Herbert Baker, quoted in Mack, *Prince of Our Disorder*, 320; Jarvis, *Arab Command*, 83. Lawrence later exaggerated, "As soon as I was able to have my own way in the Middle East I approached Trenchard on this point, converted Winston easily, tricked the Cabinet into approving…" (to Liddell Hart, 1933, in *Letters of T. E. Lawrence*, 323). Churchill was certainly also influenced by his cousin Frederick Sykes, chief of Air Staff until 1919, who had urged the creation of an "Imperial" air force (austerity had intervened at that point). On the creation of the Royal Air Force, see, for instance, Ferris, *British Strategic Policy*.

4. Air Staff, "On the Power of the Air Force," March 1920; AIR 20/526: "Memorandum on the scheme for…Mesopotamia," n.d.; AIR 23/807: Robinson to GSI, 6 Feb. 1919; Salmond, report, [c. April 1924]; Churchill, Cabinet Memorandum, "Policy and Finance in Mesopotamia, 1922–23," 4 Aug. 1921, in *Churchill*, 4/3:1576–81; A. T. Wilson, memo, 16 Feb. 1921, Churchill to Trenchard, 29 Feb. 1920, and Churchill, memo, 1 May 1920, quoted in Gilbert, *Churchill*, 4:217, 481, 532; AIR 5/1253: Haldane to WO, 25 Nov. 1920, Cabinet Paper, Feb. 1921; John Glubb, *War in the Desert: An R. A. F. Frontier Campaign*, 69; AIR 9/14: "Notes on…the air route between Cairo and Baghdad…," n.d.; Edmonds, Diary 1915–1924, 22 Nov. 1924; H. R. Brooke-Popham, lecture, 3 Dec. 1919, in *JRUSI* 65 (1920), 57, 60; Lawrence to Liddell Hart, 1933. Keith Jeffrey speculates with respect to the decision against using air control in Ireland, "Perhaps…the natives were more impressionable than the Irish" (!) (*British Army and the Crisis*, 67–70).

5. Lawrence, quoted in Liddell Hart, "*T. E. Lawrence*," 438; Rolls, *Steel Chariots*, 166; Lawrence to Trenchard, 5 Jan. 1922, quoted in Phillip Knightley and Colin Simpson, *The Secret Lives of Lawrence of Arabia*, 166; Andrew Boyle, *Trenchard*, 515; AIR 2/155: Glubb to Adviser to Ministry of Interior, Baghdad, 15 Jan. 1929; Philby, "Mesopotage," chap. 7; Bell, quoted in Laffin, *Swifter Than Eagles*, 176; Brooke-Popham Papers: Brooke-Popham, "Aeroplanes in Tropical Countries," lecture, 6 Oct. 1921, at Royal Aeronautical Society, in *Aeronautical Journal* 25 (March 1922) and File 2/3: Notes for a lecture at Downside, 7 Feb. 1932; Arthur Harris, *Bomber Offensive*, 54; Strachan, "British Way," 461; R. M. Hill, lecture at Royal Aeronautical Society, quoted in F. V. Monk and H. T. Winter, *The Royal Air Force*, 47.

6. Mackay, "Influence in the Future of Aircraft," 298–300; Wing Commander J. A. Chamier, "The Use of the Air Force for Replacing Military Garrisons," *JRUSI* 66 (1921), 210; AIR 9/12: "Old notes on 'substitution'…21st June, 1932"; "Notes on…the air route"; AIR 5/476: CAS, Scheme for the Control of Mesopotamia…, 12 March[?] 1921; AIR 1/21/15/1/102: Deputy Chief of the Air Staff to GOC, RAF, Cairo, 22 April 1919, and RAF, Cairo to Salmond, 10 April 1919; IOR: L/MIL/17/15/59: *An Amplification of a Report Previously Rendered by Col. P. R. Chambers in Nov. 1924* (Simla: Government Press, 1926); AIR 20/516: Minutes of inter-departmental conference…, 11 Jan. 1919; CO 730/34: 61243: [Shuckburgh], Middle East Department, note for Cabinet Committee on Iraq, 12 Nov. 1922; FO 882/XIII: MES/18/6: A. T. Wilson to HC Cairo, 22 Dec. 1918; [Lawrence], "Changing East," 88; Churchill to Hankey, 13 April

1921, in *Churchill*, 4/3:1438; AIR 2/830: Salmond to Brooke-Popham, 13 Feb. 1930; Lawrence to Clayton, 27 Aug. 1917, in *Selected Letters*, 120. On the air route and British strategy, see Hughes, *Allenby and British Strategy*, 135–37. On interwar British military strategy generally, see Jeffrey, *British Army and the Crisis*, chap. 8; Anthony Clayton, *The British Empire as a Superpower, 1919–39*.

7. Air Staff, "On the Power of the Air Force," March 1920; AIR 23/801: correspondence, 1921; AIR 5/476: CAS, memo, 5 Aug. 1921; Glubb, Part 3, in report, 16 April 1925; AIR 1/426/15/260/3: "Scheme for...Mesopotamia," n.d.; Robinson to GSI, 6 Feb. 1919; Salmond, report, [c. April 1924]; AIR 23/807: Report on the operations on the Euphrates above Hit, [after Dec. 1919]; Chamier, "Use of the Air Force," 212; IOR: L/PS/11/154: Bray to Shuckburgh, 4 Aug. 1919.

8. Rolls, *Steel Chariots*, 164–65; J. F. C. Fuller, *Memoirs of an Unconventional Soldier*, 396–97; CAS, memo, 5 Aug. 1921; AIR 5/476: Air Staff, notes, 20 June 1923. For a narrative of the adoption of the scheme, see J. Cox, "Splendid Training Ground."

9. CAS, Scheme, 12 March[?] 1921; Ferrier, "Trans-Desert Route"; *Illustrated London News*, 1 Feb. 1919, 149 (quoting without attribution from Stephen Phillips, "Marpessa," a poem dating from 1897); O. G. S. Crawford, "Air Photographs of the Middle East," *Geographical Journal* 73 (1929): 497–509; AIR 8/57: Extracts from First Lord of the Admiralty, letter, 26 Dec. 1922; AIR 1/2132/207/133/1: H. T. Montague Bell, "By Air to Baghdad: A Tribute to a Notable Achievement of the Royal Air Force," *Near East* 21 (1922); Caddell, comment, on Brooke-Popham, "Aeroplanes in Tropical Countries"; Young, *Independent Arab*, 338; Wing Commander R. H. Peck, "Aircraft in Small Wars," 1 Feb. 1928, in *JRUSI* 73 (1928), 541.

10. AIR 5/202: Fraser to WO, 3 Aug. 1922; John Glubb, *The Changing Scenes of Life: An Autobiography*, 60, and *Arabian Adventures: Ten Years of Joyful Service*, 135; AIR 23/800: Report regarding...aeroplanes as main weapon of an Administration...in Mesopotamia, n.d.; C. H. Keith, 29 Oct. 1926, in *Flying Years*, 16; CO 730/4: 4881: SSO Basrah to GHQ, 19 July 1921; AIR 1/432/15/260/23 (A-B): 18th Division, Intelligence report, 15 June 1921 (and many similar); W. A. Wigram, "Problems of Northern Iraq," *JCAS* 15 (1928), 331; Haldane to WO, 25 Nov. 1920 and Air Staff comments thereon, Jan. 1921; Glubb Papers: Box 1: Iraq S. Desert (3): "Conduct of the operations: 1928–29 Year of Sibilla," draft; CO 730/20: 14464: E. A. S., minute, 30 March 1922; AIR 5/476: Wilson, note, 26 Feb. 1921; AIR 20/521: Office of no. 30 Squadron, Baghdad to GOC, 8 April 1919; CO 730/2: 39645: Divisional Adviser, Nasiriyah to the adviser to the Ministry of Interior, Baghdad, 22 June 1921; FO 371/13027: E754: Iraq Intelligence Report, 1 Feb. 1928; Air Staff, "On the Power of the Air Force," March 1920; Chamier, "Use of the Air Force," 207; Philby, Note, c. July 1919; CO 727/9: 16383: Knox, report, 3 April 1924; AIR 5/1253: Salmond, Iraq Command Report, Nov. 1924; "Thomson's Defence of Bombing," *Times*, 11 Oct. 1924, 7; Squadron-Leader J. C. Slessor, "The Development of the Royal Air Force," *JRUSI* 76 (1931), 332; Peck, "Aircraft in Small Wars," 545. On Arab tactics against air control, see Omissi, *Air Power*, chap. 6. Some historians nevertheless believe air control actually worked against the "clearly defined, completely visible targets" of desert regions (Lindqvist, *History of Bombing*, 68; Malcolm Smith, *British Air Strategy between the*

Wars, 29). On air control elsewhere, see Churchill to Shuckburgh, 11 Jan. 1922, in *Churchill*, 4/3:1723; David Killingray, " 'A Swift Agent of Government': Air Power in British Colonial Africa, 1916–1939," *Journal of African History* 25 (1984); Omissi, *Air Power*, 28–29, 39–59; Charles Townshend, *Britain's Civil Wars: Counterinsurgency in the Twentieth Century*, 99–113.

11. Lawrence, *Seven Pillars*, 196; Buchan, *Memory Hold the Door*, 214; Air Staff, "On the Power of the Air Force," March 1920; CAS, memo, 5 Aug. 1921; Deputy Director of Operations, memo on "Forms of Frightfulness," 1922, quoted in C. Townshend, "Civilization and 'Frightfulness,' " 148–51; C. Townshend, *Britain's Civil Wars*, 98. On the play of this theory among contemporary military theorists, see Lindqvist, *History of Bombing*, 46–47.

12. C. Townshend, "Civilization and 'Frightfulness,' " 149–50; Chamier, "Use of the Air Force," 210; AIR 1/432/15/260/23 (A-B): Commanding Officer, 17th Division, report, 26 June 1921; FO 371/5230: E11758: Thomas to PO Muntafik, 13 July 1921; CO 730/2: 39645: [Hall?], minute, 11 Aug. 1921; SSO Basrah to GHQ, 19 July 1921; CO 730/7: 58013: Cox to Churchill, 6 Oct. 1921; WO 32/5745: General Staff, memo, 27 July 1920. See also Omissi, *Air Power*, 174; C. Townshend, "Civilization and 'Frightfulness,' " 148, 153. Cf. Anthony Clayton, " 'Deceptive Might': Imperial Defence and Security, 1900–1968," 291. By 1923, official procedure was: the British divisional adviser's request for bombers went to the Ministry of Interior, then the high commissioner, and then the AOC. See FO 371/9002: E741: Air Ministry to AOC, 22 Feb. 1923 and reply, 24 Feb. 1923. For exemplary episodes, see Sluglett, *British in Iraq*, 262–70; Dodge, *Inventing Iraq*, 150–54; Corum, "Myth of Air Control," 67.

13. Young, memo, 18 June 1920; Meinertzhagen, minute, 10 Oct. 1921, on SSO Basrah to GHQ, 19 July 1921; FO 371/5076: E8608: minutes on Leachman, Diary of Events, 1–20 May 1920; Worthington-Evans, quoted in C. Townshend, "Civilization and 'Frightfulness,' " 147. See also Omissi, *Air Power*, 151–83; Sluglett, *British in Iraq*, 262–70. For critiques stemming from interservice rivalry, see, for instance, FO 371/7781: E11529: Bentnick and J. Murray, minutes, 25 Oct. 1922; FO 371/7770: E1561: WO, memo, 8 Feb. 1922. Criticism intensified under Labour in 1924 (prompting greater official secrecy), but it started earlier (cf. Corum, "Myth of Air Control," 66).

14. CO 730/18: 58212: Air Staff, memorandum, n.d., in Air Ministry to CID [Committee of Imperial Defence], 26 Nov. 1921; Brooke-Popham, "Some Notes on Aeroplanes, with Special Reference to the Air Route from Cairo to Bagdad," *JCAS* 9 (1922), 139; Basil Embry, *Mission Completed*, 29; Gerald Gibbs, *Survivor's Story*, 38; Harris, *Bomber Offensive*, 23; Chairman [Lord Peel?], comment on Lord Thomson, "My Impressions of a Tour in Iraq," *JCAS* 12 (1925), 211.

15. See Basil Liddell Hart, *Paris, or The Future of War*, 44; Fussell, *Great War*, 190. At the same time, as Nicoletta Gullace has argued, propaganda about German atrocities had helped rehabilitate the Hague conventions, giving them an unambiguously "gendered, humanitarian cast" ("Sexual Violence and Family Honor: British Propaganda and International Law during the First World War").

16. Thomson, House of Lords, 9 April 1930, reported in *Times*, 10 April 1930, 8; Thomson, "Impressions of a Tour," 211; AIR 5/1298: officer, quoted in "With the RAF in Iraq," *Basrah Times*, 3 May 1924. Geoffrey Best and Charles Townshend also find

the Air Staff defense specious, but, oddly, others find it compelling: Omissi, *Air Power*, 169; Philip S. Meilinger, "Trenchard and 'Morale Bombing': The Evolution of Royal Air Force Doctrine before World War II," 259; James S. Corum and Wray R. Johnson, *Airpower in Small Wars*, 59.

17. J. Lawrence, "Forging a Peaceable Kingdom," 558. On the airplane's centrality to interwar militarism, see Edgerton, *England and the Aeroplane*.

18. Cf. C. Townshend, "Civilization and 'Frightfulness,'" 159; Omissi, *Air Power*, 109; Lindqvist, *History of Bombing*; Dodge, *Inventing Iraq*, 64. True, when critics appealed to British memories of bombardment in the war, the RAF replied that it was "fantastic to suggest that the psychology of the tribesmen, who spend half their lives shooting each other, is similar to that of an English villager" (1936, quoted in "Civilization and 'Frightfulness,'" 158), but the particularism here applies not to bombardment's power to enforce submission but to the tribes' ability to cope with it.

19. Salmond on universal psychology, in C. Townshend, "Civilization and 'Frightfulness,'" 149–50 and Omissi, *Air Power*, 110; Glubb Papers: Box 1: File Iraq S. Desert (1): Note on the Southern Desert Force, [c. 1930s]; Keith, 29 Oct. 1926, in *Flying Years*, 18; Thomas, *Alarms and Excursions*, 63; Mackay, "Influence in the Future," 299; Aylmer Haldane, "The Arab Rising in Mesopotamia, 1920," 29 Nov. 1922, in *JRUSI* 68 (1923), 65; Glubb, *Story of the Arab Legion*, 149, and *Arabian Adventures*, 148; John Slessor, *The Central Blue*, 54–55; Wilson to the CGS, 4 March 1920, in Air Staff, memo, n.d.; Sykes to Browne, 3 Dec. 1907, quoted in Leslie, *Mark Sykes*, 178–79; Trenchard in the House of Lords, 9 April 1930, reported in *Times*, 10 April 1930, 8; Spaight, *Air Power*, 23–24, 102–03; Haldane to Churchill, 26 Nov. 1921, in *Churchill*, 4/3:1676; Lawrence to Liddell Hart, June 1930, quoted in Mack, *Prince of Our Disorder*, 385; Hoare in House of Commons, 1 March 1923, reported in *Times*, 2 March 1923, 6. Lawrence seems to have reformed his view of air control later—see Lawrence to Thurtle, 1933, quoted in *Prince of Our Disorder*, 395.

20. WO 32/5806: "Note on Secretary of State's Requirements," n.d., and the accompanying table; AIR 8/94: Humphrys to Simon, 15 Dec. 1932; CO 730/18: Air Ministry to CID, 26 Nov. 1921; Arthur Gould Lee, *Fly Past: Highlights from a Flyer's Life*, 53; Laffin, *Swifter Than Eagles*, 181; Lawrence, *Seven Pillars*, 189, 194. Since the turn of the century Social Darwinians like Herbert Spencer had argued that in "rude societies," "all adult males are warriors; consequently, the army is the mobilized community, and the community is the army at rest" (quoted in Daniel Pick, *War Machine: The Rationalisation of Slaughter in the Modern Age*, 77). For a similar argument about the links between paranoia and colonial violence, see Michael Taussig, "Culture of Terror—Space of Death: Roger Casement's Putumayo Report and the Explanation of Torture."

21. Lionel Evelyn Charlton, *Charlton*, 271. Major General Sir N. M. Smyth, while chairing at the United Service Institute in 1921, similarly cautioned that Arabs were "very highly civilized and fight as gentlemen always" (comment on Chamier, "Use of the Air Force," 216). George Lloyd was also a vocal critic of air control's inability to distinguish between the innocent and guilty. Claude Hilton Keith attests to pilots' general distaste for bombing anyone but the Ikhwan (*Flying Years*). Curiously, although many of the bombing operations were directed against Kurds, British

experts, despite their taste for fine ethnographic distinctions, habitually referred only to "Arabs" or, more generally, "semicivilised" tribes in their pronouncements on airpower's suitability to the region. This says much about the degree to which these officials had come to imagine Iraq as a uniformly flat and desert terrain—as "Arabia."

22. As, for instance, in Divisional Adviser, Nasiriyah to the adviser to the Ministry of Interior, 22 June 1921. See Young to Trenchard, 20 Aug. 1921 in the same file on Churchill's feeling.

23. CO 730/2: 39645: Trenchard to Young, 22 Aug. 1921; CO 730/20: 14464: Meinertzhagen and Bullard, minutes, 29 March 1922; telegram reported in Bell to her father, 12 Dec. 1920, quoted in Burgoyne, *Gertrude Bell*, 2:190. The RAF also doctored its reports to make casualties look smaller (C. Townshend, "Civilization and 'Frightfulness,'" 147). On Trenchard and intuition, see Tami Davis Biddle, "British and American Approaches to Strategic Bombing: Their Origins and Implementation in the World War II Combined Bomber Offensive," 92. On Meinertzhagen's East African past, see Elkins, *Imperial Reckoning*, 3.

24. Humphreys to Simon, 15 Dec. 1932. Stanley Baldwin began to find air warfare utterly repugnant after the conference and called for its abolition, but others vehemently protested its importance in the colonies. The conference achieved little—particularly after Hitler came to power in 1933.

25. [Lawrence, June 1930], quoted in Liddell Hart, *British Way*, 159; Chamier, "Use of the Air Force," 209–10; Edmonds Papers: Box 1: File 1: Edmonds (Administrative Inspector Kirkuk) to Adviser to the Ministry of Interior, 29 Dec. 1923. Cars—only the most heavily and awesomely armed—were also favored over camels for defense patrols partly for this reason. See AIR 23/300: SSO Nasiriyah to AI, 3 March 1926; G. E. Godsave, "Armoured Cars in Desert Warfare," lecture, 14 Jan. 1931, *JRUSI* 76 (1931), 397.

26. Glubb, *Arabian Adventures*, 148, and *Story of the Arab Legion*, 149, 159, 161; Genstaff, "Notes on Modern Arab Warfare Based in the Fighting round Rumaithah and Diwaniyah, July–August 1920," appendix 9, in Haldane, *Insurrection in Mesopotamia*, 333; Lawrence, *Seven Pillars*, 586; Maguire, comment on Borton, "Use of Aircraft," 317. Bell to her parents, 16 March 1922, quoted in Burgoyne, *Gertrude Bell*, 2:266; AIR 8/94: "The Akhwan Operations (1928) and the General Service Medal," 6 May 1929; Glubb, *War in the Desert*, 216; Lee, *Fly Past*, 77. That Wahhabis were somehow beyond the pale is mutely accepted in Omissi, *Air Power*, 170. In fact, not all the victims of bombings in Wahhabi raiding areas were Wahhabis, and bombing was often used there for tax collection.

27. Leachman, 20 July 1920, quoted in Bray, *Paladin of Arabia*, 391; *Paladin of Arabia*, 406. My italics. Dhari's arrest was announced with fanfare in 1927. He became something of a folk hero in Iraq.

28. Quoted in J. Cox, "Splendid Training Ground," 174–75. Omissi puts the ethical debates down to interservice rivalry (*Air Power*, 163).

29. Air Staff, 1921, quoted in C. Townshend, "Civilization and 'Frightfulness,'" 159; John Salmond, "The Air Force in Iraq," *JRUSI* 70 (1925), 497, and *Times* report, 26 March 1925, 13; AIR 1/426/15/260/4: Air Staff, "On the Policy Which Should

Govern the Distribution of Air Forces…," April 1920, Cabinet Paper, June 1920. Cf.
Roger Beaumont, who argues that "the further from visiblity, the more the tendency to
take off the gloves" ("A New Lease on Empire: Air Policing, 1919–1939," 89; and
Corum, "Myth of Air Control," 66). See also chapter 9.

30. Harris, quoted in Omissi, *Air Power*, 154; Churchill, quoted in Gerard J. De
Groot, "Why Did They Do It?" *Times Higher Education Supplement*, 16 Oct. 1992, 18;
W. G. Sebald, *On the Natural History of Destruction*, 19–24; Harris, *Bomber Offensive*,
9–33; First Lord of the Admiralty, letter, 26 Dec. 1922; R. Graves, *Lawrence and the
Arabs*, 395; J. Cox, "Splendid Training Ground," 176; [Glubb?], "The Iraq-Najd
Frontier," *JCAS* 17 (1930), 85; Lindqvist, *History of Bombing*, 54, 57; Matless, *Landscape
and Englishness*, 113; Uri Bialer, *The Shadow of the Bomber: The Fear of Air Attack and
British Politics, 1932–1939*, 40. Omissi claims air policing had little influence on the
RAF's development, partly because he, like others, is refuting a historiography that
blames the RAF's inadequate preparation for World War Two on its imperial
preoccupations (*Air Power*, 134–49, 210; Meilinger, "Trenchard and 'Morale
Bombing,'" 244; "Splendid Training Ground," 176; A. Clayton, "'Deceptive Might,'"
286). On British versus American approaches to strategic bombing, see Biddle,
"British and American Approaches," 115–16; W. Hays Parks, "'Precision' and 'Area'
Bombing: Who Did Which, and When?" To be sure, this is not the whole story of how
bombardment became part of this world—it cannot explain the Japanese attacks on
China, the Spanish Civil War, the Italians in Ethiopia, the Blitz, Hiroshima, and the
rest—but it is striking that Erich Ludendorff had British colonial bombings in mind
when he wrote *Der Totale Krieg* (1935) (*History of Bombing*, 68).

31. Air Staff, "On the Policy Which Should Govern," April 1920.

32. Ormsby Gore, "Organization of British Responsibilities," 95–96; IOR: L/PS/
10/766: Hirtzel, minute, 16 Aug. 1920; Glubb, report, 16 April 1925; FO 371/4144:
4370: Philby to Wilson, 12 Nov. 1918; MECA: Elphinston Papers: File "Kurds":
W. G. Elphinston, "Shaikh Mahmud of Kurdistan," annotated TS of lecture, n.d.
[interwar]; IOR: Eur Mss F118/86: Reading Papers: Trenchard to Tyrrell, 8 May 1928,
CP 160 (28) and Trenchard to Reading, 13 April 1931; Glubb, *War in the Desert*, 69–70,
and *Arabian Adventures*, 32; AIR 5/1203: Draft Chapters of RAF manual, in Air
Ministry to AOC RAF Uxbridge, 5 July 1933.

33. CO 730/3: 37169: Cox to Churchill, 23 July 1921, and [Hall?], minute, 26 July
1921, thereon; AIR 2/1196: Wing Commander K. C. Buss, memorandum, in AOC Iraq
to Air Ministry, 8 Sept. 1930; Boyle, *Trenchard*, 390; Keith, 20 Jan. 1928, in *Flying
Years*, 155. In the postwar dyarchy scheme, each division was administered by a
mutassarif (governor) with an "Admintor" (administrative inspector) representing the
high commissioner at his side. In August 1920, there were 1,022 British, 2,216
Indian, and 8,566 Arab officials in the administration. After the creation of the
constitutional monarchy under Faisal, few British officers were left behind.
G. Buchanan, *Tragedy of Mesopotamia*, 269.

34. Glubb, *Arabian Adventures*, 125; Draft Chapters of RAF manual; War Office,
Manual of Military Intelligence, 197–98, 204–07; Wheeler, "50 Years of Asia," chap. 7;
Colonel Wing, diary, quoted in Bray, *Paladin of Arabia*, 385; Lee, *Fly Past*, 53; AIR
23/433: Dent to Codrington, 29 Dec. 1927 and Air Ministry to AOC Iraq, 24 May 1928;

A. T. Wilson, *Mesopotamia*, 2:161–62; Gilbert Clayton, *An Arabian Diary*, 268; Mack, *Prince of Our Disorder*, 308; WO 106/200: Bray, memo, 15 Oct. 1920; Young, *Independent Arab*, 327–37; Presland, *Deedes Bey*, 335–36, 346; AIR 23/6: [Glubb], memo, in Aviation Baghdad to Abu Ghar, 14 Feb. 1925; Wilson, note, 26 Feb. 1921; AIR 9/12: CAS to Maconachie, 10 Jan. 1933; Codrington to Dent, 5 Jan. 1928; Codrington, "Gathering Moss," 282, 332; AIR 10/1348: Air Ministry, "Handbook of the Southern Desert of Iraq," Jan. 1930; Glubb, *War in the Desert*, 144, 202–03, 228–31; Keith, 25 April 1927 and 20 Sept. 1928, in *Flying Years*, 82, 197; Glubb Papers: Box 1: File Iraq S. Desert (1): "Police work in the desert," 3 July 1928; AIR 23/807: Robinson to RAF, GHQ, MEF, 7 Jan. 1919; Glubb, "Conduct of the operations"; Jarvis, *Arab Command*, 101, 129; IOR: L/PS/10/755: Howell, Deputy Civil Commissioner, personal letter, 4 Dec. 1918; Thomas, *Alarms and Excursions*, 75, 85; *Paladin of Arabia*, 385, 400; Kinch, autobiographical notes; Glubb, *Changing Scenes*, 105; Dobbs to CO, quoted in Bell to Florence Bell, 28 Feb. 1924, in *Letters of Gertrude Bell*, 2:685–86; AIR 2/1196: [Flight Lieutenant?, AI5], Future Intelligence Organisation in Iraq, 21 July 1930 and [undated document on air intelligence in Iraq]; AIR 5/1254: Higgins, AOC Iraq to Air Ministry, 19 Nov. 1926; AIR 23/3: Administrative Inspector, Nasiriya to Advisor to the Ministry of the Interior, 3 Jan. 1925; Glubb Papers: Iraq S. Desert (3): handwritten chapter on the conference at Jidda in 1928.

35. CO 730/5: 48218: Bullard and Meinertzhagen, minutes, Sept. 1921; Thomas, *Alarms and Excursions*, 85.

36. CAS to Maconachie, 10 Jan. 1933; AIR 9/14: S/S War, memo, 17 Aug. 1921, CP 3240, quoted in DCAS, Extracts showing attitude of WO . . . re Air Control in Iraq, July 1933; Slessor, *Central Blue*, 57; Glubb, *Changing Scenes*, 105; Towle, *Pilots and Rebels*, 54. Towle is cited in, for instance, Captain David Willard Parsons, USAF, "British Air Control: A Model for the Application of Air Power in Low-Intensity Conflict," *Airpower Journal* (Summer 1994), available at http://www.airpower.maxwell. af.mil/ airchronicles/apj/apj94/parsons.html. For other American works looking to the Iraqi model, see Lt. Col. David J. Dean, USAF, *The Air Force Role in Low-Intensity Conflict*, chap. 2; Corum, "Myth of Air Control," 62 n. 2, 73 nn. 76, 79, 84.

37. Glubb, *War in the Desert*, 66–67, 87, 92–95, 104, 179, 215, 255; *Arabian Adventures*, 63, 93, 94, 147; report, 16 April 1925; Keith, 24 and 26 Oct. 1926, 28 Dec. 1926, 3 Dec. 1927, 10 March 1928, in *Flying Years*, 9, 15, 42, 137–38, 168; Codrington, "Gathering Moss," 195, 211, 215, 332; Glubb, *Changing Scenes*, 55–56, 71; Mann to Cumberbatch, 31 Aug. 1919, and to his mother, 11 Nov. 1919, in *Administrator in the Making*, 149, 168; Edmonds Papers: Box 12: File 2: Edmonds to "Chick," 8 Dec. 1926, and 12 March 1923, in diary; Curzon, 1921, quoted in Aaron Klieman, "Lawrence as Bureaucrat," 248; Prudence Hill, *To Know the Sky: The Life of Air Chief Marshal Sir Roderic Hill*, 93, 97; Embry, *Mission Completed*, 45; Thomas, *Alarms and Excursions*, 112, 143; Liddell Hart, "T. E. Lawrence," 26, 436; Tennant, *In the Clouds*, 3; Flight Lieutenant, *Reminiscences of the Royal Air Force*, 46; Meinertzhagen, 2 Nov. 1922, in *Middle East Diary*, 125; Lee, *Fly Past*, 61, 64, 66–71, 76–79.

38. Brooke-Popham, "Aeroplanes in Tropical Countries"; Keith, 16 March 1927, 3 Dec. 1927, 30 April 1929, in *Flying Years*, 66–67, 137–38, 240–41; CO 730/16: 56181: Young to Shuckburgh, 23 Oct. 1921; Frederick Maurice and Chairman, comments on

Brooke-Popham, "Some Notes on Aeroplanes," 142, 146; Herbert Baker, in *Lawrence, by His Friends*, 206; P. Hill, *To Know the Sky*, 95, 96–97, 100; Glubb, appendix 1, in report, 16 April 1925; *Charlton*, 269, 277–79; AIR 1/2120/207/72/6(A): W. G. H. Salmond to [General?], [16 Feb. 1929]; S. F. Vincent, *Flying Fever*, 64. For a similar argument about colonial violence and alternative moral universes, see Sayer, "Reaction to the Amritsar Massacre." British criticism of such moral relativism is also as old as the Eastern empire—see Edmund Burke's words at the start of this book's introduction. In 1959, the even more controversial, if less philosophically subtle, Enoch Powell similarly proclaimed in a Commons debate on counterinsurgency in Kenya: "We cannot say, 'We will have African standards in Africa, Asian standards in Asia and perhaps British standards here at home'" (quoted in Elkins, *Imperial Reckoning*, 352).

39. Official document quoted in Omissi, *Air Power*, 157; AIR 23/433: Dent to Codrington, 29 Dec. 1927; Presland, *Deedes Bey*, 346; [Hall?], minute, 11 Aug. 1921; Air Staff, "On the Policy Which Should Govern," April 1921; Peck, "Aircraft in Small Wars," 544; Michael Asher, *Lawrence: The Uncrowned King of Arabia*, 98; Lawrence, "Changing East," 95–96. Aerial violence conformed with a British penal tradition that had long associated impersonality with humaneness; the ruling image here as in the Victorian penitentiary was "the eye of the state—impartial, humane, and vigilant—holding the 'deviant' in thrall of its omniscient gaze" (Michael Ignatieff, *A Just Measure of Pain: The Penitentiary in the Industrial Revolution, 1750–1850*, 113). This John Howardian paternalism (echoing the ostensibly impersonal rewards and punishments of the Smithian "invisible hand") deserves a cultural history of its own.

40. See Tackett, "Conspiracy Obsession."

41. Cox to Churchill, 19 April 1921 and Churchill to Cox, 14 Nov. 1921, quoted in Gilbert, *Churchill*, 4:796, 809; Laffin, *Swifter Than Eagles*, 167; Churchill, "Policy and Finance"; Salmond, "Air Force in Iraq," 486; CO 730/33: 7269: Meinertzhagen, memo, 10 Feb. 1922.

42. CO 732/8: 52945: Meinertzhagen, minute, 13 Aug. 1922 and Trenchard to Young, 25 Oct. 1922; Third meeting of the Joint Political and Military Committee at the Cairo Conference, 16 March 1921, quoted in Gilbert, *Churchill*, 4:550; Air Staff, "On the Power of the Air Force," March 1920; AIR 9/14: "Notes on the value of the air route," n.d.; AIR 9/15: "Notes on the...RAF abroad," Jan. 1929; [Shuckburgh], note, 12 Nov. 1922; AIR 2/2816: "Iraq—Reorganisation of Defence Forces," CID [Committee of Imperial Defence] 770-B, 23 Feb. 1927; Cox to Cabinet Committee on Iraq, Feb. 1923.

43. FO 371/17864: E2107: Air Ministry to FO, 3 April 1934; AIR 9/14: Air Staff, draft, "The strategical importance of Iraq," Nov. 1926; AIR 2/1196: AOC Iraq to Air Ministry, 15 Nov. 1926. The Iraqi government and Arabic newspapers stressed the role of Iraqi forces in maintaining security, but British observers stressed the power of the bomber, as does Omissi (*Air Power*, 35, 37; Liddell Hart, *British Way in Warfare*, 153, 155; Air Ministry to FO, 3 April 1934).

44. AIR 2/2816: HC to S/S CO, 28 Feb. 1927 and CID [Committee of Imperial Defence] minutes of meeting of 25 Feb. 1927; "Notes on the...RAF abroad," Jan. 1929. For Iraqi reaction, see documents in AIR 2/931.

45. FO 371/15303: E5751: Hall, note, 12 Nov. 1931; Buss, memorandum; FO 371/14504: E2176: Humphrys to British Officers, draft, 1930; FO 371/14503: E670: Young, note, in Humphrys to CO, 19 Dec. 1929; Humphrys to S/S CO, 8 July 1930, quoted in Air Ministry to FO, 3 April 1934; AIR 2/830: Air Policy with Regard to Iraq, [Oct.–Nov. 1929] and Air Staff, Note on the . . . RAF in Iraq . . . League of Nations, 7 Sept. 1929. On the logic determining Britain's (nominal) departure from Iraq in 1932, see Dodge, "International Obligation," 162.

46. Glubb, *War in the Desert*, 221.

47. Omissi, *Air Power*, 37; consultant quoted in Seymour Hersh, "Up in the Air: Where Is the Iraq War Headed Next?" *New Yorker*, 5 Dec. 2005, available at http://www.newyorker.com/fact/content/articles/051205fa_fact. On "control without occupation," see A. Clayton, *British Empire*, 11, 80.

CHAPTER 8

1. Sykes, quoted in Adelson, *Mark Sykes*, 233; S/S IO, instructions for Civil Administration in Baghdad, quoted in Marlowe, *Late Victorian*, 120, 140; Said, *Orientalism*, 246.

2. FO 371/4230: 95339: WO to FO, 7 July 1919; FO 371/5196: E9979: Thwaites to FO, 16 Aug. 1920; IOR: L/PS/10/576: Allenby to S/S WO, 17 May 1919.

3. Westrate, *Arab Bureau*, 191; Adelson, *Mark Sykes*, 251–55; Wingate, *Wingate*, 208; Sykes Papers: Box 2: File 8: Doc 118: Sykes, personal and private, 2 Sept. 1918; FO 371/5196: E9979: minute, 30 Aug. 1920; FO 371/5248: E16148: Cornwallis, minute, 29 Dec. 1920.

4. Leith-Ross, "Tactical Side," 21; FO 371/4230: 95339: WO to FO, 17 Oct. 1919; FO 882/XXII: IND/19/2 and IND/19/3: Extract from Circular, 12 April 1920 and "Summaries of Replies," 23 April 1919; WO 32/3528: General Staff memo, [late 1924] and FO to Loraine, 22 Jan. 1925; AIR 1/431/15/260/20: Genstaff, Iraq to Mosul District, 20 Feb. 1922.

5. [Clark?] to Courtney, 10 Feb. 1919; AIR 23/800: lecture, Northern Command Intelligence class, 30 Aug. 1921; FO 371/4230: 95339: Minute on WO to FO, 7 July 1919; AIR 23/800: CGS, memo, 12 May 1920; FO 371/16010: E2126: Lamington, in extract of Lords debates, 27 April 1932; Philby, Note, c. July 1919; "The Highways of Central Arabia," lecture, anniversary meeting of Central Asian Society, *JCAS* 7 (1920), 113; IOR: L/PS/10/866 Part 2: Bray to Wakely, 3 March 1921; Bell to Chirol, late Dec. 1921, quoted in Burgoyne, *Gertrude Bell*, 2:258; IOR: L/PS/11/154: Garbett, minute, 5 Feb. 1920, on Bray, memo, "panorientalism"; FO 371/5232: E16278: Bray, appendix 1 of memo, 30 Dec. 1920; Lawrence, "Changing East," 72; FO 371/10110: E9788: IDCEU, Minutes for meeting, 7 Nov. 1924; Wheeler, "50 years of Asia," chap. 7; FO 371/5255: E13520: minutes, 2–3 Nov. 1920; FO 371/6348: E8592: Cox to Churchill, 23 July 1921; Cox to Cabinet Committee on Iraq, Feb. 1923; CO 730/13: Interdepartmental committee on the Middle East to Churchill, 31 Jan. 1921.

6. FO 371/4234: 117491: H. F. Jacob, "A Plea for a Moslem Bureau," Arab Bureau Supplementary Paper no. 6, 1 July 1919; WO to FO, 7 July 1919; FO 371/5284: E12297: minutes, 7 Oct. 1920; Thwaites to FO, 16 Aug. 1920. Allenby still considered

Cairo "the most appropriate center" (quoted in Westrate, *Arab Bureau*, 198), understandably, given its value as a surveillance arm for the Egyptian government where he was high commissioner.

7. [Clark?] to Courtney, 10 Feb. 1919; Thwaites to FO, 16 Aug. 1920; Pirie-Gordon and Mackintosh, proposal, early 1918, described in Westrate, *Arab Bureau*, 195; Jacob, "Plea for a Moslem Bureau"; minutes, 2–3 Nov. 1920.

8. FO 371/4230: 95339: FO to Secretary to the Army Council, 15 Sept. 1919, FO to WO, 31 Oct. 1919, and Curzon, note, Sept. 1919; IOR: L/PS/10/576: Shuckburgh, Seton, Hirtzel, minutes, 25 and 26 Aug. 1919; Montagu, note, [c. 25 Aug. 1920]; FO 371/5229: E10912: WO to Political Department, IO, 4 Sept. 1920; Bell to Chirol, 12 Feb. 1920, and to her father, 12 Sept. 1920, quoted in Burgoyne, *Gertrude Bell*, 2:127–28, 163; FO 371/6344: E10139: Palmer to FO, 24 Aug. 1921; Bray, Note, 28 July 1919; Bray, report, [Oct. 1920].

9. Philby Papers: Box 17: File 1: Bell to Philby, 19 Dec. 1921; Wilson to Hirtzel, March 1920, quoted in Marlowe, *Late Victorian*, 183–84; FO 371/5284: E11440: Wilson to IO, 10 Sept. 1920, and E15812: Cornwallis, minute, 21 Dec. 1920, Courtney to Cairo Residency, 1 Dec. 1920; Palmer to FO, 24 Aug. 1921; CO 727/7: Wakely, IO to CO, 4 Dec. 1923, and reply, 11 Dec. 1923; FO 371/9046: E2894: correspondence, March 1923; AIR 5/269: Air Ministry to GOC-in-C Egypt and Constantinople and AOC's in Iraq and Palestine, 10 Oct. 1922; AIR 8/34: James Masterton Smith, Young, Shuckburgh, et al., Report to Churchill, 31 Jan. 1921, appendix 1 of Report on Cairo Conference (CP 3123), June 1921; Curzon, quoted in Klieman, *Foundations of British Policy*, 223; FO 371/16011: E2127: Rendel, report, 29 April 1932, and Rendel and Oliphant, minutes, 2 May 1932; Bell to her parents, 30 Jan. 1922, quoted in Burgoyne, *Gertrude Bell*, 2:261; Winterton, foreword to Jarvis, *Arab Command*, 3; *Arab Command*, 6, 87.

10. WO 32/5728: IO to FO, 4 Jan. 1921, Montagu to S/S, 24 June 1921, FO to IO, 27 June 1921, and second report of Interdepartmental Committee on Bolshevik menace, [June 1921]; FO 371/7790: E14032: IDCEU Report, and E1867: Minutes of meeting, 18 Feb. 1922; Oliphant, minute, 15 Dec. 1921, on IO to FO, 9 Dec. 1921; CO 537/838: IO to CO, 7 April 1926; FO 371/11475: E3586: Minutes of meeting of 28 May 1926.

11. Curzon, note, Sept. 1919; CO 730/11: 27952: Meinertzhagen, minute, 9 June 1921.

12. [AI5], Future Intelligence, 21 July 1930; AIR 2/1196: Draft Air Ministry letter, 10 Jan. 1927; CO 730/10: 56271: Oliphant, FO to CO, 10 Nov. 1921; FO 371/7770: E1441: CO to FO, 13 Jan. 1922, and Shuckburgh, CO to FO, 8 Feb. 1922; AOC Iraq to Air Ministry, 9 June 1927; AIR 23/433: Dent to Codrington, 19 May 1927, Codrington to Dent, 13 June 1927, Dent to Codrington, 6 Oct. 1927, Codrington to Dent, 21 Dec. 1927, Dent to Codrington, 29 Dec. 1927, Dent to Codrington, 12 Jan. 1928, Extracts of Dent to BMA Constantinople and Blunt, 19 Aug. 1927 to Carmichael, 24 Aug. 1927, to Saunders, 1 Sept. 1927, and Codrington to Dent, 5 March 1928; Codrington, "Gathering Moss," 282.

13. AOC Iraq to Air Ministry, 9 June 1927; AIR 23/433: AOC Iraq to Air Ministry, 23 March 1928, and Dent to Carmichael, 4 Nov. 1927; AIR 5/485: Air Ministry, notes, 15 July 1927; AIR 23/433: Carmichael to Dent, 7 Oct. 1927, and Dent's comments thereon; WO, *Manual of Military Intelligence*, 204–07. On the Jeddah agency, see FO

686/26: Intelligence and Political Reports of 1919 and 1920, especially by Captain Ajab Khan; FO 882/XXII: KH/20/41 and 46 Captain Nasiruddin Ahmad, reports, 24 June and 9 July 1920; FO 371/6252: E329 and E580: BA Jeddah, telegrams, 6 Jan. and 10 Oct. 1921. On Damascus, see FO 371/10005: E901: reports from Palmer, Vaughan Russell, and Smart in early 1924 and correspondence thereon.

14. AIR 23/433: AOC Iraq to Air Ministry, 23 March 1928, DOI to OC Aden, 24 May 1928, Buss to Mitchell, 22 June 1928, Air Ministry to AOC Iraq, 24 May 1928; AIR 2/1212: [Transjordania command] to Palestine Command, July 1926, Rees to Burnett, 4 Jan. 1927, DDOI to Rees, 31 May 1927, AOC Palestine to Air Ministry, 5 June 1926, and Burnett, minute thereon, 13 May 1925, Air Ministry to AOC Palestine, 17 June 1926, extract from Wadham to AI2a, 25 Nov. 1926, Wadham to Carmichael, 10 Jan. 1927, Carmichael to DDOI, 26 May 1927, extract from Rees, letter, 27 Feb. 1928, Rees to AOC Cairo, 17 May 1928; AIR 5/269: DOI to AOC Transjordan and Palestine, 24 May 1928, and Rees's reply, n.d.; AIR 2/1212: Minutes of conference on 9 July 1928; FO 371/14458: E1408: Webster, Air Ministry to CO, 18 March 1930; FO 371/14459: E5157: Resident, Amman to Acting HC Transjordania, 28 Aug. 1930, Ryan to Rendel, 22 Sept. 1930, and E4898: Warner, minute, 12 Sept. 1930, and E4365: Warner, minute, 25 Aug. 1930, and Chancellor, dispatch, 26 June 1930; Glubb, *Changing Scenes*, 99; FO 371/16017: E5810: extract from Resident to HC Transjordania, 12 Aug. 1832, and extract from Glubb, note; FO 371/14482: E6564: Rendel, minute, 17 May 1930, and Young to Shuckburgh, 1 Aug. 1930; AIR 2/1212: Newall to G. Salmond, Webb-Bowen, Clark-Hall, 15 May 1928, and Webb-Bowen to Newall, 1 June 1928; FO 371/16239: F168: WO to FO, 23 Dec. 1931.

15. FO 371/14455: E4247: Ryan, dispatch, 6 Aug. 1930, and minutes thereon; FO 371/14460: E5396: Oliphant, minute to Gaselee, 27 Jan. 1931, and Rendel, minute, 27 Nov. 1930; IDCEU report, 12 April 1927; CO 730/105/01: Dobbs to Shuckburgh, 22 July 1926, and Hall, minute, 6 Aug. 1925; FO 371/15298: E1185: Warner, minute, 12 March 1931, on Ryan to Warner, 7 Feb. 1931, and FO to Ryan, 11 Sept. 1931; FO 371/14482: E4191: Ryan to Warner, 12 April 1927 (and Warner's minute, 21 Oct. 1931) and 15 July 1930.

16. AIR 4/485: Carmichael, AI, minute, 24 Sept. 1926, MO2a to Carmichael, 29 Sept. 1926, minutes of 3rd Meeting of IDCEU sub-committee, 24 Sept. 1926, and Jordan, quoted in minutes of 4th Meeting, 5 Oct. 1926.

17. Philby, *Arabian Days*, 210; Leith-Ross Papers: Leith-Ross, "Character and Qualifications of Intelligence Personnel," n.d., 8. By contrast, in the Far East, interwar paranoid agents were not taken seriously, and intelligence arrangements were severely cut back. Anthony Best, *British Intelligence and the Japanese Challenge in Asia, 1914–1941*, 52–54.

18. AOC Iraq to Air Ministry, 15 Nov. 1926; Buss, memorandum; FO 371/16925: E7529: Air Ministry to Rendel, 4 Dec. 1933; AIR 2/1196: "Notes on Future Intelligence Organisation in Iraq," [early 1927], AOC Iraq to Air Ministry, 2 April 1931, and Ludlow-Hewitt to Humphrys, 3 May 1931; FO 371/16925: E7529: Rendel, note for Eden, and Air Ministry memo, 5 Dec. 1933.

19. AOC Iraq to Air Ministry, 15 Nov. 1926 (and draft, 10 Jan. 1927); "Notes on Future Intelligence," [early 1927]; Buss, memo; Young, note, in Humphrys to FO,

19 Dec. 1929; AIR 2/1196: Annexure B in Ludlow-Hewitt to Air Ministry, 26 June 1931; [AI5], Future Intelligence, 21 July 1930; FO 371/16041: E4224: Sterndale-Bennett, minute, 22 Aug. 1932, and draft memo based on Flood, draft letter, 7 Oct. 1932, and E5086: FO to Humphrys, 8 Dec. 1932; FO 371/16889: E5374: Humphrys to Rendel, 6 Sept. 1933; AIR 2/1196: Ross, Air Ministry to AOC, 21 Aug. 1931.

20. Buss, memo; AIR 2/1196: [unreadable], Air HQ, Hinaidi to Newall, Air Ministry, 19 Feb. 1930, and Brooke-Popham to S/S AIR, 8 Sept. 1930; [AI5], Future Intelligence, 21 July 1930; AIR 2/1196: Webster, Air Ministry to AVM Iraq, 19 Nov. 1930, Ludlow-Hewitt, AOC Iraq to Air Ministry, 2 April 1931 and 22 May 1931, and Annexure B in Ludlow-Hewitt to Air Ministry, 26 June 1931; FO 371/20794: E5095: Scott to Rendel, 13 Aug. 1937.

21. AIR 2/1196: Air Ministry to G. W. Rendel, FO, 4 Dec. 1933; FO 371/16925: E7529: Barnes, minute to Rendel, 1 Dec. 1933; Helm, minute, 12 April 1934, on Air Ministry to FO, 3 April 1934; Air Ministry to Rendel, 4 Dec. 1933; Rendel to Eden, 5 Dec. 1933.

22. Young, memo, 18 June 1920; FO 371/10013: E7624: minutes on Jeddah reports of Sept. 1924; CO 727/8: 49699: Bullard to Macdonald, 21 Sept. 1924.

23. Cf. (for instance) A. Clayton, *British Empire*, 120.

24. Young, memo, 18 June 1920. Timothy Paris argues that the India Office *switched* to a pro-annexation position mostly to defend Wilson against Lawrence's press attacks; such was the force of personality ("British Middle East Policy-Making after the First World War: The Lawrentian and Wilsonian Schools"). Unfortunately, there is not space here to finely dissect the agents' divergent politics.

25. Orwell, "Lion and the Unicorn"; Arendt, *Totalitarianism*, 101, 127.

26. WO 106/201: "Les jeunes turcs et l'agitation panislamique," French intelligence, 15 Oct. 1920; WO 106/196: Butler to de Robeck, 24 Feb. 1920; FO 371/9016: E9151: Rodd, minute, 14 Sept. 1923; FO 371/16188: F6141: Walton, IO to Orde, FO, 19 Aug. 1932, and Mackillop, minute, 11 Aug. 1932; FO 371/14579: E2185: Clive to Humphrys, 16 April 1930; FO 371/14539: E4770: Tehran Intelligence Summary no. 17, 26 Aug. 1930; FO 371/14472: E596: Bordenaro in conversation with Oliphant, 31 Jan. 1930; FO 371/14680: E4863: Meade to Henderson, 24 Aug. 1930; FO 371/14524: E4509: *Times* clipping, 14 Aug. 1930, and minutes; FO 371/14521: E4976: minutes, 16–18 Sept. 1930; FO 371/14483: E5777: "Aux pays torrides des pêcheurs de perles," *Petit Parisien*, 24 Oct. 1930; "Great Britain and Afghan Rising" and "False Reports Published in Germany," *Times*, 7 Jan. 1929, 14; "Afghan Rising. The Lawrence Canard," *Times*, 9 Jan. 1929, 11, and similar reports, 11–16 Jan. 1929, 2 Oct. 1930, and 12 March 1931; FO 371/10118: E7962: Salisbury Jones, Syria, to Genstaff, Palestine, 4 Sept. 1924; FO 371/9016: E9151: Rodd, minute, 14 Sept. 1923; AIR 23/374: Jardine to Adviser to the Ministry of the Interior, 29 May 1927 and 20 Nov. 1927; FO 371/9016: E10855: Smart to Curzon, 14 Oct. 1923, E11395: McCallum to Palestine Command, 9 Nov. 1923, and E12166: Smart to Curzon, 7 Dec. 1923; FO 371/9056: Satow to S/S, 18 May 1923, E7390: 5 July 1923, E8254: 1 Aug. 1923, E9979: 25 Sept. 1923, and E8254: McCallum to GHQ Palestine, 30 July 1923.

27. FO 371/13027: E1950: Irak Intelligence Report no. 7, 28 March 1928; FO 371/13010: E994: Stonehewer-Bird, Jeddah Report of 1–31 Jan. 1928, E994/484/91/1928;

CO 727/10: 1158: Woodward, report, 22 Nov. 1924; Glubb Papers: Box 1: File Iraq S. Desert (1): "The Lord of the Earth," *Al Istiqlal*, 16 Nov. 1928; Box 3: *Al Taqaddum*, 22 Nov. 1928.

28. Scott to Rendel, 13 Aug. 1937; CO 537/815: Dobbs to Shuckburgh, 2 Aug. 1923, and FO 371/11515: E345: 18 Nov. 1925; Review of Stevens, *Times*, 14 Dec. 1923, 8; Dickson Papers: Box 2: File 4: Wilson to Dickson, 8 Aug. 1925.

29. FO 371/21849: E457: memo in Clark Kerr to Courtney, 20 Dec. 1937 (and Courtney's note, 31 Dec. 1937), and Local Press Extracts, 26 Nov. 1937 (and other correspondence in this file); AIR 2/1196: Local Press Extracts, 8 May 1933; [unreadable], minute, 28 Jan. 1938, on E457.

30. FO 371/21850: E1596: minutes of Feb.–March 1938; FO 371/21865: E6507: minutes, Oct.–Nov. 1938, and Chancery Baghdad to Egyptian Department, 7 Oct. 1938; FO 371/20794: E3042: Clark Kerr to Rendel, 28 May 1937.

31. FO 371/34940: E4926: Thompson to Clayton, 5 and 10 Aug. 1943, and Clayton to Thompson, 29 Aug. 1943; Nigel Clive, interview, 9 Nov. 1994, in *The Role of the Intelligence Services in the Second World War*, ed. Christopher Andrew et al., 42–43; H. O. Dovey, "The Middle East Intelligence Centre"; H. W. [Holt-Wilson?] to the DSS, 6 March 1939, note on "Intelligence Methods in Peace Time."

32. See Hynes, *Soldier's Tale*, 124, 138, 140.

33. Middle East Department, note for Cabinet, quoted in Dodge, *Inventing Iraq*, 17. On deception of the Permanent Mandates Commission, see *Inventing Iraq*, 28–31, 36–41.

CHAPTER 9

1. Lord Peel, comment on Haldane, "Arab Rising," 80; Coke, *Heart of the Middle East*, 11.

2. Dodge, *Inventing Iraq*, 23–24; Salmond, report, [c. April 1924].

3. See Colls, "Constitution of the English," 114–15; D. Vincent, *Culture of Secrecy*, 122–23, 170.

4. On the loss of faith in official news, see E. D. Morel, *Truth and the War*; Fussell, *Great War*, 115. On the interwar expansion of imperial propaganda, see J. Mackenzie, *Propaganda and Empire*, 10–11. On state control of press on Indian issues, see Chandrika Kaul, *Reporting the Raj: The British Press and India, c. 1880–1922*.

5. "Why Is the Persian Gulf Campaign Ignored?" and "The Middle East and the War," *Times*, 10 and 22 Sept. 1915, 9 (both also found in LCLUL: MES 082: Box 4: Annie Phillips, scrapbook about the Mesopotamian war, in which her son William served); Candler, *Long Road*, 1:65–69; review of *Long Road*, by Candler, in *Spectator*, 8 Feb. 1919, 166–67; A. T. Wilson, *Loyalties*, 1:166.

6. Chesney, "Mesopotamian Breakdown," 247; A. T. Wilson, *Loyalties*, 177; Mariel Grant, *Propaganda and the Role of the State in Inter-War Britain*, 11–12, 15; F. W. Leland, *With the M. T. in Mesopotamia*, vii; Harold Finlinson, *With Pen and Ink in Iraq*; Bar-Yosef, "Last Crusade?" 88.

7. Bell to Florence Bell, 5 Sept. 1918, in *Letters of Gertrude Bell*, 2:461–62; IOR: CPO, IEF "D," *Sketch of the Political History*, chap. 1; Hogarth to Billy, 30 May 1918;

Sykes to Clayton, 16 Jan. 1918, quoted in J. Wilson, *Lawrence of Arabia*, 466–67; Sykes, *Observer*, mid-Dec. 1917, quoted in Adelson, *Mark Sykes*, 246.

8. Lovat Fraser, "The War-Mongers. 'Sack the Lot!'" *Daily Mail*, 12 July 1920; "Outlook in the Middle East," *Round Table* 37 (Dec. 1919), 82; Monroe, *Britain's Moment*, 142; G. Buchanan, "The Development of Mesopotamia," *Times*, 23–26 Sept. 1920, 9; G. Buchanan to the editor, *Times*, 21 June 1920, 10; Candler, "Lawrence and the Hejaz," *Blackwood's* (Dec. 1925), 761; A. S. Elwell-Sutton, "Some Reminiscences of the Arabs of Mesopotamia," in *Spectator*, 27 Nov. 1920, 698; *Spectator*, 15 July 1922, 66; "The Need to Withdraw from Mesopotamia and Palestine," *Spectator*, 24 Feb. 1923, 317–18; "The Arab and Oil," *Guardian*, 5 Feb. 1921, 6; Haldane, "Arab Rising," 72; Churchill to Lloyd George, 31 Aug. 1920; J. de V. Loder, *The Truth about Mesopotamia, Palestine and Syria*, 5. The saying "that blessed word Mesopotamia" has been traced to stories about the power of the voice of the Methodist preacher George Whitefield, who could make his followers weep merely by uttering the word "Mesopotamia." Other versions attribute the saying to an old woman (sometimes English, sometimes Scotch) who told her pastor she found "great support in that blessed word Mesopotamia." Still other versions have it that she was an invalid who begged her preacher to read from the Act of Apostles so that she might derive comfort from "that blessed word Mesopotamia." Some say she died during the Great War.

9. Haldane, "Arab Rising," 64; [An Eastern Trader], "The Mosul Problem," *JRUSI* 71 (1926), 144; Atiyyah, *Iraq*, 264; CO 727/10: 25123: correspondence about A. W. Upcher, 1925; CO 732/42/2: correspondence regarding Italian explorations, 1930; AIR 20/523: Palmer's reports, 1921; IOR: L/PS/11/264: "Travellers:—Arabia," correspondence, 1925–30; FO 686/26: Jeddah, Report, 11–21 Feb. and 1–10 Dec. 1920; AIR 20/645: "Prisoners and Revolutionists: From 8th Mar. 1919 to 6th Mar. 1920"; AIR 23/387: "Suspicious Characters. 6-5-1925"; AIR 23/333: SSO Baghdad, reports, 1925; AIR 23/388: Air Intelligence correspondence about "Suspicious Characters," 1926–27; FO 371/5074: E5419: Acting C. C. Baghdad, Quarterly Return of Arrivals and Departures from Basrah, 1919–1920, and minutes thereon; FO 371/14482: E4009: Baxter, minute, 1 Sept. 1930; Shuckburgh to Masterton Smith, 31 Jan. 1922, and Churchill, quoted in Klieman, *Foundations of British Policy*, 233–35.

10. "The Problem of Mesopotamia," *Times*, 8 Nov. 1919, 13 (my italics); Colonel Hodge, 1 March 1923, reported in *Times*, 2 March 1923, 6; *Spectator*, 5 May 1923, 742; "Policy in Mesopotamia," *Guardian*, 19 Oct. 1920, 6; Lloyd George in Commons, reported in *Times*, 24 June 1920, 9; Herbert to the editor, *Times*, 15 July 1920, 10.

11. "Problem of Mesopotamia"; "Mesopotamia," *Times*, 31 Dec. 1919, 11; "More Trouble in Mesopotamia," *Times*, 12 June 1920, 17; "The Risings in Mesopotamia," *Times*, 7 Aug. 1920, 11; "Mesopotamia," *Guardian*, 24 June 1920, 6, and report on Lords, 26 June 1920, 13. On fears about the brutalization of the state, see also J. Lawrence, "Forging a Peaceable Kingdom."

12. "A Case for Frankness," *Times*, 15 June 1920, 17; "Mesopotamia and Anatolia," *Times*, 23 June 1920, 17; Fraser, "War-Mongers"; "Policy in the Middle East," *Guardian*, 30 Sept. 1920, 6; "Risings in Mesopotamia"; "Mesopotamia and Economy," *Guardian*, 12 March 1921, 8; "Conspiracies and Common Sense" and "Publicity the True Remedy," *Spectator*, 4 Dec. 1920, 728–30; "The Burden of

Mesopotamia," *Times*, 31 Aug. 1922, 13; "The War in Mesopotamia," *Times*, 21 Aug. 1920, 11; "Mesopotamia," *Times*, 18 July 1921, 11; *Spectator*, 21 Oct. 1922, 543; Barron, "New Responsibilities," 256.

13. "Case for Frankness"; "Our Oriental Empire," *Spectator*, 28 Aug. 1920, 260; "Ministers at Mosul," *Times*, 6 April 1925, 15; "The Question of the Mandates," *Times*, 4 March 1921, 11.

14. "Imperial and Foreign News," *Times*, 10 June 1924, 11; "The Allies and the Arabs," *Guardian*, 6 Aug. 1920, 6; "An Imperial Secretary of State," *Times*, 20 Jan. 1921, 11; E. Alexander Powell, *The Struggle for Power in Moslem Asia*, xi, 5–6 (an American author aligning himself with similarly minded "English critics"). See also my "Developing Iraq."

15. Thornton, *Imperial Idea*, 150, 279–81.

16. Asquith, reported in "Reckless Waste," *Times*, 21 June 1920, 5; "Risings in Mesopotamia"; "What Is Our Mesopotamian Policy," *Times*, 16 Aug. 1920, 11; "Mesopotamian Trouble," *Times*, 19 Aug. 1920, 10; "Mesopotamia," *Times*, 19 Aug. 1920, 11; "War in Mesopotamia"; "British Policy in Mesopotamia," *Times*, 24 Aug. 1920, 11; "What Is Happening in Mesopotamia?" *Times*, 8 Sept. 1920, 11; "The Government and the Middle East," *Times*, 21 Sept. 1920, 11; "Our Military Expenditure Overseas," *Times*, 29 Oct. 1920, 13; "India and the Middle East," 5 Nov. 1920, 13; "The Army Estimates and Mesopotamia," *Times*, 15 and 17 Dec. 1920, 13; Frank Swettenham to the editor, *Times*, 24 June 1920, 12; Lawrence, "Suppressed Introductory Chapter," 144–45; Lawrence to the *Sunday Times*, 22 Aug. 1920, in *Letters of T. E. Lawrence*, 315; Zetton Buchanan, *In the Hands of the Arabs*, 4, 229, 233; "Captured Englishwoman," letter to her sister, *Times*, 23 Aug. 1920, 9; "In the Hands of the Arabs," *Times*, 25 May 1921, 11; "The Middle Eastern Department," *Guardian*, 16 Feb. 1921, 6; "The Air Ministry," *Guardian*, 18 Feb. 1921, 6; A. T. Wilson to the editor, *Times*, 17 Oct. 1924, 15; "The Change in Arabia," *Guardian*, 5 Nov. 1924, 8.

17. "Mesopotamia," *Times*, 1 June 1920, 17; "The Mandates," *Spectator*, 2 April 1921, 419; "The Iraq Raids," *Times*, 27 Sept. 1924, 12; Commons debate, reported in *Times*, 17 Nov. 1925, 8; Kenworthy to the editor of the *Times*, 4 Feb. 1921, 6; "The Mandate for Mesopotamia," *Times*, 4 Feb. 1921, 11; "Mesopotamia and Mr. Churchill," *Times*, 23 Feb. 1921, 11; "Parliament and the Mandates," *Times*, 22 March 1921, 11 (and subsequent letters to the editor); "Parliament and Mandates," *Guardian*, 24 Feb. 1921, 6, and 15 March 1921, 6; "Iraq," *Guardian*, 4 May 1923, 8; Clynes in Commons, 2 Feb. 1926, reported in *Times*, 3 Feb. 1926, 8; "The Arab and Oil," *Guardian*, 5 Feb. 1921, 6; "Mesopotamia," *Guardian*, 26 June 1920, 10, "The League and Mosul," *Guardian*, 16 Dec. 1925, 10. On concerns about the league and secret diplomacy, see also James Hinton, *Protests and Visions: Peace Politics in Twentieth-Century Britain*, 77–80; and Thornton, *Imperial Idea*, 283.

18. Morel in Commons, reported in *Times*, 25 Nov. 1922, 16; Lords debate, reported in *Times*, 2 March 1923, 6; Commons debate, reported in *Times*, 21 March 1923, 7; Commons debate, reported 23 Feb. 1923, 6. See also Thornton, *Imperial Idea*, 273; Howe, *Anticolonialism in British Politics*, 47–48.

19. Thornton, *Imperial Idea*, 279–81; "Mesopotamia," *Times*, 1 June 1920; "Risings in Mesopotamia"; "Case for Frankness"; "A Recent Retirement," *Times*,

5 March 1921, 11; "The Case of Sir Arnold Wilson," *Times*, 26 March 1921, 9; "Reckless Waste"; "Mesopotamia," *Guardian*, 24 June 1920, 6; Macdonald and Bonar Law in Commons, reported in *Times*, 24 Nov. 1922, 7; "Mesopotamia," *Guardian*, 26 June 1920, 10; "Mesopotamia," *Times*, 18 July 1921, 11; "Mesopotamia," *Guardian*, 21 Feb. 1923, 6; "Iraq," *Guardian*, 31 July 1924, 8; Commons debate, reported in *Times*, 6 July 1926, 9.

20. "The Position in Mesopotamia," *Times*, 6 Sept. 1920, 11; Tweedy, 28 Feb. 1927 and 20 March 1920, in *Gathering Moss*, 123, 170–71.

21. See, for instance, "The War in Mesopotamia," *Times*, 21 Aug. 1920, 11, and "Sir Percy Cox and His Task," 30 Aug. 1920, 11.

22. "Mesopotamia," *Guardian*, 24 June 1920, 6; J. Wilson, *Lawrence of Arabia*, 621; Lawrence, quoted in Knightley and Simpson, *Secret Lives of Lawrence*, 138; Monroe, *Philby of Arabia*, 138; G. Buchanan, *Tragedy of Mesopotamia*, 222; Herbert, *Ben Kendim*, 75; "The Problem of Mesopotamia," *Guardian*, 24 July 1920, 8. Knightley and Simpson juxtapose Lawrence's statement about gas with the "grim truth" that Churchill had actually considered something on these lines (157); indeed, given his druthers, Churchill would have used *nonlethal* gas bombs (see C. Townshend, "Civilization and 'Frightfulness,' " 148), but the gas shells available caused such injuries as to prove effectively lethal. Jonathan Steele similarly misreads the quote in "A Mess of Our Making," *Guardian*, 25 Jan. 2003.

23. "Iraq's 'Little War,' " *Times*, 6 April 1932, 16; "Bombing in Iraq," *Guardian*, 21 April 1925, 8; "Outlook in the Middle East," 85; *Spectator*, 11 Nov. 1922, 682; "Aeroplanes as Tax Collectors," *Guardian*, 17 Jan. 1923, 6.

24. Commons debate, reported in *Times*, 21 Feb. 1923, 6; debate, reported 21 March 1923, 7; debate, reported 23 Feb. 1923, 6; debate, reported 13 April 1924, 7; debate, reported 1 July 1924, 9; paraphrase of debate, reported 4 July 1924, 8; debate, reported 11 July 1924, 8; White Paper, excerpted in "Iraq Bombing Operations," *Times*, 7 Aug. 1924, 11.

25. Atlee, Commons debate, 8 March 1926, reported in *Times*, 9 March 1926, 8; Captain Guest, in debate reported 13 March 1928, 8–9.

26. Sir Charles W. Gwynn, *Imperial Policing*, 1–2, 34; Herbert, *Ben Kendim*, 75; Mary Lago, *"India's Prisoner": A Biography of Edward John Thompson*, 205–27.

27. Commons debate, reported in *Times*, 3 April 1928, 8; "What Is Our Mesopotamian Policy," 11; Edward Bernays, *Propaganda* (1928), quoted in Grant, *Propaganda and the Role of the State*, 16–17.

28. "Air Pageant at Hendon," *Times*, 19 June 1923, 11; "The Royal Air Force," *Times*, 2 July 1927, 13; "The Hendon Air Display," *Times*, 28 June 1930, 13; Dodge, *Inventing Iraq*, 35–36; Air Vice-Marshal Sir W. S. Branker, "Air Communications in the Middle East," 16 Dec. 1925, *JRUSI* 71 (1926), esp. 338–40. On the pageants, see also Omissi, *Air Power*, 171–77, and "The Hendon Air Pageant, 1920–37," in John Mackenzie, ed., *Popular Imperialism and the Military, 1850–1950*; M. Paris, *Warrior Nation*, 158.

29. See, for instance, Leach to the Bradford ILP, reported in "The Air Force in Iraq," *Times*, 30 Sept. 1924, 10; "Thomson's Defence of Bombing," *Times*, 11 Oct. 1924, 7, and similar articles in November. See also contemporaneous coverage of Labour

criticisms of party leaders' imperialist policy in Iraq. On the divides within Labour, see Thornton, *Imperial Idea*, 299–300; Howe, *Anticolonialism in British Politics*, 68; Hinton, *Protests and Visions*; and Barry Powers, *Strategy without Slide-Rule: British Air Strategy, 1914–1939*, 172. Lansbury had to step down from his position as president of the Congress of Oppressed Nationalities at Brussells in 1926.

30. Charlton, *Deeds That Held*, 2, 205–06, 274–75.

31. M. Paris, *Warrior Nation*, 167–68, 171; R. F. Foster, *W. B. Yeats: A Life II. The Arch Poet, 1915–1939*, 557–58. See also Hynes, *Soldier's Tale*, 92.

32. CO 730/17: 49826: Bell to Shuckburgh, 13 Aug. 1921, and Bullard, minute, 7 Oct. 1921 (and enclosed article by Bell for *Graphic* [Oct. 1921]); CO 730/46: 54223: Hall and Shuckburgh, minutes, 9 Nov. 1923; Fulanain [pseud.], *The Marsh Arab: Haji Rikkan*, 7; Philby Papers: Box 4: File 7: H. T. Montague Bell, introduction to catalogue for Walker's Galleries, 15–18 Nov. 1922; "Great Britain and the Iraq: An Experiment in Anglo-Asiatic Relations," *Round Table* 53 (1923), 64–83; Buchan, "The 'Liberties' of the Air III," *Spectator*, 20 March 1926, 518; "Emir Feisal," *Times*, 7 Aug. 1920, 9; "W.," "Arabian Nights and Days," *Blackwood's* (1920), 588; "British Advisers in Iraq," *Times*, 18 Feb. 1928, 11; Cox, "Mesopotamia," *Times*, 10 Nov. 1928, xvii.

33. "State-making in Eden," *Times*, 16 Dec. 1919, 13; Commons debate, reported in *Times*, 10 July 1920, 17.

34. Commons debate, reported in *Times*, 13 March 1928, 8–9; "Wahabis and Iraq," *Times*, 13 March 1928, 15; "Order in Iraq," 14 April 1928, 10; Philby to the editor, *Times*, 24 June 1932, 8; Correspondent in Arabia, "Arab Border Raids," *Times*, 27 April 1932, 13; Wilson Papers: 52459A: Pennington to Wilson, 2 June 1920.

35. Ruck, comment on H. R. Brooke-Popham, lecture on the uses of airpower in the war, 3 Dec. 1919, in *JRUSI* 65 (1920), 69; comments on Webster, "Bolshevism and Secret Societies," Nov. 1921, *JRUSI* 67 (1922), 1–15; FO 371/13736: E3490: Monteagle, minute, 8 July 1929; Captain Eden, "The Annual Dinner of the Central Asian Society," *JCAS* 13 (1926), 320; A. T. Wilson, "Mesopotamia, 1914–1921," 155; Barrow and Peel, comments on Haldane, "Arab Rising," 79–80; Peel, comment on Eden, "Annual Dinner," 320, 325; Captain Acland, comment on Col. H. Burchall, "The Air Route to India," 20 Oct. 1926, *JCAS* 14 (1927), 17; Dickson Papers: Box 2: File 4: Thomas to Violet Dickson, 2 Feb. 1925; FO 371/13736: E3490: Rendel, minute, 6 July 1929; CO 730/18: 19794: Wilson to Shuckburgh, 26 April 1921, and Young and Bullard, minutes, 23 and 25 April 1921; CO 730/18: 28620: D. Campbell Lee, "The Mandate for Mesopotamia and the Principle of Trusteeship in English Law," lecture, University College, London University, 23 May 1921, and Young's corrections, 23 May 1921; Glubb Papers: Box 2: Iraq S. Desert (3): Edmonds to Glubb, 21 Nov. 1929; [Glubb?], "Iraq-Najd Frontier."

36. Maguire, comment on Borton, "Use of Aircraft," 317; F. H. Tyrrell: "The Arab Soldier," *JRUSI* 68 (1923), 82–88; R. H. Beadon, "The Iraq Army," *JRUSI* 71 (1926), 343–54.

37. See Fussell, *Great War*, 316; Nicoletta Gullace, *"The Blood of Our Sons": Men, Women, and the Renegotiation of British Citizenship during the Great War*, 29–33.

38. Bray, appendix I of memo, 30 Dec. 1920; WO 32/5728: Montagu to S/S WO, 24 June 1921; IOR: L/PS/10/866 Part 2: Bray to Wakely, 22 Feb. 1921; FO 371/5232: E15068: IO to FO, 1 Dec. 1920, and minutes thereon; and IO, Statement for

press release, in IO to FO, 1 Dec. 1920; Reuters, "'England the Enemy,'" *Times*, 22 Dec. 1920, 9; Valentine Chirol, "The Reawakening of the Orient," in *The Reawakening of the Orient and Other Addresses*, 6; Lyell, *Ins and Outs*, 226, 214; "Kurdistan Conspiracy," *Times*, 7 July 1919, 11, and similar reporting on Soviet conspiracies in August; "Revolutionary Conspiracy," *Times*, 19 June 1920, 13; "Anti-British Conspiracy," *Times*, 8 July 1920, 16; "Bolshevist Threat to the Empire," *Times*, 5 Nov. 1920, 9; Neilson, "Tsars and Commissars," 490; "Persia and Mesopotamia" and "S" to the editor, *Times*, 10 June 1920, 12, 17.

39. FO 371/5422: E2435: H. G. Wells, "Blundering Bolshevism," *Sunday Express*, 14 Nov. 1920; IOR: L/PS/11/154: "The Cause of World Unrest," n.d., newsclipping; Duke of Northumberland, "The Conspiracy against the British Empire: Some Leading Facts," pamphlet presented to Members of Parliament in May 1921.

40. "The Palestine Mandate," *Guardian*, 23 June 1922, 6; "Lord Balfour and Palestine," *Guardian*, 13 April 1925, 6; Percival Landon, "Mesopotamia," *Daily Telegraph*, 3 May 1921; Gisela Lebzelter, "The *Protocols* in England," 116; "Musings without Method," *Blackwood's* (Aug. 1920), 265.

41. Lyell, *Ins and Outs*, 214; "Battlefields of Iraq," *Times*, 12 Dec. 1923, 11; "Battlefields of Iraq. II," 18 Jan. 1924, 11.

42. See also Grant, *Propaganda and the Role of the State*, 11–15, and, on a later period, Susan L. Carruthers, *Winning Hearts and Minds: British Governments, the Media, and Colonial Counter-Insurgency, 1944–1960*.

43. Cicely Hamilton, *Theodore Savage: A Story of the Past or the Future*, 18–24, 86–89, 316; "National Defence in the Air," *Times*, 15 March 1923, 13; "The Hendon Air Display," *Times*, 28 June 1930, 13. See also chapter 7 on British fears of bombardment.

44. Commons debate, reported in *Times*, 3 July 1926, 9; Edgerton, *England and the Aeroplane*, 107; Orwell, *Tribune* column, 12 May 1944, reprinted in *As I Please* (1943–1945), available at http://orwell.ru/library/articles/As_I_Please/english/eaip_03.html.

45. "Iraq and the Treaty," *Times*, 10 June 1924, 11; Commons debate, reported *Times*, 19 Feb. 1926, 9; "The Rebirth of a Nation," *Guardian*, 6 July 1925, 8; "Britain and Iraq," *Times*, 21 Sept. 1929, 11; "Ten Years of Mandates," *Times*, 31 May 1930, 13; "New Session Opened," *Times*, 3 Feb. 1926, 14; Coke, *Arab's Place*, 13, 305–07; *Heart of the Middle East*, 222.

46. On this political shift, see Dodge, *Inventing Iraq*, 35–36.

47. Young, note, in Humphrys to CO, 19 Dec. 1929; "Iraq and Its Minorities," *Times*, 23 Sept. 1932, 13; Dobbs to the editor, *Times*, 29 Sept. 1932, 6. On similar concerns today about an independent Iraqi government misusing the U. S. Air Force, see Hersh, "Up in the Air."

48. Coke, *Arab's Place*, 13, 305–07.

49. Commons debate, reported in *Times*, 29 Jan. 1929, 8.

50. "British Policy in Mesopotamia," *Times*, 24 Aug. 1920, 11; special correspondent in the Middle East, "Mesopotamia," *Times*, 23 Aug. 1920, 15; "Mesopotamian Misrule," *Times*, 20 Sept. 1920, 14; "Mesopotamian Mystery I," *Times*, 27 Dec. 1921, 3; II. 28 Dec. 1921, 3; III. 29 Dec. 1921, 7; CO 730/16: 4311: minutes, 29 Dec. 1921, 1 and 23 Jan. 1922; CO 730/35: 5819: Cox to Shuckburgh, 20 Jan. 1922.

51. Montagu, note, [c. 25 Aug. 1920]; Kidston, quoted in J. Wilson, *Lawrence of Arabia*, 619; FO 371/4141: Hirtzel to Curzon, 24 June 1919.

52. Mann, *Administrator in the Making*, 257; CO 730/9: correspondence about Stitt, 1921; FO 371/9016: E9605: correspondence about Jackman, 1923; FO 371/16878: E3999: Warner, minute, 25 July 1933; R. Graves, *Lawrence and the Arabs*, 54; review of *Lawrence and the Arabs*, *Times*, 18 Nov. 1927, 8; J. Wilson, *Lawrence of Arabia*, 858; clippings of Philby's journalism in FO 371/10017 and 10807, FO 967/38, and WO 181/3; FO 371/3718: 104620: Basil Thomson, Special Report no. 3, 1919; FO 371/5202: E1073: [Thomson], précis, 5 March 1920; IDCEU, "Pan-Islamism and the Caliphate."

53. "Musings without Method," *Blackwood's* (Sept. 1919), 434–37; Meinertzhagen, *Black Sheep*, 73.

54. CO 730/18: 63592: Young to Shuckburgh, 8 Dec. 1921; CO 730/3, 20, 21, 26: correspondence about agent to Najd, 1920–22; Jeddah reports of mid–1920s, e.g., FO 371/11431: E1597: 15 Feb. 1926; FO 371/13734: E3857: Monteagle, minute, 17 Aug. 1929; FO 967/16: Oliphant to Stonehewer-Bird, 3 May 1928; FO 967/38: RMS to Hope Gill, 27 Nov. 1930; FO 371/13740: E3737: Thomas to Shuckburgh, 30 June 1929, and to Laithwaite, 1 July 1929; Dickson Papers: Box 2: File 2: Cox to Dickson, 4 Sept. 1928; CO 732/41/11: Moore to FO, 25 June 1929; CO 727/5: [Shuckburgh?], minute, 26 Sept. 1923, on Knox to CO, 20 Sept. 1923; CO 727/11: Vernon, CID to S/S, 25 June 1925; FO 371/10005: E1984: Mallet, memo, 3 March 1924; FO 371/13741: E5405: Rendel, minute, 22 Oct. 1928; Wilson Papers: 52457B: Hogarth to Bell, 15 Feb. 1918; Lyell, *Ins and Outs*, 206.

55. Bray, *Paladin of Arabia*, 367; CO 730/6: 55824: Meinertzhagen, minute, 10 Nov. 1921; Abdullah Achmed and T. Compton Pakenham, *Dreamers of Empire*, xiii; Philby, preface, 1945, Riyadh, in *Arabian Days*, xvi; "The Mesopotamian Imbroglio," *Spectator*, 31 July 1920, 133; Jarvis, *Arab Command*, 129; Stirling, *Safety Last*, 117; Shaw to Lawrence, 1 Dec. 1922, in *Letters to T. E. Lawrence*, 161–63.

56. Yeats, "The Second Coming," appeared first in *Nation*, Nov. 1920; Yeats to Ethel Manning, 6 April 1936, quoted in Foster, *Yeats*, 2:542 (see also 146–51, 274); Tabachnick, "Art and Science," 8; Bushrui, "Yeats's Arabic Interests," 313; R. Graves, *Lawrence and the Arabs*, 272. On Medina, see Stafford, "John Buchan's Tales."

57. Thornton, *Imperial Idea*, 279; headlines from Beaverbrook and Rothermere newspapers, quoted in Monroe, *Britain's Moment*, 142; Lady Bell, conclusion, in *Letters of Gertrude Bell*, 2:776; J. Wilson, *Lawrence of Arabia*, 706, 875; "Arrested Russian Professors," *Times*, 14 Nov. 1930, 14, and follow-ups on 17, 25, and 27 Nov. 1930, 14, 15, and 8 Dec. 1930, 13; *Daily Herald*, 5 Jan. 1929, quoted in Brown, *Selected Letters*, 311; Commons debate, reported in *Times*, 7 Feb. 1929, 8; "Great Britain and Afghan Rising," *Times*, 7 Jan. 1929, 14; *Sunday Chronicle*, quoted in J. Wilson, *Lawrence of Arabia*, 894–95; Edward Thompson, "America and India," *Times*, 22 July 1930, 15; Jeffrey Richards and Jeffrey Hulbert, "Censorship in Action: The Case of *Lawrence of Arabia*"; FO 371/10017: E9603: Shuckburgh to Osborne, 4 Nov. 1924 passim, and minute to Spring-Rice, 5 Nov. 1924; Thurtle, quoted in Marlowe, *Late Victorian*, 243–44; C. E. Montague, "The Duty of Lying," in *Disenchantment*, 154–55; G. T. Garratt to the editor, *Times*, 20 April 1921, 6; "A Recent Retirement"; "The Case of Sir Arnold Wilson," *Times*, 26 March 1921, 9. If Lawrence was not involved in the Afghani

revolution, it was not because Britain was not interested in sending special agents there. Immediately after the war, unsupervised agents inspired by Buchan and the Arab Revolt were dispatched to Central Asia to combat Bolshevik and "Turco-German" influence. See L. P. Morris, "British Secret Missions in Turkestan, 1918–1919." Lawrence and Thurtle eventually joined forces in the campaign to abolish the death penalty for military offenses.

58. *Sunday Chronicle*, quoted in J. Wilson, *Lawrence of Arabia*, 894–95.

59. Jarvis, *Arab Command*, 112.

60. Hynes, *Soldier's Tale*, 103–04.

61. Buchan, dedication to Caroline Grosvenor, in *Greenmantle*; Max Horkheimer and Theodor Adorno, *Dialectic of Enlightenment*, 78.

CONCLUSION

1. John D. Fair, "The Conservative Basis for the Formation of the National Government of 1931"; Satia, "'The Acid Test of Democracy': Britain's Devaluation in 1931."

2. Harvey Mitchell, "Hobson Revisited"; Grant, *Propaganda and the Role of the State*, 11–12, 15; M. Taylor, "Patriotism, History, and the Left," 981. On the documentary impulse, see John Baxendale and Chris Pawling, *Narrating the Thirties*, chap. 2.

3. E. P. Thompson, quoted in Dennis Dworkin, *Cultural Marxism in Postwar Britain*, 17; E. P. Thompson, "The Secret State," esp. 225–26, and "An Alternative to Doomsday." On his and contemporary historians' relationship to older social investigatory practice, see M. Taylor, "Patriotism, History, and the Left."

4. See, for instance, Bernard Porter, *The Absent-Minded Imperialists: Empire, Society, and Culture in Britain*; David Cannadine, *Ornamentalism: How the British Saw Their Empire*; BBC Radio, "Start the Week," series on "This Sceptred Isle: Empire," with Eric Hobsbawm, Niall Ferguson, Priyamvada Gopal, Linda Colley, and Robert Beckford, 12 June 2006, available at http://www.bbc.co.uk/radio4/factual/starttheweek_20060612.shtml.

5. Coke, *Heart of the Middle East*, 143, 251; G. Buchanan, *Tragedy of Mesopotamia*, 276, 285.

6. Dawson, *Soldier Heroes*, 190, 229; Hynes, *Soldier's Tale*, 124, 138, 140; Dennis Oldham, "A Boy's War—London, Leicestershire and Warwickshire," 29 June 2003, in "WW2 People's War: An Archive of World War Two Memories—Written by the Public, Gathered by the BBC," available at http://www.bbc.co.uk/ww2peopleswar/stories/45/a1092845.shtml; Djilas, quoted in Phillip Knightley, *The Second Oldest Profession: The Spy as Bureaucrat, Patriot, Fantasist and Whore*, 121, also chap. 6; Judd, *Quest for C*, 432–33.

7. Tidrick, *Heart-Beguiling Araby*, 201; obituary, *Economist*, 28 Aug. 2003.

8. Phillip Knightley, personal communications, 21 and 23 April 2007; Anthony Cave Brown, *Treason in the Blood*. A recent book argues that Kim Philby & Co. were in fact being used in a disinformation tactic organized by his higher-ups. See S. J. Hamrick, *Deceiving the Deceivers: Kim Philby, Donald Maclean, and Guy Burgess*. See also *Treason in the Blood*, 265, 387.

9. John Cairncross, *The Enigma Spy*, 23; John Le Carré, *Tinker, Tailor, Soldier, Spy*, 26, 147, 175, 296, 390, 403. On Le Carré's style, see William Finnegan, "Double-Cross in the Congo," *New York Review of Books* 54 (2007), 38.

10. See Renda, *Taking Haiti*, 4–5.

11. Peter Maass, "Professor Nagl's War," *New York Times Magazine*, 11 Jan. 2004, 23–31, 38, 49, 56, 62; Interview with Dr. Duncan Anderson, 19 May 2005, BBC Radio 4; Oliver Poole, *Daily Telegraph*, 6 July 2005, 14. On the CIA and knowledge about the Middle East, see T. Mitchell, *Rule of Experts*, 148–51.

12. Deleuze and Guattari, *Thousand Plateaus*, 380–94. See also J. Scott, *Seeing Like a State*, 1; T. Richards, *Imperial Archive*, 19–20. Both Richards and Deleuze and Guattari rely heavily on Lawrence's (and other agents') writings.

13. John Le Carré, *Absolute Friends*, 190.

14. See, for instance, Robert Fisk, "One Year On—War Without End," *Independent*, 14 March 2004.

15. See, for instance, John Keegan, "In This War of Civilizations, the West Will Prevail," *Daily Telegraph*, 8 Oct. 2001, Opinion; John Burns, "Remote Yemen May Be Key to Terrorist's Past and Future," *New York Times*, 5 Nov. 2000, 1, 24; Neil MacFarquhar, "Unmanned U. S. Planes Comb Arabian Desert for Suspects," *New York Times*, 23 Oct. 2002, A14; Anthony Swofford, "Fighting the First Gulf War," *New York Times*, 2 Oct. 2002, A27; Ken Ringle, "The Crusaders' Giant Footprints," *Washington Post*, 23 Oct. 2001, C 01.

16. Robert Baer, *See No Evil: The True Story of a Ground Soldier in the CIA's War on Terrorism*, 81, 178. See also "MI5 Men Posed as Arabs to Catch Terror Gang," *Sunday Times*, 15 July 2002, 1. On post–World War Two American orientalism and covert activity in the Middle East, see the work of Douglas Little.

17. See, for instance, Michael Ignatieff, "The Burden," *New York Times Magazine*, 5 Jan. 2003 (cover story); Niall Ferguson's error-ridden "The Last Iraqi Insurgency," *New York Times*, 18 April 2004, Sec. 4, 13; Paul Ehrlich and Anne Ehrlich, *One With Nineveh: Politics, Consumption, and the Human Future*.

Selected Bibliography

PRINCIPAL ARCHIVAL SOURCES

Parliamentary Papers

Public Record Office (now The National Archives), Kew

Foreign Office Records: FO 78, 195, 371, 373, 395, 406, 602, 685, 686, 800, 967
Colonial Office Records: CO 537, 727, 730, 732
War Office Records: WO 32, 33, 106, 157, 158, 160, 181, 208, 287, 837
Security Service Records: KV 1
Air Ministry Records: AIR 1, 2, 4, 5, 8, 9, 10, 19, 20, 23, 75
Cabinet Office Records: CAB 16, 21, 27, 51

British Library, London

Map Collections
Manuscript Collections: The Macmillan Archive, Letters from T. E. Lawrence
    to the Shaws, Papers of A. T. Wilson, Shaw Papers, The Wentworth
    Bequest, Northcliffe Papers, Diaries of Gertrude Bell
India Office Records: IOR L/PS, L/MIL, R
India Office Private Papers: Papers of Emily Lorimer, Ilay Ferrier, Lord Reading,
    Sir Walter Lawrence, Lord Curzon, Sir Malcolm Seton, Henry Ross, Terence
    Stokes, Ronald Wingate, Stanley Taylor, Herbert Vernon, Arthur Peckham

National Army Museum, London

Papers of William Leith-Ross

Middle East Centre Archive, St. Antony's College, Oxford

Papers of Gertrude Margaret Lowthian Bell, Reader W. Bullard, Percy Cox, Charles R. Crane, J. D. Crowdy, Harold R. P. Dickson, John Dickson, Harold Frederick Downie, Cecil John Edmonds, W. G. Elphinston, John Bagot Glubb, William Rupert Hay, David George Hogarth, Edward Alec Kinch, Gerard Evelyn Leachman, Harry St. John Bridger Philby, Andrew Ryan, Mark Sykes, Owen M. Tweedy, Geoffrey Edleston Wheeler, Hubert W. Young, J. W. A. Young

Liddell Hart Centre for Military Archives, King's College, London

Papers of Alexander Bishop, Pierce C. Joyce, John Alfred Codrington, Robert Brooke-Popham, Hubert W. Young

Liddle Collection, Leeds University Library, Leeds

Papers of Lord Ailwyn, A. Archdale, Thomas Noel Arkell, J. L. M. Armitage, F. S. G. Barnett, Eric Bellers, L. Bell-Syer, T. R. Bennett, Alec Bishop, Robert Stewart Blucke, Owen Tudor Boyd, F. E. Bradbury, H. Vyner Bragg, Patrick Alfred Buxton, Robert Stewart Campbell, I. E. Cliffe, D. A. Clifton, H. J. Coombes, A. A. Cullen, J. Davey, Norman S. Dyson, Evelyn Dalrymple Fanshawe, Ilay Ferrier, H. L. O. Flecker, W. R. Forrester, J. P. Fullerton, Walter Gordon Gledhill, F. L. Goldthorpe, Ernest William Goodale, John Grimshaw, J. F. Haigh, J. H. Harris, George Bagshaw Harrison, B. L. Holme, G. S. Hooper, T. E. Hulbert, John Eric Birdwood Jardine, Lionel Westropp Jardine, Peter Gilbert Kennedy, Stanley Van Buren Laing, A. B. Lee, L. A. Lynden-Bell, Robert Levitt, Lauchlan G. T. MacDonald, Reginald Willows Hildyard Marris, W. G. Martin, Wilfred Richard Matthews, T. R. Milford, Charles Disney Milward, Leslie R. Missen, R. C. Morton, Joseph Napier, Mabel Napier, Kenneth Kennedy O'Connor, Thomas E. Osmond, Charles H. K. Phillips, William Watt Addison Phillips, A. H. Philpot, C. R. S. Pitman, R. B. Rathbone, Alec T. P. Robertson, H. T. Rohde, P. J. Rolt, Ernest Charles Rycroft, Frank Salisbury, T. Sampson, Reginald Savory, D. A. Simmons, William C. Spackman, J. R. Starley, John Stevenson, T. E. Tate, Roland Taylor, M. M. Thorburn, H. S. Thuillier, Henry Robert Warren, Josiah Clement Wedgwood

Firestone Library, Princeton University

Arab Bureau Papers (FO 882)

Electronic Manuscript Collections

The Gertrude Bell Project. University of Newcastle. http://www.gerty.ncl.ac.uk/
Unpublished letters of W. B. Yeats. In *The Collected Letters of W. B. Yeats.* Edited by John Kelly. Oxford University Press. http://library.nlx.com.

MAIN PERIODICALS

Blackwood's Magazine
Economist
Geographical Journal
Illustrated London News
Journal of the Central Asian Society
Journal of the Royal United Service Institute
Manchester Guardian
Nation
New Statesman
Round Table
Spectator
Times (London)
Times Literary Supplement

UNPUBLISHED SECONDARY SOURCES

"Christie and Mesopotamia." Exhibition, Museum of the British Library, London, 2001.
Fullagar, Kate. "The Bimbo and the Bedouin: Sexuality, Gender, and the 'Sheik Mystique' in 1920s Britain." The Australian National University, Canberra, [1998?].
Hanioglu, M. Sükrü. "Invention of Traditions: Pan-Islamism and Espionage." Lecture, Princeton University, 15 Oct. 2000.
Lake, Peter. "Buckingham Does the Globe: Shakespeare's Henry VIII and the Origins of the Personal Rule." Lecture, Stanford University, 12 April 2007.
Lindsley, B. "W. B. Yeats's Encounters with His Daimon, Leo Africanus: The Daimon and Anti-Self Concepts in *Per Amica Silentia Lunae*." California State University, Northridge, 1995. http://www.csun.edu/~hcengo29/yeats/lindsley.html.
Price, Richard. "Is Bernard Porter's *Absent-Minded Imperialists* Useful for the Study of Empire and British National Culture?" Paper presented at North American Conference on British Studies, Boston, 17–19 Nov. 2006.
Satia, Priya. "'The Acid Test of Democracy': Britain's Devaluation in 1931." University of California, Berkeley, 1999.
———. "The Secret Center: Arabia Intelligence in British Culture and Politics, 1900–1932." Ph.D. diss., University of California, Berkeley, 2004.
Sinha, Meeta. "'Where Electricity Dispels the Illusion': The British and the Modern in Interwar India." Paper presented at the Pacific Coast Conference on British Studies, Irvine, CA, 24–26 March 2006.

PUBLISHED PRIMARY AND SECONDARY SOURCES

Achmed, Abdullah, and T. Compton Pakenham. *Dreamers of Empire*. New York: Frederick A. Stokes, 1929.
Adam, Colin Forbes. *The Life of Lord Lloyd*. London: Macmillan, 1948.

Adelson, Roger. *London and the Invention of the Middle East: Money, Power, and War, 1902–1922*. New Haven, CT: Yale University Press, 1995.

———. *Mark Sykes: Portrait of an Amateur*. London: Cape, 1975.

Adorno, Theodor, and Max Horkheimer. *Dialectic of Enlightenment*. Translated by John Cumming. 1944. Reprint, New York: Continuum, 1998.

Aldrich, Richard. "Britain's Secret Intelligence Service in Asia during the Second World War." *Modern Asian Studies* 32:1 (1998): 179–217.

Allen, James Lovic. "The Road to Byzantium: Archetypal Criticism and Yeats." *Journal of Aesthetics and Art Criticism* 32 (1973): 53–64.

Allen, M. D. *The Medievalism of Lawrence of Arabia*. University Park: Pennsylvania University Press, 1991.

Andrew, Christopher. *Her Majesty's Secret Service: The Making of the British Intelligence Community*. 1985. Reprint, New York: Viking, 1986.

Andrew, Christopher, Richard J. Aldrich, Michael D. Kandiah, and Gillian Staerck, eds. *The Role of the Intelligence Services in the Second World War*. ICBH Witness Seminar Programme. London: Institute of Contemporary British History, 2003.

Anscombe, Frederick. *The Ottoman Gulf: The Creation of Kuwait, Saudi Arabia, and Qatar, 1870–1914*. New York: Columbia University Press, 1997.

Antliff, Mark. *Inventing Bergson: Cultural Politics and the Parisian Avant-Garde*. Princeton, NJ: Princeton University Press, 1993.

Arendt, Hannah. *The Origins of Totalitarianism*. 1951. Reprint, New York: Harvest, 1968.

Armstrong, H. C. *Lord of Arabia: Ibn Saud; An Intimate Study of a King*. Beirut: Khayats, 1966.

Asher, Michael. *Lawrence: The Uncrowned King of Arabia*. Woodstock, NY: Overlook, 1999.

Asprey, Robert. *War in the Shadows: The Guerrilla in History*. New York: William Morrow, 1994.

Atiyyah, Ghassan. *Iraq, 1908–1921: A Socio-Political Study*. Beirut: Arab Institute for Research and Publishing, 1973.

Audoin-Rouzeau, Stephane, and Annette Becker. *14–18: Understanding the Great War*. Translated by Catherine Temerson. New York: Hill & Wang, 2002.

Bachchan, Harbans Rai. *W. B. Yeats and Occultism: A Study of His Works in Relation to Indian Lore, the Cabbala, Swedenborg, Boehme and Theosophy*. Delhi: Motilal Banarsidass, 1965.

Baer, Robert. *See No Evil: The True Story of a Ground Soldier in the CIA's War on Terrorism*. New York: Three Rivers, 2003.

Baldensperger, Philip. *The Immovable East: Studies of the People and Customs of Palestine*. Boston: Small, Maynard, 1913.

Baldry, John. "Soviet Relations with Saudi Arabia and the Yemen, 1917–1938." *Middle Eastern Studies* 20 (1984): 53–80.

Balfour-Paul, Glen. "Britain's Informal Empire in the Middle East." In *The Oxford History of the British Empire*. Vol. 4, *The Twentieth Century*, ed. Judith M. Brown and Wm. Roger Louis, 490–514. New York: Oxford University Press, 1999.

Banfield, Ann. *The Phantom Table: Woolf, Fry, Russell, and the Epistemology of Modernism*. New York: Cambridge University Press, 2000.

Barber, Major Charles H. *Besieged in Kut and After*. London: William Blackwood, 1918.

Barker, A. J. *The Bastard War: The Mesopotamian Campaign of 1914–1918*. New York: Dial, 1967.

Bar-Yosef, Eitan. "The Last Crusade? British Propaganda and the Palestine Campaign, 1917–18." *Journal of Contemporary History* 36 (2001): 87–109.

Batatu, Hanna. *The Old Social Classes and the Revolutionary Movements of Iraq: A Study of Iraq's Old Landed and Commercial Classes and of Its Communists, Ba'thists, and Free Officers*. Princeton, NJ: Princeton University Press, 1978.

Baxendale, John, and Chris Pawling, *Narrating the Thirties: A Decade in the Making: 1930 to the Present*. New York: St. Martin's, 1996.

Bayly, C. A. *Empire and Information: Intelligence Gathering and Social Communication in India, 1780–1870*. Cambridge: Cambridge University Press, 1996.

———. " 'Knowing the Country': Empire and Information in India." *Modern Asian Studies* 27 (1993): 3–43.

Beaumont, Roger. "A New Lease on Empire: Air Policing, 1919–1939." *Aerospace Historian* (June 1979): 84–90.

Beer, Gillian. "The Island and the Aeroplane: The Case of Virginia Woolf." In *Nation and Narration*, ed. Homi Bhabha, 265–290. London: Routledge, 1990.

Behdad, Ali. *Belated Travelers: Orientalism in the Age of Colonial Dissolution*. Durham, NC: Duke University Press, 1994.

Bell, Gertrude. *Amurath to Amurath*. New York: Dutton, 1911.

[———.] *The Arab of Mesopotamia*. Basrah: Government Press, 1917.

———. *The Desert and the Sown*. London: W. Heinemann, 1907.

———. *The Earlier Letters of Gertrude Bell*. Edited by Elsa Richmond. New York: Liveright, 1937.

———. *Gertrude Bell: The Arabian Diaries, 1913–1914*. Edited by Rosemary O'Brien. Syracuse, NY: Syracuse University Press, 2000.

———. *The Letters of Gertrude Bell*. 2 vols. Edited by Lady Bell. London: E. Benn, 1927.

———. *Palace and Mosque at Ukhaidir*. Oxford: Clarendon, 1914.

Bell, Morag, Robin Butlin, and Michael Heffernan. *Geography and Imperialism, 1820–1940*. Manchester, UK: Manchester University Press, 1995.

Benjamin, Walter. "The Work of Art in the Age of Mechanical Reproduction." 1937. In *Illuminations*. Edited by Hannah Arendt. Translated by Harry Zohn, 217–52. New York: Schocken Books, 1968.

Bennett, Edward. "Intelligence and History from the Other Side of the Hill." *Journal of Modern History* 60 (1988): 312–37.

Bent, Theodore, and Mrs. Theodore Bent. *Southern Arabia*. 1899. Reprint, Reading, UK: Garnet, 1994.

Benton, Lauren. *Law and Colonial Cultures: Legal Regimes in World History, 1400–1900*. Cambridge: Cambridge University Press, 2002.

Béraud-Villars, Jean M. E. *T. E. Lawrence; or, The Search for the Absolute*. Translated by Peter Dawnay. London: Sidgwick & Jackson, 1958.

Best, Anthony. *British Intelligence and the Japanese Challenge in Asia, 1914–1941.* New York: Palgrave Macmillan, 2002.

Best, Geoffrey. *Humanity in Warfare.* New York: Columbia University Press, 1980.

Betts, Ernest. *The Bagging of Baghdad.* London: John Lane, 1920.

Bevan, Edwyn. *The Land of the Two Rivers.* London: E. Arnold, 1918.

Bevis, Richard. "Desert Places: The Aesthetics of *Arabia Deserta.*" In *Explorations in Doughty's* Arabia Deserta, ed. Stephen Tabachnick, 62–76. Athens: University of Georgia Press, 1987.

———. "Spiritual Geology: C. M. Doughty and the Land of the Arabs." *Victorian Studies* 16:2 (1972): 163–81.

Bialer, Uri. *The Shadow of the Bomber: The Fear of Air Attack and British Politics, 1932–1939.* London: Royal Historical Society, 1980.

Biddle, Tami Davis. "British and American Approaches to Strategic Bombing: Their Origins and Implementation in the World War II Combined Bomber Offensive." In *Air Power in Theory and Practice,* ed. John Gooch, 91–144. London: Frank Cass, 1995.

Bird, W. D. *A Chapter of Misfortunes: The Battles of Ctesiphon and of the Dujailah in Mesopotamia, with a Summary of the Events Which Preceded Them.* London: Forster Groom, 1923.

Bivona, Daniel. *British Imperial Literature, 1870–1940: Writing and the Administration of Empire.* Cambridge: Cambridge University Press, 1998.

Blacker, L. V. S. *On Secret Patrol in High Asia.* London: J. Murray, 1922.

Bloch, Ernst. "A Philosophical View of the Detective Novel." 1974. In *The Utopian Function of Art and Literature: Selected Essays.* Translated by Jack Zipes and Frank Mecklenburg. Cambridge: MIT Press, 1988.

Bloch, Jonathan, and Patrick Fitzgerald. *British Intelligence and Covert Action: Africa, Middle East, and Europe since 1945.* London: Junction, 1983.

Blunt, Lady Anne. *Bedouin Tribes of the Euphrates.* New York: Harper, 1879.

———. *Journals and Correspondence, 1878–1917.* Edited by Rosemary Archer and James Fleming. Cheltenham, UK: Heriot, 1986.

———. *A Pilgrimage to Nejd, the Cradle of the Arab Race. A Visit to the Court of the Arab Emir, and "Our Persian Campaign."* London: J. Murray, 1881.

Boehmer, Elleke. "'Immeasurable Strangeness' in Imperial Times: Leonard Woolf and W. B. Yeats." In *Modernism and Empire,* ed. Howard J. Booth and Nigel Rigby, 93–111. Manchester, UK: Manchester University Press, 2000.

Booth, Howard J., and Nigel Rigby, eds. *Modernism and Empire.* Manchester, UK: Manchester University Press, 2000.

Boscawen, W. St. Chad. *The First of Empires: "Babylon of the Bible" in the Light of Latest Research.* London: Harper, 1903.

Bose, Sugata. *A Hundred Horizons: The Indian Ocean in the Age of Global Empire.* Cambridge, MA: Harvard University Press, 2006.

Boyle, Andrew. *Trenchard.* New York: Norton, 1962.

Brantlinger, Patrick. *Rule of Darkness: British Literature and Imperialism, 1830–1914.* Ithaca, NY: Cornell University Press, 1988.

Bray, N. N. E. *A Paladin of Arabia: The Biography of Brevet Lieut.-Colonel G. E. Leachman*...London: Unicorn, 1936.

———. *Shifting Sands*. London: Unicorn, 1934.

Brecher, F. W. "Charles R. Crane's Crusade for the Arabs, 1919–1939." *Middle Eastern Studies* 24:1 (1998): 42–55.

Brent, Peter. *Far Arabia: Explorers of the Myth*. London: Weidenfeld & Nicolson, 1977.

Brown, Anthony Cave. *Treason in the Blood: H. St. John Philby, Kim Philby, and the Spy Case of the Century*. New York: Houghton Mifflin, 1994.

Buchan, John. *Greenmantle*. 1916. Reprint, Oxford: Oxford University Press, 1993.

———. *Memory Hold the Door*. London: Hodder & Stoughton, 1940.

———. *The Moon Endureth: Tales and Fancies*. London: Hodder & Stoughton, 1912.

———. *The Thirty-Nine Steps*. 1915. Reprint, Ware, Hertfordshire: Wordsworth, 1996.

Buchanan, Sir George. *The Tragedy of Mesopotamia*. London: W. Blackwood, 1938.

Buchanan, Zetton. *In the Hands of the Arabs*. London: Hodder & Stoughton, 1921.

Bullard, Reader. *Britain and the Middle East: From Earliest Times to 1952*. London: Hutchinson, 1952.

———. *The Camels Must Go: An Autobiography*. London: Faber & Faber, 1961.

———. *Two Kings in Arabia: Letters from Jeddah: 1923–5 and 1936–9: Reader Bullard*. Edited by E.C. Hodgkin. Reading, UK: Ithaca, 1993.

Bunyan, Tony. *The History and Practice of the Political Police in Britain*. London: Julian Friedmann, 1976.

Burdett, A. L. P., ed. *Records of the Hijaz, 1798–1925*. 8 vols. Oxford: Archive Editions, 1996.

Burgoyne, Elizabeth. *Gertrude Bell: From Her Personal Papers*. 2 vols. London: E. Benn, 1958–1961.

Burke, Keast, ed. *With Horse and Morse in Mesopotamia: The Story of Anzacs in Asia*. Sydney: Arthur McQuitty, 1927.

Bury, G. Wyman. *Arabia Infelix, or The Turks in Yamen*. London: Macmillan, 1915.

———. [Abdullah Mansur, pseud.] *The Land of Uz*. London: Macmillan, 1911.

———. *Pan-Islam*. London: Macmillan, 1919.

Busch, Briton. *Britain, India, and the Arabs, 1914–1921*. Berkeley: University of California Press, 1971.

———. *Britain and the Persian Gulf, 1894–1914*. Berkeley: University of California Press, 1967.

Bushrui, S. B. "Yeats's Arabic Interests." In *In Excited Reverie: A Centenary Tribute to William Butler Yeats, 1865–1939*, ed. A. Norman Jeffares and K. G. W. Cross, 280–314. New York: Macmillan, 1965.

Butt, Gerald. *The Lion in the Sand: The British in the Middle East*. London: Bloomsbury, 1995.

Byron, Robert. *The Road to Oxiana*. London: J. Lehmann, 1950.

Cairncross, John. *The Enigma Spy: The Story of the Man Who Changed the Course of World War Two*. London: Century, 1997.

Callaghan, John. "The Communists and the Colonies: Anti-Imperialism between the Wars." In *Opening the Books: Essays on the Social and Cultural History of British*

Communism, ed. Geoff Andrews, Nina Fishman, and Kevin Morgan, 4–22. London: Pluto, 1995.

Callwell, C. E. *Field-Marshal Sir Henry Wilson*. London: Cassell, 1927.

———. *Small Wars: Their Principles and Practice.* 3rd ed. London: Harrison & Sons (for H. M.'s Stationery Office), 1906.

Campbell-Thompson, Reginald. *A New Decipherment of the Hittite Hieroglyphics.* Oxford: Horace Hart (for the Society of Antiquaries of London), 1914.

———. *Semitic Magic, Its Origins and Development.* London: Luzac, 1908.

Candler, Edmund. *The Long Road to Baghdad.* 2 vols. New York: Houghton Mifflin, 1919.

Cannadine, David. *Ornamentalism: How the British Saw Their Empire.* New York: Oxford University Press, 2001.

Carr, Helen. "Imagism and Empire." In *Modernism and Empire*, ed. Howard J. Booth and Nigel Rigby, 64–92. Manchester, UK: Manchester University Press, 2000.

Carruthers, Douglas. *Arabian Adventure: To the Great Nafud in Quest of the Oryx.* London: H. F. & G. Witherby, 1935.

Carruthers, Susan. *Winning Hearts and Minds: British Governments, the Media, and Colonial Counter-Insurgency, 1944–1960.* New York: Leicester University Press, 1995.

Casey, Edward. *The Fate of Place: A Philosophical History.* 1997. Reprint, Berkeley: University of California Press, 1998.

Casey, Roger. *Baghdad and Points East.* London: Hutchinson, 1928.

Cato, Conrad. *The Navy in Mesopotamia.* London: Constable, 1917.

Cawelti, John, and Bruce Rosenberg. *The Spy Story.* Chicago: University of Chicago Press, 1987.

Cell, John W. "Colonial Rule." In *The Oxford History of the British Empire.* Vol. 4, *The Twentieth Century*, ed. Judith M. Brown and Wm. Roger Louis, 232–54. New York: Oxford University Press, 1999.

Chace, William M. "T. E. Lawrence: The Uses of Heroism." In *Lawrence: Soldier, Writer, Legend*, ed. Jeffrey Meyers, 128–60. Hampshire, UK: Macmillan, 1989.

Chapple, Joe Mitchell. *To Bagdad and Back.* Boston: Chapple, 1928.

Charlton, Lionel Evelyn. *Charlton.* London, Faber & Faber, 1931.

———. *Deeds That Held the Empire, by Air.* London: J. Murray, 1940.

———. *The Next War.* London: Longman's, Green, 1937.

Cheesman, R. E. *In Unknown Arabia.* London: Macmillan, 1926.

Chesney, G. M. "The Mesopotamian Breakdown." *Fortnightly Review* 108 (1917): 247–56.

Chesterton, G. K. *The Essential G. K. Chesterton.* New York: Oxford University Press, 1987.

Childers, Erskine. *Common Sense about the Arab World.* London: Victor Gollancz, 1960.

———. *The Riddle of the Sands.* 1903. Reprint, Mineola, NY: Dover, 1999.

———. *The Road to Suez.* London: MacKibbon & Kee, 1962.

Chirol, Valentine. *The Middle Eastern Question, or Some Political Problems of Indian Defence.* New York: Dutton, 1903.

———. *The Occident and the Orient: Lectures on the Harris Foundation, 1924.* Chicago: University of Chicago Press, 1924.

———. *The Reawakening of the Orient and Other Addresses by Valentine Chirol, Yusuke Tsurumi, Sir James Arthur Salter.* New Haven, CT: Yale University Press, 1925.

———. *The Turkish Empire from 1288 to 1914, by Lord Eversley, and from 1914 to 1922, by Sir Valentine Chirol,* 2nd ed. New York: Dodd, 1923.

Churchill, Winston. *Great Contemporaries.* 1937. Reprint, London: Odhams, 1949.

———. *The Story of the Malakand Field Force, an Episode of Frontier War.* New York: Longmans, 1898.

———. *The World Crisis.* Vol. 5. New York: Scribner's, 1929.

Clark, Arthur Tillotson. *To Bagdad with the British.* New York: D. Appleton, 1918.

Clayton, Anthony. *The British Empire as a Superpower, 1919–39.* London: Macmillan, 1986.

———. "'Deceptive Might': Imperial Defence and Security, 1900–1968." In *The Oxford History of the British Empire.* Vol. 4, *The Twentieth Century,* ed. Judith M. Brown and Wm. Roger Louis, 280–305. New York: Oxford University Press, 1999.

———. *Forearmed: A History of the Intelligence Corps.* London: Brassey's, 1993.

Clayton, Sir Gilbert. *An Arabian Diary.* Edited by Robert O. Collins. Berkeley: University of California Press, 1969.

Cocker, Mark. *Richard Meinertzhagen: Soldier, Scientist, and Spy.* 1989. Reprint, London: Mandarin, 1990.

Cohen, Michael, and Martin Kolinsky, eds. *Britain and the Middle East in the 1930s: Security Problems, 1935–39.* Basingstoke, UK: Macmillan (in association with King's College, London), 1992.

Cohen, Stuart A. *British Policy in Mesopotamia, 1903–1914.* London: Ithaca, 1976.

———. "The Genesis of the British Campaign in Mesopotamia, 1914." *Middle Eastern Studies* 12:2 (1976): 119–32.

Coke, Richard. *The Arab's Place in the Sun.* London: Thornton Butterworth, 1929.

———. *Baghdad: The City of Peace.* London: Thornton Butterworth, 1927.

———. *The Heart of the Middle East.* London: Thornton Butterworth, 1925.

———. *Passenger by Air.* London: J. Hamilton, 1937.

Coldicott, Rowlands. *London Men in Palestine, and How They Marched to Jerusalem.* London: E. Arnold, 1919.

Cole, Juan. *Roots of North Indian Shi'ism in Iran and Iraq: Religion and State in Awadh, 1722–1859.* Berkeley: University of California Press, 1988.

Colls, Robert. "The Constitution of the English." *History Workshop Journal* 46 (1998): 97–128.

Connell, John. *Wavell, Scholar and Soldier.* New York: Harcourt, Brace & World, 1964.

Conrad, Joseph. *Lord Jim.* 1900. Reprint, London: Penguin, 1989.

———. *The Secret Agent.* 1907. Reprint, New York: Signet, 1983.

Constantine, Stephen. *The Making of British Colonial Development Policy, 1914–1940.* London: F. Cass, 1984.

Cook, Albert. "*Seven Pillars of Wisdom*: Turns and Counter-Turns." In *Lawrence: Soldier, Writer, Legend,* ed. Jeffrey Meyers, 87–109. Hampshire, UK: Macmillan, 1989.

Cooper, Frederick. "Modernizing Bureaucrats, Backward Africans, and the Development Concept." In *International Development and the Social Sciences: Essays on the History and Politics of Knowledge*, ed. Frederick Cooper and Randall Packard, 64–92. Berkeley: University of California Press, 1997.

Cooper, Frederick, and Randall Packard, eds. *International Development and the Social Sciences: Essays on the History and Politics of Knowledge*. Berkeley: University of California Press, 1997.

Corum, James S. "The Myth of Air Control: Reassessing the History." *Aerospace Power Journal* 14:4 (2000): 61–77.

Corum, James S., and Wray R. Johnson. *Airpower in Small Wars: Fighting Insurgents and Terrorists*. Lawrence: University Press of Kansas, 2003.

Cowper, H. Swainson. *Through Turkish Arabia: A Journey from the Mediterranean to Bombay by the Euphrates and Tigris Valleys and the Persian Gulf*. 1894. Reprint, London: Darf, 1987.

Cox, Jafna. " 'A Splendid Training Ground': The Importance to the Royal Air Force of Its Role in Iraq, 1919–32." *Journal of Imperial and Commonwealth History* 13 (1985): 157–84.

Craig, Gordon, and Felix Gilbert, eds. *The Diplomats*. 2 vols. 1953. Reprint, New York: Atheneum, 1972.

Crush, Jonathan, ed. *Power of Development*. London: Routledge, 1995.

Curzon, George Nathaniel. *Tales of Travel*. London: Hodder & Stoughton, 1923.

Dane, Edmund. *British Campaigns in the Nearer East, 1914–1918: From the Outbreak of War with Turkey to the Armistice*. London: Hodder & Stoughton, 1919.

———. *British Campaigns in the Nearer East, 1914–1918: From the Outbreak of War with Turkey to the Taking of Jerusalem*. London: Hodder & Stoughton, 1917.

Dann, Uriel, ed. *The Great Powers in the Middle East, 1919–1939*. New York: Holmes & Meier, 1988.

Darwin, John. *Britain, Egypt and the Middle East Imperial Policy in the Aftermath of War, 1918–1922*. London: Macmillan, 1981.

Davis, Natalie Zemon. *Trickster Travels: A Sixteenth-Century Muslim between Worlds*. New York: Hill & Wang, 2006.

Davis, Paul K. *Ends and Means: The British Mesopotamian Campaign and Commission*. London: Associated University Presses, 1994.

Dawn, C. Ernest. "The Influence of T. E. Lawrence on the Middle East." In *T. E. Lawrence: Soldier, Writer, Legend*, ed. Jeffrey Meyers, 58–86. Hampshire, UK: Macmillan, 1989.

Dawson, Graham. *Soldier Heroes: British Adventure, Empire, and the Imagining of Masculinities*. London: Routledge, 1994.

Dean, David J. *The Air Force Role in Low-Intensity Conflict*. Maxwell Air Force Base, AL: Air University Press, 1986.

De Gaury, Gerald, and H. V. F. Winstone, eds. *The Road to Kabul: An Anthology*. New York: Macmillan, 1982.

De la Mare, Walter. *The Collected Poems of Walter de la Mare*. London: Faber, 1979.

Deleuze, Gilles. *Bergsonism*. Translated by Hugh Tomlinson and Barbara Habberjam. New York: Zone Books, 1988.

Deleuze, Gilles, and Félix Guattari. *A Thousand Plateaus: Capitalism and Schizophrenia.* 1980. Translated by Brian Massumi. Minneapolis: University of Minnesota Press, 1987.

De V. Loder, J. *The Truth about Mesopotamia, Palestine and Syria.* London: George Allen & Unwin, 1923.

Dewar, Michael. *The Art of Deception in Warfare.* Newton Abbot, Devon: David & Charles, 1989.

Dickson, H. R. P. *The Arab of the Desert: A Glimpse into Badawin Life in Kuwait and Sau'di Arabia.* London: George Allen & Unwin, 1949.

Dickson, Violet. *Forty Years in Kuwait.* London: Allen & Unwin, 1971.

Dirks, Nicholas. *Castes of Mind: Colonialism and the Making of Modern India.* Princeton, NJ: Princeton University Press, 2001.

———. *Scandal of Empire: India and the Creation of Imperial Britain.* Cambridge, MA: Belknap, 2006.

Dodge, Toby. *Inventing Iraq: The Failure of Nation Building and a History Denied.* New York: Columbia University Press, 2003.

———. "International Obligation, Domestic Pressure, and Colonial Nationalism: The Birth of the Iraqi State under the Mandate System." In *The British and French Mandates in Comparative Perspectives,* ed. Peter Sluglett and Nadine Méouchy, 143–64. Leiden, Netherlands: Brill, 2004.

Doughty, Charles. *Travels in Arabia Deserta.* 1888. Reprint, London: J. Cape, 1924.

Dovey, H. O. "Cheese." *Intelligence and National Security* 5 (1990): 176–83.

———. "The Middle East Intelligence Centre." *Intelligence and National Security* 4 (1989): 800–12.

Dreisiger, N. F., ed. *Mobilization for Total War: The Canadian, American and British Experience, 1914–1918, 1939–1945.* Waterloo, ON: Wilfrid Laurier University Press, 1981.

Driver, Felix. *Geography Militant: Cultures of Exploration and Empire.* Oxford: Blackwell, 2001.

Drobutt, Richard. *I Spy for the Empire.* London: S. Low, Marston, 1939.

Dunsterville, L. C. *The Adventures of Dunsterforce.* 1920. Reprint, London: E. Arnold, 1932.

———. *Stalky's Reminiscences.* London: Jonathan Cape, 1928.

Dworkin, Dennis. *Cultural Marxism in Postwar Britain: History, the New Left, and the Origins of Cultural Studies.* Durham, NC: Duke University Press, 1997.

Earle, Edward Mead. *Turkey, the Great Powers, and the Baghdad Railway: A Study in Imperialism.* New York: Macmillan, 1923.

Edgerton, David. *England and the Aeroplane: An Essay on a Militant and Technological Nation.* Basingstoke, UK: Macmillan (in association with the Centre for the History of Science, Technology and Medicine, University of Manchester), 1991.

———. *Warfare State: Britain, 1920–1970.* Cambridge: Cambridge University Press, 2006.

Edney, Matthew. *Mapping an Empire: The Geographical Construction of British India, 1765–1843.* Chicago: University of Chicago Press, 1997.

Egan, Eleanor Franklin. *The War in the Cradle of the World: Mesopotamia.* New York: Harper, 1918.

Ehrlich, Paul R., and Anne H. Ehrlich. *One with Nineveh : Politics, Consumption, and the Human Future.* Washington, D.C.: Shearwater Books, 2004.

Eliot, T. S. *The Waste Land.* 1922. http://www.bartleby.com/201/1.html.

Elkins, Caroline. *Imperial Reckoning: The Untold Story of Britain's Gulag in Kenya.* New York: Henry Holt, 2005.

Eksteins, Modris. *Rites of Spring: The Great War and the Birth of the Modern Age.* 1989. Reprint, New York: Houghton Mifflin, 2000.

Embry, Sir Basil. *Mission Completed.* London: Methuen, 1957.

Fabian, Johannes. *Out of Our Minds: Reason and Madness in the Exploration of Central Africa.* Berkeley: University of California Press, 2000.

————. *Time and the Other: How Anthropology Makes Its Object.* New York: Columbia University Press, 1983.

Fair, John D. "The Conservative Basis for the Formation of the National Government of 1931." *Journal of British Studies* 19 (1980): 142–64.

Fergusson, Thomas. *British Military Intelligence, 1870–1914: The Development of a Modern Intelligence Organization.* Frederick, MD: University Publications of America, 1984.

Ferris, John. *The Evolution of British Strategic Policy, 1919–26.* London: Macmillan, 1989.

————. "Before 'Room 40': The British Empire and Signals Intelligence, 1898–1914." *The Journal of Strategic Studies* 12 (1989): 431–57.

Fieldhouse, D. K. *Western Imperialism in the Middle East, 1914–1958.* Oxford: Oxford University Press, 2006.

Filmer, Kath, ed. *Twentieth-Century Fantasists: Essays on Culture, Society, and Belief in Twentieth-Century Mythopoeic Literature.* New York: St. Martin's, 1992.

Finlinson, Harold. *With Pen and Ink in Iraq.* Madras: Higginbothams, 1918.

Fisher, John. *Curzon and British Imperialism in the Middle East: 1916–19.* London: Frank Cass, 1999.

————. "The Defence of Britain's Eastern Empire after World War One: The Role of the Interdepartmental Committee on Eastern Unrest, 1922–1927." *Historian* 64 (1999): 13–17.

————. *Gentleman Spies: Intelligence Agents in the British Empire and Beyond.* Stroud, UK: Sutton, 2002.

————. "The Interdepartmental Committee on Eastern Unrest and British Responses to Bolshevik and Other Intrigues against the Empire during the 1920s." *Journal of Asian History* (Germany) 34 (2000): 1–34.

————. "Major Norman Bray and Eastern Unrest in the Aftermath of World War I." *Archives* 27 (2002): 39–56.

————. "On the Baghdad Road: On the Trail of W. J. Childs; A Study in British Near Eastern Intelligence and Historical Analysis, c. 1900–1930." *Archives* 24 (1999): 53–70.

Fitzherbert, Margaret. *The Man Who Was Greenmantle: A Biography of Aubrey Herbert.* London: Murray, 1983.

Flecker, James Elroy. *The Collected Poems of James Elroy Flecker*. 1916. Reprint, London: M. Secker, 1935.

———. *Hassan: The Story of Hassan of Bagdad and How He Came to Make the Golden Journey to Samarkand*. London: William Heinemann, 1922.

———. *Some Letters from Abroad of James Elroy Flecker*. Edited by Hellé Flecker. London: W. Heinemann, 1930.

Flight Lieutenant. *Reminiscences of the Royal Air Force*. New York: Pegasus, 1940.

Fogg, G. E. *A History of Antarctic Science*. Cambridge: Cambridge University Press, 1992.

Forbes, Rosita. *Conflict: Angora to Afghanistan*. New York: F. A. Stokes, 1931.

———. *Quest: The Story of Anne, Three Men, and Some Arabs*. New York: H. Holt, 1923.

Foster, R. F. *W. B. Yeats: A Life*. 2 vols. New York: Oxford University Press, 1997–2003.

Foucault, Michel. "Of Other Spaces." *Diacritics* 16 (1986): 22–27. Originally lecture of 1967.

Fraser, David. *The Short Cut to India; The Record of a Journey along the Route of the Baghdad Railway*. London: W. Blackwood, 1909.

French, David. "Spy Fever in Britain, 1900–1915." *Historical Journal* 21 (1978): 355–70.

Fromkin, David. *A Peace to End All Peace: The Fall of the Ottoman Empire and the Creation of the Modern Middle East*. New York: Avon, 1989.

Fulanain [pseud.]. *The Marsh Arab: Haji Rikkan*. Philadelphia: J. B. Lippincott, 1928.

Fuller, J. F. C. *Memoirs of an Unconventional Soldier*. London: I. Nicholson & Watson, 1936.

Fussell, Paul. *The Great War and Modern Memory*. London: Oxford University Press, 1975.

Galbraith, John S. "No Man's Child: The Campaign in Mesopotamia, 1914–1916." *International History Review* 6:3 (1984): 358–85.

Gardner, Brian. *Allenby*. London: Cassell, 1965.

Gat, Azar. *Fascist and Liberal Visions of War: Fuller, Liddell Hart, Douhet, and Other Modernists*. Oxford: Clarendon, 1998.

Gavish, Dov. "Wadi Fari'a—The 'Valley of Death' in the Great War." *Over the Front* 15 (2000): 360–66.

Gera, Gideon. "T. E. Lawrence: Intelligence Officer." In *The T. E. Lawrence Puzzle*, ed. Stephen Tabachnick, 204–19. Athens: University of Georgia Press, 1984.

Gershoni, Israel, and James Jankowski, eds. *Rethinking Nationalism in the Arab Middle East*. New York: Columbia University Press, 1997.

Gibbs, Sir Gerald. *Survivor's Story*. London: Hutchinson, 1956.

Gilbert, Vivian. *The Romance of the Last Crusade: With Allenby to Jerusalem*. 1923. Reprint, London: D. Appleton, 1925.

Gilbert, Martin. *Winston S. Churchill*. 8 vols. London: Heinemann, 1966–88.

———. *Winston S. Churchill: Companion Volume 4*. 3 parts. London: Heinemann, 1977.

Gillard, David. *The Struggle for Asia, 1828–1914: A Study in British and Russian Imperialism*. London: Methuen, 1977.

Gillies, Mary Ann. *Henri Bergson and British Modernism*. Buffalo, NY: McGill-Queen's University Press, 1996.

Gilmartin, David. "Imperial Rivers: Irrigation and British Visions of Empire." In *Decentring Empire: Britain, India and the Transcolonial World*, ed. Durba Ghosh and Dane Kennedy. New Delhi: Orient Longman, 2006.

Glen, Douglas. *In the Steps of Lawrence of Arabia*. London: Rich & Cowan, 1940.

Glubb, John Bagot. *Arabian Adventures: Ten Years of Joyful Service*. London: Cassell, 1978.

———. *Britain and the Arabs*. London: Hodder & Stoughton, 1959.

———. *The Changing Scenes of Life: An Autobiography*. London: Quartet, 1983.

———. *Story of the Arab Legion*. London: Hodder & Stoughton, 1948.

———. *War in the Desert: An R. A. F. Frontier Campaign*. London: Hodder & Stoughton, 1960.

Goldstein, Erik. "British Peace Aims and the Eastern Question: The Political Intelligence Department and the Eastern Committee, 1918." *Middle Eastern Studies* 23:4 (1987): 419–36.

Gooch, John, ed. *Air Power in Theory and Practice*. London: Frank Cass, 1995.

Gokay, B. *A Clash of Empires: Turkey between Russian Bolshevism and British Imperialism, 1918–1923*. London: Tauris Academic Studies, 1997.

Goodheart, Eugene. "A Contest of Motives: T. E. Lawrence in *Seven Pillars of Wisdom*." In *Lawrence: Soldier, Writer, Legend*, ed. Jeffrey Meyers, 110–27. Hampshire, UK: Macmillan, 1989.

Gordon, General T. E. "The Problem of the Middle East." *Nineteenth Century* 47 (1900): 413–424.

Grafftey-Smith, Sir Laurence. *Bright Levant*. London: J. Murray, 1970.

Grant, Mariel. *Propaganda and the Role of the State in Inter-War Britain*. Oxford: Clarendon, 1994.

Graves, Philip. *Briton and Turk*. London: Hutchinson, 1945.

———. *The Life of Sir Percy Cox*. London: Hutchinson, 1941.

Graves, Robert. *Good-bye to All That: An Autobiography*. 1929. Reprint, New York: Blue Ribbon, 1930.

———. *Lawrence and the Arabs*. London: J. Cape, 1927.

Graves, Robert W. *Storm Centres of the Near East: Personal Memories, 1879–1929*. London: Hutchinson, 1933.

Grosvenor, Charles. "The Subscribers' *Seven Pillars of Wisdom*: The Visual Aspect." In *The T. E. Lawrence Puzzle*, ed. Stephen Tabachnick, 159–84. Athens: University of Georgia Press, 1984.

Groves, P. R. C. *Behind the Smoke Screen*. London: Faber & Faber, 1934.

Gruen, George E. "The Oil Resources of Iraq: Their Role in the Policies of the Great Powers." In *The Creation of Iraq, 1914–1921*, ed. Reeva Spector Simon and Eleanor H. Tejirian, 110–24. New York: Columbia University Press, 2004.

Gudgin, Peter. *Military Intelligence: The British Story*. London: Arms & Armour, 1989.

Guha, Ranajit. *Dominance without Hegemony: History and Power in Colonial India*. Cambridge, MA: Harvard University Press, 1997.

———. "The Prose of Counter-Insurgency." In *Selected Subaltern Studies*, ed. Ranajit Guha and Gayatri Chakravorty Spivak, 45–88. New York: Oxford University Press, 1988.

Gullace, Nicoletta F. *"The Blood of Our Sons": Men, Women, and the Renegotiation of British Citizenship during the Great War*. New York: Palgrave, 2002.

———. "Sexual Violence and Family Honor: British Propaganda and International Law during the First World War." *American Historical Review* 102:3 (1997): 714–47.

Gwynn, Sir Charles W. *Imperial Policing*. London: Macmillan, 1939.

Haldane, Aylmer. *The Insurrection in Mesopotamia, 1920*. Edinburgh: W. Blackwood, 1922.

Hall, L. J. *The Inland Water Transport in Mesopotamia*. London: Constable, 1921.

Hamilton, Angus. *Problems of the Middle East*. London: E. Nash, 1909.

Hamilton, Cicely. *Theodore Savage: A Story of the Past or the Future*. 1927. Reprint, London: Leonard Parsons, 1922.

Hamrick, S. J. *Deceiving the Deceivers: Kim Philby, Donald Maclean, and Guy Burgess* New Haven, CT: Yale University Press, 2007.

A Handbook of Arabia. 2 vols. London: Admiralty War Staff, Intelligence Division, 1916–1917.

Handel, Michael. *Strategic and Operational Deception in the Second World War*. London: F. Cass, 1987.

Harris, Sir Arthur. *Bomber Offensive*. London: Collins, 1947.

Harrison, Paul. *The Arab at Home*. New York: Thomas Y. Crowell, 1924.

Hart, Basil Henry Liddell. *The British Way in Warfare*. New York: Macmillan, 1933.

———. *Paris, or The Future of War*. New York: E. P. Dutton, 1925.

———. *"T. E. Lawrence": In Arabia and After*. London: Jonathan Cape, 1934.

Hartcup, Guy. *Camouflage: A History of Concealment and Deception in War*. New York: Scribner's, 1980.

Harwood, John. *Olivia Shakespear and W. B. Yeats: After Long Silence*. Basingstoke, UK: Macmillan, 1989.

Haswell, Jock. *British Military Intelligence*. London: Weidenfeld & Nicolson, 1973.

Hauner, Milan. "The Last Great Game." *Middle East Journal* 38 (1984): 72–84.

Haynes, Roslynn D. *Seeking the Centre: The Australian Desert in Literature, Art and Film*. Cambridge: Cambridge University Press, 1998.

Heller, Joseph. *British Policy towards the Ottoman Empire, 1908–1914*. London: Cass, 1983.

Henderson, David. *The Art of Reconnaissance*. London: J. Murray, 1916.

Hennock, E. P. "The Measurement of Urban Poverty: From the Metropolis to the Nation, 1880–1920." *Economic History Review*, 2nd ser., 40:2 (1987): 208–27.

Herbert, Aubrey. *Ben Kendim: A Record of Eastern Travel*. Edited by Desmond MacCarthy. 2nd ed. New York: G.P. Putnam's, 1925.

———. ["an M.P."]. *Mons, ANZAC, and Kut*. London: Edward Arnold, 1919.

Hichens, Robert S. *Garden of Allah*. New York: F. A. Stokes, 1904.

Hiley, Nicholas. "Counter-Espionage and Security in Great Britain during the First World War." *English Historical Review* (UK) 101:400 (1986): 635–70.

Hill, George. *Go Spy the Land: Being the Adventures of I. K. 8 of the British Secret Service*. London: Cassell, 1932.

Hill, Prudence. *To Know the Sky: The Life of Air Chief Marshal Sir Roderic Hill*. London: W. Kimber, 1962.

Hilton, James. *Lost Horizon*. New York: W. Morrow, 1934.

Hinsley, F. H. *British Intelligence in the Second World War: Its Influence on Strategy and Operations*. 5 vols. New York: Cambridge University Press, 1979.

Hinton, James. *Protests and Visions: Peace Politics in Twentieth-Century Britain*. London: Radius, 1989.

Hofstadter, Richard. *The Paranoid Style in American Politics, and Other Essays*. New York: Knopf, 1965.

Hogarth, David G. *Arabia*. Oxford: Clarendon, 1922.

———. *The Life of Charles M. Doughty*. New York: Doubleday, Doran, 1929.

———. *The Nearer East*. London: Heinemann, 1902.

———. *The Penetration of Arabia: A Record of the Development of Western Knowledge Concerning the Arabian Peninsula*. New York: F. A. Stokes, 1904.

———. *A Wandering Scholar in the Levant*. 2nd ed. London: J. Murray, 1896.

Holmes, Colin. "Public Opinion in England and the Jews 1914–1918." In *Michael* (Israel) 10 (1986): 97–115.

Hopkirk, Peter. *Like Hidden Fire: The Plot to Bring Down the British Empire*. New York: Kodansha, 1994.

———. *Setting the East Ablaze: Lenin's Dream of an Empire in Asia*. London: J. Murray, 1984.

Hopwood, Derek, ed. *Tales of Empire: The British in the Middle East, 1880–1952*. London: Tauris, 1989.

Hourani, Albert. *Emergence of the Modern Middle East*. Oxford: Macmillan, 1981.

———. "The Myth of T. E. Lawrence." In *Adventures with Britannia: Personalities, Politics, and Culture in Britain*, ed. Wm. Roger Louis, 9–24. London: I. B. Tauris, 1995.

House, Jonathan M. *Military Intelligence, 1870–1991: A Research Guide*. Westport, CT: Greenwood, 1993.

Howard, Michael. *Restraints on War: Studies in the Limitation of Armed Conflict*. Oxford: Oxford University Press, 1979.

Howe, Stephen. *Anti-Colonialism in British Politics: The Left and the End of Empire, 1918–1964*. New York: Oxford University Press, 1993.

Hubbard, G. E. *From the Gulf to Ararat: An Expedition through Mesopotamia and Kurdistan*. New York: E. P. Dutton, 1917.

Hudson, Kenneth. *A Social History of Archaeology: The British Experience*. London: Macmillan, 1981.

Hughes, Matthew. *Allenby and British Strategy in the Middle East, 1917–1919*. London: Frank Cass, 1999.

Hull, Isabel. *Absolute Destruction: Military Culture and the Practices of War in Imperial Germany*. Ithaca, NY: Cornell University Press, 2005.

Hume-Griffith, M. E. *Behind the Veil in Persia and Turkish Arabia: An Account of an Englishwoman's Eight Years' Residence amongst the Women of the East*. London: Seeley, 1909.

Huxley, Aldous. *Arabia Infelix, and Other Poems*. London: Chatto & Windus, 1929.

Hyam, Ronald. "Bureaucracy and 'Trusteeship' in the Colonial Empire." In *The Oxford History of the British Empire*. Vol. 4, *The Twentieth Century*, ed. Judith M. Brown and Wm. Roger Louis, 255–79. New York: Oxford University Press, 1999.

Hynes, Samuel. *The Edwardian Turn of Mind*. Princeton, NJ: Princeton University Press, 1968.

———. *A Soldier's Tale: Bearing Witness to Modern War*. New York: Penguin, 1997.

Ignatieff, Michael. *A Just Measure of Pain: The Penitentiary in the Industrial Revolution, 1750–1850*. New York: Pantheon, 1978.

India's Services in the War. 2 vols. New Delhi: Low Price, 1993.

Ireland, Philip. *Iraq: A Study in Political Development*. London: J. Cape, 1937.

James, Sir William M. *The Code Breakers of Room 40: The Story of Admiral Sir William Hall, Genius of British Counter-Intelligence*. New York: St. Martin's, 1956.

Jarvis, Major C. S. *Arab Command: The Biography of Lieutenant-Colonel F. G. Peake Pasha*. 1942. Reprint, London: Hutchinson, 1946.

Jay, Martin. *Downcast Eyes: The Denigration of Vision in Twentieth-Century French Thought*. Berkeley: University of California Press, 1993.

Jebb, Louisa. *By Desert Ways to Baghdad*. Boston: Dana, Estes, 1909.

Jeffrey, Keith. *The British Army and the Crisis of Empire, 1918–22*. Manchester, UK: Manchester University Press, 1984.

Jones, H. A. *Over the Balkans and South Russia: Being the History of No. 47 Squadron Royal Air Force*. London: Edward Arnold, 1923.

———. *The War in the Air: Being the Story of the Part Played in the Great War by the Royal Air Force*. Vols. 5, 6. Oxford: Clarendon, 1935–1937.

Joyce, James. *Dubliners*. 1914. Reprint, New York: Gramercy, 1995.

———. *A Portrait of the Artist as a Young Man*. 1914. Reprint, New York: Gramercy, 1995.

Joyce, Patrick. *Visions of the People: Industrial England and the Question of Class, 1848–1914*. 1991. Reprint, Cambridge: Cambridge University Press, 1994.

Judd, Alan. *The Quest for C: Sir Mansfield Cumming and the Founding of the British Secret Service*. London: Harper Collins, 1999.

Kabbani, Rana. *Europe's Myths of Orient*. Bloomington: Indiana University Press, 1986.

Kaplan, Robert. *The Arabists: The Romance of an American Elite*. New York: Macmillan, 1993.

Kaul, Chandrika. *Reporting the Raj: The British Press and India, c. 1880–1922*. Manchester, UK: Manchester University Press, 2004.

Kedourie, Elie. *England and the Middle East: The Destruction of the Ottoman Empire, 1914–1921*. 2nd ed. Hassocks, UK: Harvester, 1978.

———. *In the Anglo-Arab Labyrinth: The McMahon-Husayn Correspondence and Its Interpretation, 1914–1939*. 2nd ed. London: Frank Cass, 2000.

Keith, C. H. *Flying Years*. Aviation Book Club ed. London: J. Hamilton, 1937.

Kent, Marian. *Moguls and Mandarins: Oil, Imperialism, and the Middle East in British Foreign Policy, 1900–1940*. London: Frank Cass, 1993.

———. *Oil and Empire: British Policy and Mesopotamian Oil, 1900–1920*. London: Macmillan, 1976.

Kent, Raymond. *A History of British Empirical Sociology*. Aldershot, UK: Gower, 1981.

Kern, Stephen. *The Culture of Time and Space, 1880–1918*. Cambridge, MA: Harvard University Press, 1983.

Kestner, Joseph. *The Edwardian Detective, 1901–1915*. Brookfield, VT: Ashgate, 2000.

Keynes, John Maynard. *Essays in Persuasion*. 1931. Reprint, New York: Norton, 1963.

Khalidi, Rashid. *British Policy towards Syria and Palestine, 1906–1914: A Study of the Antecedents of the Hussein-McMahon Correspondence, the Sykes-Picot Agreement, and the Balfour Declaration*. London: Ithaca, 1980.

Kiberd, Declan. *Inventing Ireland*. London: J. Cape, 1995.

Kiernan, R. H. *The Unveiling of Arabia: The Story of Arabian Travel and Discovery*. London: George G. Harrap, 1937.

Killingray, David. "'A Swift Agent of Government': Air Power in British Colonial Africa, 1916–1939." *Journal of African History* 25 (1984): 429–44.

King, L. W. *A History of Sumer and Akkad: An Account of the Early Races of Babylonia from Prehistoric Times to the Foundation of the Babylonian Monarchy*. London: Chatto & Windus, 1910.

Kipling, Rudyard. *Kim*. 1901. Reprint, London: Penguin, 1987.

———. *The Secret Agent*. 1907. Reprint, New York: Signet, 1983.

Kippenberg, Hans G., and Guy G. Stroumsa, eds. *Secrecy and Concealment: Studies in the History of Mediterranean and Near Eastern Religions*. Leiden: E. J. Brill, 1995.

Kirkbride, Alec. *An Awakening: The Arab Campaign, 1917–1918*. London: University Press of Arabia, 1971.

———. *A Crackle of Thorns: Experiences in the Middle East*. London: John Murray, 1956.

Klieman, Aaron. *Foundations of British Policy in the Arab World: The Cairo Conference of 1921*. Baltimore: Johns Hopkins Press, 1970.

———. "Lawrence as Bureaucrat." In *The T. E. Lawrence Puzzle*, ed. Stephen Tabachnick, 243–68. Athens: University of Georgia Press, 1984.

Knightley, Phillip. *The First Casualty: The War Correspondent as Hero and Myth-Maker from the Crimea to Iraq*. 3rd ed. Baltimore: Johns Hopkins University Press, 2004.

———. *The Second Oldest Profession: The Spy as Bureaucrat, Patriot, Fantasist and Whore*. London: Andre Deutsch, 1986.

Knightley, Phillip, and Colin Simpson. *The Secret Lives of Lawrence of Arabia*. London: Nelson, 1969.

Knoepflmacher, U. C., and G. B. Tennyson, eds. *Nature and the Victorian Imagination*. Berkeley: University of California Press, 1977.

Koven, Seth. *Slumming: Sexual and Social Politics in Victorian London*. Princeton, NJ: Princeton University Press, 2004.

Kramer, Martin. *Islam Assembled: The Advent of the Muslim Congresses*. New York: Columbia University Press, 1986.

Lacey, Michael J., and Mary O. Furner, eds. *The State and Social Investigation in Britain and the United States*. Cambridge: Cambridge University Press, 1993.

Laffin, John. *Swifter Than Eagles: The Biography of Marshal of the Royal Air Force Sir John Maitland Salmond*. Edinburgh: W. Blackwood, 1964.

Lago, Mary. "India's Prisoner": A Biography of Edward John Thompson, 1886–1946. Columbia: University of Missouri Press, 2001.

Landau, Jacob M. *The Politics of Pan-Islam: Ideology and Organization*. New York: Oxford University Press, 1990.

Laqueur, Walter. *A World of Secrets: The Uses and Limits of Intelligence*. New York: Basic Books, 1985.

Lawley, Sir Arthur. *A Message from Mesopotamia*. London: Hodden & Stoughton, 1917.

Lawrence, A. W., ed. *Letters to T. E. Lawrence*. London: J. Cape, 1962.

———. *T. E. Lawrence, by His Friends*. 1937. Abridged ed. London: Jonathan Cape, 1954.

Lawrence, Jon. "Forging a Peaceable Kingdom: War, Violence, and Fear of Brutalization in Post-First World War Britain." *Journal of Modern History* 75 (2003): 557–89.

Lawrence, M. R., ed. *The Home Letters of T. E. Lawrence and His Brothers*. Oxford: B. Blackwell, 1954.

Lawrence, T. E. *The Letters of T. E. Lawrence*. Edited by David Garnett. London: Jonathan Cape, 1938.

———. *The Mint: Notes Made in the R. A. F. Depot between August and December, 1922, and at Cadet College in 1925, by T. E. Lawrence . . . 1955*. Reprint, New York: Norton, 1963.

———. *Oriental Assembly*. Edited by A. W. Lawrence. London: Williams & Norgate, 1939.

———. *Secret Despatches from Arabia: And Other Writings*. Edited by Malcolm Brown. London: Bellew, 1991.

———. *The Seven Pillars of Wisdom: A Triumph*. 1926. Reprint, New York: Anchor, 1991.

———. *T. E. Lawrence: The Selected Letters*. Edited by Malcolm Brown. New York: Paragon, 1992.

Leatherdale, Clive. *Britain and Saudi Arabia, 1925–1939: The Imperial Oasis*. London: Frank Cass, 1983.

Lebzelter, Gisela. "The *Protocols* in England." *Wiener Library Bulletin* 31 (1978): 111–17.

Le Carré, John. *Absolute Friends*. New York: Back Bay Books, 2003.

———. *Tinker, Tailor, Soldier, Spy*. New York: Pocket, 1974.

Lee, Arthur Gould. *Fly Past: Highlights from a Flyer's Life*. London: Jarrolds, 1974.

Leed, Eric. *No Man's Land: Combat and Identity in World War I*. Cambridge: Cambridge University Press, 1979.

Leland, F. W. *With the M. T. in Mesopotamia*. London: Forster Groom, 1920.

LeMahieu, D. L. *A Culture for Democracy: Mass Communication and the Cultivated Mind in Britain between the Wars*. Oxford: Clarendon, 1988.

Le Strange, Guy. *The Lands of the Eastern Caliphate*. Cambridge: Cambridge University Press, 1905.

Leslie, Shane. *Mark Sykes: His Life and Letters*. London: Cassell, 1923.

Lethem, G. J. *A History of Islamic Political Propaganda in Nigeria*. London: Waterlow & Sons, 1927.

Levenson, Michael. *The Genealogy of Modernism: A Study of English Literary Doctrine, 1908–1922*. Cambridge: Cambridge University Press, 1984.

Levine, Bernard. *The Dissolving Image: The Spiritual-Esthetic Development of W. B. Yeats*. Detroit, MI: Wayne State University Press, 1970.

Levine, George. "High and Low: Ruskin and the Novelists." In *Nature and the Victorian Imagination*, ed. U. C. Knoepflmacher and G. B. Tennyson, 137–52. Berkeley: University of California Press, 1977.

Levy, Reuben. *A Baghdad Chronicle*. Cambridge: Cambridge University Press, 1929.

Liebersohn, Henry. "Recent Works on Travel Writing." *Journal of Modern History* 68 (1996): 617–28.

Liebregts, Peter. "'Between that staring fury and the blind lush leaf': William Butler Yeats and the Occult." In *Literary Modernism and the Occult Tradition*, ed. Leon Surette and Demetres Tryphonopoulos, 51–72. Orono: The National Poetry Foundation, University of Maine, 1996.

Light, Alison. *Forever England: Femininity, Literature, and Conservatism between the Wars*. London: Routledge, 1991.

Lindqvist, Sven. *A History of Bombing*. Translated by Linda Haverty Rugg. New York: W. W. Norton, 2001.

Linehan, Thomas. *British Fascism, 1918–1939: Parties, Ideology and Culture*. Manchester, UK: Manchester University Press, 2000.

Little, Douglas. *American Orientalism: The United States and the Middle East since 1945*. Chapel Hill: University of North Carolina Press, 2002.

Litvak, Meir. "A Failed Manipulation: The British, the Oudh Bequest and the Shi'i Ulama of Najaf and Karbala." *British Journal of Middle Eastern Studies* 27 (2000): 69–89.

———. "Money, Religion, and Politics: The Oudh Bequest in Najaf and Karbala, 1850–1903." *International Journal of Middle Eastern Studies* 33 (2001): 1–21.

Lockman, J. N. *Meinertzhagen's Diary Ruse: False Entries on T. E. Lawrence*. Grand Rapids, MI: Cornerstone, 1995.

Longford, Elizabeth. *A Pilgrimage of Passion: The Life of Wilfrid Scawen Blunt*. London: Weidenfeld & Nicolson, 1979.

[Longford, J. H.] "The Consular Service and Its Wrongs." *Quarterly Review* 197 (1903): 598–626.

Longrigg, S. H. *Four Centuries of Modern Iraq*. Oxford: Clarendon, 1925.

Loomis, Chauncey C. "The Arctic Sublime." In *Nature and the Victorian Imagination*, ed. U. C. Knoepflmacher and G. B. Tennyson, 95–112. Berkeley: University of California Press, 1977.

Lorimer, J. G., ed. *Gazetteer of the Persian Gulf, Oman, and Central Arabia*. 2 vols. Calcutta: Government Press, 1908–1915.

Louis, Wm. Roger. *In the Name of God, Go!: Leo Amery and the British Empire in the Age of Churchill*. New York: W. W. Norton, 1992.

———, ed. *The Oxford History of the British Empire*. 5 vols. New York: Oxford University Press, 1998–1999.

Luke, Harry Charles. *Mosul and Its Minorities*. London: Martin Hopkinson, 1925.

Lunn, Kenneth. "Political Antisemitism before 1914." In *British Fascism: Essays on the Radical Right in Inter-War Britain*, ed. Kenneth Lunn and Richard Thurlow, 19–40. New York: St. Martin's, 1980.

Lunn, Kenneth, and Richard Thurlow, eds. *British Fascism: Essays on the Radical Right in Inter-War Britain*. New York: St. Martin's, 1980.

Lunt, James. *Glubb Pasha: A Biography*. London: Harvill, 1984.

Lyell, Thomas. *The Ins and Outs of Mesopotamia*. London: A. M. Philpot, 1923.

Macfie, A. L. "British Intelligence and the Causes of Unrest in Mesopotamia, 1919–21." *Middle Eastern Studies* 35 (1999): 165–77.

Mack, John. *A Prince of Our Disorder: The Life of T. E. Lawrence*. Boston: Little, Brown, 1976.

Mackay, Dorothy. *The Ancient Cities of Iraq*. Baghdad: K. Mackenzie, 1926.

Mackenzie, Compton. *Aegean Memories*. London: Chatto & Windus, 1940.

————. *First Athenian Memories*. London: Cassell, 1931.

————. *Gallipoli Memories*. London: Cassell, 1929.

————. *Greek Memories*. 1932. Reprint, London: Chatto & Windus, 1939.

————. *My Life and Times: Octave Five, 1915–1923*. London: Chatto & Windus, 1966.

Mackenzie, John, ed. *Popular Imperialism and the Military, 1850–1950*. Manchester, UK: Manchester University Press, 1992.

————. *Propaganda and Empire: The Manipulation of Public Opinion, 1880–1960*. Manchester, UK: Manchester University Press, 1984.

————. "T. E. Lawrence: The Myth and the Message." In *Literature and Imperialism*, ed. Robert Giddings. London: Macmillan, 1991.

MacLaren, Ian. "Exploration/Travel Literature and the Evolution of the Author." *International Journal of Canadian Studies* 5 (1992): 39–68.

Main, Ernest. *Iraq: From Mandate to Independence*. London: G. Allen & Unwin, 1935.

Mallowan, Max. *Mallowan's Memoirs*. New York: Dodd, Mead, 1977.

Malmignati, Countess. *Through Inner Deserts to Medina*. London: P. Allan, 1925.

Mangan, J. A. *Athleticism in the Victorian and Edwardian Public School: The Emergence and Consolidation of an Educational Ideology*. New York: Cambridge University Press, 1981.

[Mann, James Saumarez]. *An Administrator in the Making: James Saumarez Mann, 1893–1920*. Edited by his father. London: Longmans, Green, 1921.

Mann, Thomas. *The Magic Mountain*. Translated by John E. Woods. 1924. Reprint, New York: Vintage, 1996.

Margoliouth, D. S. *Cairo, Jerusalem, and Damascus: Three Chief Cities of the Egyptian Sultans*. New York: Dodd, Mead, 1907.

Marlowe, John. *Late Victorian: The Life of Sir Arnold Talbot Wilson*. London: Cresset, 1967.

Marshall, Sir William. *Memories of Four Fronts*. London: E. Benn, 1929.

Marwick, Arthur, Clive Emsley, and Wendy Simpson, eds. *Total War and Historical Change: Europe 1914–1955*. Buckingham, UK: Open University Press, 2001.

Masters, Anthony. *Literary Agents: The Novelist as Spy*. New York: B. Blackwell, 1987.

Materer, Timothy. "The Alchemy of Myth in Ted Hughes's *Cave Birds*." In *Literary Modernism and the Occult Tradition*, ed. Leon Surette and Demetres Tryphonopoulos, 163–77. Orono: The National Poetry Foundation, University of Maine, 1996.

Matless, David. *Landscape and Englishness*. London: Reaktion, 1998.

May, Ernest, ed. *Knowing One's Enemies: Intelligence Assessment before the Two World Wars*. Princeton, NJ: Princeton University Press, 1985.

Mazower, Mark. "Violence and the State in the Twentieth Century." *American Historical Review* 107 (2002): 1158–78.

McClure, John A. *Late Imperial Romance*. London: Verso, 1994.

Meilinger, Philip S. "Trenchard and 'Morale Bombing': The Evolution of Royal Air Force Doctrine before World War II." *Journal of Military History* 60 (1996): 243–70.

Meinertzhagen, Richard. *Army Diary, 1899–1926.* Edinburgh: Oliver & Boyd, 1960.

———. *Diary of a Black Sheep.* Edinburgh: Oliver & Boyd, 1964.

———. *Middle East Diary: 1917–1956.* London: Cresset, 1959.

Meisel, Perry. *The Myth of the Modern: A Study in British Literature and Criticism after 1850.* New Haven, CT: Yale University Press, 1987.

Mejcher, Helmut. *Imperial Quest for Oil: Iraq 1910–1928.* London: Ithaca, 1976.

Melka, R. L. "Max Freiherr von Oppenheim: Sixty Years of Scholarship and Political Intrigue in the Middle East." *Middle Eastern Studies* 9:1 (1972): 81–94.

Melman, Billie. *Women and the Popular Imagination in the Twenties: Flappers and Nymphs.* Basingstoke, UK: Macmillan, 1988.

———. *Women's Orients: English Women and the Middle East, 1718–1918: Sexuality, Religion and Work.* Basingstoke, UK: Macmillan, 1992.

Metcalf, Thomas. *Ideologies of the Raj.* The New Cambridge History of India. Cambridge: Cambridge University Press, 1995.

Meyers, Jeffrey, ed. *T. E. Lawrence: Soldier, Writer, Legend; New Essays.* Hampshire, UK: Macmillan, 1989.

Miller, Michael. *Shanghai on the Métro: Spies, Intrigue, and the French between the Wars.* Berkeley: University of California Press, 1994.

Miller, William. *The Ottoman Empire and Its Successors, 1801–1927.* Cambridge: Cambridge University Press, 1927.

Mitchell, Harvey. "Hobson Revisited." *Journal of the History of Ideas* 26 (1965): 397–416.

Mitchell, Timothy. *Rule of Experts: Egypt, Techno-Politics, Modernity.* Berkeley: University of California Press, 2002.

Moberly, F. J. *The Campaign in Mesopotamia 1914–1918.* London: His Majesty's Stationery Office, 1924–1925.

Mockaitis, Thomas. *British Counterinsurgency, 1919–60.* New York: St. Martin's, 1990.

Monk, F. V., and H. T. Winter. *The Royal Air Force.* London: Blackie & Son, 1938.

Monroe, Elizabeth. *Britain's Moment in the Middle East, 1914–1956.* London: Methuen, 1963.

———. *Philby of Arabia.* London: Faber & Faber, 1973.

Montague, C. E. *Disenchantment.* New York: Brentano's, 1922.

Morel, E. D. *Truth and the War.* 3rd ed. London: National Labour Press, 1918.

Morgan, Gerald. "Myth and Reality in the Great Game." *Asian Affairs* 60 (1973): 55–65.

Morris, L. P. "British Secret Missions in Turkestan, 1918–1919." *Journal of Contemporary History* 12 (1977): 363–79.

Morris, Peter. "Intelligence and Its Interpretation: Mesopotamia 1914–16." In *Intelligence and International Relations, 1900–1945,* ed. Christopher Andrew and Jeremy Noakes, 77–102. Exeter, UK: University of Exeter, 1987.

Moses, A. Dirk. "Conceptual Blockages and Definitional Dilemmas in the 'Racial Century': Genocides of Indigenous Peoples and the Holocaust," ed. Mark Levene. Special issue, *Patterns of Prejudice* 36:4 (2002): 7–36.

Mowat, Charles. *Britain between the Wars*. London: Methuen, 1955.

Nabers, Deak. "Spies Like Us: John Buchan and the Great War Spy Craze." *Journal of Colonialism and Colonial History* 2 (2001). http://muse.jhu.edu/journals/cch/v002/2.1nabers.html.

Nasir, Sari. *The Arabs and the English*. London: Longman, 1976.

Neilson, Keith. "'Joy Rides'? British Intelligence and Propaganda in Russia, 1914–17." *Historical Journal* 24 (1981): 885–906.

———. "'Pursued by a Bear': British Estimates of Soviet Military Strength and Anglo-Soviet Relations, 1922–1939." *Canadian Journal of History* 28 (1993): 189–221.

———. "Tsars and Commissars: W. Somerset Maugham, *Ashenden*, and Images of Russia in British Adventure Fiction, 1890–1930." *Canadian Journal of History* 27:3 (1992): 475–500.

Northumberland, Duke of. *The Conspiracy against the British Empire*. Pamphlet. London, 1921.

Nunn, Wilfred. *Tigris Gunboats: A Narrative of the Royal Navy's Co-operation with the Military Forces in Mesopotamia from the Beginning of the War to the Capture of Baghdad (1914–17)*. London: A. Melrose, 1932.

Occleshaw, Michael. *Armour against Fate: British Military Intelligence in the First World War*. London: Columbus Books, 1989.

Omissi, David. *Air Power and Colonial Control: The Royal Air Force 1919–1939*. Manchester, UK: Manchester University Press, 1990.

———. "The Hendon Air Pageant, 1920–37." In *Popular Imperialism and the Military, 1850–1950*, ed. John Mackenzie, 198–220. Manchester, UK: Manchester University Press, 1992.

One of Its Officers. *With a Highland Regiment in Mesopotamia: 1916–1917*. Bombay: Times Press, 1918.

Orwell, George. *As I Please*. 1943–1945. http://orwell.ru/library/articles/As_I_Please/english/eaip_03.html.

———. "The Lion and the Unicorn: Socialism and the English Genius." 1941. http://www.k-1.com/Orwell/index.cgi/work/essays/lionunicorn.html.

Owen, Alex. *The Place of Enchantment: British Occultism and the Culture of the Modern*. Chicago: University of Chicago Press, 2004.

Owen, Nicholas. "Critics of Empire in Britain." In *The Oxford History of the British Empire*. Vol. 4, *The Twentieth Century*, ed. Judith M. Brown and Wm. Roger Louis, 188–211. New York: Oxford University Press, 1999.

Panayi, Panikos. "'The Hidden Hand': British Myths about German Control of Britain during the First World War." *Immigrants and Minorities* (UK) 7:3 (1988): 253–72.

Parfit, J. T. *Mesopotamia: The Key to the Future*. London: Hodder & Stoughton, 1917.

———. *Serbia to Kut: An Account of the War in the Bible Lands*. London: Hunter & Longhurst, 1917.

Paris, Michael. "Air Power and Imperial Defence, 1880–1919." In "Studies on War." Special issue, *Journal of Contemporary History* 24 (1989): 209–25.

———. *Warrior Nation: Images of War in British Popular Culture, 1850–2000*. London: Reaktion, 2000.

Paris, Michael. *Winged Warfare: The Literature and Theory of Aerial Warfare in Britain, 1859–1917.* Manchester, UK: Manchester University Press, 1992.

Paris, Timothy J. "British Middle East Policy-Making after the First World War: The Lawrentian and Wilsonian Schools." *Historical Journal* 41:3 (1998): 773–93.

Parks, W. Hays. "'Precision' and 'Area' Bombing: Who Did Which, and When?" In *Air Power in Theory and Practice*, ed. John Gooch, 145–74. London: Frank Cass, 1995.

Parritt, B. A. H. *The Intelligencers: The Story of British Military Intelligence up to 1914.* 2nd ed. Ashford, KY: Intelligence Corps Association, 1983.

Parsons, David Willard. "British Air Control: A Model for the Application of Air Power in Low-Intensity Conflict." *Airpower Journal* (Summer 1994). http://www. airpower.maxwell.af.mil/ airchronicles/apj/apj94/parsons.html.

Patnaik, Eira. "Europe's Middle East: History or Invention?" *American Journal of Islamic Social Sciences* 7 (1990): 335–56.

Pears, Sir Edwin. *Forty Years in Constantinople: The Recollections of Sir Edwin Pears, 1873–1915.* New York: D. Appleton, 1916.

Perrett, Bryan. *Desert Warfare: From Its Roman Origins to the Gulf Conflict.* Wellingborough, UK: Stephens, 1988.

Peterson, J. E. "The Arabian Peninsula in Modern Times: A Historiographical Survey." *American Historical Review* 96 (1991): 1435–49.

Petrow, Stefan. "The Rise of the Detective in London, 1869–1914." *Criminal Justice History* 14 (1993): 91–108.

Philby, H. St. John B. *Arabia.* London: E. Benn, 1930.

———. *Arabia of the Wahabis.* London: Constable, 1928.

———. *Arabian Days: An Autobiography.* London: R. Hale, 1948.

———. *The Empty Quarter, Being a Description of the Great South Desert of Arabia Known as Rub' al Khali.* London: Constable, 1933.

———. *Forty Years in the Wilderness.* London: R. Hale, 1957.

———. *The Heart of Arabia: A Record of Travel and Exploration.* 2 vols. London: Constable, 1922.

———. *The Land of Midian.* London: Benn, 1957.

Pick, Daniel. *War Machine: The Rationalisation of Slaughter in the Modern Age.* New Haven, CT: Yale University Press, 1993.

Pickthall, Marmaduke. *The House of Islam.* London: Methuen, 1906.

Pierce, Steven. *Farmers and the State in Colonial Kano: Land Tenure and the Legal Imagination.* Bloomington: Indiana University Press, 2005.

Pipes, Daniel. *The Hidden Hand: Middle East Fears of Conspiracy.* New York: St. Martin's, 1996.

Pirie-Gordon, H., ed. *A Brief Record of the Advance of the Egyptian Expeditionary Force under the Command of Sir Edmund H. H. Allenby.* 2nd ed. London: H. M. Stationery Office, 1919.

Platt, D. C. M. *The Cinderella Service: British Consuls since 1825.* London: Longman, 1971.

Plotke, A. J. *Imperial Spies Invade Russia: The British Intelligence Interventions, 1918.* Westport, CT: Greenwood, 1993.

Popplewell, Richard. "British Intelligence in Mesopotamia, 1914–1916." *Intelligence and National Security* 5:2 (1990): 139–72.

———. *Intelligence and Imperial Defence: British Intelligence and the Defence of the Indian Empire, 1904–1924.* London: Frank Cass, 1995.

———. "'Lacking Intelligence': Some Reflections on Recent Approaches to British Counter-insurgency, 1900–1960." *Intelligence and National Security* 10:2 (1995): 336–52.

Porter, Bernard. *The Absent-Minded Imperialists: Empire, Society, and Culture in Britain.* New York: Oxford University Press, 2004.

———. "The Historiography of the Early Special Branch." *Intelligence and National Security* 1:3 (1986): 381–94.

———. *Plots and Paranoia: A History of Political Espionage in Britain, 1790–1988.* London: Unwin Hyman, 1989.

Powell, E. Alexander. *The Last Home of Mystery: Adventures in Nepal together with Accounts of Ceylon, British India, the Native States, the Persian Gulf, the Overland Desert Mail and the Baghdad Railway.* New York: Century, 1929.

———. *The Struggle for Power in Moslem Asia.* New York: Century, 1923.

Powers, Barry D. *Strategy without Slide-Rule: British Air Strategy, 1914–1939.* London: Croom Helm, 1976.

Prasad, Yuvraj Deva. "The Silk Letter Plot: An Anti-British Conspiracy in World War I." *Journal of the Pakistan Historical Society* 34 (1986): 153–63.

Pratt, Mary Louise. *Imperial Eyes: Travel Writing and Transculturation.* London: Routledge, 1992.

———. "Scratches on the Face of the Country; or, What Mr. Barrow Saw in the Land of the Bushmen." *Critical Inquiry* 12:1 (1985): 119–43.

Presland, John [Gladys Skelton]. *Deedes Bey: A Study of Sir Wyndham Deedes, 1883–1923.* London: Macmillan, 1942.

Preston, R. M. P. *The Desert Mounted Corps: An Account of the Cavalry Operations in Palestine and Syria, 1917–1918.* Boston: Houghton Mifflin, 1922.

Price, Thomas. "Spy Stories, Espionage, and the Public in the Twentieth Century." *Journal of Popular Culture* 30 (1996): 81–89.

Ralli, Augustus. *Christians at Mecca.* London: W. Heinemann, 1909.

Rand, Gavin. "Martial Races and Imperial Subjects: Violence and Governance in Colonial India 1857–1914." *European Review of History* 13 (2006): 1–20.

Renda, Mary. *Taking Haiti: Military Occupation and the Culture of U. S. Imperialism, 1915–1940.* Chapel Hill: University of North Carolina Press, 2001.

Reynardson, H. Birch. *Mesopotamia, 1914–15: Extracts from a Regimental Officer's Diary.* London: Andrew Melrose, 1919.

Rich, Paul. *Race and Empire in British Politics.* Cambridge: Cambridge University Press, 1986.

Richards, Jeffrey. *Films and British National Identity: From Dickens to "Dad's Army."* Manchester, UK: Manchester University Press, 1997.

Richards, Jeffrey, and Jeffrey Hulbert, "Censorship in Action: The Case of *Lawrence of Arabia*." *Journal of Contemporary History* 19 (1984): 154–170.

Richards, Thomas. *The Imperial Archive: Knowledge and the Fantasy of Empire*. London: Verso, 1993.

Richards, Vyvyan. *Portrait of T. E. Lawrence: The Lawrence of "The Seven Pillars of Wisdom."* London: J. Cape, 1936.

Robertson, David. "Mid-Victorians amongst the Alps." In *Nature and the Victorian Imagination*, ed. U. C. Knoepflmacher and G. B. Tennyson, 113–26. Berkeley: University of California Press, 1977.

Robinson, Francis. "The Muslim World and the British Empire." In *The Oxford History of the British Empire*. Vol. 4, *The Twentieth Century*, ed. Judith M. Brown and Wm. Roger Louis, 398–420. New York: Oxford University Press, 1999.

Rolls, S. C. *Steel Chariots in the Desert: The Story of an Armoured-Car Driver with the Duke of Westminster in Libya and in Arabia with T. E. Lawrence*. London: Cape, 1937.

Roosevelt, Kermit. *War in the Garden of Eden*. New York: C. Scribner's, 1919.

Ryan, Sir Andrew. *The Last of the Dragomans*. London: G. Bles, 1951.

Ryan, Simon. *The Cartographic Eye: How Explorers Saw Australia*. New York: Cambridge University Press, 1996.

Sackville-West, Vita. *Passenger to Teheran*. London: Hogarth Press, 1926.

———. *Poems of West and East*. 1917. Reprint, London: John Lane, 1918.

Said, Edward. *Orientalism*. 1978. Reprint, New York: Vintage, 1979.

Sandes, E. W. C. *In Kut and Captivity with the Sixth Indian Division*. London: J. Murray, 1919.

Satia, Priya. "The Defense of Inhumanity: Air Control and the British Idea of Arabia." *American Historical Review* 111 (2006): 16–51.

———. "Developing Iraq: Britain, India, and the Redemption of Empire and Technology in World War I." *Past and Present* 197 (2007): 211–55.

Saunders, Hilary St. George. *Per Ardua: The Rise of British Air Power 1911–1939*. London: Oxford University Press, 1944.

Savage, Raymond. *Allenby of Armageddon: A Record of the Career and Campaigns of Field-Marshal Viscount Allenby*. Indianapolis: Bobbs-Merrill, 1926.

Sayer, Derek. "British Reaction to the Amritsar Massacre, 1919–1920." *Past and Present* 131 (1991): 130–64.

Schenkel, Elmar. "Visions from the Verge: Terror and Play in G. K. Chesterton's Imagination." In *Twentieth-Century Fantasists: Essays on Culture, Society, and Belief in Twentieth-Century Mythopoeic Literature*, ed. Kath Filmer, 34–46. New York: St. Martin's, 1992.

Schwartz, Sanford. *The Matrix of Modernism: Pound, Eliot, and Early Twentieth-Century Thought*. Princeton, NJ: Princeton University Press, 1985.

Scott, James. *Seeing Like a State: How Certain Schemes to Improve the Human Condition Have Failed*. New Haven, CT: Yale University Press, 1998.

Scott, Len. "Secret Intelligence, Covert Action, and Clandestine Diplomacy." *Intelligence and National Security* 19:2 (2004): 322–41.

Scovill, Elmer B. "The RAF and the Desert Frontiers of Iraq, 1919–1930." *Aerospace Historian* (June 1975): 84–90.

Sebald, W. G. *On the Natural History of Destruction*. Translated by Anthea Bell. New York: Random House, 2003.

Seabrook, W. S. *Adventures in Arabia among the Bedouins, Druses, Whirling Dervishes, and Yezidee Devil Worshipers*. New York: Harcourt, Brace, 1927.

Sheffy, Yigal. "British Intelligence in the Middle East, 1900–1918: How Much Do We Know?" *Intelligence and National Security* 17.1 (2002): 33–52.

———. *British Military Intelligence in the Palestine Campaign, 1914–1918*. Portland, OR: F. Cass, 1997.

———. "Institutionalized Deception and Perception Reinforcement: Allenby's Campaigns in Palestine." *Intelligence and National Security* 5:2 (1990): 173–236.

Shepherd, John. "A Life on the Left: George Lansbury (1859–1940): A Case Study in Recent Labour Biography." *Labour History* 87 (2004). http://www.historycooperative. org/journals/lab/87/shepherd.html.

Silberman, Neil Asher. *Digging for God and Country: Exploration, Archaeology, and the Secret Struggle for the Holy Land, 1799–1917*. New York: Knopf, 1982.

Silver, Carole. *Strange and Secret Peoples: Fairies and Victorian Consciousness*. New York: Oxford University Press, 1999.

Silverfarb, David. *Britain's Informal Empire in the Middle East: A Case Study of Iraq, 1929–1941*. New York: Oxford University Press, 1986.

Silvestri, Michael. "The Thrill of 'Simply Dressing Up': The Indian Police, Disguise, and Intelligence Work in Colonial India." *Journal of Colonialism and Colonial History* 2:2 (2001). http://muse.jhu.edu/journals/journal_of_colonialism_and_ colonial_history/v002/2.2silvestri.html.

Simon, Reeva Spector, and Eleanor H. Tejirian, eds. *The Creation of Iraq, 1914–1921*. New York: Columbia University Press, 2004.

Sims, Charles. *The Royal Air Force: The First Fifty Years*. London: Adam & Charles Black, 1968.

Slessor, Sir John. *The Central Blue: The Autobiography of Sir John Slessor*. New York: Praeger, 1957.

Sluglett, Peter. *Britain in Iraq, 1914–1932*. London: Ithaca, 1976.

———. "Formal and Informal Empire in the Middle East." In *The Oxford History of the British Empire*. Vol. 5, *Historiography*, ed. Robin Winks, 416–36. New York: Oxford University Press, 1999.

Sluglett, Peter, and Nadine Méouchy, eds. *The British and French Mandates in Comparative Perspectives*. Leiden, Netherlands: Brill, 2004.

Smith, Clare Sydney. *The Golden Reign: The Story of My Friendship with "Lawrence of Arabia."* 1940. Reprint, London: Cassell, 1978.

Smith, Malcolm. *British Air Strategy between the Wars*. Oxford: Clarendon, 1984.

Soane, Ely B. *To Mesopotamia and Kurdistan in Disguise*. London: J. Murray, 1912.

Sonyel, Salahi R. "Mustafa Kemal and Enver in Conflict, 1919–22." *Middle Eastern Studies* 25:4 (1989): 506–15.

Spaight, J. M. *Air Power and War Rights*. London: Longmans, Green, 1924.

Spring-Rice, Sir Cecil. *The Letters and Friendships of Sir Cecil Spring-Rice, A Record*. Edited by Stephen Gwynn. Boston: Houghton Mifflin, 1929.

Stafford, David. *Churchill and Secret Service.* 1997. Reprint, London: Abacus, 2000.

———. "Conspiracy and Xenophobia: The Popular Spy Novels of William Le Queux, 1893–1914." *Europa* (Canada) 4:2 (1981): 163–86.

———. "John Buchan's Tales of Espionage: A Popular Archive of British History." *Canadian Journal of History* 18 (1983): 1–21.

———. "Spies and Gentlemen: The Birth of the British Spy Novel, 1893–1914." *Victorian Studies* 24 (1981): 489–509.

Stang, Charles, ed. *The Waking Dream of T. E. Lawrence: Essays on His Life, Literature, and Legacy.* New York: Palgrave, 2002.

Stansky, Peter. *On or about December 1910: Early Bloomsbury and Its Intimate World.* Cambridge, MA: Harvard University Press, 1996.

Stark, Freya. *Baghdad Sketches.* New York: E. P. Dutton, 1938.

———. *Beyond Euphrates: Autobiography, 1928–1933.* London: J. Murray, 1951.

Stern, Fritz. *The Politics of Cultural Despair: A Study in the Rise of the German Ideology.* Berkeley: University of California Press, 1961.

Stirling, W. F. *Safety Last.* London: Hollis & Carter, 1953.

Stone, Dan. *Breeding Superman: Nietzsche, Race, and Eugenics in Edwardian and Interwar Britain.* Liverpool, UK: Liverpool University Press, 2002.

———. "The English Mistery, the BUF, and the Dilemmas of British Fascism." *Journal of Modern History* 75 (2003), 336–58.

Storrs, Sir Ronald. *Memoirs of Sir Ronald Storrs.* New York: Putnam, 1937.

———. *Orientations.* London: I. Nicholson & Watson, 1937.

Strachan, Hew. "The British Way in Warfare Revisited." *Historical Journal* 26 (1983): 447–61.

———. "Total War in the Twentieth Century." In *Total War and Historical Change,* ed. Arthur Marwick, Clive Emsley, and Wendy Simpson, 264–66. Buckingham, UK: Open University Press, 2001.

Strachey, John St. Loe. *The Adventure of Living: A Subjective Biography.* New York: G. P. Putnam's, 1922.

Streets, Heather. *Martial Races: The Military, Race, and Masculinity in British Imperial Culture, 1857–1914.* Manchester, UK: Manchester University Press, 2005.

Surette, Leon, and Demetres Tryphonopoulos, eds. *Literary Modernism and the Occult Tradition.* Orono: The National Poetry Foundation, University of Maine, 1996.

Swayne, Martin. *In Mesopotamia.* London: Hodder & Stoughton, 1917.

Sykes, Mark. *The Caliph's Last Heritage: A Short History of the Turkish Empire.* London: Macmillan, 1915.

———. *Dar-ul-Islam; A Record of a Journey through Ten of the Asiatic Provinces of Turkey.* London: Bickers & Son, 1904.

Tab, Black [pseud.]. *On the Road to Kut; A Soldier's Story of the Mesopotamian Campaign.* London: Hutchinson, 1917.

Tabachnick, Stephen. "Art and Science in *Travels in Arabia Deserta.*" In *Explorations in Doughty's Arabia Deserta,* 1–39. Athens: University of Georgia Press, 1987.

———, ed. *Explorations in Doughty's Arabia Deserta.* Athens: University of Georgia Press, 1987.

———. "A Fragmentation Artist." In *The T. E. Lawrence Puzzle*, 1–49. Athens: University of Georgia Press, 1984.

———, ed. *The T. E. Lawrence Puzzle*. Athens: University of Georgia Press, 1984.

Tackett, Timothy. "Conspiracy Obsession in a Time of Revolution: French Elites and the Origins of the Terror, 1789–1792." *American Historical Review* 105 (2000): 691–713.

Tauber, Eliezer. *The Arab Movements in World War I*. London: Frank Cass, 1993.

———. *The Emergence of the Arab Movements*. London: Frank Cass, 1993.

———. *The Formation of Modern Syria and Iraq*. Portland, OR: Frank Cass, 1995.

———. "Secrecy in Early Arab Nationalist Organizations." *Middle Eastern Studies* 33 (1997): 119–27.

Taussig, Michael. "Culture of Terror—Space of Death: Roger Casement's Putumayo Report and the Explanation of Torture." *Comparative Studies of Society and History* 26 (1984): 467–97.

Taylor, John. *A Dream of England: Landscape, Photography, and the Tourist's Imagination*. Manchester, UK: Manchester University Press, 1994.

Taylor, Miles. "Patriotism, History and the Left in Twentieth-Century Britain." *Historical Journal* 33 (1990): 971–87.

Teague-Jones, Reginald. *The Spy Who Disappeared: Diary of a Secret Mission to Russian Central Asia in 1918*. London: Gollancz, 1990.

Tennant, J. E. *In the Clouds above Baghdad, Being the Records of an Air Commander*. London: Cecil Palmer, 1920.

Thomas, Bertram. *Alarms and Excursions in Arabia*. London: G. Allen & Unwin, 1931.

———. *Arabia Felix: Across the "Empty Quarter" of Arabia*. London: J. Cape, 1932.

Thompson, Edward J. *Damascus Lies North*. New York: Knopf, 1933.

———. *The Leicestershires beyond Baghdad*. London: Epworth, 1919.

———. *The Making of the English Working Class*. 1963. Reprint, New York: Vintage, 1966.

———. *These Men, Thy Friends*. New York: Harcourt, Brace, 1928.

Thompson, Edward P. "An Alternative to Doomsday." *New Statesman*, 21 Dec. 1979, reprinted in *Britain and the Bomb: The* New Statesman *Papers on Destruction and Disarmament*, 9–18. Manchester, UK: Manchester Free Press, 1981.

———. "The Secret State." *Race and Class* 20:3 (1979): 219–42.

———. *Whigs and Hunters: The Origin of the Black Act*. New York Pantheon, 1975.

Thompson, Jon. *Fiction, Crime, and Empire: Clues to Modernity and Postmodernism*. Urbana: University of Illinois Press, 1993.

Thornton, A. P. *The Imperial Idea and Its Enemies: A Study in British Power*. 1959. Reprint, Houndmills, Basingstoke, UK: Macmillan, 1985.

Thurlow, Richard. *Fascism in Modern Britain*. Stroud, UK: Sutton, 2000.

———. "The Powers of Darkness: Conspiracy Belief and Political Strategy." *Patterns of Prejudice* 12 (1978): 1–12.

———. "The Return of Jeremiah: The Rejected Knowledge of Sir Oswald Mosley in the 1930s." In *British Fascism*, ed. Kenneth Lunn and Richard Thurlow, 100–113. New York: St. Martin's, 1980.

———. *The Secret State: British Internal Security in the Twentieth Century*. Oxford: Blackwell, 1994.

Tidrick, Kathryn. *Heart-Beguiling Araby*. Cambridge: Cambridge University Press, 1981.

Townsend, Meredith. *Asia and Europe: Studies Presenting the Conclusions Formed by the Author in a Long Life Devoted to the Subject*... 2nd ed. New York: G. P. Putnam's, 1904.

Townshend, A. F. *A Military Consul in Turkey: The Experiences and Impressions of a British Representative in Asia Minor*. London: Seeley, 1910.

Townshend, Charles Vere Ferrers. *My Campaign*. 2 vols. New York: J. A. McCann, 1920.

Townshend, Charles. *Britain's Civil Wars: Counterinsurgency in the Twentieth Century*. Boston: Faber & Faber, 1986.

———. "Civilization and 'Frightfulness': Air Control in the Middle East between the Wars." In *Warfare, Diplomacy and Politics: Essays in Honour of A. J. P. Taylor*, ed. Chris Wrigley, 142–62. London: Hamish Hamilton, 1986.

Towle, Philip Anthony. *Pilots and Rebels: The Use of Aircraft in Unconventional Warfare 1918–1988*. London: Brassey's Defence Publishers, 1989.

Toynbee, Arnold. *Cities on the Move*. New York: Oxford University Press, 1970.

———. *Civilization on Trial*. New York: Oxford University Press, 1948.

———. *The Conduct of British Empire Foreign Relations since the Peace Settlement*. London: Oxford University Press, 1928.

———. *The Western Question in Greece and Turkey: A Study in the Contact of Civilisations*. London: Constable, 1923.

———. *The World after the Peace Conference*... London: Oxford University Press, 1925.

Toynbee, Arnold, and Kenneth P. Kirkwood. *Turkey*. New York: Scribner, 1927.

Travers, Timothy. *The Killing Ground: The British Army, the Western Front, and the Emergence of Modern Warfare, 1900–1918*. London: Allen & Unwin, 1987.

Trotter, David. "The Politics of Adventure in the Early British Spy Novel." In *Spy Fiction, Spy Films, and Real Intelligence*, ed. Wesley K. Wark, 30–54. London: Routledge, 1991.

Tryphonopoulos, Demetres. "The History of the Occult Movement." In *Literary Modernism and the Occult Tradition*, ed. Leon Surette and Demetres Tryphonopoulos, 19–49. Orono: The National Poetry Foundation, University of Maine, 1996.

Tuohy, Ferdinand. *Battle of Brains*. London: W. Heinemann, 1930.

———. *The Crater of Mars*. London: William Heinemann, 1929.

———. *The Secret Corps: A Tale of "Intelligence" on All Fronts*. London: John Murray, 1920.

Tweedy, Owen. *By Way of the Sahara: The African Odyssey of Three Men and a Grocer's Van*. London: Duckworth, 1930.

———. *Gathering Moss: A Memoir of Owen Tweedy*. Edited by Thomas Crowe. London: Sidgwick & Jackson, 1967.

Vaczek, Louis, and Gail Buckland. *Travelers in Ancient Lands: A Portrait of the Middle East, 1839–1919*. Boston: New York Graphic Society, 1981.

Vagts, Alfred. *The Military Attaché*. Princeton, NJ: Princeton University Press, 1967.

Vennesson, Pascal. "Institution and Airpower: The Making of the French Air Force." In *Air Power in Theory and Practice*, ed. John Gooch, 36–67. London: Frank Cass, 1995.

Vincent, David. *The Culture of Secrecy: Britain, 1832–1998*. Oxford: Oxford University Press, 1998.

———. "Secrecy and the City, 1870–1939." *Urban History* 22 (1995): 341–59.

Vincent, S. F. *Flying Fever*. London: Jarrolds, 1972.

Walkowitz, Judith. *City of Dreadful Delight: Narratives of Sexual Danger in Late-Victorian London*. Chicago: University of Chicago Press, 1992.

Wallach, Janet. *Desert Queen: The Extraordinary Life of Gertrude Bell, Adventurer, Adviser to Kings, Ally of Lawrence of Arabia*. New York: Doubleday, 1996.

Waller, Derek. *The Pundits: British Exploration of Tibet and Central Asia*. Lexington: University Press of Kentucky, 1990.

Wark, Wesley. "In Never-Never Land? The British Archives on Intelligence." *Historical Journal* 35 (1992): 195–203.

———. "Introduction: Fictions of History." *Intelligence and National Security* 5 (1990), 1–3.

———, ed. Special issue. *Spy Fiction, Spy Films and Real Intelligence. Intelligence and National Security* 5:4 (1990).

———, ed. *Spy Fiction, Spy Films, and Real Intelligence*. London: Frank Cass, 1991.

Watson, Bruce. *Desert Battle: Comparative Perspectives*. Westport, CT: Praeger, 1995.

Watson, Janet S. K. *Fighting Different Wars: Experience, Memory, and the First World War in Britain*. Cambridge: Cambridge University Press, 2004.

Waugh, Sir Telford. *Turkey, Yesterday, To-day and To-morrow*. London: Chapman & Hall, 1930.

Wavell, A. F. *Allenby: Soldier and Statesman*. London: George G. Harrap, 1944.

Wavell, A. J. B. *A Modern Pilgrim in Mecca and a Siege in Sanaa*. Boston: Small, Maynard, 1913.

Weale, Adrian. *Special Operations Forces from the Great Game to the SAS*. London: Coronet, 1997.

Weintraub, Stanley. "Lawrence of Arabia: The Portraits from Imagination." In *The T. E. Lawrence Puzzle*, ed. Stephen Tabachnick, 269–92. Athens: University of Georgia Press, 1984.

Weldon, L. F. B. *"Hard Lying": Eastern Mediterranean, 1914–1919*. London: Herbert Jenkins, 1925.

West, Nigel. *GCHQ: The Secret Wireless War, 1900–86*. London: Weidenfeld & Nicholson, 1986.

Westrate, Bruce. *The Arab Bureau: British Policy in the Middle East, 1916–1920*. University Park: Pennsylvania State University Press, 1992.

Wigram, W. A. *The Cradle of Mankind: Life in Eastern Kurdistan*. London: A & C Black, 1914.

Wilkinson, John. *Arabia's Frontiers: The Story of Britain's Boundary Drawing in the Desert*. London: I. B. Tauris, 1991.

Willcocks, Sir William. *From the Garden of Eden to the Crossing of the Jordan*. 3rd ed. London: E. & F. N. Spon, 1929.

Willcocks, Sir William. *Sixty Years in the East*. Edinburgh: W. Blackwood, 1935.

Wilson, Arnold T. *Loyalties: Mesopotamia, 1914–1917; A Personal and Historical Record*. London: Oxford University Press, 1930.

———. *Mesopotamia, 1917–1920: A Clash of Loyalties, A Personal and Historical Record*. London: Oxford University Press, 1931.

Wilson, Jeremy. *Lawrence of Arabia: The Authorised Biography of T. E. Lawrence*. London: Heinemann, 1989.

Wingate, Ronald. *Wingate of the Sudan: The Life and Times of General Sir Reginald Wingate*. London: John Murray, 1955.

Winstone, H. V. F. *Captain Shakespear: A Portrait*. London: J. Cape, 1976.

———. *The Diaries of Parker Pasha: War in the Desert, 1914–18…* London: Quartet Books, 1983.

———. *Gertrude Bell*. London: Constable, 1978.

———. *The Illicit Adventure: The Story of Political and Military Intelligence in the Middle East from 1898 to 1926*. London: Jonathan Cape, 1982.

———. *Leachman: "OC Desert"; The Life of Lieutenant-Colonel Gerard Leachman, D. S. O*. London: Quartet, 1982.

———. *Woolley of Ur: The Life of Sir Leonard Woolley*. London: Secker & Warburg, 1990.

Winter, Jay. *Sites of Memory, Sites of Mourning: The Great War in European Cultural History*. Cambridge: Cambridge University Press, 1995.

Wood, Alfred C. *A History of the Levant Company*. London: Oxford University Press, 1935.

Wood, Gordon. "Conspiracy and the Paranoid Style: Causality and Deceit in the Eighteenth Century." *William and Mary Quarterly* 39 (1982): 401–41.

Wohl, Robert. *A Passion for Wings: Aviation and the Western Imagination, 1908–1918*. New Haven, CT: Yale University Press, 1994.

Woolf, Leonard. *An Autobiography*. 2 vols. New York: Oxford University Press, 1980. First published in 5 vols. 1960–1969.

———. *Diaries in Ceylon, 1908–1911: Records of a Colonial Administrator…* London: Hogarth Press, 1963.

———. *The Future of Constantinople*. New York: Macmillan, 1917.

———. *In Savage Times: Leonard Woolf on Peace and War, Containing Four Pamphlets. 1925–1944*. Edited by Steven J. Stearns. New York: Garland, 1973.

———. *International Government*. London: Fabian Society/George Allen & Unwin, 1916.

———. *Stories of the East*. Richmond, UK: L. and V. Woolf, 1921.

Woolf, Virginia. *The Letters of Virginia Woolf*. 6 vols. Edited by Nigel Nicolson and Joanne Trautmann. New York: Harcourt Brace Jovanovich, 1975–1980.

———. *Mrs. Dalloway*. 1925. Reprint, London: Grafton, 1992.

———. *Night and Day*. 1920. Reprint, New York: Harvest, 1948.

———. *Orlando*. 1928. Reprint, London: Penguin, 1993.

———. *Three Guineas*. 1938. Reprint, New York: Harvest, 1963.

———. *To the Lighthouse*. 1927. Reprint, San Diego, CA: Harvest/HBJ, 1981.

———. *The Voyage Out*. 1915. Reprint, London: Triad, 1978.

———. *The Waves*. 1931. Reprint, New York: Harvest, 1950.

———. *The Years*. 1937. Reprint, London: Granada, 1982.

Woolley, Leonard. *As I Seem to Remember*. London: George Allen & Unwin, 1962.

———. *Dead Towns and Living Men: Being Pages from an Antiquary's Notebook*. London: Oxford University Press, 1920.

———. *Digging Up the Past*. New York: C. Scribner's, 1931.

———, ed. *From Kastamuni to Kedos, Being a Record of Experiences of Prisoners of War in Turkey, 1916–1918*. Oxford: B. Blackwell, 1921.

Woolley, Leonard, and T. E. Lawrence. *The Wilderness of Zin*. 1914. Rev. ed. London: Stacey, 2003.

Wratislaw, A. C. *A Consul in the East*. Edinburgh: W. Blackwood, 1924.

Yapp, M. E. *Making of the Modern Near East, 1792–1923*. New York: Longman, 1987.

Yeates, V. M. *"Winged Victory."* New York: H. Smith & R. Haas, 1934.

Yeats, W. B. *The Autobiography of William Butler Yeats, Consisting of Reveries over Childhood and Youth, The Trembling of the Veil, and Dramatis Personae*. New York: Macmillan, 1938.

———. *The Collected Letters of W. B. Yeats*. Vols. 3, 4. Edited by John Kelly. Oxford: Clarendon, 1986.

———. *The Collected Poems of W. B. Yeats*. New York: Scribner, 1996.

———. *Essays by W. B. Yeats*. New York: Macmillan, 1924.

———. *If I Were Four-and-Twenty*. Dublin: Cuala, 1940.

———. *Memoirs: Autobiography—First Draft; Journal*. Edited by Denis Donoghue. London: Macmillan, 1972.

———. *The Variorum Edition of the Plays of W. B. Yeats*. Edited by Russell K. Alspach. New York: Macmillan, 1966.

———. *A Vision*. 1938. Reprint, New York: Macmillan, 1961.

Yergin, Daniel. *Prize: The Epic Quest for Oil, Money, and Power*. New York: Simon & Schuster, 1991.

Young, Sir Hubert. *The Independent Arab*. London: J. Murray, 1933.

Young, Robert J. "The Strategic Dream: French Air Doctrine in the Inter-War Period, 1919–39." *Journal of Contemporary History* 9 (1974): 57–76.

Index

Abdullah, 39, 123
Abu el Lissan, 53
Adelson, Roger, 39
Adrianople, 48
Africa, 6, 13, 15, 29, 72, 85, 95, 107,
    214, 265, 266, 341 n.4, 394 n.38
Aden, 29, 44, 47, 52, 67, 72, 105, 122,
    245, 266, 272
administration, imperial, 24, 29–31,
    43, 45, 52, 77, 270, 278,
    296–97, 346 nn.1, 2
    Indian-Egyptian rivalry, 49, 52, 267
    See also government, Indian; covert
    empire; Whitehall
Admiralty, 28, 38, 45, 143, 158, 166,
    170, 172, 304
Adorno, Theodor and Max
    Horkheimer, 326–27
Afghanistan, 52, 202, 212, 236, 266,
    279, 312, 317, 387 n.1
air control, 7, 11, 163, 178, 182, 184,
    191, 203, 240–62, 278, 295–96,
    311, 314–15, 332–33
    alleged humanity of, 240, 246–54,
    256–58, 314, 395 n.39
    See also airpower; bombardment;
    violence, colonial
Air Ministry, 213, 247–48, 259, 260,
    268, 272–73, 276, 277–78, 283,
    303, 305, 324
air route, imperial, 184, 243, 244, 259–60
airmen, 105, 159, 161, 162–63, 184,
    187, 190, 306

and air control, 244–45, 253, 255–58,
    261, 274, 391 n.21
airpower, 158–64, 169–70, 172–73,
    184–85, 244, 249, 253–54,
    259–62, 302, 309, 314–15,
    333–34
    and covert empire, 160, 261–62,
    275, 277, 263, 265, 273, 288,
    292, 301–7, 319–20, 325, 330
    fascination with, 170, 172–73, 178,
    185–86, 193, 197, 306, 341 n.12
    See also air control; Royal Air Force;
    Royal Flying Corps
Akaba, 147, 325
Aldington, Richard, 75
Aleppo, 41, 112, 113, 155
Alexander the Great, 14, 156, 175
Alexandria, 48, 85, 190
Allenby, Edmund, 47–48, 62, 80, 84,
    143–45, 148–49, 156, 168, 181,
    190, 192, 396 n.6
Ali, Rashid, 261
Alps, 107, 133
Amara, 42, 55, 57, 137, 140
American Presbyterian Mission, 39
Amery, Leo, 177, 305
Amman, 148, 231, 256, 269, 273,
    274, 309
Amritsar Massacre, 246, 304
Anaiza, 138
Anatolia, 13, 69, 216
Anglo-Persian Oil Company, 18, 41,
    274, 282, 325

Anglo-Turkish Accord, 1901 16, 23, 25, 32
Anglo-Turkish Society, 302
Anjuman-i-Kaaba, 208
anthropology, 17, 65, 94
anti-imperialism, 9, 175–76, 179, 190,
    194, 209, 236, 246–47, 264, 279,
    288–89, 292–93, 296, 304–5, 311,
    322–26, 329, 336
  colonial, 202–3, 208–9, 225–26, 313
  and conspiracy-thinking, 300–1, 318–19
  See also nationalism
anti-Semitism, 194, 204, 212, 300, 312–13, 326
Arab Army, 47–48, 53, 104, 138, 151, 213
Arab Bulletin, 46, 51, 109–11, 124, 138, 205, 265
Arab Bureau, 44–51, 91, 123–24, 127, 154,
    180, 207, 228, 230, 264–66, 268,
    271, 284, 290
  Jeddah agency, 47
  Basra branch, 49–50, 51, 57
  Jerusalem Bureau, 54
  and the Arabs, 53–54, 160, 163
  and military operations, 56–57
  See also Arab Bulletin
Arab Legion, 231
Arab Revolt, 39, 47–49, 52, 71, 111, 153–54,
    156–57, 162, 204–5, 214, 217, 236,
    263, 361 n.2, 406 n.57
  as a covert operation, 142, 149–51, 155, 289
  Lawrence and, 83–84, 129, 163, 182, 291,
    297, 324
  See also Great War, Middle East
    campaigns of
Arabia, 81, 85, 106, 114, 273, 331
  definitions of, 3, 6, 9, 11, 13–15, 184,
    209–10, 212–13, 215–17, 237, 243,
    266, 391 n.21
  and North West Frontier, 77–78, 222,
    256, 294, 302
  fascinations with, 60–61, 64–68, 72–73,
    76, 78–81, 84–93, 95–97, 106,
    111–15, 116, 121, 125, 129, 138, 144,
    149, 155, 161, 163–64, 166, 168, 183,
    185, 193–94, 196–97, 222, 233–34,
    236, 240, 248–49, 250–53, 257,
    290–91, 297, 310
  Romantics' view of, 64–65, 72, 78, 87,
    95, 118, 178–79
  as unknown, 3, 12, 37, 70–71, 79, 87, 92,
    100–6, 126–28, 151, 159, 161, 166,
    173, 210, 220, 232, 236, 242, 245,
    250, 289, 293, 295–96, 301–2
Arabian Nights, 17, 60, 68, 77–79, 81, 91,
    109–10, 120, 166–67, 291, 297, 334
Arabian peninsula, 15–16, 18, 24, 32, 37,
    52, 102, 105, 126, 202–3, 234, 269,
    273, 309

Arabs, 13, 95, 116
  British views of, 54, 65–66, 79, 100–2,
    104, 111, 115, 117–24, 127, 134,
    145–47, 149–50, 168, 193, 196, 242,
    248–51, 310
  British sense of connection to, 89,
    120–21, 123–24, 133, 152, 195–97,
    214, 251, 257, 320–21, 340 n.5
  See also racial thinking
Arafat, 194
archaeology, 71, 85–86, 90, 95, 106, 310
  and intelligence, 34–36, 38–39, 76, 109, 191
  popularity of, 61–62, 69, 86, 183
Arendt, Hannah, 10, 142, 263, 278–79, 357
    n.30, 369 n.47
Aristotle, 86
Armenia, 216–17, 293
armored cars, 56, 126, 143, 170, 185, 190,
    242, 244–45, 261, 392 n.25
Army Quarterly, 150, 186, 190
ascetism, 74–76, 193, 197, 258, 281
Ashmolean Museum, 36, 61
Asia Minor. See Anatolia
Asquith, Herbert, 45, 294, 297, 299, 300
Asquith, Raymond, 36, 62
Assyrians, 285, 293
Astor, Nancy (Lady Astor), 319–20
Athenaeum Club, 183
Athens, 44, 81, 82
Atlantic Monthly, 183
Atlee, Clement, 62, 304
attachés, honorary, 28, 34, 38
attachés, military, 26–28, 39, 267, 272
Auden, W. H., 66, 186
austerity. See minimalism
Australia, 6, 72, 107, 111, 354 n.11, 363 n.11
Aylmer, Leycester, 28, 105
Azrak, 91

Baath Party, 336
Babylonia, 13, 86, 166, 174, 176, 192, 240
Bacon, Francis, 152
Baden-Powell, Robert, 66, 71
Baer, Robert, 336–37
Baghdad, 31–33, 36, 39, 41, 55–57, 78,
    84, 91–92, 108, 125–26, 133, 157,
    166–67, 171–73, 175, 178, 185, 191,
    206, 208, 212–13, 215, 243–44, 261,
    263, 266, 277, 289–91, 305, 307,
    309, 314–15, 324
  General Staff Intelligence at, 139
Baghdad Railway, 15, 33–35, 60, 102, 162
Bahrein, 25, 41, 180, 222, 320
Baker, Herbert, 193
Baku, 215, 271
Baldensperger, Philip, 95

Baldwin, Stanley, 188, 298, 315, 329, 392 n.24
Balfour, Arthur, 63, 130, 134, 142
Balfour Declaration, 56, 201–2
Balkans, 264, 333
Banfield, Ann, 131
Bar-Yosef, Eitan, 168, 290
Baring, Maurice, 62
Barrow, Edmund, 309
Basra, 15, 25–27, 30–32, 49–53, 57, 82, 113, 126, 157, 173, 308–9
   General Staff Intelligence at, 39–41, 43, 46, 104, 125, 159
Basra Times, 140
Batas, 250
Beach, W. H., 40, 42–43, 46, 49–50, 55, 99, 125, 157
Beaverbrook, Lord (Max Aitken), 291–92
Bedouin. *See* Arabs
Beersheba, 57, 143, 325
Beirut, 38, 61, 209, 266, 271–73, 334
Belgium, 171, 176, 179
Bell, Gertrude, 7, 14, 40, 44–46, 50–51, 55, 57, 61, 65, 70, 72–74, 76, 78–80, 82, 91–92, 94–95, 100, 102–3, 106–7, 109–12, 117–21, 123–25, 140, 159, 173–74, 176–78, 180, 185, 188, 190–91, 201, 206, 209, 220–21, 227, 230–31, 237, 241–42, 251, 265, 268–69, 306–7, 319, 322, 324, 332, 340 n.5
   as an author, 68, 86, 111, 134–35, 182, 290
   social world of, 17, 36–38, 63
Bell, Hugh, 17, 63
Bell, Florence, 17, 324
Belloc, Hilaire, 62, 63
Bengal, 319
Beni Lam, 26
Beni Sakhr, 112
Benjamin, Walter, 91, 240
Bergson, Henri, 130–31, 134
Bergsonism, 130–32, 134, 192, 195, 336
   See also epistemology
Berlin, 206, 208, 221, 224, 312
Berlin, Isaiah, 111
Bevan, Edwyn, 85, 174, 175
Bevis, Richard, 66
Bible, 80–82, 84, 109, 120, 126, 144, 168
   scholarship on, 34, 86, 90, 93
   See also Palestine Exploration Fund
Blavatsky, Helena (Madame Blavatsky), 96
Blunden, Edmund, 188, 189
Boehmer, Elleke, 87, 96
Boscawen, W. St. Chad, 86
Blackwood's Magazine, 61, 95, 174, 307
Blaker, Major W. F., 50
Bloch, Ernst, 192

Bloomsbury, 63, 131–32, 189
Blunt, Anne, 37, 63
Blunt, Anthony, 334
Blunt, Wilfrid, 63, 71, 75, 130, 191, 201, 302, 322, 334, 360 n.58, 367 n.35
Boer War. *See* South African War
Bolshevism, 194, 202, 217, 219, 221–22, 224, 226–27, 231, 233, 235, 269–71, 295, 309, 311–13, 317, 320
bombardment, aerial, 11, 162–63, 240, 244–58, 261, 302–3, 305, 314–16, 332–33
Bombay, 44, 71, 180
Bonar Law, Andrew, 292
Boy Scouts, 66, 71
Bradley, F. H., 131
Bray, Norman N. E., 28, 31, 38, 49, 52, 56, 74, 76, 91, 116, 121, 125, 126, 138, 154, 163–64, 183–84, 192, 194, 205–8, 210, 212, 216–26, 231–32, 234, 236, 252, 265, 268, 270, 301, 311–12, 319, 321–22, 333
Brent, Peter, 73, 78, 103
British Museum, 35
Britishness. *See* Englishness
Brooke, Rupert, 62
Brooke-Popham, Robert, 184, 229–30, 242, 257, 277, 309
Brookes, H. H., 283
Brown, Gordon, 329
Brown, Malcolm, 110
Browne, E. G., 36
Byron, George Gordon (Lord Byron), 63, 196
Buchan, John, 62, 68–70, 74–75, 87–89, 96, 127, 131, 133, 186, 188, 190, 193, 195, 290–91, 307, 311, 323, 326, 331, 333, 406 n.57
Buchanan, George, 43, 184, 237, 291, 302, 332
Buchanan, Zetton, 297
Bukhara, 209, 216
Bulgaria, 231
Bullard, Reader, 41, 56, 180, 184, 213, 241, 250, 306, 318
Burgoyne, Elizabeth, 63
Burke, Edmund, 3–4, 120, 394 n.38
Burma, 52, 333
Burton, Richard, 72, 82, 112, 115, 120, 322, 356 n.28
Bury, G. Wyman, 29, 32, 36–37, 47, 61, 64, 72, 76, 95, 113, 121, 123, 215, 227, 332
Bushire, 26, 180, 272
   See also Persian Gulf
Butler, S. S., 28, 37, 105
Buxton, Robin, 188

Cairncross, John, 334
Cairo, 13–14, 37, 44–45, 52, 56, 63, 71, 83,
    113, 117, 122, 125–26, 178, 187, 213–14,
    230–31, 243, 265–66, 271, 309, 323
    General Staff Intelligence at, 28, 40,
        43–50, 56–57, 71, 110, 123, 126–27,
        142, 155, 159, 190, 205, 272–73
Cairo Conference, 180, 202, 244, 259, 293,
    295, 298, 318
Callwell, C. E., 100–1, 336
Cambridge Five. See Cold War
Cambridge University, 34, 36, 75, 81
Campbell, Roy, 187
Campbell-Thompson, Reginald, 34, 36,
    40, 86
Canada, 311, 353 n.3
Candler, Edmund, 65, 84, 104, 109, 119,
    125, 143, 145, 149, 157–58, 164, 169,
    170, 172, 175, 177, 190, 214, 289
Cape, Jonathan, 187
Capitulations, 24, 74
Carchemish, 34, 38, 61
Carlyle, Thomas, 120
Carnarvon, Lord (George Herbert), 38
Carpenter, Edward, 130
Carr, Helen, 75
Carruthers, Douglas, 16, 28, 37, 73, 78,
    91–92, 102, 112, 114, 121–22, 137, 183
Casement, Roger, 322
Caspian Sea, 158
Catholicism, 85, 194
Caucasus, 207, 216
Cavan, Lord (Frederick Lambart), 247
Cecil, Edward, 40
Cecil, Robert, 40, 52, 57, 174, 180
Celtism, 89, 322–23
censorship, 289, 292, 305, 308–9, 314, 325
Central Asia, 6, 56, 107, 184, 210, 265, 309,
    406 n.57
Central Asian Society, 61, 176, 183, 302,
    309–10
Ceylon, 63, 191, 194
Chamberlain, Austen, 49, 207
Chamberlain, Joseph, 62, 172
Charlton, Lionel E. O., 162, 250, 306
Chatham House, 310
Cheesman, Edith, 307
Cheesman, R. E., 307
Chelmsford, Lord (Frederic Thesiger), 171
Chesney, Francis Rawdon, 105
Chesterton, G. K., 62–63, 69, 82, 133
Childers, Erskine, 322
    The Riddle of the Sands, 17, 69, 133–34, 194
Childs, W. J., 45
Childs, Wyndham, 231
Chirol, Valentine, 37–38, 46, 61, 95, 184, 311

Christie, Agatha, 191–92
Churchill, Winston, 62–63, 75, 108, 118,
    180, 188, 190, 225, 230, 241, 244,
    246–47, 250, 253–54, 284, 292–95,
    297–99, 312, 318–19, 403 n.22
cinema, 179, 192, 194, 306, 324, 325
    Hollywood, 82, 317
    portrayals of Arabia, 60, 182, 306, 323
Clausewitz, Carl, 153
Clayton, Gilbert, 40, 45–48, 123, 127, 134,
    142, 151, 184, 213–14, 228–29, 284,
    290, 316, 332
Clayton, Iltyd, 284, 333
Cleveland, Charles, 204, 224
Cochrane, Ralph, 253
Cockerell, Sydney, 75
Codrington, John, 271
Coke, Richard, 173, 287, 316–17, 332
Cold War, 334–36
Colls, Robert, 178
Colonial Office, 15, 180, 192, 207, 213,
    230–31, 234, 256, 268–69, 274, 295,
    297, 302, 305–7, 310, 318, 320
    Middle East Department, 15, 180, 207,
        218, 228, 241, 250, 269–70, 293,
        297, 307, 325
Committee of Union and Progress (CUP),
    203, 206–9, 217, 224, 270, 273
    See also Young Turks
Conan Doyle, Arthur, 133, 186, 193
Connell, John, 111
Conrad, Joseph, 66–67, 69–70, 188
Conservative Party, 36, 129–30, 177, 294,
    306, 308, 315–16
conspiracy thinking, 8–9, 197–98, 207–37,
    240, 243–44, 249, 252, 255, 258–59,
    260–61, 264–67, 269–70, 275,
    277–83, 295, 297, 299–301, 311–15,
    317–21, 323–26, 329, 332, 337
Constantinople, 13, 16, 27–28, 34, 36–38,
    40, 63, 66–68, 89, 127, 180, 193,
    204, 206, 213–16, 223, 236, 266,
    272, 313
consuls. See Levant Consular Service
Cooper, James Fenimore, 81
Cornwallis, Kinahan, 46–47, 180, 184, 208,
    267, 276
Cornwell, David (John Le Carré), 334–36
Cross, L. B., 193
counterespionage, counterintelligence, 13,
    48, 54–55, 139, 147, 162–63, 266, 272
counterinsurgency, 10–11, 100, 102, 137,
    163, 179, 237, 241, 243–44, 247,
    294–95, 302, 310, 331, 336
covert empire, 7–9, 43–45, 48–49, 55,
    143, 243, 249, 258, 264, 266–75,

288–89, 292–93, 297, 299–301,
  305, 316–17, 320, 324–26, 331–32,
  335, 337
denials of, 279–85
Iraqi suspicions of, 277, 279–82, 284,
  296, 314, 326, 336–37
as oriental style, 52, 54, 140–42, 277, 282,
  288, 295, 302, 318
postwar evolution of, 261–62, 264, 266–78
prewar foundations of, 23–39
wartime evolution of, 43–57, 137–39
See also airpower; air control; indirect rule;
  intelligence gathering; state secrecy
covert operations, 49, 155, 157–59, 289, 294
See also Arab Revolt; Dunsterforce
Coward, Noel, 191
Cox, Percy, 27–28, 30–31, 37–40, 43, 46,
  49–51, 53, 55–56, 124–25, 144, 157,
  162, 180, 182–84, 192, 219–21, 228,
  236, 297, 307, 310–11
Crimean War, 289
Cromer, Lord (Evelyn Baring), 63
Cromwell, Oliver, 80, 196
Crow, F. E., 26, 31, 123
Crusades, 72, 80, 84, 153, 155, 167–68, 290
Ctesiphon, 169–70
cultural history, 3–5, 10–12, 240, 248,
  261–62, 331–32, 336–37
cultural relativism, 86–87, 96–97, 248–49,
  251, 303
Curzon, George Nathaniel (Lord Curzon),
  16, 176, 180, 212, 236, 267, 269–70,
  296–97

Dahoum, 62
Daily Chronicle, 291
Daily Express, 291–92
Daily Herald, 291, 302, 324
Daily Mail, 183, 291
Daily News, 183, 196
Daily Telegraph, 151, 183, 313
Damascus, 38, 53, 56, 60, 68, 126, 162, 181,
  201, 208, 213–14, 220, 228, 232,
  271–72, 280, 335
Darwin, Charles, 62
Dawnay, Alan, 48, 57, 183, 191
Dawnay, Guy, 57, 148–49, 156, 190
Dawson, Graham, 333
Day Lewis, Cecil, 186
De Bunsen Committee, 40
deception tactics, 13, 143–49, 151, 154, 158,
  161, 333
Declaration to the Seven, 128
Deedes, Wyndham, 17, 38, 40, 47–48, 54,
  56, 75, 81, 113, 124, 128, 148, 154,
  180, 184, 258, 266

Defoe, Daniel, 240
De la Mare, Walter, 95, 150
Deleuze, Gilles and Félix Guattari, 215, 336,
  367 n.31
Delhi, 38, 44, 46, 49, 127, 207
Delhi Durbar, 37
democracy, 8–9, 181, 196, 279, 285, 288,
  293–94, 296, 298–300, 305, 308–9,
  314, 316, 318, 324–26, 329–31
See also state secrecy, critique of; Union
  for Democratic Control
Dent, Colonel (chief of Air Intelligence in
  Iraq), 271–72
Depression, Great, 18, 235, 308, 329
desert
  British view of, 64–70, 73–74, 78, 87,
    89–95, 106–7, 134, 195–96, 213, 232,
    257–58, 321, 331, 334
  effect on mind of, 103–4, 107, 118–21,
    134, 257–58
  and cartography, 102–3, 106, 158, 209, 242
  See also Arabia, fascinations with;
    intelligence gathering, peculiarities of
Desert Mounted Corps, 56
development. See imperialism and
  development; Iraq, development of
Dhari, Sheikh, 252, 392 n.27
Dickens, Charles, 110
Dickson, Harold, 41–42, 55, 81–82, 84, 92,
  113, 119–20, 128, 139–41, 145–47,
  149, 157, 180, 184, 214, 222, 229–32,
  234, 320, 333
Directorate of Military Intelligence, 45, 267
Directorate of Military Operations (DMO),
  15, 28, 34–35, 37, 40, 73, 103, 105,
  121, 266
Directorate of Naval Intelligence, 36, 39–40, 50
Dirks, Nicholas, 315
disarmament, 250, 331
disguise, 72, 77, 111–16, 122, 138, 153, 335, 336
Diwaniyah, 237, 277, 281
Djilas, Milovan, 333
Dobbs, H. R., C. 41, 43, 50, 184, 281, 285,
  308, 316
Dobson, Frank, 187
Dodd, Francis, 62
Doughty, Charles, 16, 37, 39, 60, 64–66,
  72, 75, 80, 82, 111, 185–87, 192, 196,
  201, 301–2, 323, 355 n.18, 360 n.57
Doughty-Wylie, Charles, 37, 48
Douglas, Alfred, 63
Dulaim, 56
Dundee, 299
Dunsterforce, 157–58, 289
Dunsterville, Lionel Charles, 157
Dutch East Indies, 224

Eadie, G. F., 40, 50, 157, 184, 237
East Africa, 28, 54, 125, 158, 180, 250,
　　372 n.15
East India Company, 346 n.2, 357 n.30
　　See also Hastings, Warren
Eastern Mediterranean Special Intelligence
　　Bureau. See MI5
Eastern Unrest, 8, 205–7, 313, 318
Edgerton, David, 11, 173, 315
Edmonds, C. J., 42, 184, 282
Egan, Eleanor Franklin, 375 n.5
Egypt, 13–16, 38, 44, 52, 81, 83, 85, 87, 172,
　　176, 180, 183, 203, 215–18, 221, 231,
　　237, 266, 273–74, 282–84, 312, 387 n.1
　　Egyptian Army, 29, 39–40, 45, 123
　　See also Cairo; nationalism
Elgar, Edward, 188
Eliot, George, 62
Eliot, T. S., 66, 88, 132, 188
empathy, 100, 254, 256–58, 296, 203–3, 321
　　See also intuition; colonial violence,
　　　　critique of; anti-imperialism
Empire Review, 291
empiricism, 4, 6, 17, 102–3, 121–22,
　　130–32, 135
　　skepticism about, 59–60, 73, 78, 93–95,
　　　　100–3, 106–7, 111, 118–19, 122, 153, 227
　　See also epistemology
Englishness, 73–75, 77, 112–15, 117, 123, 152,
　　178–79, 195–97, 248, 257, 288, 293,
　　298, 308, 316, 320–23, 335
Enlightenment, 4, 93, 120, 132, 236, 387 n.65
　　See also epistemology; science;
　　　　universalism
Entente, 15
Enver Pasha (Ismail Enver), 209
epistemology, 4–5, 7, 9, 12, 17–18, 92, 100,
　　107, 111, 129–35, 195, 201, 203, 205,
　　of conspiracy thinking, 218–22, 236,
　　　　313, 326
　　See also empiricism; intelligence
　　　　gathering; intuition
Eritrea, 274
Erzurum, 88, 133
Ethiopia, 89, 284, 393 n.30
Euphrates River, 39, 43, 104, 214
the expert, 44, 106, 109, 120, 122–28, 142, 155,
　　165, 171, 181, 184, 192, 195, 202, 205–6,
　　214, 217–20, 227, 230, 263, 274, 278,
　　292, 296–99, 309, 315, 317–19
　　See also intelligence community; intuition
exploration, 71, 85, 102, 122, 134
　　of Arabia, 28–29, 33, 36–38, 60–61,
　　　　63–64, 71, 76, 79–80, 102–7, 109,
　　　　111–12, 117, 138–39, 184, 242, 336
　　See also intelligence gathering

Fabian Society, 302
Faisal, 39, 47–48, 56, 123, 181, 190–91,
　　201–2, 208, 215, 221–22, 269, 278,
　　281–82, 306–8, 318, 387 n.65
Falluja, 137
al-Faruqi, Mohammed, 127
fascism, 194–95, 254, 305, 313, 330, 333, 336
　　See also anti-Semitism; Nazism
Fielding, Lieutenant, 125
Financial Times, 183
Fitzmaurice, Gerald, 35, 39, 85, 128, 204–5
FitzWilliam Museum, 75
Flanders. See Great War
Flecker, James Elroy, 38, 61–62, 66, 69, 88,
　　95, 123, 132–33, 182, 191
Foch, Ferdinand, 153
Forbes, Rosita, 319
Foreign Office, 12, 25–27, 29–38, 40,
　　44–45, 47, 52, 57, 63, 108, 127, 142,
　　180, 207, 217, 220–21, 224, 230, 232,
　　234, 245, 265–68, 273–74, 276, 278,
　　283, 291, 297, 310, 316, 318, 334
Forster, E. M., 187–91
Fortnightly Review, 183
Foucault, Michel, 287, 337
France, 6, 16, 28, 39, 55–56, 142, 159,
　　165, 169–71, 179, 189, 201–2, 206,
　　210, 219–20, 224, 228, 234, 272,
　　278–81, 320
Fraser, David, 34, 38, 61, 64, 119
Frazer, J. G., 86
Fromkin, David, 212
Fuller, J. F. C., 156, 244
Fussell, Paul, 167, 185, 326

Gabriel, Lieutenant, 32
Galton, Francis, 62
Gandhi, Mohandas Karamchand, 197
Garbett, C. C., 219–20, 227, 230, 265
Garland, Herbert, 110
Garnett, David, 189, 192
Garnett, Edward, 192
Garratt, Geoffrey, 304, 325
Gaza, 143, 148
Gazetteer of the Persian Gulf, Oman, and
　　Central Arabia, 16, 27–28, 39
gender, 73, 191, 248–50, 321, 340 n.5, 390 n.15
　　See also Arabia, fascinations with;
　　　　Englishness; heroism
General Strike of, 1926 212, 315
Geneva, 231, 251, 298
George V, 188
Germany, 6, 15–16, 25, 28, 35, 52, 56, 69,
　　72, 75, 127, 154, 176, 206–9, 212–13,
　　216–17, 224, 234–35, 249, 253–54,
　　272, 279, 289, 291, 303, 312, 333, 335

Gibbon, C. M., 28
Gibbon, Edward, 80, 89, 167, 175
Gibraltar, 266
Gilbert, Vivian, 80, 168
Glubb, John, 179, 182, 231–32, 242, 248, 251,
    255–57, 261, 273–74, 281, 292, 322
Gordon, Charles, 322
government, Indian, 41, 44, 53, 169–71,
    204, 267, 289, 324
government, Iraqi, 202, 231, 260, 270,
    275–77, 280–83, 316
Granville-Barker, Harley, 188
Graves, Philip, 37, 40, 46, 51, 57, 126, 166,
    183, 190, 302, 313
Graves, Robert W., 40, 48, 57, 180
Graves, Robert von Ranke, 74, 166, 182,
    187–89, 190–92, 196, 319, 323
Great Game, 15, 77, 229, 333, 336
    See also North West Frontier
Great War
    Gallipoli campaign of, 39, 44, 48, 127,
        154, 167
    legacies of, 4, 5, 7, 13, 129, 151, 174, 177–81,
        187–89, 193–96, 204–5, 213–14, 234,
        236, 247–48, 252, 256, 294, 298,
        306, 312, 319, 321–22, 326–27, 337
    memoirs of, 166, 185, 187–89, 190, 191,
        290, 304, 323, 326
    Middle East campaigns of, 7–8, 39, 42,
        47, 55–56, 80–84, 100, 103–4, 111,
        125–26, 129, 143–71, 173–76, 185, 240,
        289–91, 301, 314, 326, 332, 333, 335
    Western front of, 7–8, 40, 49, 81, 83,
        143–44, 149, 151–54, 158–60,
        165–67, 169–71, 174, 179, 185–86,
        189, 289–90
    See also Arab Revolt; covert operations;
        deception tactics; warfare, irregular;
        airpower
Greece, 48, 63, 85, 196, 206, 207, 217,
    219, 272
Green, Henry, 66
Gregory, Isabella Augusta (Lady Gregory), 63
Gregson, Lieutenant, 31, 184
Grey, Edward, 25, 34–35, 108
Gribbon, W. H., 40
Guest, Frederick, 241
Gwynn, Charles W., 304

haj, 204, 214–16, 235, 272, 308
    See also Islam; Mecca
Haig, Douglas, 375 n.8
Hail, 61, 63, 82, 214
Haldane, Aylmer, 227, 233, 237, 248,
    291–92, 297, 309
Hall, Reginald "Blinker," 36, 39–40

Hamilton, Angus, 61
Hamilton, Cicely, 314
Hamilton, Robert, 110
Hardinge, Charles, 45, 267
Hardy, Thomas, 188
Harris, Arthur, 253–54
Hart, Basil Liddell, 69, 113, 122, 148, 151–52,
    155–56, 186, 189, 193, 195
Hastings, Warren, 4
Hejaz, 14, 39, 50, 52, 56, 71, 103, 123–24,
    126, 150, 154–55, 159–60, 202, 213,
    215–16, 219, 221, 235, 272, 278, 297,
    308, 310
Hejaz Operations Staff, 47–48, 57
Henty, George Alfred, 81
Herbert, Aubrey, 34, 36–38, 40, 48–49,
    61–62, 66, 68, 74–75, 82, 85, 102,
    104, 119, 133, 180, 183, 186, 191, 294,
    302, 304, 332
Herodotus, 76, 80
heroism, 129, 143, 165–66, 169–70, 181–82,
    189, 192–97, 237, 321–23
    See also intelligence community; spy novel
Hillah, 27, 206, 277
Hinaidi, 178
Hiroshima, 261, 393 n.30
Hirtzel, Arthur, 45, 127, 267
Hitler, Adolf, 194, 235, 254, 392 n.24
Hoare, Samuel, 249, 314
Hobson, J. A., 300
Hofstadter, Richard, 203, 297
Hofuf, 25, 33
Hogarth, David, 15, 34–40, 44–47, 51, 57,
    61, 63–64, 68, 71–72, 76, 78, 82,
    87, 94–95, 102, 105–6, 109–10, 114,
    123, 140, 176, 180, 184, 188, 192,
    201, 205, 213–14, 264, 290, 310,
    323, 332
Hogarth, Janet, 36, 40, 65
Holdich, Thomas, 48
Holmes, Sherlock. See Conan Doyle, Arthur
Holt-Wilson, Eric, 284
Home Office, 208, 217, 319
Homer, 87, 187, 196
    Odyssey, 75, 80–82, 187
Hong Kong, 266
Hope-Johnstone, J., 119
Hourani, Albert, 83
Howeitat, 110
Huber, Charles, 16
Hull, Edith, 182
Hull, Isabel, 10
Hulme, T. E., 87
Humphrys, Francis, 261, 276
Hunter, F. Fraser, 28, 105
Hussein, Saddam, 336

Hussein, Sherif (Hussein bin Ali), 14, 39, 47, 52–53, 56, 126, 155, 210, 297, 299–300, 325, 387 n.65
Huxley, Aldous, 62–63, 66
Hynes, Samuel, 87, 192

Ibu Tayi, Auda, 83, 110
Ikhwan, 212, 232, 280, 251, 254–55, 261, 280, 391 n.21
Illustrated London News, 60, 191, 244
immersion
    as intelligence tactic, 5, 100, 112–17, 120, 125, 129, 255–56, 258, 274–75, 280, 283, 336
    as political tactic, 137–42
    in military operations, 147, 150, 155
imperialism, 5–6, 9, 157, 165, 171, 202, 233, 236, 260–62, 279, 296, 331–32, 337
    and the rule of law, 10–11, 278, 281, 307
    and popular culture, 8, 85, 115, 178, 285, 288, 306, 331–32
    and development, 8, 60, 165, 172–79, 196–97, 240, 244–45, 287, 291–92, 307, 313, 315–16
Independent Labour Party, 224, 300, 306
India, 4, 6, 13, 16, 45, 52, 54, 71–72, 77, 80, 92, 101, 105, 115, 139, 173, 176–77, 189–90, 197, 208, 210, 212–16, 221, 223, 230–31, 234, 236–37, 260, 264, 266, 273–74, 290, 293, 300, 311–12, 317, 355 n.21
    route to, 3, 14–15, 18, 64, 313
    See also Great Game; North West Frontier
India Office, 30, 32, 35–36, 44–45, 127, 180, 183, 206–7, 219–20, 227, 230, 268–70, 287, 295, 297, 307, 309, 311, 318
Indian Army, 28, 30–31, 43, 62, 167, 202, 244, 342 n.19, 347 n.11
    intelligence, 27–28, 31, 40–41, 44, 46, 272
    Indian Expeditionary Force D, 39–40, 43, 54, 146, 158, 169, 369 n.41
Indian "Mutiny" 190, 203, 304
indirect rule, 7, 264
intelligence community, 5, 23–24, 27–30, 37–57, 81–83, 115, 117, 124–25, 157, 183–84, 213–14, 223, 225, 228–30, 243, 264–76
    informality of, 30, 38, 41–43, 45–46, 50–51, 56–57, 106, 125, 155, 264, 268–75, 299, 325
    autonomy of, 23–26, 29–33, 43, 47, 50, 117, 155, 227, 232–33, 257, 264, 269, 271–72, 283–84, 297, 307
    civilians in, 33–38, 61, 183, 272, 275

social ties of, 36–38, 61–63, 74–75, 89, 130, 185–92, 232–33, 241, 269
influence of, 39–41, 45, 123–24, 127–29, 143, 148, 155–56, 178, 180, 205, 207, 218, 220, 227, 230–32, 236, 240, 263–64, 269, 278, 290, 296–97, 318–19
cultural formation of, 59–97
    See also Arabia, fascinations with
as authors, 60–62, 64–66, 76, 80, 82–83, 86, 95–96, 107, 182–83, 187–88, 222, 242, 290–91, 301–2, 306–7, 320, 334
as heroes, 74–78, 81, 83, 116, 123, 126, 141, 161, 165, 180–98, 230, 232, 257, 290–91, 301, 310, 321–22, 333, 340 n.5
    See also heroism
and "genius" 5, 9, 81, 99–100, 111, 120, 122–24, 126, 128, 135, 148–49, 156, 205, 218–20, 227–33, 256, 271, 278, 280, 309, 321
eccentricity of, 73–76, 100, 128–29, 140, 148, 156, 164, 195, 197, 205, 230–33, 257–58, 283, 320–22
and airpower, 158–61, 163, 241–44
    See also the expert; intelligence gathering
intelligence gathering, 3–4, 6, 10–13, 15–16, 24–26, 53–55, 139, 147–48, 162–64, 242, 272
    and Arabic language, 33, 41–42, 106, 113, 124–25, 139–40, 168, 280
    and diplomacy, 15, 23, 28, 34–35, 38, 47, 142, 269, 272
    failures of, 100, 278
    guides in, 38, 41, 79, 107, 120–22
    and mapping, 25, 27–28, 37, 49, 100, 102–6, 117, 242, 364 n.14
        See also desert; exploration
    peculiarities of in Middle East, 23–24, 28–29, 42–43, 47–49, 70, 72–73, 75, 78–82, 85, 90–97, 100, 103–4, 108, 111, 117, 119–20, 124–27, 129, 163, 219–21, 229–30, 252, 266, 273–74, 283–84, 336, 398 n.17
    and scholarship, 25, 29, 31–32, 34–36, 38–39, 86, 102, 109, 274
        See also archaeology
    and administration. *See* covert empire
    See also counterespionage; epistemology; intuition; propaganda; spy novel
intelligence, "operational," 143–64, 237, 240, 243, 256, 265, 332, 336
intelligence reporting
    literary style of, 99, 106–111, 222, 230, 257, 291
    See also *Arab Bulletin*; intelligence community as authors

Interdepartmental Committee on the
    Eastern Unrest (IDCEU), 207, 212,
    216, 219, 222, 225, 236, 269–71
    See also conspiracy thinking; covert
    empire; Eastern Unrest
intuition, 4–5, 70, 99–101, 117, 119–25,
    127–28, 130–35, 154–56, 158–61,
    164, 185–87, 192–93, 203, 218–21,
    230, 249–50, 254–56, 274, 331–32,
    340 n.5
    See also epistemology; modernism
investigation, social, 17, 330
Iran. *See* Persia
Iraq, 14–15, 18, 27, 38, 104, 120, 141, 147,
    159, 161–62, 173, 180, 182–83,
    190–91, 193, 202–3, 208–210,
    212–15, 218–21, 229, 231, 235–36,
    240, 242, 244–46, 248, 250–51,
    253, 257, 259, 262, 265–66, 269,
    273, 278–79, 281, 283, 292, 295–97,
    302–7, 310–11, 313–14, 317, 335
    development of, 18, 172, 177–79, 192,
    244–45, 301, 332, 369 n.41
    See also League of Nations; Mesopotamia
Iraqi Army, 124, 261, 275–76, 282
Iraqi Communist Party, 208
Iraqi Levies, 244, 285
Iraqi Revolution (1958), 261, 334, 335
Ireland, 63, 89, 202, 206–7, 219, 221, 224,
    225, 241, 244, 312, 318, 322–23
    See also Celtism
Islam, 88, 90–91, 101, 111, 114–15, 127, 211,
    214, 225, 234, 267, 311, 320, 323
    Shia, 77, 203, 210, 214–215, 293
    Wahhabi, 183, 196, 208, 212, 308, 310,
    392 n.26
Isle of Wight, 297
Italy, 128, 153, 205, 219, 234, 284, 305,
    393 n.30

Jacob, Harold Fenton, 266, 268
James, Henry, 66
James, Hindle, 282–83
James, William, 87, 129, 131
Japan, 217, 393 n.30
Jarvis, C. S., 126, 167, 186, 256, 269, 325
Java, 52, 266
Al Jawf, 105
Jebb, Louisa, 93, 103
Jeddah, 47, 49, 117, 180, 194, 215–16,
    220–22, 225, 231, 272–74, 301
Jerablus, 108
Jericho, 80, 109
Jerusalem, 13, 41, 55, 113, 144, 167, 171, 175,
    192, 266, 269, 271, 290–91, 302
Jewish Colonization Association, 34

Jiza, 111
John, Augustus, 187, 191
Johnstone, Harry, 72
Jordan. *See* Transjordan
Joyce, James, 66–67, 132
Joyce, Pierce, 47–48, 113, 124, 143, 154, 184

Kabbani, Rana, 115
Kabul, 52, 216, 317
Kadhimain, 214
Karachi, 31, 243
Karbala, 26–27, 56, 77, 91, 206, 214–16,
    218, 221, 228, 277
Kell, Vernon ("K"), 6, 23, 45, 284
Kemal, Mustafa, 203, 219
Kemalists, 203, 206–9, 215, 221, 236, 270,
    311–12
Kennington, Eric, 182, 187, 191
Kenworthy, Joseph, 298, 303, 305
Kermanshah, 215
Kern, Stephen, 85
Keynes, John Maynard, 190
Khan Baghdadi, 56, 144
Khaniqin, 56
Khartoum, 47, 52, 266
Khayyam, Omar, 120
Khilafat, 208
Khuzistan, 272
Kidston, George, 224–25
Kifri, 56
Kinch, Edward, 168
Kinglake, Alexander, 60, 76, 94
Kipling, Rudyard, 62, 66, 68–70, 76–77,
    80, 84, 157, 186, 188, 191, 289, 337
    Kim, 17, 77, 113, 115–16, 335
Kirkbride, Alec, 53, 56–57, 103, 153
Kirkuk, 56
Kitchener, Horatio Herbert, 29, 36, 39, 45,
    49, 57, 122, 126–27
knowledge, colonial, 4–8, 10–11, 18, 24, 33,
    41, 45, 53, 77, 80, 102, 106, 109, 112,
    115–16, 125, 137, 139–42, 155, 184,
    201, 227, 255, 272, 288, 309, 317,
    332, 335
    See also epistemology; intelligence
    gathering; intuition; nomadism;
    orientalism; the state
Koran, 13, 86, 91, 110
Korda, Alexander, 182, 324–35
Korea, 14
Koven, Seth, 17
Knox, S. G., 41, 122–23, 139
Kurdistan, 14, 41, 77, 116–17, 125, 157, 209,
    216, 241, 279–80, 294
Kurds, 34, 135, 183, 202, 206, 222, 244, 253,
    277, 293, 391 n.21

Kut, 39, 44, 49, 103, 126, 152, 159, 166,
    168–71, 185, 191, 289, 361 n.2,
    374 n.38
Kuwait, 16, 27, 30, 40, 82, 110, 113, 122,
    123, 180

Labour Party, 177, 179, 217, 229, 231, 271,
    288, 291, 298–300, 303, 306, 315–17,
    390 n.13
Lang, Andrew, 71
Lansbury, George, 303, 403 n.29
Lausanne, 299, 300
Lawrence, D. H., 66, 186
Lawrence, Jon, 315
Lawrence, T. E., 3, 7–8, 11, 13–14, 34–38, 40,
    43, 46–51, 56–57, 61–62, 66, 69–75,
    77, 81–84, 110–13, 115–16, 118–20,
    122–26, 128–29, 137–38, 140–43,
    146–56, 159–60, 162–63, 165, 167,
    175, 180–97, 201, 205, 212–13, 218,
    228, 230, 237, 241–42, 244, 248–50,
    256–58, 263, 265, 269–70, 274,
    278–80, 282, 284, 287–88, 290–92,
    297, 301–2, 310, 317–26, 332–36, 340
    n.5, 378 n.30, 403 n.22
    See also Arab Revolt
Leach, William, 303, 306
Leachman, Gerard, 28, 30, 31, 37–38, 41–42,
    44, 50, 56, 74, 77, 81, 101, 113,
    116–17, 124–26, 138, 140–41, 155,
    157, 160, 164, 230, 237, 252, 332
League of Nations, 202, 260, 298–99, 314–16
    Iraqi admission to, 18, 229, 259–61, 275,
    285, 315–16
    See also mandate system, Permanent
    Mandates Commission
Le Carré, John. See Cornwell, David
Lebanon, 14, 334, 337
Leith-Ross, William, 104, 139, 147–48, 161,
    163, 275
Leo Africanus, 89
Levant Consular Service, 24–32, 37, 41, 42, 75,
    78, 80, 117, 214, 272, 276, 349 n.29
Lewis, Wyndham, 66, 187
Liberal Party, 63, 129, 291, 293, 298–300
liberalism, 11, 173, 202, 245, 304, 341 n.11
Lippmann, Walter, 310
Livingstone, David, 72
Lloyd, George, 34, 36–38, 40, 46, 48–50,
    52, 81, 85, 180, 184, 191, 212, 215–16,
    231, 302, 319, 333, 391 n.21
Lloyd George, David, 143, 167, 290–91, 299
London, 17, 41, 43, 45, 49, 52, 85, 93, 133,
    180, 188, 208–9, 213, 217, 225,
    230, 258, 264, 266, 269, 290, 292,
    307–8, 310, 320, 324, 333

Lorimer, D. L. R., 41, 101
Lorimer, J. G., 24, 26–28, 30–32, 35–36, 39,
    41, 116, 123, 204, 282
Lucas, F. L., 189
Ludendorff, Erich, 393 n.30
Lyell, Thomas, 215, 313
Lynch Company, 26, 34, 39

Mackay, C. J., 242, 248
Macdonald, Ramsay, 299
Macdonogh, George, 85
Mackenzie, Compton, 36, 81–82, 128, 148
Mackenzie, John, 38, 178
Mackinder, Halford John, 15, 64
Maguire, Miller, 251
Mahan, Alfred, 14
Mallet, Louis, 36
Mallowan, Max, 191
Malory, Thomas, 82, 84, 110
Malta, 53, 266, 273
Manchester, 70
Manchester Guardian, 175, 177, 179,
    292–302, 315, 325
mandate system, 7, 11, 15, 18, 191, 202, 235,
    241, 258–60, 269, 276–77, 282, 285,
    288, 295, 298–99, 302, 313, 325, 330,
    393 n.33
    Permanent Mandates Commission, 202,
    260, 281–82, 285, 316
    See also League of Nations
Mann, James Suarez, 179, 191, 319, 332
Manning, Frederic, 75, 187, 189, 191, 192
mapping. See desert; exploration;
    intelligence gathering
Marsden, Victor, 312
Marsh, Edward, 190
Marshall, William, 157
Marx, Karl, 337
al-Masri, Aziz, 126
Matless, David, 172
Maude, Stanley, 54–55, 144, 157, 175
Maunsell, Francis Richard, 27–28, 34, 91
Maxwell, John, 127
Mazower, Mark, 10
McClure, John, 70
McMahon, Henry, 14, 47, 52, 127, 155,
    184, 230
Mead, G. R. S., 85, 134
Mecca, 70–72, 80, 90, 112, 115, 194, 210–11,
    213–16, 224, 234, 274
medievalism, 72–74, 83, 148, 152–53,
    163, 196
Medina, 60, 150, 160, 167
Mediterranean Expeditionary Force, 44, 48
Mediterranean Sea, 13, 38, 52, 69, 141, 209
Megiddo, 80, 143, 148, 161, 165

Meinertzhagen, Richard, 28, 33, 54, 62, 72,
    124, 125, 140, 143, 145, 148–49, 151,
    180, 184, 192, 194, 207, 220, 231,
    241, 250, 259, 269, 270, 320, 322,
    333, 348 n.15
Melbourne, 54
Melville, Herman, 99
Mesopotamia, 18, 24, 31–33, 41, 44, 53,
    55–57, 65, 68, 72, 81, 84–85, 93,
    99, 103, 105, 108–9, 116, 118–19,
    123, 126, 133, 138, 140, 145–46, 152,
    156–61, 166, 168, 172–80, 192, 201,
    206–7, 209–11, 215–16, 225, 236–37,
    243, 247, 263, 266, 278, 287–90,
    294–98, 301, 305, 307, 309, 311–12,
    318, 325, 334–35, 337, 401 n.8
  civil administration of, 41, 43, 55, 139,
    168, 180, 227, 241, 250, 255, 263,
    297, 305, 308, 317–18
  Political Department, 40–41, 43, 50, 55,
    125, 269, 333
  See also Iraq
Mesopotamia Commission, 171, 289
Metropolitan Police, 320
Middle East, definition of., 4, 6–8, 10,
    14–15, 213, 217, 291
  See also Arabia
Middle East Department. See Colonial Office
militarism, 11, 178, 240, 248, 279, 290,
    294, 304, 306, 315–16, 330
  See also air control; bombardment;
    violence, colonial
MI5, 6, 12, 17, 23, 45, 48, 54, 284
  Eastern Mediterranean Special
    Intelligence Bureau, 48, 54, 56,
    57, 284
MI6 (SIS), 12, 23, 29, 45, 48, 54, 228–29,
    231, 236, 256, 271–72, 274, 284,
    333–34, 336
Mill, John Stuart, 120, 177
Milner, Alfred, 296
minimalism, 59, 65–66, 76, 87, 89, 132,
    153–54, 168, 197
mirage, 93, 102–4, 118–19, 122, 145–46,
    158–60, 245
modernism, literary, 8, 66, 75, 132, 188, 192
  cult of the Arabian desert, 66–70, 88–90,
    130, 182, 191–94, 323
  and travel writing, 66, 88–90, 96–97
modernity, critique of, 59–60, 65, 69,
    71–74, 76, 78, 85–87, 90–92, 107,
    195, 334–35
Mohammerah, 37, 40
monism, 129
  See also epistemology; intuition
Mons, 40

Montagu, Edwin, 171, 176, 236, 297, 306, 313
Moore, Arthur, 308, 317–18, 322
More, J. C., 31, 40, 140, 184
Morel, E. D., 299
Morning Post, 63, 289, 291, 312–13
Morrell, Ottoline, 63, 191
Morris, William, 66, 110, 197
Moscow, 206, 210–12, 221–22, 224, 227,
    236, 271, 320, 334
Mosley, Oswald, 194–95
  See also fascism
Mossadegh, Mohammed, 335
Mosul, 25, 34–35, 39, 56, 169, 202, 210, 215,
    250, 265
  and oil, 18, 325
Mouvahiddin Society, 223
Mouwazanat il Ibad, 226
Mukhmas, 80
Muntafiq, 92, 139, 232, 234
Musaiyib, 27
mysticism. See occultism

Nadi al-Arab, 219
Nagl, John, 137
Najaf, 32, 77, 194, 214–16, 277
Najd, 15–16, 26, 32–33, 56, 72, 82, 106, 115,
    117, 202, 212, 214, 222, 231, 244, 251,
    272–73, 281, 317, 321, 325
Nairn Company, 185
Nalder, L. F., 47
Napoleon, 153, 170, 206
Nash, Paul, 187
Nasiriyah, 214
Nasiriyah Arab Scouts, 42, 157
Nation, 302, 319
nationalism, Arab, 215, 311, 321
  British assessments of, 126–28, 203–4,
    213, 225–26
  secret societies of, 127–28, 204
nationalism, Egyptian, 202, 207, 209, 217,
    224–26, 319
nationalism, Indian, 197, 202, 206–7, 209,
    217, 224–26, 262, 270, 289, 312
nationalism, Iraqi, 202, 208, 210, 260, 277–78
  See also anti-imperialism; nationalism,
    Arab; Rising, Iraqi
Natural History Museum, 61
Navy, Royal. See Admiralty
Navy, Royal Indian, 27
Nazism, 10, 194, 333
Neilson, Keith, 42
Nietzsche, Friedrich, 131, 195
Near and Middle East Association, 302
New Statesman, 304
Newcombe, Stewart, 29, 32, 35–36, 40,
    47–48, 148, 159

Newmarch, N. S., 27
Nicolson, Harold, 63, 190
Nineteenth Century and After, 183, 302
No More War Association, 302
Noel, E. W. C., 33, 41, 77, 157, 184, 230–31, 322
nomadism, 29, 38, 46, 56, 76, 94, 116–17,
        120–22, 134, 138, 150–51, 160,
        255–56, 269, 271, 274
    subversiveness of, 54, 213, 243, 265, 270,
        293, 313, 336
North Africa, 13, 24, 216, 266, 279, 330
North West Frontier, 16, 25, 39, 41, 52,
        63–64, 77–78, 108, 169, 209, 216,
        294, 317, 324, 347 n.11, 387 n.1
    See also Arabia; India, route to
Northumberland, Duke of, 311–12

Observer, 290, 302
oil, 18, 176, 260, 287, 299–300, 315, 325
O'Conor, Nicholas, 34
occultism, 59, 62, 85–92, 120–22, 125,
        130–34, 167, 193
    Hermetic Order of the Golden Dawn,
        89, 134
Odessa, 217
Oliphant, Lancelot, 38, 45
Oman, 273
Omissi, David, 253
Operation Yilderim, 55
orientalism, 5, 7, 10, 52, 63, 68, 70, 73,
        78–79, 86–88, 90, 93, 96–97, 115,
        120, 130, 132, 135, 141, 174, 191, 196,
        201, 204, 210, 222–23, 235, 249
    and development, 172–73, 181
    and social investigation, 17
    and intelligence gathering, 24, 35, 79,
        100–1, 111, 135, 309
    and warfare, 138, 147, 151, 251
Ormsby-Gore, William, 91, 124, 180, 184,
        191, 308, 310
Orwell, George, 178, 279, 315
Ottoman Empire, 6, 14, 15, 74, 141, 201, 203,
        211, 213, 266, 321, 345 n.35, 357 n.31
Oudh Bequest, 77
Owen, Alex, 85, 134
Owen, Wilfred, 189
Oxford, 34, 36, 62, 72, 75, 183, 190, 241,
        301, 334

Palestine, 14–15, 39, 55–56, 80, 125, 145, 151,
        158, 167–68, 177, 180, 186, 194, 202,
        206, 209, 212, 215, 220, 223, 226,
        228, 231, 234–35, 237, 241, 245, 258,
        269, 271–74, 313, 333
    General Staff Intelligence in, 54, 284
Palestine Exploration Fund, 29, 35

Pall Mall Gazette, 61
Palmer, C. E. S., 228
Pan-Arabism, 205, 226, 235, 318
Pan-Islam, 52, 127, 204–9, 215, 218, 223,
        225, 228–29, 231, 234–36, 267,
        312–13
Pan-Orientalism, 216
Pan-Turanianism, 205–6, 215
Paris, Michael, 306
Paris Peace Conference, 180, 190–91, 201,
        241, 291
Parker, Alfred, 47, 57, 127, 140, 184
Passchendaele. See Great War, Western front
Peacock Dinner, 75
Peake, F. G., 231, 269, 325
Peel, William Wellesley, 287, 309
People's Union for Economy, 297
Permanent Mandates Commission. See
        mandate system
Persia, 6, 13–15, 26, 28, 38, 41, 51–52, 73, 81,
        157–58, 203, 210–14, 216–17, 221,
        224, 229, 237, 260, 265, 271–73, 275,
        279, 293–94, 296, 325, 335
Persian Gulf, 13, 16, 18, 38–39, 44, 77, 214,
        216, 271, 273, 289
Petrie, Flinders, 38
Philby, H. St. John B., 41, 55, 57, 77, 105,
        110, 113, 115, 117, 119, 122, 142, 160,
        180–81, 183–84, 191, 194, 196, 201,
        220, 231–32, 242, 256, 265, 268,
        279, 281, 301–2, 308–9, 318–22, 325,
        333–35, 345 n.39
Philby, Kim, 77, 334
photography, aerial, 159, 161
Pickthall, Marmaduke, 319
pilots. See airmen
Pirie-Gordon, Harry, 36, 48, 290
Pitman, C. R. S., 175
Poles, North and South, 6, 71, 107, 355 n.19
policing, 162–63, 176, 178, 186, 203, 237,
        240–41, 243, 245, 248–49, 256, 269,
        287–88, 304–5, 319, 326, 331, 337
    See also air control; counterespionage;
        intelligence gathering
politics, paranoid. See conspiracy thinking
political officer, 39–43, 47, 50–51, 55–57,
        92, 102, 113, 117, 125, 138–41, 157,
        162–63, 179–81, 184, 206, 215, 218,
        237, 243, 250, 252, 254–56, 265, 282,
        284, 319, 321
Port Said, 82, 180
Portugal, 312
Pound, Ezra, 62, 63, 75, 88–89, 188
Pound, Omar, 62
Powell, Enoch, 394 n.38
Powell and Pressburger, 194

the press, 173, 176, 182–83, 188, 247, 281, 289–96, 298–303, 305–9, 311–12, 316, 318–19 324–26
See also censorship; intelligence community as authors; propaganda; state secrecy, critique of
Price, Richard, 11
primitivism, 59, 65, 70, 87, 88–89, 93
See also modernism; minimalism
propaganda, 44–46, 54, 56, 127, 140, 206, 211, 215–16, 225, 229, 235, 243, 280, 289–91, 304–309, 311–14, 316, 318–19, 320, 325, 375 n.5
Protocols of the Elders of Zion, 312–13, 342 n.15
Pro-Turks, 184, 217, 319
Punjab, 172, 176, 387 n.1

Qasim, Abd al-Karim, 336
Qatif, 33
Quran. *See* Koran
Qurnah, 168, 194

Rabigh, 47
racial thinking, 7, 70, 114–15, 119, 124, 135, 197, 210, 243, 248, 256–57, 356 n.24, 391 n.21
See also Arabs
al-Rahhal, Husain, 208
Ramsay, Major (Baghdad Resident), 27
Ramsay, William Mitchell, 38
al-Rashid, Harun (Haroun al Raschid), 17, 108, 126, 175, 178, 282
Rashid, House of, 37, 79, 115
Red Sea, 13, 38
Red Sea Patrol, 47
religion. *See* Arabia, fascinations with; Bible; Catholicism; haj; Koran; Islam; occultism
Reynardson, H. Birch, 103
Rhodes, Cecil, 72
Richards, Thomas, 115, 132, 203
Riding, Laura, 187
Rising, Iraqi (1920), 19, 185, 198, 202, 206, 209, 218, 222, 226–27, 233–34, 237, 243–44, 252, 255, 268, 278, 287–88, 291, 294–97, 302, 309, 311, 317–18, 323, 326, 332
Riyadh, 30, 39, 82, 142
Roberts, William, 187
Rolls, S. C., 126, 185
Romania, 82
Rome, 81, 84–85, 167, 175
Roosevelt, Kermit Jr., 335
Ross, Denison, 36
Rothermere, Lord (Harold Harmsworth), 291
Round Table, 302, 307

Royal Air Force (RAF), 159, 161–62, 178, 180, 184, 186, 188, 190, 194, 197, 211–12, 240–42, 244–46, 248–49, 251, 253–54, 257, 259–62, 269–70, 274–75, 278, 292–93, 302–6, 314, 316–17, 319–20, 324, 331, 335
intelligence in Iraq, 212, 221, 226, 229–31, 256, 270–72, 275–77, 284
Special Service Officer (SSO) organization, 255–58, 271, 273–74, 276–77, 281–83
See also Royal Flying Corps
Royal Anthropological Institute, 61
Royal Flying Corps (RFC), 57, 126, 159–64
Royal Geographical Society, 28, 37, 44, 61, 68, 71, 105, 122, 184
Rub al-Khali, 105, 183–84, 242, 336, 391 n.21
Ruck, R. M., 309
Rumm, 84, 91
Rushdie, Salman, 99
Ruskin, John, 120, 197
Russell, Bertrand, 63, 129, 131–32
Russia, 6, 15–16, 50, 56, 96, 158, 184, 201, 203, 210–14, 222, 224, 226, 235, 260, 266, 279, 294, 311–13, 320, 387 n.1
See also Bolshevism; Soviet Union
Russians, 208, 217, 293
Russian Revolution, 205, 293, 312
See also Bolshevism; Russia
Rutter, Eldon, 183
Ryan, Andrew, 222, 274

Sackville-West, Vita, 63, 67, 69, 134, 178, 179, 190–91
Sahara, 66, 111
Said, Edward, 7, 10, 70, 93, 115, 196, 201, 263
See also orientalism
al-Said, Nuri, 283, 335
Saklatvala, Shapurji, 324
Salmond, Geoffrey, 162, 241, 373 n.33
Salmond, John, 253, 259, 305
Salonika, 40, 167
Samarkand, 216
Samawa, 139
Samson, Rhys, 48
Samuel, Herbert, 313
Sannaiyat, 144
Sassoon, Philip, 319
Sassoon, Siegfried, 182, 188, 189, 190, 191, 326
Ibn Saud, Abdul Aziz, 15, 26, 30–33, 37, 39, 53, 79, 115, 194, 202, 210, 222, 225, 228, 231–32, 234–35, 251, 261, 272–74, 278, 297, 300, 308, 310, 320–21, 325, 387 n.65
Saud, House of. *See* Ibn Saud, Abdul Aziz

Saudi Arabia, 14, 18, 254, 273, 281, 334–35
  See also Najd; Hejaz; Hail
Saundby, Robert, 253
Savage, Raymond, 190
Savory, Reginald, 158
Schwartz, Sanford, 131
Scotland Yard, 228, 231
Scott, James, 5, 99
science, 92–95, 100, 106, 120, 130–33, 192,
    236, 257
  See also Arabia, fascinations with;
    empiricism; epistemology;
    exploration; intuition; occultism
Secret Intelligence Service (SIS). *See* MI6
Selfridges, 192
Shakespear, Dorothy, 62
Shakespear, Olivia, 62, 89, 132
Shakespear, William, 27, 30–33, 37–39, 44,
    61–62, 76, 80, 115, 122–23, 132, 332
Shakespeare, William, 79
Shammar, 31, 64
Shepherd, Dawson, 284
Sherrarat, 122
Shatra, 139
Shatt-al-Hai, 144
Shaw, Charlotte, 191, 192
Shaw, George Bernard, 62–63, 120, 182,
    186, 188, 191–92, 195, 320, 322
Sheffy, Yigal, 12
Sidqi, Bakr, 283
Silk Letter Plot, 52–53, 204, 218, 223
Simla, 27, 28, 52
Sinai, 16, 35, 39, 69, 122, 126
Singapore, 54, 243, 266, 351 n.44
Sinn Fein, 217, 312
Slessor, John, 257
small wars. *See* counterinsurgency
Smith, George Adam, 145
Smith, John Hugh, 79
Smith-Cumming, Mansfield ("C"), 23, 29, 45
Soane, Ely B., 28, 38, 41, 72, 73, 77, 93,
    113–14, 135, 140, 157, 332
socialism, 194–95, 208, 217, 226
Socialist Party, 207, 296, 323–24
Society for Psychical Research, 125, 134
Sofia, 205
Somaliland, 202, 387 n.1
South Africa, 54, 107, 111, 197
South African War, 15–16, 34, 73, 133, 318,
    371 n.9
South America, 66–67, 89, 107
Soviet Union, 10, 209–12, 215–16, 219, 221,
    224, 226, 229, 231, 234–35, 265, 272,
    279, 280, 311, 320, 324, 334–35
Spain, 251, 323, 393 n.30
Spanish flu, 57, 332

Special Duty agents, 26, 28–30, 32, 38–39
  See also Directorate of Military Operations
Special Operations Executive, 284, 333
Special Service Organization (SSO). *See*
    Royal Air Force
Spectator, 187, 292–93, 295, 307, 322
Spencer, Herbert, 62–63, 367 n.35, 391 n.20
Spring-Rice, Cecil, 63, 290, 375 n.5
spy novel, 17, 64, 68–69, 75, 87–88,
    132–33, 191, 204, 311, 323, 326, 331,
    333–34, 336
  and intelligence gathering, 68, 75, 77–78,
    82, 84, 96, 133–34, 357 n.31
Standard Oil Company, 206, 218–19, 236,
    334–35, 345 n.39
Stanley, Henry, 72
the state, 4–5, 7–10, 43, 99, 173, 175–76,
    179, 196, 222, 231, 264, 280,
    284–85, 287, 296–300, 309–10, 312,
    317, 321, 326, 330–32, 336
  See also covert empire; Whitehall;
    administration, imperial
state secrecy, 9, 17, 56, 77, 142, 155, 157, 182,
    194, 196, 262, 288–89, 292–95, 315
  critique of, 8–9, 165, 284–85, 288, 293–
    305, 307–8, 311, 316, 318, 324–26,
    329–31, 333, 337, 342 n.17
  See also censorship; covert empire
secret diplomacy, 126, 142, 293, 299,
    309, 321
  See also covert empire; state secrecy
Stephenson, Geoffrey, 180
Stewart, Rory, 137
Stirling, Walter, 71, 126, 153, 181–82, 191,
    322, 333
Storrs, Ronald, 37, 57, 81–82, 110, 117, 126,
    134, 140, 142, 154, 175, 201, 264
Strachan, Hew, 10, 242
Strand Magazine, 182
the sublime, 13, 66, 106–7, 257
Sudan, 44–45, 47, 123, 273
Suez Canal, 13, 39, 71, 202, 207
Suez Crisis, 334
Sulimaniyeh, 303
Sunday Chronicle, 324
Sunday Times, 297, 301
Suq al-Shuyukh, 42, 214
surveillance. *See* policing
Survey of Egypt, 29, 49
Survey of India, 27, 105
Swayne, Martin, 146
Swedenborg, 88
Switzerland, 206, 209, 213, 216–18, 231, 234
Sykes, Frederick, 388 n.3
Sykes, Mark, 7, 14, 34, 36, 40, 44–46, 49,
    51, 53, 55–57, 61–62, 64–66, 70, 73,

78–79, 85, 91–94, 106–8, 110–12, 114, 116–17, 119–20, 123, 128–29, 140, 142, 154, 161, 176, 201, 204–5, 213, 230, 249, 263–64, 290, 301, 332
Sykes-Picot Accord, 56, 142, 201, 233
Syria, 6, 14–15, 37, 39–40, 53, 69, 85, 128, 183, 190, 206, 208–9, 213, 215–16, 219–20, 226, 234–35, 272–74, 279–81, 311, 317–18

Taba, 16
Tafileh, 153
Talib, Sayyid, 15, 26, 53
tanks. *See* armored cars
Taurus mountains, 35, 40
Teesdale, Captain, 30–32
Tehran, 56, 216, 272, 294, 307
Tennant, J. E., 126, 159, 162–63
Thesiger, Wilfred, 334
Thomson, Basil, 319
Thomas, Bertram, 181, 183–84, 232, 310, 320–21
Thomas, Lowell, 180–81, 290, 375 n.5
Thompson, Edward J., 166–67, 190, 304, 324, 330–31
Thompson, Edward P., 329–31
Thompson, Jon, 84, 132
Thomson, Christopher (Lord Thomson), 245, 247–48, 306
Thornton, A. P., 304
Thucydides, 80
Thurtle, Ernest, 317, 321, 325, 406 n.57
Tibet, 279, 355 n.19
Tidrick, Kathryn, 14, 64, 83, 142, 340 n.5
Tigris River, 13, 39, 43, 104, 169, 178
Times (London), 37, 65, 71, 84, 168, 170, 172, 177, 183, 192, 203, 229, 253, 279, 287, 289, 291, 293–300, 302, 305, 307–8, 312–19, 325, 332
Times of India, 34, 61, 175
Times Literary Supplement (*TLS*), 61, 64, 68, 71, 81, 96
Tomlinson, H. M., 189
El Tor, 158
total war, 10, 41
    See also warfare
totalitarianism, 10, 178, 279, 336
tourism, 60, 78, 86–87, 93, 106, 167, 182, 185, 190–91, 292
Townsend, Meredith, 70, 86, 118–19
Townshend, Charles, 125, 145, 170
Toynbee, Arnold, 191, 210–11
Transjordan, 14–15, 180, 231, 245, 269, 273–74, 293
travel writing, 61–62, 64, 76, 95–96, 134–35, 166, 183, 185–86

See also exploration; intelligence community, as authors; spy novel
Treasury, 110
Trenchard, Hugh, 241–43, 248, 250, 305, 319–20
Trevelyan, George, 63, 185
Trollope, Anthony, 110
Trucial Coast, 273
Tuohy, Ferdinand, 124, 141, 148, 164
Turkestan, 52, 216, 279
Turkey, 25–26, 29–33, 35, 37–38, 40, 52, 101, 105–6, 202–3, 206–8, 210–14, 219, 222, 224, 226, 229, 231, 233–35, 237, 244, 247, 254–55, 260, 266, 274–75, 277, 279–80, 293–95, 299, 311–12, 317
    See also Ottoman Empire
Turkish Army, 39, 150, 154, 160, 162, 208, 277, 363 n.11
Tweedy, Owen, 183–84
Tyrell, William, 28, 30

Urabi Pasha, 63
Union for Democratic Control, 293, 299–300
    See also democracy
United Service Institute, Royal, 156, 183–84, 242, 248, 251, 253, 309–10, 361 n.4
universalism, 4, 394 n.38
    See also Enlightenment; science
United States, 18, 178–79, 187, 202, 207, 218–19, 253, 257, 290, 310, 324, 334–36
    CIA 261, 335–36
    current war in Iraq, 18, 23, 137, 201, 239, 257, 262, 336–37, 341 n.11, 405 n.47
Uqair, 33

Vagts, Alfred, 28
Valentino, Rudolph, 182
Victoria, 16
Victorianism, 70–72, 76, 85–86, 94, 102, 164, 179, 189, 256
Vienna, 217
violence, colonial, 5, 8–11, 13, 246–47, 250, 253, 261, 294, 301–4, 306, 332, 340 n.5
    critique of, 294, 302–4, 316, 323
    See also air control; bombardment; militarism
Vivian, Valentine, 223, 334
von Stotzingen mission, 52

Wadi Araba, 269
Wadi Faria, 162–63
Wahab, R. A., 105

Waheida, 53
Wahhabism. *See* Ikhwan; Islam
Walkowitz, Judith, 17
Walrond, Osmond, 127
War Committee, 44
War Office, 28–30, 32, 34, 39–40, 44, 105,
  127–28, 148, 169, 180, 207, 217, 221,
  223, 225, 231, 265–67, 268, 274,
  289–90, 295, 299, 311
warfare
  aerial. *See* airpower
  amphibious, 143, 146
  guerrilla. *See* warfare, irregular
  irregular, 143, 149–59, 162, 186, 196,
    211, 235, 242–43, 246, 248–50, 255,
    316, 336
  naval, 152, 243, 247–48, 256, 259
Wauchope, A. G., 159, 174
Waugh, Evelyn, 191
Wavell, Archibald F., 80, 144, 156, 284
Wavell, Arthur J. B., 64, 71–72, 80, 90,
  101, 111
Webb, Beatrice, 62, 320
Webb, Sidney, 192, 194, 231, 269, 320
Webster, Nesta, 309, 312
Wedgwood, Josiah, 303, 305
Wells, H. G., 62, 173, 186, 188, 195, 312
Westminster Gazette, 302
Westrate, Bruce, 48
Wheeler, Geoffrey, 229, 266
Whitehall, 15, 30, 34, 36–37, 40, 45, 47,
  50–51, 59, 83, 110, 123, 127, 129,
  142, 205, 217–18, 220, 227, 230–32,
  240, 243, 246, 265, 268–69, 271,
  273, 276, 278, 284, 288, 290, 301,
  318–19, 326
  See also Air Ministry; Admiralty; Foreign
  Office; India Office; Treasury; War
  Office; administration, imperial;
  covert empire
Wilde, Oscar, 62
Willcocks, William, 39, 60, 319
Williamson, Henry, 186, 195
Wilson, Arnold T., 18, 38, 41–42, 51, 57,
  81, 110, 125, 157, 160, 180, 183–85,

  193, 209, 218–21, 226–27, 230, 237,
  241, 245, 248, 250, 278, 282, 289,
  296–97, 309–10, 320, 325, 333
Wilson, Cyril E., 47–49, 53
Wilson, Jeremy, 142
Wilson, Woodrow, 202
Wingate, Orde, 333
Wingate, Reginald, 29, 40, 47–48, 52, 55,
  57, 123, 134, 175, 184
Wingate, Ronald, 57, 333
Winstone, H. V. F., 76, 110
Winterton, Lord (Edward Turnour), 196,
  308, 317
Wireless, 103, 118, 130, 143, 147, 161, 170,
  243, 256, 257, 261, 315
Wood, Gordon, 236
Woolf, Leonard, 63, 183, 190–91, 314
Woolf, Virginia, 63, 66, 70, 89, 132, 182,
  190–91, 193
Woolley, Leonard, 34–36, 38, 40, 46,
  61–62, 108, 183, 191
World War One. *See* Great War
World War Two, 80, 144, 151, 194, 253–54,
  261, 279, 283–84, 315, 330, 333–36,
  341 n.12
Wyndham, George, 62

Xenophon, 80, 167

Yanbo, 47
Yeats, W. B., 62, 63, 66, 75, 88–89, 94, 123,
  132, 134, 186–87, 192–93, 306, 323
Yemen, 13
Yorkshire, 62
Young, Hubert, 28, 31, 33, 41, 48, 50, 56, 63,
  72, 104, 126, 138, 143, 151, 154, 180,
  208, 211, 214–15, 227–30, 241, 245,
  247, 278, 316
Young, J. W. A., 47
Young Turks, 14–15, 60, 204, 209
  See also Committee of Union and
  Progress

Zionism, 56, 194, 215, 217, 313
Zubair, 27

CPSIA information can be obtained at www.ICGtesting.com
Printed in the USA
BVOW071155171111

276235BV00001B/6/P